European Review
of Social Psychology

European Review of Social Psychology

Editors

Gordon Hodson - *Brock University, Canada*
Rhiannon Turner - *Queen's University Belfast, UK*

Editorial Board

Julia Becker - *University of Osnabrück, Germany*
Monica Biernat - *University of Kansas, USA*
Lindsey Cameron - *University of Kent, UK*
Dora Capozza - *University of Padova, Italy*
John Dovidio - *Yale University, USA*
Belle Derks - *Utrecht University, the Netherlands*
Bertram Gawronski - *University of Texas at Austin, USA*
Tobias Greitmeyer - *University of Innsbruck, Austria*
Lasana Harris - *University College London, UK*
Nick Haslam - *University of Melbourne, Australia*
Miles Hewstone - *University of Oxford, UK*
Alain van Hiel - *Ghent University, Belgium*
Michael Hogg - *Claremont Graduate University, USA*
Aarti Iyer - *University of Sheffield, UK*
Jolanda Jetten - *University of Queensland, Australia*
John Jost - *New York University, USA*
Małgorzata Kossowska - *Jagiellonian University, Poland*
Barbara Krahe - *University of Potsdam, Germany*
Colette van Laar - *University of Leuven, Belgium*
Antony Manstead - *Cardiff University, UK*
Elizabeth Page-Gould - *University of Toronto, Canada*
Monica Rubini - *University of Bologna, Italy*
Linda Tropp - *University of Massachusetts, Amherst, USA*
Ayse K. Uskul - *University Kent, UK*
Jacquie Vorauer - *University of Manitoba, Canada*
Fiona White - *University of Sydney, Australia*

European Review of Social Psychology

Volume 31

Edited by

Gordon Hodson
Brock University, Canada

and

Rhiannon N. Turner
Queen's University Belfast, UK

First published 2020 by Routledge

4 Park Square, Milton Park, Abingdon, Oxon OX14 4RN, UK.

http://www.tandfonline.com/pers

Simultaneously published in the USA and Canada by Routledge

711 Third Avenue, New York, NY 10017

Routledge is part of the Taylor & Francis Group, an Informa business

British Library Cataloguing in Publication Data

A catalogue record for this book is available from the British Library

ISBN 13: 978-1-138-67268-0 (hbk)

IBSN 13: 978-1-138-67270-3 (pbk)

ISSN 1046-3283

Cover design by Jim Wilkie

SUBSCRIPTION INFORMATION

***European Review of Social Psychology*, Print ISSN 1046-3283, Online ISSN 1479-277X, Volume 31, 2020.**

European Review of Social Psychology (www.tandfonline.com/PERS) is a peer-reviewed journal published annually for the European Association of Social Psychology (www.easp.eu) by Taylor & Francis, 4 Park Square, Milton Park, Abingdon, Oxon, OX14 4RN, UK.

Institutional Subscription Rate (print and online): $305/£199/€245
Institutional Subscription Rate (online-only): $267/£174/€214 (+ VAT where applicable)

Taylor & Francis has a flexible approach to subscriptions enabling you to match individual libraries' requirements. This journal is available via a traditional institutional subscription (either print with online access, or online only at a discount) or as part of our libraries, subject collections or archives. For more information on our sales packages please visit www.tandfonline.com/page/librarians

All current institutional subscriptions include online access for any number of concurrent users across a local area network to the currently available backfile and articles posted online ahead of publication.

The US annual subscription price is $305. Airfreight and mailing in the USA by agent named Air Business Ltd, c/o Worldnet Shipping Inc., 156-15, 146th Avenue, 2nd Floor, Jamaica, NY 11434, USA. Periodicals postage paid at Jamaica NY 11431. US Postmaster: Send address changes to *European Review of Social Psychology*, Air Business Ltd, c/o Worldnet Shipping Inc., 156-15, 146th Avenue, 2nd Floor, Jamaica, NY 11434, USA.

Subscription records are maintained at Taylor & Francis Group, 4 Park Square, Milton Park, Abingdon, OX14 4RN, United Kingdom.

Ordering information:
Please contact your local Customer Service Department to take out a subscription to the Journal: USA, Canada: Taylor & Francis, Inc., 530 Walnut Street, Suite 850, Philadelphia, PA 19106, USA. Tel: +1 800 354 1420; Fax: +1 215 207 0050. UK/Europe/Rest of World: T&F Customer Services, Informa UK Ltd, Sheepen Place, Colchester, Essex, CO3 3LP, United Kingdom. Tel: +44 (0) 20 7017 5544; Fax: +44 (0) 20 7017 5198; Email: subscriptions@tandf.co.uk.

Dollar rates apply to all subscribers outside Europe. Euro rates apply to all subscribers in Europe, except the UK and the Republic of Ireland where the pound sterling rate applies. If you are unsure which rate applies to you please contact Customer Services in the UK. All subscriptions are payable in advance and all rates include postage. Journals are sent by air to the USA, Canada, Mexico, India, Japan and Australasia. Subscriptions are entered on an annual basis, i.e. January to December. Payment may be made by sterling cheque, dollar cheque, euro cheque, international money order, National Giro or credit cards (Amex, Visa and Mastercard).

Back issues: Taylor & Francis retains a two-year back issue stock of journals. Older volumes are held by our official stockists to whom all orders and enquiries should be addressed: Periodicals Service Company, 351 Fairview Ave., Suite 300, Hudson, New York 12534, USA. Tel: +1 518 537 4700; fax: +1 518 537 5899; email: psc@periodicals.com

Taylor & Francis grants authorization for individuals to photocopy copyright material for private research use, on the sole basis that requests for such use are referred directly to the requestor's local Reproduction Rights Organization (RRO). The copyright fee is £26.00/US$33.00/€41.00 exclusive of any charge or fee levied. In order to contact your local RRO, please contact International Federation of Reproduction Rights Organizations (IFRRO), rue du Prince Royal, 87, B-1050 Brussels, Belgium; email ifrro@skynet.be; Copyright Clearance Center Inc., 222 Rosewood Drive, Danvers, MA 01923, USA; email info@copyright.com; or Copyright Licensing Agency, 90 Tottenham Court Road, London, W1P 0LP, UK; email cla@cla.co.uk. This authorization does not extend to any other kind of copying, by any means, in any form, for any purpose other than private research use.

Copyright © 2021 European Association of Social Psychology. All rights reserved. No part of this publication may be reproduced, stored, transmitted, or disseminated, in any form, or by any means, without prior written permission from Taylor & Francis, to whom all requests to reproduce copyright material should be directed, in writing.

European Association of Social Psychology and our publisher Taylor & Francis make every effort to ensure the accuracy of all the information (the "Content") contained in our publications. However, European Association of Social Psychology and our publisher Taylor & Francis, our agents, and our licensors make no representations or warranties whatsoever as to the accuracy, completeness, or suitability for any purpose of the Content. Any opinions and views expressed in this publication are the opinions and views of the authors, and are not the views of or endorsed by European Association of Social Psychology and our publisher Taylor & Francis. The accuracy of the Content should not be relied upon and should be independently verified with primary sources of information. European Association of Social Psychology and our publisher Taylor & Francis shall not be liable for any losses, actions, claims, proceedings, demands, costs, expenses, damages, and other liabilities whatsoever or howsoever caused arising directly or indirectly in connection with, in relation to or arising out of the use of the Content. Terms & Conditions of access and use can be found at http://www.tandfonline.com/page/terms-and-conditions.

European Review of Social Psychology

Volume 31   Number 1   December 2020

CONTENTS

Articles

1   Fitting in: How the intergroup context shapes minority acculturation and achievement
Karen Phalet and Gülseli Baysu

40   It's not just "us" versus "them": Moving beyond binary perspectives on intergroup processes
John Dixon, Guy Elcheroth, Philippa Kerr, John Drury, Mai Al Bzour, Emina Subašić, Kevin Durrheim and Eva G. T. Green

76   Text-based E-contact: Harnessing cooperative Internet interactions to bridge the social and psychological divide
Fiona A. White, Rachel Maunder and Stefano Verrelli

120   How static facial cues relate to real-world leaders' success: a review and meta-analysis
Miranda Giacomin and Nicholas O. Rule

149   Bystanders' reactions to intimate partner violence: an experimental approach
Stefano Pagliaro, Maria Giuseppina Pacilli and Anna Costanza Baldry

183   A meta-analytic integration of research on the relationship between right-wing ideological attitudes and aggressive tendencies
Alain Van Hiel, Emma Onraet, Dries H. Bostyn, Jonas Stadeus, Tessa Haesevoets, Jasper Van Assche and Arne Roets

222   Social game theory: Preferences, perceptions, and choices
Joachim I. Krueger, Patrick R. Heck, Anthony M. Evans and Theresa E. DiDonato

254   Harm inflation: Making sense of concept creep
Nick Haslam, Brodie C. Dakin, Fabian Fabiano, Melanie J. McGrath, Joshua Rhee, Ekaterina Vylomova, Morgan Weaving and Melissa A. Wheeler

287   A communal approach to sexual need responsiveness in romantic relationships
Emily A. Impett, James J. Kim and Amy Muise

319   Ideological differences in attitude and belief similarity: distinguishing perception and reality
Chadly Stern

350   Changing prejudiced attitudes, promoting egalitarianism, and enhancing diversity through fundamental processes of persuasion
Pablo Briñol and Richard E. Petty

List of contributors

Dominic Abrams, *Centre for the Study of Group Processes, School of Psychology, University of Kent, Canterbury CT2 7NP, UK*

Hans Alves, *Social Cognition Center Cologne, Universität zu Köln, Köln, Germany*

Katarina Blask, *Department of Psychology, University of Trier, Trier, Germany*

Susan E. Cross, *Department of Psychology, Iowa State University, Ames, Iowa, USA*

Tegan Cruwys, *Research School of Psychology, The Australian National University, 39 Science Road, ACT 0200, Australia*

Christian Frings, *Department of Psychology, University of Trier, Trier, Germany*

Roger Giner-Sorolla, *School of Psychology, University of Kent, Keynes College, Canterbury, UK*

Georg Halbeisen, *Department of Psychology, University of Trier, Trier, Germany*

Jolanda Jetten, *School of Psychology, McElwain Building University of Queensland, St Lucia, QLD 4072, Australia*

Michelle Kearns, *Centre for Social Issues Research, Department of Psychology, University of Limerick, Limerick V94 T9PX, Ireland; International Rescue Committee, Freetown, Sierra Leone*

Alex Koch, *Booth School of Business, University of Chicago, Chicago, IL, USA*

S. Alexander Haslam, *School of Psychology, McElwain Building University of Queensland, St Lucia, QLD 4072, Australia*

Catherine Haslam, *School of Psychology, McElwain Building University of Queensland, St Lucia, QLD 4072, Australia*

Orla T. Muldoon, *Centre for Social Issues Research, Department of Psychology, University of Limerick, Limerick V94 T9PX, Ireland*

Kai Sassenberg, *Leibniz-Institut für Wissensmedien; University of Tuebingen, Tübingen, Germany*

Annika Scholl, *Leibniz-Institut für Wissensmedien*

Constantine Sedikides, *Psychology Department, University of Southampton, Southampton, UK*

Giovanni A. Travaglino, *School of Humanities and Social Science, The Chinese University of Hong Kong, Shenzhen 518100, China; Centre for the Study of Group Processes, School of Psychology, University of Kent, Canterbury CT2 7NP, UK*

Christian Unkelbach, *Social Cognition Center Cologne, Universität zu Köln, Köln, Germany*

Ayse K. Uskul, *School of Psychology, Keynes College, University of Kent, Canterbury, UK*

Eva Walther, *Department of Psychology, University of Trier, Trier, Germany*

Tim Wildschut, *Psychology Department, University of Southampton, Southampton, UK*

Acknowledgments

We would like to thank the following reviewers who helped us and the authors to shape these articles into their final versions:

Analia Albuja

Michael Ashton

Daniel Balliet

John Banas

Maik Bieleke

Kwan Lamar Blount-Hill

Mark Brandt

Marilynn Brewer

Nicholas Buttrick

Dora Capozza

James Cornwell

Shai Davidai

Daniel Decaro

Marieke Dewitte

Lindsay Dillingham

Ronald Fischer

Amber Gaffney

Teresa Garcia Marques

Guido Gendolla

Theofilos Gkinopoulous

Jin Xun Goh

Seval Gundemir

Paul Hanel

Emily Harris

Astrid Homan

Wiebren Jansen

Jolanda Jetten

Barbara Krahe

Inna Ksenofontov

Lisa Legault

Gunnar Lemmer

David Levari

Scott Lilienfield

Robyn Mallett

Nora Murphy

Christopher Olivola

Rebecca Pinkus

Mike Prentice

Andrew Prestwich

David Rast

Michael Schmitt

Schwartz Shalom

Lisa Sinclair

Alain Van Hiel

Erika Weisz

Arnaud Wisman

Lukas J. Wolf

Preface

The *European Review of Social Psychology (ERSP)* is an international journal which, for nearly 30 years, has sought to further the exchange of ideas by providing an outlet for substantial reviews of theoretical and empirical work. ERSP is a premium outlet for publishing theoretically interesting and empirically supported ideas that shape and guide the field. The previous editors (Miles Hewstone and Antony Manstead) are leaving the journal in excellent shape, with a 2020 Impact Factor of 7.353. We are grateful for their stewardship of the journal, and for their mentorship as the journal has transitioned to a new editorial team.

ERSP is a unique and special journal, where authors enjoy the opportunity to fully explore their ideas and to discuss the implications of their research programme. This outlet allows authors to consolidate a body of research and to disseminate new ideas, grounded in their research findings. It is our intention that any paper published here would be among those that authors themselves consider special and cherish.

The discipline of social psychology is an international endeavour and this fact underpinned the decision of the previous editors, and ourselves, to make the *European Review of Social Psychology* an international review that published outstanding work of authors from all nations, rather than restricting it to Europeans. We are 'European' in that, like our sister journal, the *European Journal of Social Psychology*, we are published under the auspices of the European Association of Social Psychology (EASP).

The emphasis of the contributions we publish in *ERSP* is on integrative reviews of authors' substantial programmes of research, which will already have appeared (or be accepted for publication) in several individual articles in leading peer-reviewed journals of our discipline. We also publish articles on topics and initiatives of contemporary interest and originality, and broader integrative reviews on an issue to which the author will have made substantive primary contributions.

All articles published by the *European Review*, whether commissioned by the editors or spontaneously submitted by authors, are externally reviewed and publication is subject to a positive outcome of the review process. In making their decisions, the editors are assisted by an international Editorial Board consisting of senior scholars, as well as by ad hoc reviewers. Thanks to the

X PREFACE

quality both of the authors and of the editorial process, the *European Review* has become internationally renowned and widely cited.

Originally an annual series, the *European Review of Social Psychology* was re-launched in 2003 as an 'e-first journal'. Each article is published electronically as soon as the editorial process has been completed; this procedure not only considerably reduces the publication lag, but it also allows libraries to subscribe to the *European Review*, rather than having to order volume by volume via standing orders. For authors, this means that accepted papers are accessible to research peers almost immediately, facilitating the access and citation of the paper. As a journal we are accessed by all important abstracting and indexing services, such as *Current Contents/Social and Behavioral Sciences (CC/S&BS); PsycINFO; Social Sciences Citation Index (SSCI)* and *Social Scisearch*. Subscribers (among them the more than 1000 members and affiliates of the EASP) also receive their familiar blue volume when, at the start of each year, the set of e-first published articles from the previous year is published as a printed volume.

Our goal is to make ERSP one of the first outlets that scholars turn to, in their efforts to better understand contemporary social psychology, and in adding their own unique voices to a discipline that is becoming increasingly relevant in the 21st century.

Gordon Hodson & Rhiannon Turner

ARTICLE

Fitting in: How the intergroup context shapes minority acculturation and achievement

Karen Phalet[a] and Gülseli Baysu[b]

[a]Faculty of Psychology and Educational Sciences, Center for Social and Cultural Psychology, Leuven, Belgium; [b]School of Psychology, Queen's University Belfast, Belfast, UK

ABSTRACT
Children of immigrants are at risk of underachieving in school with long-lasting consequences for future life-chances. Our research contextualises the achievement gap by examining minority acculturation experiences in daily intergroup contact across different intergroup contexts. Acculturation researchers often find an adaptive advantage for minority youth with an integration-orientation (combining both cultures). But findings from Europe are inconclusive. Looking beyond individual differences in acculturation-orientations, this review shifts focus to the intergroup context of minority acculturation and achievement. We discuss longitudinal, multi-group, multi-level and experimental evidence of the up- and downsides of integration for minority inclusion and success in European societies. Our studies show that both (1) intergroup contact experiences and (2) intergroup ideologies affect achievement – either directly or through the interplay of (3) acculturation-norms, defined as shared views on acculturation in social groups, with individual acculturation-orientations. The findings suggest how schools can reduce achievement gaps through improving intergroup relations.

ARTICLE HISTORY Received 20 February 2018; Accepted 2 January 2020

KEYWORDS Acculturation; integration; intergroup relations; achievement; diversity

Introduction

Estimated numbers of international migrants worldwide have increased from 173 million in 2000 to 244 million in 2015 (UN, 2015). In Europe 34.3 million people or 6.7% of the total population were born outside of the EU (Eurostat, 2016). The new scale of migration-related diversity has fuelled public debates over the inclusion of immigrant minorities in European societies. A major hurdle to the inclusion and success of minority youth is the overlap of cultural diversity with persistent educational inequalities. In North-America and in Europe, disadvantaged minority youth lag behind majority peers in school (OECD, 2015) – with far-reaching consequences for their future life chances (Motti-Stefanidi & Masten, 2013). Especially in most stratified and ethnically

CONTACT Karen Phalet ✉ karen.phalet@kuleuven.be Faculty of Psychology and Educational Sciences, Center for Social and Cultural Psychology, KULeuven, Tiensestraat, 102, Leuven 3000, Belgium
© 2020 European Association of Social Psychology

segmented European educational systems, achievement gaps widen throughout school careers even when minority and majority students enter at the same level (Baysu & de Valk, 2012; Baysu & Phalet, 2012). A growing body of research addresses the question, which psychological processes connect minority status to school failure? Against the backdrop of mounting assimilationist pressures in Europe (Phalet, Baysu, & van Acker, 2015), our research inquires into the acculturation experiences of minority youth, and how they affect their school achievement.

This review identifies a significant problem with a predominant individual-differences approach in psychological acculturation research. The empirical focus of this approach is on the assessment of individual acculturation-orientations, distinguishing the orientations of minority people towards the heritage culture and the mainstream culture and towards the combined cultures (Sam & Berry, 2010). As will be illustrated below, acculturation-orientations refer broadly to individual differences in cultural preferences (such as one's attachment to heritage cultural values or customs), behaviours (such as language use and religious practice), or identifications (such as ethnic and national identities). In view of persistent ethnic educational inequalities across Europe (Heath & Brinbaum, 2014), this review highlights minority achievement as a critical adaptation outcome. The first part of this article exposes the limits of an individual-differences approach, reviewing mainly cross-sectional evidence that relates the achievement of minorities to their individual acculturation-orientations. We posit that mixed evidence for the acculturation-achievement relationship reflects the fact that social context, in particular intergroup dynamics, has received scant attention in traditional acculturation research. We propose that the intergroup context considered at multiple levels, both from the bottom up and from the top down, must be taken into account.

The main part of the review articulates an alternative contextual approach to minority acculturation and achievement. This approach spells out how the intergroup context affects minority achievement *directly* as well as *indirectly* through the interplay with individual acculturation-orientations. We present illustrative findings from a series of large-scale field studies with minority samples in educational settings, combining comparative, multi-level, longitudinal and experimental research designs. The studies establish contextual variation in minority achievement and in the associations with acculturation-orientations. They identify critical conditions and test connecting processes in the intergroup context. Across the studies, minority participants are immigrant-origin youth – "youth" refers broadly to older children, adolescents and young-adults. Participants are sampled from major disadvantaged minorities – Turkish, Moroccan and other Muslim minorities – in North-West Europe – Belgium, Netherlands, Austria, Sweden, Germany and England.

To assess achievement we use various measures of motivated learning and school success, such as behavioural and affective (dis)engagement, academic self-competence, verbal and non-verbal achievement tests, school grades, progress and attainment. The success of minority youth is premised on their inclusion in academic contexts (Juang et al., 2018; Schachner, Van de Vijver, & Noack, 2017). As measures of minority inclusion we assess school belonging (O'Neel & Fuligni, 2013) and feelings of peer acceptance or rejection (Eccles, Wong & Peck, 2006). Lack of belonging is a critical developmental risk factor for minority youth (Motti-Stefanidi & Masten, 2013). Thus, academic contexts that threaten minorities' sense of belonging undermine their achievement (Inzlicht, Good, Levin, & Van Laar, 2006). Conversely, felt acceptance by other students enables academic achievement for minority students (Cook, Purdie-Vaughns, Garcia, & Cohen, 2012). Either way, school success or failure hinges upon the inclusion of minority students in the school environment (Schachner, Juang, Moffit, & Van de Vijver, 2018; Walton & Cohen, 2007). Therefore, both success and inclusion are key components of a context-sensitive assessment of minority achievement. Our main interest here, however, is less how inclusion and success are interrelated, and more how schools as intergroup contexts shape both outcomes.

Acculturation and achievement: an individual-differences approach

Psychological acculturation research seeks to explain minority adaptation from the experience of acculturation: the process through which people from different cultures who are engaging in sustained contact adapt to one another (Berry, Phinney, Sam, & Vedder, 2006). To study acculturation, researchers typically ask individual members of minority groups to report their own orientations towards the heritage culture of their country of origin and towards the mainstream culture in their country of residence: Do they prefer to maintain the heritage culture, to adopt the mainstream culture, or to combine both cultures? Individual acculturation-orientations are measured to predict individual differences in the adaptation of immigrant minorities (Dimitrova, Chasiotis, & van de Vijver, 2016). Although early acculturation researchers were clear that the adaptive value of individual acculturation-orientations also depends on the wider intergroup context (Berry, 1980; Bourhis, Moise, Perreault, & Senecal, 1997), this concern has only recently received systematic empirical attention (Brown & Zagefka, 2011). Instead, an individual-differences approach to acculturative adaptation examines which individual acculturation-orientations help minorities adjust to cross-cultural transitions (Berry et al., 2006). Due to predominant single-group and single-country studies of acculturation, contextual variability in acculturation experiences and outcomes has long been overlooked. Most research predicts health and wellbeing aspects of psychological adjustment – conceiving of acculturation as a source of psychological strain or "acculturation stress" (Berry, 1980). A parallel line of research predicts individual differences in socio-cultural adaptation, which refers to competence aspects such as task performance and social skills (Van De Vijver & Phalet, 2004; Ward & Kennedy, 1993). Although minority achievement as our main outcome of interest has received less attention in acculturation research, it is commonly subsumed under the heading of socio-cultural adaptation (Schachner et al., 2018).

An influential bi-dimensional model by Berry (1980) distinguishes acculturation-orientations towards maintaining the heritage culture and towards contact with the mainstream culture. Both dimensions combine into four theoretical groups: integration is a combination of maintaining one's heritage culture and seeking contact with the mainstream culture; assimilation denotes relinquishing one's heritage culture in favour of mainstream culture contact; separation is defined as maintaining the heritage culture at the expense of mainstream culture contact. Finally, marginalisation rejects both one's heritage culture and contact with the mainstream culture. Berry's (1980) famous model was seminal in stimulating a continuing stream of cross-cultural acculturation research that developed multiple measures, modifications and extensions of the four groups distinguished by their distinct acculturation orientations (see below).

Assessing individual acculturation-orientations

Early research defined acculturation as a unidimensional process, that is, a change from the heritage culture of the country of origin towards the mainstream culture in the country of residence (Gordon, 1964). More recently, a well-established bidimensional conceptualisation of the acculturation process distinguished minority orientations towards both heritage and mainstream cultures (Ryder, Alden, & Paulhus, 2000). The most commonly used bidimensional model was proposed by Berry (see above). Another bidimensional acculturation model combines heritage culture maintenance with the adoption of the mainstream culture instead of the desire for contact (Bourhis et al., 1997). Still others extend acculturation-orientations beyond attitudinal measures to minorities' behavioural involvement in heritage and mainstream cultural domains, such as their language use or religious practice (Phalet, Hillekens, & Fleischmann, 2018; Ryder et al., 2000).

Yet another approach defines acculturation-orientations as cultural identifications, or minorities' commitment to heritage and mainstream cultural groups (Liebkind, 2006; Phinney, 2003). Applying the bidimensional acculturation model to cultural identifications, dual identifiers are strongly committed to both ethnic and national identities; those with a separated identity combine strong ethnic identification with weak national identification; those with an assimilated identity combine strong national identification with weak ethnic identification; and a marginalised identity is detached from both national and ethnic groups. Typically, dual identification does not require that both identities are *equally* important parts of the self. More often minorities' national identity is psychologically significant against the background of strong ethnic identities (Fleischmann & Phalet, 2015).

Acculturation-orientations are assessed using various procedures. One common procedure creates four statements for the four theoretical attitude groups (Berry et al., 2006; Van de Vijver, Helms-Lorenz, & Feltzer, 1999; but see problems with this procedure, Brown & Zagefka, 2011). Another procedure uses separate statements for heritage and mainstream cultural orientations (Ryder et al., 2000). Individuals are classified into four groups by combining their scores on both acculturation-orientations, using median-split or cutting off at the scale-midpoint (Berry & Sabatier, 2010). Still other procedures test the statistical interaction of both acculturation-orientations to identify attitude-groups (Baysu, Phalet, & Brown, 2011); or use person-centred methods to assign individuals to inductively derived distinct groups (Berry et al., 2006; Schwartz & Zamboanga, 2008).

Measures also vary in how they operationalise both cultures. Some researchers assess cultural preferences globally ("How important to you is it to adopt the mainstream culture?"; Van Acker & Vanbeselaere, 2012). Others select specific cultural contents such as customs, language, food, friends, values or norms (Berry & Sabatier, 2010; Santiago, Gudiño, Baweja, & Nadeem, 2014). Some measures are domain-specific, so that minorities can combine integration in school or at work, for instance, with separation in the private domain (Arends-Tóth & van de Vijver, 2006; Navas, Rojas, Garcia, & Pumares, 2007). Still other measures reflect more complex forms of multiplicity or hybridity in the hyperdiverse environments of today's minority youth (Doucerain, Dere, & Ryder, 2013). For instance, Ferguson, Bornstein, and Pottinger (2012) distinguished three acculturation-orientations towards ethnic-Jamaican, African-American and European-American cultures for Jamaican immigrants to the U.S. and in Switzerland, Hoti, Heinzmann, Müller, and Buholzer (2017) redefined integration as the combination of minority cultural and multicultural orientations – including other minority cultures as well.

The various ways acculturation-orientations are conceptualised and measured have implications for their associations with minority inclusion and success. For our purposes acculturation-orientations refer broadly to both mainstream and heritage cultural orientations (attitudes, practices, identifications) with specific studies using different measures. Our studies supplement separate measures of mainstream and heritage cultural orientations with alternate direct measures of integration. Our primary interest in this review is in replicating acculturation–achievement associations across multiple measures.

Do individual acculturation-orientations predict achievement?

In line with Berry's "integration hypothesis", many acculturation studies find that integration is most adaptive, with marginalisation being least adaptive, and with assimilation and separation falling in between (Berry et al., 2006; Liebkind, 2006; Nguyen & Benet-Martínez, 2013; Ward & Kennedy, 1993). Specifically, benefits of integration (when minorities combine heritage and mainstream cultural orientations) have been attributed to increased social support and resources in culturally diverse social networks, as well as enhanced perspective taking, cognitive complexity, counter-stereotypical thinking, and creativity through repeated diversity experiences (Nguyen & Benet-Martínez, 2013). When integrated minorities find their dual identities denied, however, this undercuts the social and cognitive gains of culture contact and learning (Gharaei, Phalet, & Fleischmann, 2018). Reviews and meta-analyses of acculturation studies show that acculturative adaptation varies with specific outcome measures for specific minority groups in specific receiving contexts (Bornstein, 2017). Below we review mixed evidence of the benefits of integration for minority inclusion and success.

The associations of individual acculturation-orientations with sociocultural adaptation show some robust general trends alongside less conclusive or seemingly inconsistent findings (Berry et al., 2006; Makarova & Birman, 2015; Mesquita, De Leersnyder, & Jasini, 2017; Nguyen & Benet-Martínez, 2013). Thus, minorities who are more oriented towards mainstream culture contact or adoption consistently report better sociocultural adaptation. The adjustment benefits of minorities' heritage cultural orientation, however, vary considerably across contexts. Similar general trends appear from a handful of acculturation studies that specifically assessed minority achievement (Frankenberg, Kupper, Wagner, & Bongard, 2013; Makarova & Birman, 2015; Schachner et al., 2017; Suinn, 2010). While mainstream cultural orientations consistently and positively predict school outcomes, evidence for the benefits of heritage cultural orientations is mixed.

Combining mainstream and heritage cultural orientations, several studies assessed a distinct integration-orientation. Cross-sectional studies of over 5,000 minority adolescents in 13 Western countries reveal generally positive associations between integration and sociocultural adaptation (Berry et al., 2006). However, associations were rather weak; and integration was not significantly more adaptive than separation. Also in line with Berry's integration hypothesis, a meta-analysis of 83 cross-sectional acculturation studies concludes that integration is more adaptive than monocultural mainstream or heritage orientations (Nguyen & Benet-Martínez, 2013). Yet, integration effects on adaptation varied widely in direction and size from −.78 to +.87 across countries and minority groups. Integration was less adaptive in European countries than in the U.S. – and less so for historically-disadvantaged African and indigenous minorities than for Latino, Asian or European minorities.

The evidence of an integration advantage is also less clear-cut for achievement than for well-being. In Germany, for instance, there is mixed evidence of an integration–achievement association (Spiegler, Sonnenberg, Fassbender, Kohl, & Leyendecker, 2018: higher motivation) as well as an alternate assimilation-achievement association (Schotte, Stanat, & Edele, 2018: higher achievement). Makarova and Birman (2015) reviewed 29 acculturation studies focusing narrowly on minority school success as adaptation outcome. Whereas cross-sectional findings support achievement benefits of minorities' mainstream cultural orientation, associations with their heritage cultural orientation range from positive to null or negative. Also associations with a distinctive integration-orientation vary. Repeated findings of achievement gains for assimilationist minorities in Europe suggest the adaptive advantage of integrationists may depend on the acceptance of integration in the intergroup context. In line with prevailing assimilationism in today's Europe, however, schools often expect minorities to assimilate rather than integrate (Gharaei, Phalet, & Fleischmann, 2018).

Cross-sectional evidence of individual acculturation-achievement associations leaves room for alternative interpretations (but see Asendorpf & Motti-Stefanidi, 2017; Spiegler et al., 2018, for recent longitudinal studies). In a *longitudinal* study of British minority children, we found evidence of benefits as well as costs of integration for their inclusion in school (Brown et al., 2013). The study administered repeated measures of acculturation-orientations and adaptation to Asian minority children (Mean age = 8, N = 215) who were surveyed three times with six-month intervals. To assess their inclusion in school, age appropriate self-report measures of peer acceptance and self-esteem in the school context were used, as well as teacher reports of emotional vulnerability. Heritage culture maintenance was measured by asking whether British-Asian children should learn the heritage language, dress according to cultural traditions, eat heritage cultural foods, celebrate their culture's holidays, and listen to traditional music. To measure children's orientations towards mainstream culture contact we inquired whether British-Asian children should be friends, eat lunch, and play together with White-English children.

In this study integration was the most prevalent acculturation-orientation. Older children (8–11 years) more often endorsed integration than younger children (5–7 years) (86% vs. 68.5%), while younger children were more often in favour of separation than older peers (18.5% vs. 2.8%). Moreover, children's acculturation-orientations longitudinally affected their school inclusion. Integrated children reported higher peer acceptance and self-esteem in the school context than other children, yet teacher reports also evinced more negative emotions. In less supportive intergroup contexts, maintaining heritage cultural practices can be psychologically challenging for minority children who are more oriented towards majority peers as well, because they are more vulnerable to negative contact experiences (Asendorpf & Motti-Stefanidi, 2017). In summary, first longitudinal findings of adaptive gains *and* costs hint at a possible downside of integration.

> To conclude, cross-sectional findings from comparative studies and reviews reveal considerable contextual variation in the adaptive value of integration. Moreover, we found first longitudinal evidence of the potential (delayed) costs of early integration for minority children in British schools. Few acculturation studies directly address the intergroup context that enables (or undermines) potential benefits of integration. The next section develops a contextual approach from the intergroup context and its interplay with individual acculturation-orientations.

Acculturation and achievement: towards a contextual approach

Schools are key acculturation contexts where minorities learn to negotiate their minority status and cultural difference in daily intergroup contact (Umaña-Taylor et al., 2014). As the school environment makes salient the distinct cultural identities of minority youth, it adds on an intergroup level to their interpersonal relations with teachers and peers (Rutland et al., 2012). According to Social Identity Theory (Tajfel & Turner, 1986), people derive self-worth from their membership of valued in-groups. When their in-group is devalued in particular intergroup contexts, people experience identity-threat (Ellemers, Spears, & Doosje, 2002). Identity-threat was shown to undermine achievement when minority identities are disregarded or devalued in mainstream settings (Ellemers et al., 2002), such as when their minority group is associated with low academic ability (Steele, Spencer, & Aronson, 2002). Conversely, in intergroup contexts that value minority identities and see them as compatible with academic excellence, minorities do better (Derks, van Laar, & Ellemers, 2007).

Minority achievement is thus contingent on various sources of identity-threat *and* protection at multiple levels of real-life intergroup contexts (see Figure 1). At the micro-level of face-to-face social interactions and relationships, minorities experience identity-threat in negative intergroup contact, such as discrimination or negative stereotyping, as well as valuation in positive intergroup contact, such as friendship or support from teachers. In parallel, at the macro-level of intergroup relations, schools as institutional settings differ in the intergroup ideologies they communicate, for instance

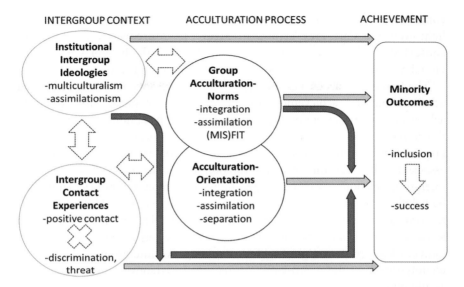

Figure 1. Conceptual framework: How the intergroup context shapes minority acculturation and achievement.

through the diversity policies and practices that are in place. Intergroup ideologies are defined here as the institutional values and rules that evaluate and regulate how different groups relate to each other and to the school (Thapa, Cohen, Guffey, & Higgins-D'Alessandro, 2013). Thus, assimilationist policies such as banning the headscarf can threaten minority identity, whereas multicultural policies aim to protect minorities from identity-threat. At an intermediate meso-level of intergroup context, we define acculturation-norms as different ways in which social groups collectively define and manage acculturation issues. Acculturation-norms may refer to minority group as well as majority group views on acculturation. We distinguish acculturation-norms from individual acculturation-orientations, which can conflict with minority or majority group acculturation-norms – such as when individual integration conflicts with assimilationist majority group norms. While group members can come to share similar views on acculturation through intergroup contact (bottom-up), acculturation-norms also reflect prevailing intergroup ideologies (top-down).

The integrative conceptual framework in Figure 1 articulates hypothetical processes connecting minority acculturation (in the middle of Figure 1) and achievement (on the righthand-side) to the intergroup context (on the lefthand-side). The intergroup context refers to the quality of intergroup relations in schools. It is multi-layered, so that day-to-day intergroup contacts (micro-level) *and* protective or threatening intergroup ideologies (macro-level) *and* their interplay – such as when integration policies buffer negative contact experiences (cross-level) – jointly shape minority achievement (see light-grey and dark-grey arrows in Figure 1). Moreover, the intergroup context also affects achievement indirectly through the interplay with individual acculturation-orientations (in the middle of Figure 1).

The framework articulates the hypothetical processes connecting individual acculturation and achievement to the intergroup context. First, minority achievement is contingent on the *quality of intergroup relations*, so that identity-threat undermines, and valuation ultimately enables inclusion and succes (light grey arrows indicate main effects of intergroup context in Figure 1). Second, associations between minority acculturation and achievement also depend on intergroup relations, so that the same individual acculturation-orientation can be helpful or harmful depending on the intergroup context. The interplay of minority acculturation-orientations with intergroup relations intersects multiple levels of context (moderation is indicated by dark grey arrows in Figure 1). Thus, individual integration might backfire when negative intergroup contact elicits identity-threat (at the micro-level). Moreover, the adaptive value of individual acculturation-orientations depends critically on acculturative *fit with group norms of acculturation*. While acculturative fit has been studied mainly with (perceived) majority group norms, in diverse schools minority group norms play a role too.

To flesh out the proposed contextual approach to acculturation, we review below relevant research on acculturation and intergroup relations and our own research at the intersection of both fields. The review is organised around multiple levels of intergroup context as hypothetical sources of identity-threat vs. valuation for minorities: from intergroup contact experiences (micro), to intergroup ideologies (macro), to group norms of acculturation (meso).

Intergroup contact experiences: positive and negative contact and threat

Schools shape minorities' acculturation experiences and outcomes through the quantity and quality of daily social interactions and relationships. While supportive relationships with school teachers and peers benefit all students, minorities especially profit from positive contact (Juang et al., 2018; Thijs & Verkuyten, 2014). Due to their minority status they are sensitive to contact quality in school, which they see as diagnostic of academic fit or merit (Walton & Cohen, 2007). Asymmetric effects of contact quality on minority vs. majority outcomes resonate with a social identity perspective on intergroup contact (Brown & Hewstone, 2005). For minorities the quality of intergroup contact with peers and teachers signals whether they are insiders or outsiders, good or not so good students. Negative experiences of discrimination or negative stereotypes convey that their minority identity is devalued (Derks et al.,

2007; Purdie-Vaughns, Steele, Davies, Ditlmann, & Randall-Crosby, 2008). Such experiences induce identity-threat and leave minorities vulnerable in performance situations. In contrast, experiences of positive contact with intergroup friends or supportive teachers are vital sources of identity-protection (Derks et al., 2007). Our research relates the quality of intergroup contact in school to minority achievement (see Figure 1: main effects of contact). Extending an intergroup relations line of acculturation research (Brown & Zagefka, 2011), we further examine how minority contact experiences affect the achievement benefits of integration (see Figure 1: moderation effect of contact). In particular, we ask whether negative contact might undercut the adaptive value of integration through eliciting identity-threat.

Contingent minority outcomes

Positive and negative intergroup contact have mostly been studied separately. But minorities in diverse schools are simultaneously exposed to positive and ambivalent or negative contact experiences (Baysu, Phalet, & Brown, 2014). Moreover, different sources of intergroup contact matter (e.g., from teachers or peers; Byrd & Andrews, 2016). Enduring relationships with teachers or peers matter more than less frequent or more distant forms of contact (Brown & Chu, 2012). Minorities experience positive contact when they spend time with majority friends or feel supported by teachers. From a social identity approach to intergroup contact (Brown & Hewstone, 2005), such positive contact signals the acceptance of minorities' cultural heritage in an academic context and should therefore protect academic achievement. Accordingly, intergroup friendship with peers in school or on campus positively predicted minority outcomes both cross-sectionally and longitudinally (Rutland et al., 2012; Shook & Fazio, 2008). Conversely, negative contact conveys disregard or derogation of minorities' cultural heritage and social standing, eliciting identity-threat and undermining achievement (Derks et al., 2007; Purdie-Vaughns et al., 2008; Verkuyten, Thijs, & Gharaei, 2019). Thus, minorities who experience discrimination from teachers or peers do less well, as shown in both cross-sectional and longitudinal studies in the US (Benner & Kim, 2009; Levy, Heissel, Richeson, & Adam, 2016) and Europe (D'hondt, Eccles, Van Houtte, & Stevens, 2016; Özdemir & Stattin, 2014). Also in the absence of overt discrimination, academic settings expose minorities to identity-threat whenever situational cues – implicitly – signal that their group is less valued (Derks et al., 2007; Purdie-Vaughns et al., 2008). Stereotype-threat as a situational form of identity-threat refers to the presence of salient negative stereotypes about a minority group's academic competence (Steele et al., 2002). Much experimental evidence links stereotype-threat to performance-decrements in minority students across Europe and the US (Appel, Weber & Kronberger, 2015). Our research relates minority achievement to intergroup contact experiences with peers and teachers, looking at friendship and support, discrimination and negative stereotypes (see Figure 1: main effects of contact).

To set the stage, we compared the school careers of local-born Turkish and Moroccan minorities in seven European cities with those of majority reference samples (Baysu & de Valk, 2012; Baysu & Phalet, 2012). Drawing on large-scale TIES surveys ("The Integration of the European Second generation") in Belgium, Sweden, Austria and Germany (N = 4022; M ages = 24–27), we longitudinally documented widening achievement gaps between majority and minority youth through secondary and into higher education. Extensive face-to-face interviews retrospectively reconstructed individual school careers: whether students were ever held back (i.e., forced to repeat a school year), to which school track they were assigned at entry, whether they changed tracks, completed secondary education, and accessed higher education. In addition, interviewees retrospectively reported early friendships with majority peers and perceived teacher support in lower-secondary school (e.g., "My teachers took care of me when I needed additional help"; OECD, 2015), as well as perceived school diversity ("How many children of immigrant origin attended your lower-secondary school?" from 1 "almost none" up to 5 "almost all").

Baysu and Phalet (2012) compared Turkish Belgians (N = 358) to a same-age majority Belgian reference sample (N = 303) (M age = 25; SD = 4.78). Multinomial regressions revealed widening gaps between minority and majority school careers at successive transitions from lower to upper secondary and into higher education. Estimated gaps were controlled for entry levels, prior grade retention and parental education. Even Turkish Belgians who had started out in academic tracks without a history of retention were more likely to end up in vocational tracks *and* to drop-out from school than most similar majority Belgians. Next, we added measures of contact quality in relations with teachers and peers (controlling for family background and prior school careers). In support of the protective role of positive intergroup contact, later school outcomes were contingent on early contact quality. For minority and majority students alike, perceived teacher support significantly increased staying-on rates in academic tracks and reduced drop-out risks at later transitions. For minorities only, early friendships with majority Belgians further protected staying-on rates and reduced drop-out risks later on. In line with identity-protection, this finding highlights intergroup friendship as a powerful form of positive contact for minorities (Davies & Aron, 2016).

In a second study, Baysu and de Valk (2012) used cross-national extensions of the TIES surveys (see above) to compare Turkish and Moroccan Belgians with Turkish-heritage students in Sweden, Austria and Germany and majority reference samples in seven cities (sample sizes ranged from N = 230 to N = 322 with approximately equal numbers of majority and minority young adults in each city). By way of sequential analysis of their retrospective school careers minorities were clustered in longitudinal trajectories through the different school systems. Across countries they were less likely than the majority reference group to follow "straight academic trajectories" (starting in academic tracks and going on to university). Conversely, they were more likely to end up in "short trajectories" (not completing secondary school) or "straight vocational trajectories" (starting and completing vocational training). While national school systems differ (with least minority disadvantage in the comprehensive Swedish system), trajectories that over-represent minorities give less access to stable and well-paid jobs across countries (Heath & Brinbaum, 2014). Looking beyond unequal chances, the cross-national analysis replicates the protective role of positive intergroup contact. Across groups and cities and conditional on school composition (self-reported school diversity), minorities with at least one early majority friend were significantly more likely to stay on in academic trajectories (versus vocational or short trajectories) than those without majority friends. Plausibly, less restricted contact opportunities in more comprehensive school systems explain in part why achievement gaps were smaller in Sweden than in Belgium, Austria or Germany.

In summary, these cross-cultural and longitudinal findings suggest longterm benefits of early experiences of positive intergroup contact for later achievement (see Figure 1, main effects of contact). They corroborate a hypothetical identity-protection function of positive contact with majority friends and teachers for minority students. On a cautionary note, associations with perceived school diversity should be replicated with proper composition measures. Also, retrospective findings should ideally be replicated with prospective longitudinal data, following up the future school careers of minority children. While controls for prior school careers make reverse causation less likely, possible retrospective bias in self-reported contact quality cannot be ruled out.

Expanding the explanatory focus, Baysu et al. (2014) asked how positive and negative intergroup contact jointly affect minority achievement (see Figure 1, main effects of contact). Drawing on the same large-scale cross-cultural TIES surveys (see above) in Belgium and Austria, we compared Turkish minorities in two Belgian and two Austrian cities with moderate to high levels of ethnic segregation (N = 1060). To test the additive associations of friendship *and* discrimination experiences with minority achievement, we supplemented the same perceived school diversity and intergroup friendship measures (see above) with measures of personal discrimination. Participants rated how often they had experienced discrimination ("hostility or unfair treatment") from teachers, headmasters or peers. They also reported any experiences of verbal harassment ("offensive words") due to their origin or background. School success was assessed as minorities' academic attainment (from higher education, over upper secondary, to less than full secondary), satisfaction ("How satisfied are you with the level of education that you have achieved?"), and self-efficacy (4 items; e.g., "It is easy for me to stick to my plans and accomplish my goals."). In multi-group structural-equation models, minority youngsters who reported higher percentages of minority peers in lower secondary school were less successful across cities (lower attainment, satisfaction and efficacy). Moreover, both positive and negative contact measures mediated the association of (perceived) school diversity with minority achievement. In line with hypothetical identity-protection, minority youth with more majority friends were more successful; and friendships were more frequent in schools with more contact opportunities (lower perceived percentages of minority students). As expected from identity-threat, minority youth who experienced personal discrimination in school were less successful. Interestingly, the association of discrimination experiences with percentages of minority students in school was curvilinear – with most frequent (self-reported) discrimination at intermediate levels of (perceived) diversity. Plausibly, highly diverse schools where minorities (were seen to) outnumber majority students offer some protection from discrimination. Along those lines, Latinx children in the U.S. who experienced discrimination from teachers did less well in predominantly White schools, yet no such association was found in predominantly Latinx schools (Brown & Chu, 2012). Restricted exposure or reduced vulnerability to discrimination in schools with fewer majority peers comes at a price, however, because minorities in those schools miss out on the achievement benefits of intergroup friendship. Note that the retrospective design of our data warrants due caution (see above).

As a rigorous test of contingent minority achievement, two large-scale field-experiments extend retrospective correlational evidence by applying a stereotype-threat paradigm in Belgian schools (Baysu, Celeste, Brown, Verschueren & Phalet, 2016; Baysu & Phalet, 2019; Baysu, 2011). Both experiments randomly assigned Turkish and Moroccan minorities (and their majority classmates) to stereotype-threat vs. control conditions preceding verbal or non-verbal cognitive tests. In follow-up questionnaires, they also reported their experiences of discrimination in school (see below). We were specifically interested in the interplay of personal discrimination experiences as a chronic source of identity-threat with situationally induced stereotype-threat (Whaley, 1998). We asked whether early discrimination experiences affect later achievement over and above stereotype-threat in the achievement situation. In addition, we explored how discrimination may leave minorities vulnerable in the long run through making them susceptible to stereotype-threat. If we find that minorities with early discrimination experiences are the ones who underperform under stereotype-threat, this would strongly support an identity-threat explanation of contingent minority achievement.

One major field experiment by Baysu, Celeste, Brown, Verschueren, and Phalet (2016) targeted Turkish and Moroccan Belgians (M age = 14; N = 735) in secondary schools (n = 47). The experiment was embedded in large-scale school-based surveys in Belgian schools with moderate to high diversity levels (partial data from CILS Belgium). The sampling design was modelled on the international CILS4EU project (CILS4EU, 2016). Schools were randomly assigned to either stereotype-threat (272 minority students in 23 schools) or control-conditions (425 minority students in 24 schools). A nonverbal inductive-reasoning test assessed cognitive performance; and post-test questions indicated cognitive-behavioural disengagement from the test (4 items, e.g., "During the test I acted as if I was working; ... my thoughts were wandering off."). Stereotype-threat was induced by making salient the minority identity and related negative stereotypes of low academic competence. In the experimental condition we asked ethnic (about their Turkish or Moroccan origin) and religious background questions (about their Islamic faith) *immediately preceding* the test; in the control condition the same questions were answered *after completing* the test. In addition, students reported their personal discrimination experiences (7 items, e.g., "How often are you treated unfairly or in a hostile way; threatened or bothered; insulted or called names ... in school?"). In line with expected identity-threat, minorities underperformed on the test in the stereotype-threat condition (relative to the control condition). There were no significant performance differences between schools in both conditions for majority students. Likewise, minorities who experienced more personal discrimination in school performed less well. Adding disengagement from the test as a motivational mediator, we estimated cross-level moderated mediation with stereotype-threat (manipulated at the school-level) and discrimination experiences (measured at the individual level) as predictors of test performance. Both stereotype-threat and discrimination experiences harmed minority achievement through eliciting disengagement. Minorities who had experienced discrimination in school or who were exposed to stereotype-threat in the test situation would sooner disengage from the test, and hence underperformed. The findings provide a stringent test of contingent minority achievement. They show how situational and chronic sources of identity-threat in real-life academic intergroup contexts add up to undermine minority achievement.

Another field-experiment by Baysu and Phalet (2019) randomly assigned individual students to stereotype-threat vs. control conditions to elucidate the interplay of stereotype-threat with their personal experiences of discrimination. We specifically targeted high-achieving Turkish and Moroccan Belgians in academic tracks of upper secondary education (M age = 18; N = 174). We asked whether early discrimination experiences might have long-term consequences through recursive cycles of threat whenever students' minority identity and related negative stereotypes are situationally salient. Immediately preceding a verbal cognitive test (selected difficult items from the "Groningen Intelligence Test", GIT), we made ethnic and religious minority identities salient (see above). Students also reported their personal experiences of discrimination in school (see above). We found the expected interaction of prior discrimination experiences with stereotype-threat, so that minorities who reported more discrimination in the past did significantly worse in the threat (vs. control) condition, $B = -.90$; $p = .02$ at high discrimination (+1 SD). On the positive side, stereotype-threat effects were non-significant when (high-achieving) minorities reported less discrimination, $B = .70$; $p = .11$ at low discrimination (−1 SD). In line with cumulative identity-threat, this finding suggests that personal discrimination experiences can have long-lasting consequences for minority achievement through sensitising minorities to situational stereotype-threat (Baysu, 2011). Distinctive strengths of both field experiments are the stereotype-threat manipulation and the objective performance measures – in combination with ecological validity in real-life academic settings. Still, causal inferences should be qualified in light of the correlational nature of discrimination-achievement associations.

In another extension of this line of inquiry, Heikamp, Phalet, Van Laar, and Verschueren (2019) replicated the achievement costs of discrimination experiences in school. We specifically tested whether such costs were mediated through school belonging as a measure of inclusion. Participants were Turkish and Moroccan minorities (M age = 15; N = 1050) and their classmates in 52 Belgian schools (subsamples from CILS Belgium, see above). Students reported how often they experienced discrimination from teachers (6 items, e.g. "How often do your teachers discriminate against you or favour others over you?") and how strongly they felt they belonged in their school (5 items, e.g., "I feel at home in this school"). In addition, a measure of academic engagement gauged students' cognitive (attention) and behavioural involvement (effort) in classroom activities (3 items, e.g., "I work as hard as I can in class.") as a reliable indicator of school success (Skinner, Kindermann, & Furrer, 2008). Multi-level structural-equation models (controlling for student background and school composition) confirmed the expected achievement costs of discrimination: minority students who experienced more discrimination from teachers were less engaged in class. They also felt less school belonging which, in turn, predicted less engagement. In line with identity-threat in negative contact with teachers, discrimination experiences put minorities at risk of academic disengagement by threatening belonging. Conversely, disengaged students might also not feel that they belonged in school and hence experience more discrimination in recursive cycles of disengagement. In the absence of longitudinal evidence of mediation, associations may work both ways.

Summing up, across multiple data sources and intergroup settings discrimination experiences were revealed to be chronic sources of identity-threat undermining minority inclusion and success (see Figure 1, main effects of contact). Discrimination was harmful over and above – and in part through activating – situational stereotype-threat in academic settings. On the positive side, retrospective longitudinal evidence corroborates robust and long-lasting protective effects of intergroup contact quality on minority achievement. Confirming theoretical expectations from identity-protection, intergroup friendship in particular mitigated identity-threat and enabled sustained academic engagement.

The interplay of intergroup contact with acculturation-orientations

In their review of acculturation research, Sam and Berry (2010) identified a close triangular relationship among contact, acculturation and adaptation. To the extent that contact quality signals the acceptance of minorities' cultural heritage in mainstream settings, contact experiences shape minority achievement directly as well as indirectly through their interplay with individual acculturation-orientations (see Figure 1: moderation by contact). In view of mixed evidence of an adaptive advantage of integration (see above), we examined the adaptive value of integration as a function of the quality of intergroup contact in school. In line with Berry's integration hypothesis (see above), integrated minority individuals – or dual identifiers – should ideally be most successful in school, since they combine bicultural competences and support networks from both minority and majority cultural groups (Nguyen & Benet-Martínez, 2013). In the presence of identity-threat, however, negative intergroup experiences may counteract a potential integration advantage.

Revisiting the same retrospective school career data on second-generation Turkish-Belgian youngsters (N = 576; TIES Belgium, see above), Baysu, Phalet, and Brown (2011) examined the interplay of their individual acculturation-orientations with discrimination experiences in school. We used the same measure of personal discrimination in interactions with teachers, headmasters or peers (see above). Individual acculturation-orientations were measured as the relative strength of identification with Turkish and Belgian cultural groups. Applying Berry's bidimensional model, we operationalised integration as the statistical interaction of ethnic and national identification (see above). We distinguished academic, vocational, and short careers as categorical outcomes, i.e., whether participants accessed higher education, completed secondary education, or left school early – conditional on their entry-levels at the start of secondary education (academic or vocational). We hypothesised that assimilated youth (weak ethnic identification) would do better than dual identifiers in the face of discrimination, because they distance themselves from the minority as target of threat. Separated youth (weak national identification) might also be less affected by discrimination than dual identifiers, because they are more distant from the majority group as source of threat. To test interactions with discrimination we contrasted dual, assimilated and separated identifiers with low identifiers (Berry's marginalisation) as a reference-category.

In line with identity-threat for integrated identifiers in particular, they were less successful when they experienced more discrimination in school (see Figure 2). Relative to assimilated and separated individuals, integrated identifiers were at once most at risk of early school leaving when they experienced discrimination *and* most likely to enter university when they did not. As expected, achievement costs vs. benefits of integration were contingent on identity-threat in the intergroup context. Whereas Berry's integration hypothesis was confirmed in the absence of discrimination, integration is associated with significant achievement costs in discriminatory intergroup contexts. In contrast, the achievement of assimilated identifiers was unaffected by discrimination; and separated identifiers did slightly better with more discrimination. Overall, separated individuals were least likely, and assimilated individuals most likely, to succeed, in line with prevailing assimilationism in Belgium (see below). On a cautionary note, cross-sectional associations do not warrant causal inferences and retrospective bias in self-reported discrimination cannot be ruled out.

As a rigorous test of the contingent achievement benefits of integration, Baysu and Phalet (2019) replicated the above findings in their field-experiment with (N = 174) high-achieving Turkish- and Moroccan-Belgian

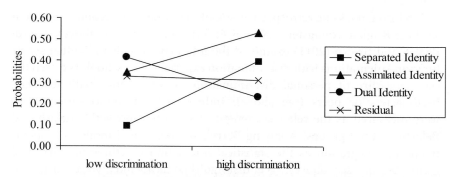

Figure 2. High (vs. Low) Achievement as a function of Experienced Discrimination and Acculturation-Orientations: Estimated Probabilities for Turkish Belgians.
Associations are controlled for Entry Level, Early School Segregation, Age, and Student Status. This figure is taken from BAYSU et al. (2011).

minority students in selective academic tracks. The experiment induced stereotype-threat by making salient participants' ethnic and religious (Muslim) identities immediately preceding a verbal achievement test (see above). A composite measure of bicultural identity integration (e.g., "I feel part of a combined Turkish and Belgian culture") was used here to measure individual integration. We hypothesised that high-integration individuals would outperform low-integration individuals only in the absence of threat (control condition) but not under stereotype-threat. A significant interaction of individual integration with stereotype-threat revealed the expected achievement costs for high-integration (vs. low-integration) individuals under threat. In contrast, we found a significant achievement advantage for high-integration (vs. low-integration) individuals in the absence of threat. The experimental findings fully replicate correlational evidence of the interplay between individual acculturation-orientations and identity-threat in academic contexts. While the experimental design and the objective achievement measure are distinctive strengths, we would ideally need repeated measures of acculturation before and after the experiment.

To conclude, we find first systematic evidence of the interplay between intergroup contact experiences and minorities' individual acculturation-orientations (see Figure 1, moderation by contact). Correlational and experimental findings support a contextual approach to the adaptive value of integration – or dual identification – from identity-threat in intergroup relations. They elucidate existing findings relating threat-related vulnerabilities of minority students to their national or ethnic identification. In German schools, for instance, assimilated identifiers outperformed less strongly German-identified peers on an achievement test under stereotype-threat (Weber, Appel, & Kronberger, 2015). In the US, in contrast, strong (vs. weak) Mexican identification buffered positive school outcomes for Mexican minority children who experienced teacher discrimination (Brown & Chu, 2012). The findings resonate with our own finding that assimilated as well as separated minorities were less vulnerable than dual identifiers in the face of discrimination. At the same time, they suggest country differences between German and American schools as intergroup contexts. The next section shifts focus from minorities' own intergroup experiences at the micro-level to the intergroup ideologies that define intergroup relations at the macro-level (see Figure 1, institutional intergroup ideologies).

Institutional intergroup ideologies: multiculturalism vs. assimilationism

Early acculturation researchers pointed out that for integration to be psychologically viable it may require a sympathetic societal climate, exemplified by Canadian multicultural policies (Berry, 1997). However, the intergroup ideologies that make up the societal climate have long remained invisible in acculturation research (Guimond, de la Sablionniere, & Nugier, 2014; Phalet et al., 2015). Our primary interest is in the institutional support for multi-culturalism in schools as macro-affordances of minority acculturation and achievement. Specifically, we contrast multiculturalism versus assimilationism as distinct intergroup ideologies that inform institutional views and practices pertaining to school diversity (see Figure 1, institutional intergroup ideologies). Other possible views such as colorblindness, alternate vocabularies, or more finegrained distinctions are beyond the scope of this review (e.g., Schwarzenthal, Schachner, Juang, & Van de Vijver, 2019). Multiculturalism here refers broadly to intergroup ideologies that value cultural diversity and promote equal treat-ment in intergroup relations (Guimond et al., 2014; Verkuyten & Thijs, 2013). Such multicultural ideologies generally support positive intergroup relations in diverse schools, because they include minorities on an equal footing and value their distinct cultural heritage (Schachner, Noack, Van de Vijver, & Eckstein, 2016; Schwarzenthal et al., 2019). In contrast, assimilationism is antithetical to multiculturalism. Assimilationist ideologies reject cultural difference and justify unequal treatment of culturally different immigrant minorities (Guimond et al., 2014). Such ideologies tend to strain intergroup relations, because they put pressure on minorities to relinquish their heritage culture and turn a blind eye to discrimination, "blaming the victim" instead for not fully adopting the main-stream culture (Van Acker, Phalet, Deleersnyder & Mesquita, 2014).

Contingent minority outcomes

Schools develop different policies and practices with a view to reducing costs and maximising benefits of cultural diversity in an academic setting. These policies reflect the wider societal climate only in part and vary considerably across schools within the same country, giving rise to distinct intergroup ideologies at the school level. For instance, when schools ban headscarves or penalise multilingual practices they apply an assimilationist ideology, putting pressure on minority students to conform to the majority culture. Alternatively, when school curricula cover materials from different heritage cultures or when minority religious practices or languages are accommo-dated, schools apply a multiculturalist ideology, signalling to minorities that the school values their heritage cultural identity. Thus, assimilationism should exacerbate, and multiculturalism dilute, identity-threat for minority students, enabling or undermining their inclusion and success (see Figure 1, main effect of ideology). Accordingly, applied research on multiculturalism in organisations (Rattan & Ambady, 2013) and multicultural education in schools (Aronson & Laughter, 2016) documents potential benefits for min-ority inclusion and success. Specific multicultural policies and practices vary widely (Zirkel, 2008), but they share a common core that values cultural diversity and ensures equal treatment (Verkuyten & Thijs, 2013). The few studies that empirically tested cross-sectional associations of multiculturalism vs. assimilationism with minority school outcomes relied mainly on student perceptions of intergroup ideologies (Brown & Chu, 2012; Hoti et al., 2017). For instance, Schachner et al. (2016) related student perceptions of different intergroup ideologies in German schools to their adaptation outcomes. In line with identity-valuation, minority children who perceived their teachers to promote equality and to include cultural difference reported better adjustment.

Looking beyond individual student perceptions, Celeste, Baysu, Phalet, Meeussen, and Kende (2019) content-analysed actual school policies as an external contextual measure of institutional intergroup ideologies. Sixty-six schools were randomly sampled to take part in CILS Belgium (see above) with school composition ranging from below 10% to over 60% of immigrant minority students. This large-scale school-based longitudinal survey followed N = 3131 students (mean age 15) over two years (waves 1 and 2 of CILS data), of whom 1747 were minorities of various immigrant origins and 1384 majority Belgians. Repeated self-report measures of school belonging (e.g., "I feel at home at this school") and school grades (standardised language and maths exam scores) assessed inclusion and success, respectively. Relative to majority students, minorities evinced lower overall levels of belonging and performance. The size of belonging and achievement gaps varied between schools, however. We hypothesised that multiculturalist school policies would reduce, and assimilationist policies could widen, the gaps (over and above school composition). Multiculturalism and assimilationism ideologies were assessed at the school-level. We content-analysed policy documents (school rules and mission statement) and identified distinct and coherent multiculturalism and assimilationism policy clusters. Assimilationist policies referred mainly to restrictions on minority languages and religious expression, such as a headscarf ban or penalties on minority language use. Multiculturalist policies included teaching about other cultures in class, respecting and valuing other cultures, and accommodating religious diets or holidays. As expected, multi-level models with school composition and policies as contextual predictors of minority and majority outcomes revealed significant interactions of minority status with the policy clusters. As expected from identity-valuation, schools that were more (vs. less) multiculturalist in their ideological orientation were associated with smaller gaps in both belonging and performance over time through higher minority belonging and success. Conversely, more (vs less) assimilationist schools significantly widened the belonging gap through alienating minorities, in line with identity-threat. Neither policy significantly affected majority outcomes. Finally, belonging longitudinally predicted student grades, highlighting inclusion as a mediator of minority achievement (Walton & Cohen,

2007). Though other school policies are beyond the scope of this review, assimilationism and multiculturalism did not cover all relevant policies in our data. For instance, policies promoting secularism were relatively frequent and distinct from assimilationism proper. Nor did multiculturalism include policies that merely tolerated religious difference. Multi-level analysis allows a stringent test of policy effects across many schools, yet its reliance on broad clusters of most frequent formal policies limits our understanding of applied ideologies in schools.

The interplay of intergroup ideologies with contact

To understand how schools as institutional settings afford minority achievement, a key question is how intergroup ideologies mesh with minorities' own experiences of day-to-day intergroup contact in school. Institutional support is essential to Allport's (1954) original conception of optimal conditions for intergroup contact to be truly inclusive. Since multiculturalist ideologies convey institutional support for equality and cultural diversity, we zoom in on the interplay of multiculturalism with minorities' own experiences of intergroup contact in school (see Figure 1, moderation by ideology). Moreover, minorities are likely targets of discrimination even as they engage in positive intergroup contact. Accordingly, two studies specifically examined whether multiculturalist ideologies effectively buffer minorities from identity-threat in the face of discrimination or negative stereotypes.

The empirical starting point was a large-scale field experiment by Baysu (et al., 2016) as part of CILS Belgium. The experiment established significant performance decrements of Turkish and Moroccan minority students with personal discrimination experiences and under stereotype-threat (see above). In follow-up analyses, Baysu et al. (2016) added the equality component of multiculturalism at the school-level as a hypothetical buffer of identity-threat. Intergroup equality was measured as shared student perceptions of equal treatment in school (2 items, e.g., "In my school some students are allowed to do more than others", reversed) and aggregated across majority and minority peers in the same schools. Next, perceived equality was specified as a contextual moderator of the associations between negative intergroup experiences (discrimination, stereotype-threat) and minority achievement (test performance, disengagement) in multi-level moderated mediation models. In support of institutional identity-protection, perceived intergroup equality enabled minority students to persist and perform better on the test. Moreover, more egalitarian schools (in terms of shared student perceptions of equal treatment) effectively buffered minority achievement under threat (see Figure 3). One limitation is that perceived equal treatment is only one component of multiculturalism as an intergroup ideology, which was aggregated across minority and majority students within each school and which might

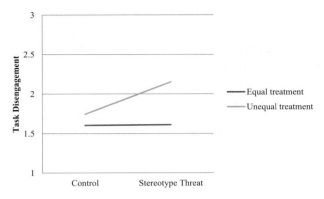

Figure 3. School-level interaction between Equal Treatment and Stereotype-Threat on Task-Disengagement. The slope for unequal treatment (between control and ST conditions) and the difference between equal and unequal treatment in the Stereotype-Threat condition are significant ($p = .004$, $p < .001$, respectively).
This figure is taken from BAYSU et al. (2016)

have a different, more colorblind meaning for majority than minority students. Another limitation is that the school-level analysis bypasses the varying classroom contexts of minorities' intergroup experiences.

In a follow-up study with Turkish and Moroccan minority subsamples from CILS Belgium (N = 1050; see above), Heikamp et al. (2019) aimed to replicate the interplay of minorities' discrimination experiences with institutional identity-protection. The study assessed perceived multiculturalism by minority peers as a contextual protective factor in multi-level analysis of school belonging as a measure of minority inclusion. Specifically, perceived institutional support for equality (2 items, see above) and cultural diversity (2 items, e.g., "In my school different cultures and religions are treated with respect.") formed one construct, perceived multiculturalism for minority students. Next, individual perceptions were aggregated over Turkish and Moroccan minority students within the same classroom (n = 274 classrooms in 52 schools). Multi-level moderated mediation analysis supported the hypothesised interplay of perceived institutional support for multiculturalism (classroom-level) with minorities' own experiences of discrimination (individual-level). In classrooms where minority peers perceived their school to support equal treatment and to value cultural diversity, minority students not only reported more school belonging overall, but their belonging was also dissociated from personal experiences of discrimination, hence was more stable. In accordance with institutional identity-protection, we conclude that minority perceptions of multiculturalism effectively buffered school belonging, thus enabling sustained academic engagement in the presence of discrimination (see above). Neither minorities' own individual perceptions, nor majority peer perceptions of multiculturalism significantly buffered minority belonging. Note that associations between discrimination, belonging and engagement are cross-sectional rather than causal.

We conclude that minority achievement is critically afforded by institutional intergroup ideologies and their interplay with minorities' own contact experiences (see Figure 1, main effects of ideology and moderation by ideology). To sum up, two components of multiculturalism – institutional support for equality and value in diversity – protected minority inclusion and success in the presence of discrimination or stereotype-threat. The last part of this review turns to acculturation-norms within majority, minority and mixed peer groups as an understudied intermediate level of intergroup context.

Acculturation-norms: integration vs. assimilation as group norms

This section seeks to explain minority inclusion from group norms of acculturation and from the acculturative fit of minorities' individual acculturation-orientations with group norms (see Figure 1, main effects of norms and moderation by norms). Acculturative fit has mainly been studied in relation to (perceived) majority group norms. Thus, minority individuals who prefer integration may deviate from an assimilationist majority group norm (cf. Brown & Zagefka, 2011, for a review). Fit consistently predicts more positive intergroup relations on both sides, yet our interest here is how acculturative fit relates to minority achievement.

Acculturative fit: the interplay with majority group norms

Majority acculturation-norms refer to shared views among majority members about how minorities should acculturate. Since majority groups powerfully define intergroup relations in society, minority acculturation interacts with majority acculturation-norms in the intergroup context. An intergroup relations tradition of acculturation research examined whether majorities expect members of minority groups to maintain the heritage culture, adopt the mainstream culture, or combine the cultures (cf. Brown & Zagefka, 2011). Perceived majority norms not only predicted minorities' own acculturation-orientations – for instance, when minorities perceived majority assimilation-norms, they preferred integration less. Majority norms also conditioned the psychological benefits of minorities' acculturation-orientations – for instance, when minorities perceived majority integration-norms, their own integration was more adaptive.

The relational acculturation model proposed by Bourhis et al. (1997) builds on Berry's (1980) model and centres on concordant or discordant majority and minority acculturation-norms and their relational outcomes.

Thus, majority integration-norms accept that minorities maintain the heritage culture and simultaneously adopt the mainstream culture, whereas alternate assimilation-norms expect minorities to adopt the mainstream culture and relinquish the heritage culture (Berry & Sabatier, 2010). Concordance (fit) is achieved when both minority and majority groups endorse an integration-norm. When minorities prefer integration and majorities expect assimilation, however, discordance (lack of fit) would lead to problematic intergroup relations. Accordingly, (perceived) discordance predicted ambivalent or negative majority emotions (threat) and attitudes (prejudice) towards immigrant minorities (Brown & Zagefka, 2011). Our own research looks beyond general intergroup attitudes as relational outcomes into the associations of acculturation-norms and acculturative fit with minority achievement.

Acculturative fit revisited: the interplay with multiple group norms

In today's highly diverse schools as key intergroup contexts for minority achievement, we conceive of acculturative fit as negotiated in relation to acculturation-norms in mixed minority and majority peer groups. Along those lines, Titzmann and Jugert (2015) measured acculturation-norms in mixed peer groups in German secondary schools and tested the interplay of both minority and majority group norms with immigrant minorities' individual acculturation-orientations and their socio-cultural adaptation. Using multi-level analysis, they specified actual group norms as school-level contextual moderators of individual-level acculturation-adaptation associations. As expected from acculturative fit with multiple group norms, both minority and majority acculturation-norms affect the adaptive value of minorities' own acculturation-orientations. Thus, minority students who prefer to adopt the German culture benefit only when they fit with acculturation-norms of their minority peer group in school: when the minority group rejects minority adoption of the German culture, individual acculturation-orientations towards the German culture were not adaptive. Likewise, minority students who prefer to maintain the heritage culture benefit less when they deviate from acculturation-norms of their majority peer group in school: when the majority group values minority contact with the German culture, individual acculturation-orientations towards the heritage culture were not adaptive.

Likewise, Celeste, Meeussen, Verschueren, and Phalet (2016) assessed actual acculturation-norms in mixed peer groups at the level of diverse classrooms as immediate intergroup contexts in Belgian schools. Using subsamples of Turkish and Moroccan minority students from CILS Belgium (age $M = 15$; N = 681 students, n = 230 classes), we related their own acculturation-orientations to experiences of peer rejection as a measure of (the lack of) inclusion in school. Acculturation-orientations were measured by single indicators of the preference for heritage culture maintenance and mainstream culture adoption: "How important is it for you to maintain the customs from Turkey or Morocco in school; and to adopt the Belgian customs in school?" Individual integration was distinguished from assimilation and separation by adding the interaction of both indicators (see above). Our self-report measure of peer rejection combined experiences of peer avoidance and victimisation (6 items; e.g., "How often do you experience that other students shut you out; ... bully you?"). In multi-level analysis, we distinguished crossgroup acculturation-norms (aggregated over all peers in each class) from minority subgroup norms (aggregated over Turkish or Moroccan peers in each class) as contextual moderators. Acculturation-norms were indicated by the average agreement with heritage culture maintenance ("Migrants should do everything possible to maintain the heritage culture.") and mainstream culture adoption (" ... should adopt the Belgian customs in this country."). Majority group norms could not be modelled separately due to very high levels of segregation at the classroom level (i.e., the absence of majority peers from many otherwise diverse classrooms).

The findings support the costs of a lack of acculturative fit with crossgroup as well as minority group norms of acculturation for minority inclusion (see Figure 4a,b). In classes with stronger cross-group norms that minorities should adopt the Belgian culture, minority students with an integration-orientation experienced significantly more peer rejection. Conversely, in classes with stronger minority group norms that minorities should maintain the heritage culture, students with an assimilation-orientation experienced most rejection. The costs of a lack of acculturative fit for minorities establish the injunctive force of actual acculturation-norms in the intergroup context. Specifically, the adaptive value of individual integration for minorities depends on its interplay with both majority and minority acculturation-norms (see Figure 1, moderation by norms). On the one hand, individual minority students who prefer integration can get caught between conflicting majority group or cross-group norms and minority group norms in school. On the other hand, minorities can collectively challenge prevailing acculturation-norms and redefine acculturative fit from the bottom up, especially in highly diverse intergroup contexts. As cross-sectional associations of acculturation-orientations with rejection experiences may work both ways, longitudinal analyses should further examine when minorities longitudinally increase acculturative fit – and avoid rejection – by conforming to group norms or by collectively redefining the norms. To trace complex norming processes in multiple-group contexts, future research may exploit more precise sociometric measures of who befriends or rejects whom within and across groups (e.g., Meeussen, Agneessens, Delvaux, & Phalet, 2017).

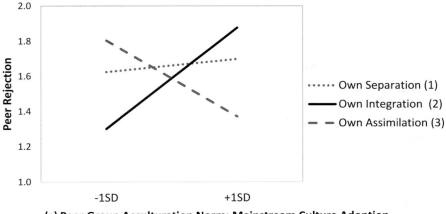

(a) Peer Group Acculturation Norm: Mainstream Culture Adoption

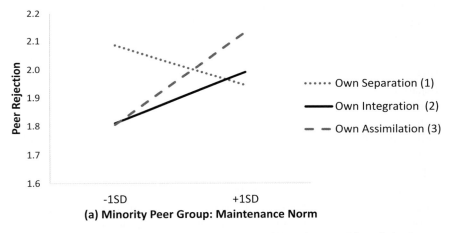

(a) Minority Peer Group: Maintenance Norm

Figure 4. (a) Minority Acculturation-Orientations and Experiences of Peer Rejection as a function of Peer Group Acculturation Norms of Mainstream Culture Adoption. (b) Minority Acculturation Attitudes and their Experience of Peer Rejection as a function of Minority Peer Group Norms of Heritage Culture Maintenance.

The figures are taken from CELESTE et al. (2016)

Discussion

In view of persistent and often widening achievement gaps between immigrant minority and majority school careers in Europe, our research inquires into the acculturation and achievement of minority youth in schools. Berry's well-established bidimensional model of acculturation-orientations distinguishes between minority individuals who prefer to adopt the mainstream culture, or to maintain the heritage culture, or to integrate both cultures. We reviewed extensive evidence across different immigrant groups and receiving countries associating the inclusion and success of immigrant minorities with their acculturation-orientations. The evidence for an alleged adaptive advantage of integration was mixed, with achievement benefits *as well as costs* for youngsters who integrate both cultures. Considerable contextual variability in the adaptive value of integration exposes limitations of a prevailing individual-differences approach and points to the need to account for the contextual affordances of successful integration.

Looking beyond individual acculturation-orientations, therefore, we proposed an integrative contextual framework that anchors minority acculturation and achievement in the intergroup context (see Figure 1). The framework takes a social identity approach to spell out hypothetical processes of identity-threat and protection for minority persons at multiple levels of intergroup relations. We applied this framework to schools as intergroup contexts of minority acculturation and achievement. In a nutshell, we established distinct sources of identity-protection and threat – and their interplay – both at the micro-level of intergroup contact and at the macro-level of institutional intergroup ideologies. As expected, our findings reveal that integration is psychologically costly in the presence of identity-threat – such as when minority students experience discrimination or face negative stereotypes in their school. Also, minority students who integrate both cultures are at risk when they deviate from acculturation-norms of either minority or majority group peers in shool. Conversely, we expected and found that positive contact experiences and school policies of multiculturalism (vs. assimilationism) buffer identity-threat and boost minority achievement. Moreover, fit with peer group acculturation-norms protects individual minority students who integrate both cultures. Below we discuss what these key findings add to the state of the art in intergroup contact, stereotype-threat, and acculturation research. We acknowledge limitations and suggest some avenues for future research as well as applied implications.

Intergroup contact experiences

At the micro-level of minority students' daily contact experiences, school segregation sets the stage for their future school careers through restricting the quantity and quality of early intergroup contact experiences (Baysu et al., 2014). In particular, cross-national (retrospective) longitudinal findings reveal long-lasting achievement benefits of early intergroup friendship for minority students in less segregated schools (Baysu & de Valk, 2012; Baysu & Phalet, 2012). Conversely, early experiences of discrimination cast a long shadow over minority school careers. Essentially, they gave rise to chronic identity-threat through leaving minority students vulnerable to recurrent stereotype-threat in assessment situations (Baysu, 2011). Moreover, longitudinal and experimental findings show how identity-threat puts minority students at risk of school failure by undermining their sense of school belonging and by eliciting affective or behavioural disengagement from academic activities or tasks (Baysu et al., 2016; Baysu & Phalet, 2019; Baysu et al., 2014; Heikamp et al., 2019).

Our research adds a distinct minority perspective to the extensive research literature on intergroup contact, which has mainly focused on the reduction of majority prejudice. Although intergroup contact is generally less effective in bringing about attitude change on the minority side (Tropp & Pettigrew, 2005), less is known about whether and how intergroup contact relates to actual disparities in minority inclusion and success. Against the background of real gaps in minority versus majority inclusion and success (Celeste et al., 2019), robust evidence of a protective function of early intergroup friendship in minority school careers opens up new avenues for future intergroup contact research. Also, applied research screening and monitoring achievement gaps would benefit from including psychological measures of intergroup contact frequency and quality – in addition to school composition.

Beyond the ecological validation of stereotype-threat experiments with large immigrant minority samples in Europe (Appel, Weber, & Kronberger, 2015), our findings articulate the interplay of identity-threat with the schooling experiences of minority youth. Whereas stereotype-threat is conceived as a situational source of threat "in the air", we found that it operates in conjunction with minorities' early experiences of discrimination. Such negative experiences may linger on and switch on stereotype-threat during tests or exams, thus resulting in chronic identity-threat. In addition, the combination of positive contact with discrimination measures integrates largely separate research lines on contact and threat in intergroup relations. First evidence that intergroup friendship buffers minority achievement in the face of discrimination highlights a critical identity-protection function of majority friends when minorities also experience discrimination. So far, the evidence for identity-protection was limited by the retrospective nature of our longitudinal design. Prospective longitudinal and experimental designs should test more rigorously hypothetical protective effects of early contact experiences. Future research may also complement self-report measures of contact with social network data on intergroup ties (Wölfer & Hewstone, 2017). Such data can elucidate early intergroup contact and discrimination effects by modelling how valenced intergroup interactions evolve over time.

Turning to the acculturation literature, we found that integration – combining heritage and mainstream cultural practices and social ties – can be psychologically demanding for minority youth (Brown et al., 2013); and we raised the question when the school environment affords successful integration. Longitudinal and experimental studies revealed integration as a two-edged sword, so that integrated minority students underperformed under threat, yet they outperformed their peers in the absence of threat (Baysu & Phalet, 2019; Baysu et al., 2014). The latter finding replicates a well-documented adaptive advantage of integration (Nguyen & Benet-Martínez, 2013), establishing significant achievement benefits for integrated minority youth in the absence of discrimination or stereotype-threat. When schools fail to effectively protect minority identities, however, this "integration advantage" cannot be taken for granted – as evident from a downside of integration for minority achievement under threat. To increase its explanatory leverage, therefore, acculturation research would need to consider minority experiences of intergroup contact and discrimination and their interplay with individual integration.

To conclude, the series of studies reviewed here consistently support the explanatory potential of minorities' intergroup contact experiences and their interplay with acculturation-orientations – in line with the proposed contextual framework (see Figure 1). Despite remaining gaps and limitations, the current findings have applied implications for public policies pertaining to school (de)segregation. To the extent that positive contact experiences such as intergroup friendship are more likely in more diverse schools (that is, schools with a significant presence of both majority and minority students), public policies should encourage greater school diversity and discourage less diverse single-faith schools, as well as other majority-only or minority-only schools. However, our research also warns against mere social mixing as a simple solution, since segregation may shield minority youth from the harmful consequences of discrimination experiences in negative intergroup contact. If educational policies are to promote more diverse schools, then, policy makers will have to invest in improving intergroup relations in those schools, for instance, by educating school teachers as effective "diversity managers" who foster positive contact and act against discrimination in diverse classrooms.

Institutional intergroup ideologies

At the level of institutional ideologies as macro-level intergroup contexts, multiculturalism values cultural difference and ensures equal treatment, thus protecting minority inclusion and success. In contrast, assimilationism rejects cultural difference and hence threatens minority inclusion. Empirical evidence on intergroup ideologies in schools comes from multi-level analyses which specify shared student perceptions or actual policies of multiculturalism as contextual affordances of minority inclusion and success (Baysu et al., 2016; Celeste et al., 2019; Heikamp et al., 2019). Taking into account school composition and using multiple outcome measures within time and over time, we consistently found significant achievement benefits for minority students in more multiculturalist schools – in line with institutional identity-protection. Conversely, more assimilationist schools increased the gap with majority students – in line with asymmetric identity-threat for minority students. Last but not least, institutional support for multiculturalism effectively protected the achievement of minority students in the face of stereotype-threat or discrimination (Baysu et al., 2016; Heikamp et al., 2019). In this way, multiculturalist schools directly boost as well as buffer minority inclusion and success from identity-threat.

These multi-level findings are only beginning to disentangle multiple sources of identity-threat and identity-protection – and to articulate their interplay – across micro- and macro-levels of real-life intergroup contexts. Whereas intergroup contact research has focused mainly on the micro-level of face-to-face intergroup encounters, Allport (1954) originally advanced institutional actors as architects of his "optimal conditions" for intergroup contact. Our research builds on Allport's now classic theorising of institutional design and resonates with multi-level evidence of the additive benefits of equal status in the contact situation (micro-level) and egalitarian intergroup ideologies (macro-level) for effective intergroup contact (Kende, Phalet, Van Den Noortgate, Kara, & Fischer, 2018). Similarly, extensive social-psychological research on stereotype-threat and discrimination has largely bypassed the institutional level of intergroup ideologies. Our findings add to this research tradition by bringing in institutional ideologies as macro-level social forces that can (aggravate or) buffer identity-threat in the immediate contact or task situation (micro-level). Finally, our multi-level approach complements and corrects common individualistic biases in applied acculturation research, which rarely takes into account how intergroup relations are defined at the institutional level. Whereas assimilation may be more adaptive than integration at the individual level, for instance, we find that minorities consistently benefit from more multiculturalist policies at the institutional level.

Future research on intergroup ideologies should test the external validity of our findings and find out what is distinctive about "multicultural education" (Zirkel, 2008) – or whether school policies reflect similar ideologies in other applied settings or in the wider society. Within educational settings, more finegrained instruments and multiple methods should better capture and contextualise the applied intergroup ideologies that are communicated by actual teaching practices. Such an in-depth analysis should elucidate further seemingly contradictory yet commonly observed mixed policies of multiculturalism *and* assimilationism within the same schools. Extending a multi-level approach to institutional ideologies, there is room to articulate further cross-level interactions with minorities' own acculturation-orientations and with their experiences of intergroup contact and discrimination. For instance, multiculturalist teaching practices such as learning about other cultures as part of the curriculum might be most protective for integrated (vs. assimilated) minority students or in high (vs. low) diversity classrooms.

In spite of many remaining questions, the research on institutional intergroup ideologies has direct applied implications for educational policies and practices. To be effective, concerted efforts to improve intergroup relations in increasingly diverse schools need to be institutionally supported from the top down. Especially assimilationist policies, such as banning headscarves or penalising immigrants' use of their mothertongue, were clearly detrimental for minority students. Conversely, multiculturalist policies that promote equality and value in diversity, created inclusive learning environments that reduced the gap between minority and majority students.

Group norms of acculturation

Institutional ideologies are communicated through written and unwritten school rules and policies that define intergroup relations from the top down. Such ideologies may or may not reflect acculturation-norms or the shared views of acculturation that define intergroup relations from the bottom up. These group norms may cumulatively reproduce or challenge intergroup ideologies. Assessing group norms of acculturation in diverse classrooms (Celeste et al., 2016), we were able to predict the inclusion of majority and minority youth from their fit with acculturation-norms. First findings suggest that especially minority youth who integrate both cultures, can be caught in a crossfire between distinct majority and minority group norms of acculturation. These findings build on a rich intergroup relations tradition of acculturation research, which established the key role of acculturation-norms in the majority society, albeit measured at the individual level, as well as the benefits of normative fit with (perceived) minority acculturation-orientations for positive intergroup relations (Brown, & Zagefka, 2011). We have added substantially to this research stream by relating normative fit to minority perspectives and outcomes, by assessing actual acculturation-norms in schools as real-life intergroup contexts, and by establishing the injunctive force of minority as well as majority group norms in these often highly diverse contexts.

To conclude, the new scale of migration-related diversity in our societies opens up prevailing acculturation-norms for intergroup negotiation or conflict when minority youth deviate from majority group norms. Future research could use daily diaries or panel surveys to examine longitudinally when minorities align their acculturation-orientations over time, and when they resist majority group norms, or converge around distinct minority group norms. In addition, longitudinal social network data could map the flows of social influence in networked social interactions that give rise to evolving acculturation-norms in diverse settings. Finally, understanding the micro-dynamics of normative fit in diverse peer groups seems essential from an applied angle to promote or amplify acculturation-norms that support integration and thus enable minority inclusion and success.

Conclusion

Looking back at where we started our review, most evidence for Berry's integration hypothesis is restricted to an individual-difference approach to acculturation-orientations and adaptation. Such an individualistic approach seems to assume that immigrant minorities mainly experience positive intergroup contact with the majority society; and that sympathetic institutional ideologies and supportive group norms are already in place in most schools. Given that immigration and integration have become deeply divisive issues in many societies the contextual affordances that make individual integration a psychologically sustainable and potentially successful pathway for individual members of minority groups cannot be taken for granted, however. Our current findings suggest much scope for schools as institutional actors, and for teachers as diversity managers on the ground, to foster more inclusive and more enabling intergroup interactions, policies and norms. We hope that this review may help boost an emerging stream of acculturation studies that pioneer truly contextual and interactive approaches to the study of co-evolving acculturation-orientations across a wider range of naturalistic intergroup contexts.

Funding

This work was supported by The Research Foundation-Flanders (Fons Wetenschappelijk Onderzoek-FWO G.0747.13) and The Advanced Research Collaborative (ARC) Distinguished Visiting Fellowship the Graduate Center CUNY.

References

Allport, G. W. (1954). *The nature of prejudice*. Reading, MA: Addison-Wesley.
Appel, M., Weber, S., & Kronberger, N. (2015). The influence of stereotype threat on immigrants: Review and meta-analysis. *Frontiers in Psychology*, 6, 900.
Arends-Tóth, J., & van de Vijver, J. R. (2006). Assessment of psychological acculturation. In D. L. Sam & J. W. Berry (Eds.), *The Cambridge handbook of acculturation psychology* (pp. 142–160). New York: Cambridge University Press.
Aronson, B., & Laughter, J. (2016). The theory and practice of culturally relevant education: A synthesis of research across content areas. *Review of Educational Research*, 86(1), 163–206.
Asendorpf, J. B., & Motti-Stefanidi, F. (2017). A longitudinal study of immigrants' peer acceptance and rejection: Immigrant status, immigrant composition of the classroom, and acculturation. *Cultural Diversity & Ethnic Minority Psychology*, 23 (4), 486–498.

Baysu, G. (2011). *An intergroup perspective on school success: Turkish & Moroccan minorities in Western Europe*. Doctoral dissertation: KU Leuven

Baysu, G., Celeste, L., Brown, R., Verschueren, K., & Phalet, K. (2016). Minority adolescents in ethnically diverse schools: Perceptions of equal treatment buffer threat effects. *Child Development, 87*(5), 1352–1366.

Baysu, G., & de Valk, H. (2012). Navigating the school system in Sweden, Belgium, Austria and Germany: School segregation and second generation school trajectories. *Ethnicities, 12*(6), 776–799.

Baysu, G., & Phalet, K. (2012). Staying on or dropping out: The role of the school environment in minority and non-minority school careers. *Teachers College Record, 114*(5), 1–25.

Baysu, G., & Phalet, K. (2019). The up- and downside of dual identity: Identity-threat and minority performance. *Journal of Social Issues, 75*(2), 568–591.

Baysu, G., Phalet, K., & Brown, R. (2011). Dual identity as a two edged sword: Identity threat and minority school performance. *Social Psychology Quarterly, 74* (2), 121–143.

Baysu, G., Phalet, K., & Brown, R. (2014). Relative group size and minority school success: The role of intergroup friendship and discrimination experiences. *British Journal of Social Psychology, 53*(2), 328–349.

Benner, A. D., & Kim, S. Y. (2009). Experiences of discrimination among Chinese-American adolescents and the consequences for socioemotional and academic development. *Developmental Psychology, 45*(6), 1682–1694.

Berry, J. W. (1980). Acculturation as varieties of adaptation. In A. M. Padilla (Ed.), *Acculturation: Theory, models, and some new findings* (pp. 9–25). Boulder, CO: Westview.

Berry, J. W. (1997). Immigration, acculturation, adaptation. *Applied Psychology: An International Review, 46*(1), 5–68.

Berry, J. W., Phinney, J. S., Sam, D. L., & Vedder, P. (2006). *Immigrant youth in cultural transition: Acculturation, identity and adaptation across national contexts.* Mahwah, NJ: Lawrence Erlbaum.

Berry, J. W., & Sabatier, C. (2010). Acculturation, discrimination, and adaptation among second generation immigrant youth in Montreal and Paris. *International Journal of Intercultural Relations, 34*(3), 191–207.

Bornstein, M. H. (2017). The specificity principle in acculturation science. *Perspectives on Psychological Science, 12*(1), 3–45.

Bourhis, R. Y., Moise, L. C., Perreault, S., & Senecal, S. (1997). Towards an interactive acculturation model: A social psychological approach. *International Journal of Psychology, 32*(6), 369–389.

Brown, C. S., & Chu, H. (2012). Discrimination, ethnic identity, and academic outcomes of Mexican immigrant children: The importance of school context. *Child Development, 83*(5), 1477–1485.

Brown, R., Baysu, G., Cameron, L., Nigbur, D., Rutland, A., Watters, C., ... Landau, A. (2013). Acculturation attitudes and social adjustment in British South Asian children: A longitudinal study. *Personality and Social Psychology Bulletin, 39*(12), 1656–1667.

Brown, R., & Hewstone, M. (2005). An integrative theory of intergroup contact. *Advances in Experimental Social Psychology, 37*, 255–343.

Brown, R., & Zagefka, H. (2011). The dynamics of acculturation: An intergroup perspective. *Advances in Experimental Social Psychology, 44*, 129–184.

Byrd, C. M., & Andrews, D. J. C. (2016). Variations in students' perceived reasons for, sources of, and forms of in-school discrimination: A latent class analysis. *Journal of School Psychology, 57,* 1–14.

Celeste, L., Baysu, G., Phalet, K., Meeussen, L., & Kende, J. (2019). Can school diversity policies reduce belonging and achievement gaps between minority and majority students? Multiculturalism, colorblindness and assimilationism assessed. *Personality and Social Psychology Bulletin, 45*(11), 1603–1618.

Celeste, L., Meeussen, L., Verschueren, K., & Phalet, K. (2016). Minority acculturation and peer rejection: Costs of acculturation misfit with peer-group norms. *British Journal of Social Psychology, 55,* 544–563.

CILS4EU (2016). Children of Immigrants Longitudinal Survey in Four European Countries. Technical Report. Wave 1 – 2010/2011, v1.2.0. Mannheim: Mannheim University.

Cook, J. E., Purdie-Vaughns, V., Garcia, J., & Cohen, G. L. (2012). Chronic threat and contingent belonging: Protective benefits of values affirmation on identity development. *Journal of Personality and Social Psychology, 102*(3), 479–496.

D'hondt, F., Eccles, J. S., Van Houtte, M., & Stevens, P. A. (2016). Perceived ethnic discrimination by teachers and ethnic minority students' academic futility. *Journal of Youth and Adolescence, 45*(6), 1075–1089.

Davies, K., & Aron, A. (2016). Friendship development and intergroup attitudes: The role of interpersonal and intergroup friendship processes. *Journal of Social Issues, 72*(3), 489.

Derks, B., van Laar, C., & Ellemers, N. (2007). The beneficial effects of social identity protection on the performance motivation of members of devalued groups. *Social Issues and Policy Review, 1*(1), 217–256.

Dimitrova, R., Chasiotis, A., & van de Vijver, F. (2016). Adjustment outcomes of immigrant children and youth in Europe. *European Psychologist, 21,* 150–162.

Doucerain, M., Dere, J., & Ryder, A. G. (2013). Travels in hyper-diversity: Multiculturalism and the contextual assessment of acculturation. *International Journal of Intercultural Relations, 37*(6), 686–699.

Eccles, J. S., Wong, C. A., & Peck, S. C. (2006). Ethnicity as a social context for the development of African-American adolescents. *Journal of School Psychology, 44,* 407–426. doi:10.1016/j.jsp.2006.04.001

Ellemers, N., Spears, R., & Doosje, B. (2002). Self and social identity. *Annual Review of Psychology, 53,* 161–186.

Eurostat. (2016).Migration and migrant population statistics. Retrieved from: http://ec.europa.eu/eurostat/statistics-explained/index.php/Migration_and_migrant_population_statistics#Migrant_population

Ferguson, G. M., Bornstein, M. H., & Pottinger, A. M. (2012). Tridimensional acculturation and adaptation among Jamaican adolescent–Mother dyads in the United States. *Child Development, 83*(5), 1486–1493.

Fleischmann, F., & Phalet, K. (2015). Identity conflict or compatibility: A comparison of Muslim minorities in five European cities. *Political Psychology, 37*(4), 445–517.

Frankenberg, E., Kupper, K., Wagner, R., & Bongard, S. (2013). Immigrant youth in Germany. *European Psychologist, 18*(3), 158–168.

Gharaei, N., Phalet, K., & Fleischmann, F. (2018). To be a real national: Perceived national fit of culturally different minority peers predicts belonging of minority youth. *Frontiers in Psychology, 9,* 1975.

Gordon, M. M. (1964). *Assimilation in American life.* New York: Oxford University.

Guimond, S., de la Sablionniere, R., & Nugier, A. (2014). Living in a multicultural world: Intergroup ideologies and the societal context of intergroup relations. *European Review of Social Pychology*, *25*(1), 142–188.

Heath, A., & Brinbaum, Y. (Eds.). (2014). *Unequal attainments*. London, UK: British Academy.

Heikamp, T., Phalet, K., Van Laar, C., & Verschueren, K. (2019). To belong or not to belong? Protecting minority engagement in the face of discrimination. *International Journal of Psychology (Forthcoming)*.

Hoti, A. H., Heinzmann, S., Müller, M., & Buholzer, A. (2017). Psychosocial adaptation and school success of Italian, Portuguese and Albanian students in Switzerland. *Journal of International Migration and Integration*, *18*(1), 85–106.

Inzlicht, M., Good, C., Levin, S., & Van Laar, C. (2006). How environments can threaten academic performance, self-knowledge, and sense of belonging. In S. Levin & C. Van Laar (Eds.), *Stigma and group inequality: Social psychological perspectives* (pp. 129–150). Mahwah, NJ: Erlbaum.

Juang, L. P., Simpson, J. A., Lee, R. M., Rothman, A. J., Titzmann, P. F., Schachner, M. K., & Betsch, C. (2018). Using attachment and relational perspectives to understand adaptation and resilience among immigrant and refugee youth. *American Psychologist*, *73*(6), 797–811.

Kende, J., Phalet, K., Van Den Noortgate, W., Kara, A., & Fischer, R. (2018). Equality revisited: A cultural meta-analysis of intergroup contact and prejudice. *Social Psychological and Personality Science*, *9*(8), 887–895.

Levy, D. J., Heissel, J. A., Richeson, J. A., & Adam, E. K. (2016). Psychological and biological responses to race-based social stress as pathways to disparities in educational outcomes. *American Psychologist*, *71*(6), 455.

Liebkind, K. (2006). Ethnic identity and acculturation. In D. L. Sam & J. W. Berry (Eds.), *The Cambridge handbook of acculturation psychology* (pp. 78–96). New York: Cambridge University Press.

Makarova, E., & Birman, D. (2015). Cultural transition and academic achievement of students from ethnic minority backgrounds: A content analysis of empirical research on acculturation. *Educational Research*, *57*(3), 305–330.

Meeussen, L., Agneessens, F., Delvaux, E., & Phalet, K. (2017). Ethnic diversity and value sharing: A longitudinal network perspective on interactive group processes. *British Journal of Social Psychology*, *57*(2), 428–447.

Mesquita, B., De Leersnyder, J., & Jasini, A. (2017). The cultural psychology of acculturation. In S. Kitayama & D. Cohen (Eds.), *The handbook of cultural psychology* (pp. 502–535). New York, NY: Guilford Press.

Motti-Stefanidi, F., & Masten, A. S. (2013). School success and school engagement of immigrant children and adolescents. *European Psychologist*, *18*, 126–135.

Navas, M., Rojas, A. J., Garcia, M., & Pumares, P. (2007). Acculturation strategies and attitudes according to the Relative Acculturation Extended Model (RAEM). *International Journal of Intercultural Relations*, *31*, 67–86.

Nguyen, A. M. D., & Benet-Martínez, V. (2013). Biculturalism and adjustment: A meta-analysis. *Journal of Cross-Cultural Psychology*, *44*(1), 122–159.

O'Neel, C. G., & Fuligni, A. (2013). A longitudinal study of school belonging and academic motivation across high school. *Child Development*, *84*(2), 678–692.

Özdemir, S. B., & Stattin, H. (2014). Why and when is ethnic harassment a risk for immigrant adolescents' school adjustment? Understanding the processes and conditions. *Journal of Youth and Adolescence*, *43*(8), 1252–1265.

OECD. (2015). *Immigrant students at school: Easing the journey towards integration, OECD Reviews of Migrant Education*. Paris: OECD Publishing. doi:10.1787/9789264249509-en

Phalet, K., Baysu, G., & van Acker, K. (2015). Ethnicity and migration in Europe. In J. Wright & X. Chryssochoou (Eds.), *International encyclopaedia of the social and behavioral sciences* (2nd ed.). Elsevier. Retrieved from http://www.sciencedirect.com/science/article/pii/B9780080970868240403

Phalet, K., Hillekens, J., & Fleischmann, F. (2018). Religious identity and acculturation of immigrant minority youth: Towards a contextual and developmental approach. *European Psychologist, 23*, 32–43.

Phinney, J. S. (2003). Ethnic Identity and acculturation. In K. M. Chun (Ed.), *Acculturation: Advances in theory, measurement and applied research* (pp. 63–81). Washington DC: APA.

Purdie-Vaughns, V., Steele, C. M., Davies, P. G., Ditlmann, R., & Randall-Crosby, J. (2008). Social identity contingencies: How diversity cues signal threat or safety for African Americans in mainstream institutions. *Journal of Personality and Social Psychology, 94*, 615–630.

Rattan, A., & Ambady, N. (2013). Diversity ideologies and intergroup relations: An examination of colorblindness and multiculturalism. *European Journal of Social Psychology, 43*(1), 12–21.

Rutland, A., Cameron, L., Jugert, P., Nigbur, D., Brown, R., Watters, C., & Touze, D. (2012). Group identity and peer relations: A longitudinal study of group identity, perceived peer acceptance and friendships amongst ethnic minority English children. *British Journal of Developmental Psychology, 30*, 283–302.

Ryder, A. G., Alden, L. E., & Paulhus, D. L. (2000). Is acculturation unidimensional or bidimensional? A head-to-head comparison in the prediction of personality, self-identity, and adjustment. *Journal of Personality and Social Psychology, 79*(1), 49–65.

Sam, D. L., & Berry, J. W. (2010). Acculturation: When individuals and groups of different cultural backgrounds meet. *Perspectives on Psychological Science, 5*(4), 472–481.

Santiago, C. D., Gudiño, O. G., Baweja, S., & Nadeem, E. (2014). Academic achievement among immigrant and US-born Latino adolescents: Associations with cultural, family, and acculturation factors. *Journal of Community Psychology, 42*(6), 735–747.

Schachner, M., Noack, P., Van de Vijver, F., & Eckstein, K. (2016). Cultural diversity climate and psychological adjustment at school: Equality and inclusion versus cultural pluralism. *Child Development, 87*(4), 1175–1191.

Schachner, M. K., Juang, L. P., Moffit, U., & Van de Vijver, F. J. R. (2018). Schools as acculturation and developmental contexts for youth of immigrant and refugee background. *European Psychologist, 23*, 44–56.

Schachner, M. K., Van de Vijver, F. J. R., & Noack, P. (2017). Contextual conditions for acculturation and adjustment of adolescent immigrants: Integrating theory and findings. *Online Readings in Psychology and Culture, 8*, 1.

Schotte, K., Stanat, P., & Edele, A. (2018). Is integration always most adaptive? The role of cultural identification in academic achievement and in psychological adjustment of immigrant students in Germany. *Journal of Youth and Adolescence, 47*(1), 16–37.

Schwartz, S. J., & Zamboanga, B. L. (2008). Testing Berry's model of acculturation: A confirmatory latent class approach. *Cultural Diversity & Ethnic Minority Psychology, 14*(4), 275–285.

Schwarzenthal, M., Schachner, M., Juang, L., & Van de Vijver, F. (2019). Reaping the benefits of cultural diversity: Classroom cultural diversity climate and students' intercultural competence. *European Journal of Social Psychology.* doi:10.1002/ejsp.2617

Shook, N. J., & Fazio, R. H. (2008). Roommate relationships: A comparison of interracial and same-race living situations. *Group Processes and Intergroup Relations, 11*, 425–437.

Skinner, E. A., Kindermann, T. A., & Furrer, C. J. (2008). A motivational perspective on engagement and disaffection: Conceptualization and assessment of children's behavioral and emotional participation in academic activities in the classroom. *Educational and Psychological Measurement, 69*, 493–525.

Spiegler, O., Sonnenberg, K., Fassbender, I., Kohl, K., & Leyendecker, B. (2018). Ethnic and national identity development and school adjustment: A longitudinal study with Turkish-immigrant origin children. *Journal of Cross-Cultural Psychology, 49*(7), 1009–1026.

Steele, C. M., Spencer, S. J., & Aronson, J. (2002). Contending with group image: The psychology of stereotype and social identity threat. *Advances in Experimental Social Psychology, 34*, 379–440.

Suinn, R. M. (2010). Reviewing acculturation and Asian Americans: How acculturation affects health, adjustment, school achievement, and counseling. *Asian American Journal of Psychology, 1*(1), 5.

Tajfel, H., & Turner, J. (1986). Social identity theory of intergroup behavior. In S. Worchel & W. G. Austin (Eds.), *Psychology of intergroup relations* (pp. 7–24). Chicago: Nelson-Hall.

Thapa, A., Cohen, J., Guffey, S., & Higgins-D'Alessandro, A. (2013). A review of school climate research. *Review of Educational Research, 83*(3), 357–385.

Thijs, J., & Verkuyten, M. (2014). School ethnic diversity and students' interethnic relations. *British Journal of Educational Psychology, 84*(1), 1–21.

Titzmann, P. F., & Jugert, P. (2015). Acculturation in context: The moderating effects of immigrant and native peer orientations on the acculturation experiences of immigrants. *Journal of Youth and Adolescence, 44*, 2079–2094.

Tropp, L. R., & Pettigrew, T. F. (2005). Relationships between inter group contact and prejudice among minority and majority status groups. *Psychological Science, 16*(12), 951–995.

Umaña-Taylor, A. J., Quintana, S. M., Lee, R. M., Cross, W. E., Rivas-Drake, D., Schwartz, S. J., ... Seaton, E. (2014). Ethnic and racial identity during adolescence and into young adulthood: An integrated conceptualization. *Child Development, 85*(1), 21–39.

United Nations (UN) (2015). International Migration Report 2015: Highlights (ST/ESA/SER.A/375). Retrieved from https://www.un.org/en/development/desa/population/migration/publications/migrationreport/docs/MigrationReport2015_Highlights.pdf

Van Acker, K., Phalet, K., De Leersnyder, J., & Mesquita, B. (2014). Do "they" threaten "us" or do "we" disrespect "them"? Majority perceptions of intergroup relations and everyday contacts with immigrant minorities. *Group Processes and Intergroup Relations, 17*(5), 617–628.

Van Acker, K., & Vanbeselaere, N. (2012). Heritage culture maintenance precludes host culture adoption and vice versa: Flemings' perceptions of Turks' acculturation behavior. *Group Processes & Intergroup Relations, 15*(1), 133–145.

Van De Vijver, F. J., & Phalet, K. (2004). Assessment in multicultural groups: The role of acculturation. *Applied Psychology, 53*(2), 215–236.

Van de Vijver, F. J. R., Helms-Lorenz, M., & Feltzer, M. J. A. (1999). Acculturation and cognitive performance of migrant children in the Netherlands. *International Journal of Psychology, 34*(3), 149–162.

Verkuyten, M., & Thijs, J. (2013). Multicultural education and inter-ethnic attitudes. *European Psychologist, 18*, 179–190.

Verkuyten, M., Thijs, J., & Gharaei, N. (2019). Discrimination and academic (dis) engagement of ethnic-racialminority-students: A social-identity threat perspective. *Social Psychology of Education.* doi:10.007/51128-018-09476-0

Walton, G. M., & Cohen, G. L. (2007). A question of belonging: Race, social fit, and achievement. *Journal of Personality and Social Psychology, 92*, 82–96.

Ward, C., & Kennedy, A. (1993). Acculturation strategies, psychological adjustment, and sociocultural competence during cross-cultural transitions. *International Journal of Intercultural Relations, 18*, 329–343.

Weber, S., Appel, M., & Kronberger, N. (2015). Stereotype threat and the cognitive performance of adolescent immigrants: The role of cultural identity strength. *Contemporary Educational Psychology, 42*, 71–81.

Whaley, A. L. (1998). Issues of validity in empirical tests of stereotype threat theory. *American Psychologist, 53*, 679–680.

Wölfer, R., & Hewstone, M. (2017). Beyond dyadic interactions: 10 reasons to use social network analysis in intergroup contact research. *British Journal of Social Psychology, 56*(3), 609–617.

Zirkel, S. (2008). The influence of multicultural educational practices on student outcomes and intergroup relations. *Teachers College Record, 110*(6), 1147–1181.

ARTICLE

It's not just "us" versus "them": Moving beyond binary perspectives on intergroup processes

John Dixon[a], Guy Elcheroth[b], Philippa Kerr[c], John Drury[d], Mai Al Bzour[e,f], Emina Subašić[g], Kevin Durrheim[h] and Eva G. T. Green[b]

[a]School of Psychology, Open University, Milton Keynes, UK; [b]Life Course and Social Inequality Research Center (LINES), University of Lausanne, Lausanne, Switzerland; [c]Higher Education and Human Development Research Programme, University of the Free State, Bloemfontein, South Africa; [d]School of Psychology, University of Sussex, Brighton, UK; [e]University of Lausanne, Life Course and Social Inequality Research Center, Switzerland; [f]Department of Social and Behavioral Science, University of Birzeit, Lebanon; [g]School of Psychology, University of Newcastle, Australia; [h]School of Applied Human Sciences, University of KwaZulu-Natal, Durban, South Africa

ABSTRACT
The social psychology of intergroup relations has emerged largely from studies of how one group of people (e.g., whites) think and feel about another (e.g., blacks). By reducing the social world to binary categories, this approach has provided an effective and efficient methodological framework. However, it has also obscured important features of social relations in historically divided societies. This paper highlights the importance of investigating intergroup relationships involving more than two groups and of exploring not only their psychological but also their political significance. Exemplifying this argument, we discuss the conditions under which members of disadvantaged groups either dissolve into internecine competition or unite to challenge the status quo, highlighting the role of complex forms of social comparison, identification, contact, and third-party support for collective action. Binary conceptualizations of intergroup relations, we conclude, are the product of specific sociohistorical practices rather than a natural starting point for psychological research.

ARTICLE HISTORY Received 6 April 2019; Accepted 7 February 2020

KEYWORDS Intergroup relations; social comparison; contact; social change; divide and rule

Intergroup relations refer to relations between *two or more* groups and their members. Whenever individuals belonging to one group interact, collectively or individually, with another group or its members in terms of their group identifications, we have an instance of intergroup behaviour. (Sherif, 1962, p. 12, our emphasis).

In his classic definition of intergroup behaviour, Sherif emphasised the importance of distinguishing between individuals who are interacting on

CONTACT John Dixon ✉ john.dixon@open.ac.uk 🏫 School of Psychology, Open University, Walton Hall, Milton Keynes MK7 6AA, UK

© 2020 European Association of Social Psychology

an interpersonal level, as discrete personalities, and individuals who are interacting as group members, in terms of their group identities. In so doing, he laid the foundations for a renaissance of psychological work that was to "rediscover" the social group (Turner et al., 1987), inspiring important new perspectives on processes such as stereotyping, prejudice, attraction, social influence, and leadership (e.g., Haslam et al., 2011; Oakes et al., 1994; Turner, 1991). As the phrase italicised in the above quotation indicates, Sherif also recognised that intergroup relations were not necessarily just a matter of "us" versus "them". They could involve more complex patterns of intergroup dynamics and, presumably, more variegated forms of group identification and intergroup behaviour. It is perhaps revealing, however, that in the closing sentence of his classic definition Sherif defaulted to a simpler binary conception. That is, he limited intergroup relations to a question of how individuals belonging to "one group" interact with those belonging to "another group".

In this paper, we argue that this kind of binary conception of intergroup relations has also become the default unit of analysis for social psychology and that, whatever advantages it has conferred, it has also obscured some fundamental features of social relations in historically divided and unequal societies. By way of contrast, we highlight the importance of (re)discovering the *complex relationality* of intergroup processes that involve more than two groups. Failure to do so, we argue, impoverishes our discipline's capacity to understand the dynamics of conflict, inequality and social change.

In the opening sections of the paper, we discuss the nature, strengths and inherent limitations of a binary perspective on intergroup dynamics. Here we use as an example the legacy of colonial "divide and rule" structures, which continue to shape intergroup relations in many "post-colonial" societies. Next, we outline some emerging strands of psychological research that have already begun to transcend such limitations by acknowledging: (1) the multi- group patterning of racial policy attitudes in complexly stratified societies (Dixon, Durrheim et al., 2017); (2) the significance of "intermediary" status (Caricati, 2018) groups in promoting or undermining social change; (3) the complex effects of intergroup contact experiences on both vertical and horizontal relations of political solidarity between historically advantaged and disadvantaged groups (Dixon, Cakal et al., 2017); and (4) the role of emergent social identities and third party interventions in shaping collective action (Drury & Reiche 2000; Klavina & van Zomeren, 2018; Subašić et al., 2008). We focus on the implications of such work for understanding the transformation of power relations and social inequality in historically divided societies. Our paper concludes by arguing that the self-evident nature of intergroup binaries should be treated as a problem to be explained rather than a pre-given starting point for psychological research. This requires us to adopt a dynamic, contextual and historical approach to understanding their emergence and conditions of reproduction. We also outline some integrative themes of our review and make suggestions for future research.

The two-group perspective on intergroup relations: nature, strengths, and limitations

Our argument is that most psychological research on intergroup relations has framed such relations in binary terms, and this claim needs to be unpacked and substantiated. In the vast majority of studies, we would contend, researchers have focused on pairs of groups whose relevance to relations in particular contexts have come to appear self-evident or even inevitable: white versus African-Americans (the US), Arabs versus Jews (Israel and Palestine), Catholics versus Protestants (Northern Ireland), and so on. In many other studies, researchers have adopted more generic binary categories, as captured by terminology such as minority-majority, ingroup-outgroup, immigrant-host, and high status-low status groups.

In several respects, the two-group perspective on intergroup relations has served the discipline well. In many historically divided societies, for example, binary oppositions have indeed acquired an overwhelming social, psychological and political salience: one thinks of the profound significance of sectarian identities in Northern Ireland or ethnic identities in the so-called "Arab-Israeli" conflict. Although we will ultimately argue that this significance is as much problem to be explained as a pre-given starting point for psychological research, it is undeniable that intergroup conflicts often do crystallise around stark "us" versus "them" dichotomies.

In addition, the two-group perspective has offered the (considerable) advantage of conceptual and methodological simplicity. It has facilitated the development of theoretical models that are at once parsimonious and of ostensibly general relevance to the explanation of intergroup relations across varying social contexts (e.g., between "minorities" and "majorities"). Moreover, by decomposing social relations into their most elementary constituents, such models have also expressed intergroup dynamics in their most accessible, lucid and researchable form. They have thus enabled the development of experimental designs that make economical use of human participants and other resources.

Perhaps for these reasons, the two-group perspective has also underpinned the vast majority of canonical experiments on intergroup relations in psychology. In their classic "Summer camp studies", for instance, Sherif et al. (1961) conducted arguably the most brilliant and widely cited experiment on groups locked into violent, binary, conflict, laying the foundations for Realistic Conflict Theory. The struggle between the "Rattlers" and the "Eagles" has become a mainstay of our field's textbooks. Similarly, extending

Sherif's et al.'s work, Tajfel and colleagues famously showed how dividing participants into arbitrary pairs of categories was sufficient to engender intergroup bias (e.g., Tajfel et al., 1971). The behaviours of those divided in terms of their supposed preferences for the artists Klee or Kandinksy inspired the development of Social Identity Theory (Tajfel & Turner, 1979), which powerfully demonstrated how intergroup discrimination may result from categorisation and differentiation processes, generally involving members of dichotomous social categories. More recently, work on implicit prejudices has been built around methodological paradigms that likewise rely on a two-group framework. The Implicit Association Test, which has informed several hundred experiments on the "hidden biases of good people" (Greenwald & Banaji, 2013), investigates how binary category distinctions such as "Black" versus "white" invoke automatic associations with qualities such as "good" and "bad". In sum, in each of these classic methodological paradigms – as in the vast majority of psychological research – an "us" versus "them" conception of intergroup processes has become the baseline unit of analysis, often without critical reflection on its potential limitations.

What are those potential limitations? To begin with, the majority of intergroup contexts involve multiple social groups – whether co-present, imagined or implied – implicated in multiple kinds of relationships. As such, the capacity of research that decomposes intergroup relations into dyadic units to explain more complicated webs of collective relations remains unclear. In many areas of research, we simply lack meaningful evidence on this issue; in other areas, the available evidence raises questions.

As an example, consider Hartstone and Augoustinos (1995) variation on the minimal group paradigm. In Experiment 1, which employed a sample of 31 secondary school pupils, they simply replicated Tajfel et al.'s (1971) classic two-group experiment and reported patterns of ingroup bias comparable to previous minimal group experiments. In Experiment 2, which employed a sample of 41 pupils drawn from the same school, they followed a similar methodology, but used three rather than two groups. They also manipulated power relations between these three groups, with status differences between group members being cued in one three-group condition and not cued another. Their results showed that only the two-group condition elicited significant displays of ingroup bias; in the three-group condition, the majority of participants did not display such bias. Moreover, manipulating the status of the three groups did not appear to moderate this effect. Interpreting their results, Harstone and Augoustinos highlighted, among other factors, the unique cultural significance of dichotomous categorisations, which tend to cue more readily competitive norms and behaviours, thereby fostering "us" versus "them" forms of differentiation.

In a comparable programme of research, Spielman (2000) employed a minimal group methodology using both two and three-group conditions and working with samples of young kindergarten students (n = 113; Study 1) and undergraduate students (n = 64; Study 2). In both studies, he also manipulated intergroup competition by providing participants with competitive primes in some experimental conditions and neutral or no primes in others. In a nuanced set of results, Spielman found that the kindergarten children displayed no ingroup bias in *either* two group or three group conditions unless competition was primed. By contrast, undergraduate students generally displayed bias in the two-group condition; however, again, they displayed bias in the three-group condition only when competitive norms were primed. In sum, these findings suggest that the supposedly "basic" pattern of intergroup bias revealed by minimal group research may be shaped not only by participant age and cultural experience, but also – and more directly relevant to our argument here – by the culturally specific significance of dichotomous forms of categorisation.

This kind of complexity was, of course, also anticipated in earlier work. When Deschamps and Doise (1978) made salient two different binaries in the same situation, for example, they observed that intergroup bias was neutralised by the resulting crossed category memberships. Subsequent studies replicated this finding and highlighted that bias created in two-group situations is often diminished when memberships of comparable social significance are crossed (e.g., Urban & Miller, 1998). Along similar lines, more recent work has shown that "us" versus "them" distinctions are often complicated by multiple (Crisp & Hewstone, 2007), complex (Brewer & Pierce, 2005) and superordinate (Gaertner & Dovidio, 2000) patterns of identification, which in turn shape the nature of intergroup cognitions, emotions and behaviours in ways that may be irreducible to simpler dyadic processes (see also Levy et al., 2017). In sum, experimental scenarios based on binary category distinctions and relationships highlight the effectiveness of binary divisions in fuelling intergroup antagonism, but also show that these results do not necessarily generalise to more complex forms of intergroup relations.

These insights from the experimental laboratory raise two questions of broader relevance: First, how is the cultural significance of binary categories exploited and nurtured in real world conflicts? Second, what are the associated pitfalls of using such binaries as a pre-given conceptual grid to analyse these conflicts? Critical to answering both questions is research on how key conflict agents employ the cultural significance of binaries to mobilise support for their own cause, often by singling out the binaries that make the course of action they are promoting appear legitimate or natural.

To clarify how such "entrepreneurs of identity" actively invoke categorical oppositions, Elcheroth and Reicher (2014) conducted a systematic analysis of

106 speeches made in the Scottish parliament, shortly before the UK took part in the US-led invasion of Iraq in 2003 and in its immediate aftermath. Their findings showed that while binary oppositions were discernible in all speeches, the conflict was defined in very different terms depending on how it was defined, when, and by whom. On the one hand, supporters of the invasion constructed their argument around an opposition between the world's democrats and (isolated) autocrats, which ultimately evolved into an opposition between the whole (democratic) world and a single tyrannical figure, Saddam Hussein. On the other hand, opponents to the invasion divided the world into dominant and subordinate groups: "at the start of the debate, English warmongers dragging the Scots into conflict; later, social elites against ordinary people; or, a hegemonic US/British West against Eastern/Arabic peoples" (p.10–11). Interestingly, Elcherot and Reicher (2014) argue, the anti-war camp invested more rhetorical efforts than the pro-war camp in the active construction of intergroup binaries; it also displayed more collective consistency in its categorical constructions and adapted them more flexibly to changing circumstances. In sum, their findings highlighted not only how binary oppositions pervade political discourse about conflict but also, and more important, how any given binary typically forms only one element in a larger system of contested and evolving categorical constructions. It follows that whenever researchers focus attention on a particular two-group dynamic, they are also at risk of perpetuating a particular window on the nature and origins of intergroup conflict.

Kerr et al. (2017) field study of xenophobic violence in a South African farming town avoids this pitfall, demonstrating how intergroup dynamics obfuscated by a binary grid may be revealed when a multi-group perspective is adopted. Their research focused on an event of anti–immigrant violence in which Zimbabwean farm workers were violently evicted from their homes by their black South African neighbours. Their methodology consisted of two rounds of interview-based fieldwork conducted in 2009 and in 2012–2013 respectively. Kerr and four research assistants conducted 65 interviews with various townspeople, including farm workers, farm owners, labour brokers, unemployed people, other workers, and local government officials.

This fieldwork produced some challenging findings. First, whereas many academic accounts of xenophobic violence in South Africa have prioritised the two-way relationship between perpetrators/citizens and victims/immigrants, close analysis of participants' own accounts of their relationships with other groups in the town revealed a more complex array of relationships were implicated in the Zimbabweans' eviction: that is, relationships between Zimbabwean workers and South African workers, Zimbabwean workers and local white farmers, and South African workers and white farmers. For instance, all groups were aware of the "good" (if highly unequal) relationship between white farmers and Zimbabwean workers, but they judged this "good" relationship as legitimate or illegitimate according to different criteria. Farmers and Zimbabwean workers argued that the relationship they enjoyed was completely legitimate as Zimbabweans were more reliable, compliant and efficient workers. For many South African farm workers, however, the recent arrival of migrant Zimbabwean workers (in the early 2000s), and farmers' apparent shift of favour to this new group, was seen as an unwanted interference in their own long-standing economic relationship with farmers. Many South Africans workers constructed *themselves* as the aggrieved party – initially exploited, and now abandoned, by farmers. In the process, Zimbabweans were perceived as the "favoured" or "advantaged" group of workers, and this legitimated forcible attempts to make them leave the area. In other words, what seemed initially to be a simple expression of local versus foreign "xenophobia" ultimately revealed a series of intersecting and nested conflicts, implicating relations of race, class and nationality and revealing complex " ... patterns of allegiance, collusion, solidarity, and resistance that seldom feature in social psychological work" (Kerr et al., 2017, p. 15).

The limitations of treating complex forms of intergroup relations as binaries are arguably illustrated even more starkly within societies where policies of "divide and rule" (cf. Christopher, 1988) have been systematically implemented during their colonial past. The underlying logic of such policies, in effect, displays an intuitive grasp of intergroup processes that social psychologists have often underplayed. This logic is captured in Figure 1 panel (a), while panel (b) captures some countervailing processes through which members of different historically disadvantaged communities may build political solidarity.

To use an iconic example: the apartheid system in South Africa installed material and status divisions not only between "whites" and "non-whites", but also between all four of the officially classified population groups – "whites", "blacks", "coloureds" and "Indians". From the outset, the legal segregation of residential, educational, social and occupational spaces was designed to prevent contact between these varying racial groups. Legislation such as the Group Areas Act of 1950 was in effect designed to dismantle *multi*racial neighbourhoods in cities such as Cape Town and Durban (e.g., see Kuper et al., 1958; Western, 1981; see Figure 2 below). Practices of segregation were also harnessed as a tool to widen cultural and linguistic divisions between sub-groups of black Africans in the workplace, pre-empting processes of unionisation in industries such as mining (e.g., see Crush, 1992). At the same time, policies granting concessionary privileges to some disadvantaged groups but not others – such as the so-called 'Coloured Labour Preference Policy'[1] – again widened the gap between communities who were common victims of Apartheid. They effectively created *hierarchies of*

---

[1]Formally instituted by the nationalist government in 1955, this policy originated in a longer historical process through which the white ruling class sought " ... to deflect the challenge of a mass opposition against the state." (Goldin, 1984, p. 112). In effect, it fostered and protected employment opportunities for "Coloured" workers, primarily in the Western Cape region, whilst denying such opportunities to "black Africans", who were subject to policies of influx control and deportation.

(a) Divide and Rule

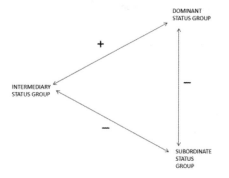

(b) Unite and resist

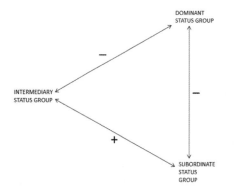

Figure 1. Intergroup attitudes and political solidarity between historically divided communities.

Note: In panel (a) in this figure the signs – and + indicate the broad pattern of intergroup attitude valences that "divide and rule" systems are generally designed to encourage. In panel (b), the signs – and + indicate the broad pattern of intergroup attitude valences under which subordinate groups are generally predisposed to act together to challenge the status quo.

subordination in which groups became embedded in a positional matrix of power relations that was irreducible to the dynamics of white versus black segregation and that arguably continues to find expression in local "race relations" (Adhikari, 2006). In sum, as Dixon et al. (2015, p. 578) observe,

> ... apartheid was based on a 'divide and rule' strategy that sought to pre-empt the formation of seditious allegiances. This strategy was accomplished through numerous tactics: from the selective conferral of economic privileges to the

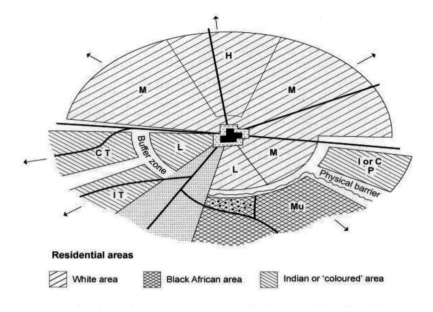

Figure 2. The Apartheid city.
Note: Economic status: H: High; M: Middle; L: Low; Mu: Municipal townships; T: Township; P: Privately developed; C: Coloured; I: Indian.

'preservation' of cultural differences to sponsorship of internecine violence. However, the segregation of different factions of the disadvantaged was fundamental. The apartheid authorities felt that too much contact between historically disadvantaged communities posed a risk to the system. They worried that it might enable the development of political solidarity between them.

What is true of the South African context, we would argue, is also true of many other "post-colonial" contexts. After all, colonialism is not so much a singular event as an evolving structure designed to shape a society's political future, and in many societies that structure has evolved around the problem of governing colonial subjects embedded within complex webs of intragroup and intergroup relations. As such, in "post-colonial" contexts such as Rwanda, Sri Lanka and Palestine, amongst others, a binary frame of reference provides a limited starting point for understanding either past, present or future relations between groups. In Rwanda, for example, it risks effacing the role of Belgian colonists in systematically accentuating category and status divisions between Tutsis and Hutus (e.g., via the establishment of ethnic identity documents), leaving a legacy that is now a focus of interventions to transform the society in the wake of its genocide (Moss, 2014; Moss & Vollhardt, 2016). In Sri Lanka, it risks reducing the civil war that has ravaged the island over decades to an ethnic strife between the Singhalese majority and the Tamil minority. As well as grossly simplifying the range of domestic actors and groups involved (e.g., Tamil-speaking Muslims, Indian Tamils, Christian minorities on both sides, cross-ethnic political parties and social movements), this overlooks how, historically, the conflict originated in British colonial policies of divide-and-rule, which marginalised the Singhalese and created a sense of collective grievances among the majority (De Votta, 2004). In Palestine, it risks neglecting how colonial rule effectively created and reproduced sectarian identities and citizenship criteria (Banko, 2016; Haiduc-Dale, 2013), whilst also ignoring the current third-party role of the Palestinian authority as an institutional mediator between Palestinian people and Israeli government (Albzour et al., 2019).

On a broader level, as we have barely begun to demonstrate, a binary perspective may provide a limited starting point for understanding the social psychology of intergroup relations in *any* complexly stratified society and not just in post-colonial contexts. In the next section, we discuss some areas of psychological and sociological research that have recently started to move beyond such a perspective. The aim here is to review several emerging strands of work, laying some foundations for future research on the complex relationality of intergroup dynamics in historically unequal societies.

Moving beyond a binary perspective on intergroup processes

Understanding policy attitudes in complexly stratified societies

Research on attitudes towards policies designed to tackle ethnic and racial inequality has been structured around a paradox: support for the ideal of equality has steadily grown over the past 60 years, but resistance to its concrete implementation has endured (e.g., see Dixon, Durrheim et al., 2017 for a review). Work on this "Principle-Implementation" gap (cf. Protho & Grigg, 1960) has largely focused on how, when and why members of historically advantaged groups resist interventions such as affirmative action, welfare subsidies and school desegregation, seeking to explain, for example, the stark disjunction between white Americans' " ... gradual elevation to lofty racial policy principles and their meagre support for policies designed to implement those principles (Jackman, 1996, p. 760)." Among other factors, such work has highlighted the role played by intergroup competition, symbolic and old-fashioned prejudice, and attributions about the nature of inequality in explaining why historically advantaged group members resist race-targeted policies (see Dixon, Durrheim et al., 2017).

The factors shaping the policy attitudes of historically disadvantaged communities have received considerably less attention; nevertheless, available evidence has identified some important trends. Perhaps unsurprising, black Americans show significantly higher levels of support for race-targeted policies than white Americans, a finding that may reflect the role of group interests as well as intergroup differences in beliefs about the nature, extent and causes of racial inequality (e.g., see Bobo, 2011). At the same time, the policy attitudes of black Americans display a principle-implementation gap similar to, though generally less extreme, than that of white Americans. For example, black Americans' support for the ideal of desegregated education is virtually 100%; however, their support for policies designed to accomplish that ideal has been significantly lower (e.g., see Krysan & Moberg, 2016). Historically, for instance, research on black attitudes towards school bussing programmes indicates that support has hovered between 50 and 60% (Sigelman & Welch, 1991), suggesting that a substantive minority rejected this means of achieving school desegregation. Moreover, *race preferential* policies (e.g., affirmative action), which directly confront whites' socioeconomic advantages, produce more opposition amongst black Americans than *race compensatory* policies (e.g., job training programmes), which focus on improving future opportunities (Tuch & Hughes, 1996).

According to Jackman (1994), the latter pattern reflects the inherently relational nature of policy attitudes, as expressed via subordinate group members' vigilance about how dominant group members think, feel and respond in hierarchical social systems. Supporting policies that directly challenge the status quo carries, among other risks, the threat of reprisal and potential erosion of current and future benefits. Arguably for this reason, such policies are evaluated cautiously by groups such as black Americans, who " ... learn to throw more energy into issues that keep a safer distance from core redistributive concerns." (Jackman, 1994, p. 259).

Whereas most research relevant to this theme has focused on binary relations (e.g., between whites and blacks), some emerging work has treated it as a more complex, multigroup problem. In this respect, research on the policy attitudes of intermediary status groups, such as Asian and Latino Americans in the US, is particularly revealing. Lopez and Pantoja (2004) reported that racial attitudes towards affirmative action policies in the US display a clear rank ordering: black Americans display most support, whites least, and Latinos and Asians are positioned between these two extremes. Drawing on data collected as part of the Los Angeles County Social Survey, Bobo (2000) similarly reported that racial minorities in the US, including Asians and Latinos, displayed less negative attitudes towards affirmative action than whites, particularly when interventions were perceived as benefitting their own group. However, he reported that black Americans again generally displayed least opposition to such policies. Although such effects are moderate in size, Bobo argued that they nevertheless represent an "American racial hierarchy" in terms of opposition to affirmative action policies, with group differences remaining statistically significant even when potentially associated variables such as conservatism, socioeconomic status, and individualism are controlled.

The "in betweenness" of Asian and Latino Americans' policy attitudes is at once intuitively obvious and potentially vital for understanding the dynamics of social change in complexly stratified societies. On the one hand, given the intergroup distribution of power, opportunity and resources in societies such as the US, is it surprising that intermediary status groups' attitudes towards race-targeted policies fall between the poles anchored by whites (least supportive) and blacks (most supportive)? Arguably, such attitudes reflect the underlying dynamics of intergroup competition in which intermediary groups have as much to lose as they have to gain by challenging the racial hierarchy. To maintain material privileges and avoid downwards assimilation, members of such groups may both distance themselves from those positioned "beneath" them in the racial hierarchy and treat race-targeted policies that threaten to disrupt the status quo with due caution (though see Wodtke, 2012, for a useful summary and critique of this perspective).

On the other hand, the "in betweenness" of the policy attitudes of intermediary status group members may reflect social, psychological and political dynamics that are ultimately irreducible to a simple intergroup competition model, opening up opportunities for promoting political solidarity and coalition-building. In their research on the voting patterns of Asian Americans, for instance, Kuo et al. (2014) have highlighted when and why such groups tend to favour Democrat political candidates and associated policies. To summarise a richer pattern of results, their attitude survey and experimental studies identified number of key trends. First, Asian Americans (over 70%) by and large identify as Democrats, and this trend has steadily grown over the past decade. This is perhaps surprising given their relatively strong economic status in the US, a factor that tends to correlate with support for Republicanism and related conservative social policies. Second, Asian Americans' identification as Democrats is partly explained by their experiences of racial victimisation, bearing in mind that the Democratic party has historically been associated with more tolerant and inclusive attitudes towards ethnic and racial minorities in the US. Third, this identification is also partly explained by perceptions of political solidarity with other ethnic minority groups vis à vis the white majority. That is, Asian Americans who perceive commonality with other ethnic minority groups tend to align themselves with these groups rather than with whites; as such, they tend to endorse Democrat political candidates and associated policy programmes.

In sum, work on the principle-implementation gap in public support for policies for redressing racial inequality in the US has historically focused on the attitudes of the historically advantaged community, namely white Americans. However, researchers have recently acknowledged the relational nature of such attitudes, investigating not only how binary relations (e.g., between white and black Americans) may affect policy attitudes, but also how such attitudes express more complex ethnic and racial dynamics. This shift is important not least because the establishment of political coalitions between disadvantaged communities may affect whether or not race-targeted policies such as affirmative action are implemented successfully, if at all (see also Lopez & Pantoja, 2004).

Complex social comparisons: the role of intermediary status groups in (resisting) social change

Caricati and colleagues have also sought to elucidate the intergroup attitudes and behaviours of group members who occupy an intermediary position within social hierarchies, proposing a Triadic Model of Social Stratification (see Caricati, 2018, for an overview). Drawing broadly on Social Identity Theory (Tajfel & Turner, 1979), this model emphasises the importance of ingroup identification (our sense of who *we* are), positive distinctiveness (our desire to maintain a positive collective self-image) and perceived system stability (our sense of the degree to which the current status hierarchy is secure) in determining when and why such members act in ways that shore up the social order. In so doing, it also clarifies some of the conditions under which intermediate status groups might seek to challenge the status quo.

Intermediary status groups, Caricati (2018) argues, occupy a unique position with the social hierarchy in terms of maintaining a positive social identity. On the one hand, "upwards" social comparisons with higher status groups may provoke identity threat and an associated loss of positive distinctiveness, social status and self-esteem. On the other hand, "downwards" social comparisons with lower status groups may bolster ingroup identity and distinctiveness. Given that group members are generally motivated to maintain rather than lose social status, Caricati (2018) proposes, they will generally favour downwards over upwards social comparison and this may, in turn, foster reactionary attitudes towards social change. This outcome is particularly likely when such group members perceive extant status relations to be unstable, with the resulting potential for erosion of their group's social standing. Under such conditions, the "in betweenness" of middle status group members in the social hierarchy creates "a fear of falling" (cf. Ehrenreich, 1989) and, more acutely, a "last place aversion effect" (Caricati, 2018). This may lead them to resist even forms of social change that are materially beneficial to their own group, yet also threaten to alter the intergroup status hierarchy.

In a series of experimental studies, Caricati and colleagues have sought to test empirically varying elements of their Triadic Model of Social Stratification. Examining the responses of nurses in a health care context, for example, Sollami and Caricati (2015) manipulated status relations between physicians (higher status group), nurses (intermediary status group) and health care operators (lower status group). To do so, they fostered perceptions that such relations were either stable (unlikely to change), unstable-ameliorative (likely to change in a way that improved nurses' standing) or unstable-detrimental (likely to change in a way that reduced nurses' standing). They found that nurses associated the unstable status-detrimental condition with identity threat, but that *neither* the stable nor unstable-ameliorative conditions invoked such threat. In a follow up study that used a similar design, Caricati and Sollami (2017) investigated nurses' perceptions of the legitimacy of the professional status hierarchy, a variable that has been consistently associated with systems justification. In this case, unsurprisingly, the unstable-detrimental condition produced highest levels of perceived illegitimacy and the unstable-ameliorative lowest levels. However, perhaps more interesting, in the stable status condition system legitimacy ratings were also comparatively high, arguably sustaining nurses' acceptance of the existing professional hierarchy and reducing the likelihood they develop political solidarity with other low status health care workers.

The potential effects of status stability on patterns of relations between groups embedded in triadic hierarchies have been clarified by Caricati and Moncelli (2012). Specifically, they found that when intermediate status group members believed their social status would improve in an unstable hierarchy, they espoused more negative attitudes towards high status group members. Conversely, when they believed their status would deteriorate in an unstable hierarchy, they espoused more negative attitudes towards lower status group members. In so far as such intergroup attitudes help to shape members' willingness to recognise and challenge social inequality, they again carry potential implications for achieving social change in historically unequal societies.

In sum, Caricati and colleagues' work has brought to centre stage questions that have been neglected by social psychologists. Notably, when and why do intermediary status group members either acquiesce to an established intergroup hierarchy or strive to improve their own and others' position within this hierarchy? In so doing, they have highlighted the central role of complex forms of (upwards and downwards) social comparison and identification as well as ideological beliefs about the stability of the status quo. Building on Social Identity Theory (Tajfel & Turner, 1979), they have also complicated the common sense, but potentially limiting, supposition that group interests in complexly stratified societies are purely instrumental, being designed to maximise material gain. The dynamics of social identification associated forms of social competition may play an equally important role.

Caricati and colleagues' work, however, also carries some potentially pessimistic implications for transforming social inequality. If political solidarity between intermediary and lower status groups is only likely to emerge when the former are reassured that their social status will not deteriorate during episodes of social change, which may entail unpredictable conditions of mass mobilisation, institutional reform and sometimes violent struggle, then how likely is such solidarity to emerge in practice? What social and psychological processes might encourage members of groups located at various positions in a political hegemony to abandon the presumption that they are locked in a zero-sum, struggle for status and resources? How might "us" versus "them" categorisations give way to "we" categorisations? In the next section, addressing such questions, we explore the potential role of intergroup contact in (re)configuring complex relations of political solidarity.

Intergroup contact and relations of political solidarity

The "contact hypothesis" (Allport, 1954) is often portrayed as one of social psychology's most significant contributions to improving intergroup attitudes and reducing discrimination. The empirical literature on this hypothesis now runs to several hundred studies (e.g., see Pettigrew & Tropp, 2011; Vezzali & Stathi, 2017). Many of them elaborate a deceptively simple idea: when members of conflicting groups are afforded the opportunity to experience positive interactions with one another, their prejudices decline and, by implication, wider forms of social change are promoted. We now know that under the "right" conditions (e.g., equality of status) contact is likely to improve negative attitudes and stereotypes and that this effect holds across a range of social contexts and types of intergroup relations (Pettigrew & Tropp, 2011). We know, too, that intergroup contact works primarily via its effects on positive emotions such as empathy and forgiveness and negative emotions such as threat and anxiety (e.g., Pettigrew & Tropp, 2011).

Like other areas of prejudice research, research on intergroup contact has focused mainly on transforming the attitudes and stereotypes held by historically advantaged groups. Research on the effects of contact for historically disadvantaged groups remains comparatively limited and suggests the effects of contact tend to be weaker than for advantaged groups (Tropp & Pettigrew, 2005). Research on forms of contact involving more than two groups is more limited still. That being said, work on the so-called "secondary transfer" effects of contact (Pettigrew, 2009) offers a promising line of inquiry that has begun to move the field beyond a binary conception of intergroup relations.

The concept of "secondary transfer" highlights how the social psychological impact of contact may generalise to groups not directly involved in such contact. Thus, for example, positive contact with "illegal" immigrants might improve local residents' attitudes towards other social groups, such as legal immigrants, political refugees and homeless people (see Harwood et al., 2011). Similarly, positive contact with black or Latino Americans might improve white Americans' attitudes towards other ethnic minorities (e.g., see Shook et al., 2016; Van Laar et al., 2005). Evidence suggests that such effects are not confined to reductions in prejudice (e.g., as measured using scales such as the "feeling thermometer"), but also may impact on wider political beliefs and policy attitudes. Flores (2015), for instance, reported that experiences of interacting with members of the gay or lesbian community shaped participants' acceptance of Trans-persons' rights in the United States, including policies to protect against discrimination in the workplace. Tee and Hegarty (2006) likewise reported that support for Trans-persons civil rights in the United Kingdom (e.g., the right to have medical treatment appropriate to a "new" gender) was positively associated with experiences of contact with the gay and lesbian community. Secondary transfer effects, in other words, may facilitate activism that extends beyond the social category memberships directly involved in social contact, creating wider patterns of political solidarity.

This optimistic picture is qualified, however, by some additional considerations. First, the degree to which secondary transfer effects generalise is strongly shaped by the perceived similarity of the target group "in contact" relative to potential secondary groups (Tausch et al., 2010). Indeed, there seems to be a *generalisation gradient* (Harwood et al., 2011) in that " … secondary transfer effects do not increase tolerance across the board: they are stronger for more similar groups and weaker for less similar groups" (p. 186).

Second, and perhaps more important, the secondary transfer effects of *vertical contact* between historically advantaged and disadvantaged groups on political attitudes and behaviours may, paradoxically, have both positive and negative implications for social change, particularly if we conceive contact in terms of its complex relationality. Positively, as evidenced above, such contact may promote generalised activism amongst the historically advantaged in support of a range of lower status groups (and not just those directly involved in contact). In addition, it may not only encourage members of disadvantaged groups to like the advantaged more but also, in some circumstances, also to like fellow subordinate group members more (e.g., Brylka et al., 2016). Negatively, however, the secondary transfer effects of positive vertical contact may carry some surprising and perhaps even ironic consequences for social change (cf. Dixon et al., 2012), which have been neglected by all but a handful of psychological studies.

In an experimental study, Glasford and Calcagno (2011) investigated political solidarity amongst members of two historically disadvantaged groups, namely African American and Latino communities in the US. They anticipated that experimentally priming a sense of common identity amongst a sample of Latinos (n = 41) would increase their readiness to collaborate with African Americans to improve their joint socio-political situation in the US. Their results suggested that this was indeed the case. Latino participants in a condition that primed common identification reported greater (p <.05) political solidarity (M = 5.97, SD = 1.51) than participants in either a control condition (M = 4.51, SD = .92) or in a condition that flagged Latino-African American group differences (M = 4.43, SD = 1.40). However, the effect of this common identity prime was also moderated by (triadic) contact with members of the historically advantaged white community. That is, the more intergroup contact Latinos had previously experienced with white Americans, the less effective this experimental prime was in fostering their political solidarity with African Americans. In other words, positive contact with an historically advantaged group effectively "sedated" (cf. Cakal et al., 2011) the impact of an intervention designed to foster solidarity between two historically disadvantaged communities.

Dixon, Cakal et al. (2017) reported a related set of findings, based on a cross-sectional survey conducted in India that focused on relations between Hindus, Muslims, and other lower status groups.[2] They found that contact between Muslims and other disadvantaged groups was associated with Muslims' motivation to engage in common collective action, an effect partially explained by a heightened recognition of shared grievances. However, they also found this tendency was itself moderated by Muslims' past experiences of positive contact with the Hindu majority. Once again, the more positive contact Indian Muslims experienced with an historically advantaged group, the less willing they were to engage in collective action to benefit the disadvantaged of India more broadly defined.

In sum, in so far as forming political coalitions of the disadvantaged who engage in unified action to transform society is often fundamental to social change, then ironically the secondary transfer effects of contact may both facilitate and inhibit the transformation of intergroup power relations (see also Dixon et al., 2012; Wright & Lubensky, 2009). Their positive ramifications in terms of *diffusing* prejudice reduction through a wider network of intergroup relations is now well-established, particularly when augmented by perceived intergroup similarity. At the same time, such benefits may be offset by their negative ramifications in terms of *defusing* collective activism and bonds of political solidarity amongst varying disadvantaged communities.

We will revisit some of these tensions further in our closing section on "future directions". However, the next section will focus on the role of third parties in collective action to achieve social change.

Common identification, third parties and collective action

Relational models of collective protest are increasingly *de rigeur* in social psychology. Whereas once collective action, particularly mass collective

---

[2]The highly complex cultural context of India, of course, also illustrates the inherent limits of shifting from dyadic to triadic intergroup relations. The challenge is ultimately not simply to move beyond binaries, but also to understand how far more complex and intersecting social category memberships shape individuals' thoughts, feelings and behaviours within specific contexts.

action, was treated mainly as an irrational by-product of group psychology – an endemic feature of intragroup processes such as "deindividuation", loss of identity and contagion (see S. D. Reicher, 1984) – our discipline has gradually evolved a less reactionary perspective. Growing recognition of the relational nature of mass collective action has revealed how its origins typically reflect intergroup as well as intragroup dynamics, heightened group identification rather than "loss" of identity, and behaviours that are contextually constrained rather than unbridled expressions of irrational impulses (Postmes & Spears, 1998). As a result, the field has evolved a richer perspective on collective action than hitherto existed.[3]

The majority of relational work on collective action, however, remains limited by the two-group focus that we have discussed in the present paper; that is, it typically continues to pit a single outgroup against a single ingroup. Again, this work carries the decided advantage of furnishing clear predictions and powerful demonstrations of the intergroup nature of collective action. However, as Drury, Stott and colleagues (e.g., Stott & Drury, 2000), Subašić et al. (2008), and Klavina and van Zomeren (2018) have argued, it also disregards the relational complexity of collective action and, more specifically, the crucial role that third parties may play in shaping how such action unfolds.

Work on crowd behaviour provides a particularly rich source of new understandings of the nature of collective action in general and of the dynamics of relations between more than two groups in particular. An example is Stott and Drury (2000) ethnographic study of the 1990 anti-poll tax demonstration in the UK. Field notes, video data and police and media reports were used to construct a narrative of events, and interviews with police and with 35 protest participants were used to examine experiences and perceptions. The analysis found that, at the same time that people were united by the anti-poll tax cause, the protest crowd was characterised by a number of divisions (including different regional groups, political groups, and other identities – "nuns against the poll tax", "bikers against the poll tax" etc.). A more fundamental division was between the small minority who sought conflict with the police, and the rest, though the majority largely ignored this minority and regarded them as largely irrelevant.

Yet there was an *asymmetry of categorical representations* in that the police's perception of the crowd differed from the crowd's own view of itself in crucial ways. First, the police saw the "troublesome minority" as representative, rather than unrepresentative, of the crowd as a whole. Second, police saw this small

---

[3]It is difficult to imagine, for example, many social psychologists nowadays endorsing Le Bon's (1895) famous observation – based partly on his assessment of collective action during the French revolution – that during events of mass revolution participants undergo a "loss" of personality, resulting in behaviours " ... almost always observed in beings belonging to inferior forms in evolution – in women, savages and children for instance" (p. 24). To the contrary, collective action is now increasingly viewed as motivated by social identity dynamics, thus being limited by category-relevant norms and values as well as the historical patterning of intergroup relationships.

group as especially powerful and able to influence the gullible "mass" (Stott & Reicher, 1998). Third, police saw actions that the crowd regarded as traditional and legitimate – such as a sit-down protest – as threatening incipient disorder. Importantly, the police had the capacity to act upon these perceptions and impose themselves on the crowd – by riding police horses into the crowd and moving against the crowd with officers in "riot gear".

This intervention inadvertently began a dynamic that transformed relations in the event as a whole. Not only was the police incursion seen as illegitimate (since crowd members felt they were doing nothing wrong), but critically it was also experienced as indiscriminate: everybody in the crowd as a whole was at risk from the police action. The sense of common fate engendered was the basis of a new and inclusive self-categorisation. The "us" that now faced the hostile police "outgroup" comprised all the previous subgroups, including the "violent minority". Indeed, since the overall relationship was now one of conflict, the actions of those seeking violence were now seen as more proto-typical of the ingroup. Thus, collective action had changed in form (who was included) and in content (what was normative).

The same kinds of complex relational dynamics have been observed in social movement phenomena, including anti-roads protests where new alliances between activists and locals developed as a result of unexpected police interventions against a crowd (Drury, Reicher, & Stott, 2003; Drury & Reicher, 2000). More recently, research has shown some parallel processes operating in the 2011 English riots. Similar to the earlier studies, Stott et al. (2018) used data triangulation of multiple sources (including police crime figures, 60 online videos, news articles, Tweets, and official reports) and thematic analysis of 41 interviews with rioters carried out as part of the *Guardian*/LSE *Reading the Riots* project (Guardian/LSE 2011). This combined analysis allowed Stott et al. to examine both the contours of collective action and the experiences of rioters in Tottenham, North London. Here, the initial fear among rioters was not the police but other marginalised groups. Their lives were normally governed by long-standing "post-code rivalries", whereby young people are constrained by territorial codes preventing them from moving freely across different London districts. Within the riots, however, shared antagonism towards the police allowed a sense of collective identity to be recognised that superseded these prior hostilities. This common identity was characterised not merely as a reaction to police action in the immediate context of the riot, but also as a consequence of their shared historical day-to-day experiences of illegitimate policing, including regular harassment. This emergent, shared, anti-police identity enabled collective action against the police as well as other targets:

Q . Did you see people that you knew there?

A . Yeah. Some people that I didn't really speak to – 'cause we're on opposite postcodes. But it didn't really matter.

Q. Why did it not matter?

A. Coz it's the lesser of two evils.

Q. What do you mean?

A. The police are the biggest crime ever. It doesn't matter where you're from anymore. So, who's the greater evil? Your enemy's enemy?
(as cited in Stott et al., 2018, p. 843)

In related work, Subašić et al. (2008) have highlighted the inherent limitations of a model of social change focused exclusively either on top down processes of prejudice reduction, emphasising attitude change amongst members of historically advantaged groups, or bottom up processes of collective resistance, emphasising the mass mobilisation of members of historically disadvantaged groups. By contrast, their Tripolar Model of Political Solidarity explores when and why historically advantaged and disadvantaged communities form alliances, acting together to challenge the hegemony of political elites. A key assumption here is that collective action is often most effective when it establishes political solidarity between members of both dominant and subordinate groups (see also Mallet et al., 2008) – as evidenced to some extent, for example, during the collapse of slavery in the US and the fall of the apartheid system in South Africa.

According to Subašić et al. (2008), this kind of solidarity tends to follow underlying shifts in the perceived nature of social identity and associated forms of intergroup behaviour. Specifically, when the collective values, norms and everyday practices of political elites become discrepant from how historically advantaged communities themselves conceive their identities, then alternative (e.g., pro-social change) sources of influence start to gain traction and the development of new forms of identification with the disadvantaged becomes possible. That is, a new common sense of "we" emerges defined by the desire to challenge collectively the status relations and forms of discrimination enforced by political authorities (see also Ferguson et al., 2018, whose "Emergent Ingroup Identity" model offers a related theoretical perspective).

To examine these processes, Subašić et al. (2011) experimentally manipulated whether or not participants thought of themselves in terms of an inclusive superordinate identity (Canadian), which was explicitly defined by egalitarian norms and values, or a subgroup identity devoid of such values (consumer). They showed that under conditions in which the inclusive superordinate identity was salient, participants (i.e., the majority in the context of the study) were more likely to engage in collective action in solidarity with sweatshop workers (Canadian Identity Salient: $M = 5.69$, $SD = 1.63$; Consumer Identity Salient: $M = 4.72$, $SD = 1.94$). In line with findings from crowd action research, this experimental work shows that when power is used in a way that violates self-defining norms and values, political solidarity with groups disadvantaged by such mistreatment is more likely (Subašić et al., 2011).

Further, Subašić et al. (2018) investigated how both men and women may be mobilised to act in solidarity for gender equality. Traditionally, psychological research primarily examines why gender inequality persists, positioning men as perpetrators and women as victims of various forms of prejudice and bias. In contrast, Subašić et al. (2018) examined how men and women can be mobilised for gender equality as agents of social change who are willing to challenge the status quo. The struggle for gender equality does not simply involve men and women (a bipolar context), but is (at least) tripolar once we consider people's orientation towards the status quo and political authorities. As such, a key question in explaining action for gender equality may instead concern whether one is willing to defend the status quo, actively challenge it, or yet to be engaged with the issue. Paradoxically, when it comes to gender equality it is necessary to look beyond gender to explain when people (and men in particular) may be willing to actively support this issue. Given that those willing to defend the status quo are typically (a) men and (b) in position of leadership and authority, men's mobilisation may rest on the availability of male exemplars prepared to challenge inequality and lead for change in solidarity with women.

To test these ideas, across three experiments gender equality was described either as a "women's issue" or a "common cause" concerning both men and women. When gender equality was framed as an issue that concerns us all (not just women), gender differences in support for collective action disappeared, so that men became just as likely as women to support change (Subašić et al., 2018). However, this effect was qualified by whether the solidarity message was attributed to a male or female leader (Experiment 3; see Figure 3). That is, men were more likely to act in solidarity with women when the common cause message was espoused by a male rather than a female leader. Male leaders' willingness to challenge the status quo signals a viable pathway towards change but also that those who support the status quo may be out of step with who "we" are. As such, to explain how people are mobilised for social change (including mobilisation across intergroup divides), it seems necessary to consider the nexus of social identity and social influence (see also S. Reicher et al., 2005; Subašić et al., 2012).

Klavina and van Zomeren (2018) have likewise conceptualised social identity processes as central to understanding the role of collective action involving third parties. Their research does not focus exclusively on the minority-majority-authority triad targeted by Subašić et al. (2008). Instead, more broadly, it explores when and why identity-related processes may facilitate (or impede) *any* form of third-party collective action on behalf of another group. To do so, they have extended the Social Identity Model of

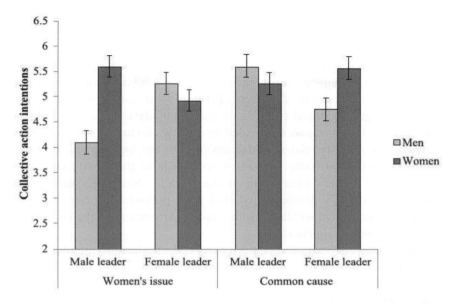

Figure 3. Mean collective action intentions as a function of participant gender, leader gender, and message framing. Error bars represent standard errors.

Collective Action (or SIMCA) developed by van Zomeren and colleagues (e.g., see Van Zomeren et al., 2008, 2004), which is itself built on seminal work in the social identity tradition (see especially S. D. Reicher, 1982, 1984). The SIMCA model holds that strong ingroup identification tends to impel collective action by encouraging group members to develop a shared sense of injustice, efficacy and anger at their mistreatment – all of which motivates them to struggle, together, for social change.

According to Klavina and van Zomeren (2018), the extension of the SIMCA to encompass third party collective action involves two distinctive pathways, entailing: (1) identity-related protection of the outgroup and (2) identity-related protection of the ingroup. The two pathways invoke social psychological processes that are essentially similar. *Identity-related protection of the outgroup* expresses individuals' identification with outgroup members who are locked into wider patterns of conflict or inequality with another group. This identification intensifies perceptions that an allied outgroup is being treated unjustly by and, in turn, encourages third party collective action on the allied group's behalf. Such action is motivated directly by a sense of injustice and indirectly via a heightening of members' sense of collective anger and efficacy. *Identity-related protection of the ingroup* follows a parallel pathway. When group members perceive that an allied minority group is being subjected to discrimination by another group, then this intensifies their sense of identification with their own group. This may again encourage them to engage in third party collective action on behalf of the allied, and similarly threatened, group – in this case, as a means of ingroup protection.

Via these dual pathways, then, members of third-party groups may be motivated to engage in third party collective action. Evidencing their model, Klavina and van Zomeren (2018) present survey data gathered across a range of cultural contexts. For example, data supporting both of their proposed pathways are provided by a study conducted in Latvia. This showed how identity-related protection of both the ingroup and the outgroup predicted Lativians' willingness to engage in third party collective resistance to Russia's annexation of the Ukraine. Similarly, survey data gathered in the US demonstrated that both pathways predicted Latino Americans' collective solidarity with African Americans in the context of challenging police violence.

Interestingly, in both surveys, third party collective action intentions were predicted not only by strength of collective identification and anger, but also by respondents' sense of shared efficacy and past experiences of positive contact with an allied group. That is, Latvians and Latino Americans who believed that mobilisation involving members of both their ingroup and the affiliated outgroup – in this case Ukrainians and African Americans respectively – was more likely to be successful also expressed greater willingness to participate in collective action on their behalf. Arguably, this may reflect what Cakal et al. (2018) have recently labelled the "power in numbers" effect. Likewise, Latvians and Latino Americans who had previously experienced more frequent positive contact with affiliated groups were also more willing to act collectively on their behalf. This is arguably because such contact enables the development of a sense of shared grievance, political solidarity, and even common identity.

Supporting this idea, Dixon et al. (2015) explored relations between Indian and Black residents of Northdale, a community located in the South African city of Pietermaritzburg in the KwaZulu-Natal province. Specifically, using a door-to-door field survey (n = 365), they investigated the role of interracial contact in shaping Indian residents' willingness to act in solidarity with their black neighbours with regard to the local council's failure to provide electrification and potable water facilities for some of the poorest, largely black occupied, settlements of Northdale. Their results suggested that positive contact with black Africans predicted Indian respondents' support both for policies of social change and for collective action to pressurise the local municipality to implement such policies. As Figure 4 illustrates, this relationship was partly mediated by Indians' increased awareness of outgroup discrimination and a heightened sense of empathy with their black neighbours. Poignantly, such findings indicate communities who were historically divided as part of the broader "divide and rule" logic of apartheid –

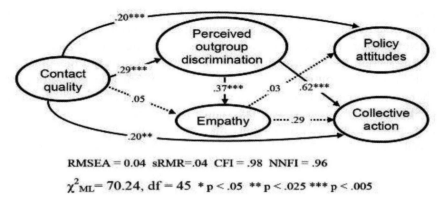

Figure 4. SEM model of the direct and indirect effects of interracial contact on Indian South Africans' political solidarity with black South Africans in Northdale, Pietermaritzburg.

Note: In this figure, the variables refer specifically to outgroup empathy, perceived discrimination against the outgroup, and support for policies and collective action designed to benefit outgroup members.

and encouraged to view one another as being locked in relations of competition and immutable difference – have the capacity to act in unison under changing conditions, potentially challenging the legitimacy of third party authorities.

In sum, although still relatively sparse and derived mainly from cross-sectional surveys, emerging evidence has clarified when and why third party and other forms of complex collective action may occur. In its focus on common identification, sense of shared injustice, joint efficacy and the role of contact between groups who share a history of disadvantage, this work elucidates social and psychological dynamics that are effectively antithetical to the "divide and rule" processes explored earlier in our paper. As Figure 1, panel b above anticipates, it offers a potential blueprint for promoting collective action grounded in a model of social change that moves beyond simple ingroup-outgroup binaries and underpins a multigroup "unite and resist" principle.

Many caveats are of course necessary at this point. In practice, for example, existing status hierarchies and structures of segregation may pre-empt the formation of political alliances between disadvantaged communities and limit the kinds of contact that might encourage their development. Moreover, as we have seen, the tenuously "in between" status of intermediary groups may generate both instrumental and identity-related motivations for rejecting joint collective action to challenge the status quo (Caricati, 2018). We would add that such motivations may often be strategically nurtured by political elites in the face of the potential threats posed by coalitions of the disadvantaged. For instance, they may adopt social policies that shore up existing status hierarchies or defuse political activism (Dixon et al., 2015).

Notwithstanding the importance of such qualifications, the broader point of this section has been to show how the nature, course and outcomes of collective action are often not merely *inter*group but also *multi*group in character. As the work of Drury, Stott and colleagues (e.g., Drury, Reicher, & Stott, 2003), Subašić et al. (2008) and Klavina and van Zomeren (2018) demonstrates, this again highlights the necessity of developing models of social change that transcend the simple two group perspective dominates social psychology.

Concluding thoughts: integrative themes and future directions

We began this paper by citing Sherif's (1962) classic definition of intergroup relations. We also noted how his "Summer Camp" studies have come to epitomise the problem of understanding why groups become locked in violent, binary conflict. As Billig (1976) pointed out more than 40 years ago, however, this characterisation of Sherif's work – dramatised in the battle between the "Rattlers" and the "Eagles" – is itself a simplification ... and we would argue a rather instructive one (see also Cherry, 1995; Perry, 2018). It effaces the role of a critically important third group in the Summer Camp studies: the team of psychologists who created the conditions under which the boys formed distinctive group identities, became embedded within relations of negative interdependence, engaged in conflictual behaviour, and ultimately had that behaviour moderated via the imposition of superordinate goals. In short, even in this classic study of binary intergroup relations, we cannot understand the nature, origins and trajectory of the conflict without appreciating the more complex web of relations between the main protagonists and a third-party authority. It is perhaps revealing, however, that textbook treatments of Sherif and colleagues' work have typically ignored role of such tripolar relations.[4]

In the present paper, we have argued that this tendency reflects a wider bias in our field. Most of what we know about the social psychology of intergroup relations has emerged from studies of how one group of people (e.g., whites) think and feel about another (e.g., blacks). By reducing the social world to binary categories, such studies have implemented an effective

---

[4]Sherif and colleagues were themselves acutely aware that the success of their field experiments required them to mask their own role as third party provocateurs. When this role became evident in the 1953 version of the summer camp, and the two groups of boys turned their attention towards the manipulative actions of the experimenters, aggressive intergroup competition between them did not emerge (Perry, 2018). From the perspective of its experimental goals, the study was deemed a failure and, probably as a consequence, fell into relative obscurity. However, from the present perspective, it is remarkable that even the most iconic of all two-group studies already contained the seeds of its own re-contextualisation as a more complex (i.e., triadic) intergroup system.

and highly efficient methodological framework. Yet, as we have sought to emphasise, they have also obscured some important features of social relations in historically divided and unequal societies. Our focus on triadic relations has itself, of course, grossly simplified intergroup relations in most societies. We have adopted this focus for heuristic reasons. Our main point has been to problematise – and potentially transcend – the standard social psychological treatment of intergroup relations in terms of even more simplistic binaries.

Proposing a complementary perspective, we have highlighted the importance of investigating intergroup relationships involving more than two groups and of exploring not only their psychological, but also their political and historical significance. We have argued that this shift in focus may illuminate patterns of domination and subordination, collusion and betrayal, solidarity and resistance that have been generally neglected in our field. Developing this argument, we have discussed the conditions under which members of historically disadvantaged groups either dissolve into internecine competition or unite to challenge the status quo, drawing on emerging work on: (1) policy attitudes in complexly stratified societies, (2) the role of "intermediary" status groups in promoting or undermining social change; (3) the consequences of vertical and horizontal forms of intergroup contact involving more than two groups, and (4) third party involvement in collective action. It is perhaps worth re-emphasising here that existing psychological research on complex forms of intergroup dynamics is limited in extent and based on evidence collected in a relatively narrow range of social contexts and using a limited range of methods. Moreover, in many societies, distinguishing between lower, intermediate and higher status groups is not as simple as it may first appear – some societies, for example, have sharply defined status boundaries, others more blurred, shifting and subtle boundaries. Bearing these limitations in mind, we will now conclude by outlining some integrative themes and highlighting potential directions for future research.

Methodological implications

A recurring theme of our paper concerns the need to develop methodological frameworks for studying intergroup dynamics beyond a simple two group scenario. Indeed, as we have noted, in many areas of research little or no evidence exists about what we've called the "complex relationality" of intergroup processes. Moreover, the work that does exist has sometimes qualified what we think we know (e.g., see Hartstone & Augoustinos, 1995; Spielman, 2000). As Zagefka (2019, p. 3) has recently emphasised: "The huge body of work on dyadic intergroup processes has undoubtedly generated a plethora of important findings and insights. Still our knowledge of intergroup processes will remain incomplete unless we do justice to relations which involve more than two entities." Developing this idea, Zagefka offers several concrete recommendations about how to investigate triadic relations that involve different combinations of observers, agents and recipients of intergroup behaviour, whilst also highlighting some potential sources of confound to avoid when designing research on such relations[5].

We want to make two additional, and somewhat broader, methodological points here. First, in our view, the self-evident nature of intergroup binaries must be treated as a problem to be explained rather than an organic starting point for psychological research. We can no longer employ such binaries unreflectingly within our research designs, e.g., as the pre-given categories of questionnaire surveys or experiments. To do so may be to unintentionally sustain the kind of historical and political amnesia that allowed, for example, colonial authorities to create the very divisions that they later attributed to the atavistic hatreds of warring factions. The point is important enough to be stressed: as soon as our methods enable us to see more complex intergroup configurations, it becomes apparent that fixed binaries are the exception rather than the rule. Treating rare instances as if they were the general case, results not only in accounts that are descriptively inaccurate – it also precludes us from explaining the very social psychological processes through which, under specific conditions, social reality crystalizes around binary oppositions. Along these lines, for example, Elcheroth and Reicher (2017) have recently reviewed research showing how collective identities and relations may change abruptly during violent confrontations. In the former Yugoslavia, reanalyses of historic survey data and related archival material have revealed that a rich configuration of social cleavages existed on the eve of war, of which ethnic differences were neither the most relevant nor salient. As ethnographic accounts and subsequent surveys show, it was only following the outburst of violence that the previous complexity was reduced and that binary divisions – notably between Croats and Serbs in Croatia, and Muslims and Serbs in large parts of Bosnia – gradually overrode more complex social cleavages.

Second and related, we want to advocate a methodological approach that can capture the dynamic practices of category construction through which such binaries, over time, become reified as normal or even "natural" ways to frame intergroup relations (cf. Reicher & Hopkins, 2001). Some of these practices are discursive in nature: invoking binary oppositions, constructing them as normative, and silencing other constructions of social relations (Reicher & Hopkins, 2001). Others are about creating material conditions

---

[5]Zagefka's (2018) work explores specifically how onlookers understand and evaluate the actions they witness between an actor and the recipient of such actions. This triadic relationship, she argues, is complexly shaped by the group memberships of all three.

under which social relations become experienced in binary terms, e.g., through systems of segregation or the distribution of social benefits and risks along binary cleavages (Elcheroth & Reicher, 2017). Correspondingly, we need to recover alternative ways of understanding and (re)contextualising such binaries, exploring where they come from, what sustains them, and what social relations they are obscuring. As it turns out, the accounts of ordinary participants in intergroup struggles often provide rich material in this respect. Kerr et al.'s (2017) work on so-called "black on black" xenophobia in South Africa provides one example of how studying such accounts might enrich our field. As this work illustrates powerfully, what may initially look like a case of binary violence may result from more complex patterns of intergroup power relations.

Identity complexity, intergroup relations and political attitudes

The importance of complex social identity dynamics in shaping social inequality and discrimination is another integrative theme of this review, extending related social psychological work on intergroup relations (e.g., see Brewer & Pierce, 2005; Gaertner & Dovidio, 2000). As we have seen, for example, attitudes towards policies designed to address racial inequality in multiracial societies reflect not only citizens' material interests, but also how they draw the very boundaries of their collective identities (Dixon, Durrheim et al., 2017). Likewise, the social change orientations and intergroup attitudes of intermediary group members tend to reflect identity-related concerns that arise from their fragile "in between" position within status hierarchies (Caricati, 2018). The likelihood that individuals belonging to "third party" groups will engage in collective action to support affiliated outgroups is likewise shaped by their common identification with members of such groups (Subašić et al., 2008), as well as an associated motivation to protect ingroup and outgroup identity (Klavina & van Zomeren, 2018).

Such work speaks to the complexity of identity formation and expression in contexts involving more than two groups. It shows how social identities may be constructed via both upwards and downwards processes of social comparison. This process may implicate varying expressions of differentiation from higher status groups "above" and lower status groups "below", the nature and consequences of which, as work on Social Identity Theory has demonstrated (Tajfel & Turner, 1979), are linked to factors such as the perceived ideological stability and legitimacy of the social order. Crucially, such identity-related processes have potentially profound implications for understanding when and why intermediary status groups either defend the status quo or express political solidarity with lower status groups and seek to challenge social inequality. As we have seen, Caricati and colleagues' studies (e.g., see Caricati's 2018 review) are an important touchstone in this respect.

We would also flag here emerging work on the transformative role played by so-called "gateway" groups – that is, groups whose members embody identity complexity and fusion (e.g., biracial or bi-ethnic group members) – in shaping the affective trajectory of intergroup relations in contexts where multiple groups and social identities coexist (see Levy et al., 2017).

Our more general point is that research on intermediate or "in between" groups remains comparatively neglected. Existing research evidence, though suggestive and important (as reviewed by Caricati, 2018), is based on small-scale opportunity samples and focused on a relatively narrow range of social contexts and forms of intergroup relations. Specifically, the conditions under which intermediary groups participate in collective action to promote social change merits further inquiry. The nature of intergroup contact within complexly stratified societies represents one such condition.

Contact, collective action and social change revisited

The majority of work on intergroup contact has focused on its potential to reduce the prejudices of members of historically groups towards members of historically disadvantaged groups and, albeit less commonly, vice versa (Pettigrew & Tropp, 2011). However, the effects of contact implicate relationships that are more complex than simple dichotomies such as "advantaged" versus "disadvantaged" or "minority" versus majority' and extend beyond the immediacy of participating groups.

Two potential areas of future research are worth underlining here. The first complicates the now well-established finding that positive contact has a stronger effect on the prejudices of majority group members than it does on the prejudices of minority group members, as evidenced by Tropp and Pettigrew (2005) influential meta-analysis. What has not yet been explored, to our knowledge, is how more complex forms of social stratification shape the contact-prejudice relationship. To give an example: how, if at all, is this relationship affected by belonging to an intermediate status group, whose members may experience contact that involves interaction with outgroups who are *both* higher and lower in status? Conversely, how might contact dynamics operating within a relatively "flat" hierarchy of subordination – in which several groups of roughly equivalent levels of low status interact both with one another and a clearly dominant group – shape related patterns of intergroup attitudes?

The second and related area of future research concerns the apparently paradoxical effects of intergroup contact on collective action involving third parties. On the one hand, vertical contact between dominant and subordinate group members may, ironically, sometimes reduce the latter's readiness to form political alliances with members of other subordinate groups (Dixon, Cakal et al., 2017). In this sense, to borrow Cakal et al.'s (2011) metaphor, it may exercise a "sedative" effect on social change. We need to know more about the nature and boundary conditions of this effect.

On the other hand, horizontal contact between disadvantaged communities may work in precisely the opposite direction, encouraging them to form a sense of shared injustice and collective efficacy and thus to unite to mount a challenge to political authorities (Dixon et al., 2015). Klavina and van Zomeren (2018) extension of the SIMCA has hinted at the potential value of this kind of integration of work on contact and third-party collective action. It suggests that positive interactions between communities who share a common history of discrimination and who thus can, via such interactions, forge a shared belief in their capacity to achieve social change may increase the likelihood of joint resistance to a third-party dominant group.

Again, however, we would emphasise that this area of research is very much in its infancy. In particular, research on the effects of contact between historically disadvantaged groups on their political attitudes and behaviours remains rare (see also Dixon, Cakal et al., 2017; Dixon et al., 2015), and the theoretical mechanisms that might link positive – and indeed negative (cf. Reimer et al., 2017) – contact experiences to joint collective action in relation to third party authorities remain under-specified. In our view, such experiences are likely to involve social psychological processes that are quite distinct from those specified within classic prejudice reduction models, which tend to emphasise processes of stereotype reduction and promotion of positive outgroup emotions. They require us to work towards an integration of theories of intergroup contact with theories of subordinate group solidarity and third-party collective action. In other words, we need to know more about what kinds of contact experiences might lead members of groups who share a history of disadvantage, vis à vis a dominant group, to unite to challenge the status quo.

In this regard, research on the contact experiences of protesters *within* unfolding events of collective action may prove particularly revealing and constitute another important topic for future research. As illustrated by the work of Drury, Stott and colleagues, protest marches, riots and other forms of crowd behaviour often initially comprise multiple groups, divided by different identities, rallying against one or more authorities with aim of resisting or promoting social change (e.g., Stott et al., 2018). More broadly, it is plausible that dynamics similar to those described in crowd research play a key role in a wider range of intergroup histories. The varying forms of intergroup interaction through which this kind of ideological process is either enacted or thwarted, and the social psychological processes that it implicates, once more requires us to grapple with the group processes beyond a simple "us" versus "them" dichotomy.

Funding

Part of the preparation of this publication was financially supported by the Swiss National Science Foundation (r4d –Swiss Programme for Research on Global Issues for Development, Project Pluralistic Memories, SNSF grant numbers: 400240_146955 /400240_171188).

ORCID

John Drury http://orcid.org/0000-0002-7748-5128
Kevin Durrheim http://orcid.org/0000-0003-2926-5953

References

Adhikari, M. (2006). Hope, fear, shame, frustration: Continuity and change in the expression of coloured identity in white supremacist South Africa, 1910–1994. *Journal of Southern African Studies*, *32*(3), 467–487. https://doi.org/10.1080/03057070600829542

Albzour, M., Penic, S., Randa, N., & Green, E. G. T. (2019). Support for 'Normalization' of relations between Palestinians and Israelis and how it relates to contact and resistance in the West Bank. *Journal of Social and Political Psychology*, 7(2), https://doi.org/10.5964/jspp.v7i2.877.

Allport, G. W. (1954). *The nature of prejudice*. Doubleday.

Banko, L. (2016). *The invention of palestinian citizenship, 1918–1947*. Edinburgh University Press.

Bobo, L. D. (2000). Race and beliefs about affirmative action: Assessing the effects of interests, group threat, ideology and racism. In D. O. Sears, J. Sidanius, & L. Bobo (Eds.), *Racialized politics: The debate about racism in America* (pp. 137–164). University of Chicago Press.

Bobo, L. D. (2011). Somewhere between Jim Crow & post-racialism: Reflections on the racial divide in America Today. *Daedalus: Journal of the American Academy of Arts & Sciences*, *140*(2), 11–36. https://doi.org/10.1162/DAED_a_00091

Brewer, M. B., & Pierce, K. P. (2005). Social identity complexity and outgroup tolerance. *Personality and Social Psychology Bulletin*, *31*(3), 428–437. https://doi.org/10.1177/0146167204271710

Brylka, A., Jasinskaja-Lahtia, I., & Mähönen, T. A. (2016). The majority influence on interminority attitudes: The secondary transfer effect of positive and negative contact. *International Journal of Intercultural Relations*, *50*, 76–88. https://doi.org/10.1016/j.ijintrel.2015.12.007

Cakal, H., Hewstone, M., Schwar, G., & Heath, A. (2011). An investigation of the social identity model of collective action and the "sedative" effect of intergroup contact amongst Black and White students in South Africa. *British Journal of Social Psychology*, *50*(4), 606–627. https://doi.org/10.1111/bjso.2011.50.issue-4

Cakal, H., van Zomeren, M., Nadhmi, F., Chauhan, A., & Dixon, J. (2018). The 'power in numbers' (or PIN) hypothesis: The benefits of common ingroup identity for collective action among groups that face violent existential threat. *Manuscript Submitted for Publication*.

Caricati, L. (2018). Considering intermediate-status groups in intergroup hierarchies: A theory of triadic social stratification. *Journal of Theoretical Social Psychology*, 2(2), 58–66. https://doi.org/10.1002/jts5.2018.2.issue-2

Caricati, L., & Monacelli, N. (2012). Intergroup biases of the intermediate-status group: The effect of stability and instability of social stratification. *Journal of Social Psychology*, 152(6), 713–726. https://doi.org/10.1080/00224545.2012.691572

Caricati, L., & Sollami, A. (2017). Perceived legitimacy follows in-group interests: Evidence from intermediate-status groups. *British Journal of Social Psychology*, 56 (1), 197–206. https://doi.org/10.1111/bjso.2017.56.issue-1

Cherry, F. (1995). *The 'stubborn particulars' of social psychology: Essays on the research process*. Routledge.

Christopher, A. J. (1988). "Divide and rule": The impress of British separation policies. *Area*, 20(3), 233–240.

Crisp, R. J., & Hewstone, M. (2007). Multiple social categorization. In M. P. Zanna & M. P. Zanna (Eds.), *Advances in experimental social psychology* (Vol. 39, pp. 163–254). Elsevier Academic Press.

Crush, J. (1992). Power and surveillance on the South African gold mines. *Journal of Southern African Studies*, 18(4), 825–844. https://doi.org/10.1080/03057079208708340

Deschamps, J.-C, & Doise, W. (1978). Crossed category memberships in intergroup relations. In (Ed.), *Differentiation between social groups* (pp. 141-158). Cambridge, UK: Cambridge University Press.

DeVotta, N. (2004). *Blowback: linguistic nationalism, institutional decay, and ethnic conflict in sri lanka*. Stanford, California: Stanford University Press.

Dixon, J., Durrheim, K., Stevenson, C., & Cakal, H. (2016). From prejudice reduction to collective action: Two psychological models of social change (and how to reconcile them). In F. Barlow & C. Sibley (Eds.), *Cambridge handbook of the psychology of prejudice*. Cambridge University Press.

Dixon, J., Cakal, H., Kahn, W., Osmany, M., & Majumdar, S. (2017b). Contact, collective action and political solidarity: An Indian case study of relations between historically disadvantaged communities. *Journal of Applied Social and Community Psychology*, 27(1), 83–95. https://doi.org/10.1002/casp.v27.1

Dixon, J., Durrheim, K., & Thomae, M. (2017a). The principle-implementation gap in attitudes towards racial equality (and how to close it). *Advances in Political Psychology*, 38, 91–126. https://doi.org/10.1111/pops.2017.38.issue-S1

Dixon, J., Durrheim, K., Thomae, M., Tredoux, C., Kerr, P., & Quayle, M. (2015). Divide and rule, unite and resist: Contact, collective action and policy attitudes amongst historically disadvantaged groups. *Journal of Social Issues*, 71(3), 576–596. https://doi.org/10.1111/josi.12129

Dixon, J., Levine, M., Reicher, S., & Durrheim, K. (2012). Beyond prejudice: Are negative evaluations the problem and is getting us to like one another more the solution? *Behavioral and Brain Sciences*, 35(6), 411–425. https://doi.org/10.1017/S0140525X11002214

Drury, J., & Reicher, S. (2000). Collective action and psychological change: The emergence of new social identities. *British Journal of Social Psychology*, 39(4), 579–604. https://doi.org/10.1348/014466600164642

Ehrenreich, B. (1989). *Fear of falling: The inner life of the middle class*. Pantheon Books.

Elcheroth, G., & Reicher, S. (2014). 'not our war, not our country': contents and contexts of scottish political rhetoric and popular understandings during the invasion of iraq. *British Journal Of Social Psychology*, 53, 112–133.

Elcheroth, G., & Reicher, S. (2014). "Not our war, not our country": Contents and contexts of Scottish political rhetoric and popular understandings during the invasion of Iraq. *British Journal of Social Psychology*, *53*(1), 112–133. https://doi.org/10.1111/bjso.12020

Elcheroth, G., & Reicher, S. (2017). *Identity, violence, and power. Mobilising hatred, demobilising dissent*. Palgrave Macmillan.

Ferguson, M. A., Branscombe, N. R., & Reynolds, K. J. (2018). Social psychological research on prejudice as collective action supporting emergent ingroup members. *British Journal of Social Psychology*, *58*(1), 1–32. https://doi.org/10.1111/bjso.12294

Flores, A. R. (2015). Attitudes towards Transgender rights: Perceived knowledge and secondary interpersonal contact. *Politics, Groups and Identities*, *3*(3), 398–416. https://doi.org/10.1080/21565503.2015.1050414

Gaertner, S. L., & Dovidio, J. F. (2000). *Reducing intergroup bias: The common ingroup identity model*. Psychology Press.

Glasford, D. E., & Calcagno, J. (2011). The conflict of harmony: Intergroup contact, commonality and political solidarity between minority groups. *Journal of Experimental Social Psychology*, *48*(1), 323–328. https://doi.org/10.1016/j.jesp.2011.10.001

Goldin, I. (1984). The coloured labour preference policy, co-option and contradiction. Collected seminar papers. *Institute of Commonwealth Studies*, *33*, 108–120.

Greenwald, A. G., & Banaji, M. R. (2013). *Blindspot: Hidden biases of good people*. Delacorte Press.

Guardian / LSE. (2011). *Reading the riots: investigating england's summer of disorder*, London: The Guardian and LSE.

Haiduc-Dale, N. (2013). *Arab Christians in British Mandate Palestine: Communalism and Nationalism, 1917–1948*. Edinburgh University Press.

Hartstone, M., & Augoustinos, M. (1995). The minimal group paradigm: Categorization into two versus three groups. *European Journal of Social Psychology*, *25*(2), 179–193. https://doi.org/10.1002/()1099-0992

Harwood, J., Paolini, S., Joyce, N., Rubin, M., & Arroyo, A. (2011). Secondary transfer effects from imagined contact: Group similarity affects the generalization gradient. *British Journal of Social Psychology*, *50*(1), 180–189. https://doi.org/10.1348/014466610X524263

Haslam, S. D., Reicher, S. D., & Platow, M. J. (2011). *The new psychology of leadership: Identity, influence and power*. Psychology Press.

Hopkins, N. (2001). Psychology and the end of history: a critique and a proposal for the psychology of categorization. *Political Psychology*, *22*, 383-487.

Jackman, M. R. (1994). *The velvet glove: Paternalism and conflict in gender, class, and race relations*. University of California Press.

Jackman, M. R. (1996). Individualism, self-interest and white racism. *Social Science Quarterly*, *77*(4), 760–767.

Kerr, P., Durrheim, K., & Dixon, J. (2017). Beyond a 'two group' approach to intergroup conflict and inequality: Third parties and intergroup alliances in xenophobic violence in South Africa. *British Journal of Social Psychology*, *56*(1), 47–53. https://doi.org/10.1111/bjso.2017.56.issue-1

Klavina, L., & van Zomeren, M. (2018). Protesting to protect "us" and/or "them"? Explaining why members of third groups are willing to engage in collective action.

Group Processes & Intergroup Relations. 18, 45-65 https://doi.org/10.1177/1368430218796930

Krysan, M., & Moberg, S. (2016). *Trends in racial attitudes.* University of Illinois Institute of Government and Public Affairs. http://igpa.uillinois.edu/programs/racial-attitudes.

Kuo, A., Malhotra, N., & Mo, C. H. (2014). *Why do Asian Americans identify as democrats? Testing theories of social exclusion and intergroup commonality.* Working paper: 1-2014. Centre for the Study of Democratic Institutions. Vanderbilt University.

Kuper, L., Watts, H., & Davies, R. (1958). *Durban: A study in racial ecology.* Jonathan Cape.

Le Bon, G. (1895). *The Crowd: A study of the popular mind.* New York: Wallachia.

Levy, A., van Zomeren, M., Saguy, T., & Halperin, E. (2017). Intergroup emotions and gateway groups: Introducing multiple social identities into the study of emotions in conflict. *Personality and Social Psychology Compass, 11*(6), e12320. https://doi.org/10.1111/spc3.v11.6

Lopez, L., & Pantoja, A. D. (2004). Beyond black and white: General support for race-conscious policies among African Americans, Latinos, Asian Americans and Whites. *Political Research Quarterly, 57*(4), 633–642. https://doi.org/10.1177/106591290405700411

Mallett, R.K, Huntsinger, J.R, Sinclair, S, & Swim, J.K. (2008). Seeing through their eyes: when majority group members take collective action on behalf of an outgroup. *Group Processes & Intergroup Relations, 11*, 451-470.

Moss, S. M. (2014). Beyond conflict and spoilt Identities: How Rwandan leaders justify a single recategorization model for post-conflict reconciliation. *Journal of Social and Political Psychology, 2*(1), 435–449. https://doi.org/10.5964/jspp.v2i1.291

Moss, S. M., & Vollhardt, J. R. (2016). "You can't give a syringe with unity": Rwandan responses to the government's single recategorization policies. *Analyses of Social Issues and Public Policy, 1*(1), 325–359. https://doi.org/10.1111/asap.2016.16.issue-1

Oakes, P. J., Haslam, A., & Turner, J. C. (1994). *Stereotyping and social reality.* Basil Blackwell.

Perry, G. (2018). *The lost boys: Inside Muzafer Sherif's Robbers Cave experiment.* Scribe Publications.

Pettigrew, T. F. (2009). Secondary transfer effect of contact: Do intergroup contact effects spread to noncontacted outgroups? *Social Psychology, 40*(2), 55–65. https://doi.org/10.1027/1864-9335.40.2.55

Pettigrew, T. F., & Tropp, L. R. (2011). *When groups meet: The dynamics of intergroup contact.* Psychology Press.

Postmes, T., & Spears, R. (1998). Deindividuation and anti-normative behavior: A meta-analysis. *Psychological Bulletin, 123*(3), 238–259. https://doi.org/10.1037/0033-2909.123.3.238

Protho, J. W., & Grigg, C. M. (1960). Fundamental principles of democracy: Bases of agreement and disagreement. *Journal of Politics, 22*(2), 276–294. https://doi.org/10.2307/2127359

Reicher, S., Haslam, S. A., & Hopkins, N. (2005). Social identity and the dynamics of leadership: Leaders and followers as collaborative agents in the transformation of social reality. *The Leadership Quarterly, 16*(4), 547–568. https://doi.org/10.1016/j.leaqua.2005.06.007

Reicher, S. D. (1982). The determination of collective behavior. In H. Tajfel (Ed.), *Social identity and intergroup relations* (pp. 41–83). Cambridge University Press.

Reicher, S. D. (1984). The St Pauls Riot: An explanation of the limits of crowd action in terms of a social identity model. *European Journal of Social Psychology*, 14(1), 1–21. https://doi.org/10.1002/ejsp.2420140102

Reimer, N. K., Becker, J. C., Benz, A., Christ, O., Dhonk, K., Klocke, U., Neji, S., Rychlowska, M., Schmid, K., & Hewstone, M. (2017). Intergroup contact and social change: Implications of negative and positive contact for collection action in advantaged and disadvantaged groups. *Personality and Social Psychology Bulletin*, 43(1), 121–136. https://doi.org/10.1177/0146167216676478

Sherif, M. (1962). *Intergroup relations and leadership*. Wiley.

Sherif, M., Harvey, O. J., White, B. J., Hood, W. R., & Sherif, C. (1961). *Intergroup conflict and cooperation: The robber's cave experiment*. University of Oklahoma.

Shook, N. J., Hopkins, P. D., & Koech, J. M. (2016). Effects of intergroup contact on second group attitudes and social dominance orientation. *Group Processes and Intergroup Relations*, 19(3), 328–342. https://doi.org/10.1177/1368430215572266

Sigelman, L., & Welch, S. (1991). *Black Americans' views of racial inequality: The dream deferred*. Cambridge University Press.

Sollami, A., & Caricati, L. (2015). Intergroup threat perception among intermediate-status group members: The role of stability-instability of social stratification. *Psicologia Sociale*, 3, 273–282 doi: 10.1482/81372.

Spielman, D. A. (2000). Young children, minimal groups and dichotomous categorization. *Personality and Social Psychology Bulletin*, 26(11), 1433–1441. https://doi.org/10.1177/0146167200263010

Stott, C., Ball, R., Drury, J., Neville, F., Reicher, S., Boardman, A., & Choudhury, S. (2018). The evolving normative dimensions of 'riot': Toward an elaborated social identity explanation. *European Journal of Social Psychology*, 48(6), 834–849. https://doi.org/10.1002/ejsp.2376

Stott, C., & Drury, J. (2000). Crowds, context and identity: Dynamic categorization processes in the 'poll tax riot'. *Human Relations*, 53(2), 247–273. https://doi.org/10.1177/a010563

Stott, C., & Reicher, S. (1998). Crowd action as intergroup process: Introducing the police perspective. *European Journal of Social Psychology*, 28(4), 509–529. https://doi.org/10.1002/()1099-0992

Subašić, E., Hardacre, S., Elton, B., Branscombe, N., Ryan, M., & Reynolds, K. (2018). We for She: Mobilising men and women to act in solidarity for gender equality. *Group Processes and Intergroup Relations*, 21(5), 707–724. https://doi.org/10.1177/1368430218763272

Subašić, E., Reynolds, K., & Turner, J. C. (2008). The political solidarity model of social change. *Personality and Social Psychology Review*, 12(4), 330–352. https://doi.org/10.1177/1088868308323223

Subašić, E., Reynolds, K. J., Reicher, S. D., & Klandermans, B. (2012). Where to from here for the psychology of social change? Future directions for theory and practice'. *Political Psychology*, 33(1), 61–74. https://doi.org/10.1111/j.1467-9221.2011.00864.x

Subašić, E., Schmitt, M. T., & Reynolds, K. J. (2011). Are we all in this together? Co-victimization, inclusive social identity and collective action in solidarity with the disadvantaged. *British Journal of Social Psychology*, 50(4), 707–725. https://doi.org/10.1111/bjso.2011.50.issue-4

Tajfel, H., & Turner, J. (1979). An integrative theory of intergroup conflict. In W. G. Austin & S. Worchel (Eds.), *The social psychology of intergroup relations* (pp. 33–47). Brooks/Cole.

Tajfel, H., Billig, M. G., Bundy, R. P., & Flament, C. (1971). Social categorization and intergroup behaviour. *European Journal of Social Psychology, 1*(2), 149–178. https://doi.org/10.1002/()1099-0992

Tausch, N., Hewstone, M., Kenworthy, J. B., Psaltis, C., Schmid, K., Popan, J., Cairns, E., & Hughes, J. (2010). Secondary transfer effects of intergroup contact: Alternative accounts and underlying processes. *Journal of Personality and Social Psychology, 99*(2), 282–302. https://doi.org/10.1037/a0018553

Tee, N., & Hegarty, P. (2006). Predicting opposition to the civil rights of, trans persons in the United Kingdom. *Journal of Community and Applied Social Psychology, 16*(1), 70–80. https://doi.org/10.1002/casp.851

Tropp, L., & Pettigrew, T. F. (2005). Relationships between intergroup contact and prejudice amongst minority and majority status groups. *Psychological Science, 16* (12), 951–957. https://doi.org/10.1111/j.1467-9280.2005.01643.x

Tuch, S. A., & Hughes, M. (1996). Whites' racial policy attitudes. *Social Science Quarterly, 77*(4), 723–745.

Turner, J. C. (1991). *Social influence.* Brooks/cole.

Turner, J. C., Hogg, M. A., Oakes, P. J., Reicher, S., & Wetherell, M. S. (1987). *Rediscovering the social group: A self-categorization theory.* Blackwell.

Urban, L.M, & Miller, N. (1998). A theoretical analysis of crossed categorization effects: a meta-analysis. *Journal Of Personality and Social Psychology, 74,* 894-908.

Van Laar, C., Levin, S., Sinclair, S., & Sidanius, J. (2005). The effect of university roommate contact on ethnic attitudes and behavior. *Journal of Experimental Social Psychology, 41*(4), 329–345. https://doi.org/10.1016/j.jesp.2004.08.002

Van Zomeren, M., Postmes, T., & Spears, R. (2008). Toward an integrative social identity mode of collective action: A quantitative research synthesis of three socio-psychological perspectives. *Psychological Bulletin, 134*(4), 504–535. https://doi.org/10.1037/0033-2909.134.4.504

Van Zomeren, M., Spears, R., Fischer, A., & Leach, C. W. (2004). Put your money where your mouth is! Explaining collective action tendencies through group-based anger and group efficacy. *Journal of Personality and Social Psychology, 87*(5), 649–664. https://doi.org/10.1037/0022-3514.87.5.649

Vezzali, L., & Stathi, S. (Eds.). (2017). *Intergroup contact theory: Recent developments and future directions.* Routledge: Current Issues in Social Psychology Book Series.

Western, J. (1981). *Outcast Cape Town.* George Allen and Unwin.

Wodtke, G. T. (2012). The impact of education on intergroup attitudes: A multiracial analysis. *Social Psychology Quarterly, 75*(1), 80–106. https://doi.org/10.1177/0190272511430234

Wright, S. C., & Lubensky, M. (2009). The struggle for social equality: Collective action vs. prejudice reduction. In S. Demoulin, J. P. Leyens, & J. F. Dovidio (Eds.), *Intergroup misunderstandings: Impact of divergent social realities* (pp. 291–310). Psychology Press.

Zagefka, H. (2018). Triadic intergroup relations: Studying situations with an observer, an actor, and a recipient of behaviour. *Journal of Theoretical and Social Psychology.* https://doi.org/10.1002/jts5.26

Zagefka, H. (2019). Triadic intergroup relations: Studying situations with an observer, an actor and a recipient of behaviour. *Journal of Theoretical Social Psychology3* (1), 62-74.. https://doi.org/10.1002/jts5.26

ARTICLE

Text-based E-contact: Harnessing cooperative Internet interactions to bridge the social and psychological divide

Fiona A. White, Rachel Maunder and Stefano Verrelli

School of Psychology, The University of Sydney, Sydney, Australia

ABSTRACT
In order to bridge the psychological and physical divide between different groups, researchers have harnessed the positive elements of the Internet to improve intergroup contact. One new and effective Internet strategy is Electronic- or E-contact. Unlike other contact approaches, E-contact is an experimental intergroup intervention that uniquely accommodates Allport's contact theory and recategorisation processes, to create a structured, cooperative, synchronous and goal-directed online text interaction between members from different groups. E-contact has been found to successfully improve intergroup relations between Catholics and Protestants in Northern Ireland and Muslims and Catholics in Australia; and reduce bias against lesbian women and gay men, people with schizophrenia, Indigenous Australians, and transgender individuals. This paper discusses the unique engineering and advantages of E-contact interventions in comparison to existing contact strategies, identifies the theories that guide E-contact interventions, provides meta-analytic evidence of its effects, and discusses the strengths, limitations and future directions for E-contact research.

ARTICLE HISTORY Received 19 November 2018; Accepted 6 April 2020

KEYWORDS E-contact; prejudice; intergroup relations; intergroup contact; computer-mediated communication

"The Internet might be particularly well suited for optimal contact, because it creates a protected and controlled environment, and allows scheduling multiple contact experiences across time" (Dovidio et al., 2017, p. 609).

The twenty-first century has been characterised by rapid technological advancements, particularly in the domain of online communication. On average, people are now spending close to 7 hours each day on the Internet, with an increasing number of the world's population actively using social media platforms, such as Facebook, Instagram, and Twitter to stay socially connected (Kemp, 2019), suggesting that that much of our day-to-day interaction has

CONTACT Fiona A. White ✉ fiona.white@sydney.edu.au ✉ School of Psychology (A18), The University of Sydney, New South Wales 2006, Australia

© 2020 European Association of Social Psychology

shifted online. Today, communities from all over the world can connect and interact with one another in cyberspace. Through the Internet, individuals residing in even the most isolated regions can be exposed to ideas and social groups they would never have otherwise encountered. Yet, the world remains divided. Prejudice continues to exist between groups defined by nationality, ethnicity, religion, gender, age, sexuality, weight, and physical and mental health status, to the detriment of both minority and majority group members. This review paper aims to demonstrate how Internet communication technology can be utilised to reduce this prejudice, with a specific focus on text-based electronic contact or E-contact interventions. E-contact represents a novel expansion of Allport's (1954) intergroup contact hypothesis, bringing together individuals from different social groups to interact cooperatively online. As the opening quote by Dovidio and colleagues (Dovidio et al., 2017) recognises, online intergroup contact may be particularly suited to realising conditions thought to enhance the effectiveness of intergroup contact. The E-contact intervention takes up this challenge, and also provides a unique bridge between direct and indirect contact strategies.

We begin this review paper by briefly summarising Allport's (1954) original conceptualisation of the contact hypothesis and the various direct and indirect contact strategies it has inspired. We then introduce a new text-based E-contact intervention, which exists within the broader context of computer mediated communication (CMC), and describe the unique engineering and advantages of E-contact interventions. Following this, we identify the theoretical underpinnings of E-contact, and how the social mechanisms (i.e., Allport's facilitating contact conditions) interact with the cognitive mechanisms (i.e., dual identity recategorisation) to produce a cooperative, goal-directed interaction that promotes less anxiety and more positive intergroup attitudes, emotions, and behaviours. We then provide a detailed description of E-contact studies conducted, along with a meta-analysis of the main effect of E-contact on prejudice, whilst highlighting noteworthy moderators and mediators across multiple intergroup contexts. Finally, we discuss the limitations of E-contact studies and identify relevant opportunities for future research.

The contact hypothesis: challenges and (possible) solutions

Arguably one of psychology's most successful and influential contributions to the formidable challenge of social harmony is Allport's (1954) contact hypothesis. This modest hypothesis proposes that *direct* – or face-to-face – social contact between groups can reduce prejudice when the contact involves cooperation rather than competition, the achievement of a common goal, equal status between the group members, and support from authorities. In the 65 years since Allport identified direct intergroup contact as one possible solution to the interracial and interethnic tensions he observed, this hypothesis has had an enduring influence on psychological theory and practice. An impressive body of research now supports the power of direct contact to alleviate prejudice not just against racial and ethnic groups, but also against groups defined by nationality, religion, gender, sexuality, and disability (Dovidio et al., 2003; Pettigrew & Tropp, 2011; Hewstone & Swart, 2011; Tausch & Hewstone, 2010). In a meta-analytic test conducted on 36 experimental, 168 quasi-experimental, and 492 cross-sectional studies of the effect of direct contact on prejudice, Pettigrew and Tropp (2006) confirmed there to be a significant negative relationship between direct contact and outgroup prejudice ($r = -.213$). Further analyses revealed that this relationship was significantly stronger when the contact intervention was structured to include Allport's (1954) facilitating contact conditions ($r = -.287$).

Despite the promising benefits of direct intergroup contact for prejudice reduction, experiencing positive and cooperative contact with others who are different from ourselves, who we may fear, or who are physically distant from us, can be difficult to realise and maintain in the long-term. In communities in which social groups are physically segregated, such as in Northern Ireland and Israel, individuals often have very limited opportunity to socialise with outgroup members. Thus, direct contact is unlikely to occur naturally and can be challenging for contact researchers to establish and sustain (McKeown, 2013). Even in increasingly diverse and multicultural societies, opportunities for intergroup contact are limited and often missed (Dixon & Durrheim, 2003; Halualani et al., 2004). Negative expectations and anxiety or fear relating to intergroup interactions often dissuade individuals from seeking contact or may even lead them to have superficial or unpleasant experiences (Plant & Devine, 2003; Stephan, 2014). There is empirical evidence to suggest that contact occurring under these conditions worsens intergroup relations and stifles prejudice reduction (Trawalter et al., 2009). Thus, encouraging individuals to engage the outgroup in positive and cooperative intergroup interactions is a key challenge for contact researchers (Paolini et al., 2018).

Although direct contact between groups may seldom occur of its own accord in the real world, particularly under the ideal conditions for prejudice reduction to occur, the contact hypothesis is well suited to expansion into interventions that overcome many of the physical and psychological barriers described above. Researchers have devised other forms of contact, commonly referred to as *indirect* contact, which do not require groups to meet face-to-face (for lengthy reviews, see Brown & Paterson, 2016; Dovidio et al., 2011; Vezzali et al., 2014). One well-examined form of indirect contact is *extended* contact, which proposes that the knowledge of an ingroup member sharing a close friendship with an outgroup member may serve as a basis for prejudice reduction (Wright et al., 1997; for a meta-analysis, see Zhou et al., 2019). Other indirect contact interventions include *vicarious* contact, where participants observe an interaction between an ingroup and outgroup member (Mazziotta et al., 2011), and *imagined* contact, where participants visualise an interaction with an outgroup member

(Crisp & Turner, 2009; for a meta-analysis, see Miles & Crisp, 2014). In the remaining sections, we introduce and discuss an alternative contact strategy that may be used to bridge the physical and psychological divide between members of different groups, and in doing so, improve intergroup relations.

E-contact as an intervention to improve intergroup relations

One substantial aspect of social life, the possibilities of which have been neglected by intergroup contact researchers until only recently and which may provide significant opportunities for intergroup contact, is the Internet – a complex global system of interconnected networks that connects billions of computers and other digital devices to the World Wide Web. As of January 2019, over 4.39 billion people reported using the Internet (Kemp, 2019), representing 57% of the world's population. Further, 3.48 billion individuals use social media platforms, such as Facebook and Twitter, for up to multiple hours a day, and instant messaging programs, such as WhatsApp and Facebook Messenger, engage hundreds of millions of monthly users and continue to rise in popularity (Statista, 2019). Even in the developing world, almost half of the population uses the Internet and has Internet access at home (International Telecommunication Union, 2018). These statistics confirm that much of our daily contact today occurs online. Reflecting this, a large research literature has developed around CMC, which focuses on the social science of communicating via computer-based media technologies (see Walther, 1996). Developing a new contact intervention that launches from this reality is a meaningful empirical pursuit, which also brings intergroup contact research into the twenty-first century (Amichai-Hamburger & Furnham, 2007; Amichai-Hamburger & McKenna, 2006; Walther, 2009). As we will discuss below, the features of the Internet, when used appropriately, provide a unique avenue for social scientists, educators, and social policy makers interested in developing, evaluating, and implementing targeted online interventions aimed at improving intergroup relations. In order to distinguish between research examining CMC broadly and research specifically concerned with reducing prejudice, we have termed this emerging contact strategy *E-contact*.

Several research, educational, and social justice organisations have already used E-contact to promote social harmony between groups living in physical segregation or in conflict around the world (for review, see Amichai-Hamburger et al., 2015). Unfortunately, many of these programs have been largely descriptive in nature, often omit a control condition, and do not evaluate changes in intergroup outcomes, like prejudice. In contrast, one promising line of research, which forms the basis of this review, is the texted-based E-contact intervention that we have advanced (White & Abu-Rayya, 2012; White, Harvey and Abu-Rayya, 2015), which involves synchronous, goal-directed, online communication between group members who never physically meet. To date, this E-contact intervention has been implemented and evaluated in classrooms, laboratories, and online, involving a range of participants and outgroups. The duration and intensity of the intervention has also varied substantially, from hour-long, weekly sessions in 9-week programs to a single interaction spanning just 5 minutes. Moreover, researchers have matched live participants to one another, but have also connected live participants with live and pre-programmed confederates. Prior to discussing the emerging evidence in support of our texted-based E-contact intervention, we will first describe the basic structure and features we perceive as being integral to cultivating positive intergroup relations using E-contact and delineate the advantages we perceive to be associated with text-based E-contact specifically, followed by the theoretical framework underpinning its development.

Engineering texted-based E-contact: structure and features

The basic E-contact intervention comprises two phases. The first phase involves the exchange of individuating information and facilitating awareness of each party's group membership. Specifically, the participant and their interaction partner introduce themselves and provide personal information, such as their age, occupation, hobbies, and interests. It is during this phase that the group membership of each party should be made apparent. This can be achieved by having the individual supervising the interaction make note of each party's group membership (e.g., Schumann et al., 2017, Study, p. 2), having participants complete a profile to share with their interacting partner (e.g., MacInnis & Hodson, 2015), or by facilitating the self-disclosure of group membership by asking soliciting questions during the interaction. For example, in White, Turner et al. (2019), the pre-programmed confederate disclosed their group membership in their answer to one of the getting-to-know-you questions posed by the moderator: "I'm also a practicing Catholic and go to services and social events at my local church". Participants' group membership might also be illustrated through a name prototypical of their group or an image representative of their group that is visible during the interaction (e.g., national flag; Alvídrez et al., 2015). The recognition of the interacting partner belonging to a different group is critical for the interaction to be perceived as intergroup rather than interpersonal. The second phase is a cooperative, goal-directed phase, where the interacting parties are orientated towards a common goal relevant to both of their interests. Frequently, when both parties are university students, the task has been to work together to provide advice to incoming university students on how to cope with the transition from high school to university (e.g., White, Turner et al., 2019). Other tasks have included having participants discuss the importance of recycling (e.g., Berry & White, 2016) or work-life balance (e.g., Boccanfuso, White, & Maunder, under review).

It is important that the entire interaction occurs synchronously. That is, the parties involved should exchange messages in real time, without a substantial delay between messages that can occur in email or forum exchanges. In this way, E-contact fosters a more natural form of communication, similar to direct contact. Comparative studies of synchronous (e.g., instant messaging) and asynchronous (e.g., discussion board) CMC have suggested that synchronous communication may help to eliminate the difference in relationship progression between intergroup and intragroup dyads that is apparent in asynchronous CMC (Mustafa et al., 2012), as well as create a deeper sense of personal involvement in the conversation (Hrastinski, 2008) and foster a stronger sense of community between interacting parties (Schwier & Balbar, 2002). Thus, it is reasonable to expect that the synchronicity of the E-contact interaction may reduce intergroup bias significantly more than forum and email exchanges in which there is a temporal discordance in responses. Moreover, emerging technologies can allow for instantaneous translations between dominant languages to occur seamlessly without the use of mediating translators (Amichai-Hamburger & McKenna, 2006). This allows for the E-contact tool to overcome language and dialect barriers in real-time.

Although we do not believe that E-contact interventions should be limited to text-only exchanges, we perceive there to be distinct advantages to text-based E-contact in comparison to face-to-face contact and E-contact interventions incorporating video and/or audio interactions. For one, there may be less anxiety regarding intergroup interactions that occur online over text. Text-based exchanges remove the threat of visual scrutiny and allow individuals heightened control over their responses and self-presentation (Amichai-Hamburger & McKenna, 2006). Participants are afforded the time to think, type, and edit their responses before sending it to their interaction partner. Relatedly, Maunder et al. (2019) propose that text-based E-contact may be a more appropriate intergroup contact intervention compared to direct contact for some outgroups which may be stereotyped as threatening, such as people with schizophrenia. Interacting with these outgroups online rather than in person may reduce participants' anxiety regarding their safety and allow them to attend to the interaction. As well, text-only exchanges over the Internet affords participants greater anonymity in comparison to video and audio exchanges. Anonymity is advantageous for two reasons. First, it encourages greater self-disclosure and hastens liking and feelings of closeness compared to interactions that occur face-to-face (McKenna et al., 2002). Self-disclosure has been found to be a critical factor in the relationship between intergroup contact and reduced prejudice (Davies et al., 2011). Second, the deficit of non-verbal cues may increase the salience of group membership, which is crucial for positive attitudes towards a single group member to generalise to positive attitudes of the entire group (Pettigrew, 1998). Cao and Lin (2017) argued that the social cues available during video-based contact may personalise the interaction, rendering it interpersonal rather than intergroup. Indeed, they found that video-based E-contact improved perceptions of the contacted group member more than text-based E-contact, whereas text-based E-contact improved perceptions of the entire group more than video-based E-contact. Moreover, unlike audio contact, which if it suffers delays and lags, can lead to increased anxiety during intergroup contact (see Pearson et al., 2008), text-based E-contact largely avoids this complication because the typed messages can be directly observed, and any delay can be at least attributed to typing speed rather than anything anxiety-provoking. Additional advantages of E-contact over other contact interventions are discussed in further detail by Amichai-Hamburger and McKenna (2006) and White, Harvey, Abu-Rayya et al. (2015).

Although empirical evaluations of the E-contact intervention may be more feasible than those of face-to-face interventions, as participants are not required to inhabit the same physical space, E-contact with real participants nevertheless requires both groups to be available at the same time. Moreover, the content and valance of the intergroup interaction is often difficult to control. Some interactions may be more pleasant and thoughtful than others, which is problematic if we want to ensure strict standardisation across interactions. Real confederates adhering to a pre-written script (e.g., Schumann et al., 2017) can somewhat address these issues, but this is still not logistically ideal. One solution we have employed in some of our research is to utilise pre-programmed confederates. Here, prior to the intervention, the researchers input text messages to be sent to the participant by the computer to simulate the involvement of an interacting partner. Regardless of the content of the message sent by the participant, the pre-programmed confederate responds in the same manner; thus, the content of the interaction is strictly controlled across participants. In order to facilitate this exchange, a pre-programmed moderator guides the interaction by posing questions to be answered by the participant and pre-programmed confederate. Although the confederate's responses are determined prior to the interaction, the participants nevertheless experience the exchange as being synchronous: the confederate's messages appear only in response to those of the participant or moderator. To maximise perceptions of realism, the confederate can be programmed to address the participant by name (e.g., "Nice to meet you John", "Good advice John!"). Emojis, typing and grammatical errors, and contemporary text speak can also be incorporated into the scripts. Finally, consistent with commonly-used instant messaging programs, participants are notified when the moderator and their interacting partner are typing by a message on the bottom of the screen (e.g., "Moderator is typing . . . "), which appears after a delay to account for time spent reading the preceding messages. The duration for which the moderator and interaction partner are ostensibly typing is also varied to account for differing lengths of responses. An example of the scripted interaction is provided in Figure 1.

The theoretical underpinnings of E-contact

Contact theory

As detailed above, E-contact is underpinned by Allport's (1954) intergroup contact hypothesis. Moreover, text-based E-contact was specifically developed to accommodate Allport's optimal contact conditions and represents a tightly structured intervention, both of which Pettigrew and Tropp (2006) evidenced as augmenting the effectiveness of contact for reducing prejudice. First, the equal status of those involved in the interaction is achieved, as far as it can be, by carefully matching the participants and outgroup members on demographic variables, such as age, gender, and education level. Although similar efforts can be made to match the status of participants in other contact strategies, Amichai-Hamburger and McKenna (2006) point out that status differentials, such as differences in physical appearance or accent, can jeopardise such efforts. To support this claim, research by Dubrovsky et al. (1991) has demonstrated that status inequalities between interaction partners are significantly reduced when communicating online as opposed to face-to-face. Second, in the E-contact intervention, participants are encouraged to view themselves as a virtual team cooperating towards a common goal. As described previously, this goal is determined a priori by the researcher and often includes working together to find the solution for a common problem. By asking participants to contribute equally to the achievement of this shared goal, we further reinforce the equal status between the interaction partners. Finally, authority support and sanctioning is operationalised in the E-contact intervention by either a parent, a teacher or a school providing consent and support to participate in the intervention, researchers being present in the vicinity to monitor the online interaction, and/or the chat moderator directing each participant to the different phases of the online interaction. To test whether the E-contact intervention is perceived to successfully incorporate these optimal contact conditions, we have used a single item manipulation check for each of the four conditions. Here we asked participants to rate the extent to which their E-contact interaction was cooperative, goal-oriented, allowed for the interaction partners to be on an equal footing, and had the support from an authority figure (e.g., a chat moderator). The mean ratings for each contact condition are displayed in Table 1. The results indicated that participants rated all four of Allport's conditions above the midpoint of the scale, which we interpreted as satisfying Allport's conditions during the interaction.

Dual identity recategorisation

In addition to contact theory, the E-contact intervention is also underpinned by dual identity recategorisation theory (Dovidio et al., 2009). Dual identity recategorisation refers to a set of cognitive processes that incorporates the simultaneous

Figure 1. Lab-based E-contact script between participant (Mikaela), pre-programmed confederate (Jasmine), and moderator.

activation of the original subgroup identity and a common or superordinate identity, which extends favouritism of the ingroup to a superordinate group encompassing the outgroup (Dovidio et al., 2005). For example, in the first phase of the E-contact interaction, both parties disclose their group membership or subgroup identity as well as a shared or superordinate identity (e.g., university students, Australians). Following this, participants are then encouraged to solve a common problem that emphasises to this shared identity, such as transitioning to university (e.g., White, Turner, et al., 2019) or developing a water-saving solution for the Australian environment (e.g., White & Abu-Rayya, 2012). This

Table 1. Mean perception of Allport's (1954) optimal contact condition across E-contact studies.

Study	Cooperation	Common Goal	Equal Status	Authority Support
Berry and White (2016)	4.01 (0.86)	3.79 (0.82)	3.97 (0.72)	4.09 (0.78)
Boccanfuso et al. (under review)	4.08 (1.31)	4.26 (0.98)	4.12 (1.13)	3.81 (1.69)
Maunder et al. (2019)	3.96 (0.73)	3.87 (0.81)	3.94 (0.83)	4.11 (0.91)
Römpke et al. (Römpke et al., 2019, Study, p. 1)	4.00 (0.68)	3.51 (0.74)	4.39 (0.73)	3.69 (0.62)
White, Verrelli et al. (2019)	4.09 (0.73)	3.84 (0.79)	4.01 (0.75)	3.72 (0.87)

Standard deviations are shown in parentheses. Higher values represent higher scores on each variable. Range = 1–5.

shared identity is believed to break down the 'us vs them' frame of thinking and instead create an understanding of 'we' between the groups. Dovidio et al. (2005) have argued that dual identity recategorisation is advantageous to improving the attitudes of both majority and minority group members. For majority group members, group-based inequity is more likely to be recognised, making individuals more likely to respond to moral violations against minority groups. Meanwhile, minority group's outgroup attitudes can be improved because the dual identity allows them to maintain their minority group identity and distinctiveness in a context of connection and cooperation with the majority group.

A new theoretical model

A summative framework of the relationship between the theory-driven processes underpinning the E-contact intervention, mediators and moderators, and their combined impact on intergroup attitudes, emotions, and behaviours, is depicted in Figure 2. This model is comparable to the one proposed by Vezzali et al. (2014) for extended contact, facilitating the identification of similarities and differences between the two contact approaches. Figure 3 elaborates upon this general model and identifies the specific variables that have been targeted across the spectrum of E-contact interventions described below. Importantly, both Figures 2 and 3 begin with an acknowledgement of the experimental nature of the E-contact intervention, which integrates the social elements of intergroup contact theory and the cognitive elements of recategorisation. The extent of the impact of these social-cognitive processes on improving intergroup outcomes are moderated and mediated by variables commonly identified in the intergroup relations literature. By examining similar mediator and moderator variables to previous contact research, it is anticipated that cross-comparisons with the E-contact intervention will be made easier, and will help corroborate existing findings to assist researchers in targeting the underlying mechanisms, identifying groups known to benefit the most from the intervention, and designing interventions in view of factors known to make them more effective.

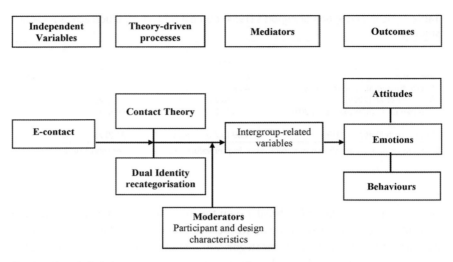

Figure 2. Theoretical model.

Empirical evidence for the text-based E-contact intervention

We and others have found the texted-based E-contact intervention described above to be effective in promoting positive intergroup relations with a range of stigmatised groups and outcome measures. A summary of these studies and their main effects is presented in Table 2, and we describe them in further detail below. This is followed by a meta-analysis calculating the average effect of texted-based E-contact on cognitive, affective, and behavioural intentions measures of prejudice, and a discussion of mediators and moderators of the E-contact effect depicted in Figure 3.

In the first investigation of the effectiveness of E-contact to promote positive intergroup relations, we (White et al., 2014; White & Abu-Rayya, 2012) recruited students from two Catholic ($n = 103$) and two Muslim ($n = 98$) single-sex high schools in Australia. Within their classes, the students were randomly allocated to either the intergroup or intragroup E-contact conditions and completed online self-report questionnaires at 4 time points (T1: six months pre-intervention, T2: two weeks post-intervention, T3: six months post-intervention, T4: 12 months post-intervention) assessing their identification with their religious group as well as intergroup bias using the Image Affective Scale, intergroup anxiety, prejudice, actual outgroup religious knowledge, and friendship in relation to the opposing religious group. In the intergroup contact condition, pairs of students from two classes from the Catholic schools were matched with live pairs of students of the same sex from two equivalent classes from the Muslim schools. These student pairs were connected to one another within an instant messaging program for 45–60 minutes once a week for 9 weeks, with the goal of completing a Harmony

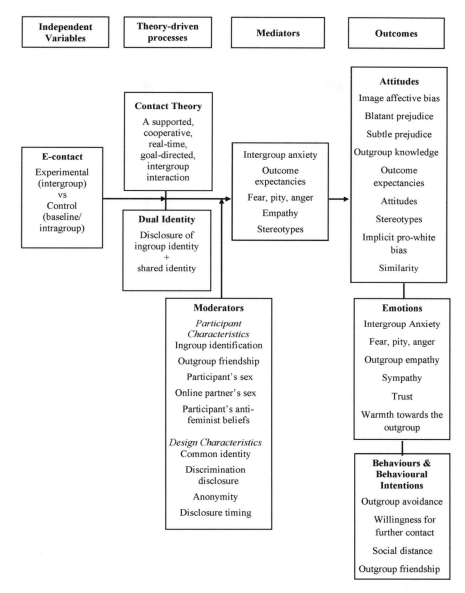

Figure 3. Theoretical model with the variables identified by the studies reviewed.

Project booklet concerned with environmental sustainability. In the first two sessions, the students exchanged personal information about their hobbies and interests and began discussing similarities and differences between Islam and Catholicism. In weeks 3–8, students were instructed to discuss how their respective religions could work together to develop a more environmentally sustainable Australia. This task constituted the common goal of the interaction and also

Table 2. Summary of E-contact studies.

Study	Participants	Outgroup	Control Condition	Moderators	Outcome (Possible Range)	Intergroup E-contact	Control
White & Abu-Rayya (2012; White et al., 2014)	98 Muslim high school students	Catholics	Intragroup contact	Ingroup identification, outgroup friendship	Intergroup bias T1 (0–70)	41.51 (18.51)	50.14 (15.71)
					Intergroup bias T2 (0–70)	20.47 (18.44)	36.40 (15.68)
					Intergroup bias T3 (0–70)	23.04 (18.56)	37.88 (15.68)
					Intergroup bias T4 (0–70)	21.13 (20.70)	35.70 (20.40)
					Intergroup anxiety T1 (0–56)	16.05 (14.87)	19.56 (13.50)
					Intergroup anxiety T2 (0–56)*	7.80 (11.16)	17.63 (13.46)
					Intergroup anxiety T3 (0–56)	11.26 (12.94)	14.98 (15.45)
					Blatant prejudice T1 (6–48)	14.51 (8.85)	17.51 (9.63)
					Blatant prejudice T2 (6–48)	13.33 (8.58)	15.53 (8.17)
					Blatant prejudice T3 (6–48)	14.74 (9.70)	18.05 (10.57)
					Subtle prejudice T1 (6–48)	18.02 (7.73)	20.44 (7.23)
					Subtle prejudice T2 (6–48)	17.47 (7.63)	21.40 (7.59)
					Subtle prejudice T3 (6–48)	16.65 (7.50)	19.43 (8.95)
					Total prejudice T1 (12–96)	32.53 (15.49)	37.95 (14.77)
					Total prejudice T2 (12–96)	30.80 (15.18)	36.93 (14.95)
					Total prejudice T3 (12–96)	31.39 (16.28)	37.48 (18.75)
					Outgroup religious knowledge T1 (0–7)	6.51 (0.57)	6.30 (0.80)
					Outgroup religious knowledge T2 (0–7)*	6.75 (0.48)	6.30 (0.77)
					Outgroup religious knowledge T3 (0–7)	6.58 (0.71)	6.28 (0.83)
					Outgroup friendship T1 (2–16)	6.58 (1.96)	5.95 (1.84)
					Outgroup friendship T2 (2–16)	7.40 (2.43)	6.28 (2.21)
					Outgroup friendship T3 (2–16)	7.29 (2.21)	6.53 (2.35)

(Continued)

Table 2. (Continued).

Study	Participants	Outgroup	Control Condition	Moderators	Outcome (Possible Range)	Intergroup E-contact	Control
White & Abu-Rayya (White & Abu-Rayya, 2012; F.A. White et al., 2014)	103 Catholic high school students	Muslims	Intragroup contact	Ingroup identification, outgroup friendship	Intergroup bias T1 (0–70)	12.49 (15.89)	12.90 (20.91)
					Intergroup bias T2 (0–70)	9.05 (12.32)	11.40 (16.57)
					Intergroup bias T3 (0–70)	8.98 (15.54)	12.33 (16.36)
					Intergroup bias T4 (0–70)	11.77 (15.14)	13.17 (21.33)
					Intergroup anxiety T1 (0–56)	10.39 (12.81)	13.21 (15.52)
					Intergroup anxiety T2 (0–56)*	8.25 (8.84)	12.07 (15.34)
					Intergroup anxiety T3 (0–56)	8.35 (12.07)	10.36 (11.37)
					Blatant prejudice T1 (6–48)	12.93 (8.50)	12.29 (8.61)
					Blatant prejudice T2 (6–48)	12.28 (7.14)	11.76 (7.82)
					Blatant prejudice T3 (6–48)	13.00 (7.88)	12.07 (8.71)
					Subtle prejudice T1 (6–48)	16.16 (7.84)	15.81 (8.28)
					Subtle prejudice T2 (6–48)	15.11 (7.41)	14.88 (8.87)
					Subtle prejudice T3 (6–48)	16.63 (7.90)	14.95 (8.38)
					Total prejudice T1 (12–96)	29.10 (15.25)	28.10 (16.27)
					Total prejudice T2 (12–96)	27.39 (14.06)	26.64 (16.21)
					Total prejudice T3 (12–96)	29.63 (14.92)	27.02 (15.94)
					Outgroup religious knowledge T1 (0–7)	4.70 (1.42)	5.24 (1.46)
					Outgroup religious knowledge T2 (0–7)*	5.79 (1.07)	5.40 (1.33)
					Outgroup religious knowledge T3 (0–7)	5.55 (1.08)	5.55 (1.11)
					Outgroup friendship T1 (2–16)	5.54 (2.34)	6.26 (3.10)
					Outgroup friendship T2 (2–16)	5.64 (2.30)	5.52 (1.85)
					Outgroup friendship T3 (2–16)	5.48 (2.14)	5.48 (1.98)

(Continued)

Table 2. (Continued).

Study	Participants	Outgroup	Control Condition	Moderators	Outcome (Possible Range)	Intergroup E-contact	Control
Abu-Rayya (2017)	85 Israeli undergraduates	Ethiopians	No contact	-	Intergrationist orientation T1 (1–6)	3.41 (0.88)	3.35 (0.84)
					Intergrationist orientation T2 (1–6)	4.84 (0.98)	3.47 (1.02)
White, Turner et al. (2019)	43 Catholic undergraduates	Protestants	No contact	-	Intergroup bias T1 (1–8)	4.22 (1.31)	4.29 (0.93)
					Intergroup bias T2 (1–8)	3.04 (1.15)	4.16 (1.20)
					Intergroup bias T3 (1–8)	3.12 (1.42)	4.41 (1.77)
					Intergroup anxiety T1 (1–8)	3.11 (1.32)	3.07 (1.07)
					Intergroup anxiety T2 (1–8)*	2.01 (1.60)	3.22 (1.96)
					Intergroup anxiety T3 (1–8)	1.93 (1.50)	3.14 (1.65)
					Positive outcome expectancies (1–5)*	3.96 (0.76)	3.68 (0.63)
					Intergroup anxiety (1–5)*	1.78 (0.64)	2.09 (0.51)
					Positive outgroup attitudes (1–8)	7.10 (1.01)	6.46 (1.09)
White, Turner et al. (2019)	43 Protestant undergraduates	Catholics	No contact	-	Positive outcome expectancies (1–5)*	3.97 (0.64)	3.51 (0.45)
					Intergroup anxiety (1–5)*	1.54 (0.45)	1.96 (0.56)
					Positive outgroup attitudes (1–8)	7.53 (0.58)	6.59 (1.33)
White, Verrelli et al. (2019)	140 heterosexual undergraduates	Gay men and lesbian women	Intragroup contact	Participant sex, Online partner's sex	Sexual prejudice (1–6)	1.88 (0.92)	1.93 (0.90)
					Intergroup anxiety (−6–+6)*	0.73 (1.00)	0.99 (1.18)
					Outgroup avoidance (1–7)	1.67 (1.16)	2.02 (1.26)
Maunder et al. (2019)	133 undergraduates	Schizophrenia	No contact, intragroup contact	-	Stereotyping (1–5)*	2.01 (1.29)	2.40 (0.51), 2.46 (0.59)
					Fear (1–7)*	2.24 (1.29)	3.38 (1.28), 3.37 (1.36)
					Pity (1–7)*	4.85 (1.08)	5.09 (0.76), 5.51 (0.87)
					Anger (1–7)*	1.93 (0.96)	2.57 (1.10), 2.60 (1.01)
					Social distance (1–4)	2.21 (0.60)	2.40 (0.51), 2.46 (0.59)

(Continued)

Table 2. (Continued).

Study	Participants	Outgroup	Control Condition	Moderators	Outcome (Possible Range)	Intergroup E-contact	Control
Berry and White (2016)	150 White and Asian undergraduates	Indigenous Australians	No contact, intragroup contact	Common student identity	Outgroup empathy (5–35); Intergroup anxiety (−24–+24)*; Prejudice (18–126); Implicit pro-White bias (−1–+1)	23.97 (4.40); 2.00 (4.26); 36.27 (13.11); 0.34 (0.44)	23.63 (4.54), 24.47 (4.56); 2.00 (4.14), 1.93 (3.80); 46.00 (15.20), 36.78 (15.98); 0.43 (0.42)
Boccanfuso et al. (under review)	77 heterosexual undergraduates, 37 heterosexual community members	Transgender people	Intragroup contact	Discrimination disclosure, participant sex, participant anti-femininity beliefs	Transgender stigma (1–6)	2.14 (0.68)	2.46 (0.86)
Römpke et al. (Römpke et al., 2019, Study, p. 1)	100 German undergraduates	Paraguayans	No contact	-	Sympathy (1–5); Trust (1–5); Similarity (1–5); Willingness for further contact (1–5)	3.69 (0.55); 3.61 (0.53); 3.16 (0.66); 3.43 (0.96)	3.38 (0.60); 3.38 (0.53); 2.80 (0.73); 3.08 (1.05)
Cao and Lin (2017)	62 Chinese students	Hong Kong	Baseline	-	Positive outgroup attitudes T1 (1–7); Positive outgroup attitudes T2 (1–7)	4.80 (0.17); 5.34 (0.17)	-; -
Mustafa and Poh (2019)	100 Chinese and Malaysian students*	Malaysian and Chinese students	Intragroup contact	-	Prejudice (1–7)	2.22 (0.44)	2.09 (0.44)

(Continued)

Table 2. (Continued).

Study	Participants	Outgroup	Control Condition	Moderators	Outcome (Possible Range)	Intergroup E-contact	Control
Schumann et al. (Schumann et al., 2017, Study)	32 non-initiated fraternity members	Initiated fraternity members	Baseline	Anonymity	Not successful at university T1 (1–7)	4.03 (1.09)	–
					Not successful at university T2 (1–7)	3.56 (0.95)	–
					Dirty T1 (1–7)	4.72 (1.59)	–
					Dirty T2 (1–7)	3.88 (1.43)	–
					Alcoholic T1 (1–7)	4.84 (1.11)	–
					Alcoholic T2 (1–7)	4.25 (1.32)	–
					Cliquey T1 (1–7)	5.66 (1.04)	–
					Cliquey T2 (1–7)	5.41 (1.01)	–
					Only interested in having a good time T1 (1–7)	6.22 (0.75)	–
					Only interested in having a good time T2 (1–7)	5.78 (0.83)	–
Schumann et al. (Schumann et al., 2017, Study)	32 initiated fraternity members	Non-initiated fraternity members	Baseline	Anonymity	Serious T1 (1–7)	4.91 (1.00)	–
					Serious T2 (1–7)	4.69 (1.00)	–
					Uptight T1 (1–7)	3.56 (1.22)	–
					Uptight T2 (1–7)	3.41 (1.16)	–
					Not interested in having a good time T1 (1–7)	3.34 (1.15)	–
					Not interested in having a good time T2 (1–7)	3.41 (1.29)	–
					Introverted T1 (1–7)	3.72 (1.11)	–
					Introverted T2 (1–7)	3.75 (1.05)	–
					Too focused on their studies T1 (1–7)	4.91 (0.73)	–
					Too focused on their studies T2 (1–7)	4.81 (0.93)	–

(Continued)

Table 2. (Continued).

Study	Participants	Outgroup	Control Condition	Moderators	Outcome (Possible Range)	Intergroup E-contact	Control
Schumann et al. (Schumann et al., 2017, Study)	37 university students	Rival university students	Baseline	Anonymity	Warmth towards the outgroup T1 (0–100)	59.25 (18.93)	-
					Warmth towards the outgroup T2 (0–100)	76.92 (22.27)	-
					Positive outgroup attitudes T1 (1–7)	4.95 (1.11)	-
					Positive outgroup attitudes T2 (1–7)	5.35 (0.96)	-

* denotes outcome variables predicted as mediators in the study. Higher values represent higher scores on all outcome variable (e.g., higher prejudice, higher knowledge, more friendship, higher implicit preference for Whites compared to the outgroup). Standard deviations are shown in parentheses. The participant groups in Mustafa and Poh (2019) could not be treated as separate studies as results were not reported separately.

emphasised the participants' individual identities as Muslim and Catholic students and their superordinate Australian identities. To conclude the program, the students created and presented a poster detailing their proposed solution to one of the environmental challenges discussed during the project. In the intragroup contact condition, pairs of students in one school were matched with a live pair of students from another school of the same religion and worked through a similar booklet which made no mention of the other religion.

We hypothesised that participants in the intergroup contact condition, compared to participants in the intragroup contact condition, would report a larger reduction in intergroup bias, intergroup anxiety, and prejudice along with a larger increase in outgroup religious knowledge and outgroup friendships from pre- to post-intervention. As displayed in Table 2 and consistent with hypotheses, between T1 and T2, the reductions in intergroup bias and intergroup anxiety and the increase in outgroup religious knowledge was significantly larger for participants in the intergroup contact condition compared to participants in the intragroup contact condition. Although the changes from pre-intervention to two weeks post intervention were not significantly different between the intergroup and intragroup conditions on prejudice or friendship, these results provided the first compelling piece of evidence in favour of text-based E-contact for improving intergroup relations. There was also evidence that this effect endured for at least one year post-intervention (see White et al., 2014). The reduction in intergroup bias between T1 and T3 and T1 and T4 was significantly greater for participants in the intergroup contact condition compared to participants in the intragroup contact condition. Few studies in the wider contact literature have confirmed the endurance of the intervention's effects two-weeks post-intervention, let alone one-year post-intervention.

Since White and Abu-Rayya (2012), the effectiveness of text-based E-contact as a prejudice-reduction intervention has been evaluated in relation to other stigmatised groups using a shorter intervention period. For example, Abu-Rayya (2017) investigated whether intergroup E-contact could improve Israeli's acceptance of Ethiopian's integration into their culture in Israel. Previous correlational studies have found that Israeli majority members who endorse an integrationist orientation towards Ethiopians report less intergroup anxiety (Abu-Rayya, 2016, as cited in Abu-Rayya, 2017), and others have found reduced intergroup anxiety to predict lower intergroup bias (e.g., Pettigrew & Tropp, 2008). Thus, a text-based intergroup E-contact intervention promoting this integrationist orientation was predicted to improve the predominantly negative attitudes held by Israelis towards this minority group through decreased intergroup anxiety.

To test these hypotheses, Abu-Rayya (2017) randomly allocated Israeli social work students from universities and colleges across Israel to intergroup E-contact or a no-contact control condition. In both conditions, participants completed measures assessing their acculturation orientation, bias against Ethiopians using the Image Affective Scale adapted from White and Abu-Rayya (2012), and intergroup anxiety two weeks pre-intervention (T1) and one- and six-weeks post-intervention (T2 and T3, respectively). In the intergroup E-contact condition, participants were paired with a live gender-matched Ethiopian student from a different institution who they interacted with in three, weekly hour-long sessions. Similar to White and Abu-Rayya, the initial session facilitated friendship-building and encouraged participants to consider the similarities and differences between their cultures. In the following two sessions, the participants were instructed to plan and devise a travel guide for a hypothetical socio-cultural trip involving both Israeli and Ethiopian students. This represented the superordinate goal of the interaction. In the control condition, participants simply completed the dependent measures without experiencing any intervention. As displayed in Table 2, participants in the intergroup E-contact condition recorded a larger improvement in their integrationist orientation from T1 to T2 and a larger decrease in intergroup bias and intergroup anxiety between T1 and T2 and T1 and T3 compared to participants in the no-contact control condition. Thus, it appears that an E-contact intervention one-third of the duration of that implemented by White and Abu-Rayya can improve intergroup relations for at least six weeks post-intervention. This result paved the way for even briefer, and therefore more practical, text-based E-contact interventions.

White, Turner et al. (2019) trialled a single session of E-contact involving a pre-programmed confederate with Catholics and Protestants in Northern Ireland. In this context, intergroup conflict continues to be a challenging social issue. Previous correlational studies have supported the inverse association between positive contact and reduced intergroup bias between these groups (e.g., Paolini et al., 2004), yet the fact that many areas in Northern Ireland remain segregated by religion makes naturalistic contact unlikely to occur. We reasoned that a text-based E-contact intervention, which does not require groups to meet face-to-face, might be effective in this context of segregation. White, Turner, et al. also expanded on the evidence for E-contact by introducing further outcome variables pertinent to intergroup relations, being participants' expectation regarding future interactions with outgroup members (i.e., outcome expectancies). It was hypothesised that participants in the intergroup E-contact condition would report more positive outcome expectancies and outgroup attitudes and lower intergroup anxiety compared to participants in the no-contact control condition.

In pursuit of these aims, White, Turner et al. (2019) randomly allocated Catholic and Protestant undergraduate university students from Northern Ireland to intergroup E-contact or a no-contact control condition. Participants in the intergroup E-contact condition engaged in a single 10-minute interaction with a gender-matched pre-programmed confederate who had a first name prototypical of the other religious group. Under the supervision of the chat moderator, the participant and confederate were first guided to share some personal information with one another (e.g., their interests and hobbies), at which point the confederate also disclosed their religiosity and church attendance. The participant and confederate were then instructed to worked together to develop one strategy to assist future first-year university students to transition from high school to university. In order to control for cognitive load, participants in the no-contact control condition visualised a positive nature scene then described what they imagined. Immediately following these activities, all participants completed questionnaires assessing outcome expectancies, intergroup anxiety, and attitudes towards the outgroup. As displayed in Table 2, participants in the E-contact condition reported more positive outcome expectancies and outgroup attitudes and lower intergroup anxiety compared to participants in the no-contact control condition. Importantly, the results demonstrate that even a very brief, single session of E-contact, and one which is strictly guided by a moderator to facilitate interaction with a pre-programmed confederate, is capable of promoting intergroup harmony between groups with a history of conflict.

The promising findings of White, Turner et al. (2019) in relation to the effectiveness of a brief, text-based E-contact intervention with a pre-programmed confederate have been replicated in relation to prejudice against lesbian women and gay men (White, Verrelli et al., 2019), people with schizophrenia (Maunder et al., 2019), transgender individuals (Boccanfuso et al., under review), and Indigenous Australians (Berry & White, 2016). In each of these studies, participants were randomly allocated to intergroup or intragroup E-contact with a pre-programmed confederate for a text-only interaction with an average duration between 15 and 18 minutes. Maunder et al. (2019) and Berry and White (2016) also utilised a no-contact control condition in which participants completed the dependent measures online without experiencing any intervention or contact with the researcher or confederate. This was done to verify that it is text-based E-contact with an outgroup member that decreases prejudice, rather than intragroup contact raising prejudice or the positive effect of an interaction in general decreasing prejudice. Following the two-phase procedure described above, the participant and the interacting partner in the intergroup and intragroup contact conditions were first guided to introduce themselves, and then cooperated towards a common goal. In White, Verrelli et al. (2019) and Maunder et al., the common goal was again related to providing advice to incoming university students. However, the common goal differed in the other two studies in order to accommodate participants and confederates who were not university students. In Boccanfuso et al. (under review), participants discussed strategies to maintain work-life balance, and in Berry and White, participants discussed strategies to increase recycling. In each study, the immediate effect of the E-contact intervention was assessed on variables relevant to the target outgroup. In each of these studies we also assessed participants' agreement with the interaction being characterised by equal status, cooperation, a common goal, and authority support using a single item for each variable (see Table 1). Given the similarity between these studies, we describe them only briefly below.

In White, Verrelli et al. (2019) heterosexual first-year psychology students were randomly allocated to one of four conditions, being intergroup contact with a confederate identified as either a lesbian woman or gay man, or intragroup contact with either a male or female heterosexual confederate. The pre-programmed confederate disclosed their sexuality by casually mentioning their boyfriend (intergroup contact/male confederate or intragroup contact/female confederate) or girlfriend (intergroup contact/female confederate or intragroup contact/male confederate). Immediately following the interaction, the participants reported their attitudes towards gay men and lesbian women, intergroup anxiety, and their desire to avoid members of this group. As displayed in Table 2, overall, participants in the intergroup E-contact condition reported significantly lower outgroup avoidance than participants in the intragroup E-contact condition. Although there was no significant main effect of E-contact on sexual prejudice or intergroup anxiety, confederate and participant sex were found to interact on these variables. This moderation effect is described in more detail below.

Maunder et al. (2019) randomly allocated first-year psychology students with no history of mental illness to an intergroup E-contact, intragroup E-contact, or no-contact control condition. In both E-contact conditions, participants engaged in a single interaction with a pre-programmed, gender-matched confederate, who was ostensibly also a first-year psychology student. In the intragroup condition, the confederate professed an interest in mental illness to be their reason for studying psychology, whereas in the intergroup condition the confederate disclosed their diagnosis of schizophrenia and intention to learn more about their illness. Immediately after the interaction, the participants completed questionnaires assessing their target-relevant emotions towards people with schizophrenia (i.e., fear, pity, anger), as well as their endorsement of stereotypes and their willingness to be in particular social relationship (e.g., work colleagues) with people with schizophrenia (i.e., social distance). As displayed in Table 2, participants in the intergroup contact condition reported significantly lower stereotype endorsement, fear, and anger, towards people with schizophrenia in the intergroup E-contact condition compared to the intragroup and no-contact control conditions. However, social distance did not significantly differ between any of the conditions, and pity was lower in the intergroup E-contact condition only compared to the intragroup E-contact condition. The authors reasoned that prejudice increased in this condition due to the ingroup confederate sympathetically framing mental illness as something that needs to be understood.

Berry and White (2016) randomly allocated White and Asian Australian first-year psychology students to intergroup E-contact, intragroup E-contact, or no-contact control condition. In both E-contact conditions, participants engaged in a single interaction with a pre-programmed, gender-matched confederate

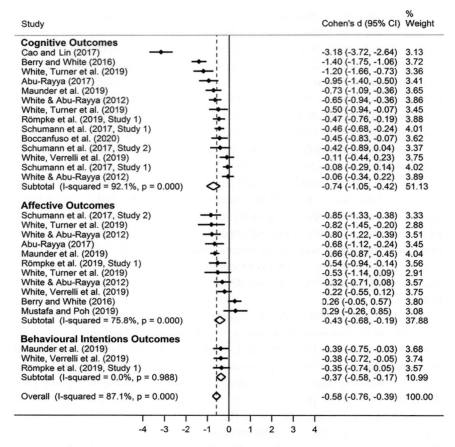

Figure 4. Forest plot of the average effect of text-based E-contact on cognitive, affective, and behavioural intentions measures of prejudice.

following the standard two-phase E-contact procedure. In the intergroup E-contact condition, the confederate's group membership was disclosed with the text statement "in my spare time i like ... hanging out with my cousins and my mob. Im a proud Aboriginal [woman/man] ... ". The confederate in the intragroup contact condition made no such reference to Indigenous culture. The researchers also manipulated whether the confederate and participant shared a common ingroup identity or not by having the confederate disclose being a first-year psychology student or having no plans to study at university, respectively. Following the interaction, participants rated their empathy, anxiety, prejudice, and implicit bias in relation to Indigenous Australians. As displayed in Table 2, participants in the intergroup E-contact condition and participants in the common identity condition reported significantly lower prejudice than participants in the no-contact condition. However, there were no significant differences on any of the dependent variables between the intergroup and intragroup E-contact conditions or the common identity conditions, and no significant interaction between the E-contact and common identity conditions. There were also no indirect effects of intergroup E-contact on prejudice through outgroup empathy or intergroup anxiety.

Boccanfuso et al. (under review) randomly allocated heterosexual and cisgender first-year psychology students and community members recruited through Facebook to intergroup or intragroup contact. Unlike previous E-contact studies, this study was conducted entirely online to facilitate the inclusion of non-student participants. All participants completed a preliminary questionnaire in which they indicated their availability and were subsequently contacted by the researcher to schedule a time to participate (ostensibly when another participant would be available). Similar to the studies described above, the participant and pre-programmed confederate were first guided to introduce themselves. In the intergroup contact condition, the confederate disclosed being a transgender woman, whereas the confederate was intended to be assumed to be a cisgender woman in the absence of this disclosure in the intragroup contact condition. The confederate also disclosed experiencing frequent, personal discrimination in relation to their gender identity (whether transgender or cisgender) in the discrimination disclosure condition, or no personal discrimination in the no disclosure condition. As depicted in Table 2, participants in the intergroup E-contact condition reported lower stigma than participants in the intragroup E-contact condition, but E-contact condition did not significantly interact with discrimination disclosure condition.

A number of studies outside of our lab have also utilised the text-based E-contact intervention to reduce prejudice between groups, demonstrating the effectiveness of E-contact in different countries, using diverging methods and participants. For example, Römpke et al. (2019, Study) randomly assigned German university students to an intergroup E-contact or no-contact control condition. In the intergroup E-contact condition, the participants were paired with a pre-programmed confederate identified as female from Paraguay, with whom they first discussed their hobbies and interests relating to art over a text-based instant messaging program for 15 messages. Unlike in the E-contact studies reported above, where participants are able to type their own replies, participants' responses during the conversation were constrained: they chose one of two pre-written replies to send to the confederate. As well, the participants knew the confederate to be pre-programmed. Following this initial conversation, the participant and confederate were guided to each complete one half of a simple puzzle which, when combined, would create a piece of abstract art. Participants in the control condition merely selected statements representing their attitude towards art and completed the puzzle independently. Immediately following the intervention, the participants reported their sympathy towards and trust of Paraguayans, their perceived similarity between Paraguayans and Germans, and their willingness for further contact with Paraguayans. Consistent with their hypotheses, the researchers found participants in the intergroup E-contact condition to report significantly higher scores on each of the outcome variables compared to participants in the no-contact control condition, with the exception of willingness for further contact, which was only marginally significantly improved.

Cao and Lin (2017), Mustafa and Poh (2019), and Schumann et al. (2017), have also found text-based intergroup E-contact to have an overall positive effect on intergroup bias. For example, Cao and Lin found Chinese university students to report more positive attitudes towards people from Hong Kong after a - 5–7 minute interaction with a male Hong Kong confederate, compared to their attitudes before the intervention. The participants interacted with the confederate either via video- or text-based E-contact. As described above, although participants in both conditions reported significantly improved attitudes towards the outgroup, attitudes towards the entire outgroup improved significantly more in the text-based contact condition compared to the video-based contact condition.

Mustafa and Poh (2019) examined changes in prejudice over four sessions in which Malaysian and Chinese undergraduate students exchanged personal information in intergroup or intragroup dyads either face-to-face or over text-based instant messaging for up to three hours at a time. Prejudice against the outgroup was measured after each session. Regrettably, the authors did not control for baseline levels of prejudice between the four groups, which appears to have been higher in the intergroup E-contact condition compared to the intragroup E-contact condition, and lower in the intergroup face-to-face condition compared to the intragroup face-to-face condition. Thus, the results give the impression that intergroup face-to-face contact significantly reduced prejudice averaged across the timepoints compared to intragroup face-to-face contact, and that there was no significant difference in prejudice between the intergroup and intragroup E-contact conditions. However, examination of mean prejudice at each timepoint suggests that prejudice increased in both of the face-to-face conditions and in the intergroup face-to-face condition especially, remained the same in the intragroup E-contact condition, and decreased over time in the intergroup E-contact condition.

Finally, across two studies which also manipulated anonymity within the text-based E-contact interaction (discussed below), Schumann et al. (2017) found stereotyping to be significantly lower and outgroup warmth to be significantly higher post-contact compared to pre-contact. Study 1 connected initiated and uninitiated study members of a fraternity at a Belgium university for a 15-minute, text-only interaction discussing the use of Facebook for studying and exam preparation. Here, the beneficial effect of E-contact was found only in the majority (uninitiated) students, which the authors attributed to the minority (initiated) students reporting less stereotyping at baseline. In Study 2, first-year psychology students from one English university were paired with a live confederate identified as a student from a rival university. The interacting parties spent 15 minutes brainstorming ideas for a cultural event to take place at both universities.

Meta-analysis of text-based E-contact studies

Given the recent growth in the number of studies empirically investigating the effects of text-based intergroup E-contact on prejudice, it is now possible to compute an average effect size. To do so, we conducted a random-effects meta-analysis on the twelve studies described above. To be included, the study must have experimentally manipulated text-based intergroup E-contact with either a live or pre-programmed outgroup member and compared it to a control condition in which there was no interaction with an outgroup member. This ruled out studies like Alvídrez at al. (2015), Dane et al. (2015), MacInnis and Hodson (2015), and Postmes, Spears, and Lea (2002), which did not utilise a no-contact control condition. We included all participant groups as well as outgroups, including rival university groups. We considered all self-report, implicit, and behavioural measures of prejudice, including outgroup stereotyping and attitudes, intergroup anxiety, and social distance, that were taken in relation to the entire outgroup rather than only the contacted outgroup member. Thus, the quantity and quality of emotion expressed during the E-contact intervention, measured by White, Abu-Rayya et al. (2015), was not considered. Knowledge relevant to the outgroup was also not considered, as it is not embodied by the generally accepted definition of prejudice.

As shown in Table 2, the type and number of control conditions, outcome measures, and assessment period differed substantially between the eligible studies. Hence, it was necessary to make decisions regarding the data to extract for analyses. Most studies employed only one eligible comparison condition, being a baseline, a no-contact, or an intragroup contact condition. However, when a baseline measure of prejudice was used in conjunction with another control condition (e.g., Abu-Rayya, 2017; White & Abu-Rayya, 2012), we chose not to utilise the pre-intervention measures as the comparison, as the participants' level of bias may have changed between pre- and post-intervention due to factors other than the intervention (e.g., direct contact). When both intragroup and no-contact control conditions were used (e.g., Berry & White, 2016; Maunder et al., 2019), we averaged across these two comparison conditions to create a single pairwise comparison. As including every outcome variable in the analysis would have violated the assumption of independent effect sizes in meta-analyses, we classified each dependent variable as being a cognitive (e.g., intergroup bias, outgroup attitudes, stereotype endorsement, similarity to the ingroup, prejudice, implicit bias), affective (e.g. intergroup anxiety, fear, anger, pity, empathy, sympathy, warmth), or behavioural intentions (e.g., outgroup friendship, social distance, outgroup avoidance, behavioural intentions) measure of prejudice, following other meta-analyses on intergroup contact (e.g., Miles & Crisp, 2014). When the study reported multiple effects within a single category, these were averaged to create one effect per category. As only one study measured the effect of intergroup E-contact on actual behaviour (i.e., White & Abu-Rayya, 2012) this outcome could not be included in the analyses. As the majority of studies only measured the effect of the intervention immediately, we extracted prejudice scores from the earliest time point post-intervention. Finally, when participants belonged to different social groups and interacted with respective outgroup members (e.g., Catholics and Protestants interacting with Protestants and Catholics, respectively; Schumann et al., 2017, Study 1; White & Abu-Rayya, 2012; White, Turner et al., 2019) these were treated as separate studies provided each group had a corresponding comparison condition and outcomes were reported separately for each group.

The meta-analysis was conducted using Stata Version 14.2 and the command *metan*. Values were adjusted so that a negative effect size would indicate less bias in the intervention condition compared to the comparison condition. We used the standardised mean difference, Cohen's *d*, as the effect size, and interpreted the results according to the new guidelines proposed by Funder and Ozer (2019) in which *r*s of .05, .10, .20, .30, and .40 (equivalent to *d*s of 0.1, 0.2, 0.4, 0.6, and 0.9) indicate very small, small, medium, large, and very large effects. The results revealed that text-based, intergroup E-contact, compared to control, had a significant and large effect on cognitive measures of prejudice, $d = -0.736$ (95% CI [−1.051, −0.420]), a significant and medium effect on affective measures of prejudice, $d = -0.434$ (95% CI [−0.678, −0.190]), and a significant and medium effect on behavioural intentions measures of prejudice, $d = -0.375$ (95% CI [−0.583, −0.167]), although the last was based on only three effect sizes. These results are displayed in Figure 4. When one substantial outlier (Cao & Lin, 2017, $d = -3.176$) was removed from the meta-analysis on the cognitive measures of prejudice, the effect size remained significant but was somewhat reduced in size, $d = -0.559$ (95% CI [−0.779, −0.339]). These results are comparable to the average effects of true experiments manipulating direct contact ($r = -.295$; T. F. Pettigrew & Tropp, 2006) and imagined contact ($d = -0.346$ on cognitive, $d = -0.410$ on affective, $d = -0.459$ on behavioural intentions; Miles & Crisp, 2014), and numerically larger than the average correlation found between extended contact and prejudice ($r = -.25$ on cognitive, $r = -.26$ on affective, $r = -.23$ on behaviour and behavioural intentions; Zhou et al., 2019). In the following sections, we discuss some of the potential mediators and moderators of the E-contact effect.

Mediators of the E-contact intervention

Intergroup anxiety

Intergroup anxiety has received the most empirical attention. Intergroup anxiety represents the discomfort an individual may feel when anticipating or experiencing intergroup encounters (Stephan, 2014). Participants who score high on intergroup anxiety report feeling uncomfortable, defensive, awkward, and self-conscious in such encounters. Multiple past studies have found intergroup anxiety to be a strong mediator of the intergroup contact effect, with both direct (Pettigrew & Tropp, 2008) and indirect (Vezzali et al., 2014) contact observed to diminish the anxiety participants feel in future intergroup encounters, which in turn reduces prejudice against the outgroup. The findings of White and Abu-Rayya (2012), White et al. (2014), Abu-Rayya (2017), White, Turner et al. (2019), and White, Verrelli et al. (2019), suggest reduced intergroup anxiety also underlies the beneficial effect of text-only E-contact. White and Abu-Rayya (2012; White et al., 2014) performed these analyses on their longitudinal datasets, finding text-based intergroup E-contact to predict reduced intergroup anxiety two weeks after the intervention, which in turn predicted reduced intergroup bias measured six months and one year post-intervention, for both their Catholic and Muslim participants. Similarly, Abu-Rayya (2017) found the effect of engaging in intergroup E-contact on intergroup bias against Ethiopians six weeks post-intervention to be partially mediated by reduced intergroup anxiety one week after the intervention. The longitudinal designs of White and Abu-Rayya (2012; White et al., 2014) and Abu-Rayya (2017) make these results particularly compelling. By comparing contact condition at Time 1 to intergroup anxiety at Time 2 and prejudice at Time 3, researchers can be more confident in the direction of the relationship between the outcome variables compared to when proposed mediator and outcome variables are measured concurrently.

E-contact researchers have also ventured a step further, exploring *how* text-based E-contact reduces intergroup anxiety. White, Turner et al. (2019) argued that participants' expectations for their ability to create a positive impression during the intergroup interaction (i.e., outcome expectancies) precedes feelings of intergroup anxiety. We reasoned that text-based E-contact provides participants with a high degree of control over how they present themselves to the outgroup, and may hence improve individuals' self-efficacy in creating the desired impression in subsequent encounters, and therefore reduce intergroup anxiety. White, Turner et al. (2019) tested this hypothesis in a serial mediation model comprised of E-contact condition, outcome expectancies, intergroup anxiety, and outgroup attitudes. Indeed, the indirect effect of intergroup contact compared to intragroup contact on outgroup attitudes through outcome expectancies and intergroup anxiety was statistically significant. It appears that E-contact may provide participants with the necessary mastery experience to increase participants' abilities in presenting a desired and well-received impression during an intergroup interaction, which in turn, may reduce the anxiety that often results when anticipating an outgroup interaction.

Intergroup emotions

Building on the importance of intergroup anxiety in explaining the effect of E-contact on prejudice, researchers have also evaluated other affective variables as potential mechanisms. Maunder et al. (2019) argued that willingness for future intergroup encounters may depend on negative outgroup stereotypes and the emotions evoked by these stereotypes being challenged in the intergroup encounter. Stereotypes regarding people with schizophrenia include group members being dangerous and unpredictable, incompetent, and not responsible for their illness, which were conjectured to relate to fear, anger, and pity, respectively. Thus, we tested a mediation model in which text-based E-contact condition predicted fear, anger, and pity towards people with schizophrenia, in turn predicting stereotyping and social distance. Stereotyping was also allowed to predict social distance. Both fear and anger were found to significantly mediate the relationship between E-contact and stereotypes, and fear and stereotyping were found to mediate the pathway to social distance. These findings reinforce the importance of intergroup emotions for bias reduction via E-contact: It was through the reduction of the group-targeted emotions of fear and anger that negative stereotypes about and social distance towards people with schizophrenia were subsequently reduced.

The text-based nature of E-contact also lends itself to the examination of the features of the contact experience the interaction can explain the subsequent reduction in prejudice. That is, the text exchanged by E-contact participants provides contact researchers with a valuable, dynamic source of data that can be qualitatively analysed to reveal underlying mechanisms of the contact-prejudice relationship. White, Abu-Rayya, et al. (2015) did exactly this, employing Linguistic Inquiry and Word Count (Pennebaker et al., 2015) software to objectively measure the quantity and quality of emotion expressed during the E-contact intervention conducted by White and Abu-Rayya (2012). The authors found reduced expressions of anger and sadness in the intergroup condition to mediate the effect of contact on intergroup bias. In the future, researchers may also be able to employ webcams and facial recognition software to monitor the nonverbal behaviour of participants as they engage in the interaction.

Although Pettigrew and Tropp (2008) also identified knowledge and empathy as important mediators in relation to direct contact, E-contact researchers have found less evidence supporting these mechanisms: White and Abu-Rayya's (2012) participants' knowledge of the outgroup's religion was found to improve in the Catholic participants in the intergroup contact condition from pre- to post-intervention, but this variable did not significantly mediate the effect of intergroup E-contact on intergroup bias. Moreover, Berry and White (2016) found neither empathy nor intergroup anxiety to be significant mediators of the effect of E-contact on prejudice against Indigenous Australians.

Moderators of the E-contact intervention

Participant characteristics

Text-based E-contact seems to be more effective when participants have more negative impressions of the outgroup initially. As outlined above, White and Abu-Rayya (2012) found contact to be effective at improving intergroup attitudes and anxiety overall. However, closer inspection of the data found crucial differences in attitude change between the Muslim and Catholic participants. Specifically, the reductions in intergroup bias and anxiety between T1 and T2 were more prominent in the Muslim participants in the intergroup contact condition, while the increase in outgroup knowledge between T1 and T2 was most apparent in the Christian participants in the intergroup contact condition in comparison to the other conditions. These differential improvements for each religious group were posited to be related to the baseline levels reported. For example, the Catholic students reported low levels of intergroup bias towards and outgroup knowledge about Muslims prior to the intervention, whereas the Muslim students reported higher bias towards and knowledge about Catholics. Similarly, as described above, Berry and White (2016) attributed the null effect of intergroup E-contact compared to intragroup E-contact to the highly favourable baseline attitudes of participants towards Indigenous Australians, and Schumann et al. (2017) attributed the non-significant change in stereotypes held by initiated fraternity students towards uninitiated fraternity students to be due to their lower stereotyping prior to the E-contact intervention. When prejudice is already low, there is limited potential for E-contact (in fact, any contact intervention) to reduce prejudice further. However, intergroup E-contact appears to be an effective means of diminishing bias in participants with higher bias to begin with.

The ability of E-contact to reduce prejudice in the participants most in need of intervention has also been investigated directly. Originally, Allport (1954) worried that intergroup contact might be ineffective for individuals prone to high levels of prejudice. Recently, a corpus of research has countered this concern, finding the association between self-reported contact and intergroup bias to be as strong, if not *stronger*, and for manipulated contact interventions to be as effective, if not *more* effective, in this population compared to individuals less prone to prejudice (for review, see Hodson, 2011). One factor that makes participants prone to prejudice is high identification with the ingroup (Riek et al., 2006). Hodson et al. (2009) found self-reported contact quantity with "homosexuals" to be significantly negatively related to bias for participants higher in ingroup identification whereas this relationship was not significant for participants lower in ingroup identification. White and Abu-Rayya (2012) replicated this in relation to text-based E-contact and bias between Catholics and Muslims. We found ingroup identification prior to the intervention moderated the effect of intergroup E-contact on intergroup bias reduction two weeks and six months after the intervention, albeit only for the Muslim participants. Specifically, the reduction in intergroup bias was significantly more pronounced for Muslim participants with high ingroup identification compared to participants with low ingroup identification.

That E-contact is more effective for prejudice-prone participants has also been found by White, Verrelli et al. (2019) and Boccanfuso et al. (under review) using variables directly related to prejudice against their target outgroups. Stigma against transgender individuals has been found to be related to both gender and gender normative beliefs, with males reporting higher prejudice than females and negative attitudes towards male femininity correlating positively with stigma (Riggs et al., 2012). In accordance with previous findings and our hypotheses, E-contact with a pre-programmed transgender confederate was found to be more effective for male participants compared to female participants and for participants higher in anti-femininity beliefs compared to participants lower in anti-femininity beliefs (Boccanfuso et al., under review). Similarly, White, Verrelli et al. (2019) found the effect of intergroup E-contact on prejudice and intergroup anxiety against lesbian women and gay men to be marginally stronger for male participants compared to female participants, in accordance with males reporting higher prejudice against sexual minorities compared to females (Kite & Whitley Jr, 1996). Moreover, the results of White, Verrelli et al. (2019) also suggest that prejudice-proneness and characteristics of the confederate can interact. Here, we found a significant three-way interaction between E-contact condition, participant sex, and confederate sex on intergroup anxiety. Compared to female participants overall and male participants in the intragroup E-contact condition, male participants reported significantly lower intergroup anxiety when they interacted with a lesbian woman but not when they interacted with a gay man. This lower intergroup anxiety also predicted lower sexual prejudice and outgroup avoidance for male participants interacting with a lesbian woman in a moderated moderated mediation model, consistent with Hodson's (2011) proposition that intergroup contact reduces prejudice in ideologically intolerant participants through established mediating processes. Conversely, female participants' intergroup anxiety did not differ according to confederate sex.

Incongruous with the proposition that intergroup contact is particularly effective for individuals more likely to be prejudiced against the outgroup, White and Abu-Rayya (2012) also found the reduction in intergroup bias to be greater for the Muslim participants who reported more friendship with Catholics prior to the intervention to compared to the Muslim participants reporting fewer Catholic friends. As outgroup friendship is a strong negative predictor of prejudice, this result somewhat contradicts the notion that intergroup contact is more effective for participants more likely to be prejudiced. As well, it is important to note that White and Abu-Rayya (2012), White, Verrelli et al. (2019), and Boccanfuso et al. (under review) relied entirely or predominantly on student samples. As student samples are routinely recognised as being more liberal-minded and less prejudiced than community members (Henry, 2008), the participants classified as highly prejudiced in these E-contact studies may only be relatively so.

Design characteristics

There are also some features unique to CMC that have been found to moderate the effectiveness of the E-contact intervention. Alvídrez et al. (2015) had participants interact via text-based E-contact with four pre-programmed Spanish ingroup members and one live Latin American outgroup member. In the depersonalised condition, the interacting parties' group membership was emphasised using an image of their national flag. In the individuated condition, the participants were identified by a photo of their face. The researchers also manipulated the stereotypicality of the outgroup member within the interaction. The interacting parties were first asked to introduce themselves and then solve a puzzle together, after which the participant was paired with the outgroup member in order to discuss, with the aim of reaching a consensus, some controversial topics in Spanish society. As expected, participants in the depersonalised condition more strongly identified with their ingroup than participants in the individuated condition. Moreover, participants in the depersonalised condition reported significantly lower subtle prejudice against Latin Americans when the outgroup member was counter-stereotypical compared to stereotypical compared to participants in the individuated condition. Similar to Cao and Lin (2017), Alvídrez et al. (2015) attributed this to the depersonalised condition increasing group salience and thereby facilitating individual-to-group generalisation from the E-contact interaction.

In contrast, other researchers have found significantly greater improvements in bias when more individuating information is available compared to less. As stated above, Schumann et al. (2017) manipulated anonymity in the E-contact interaction in two studies. The researchers hypothesised that intergroup E-contact could be less effective for participants in the anonymous intergroup contact condition compared to participants in the non-anonymous condition. In the first study, anonymity did not significantly impact stereotype reduction from pre- to post-intervention. However, there was an effect in the second study. As described above, participants in this study interacted with a live confederate from a rival university. The participant and confederate's anonymity were manipulated simultaneously: both parties were either anonymous (no photograph, no name) or non-anonymous (photograph and name). Participants completed measures of outgroup attitudes and feelings of warmth towards the outgroup before and after the interaction, as well as measures of the extent to which they believed the confederate was engaged in the chat and their willingness to meet the confederate face-to-face. Although the direct effect of anonymity condition on warmth and attitudes was not significant, the indirect effect of anonymity condition via confederate engagement was significant on both outcome variables. Specifically, confederate anonymity predicted lower perceived engagement, which in turn lowered the perceived quality and pleasantness of the interaction, resulting in lower positive attitudes and less warmth towards the outgroup and less willingness to meet the confederate in person.

The results of Postmes et al. (2002, Study 2) also suggest that depersonalisation during intergroup E-contact interactions may be harmful for intergroup attitudes. Here, 70 undergraduate psychology students interacted within a 6-person group consisting of themselves, two pre-programmed confederates identified as psychology students (ingroup members), and three pre-programmed confederates identified as being from the sociology or business school (outgroup members) in a text-based computer-conferencing system. The participants were randomly allocated to a condition in which they and the confederates were depersonalised (identified by a generic username) or individuated (identified by a photograph). Rather than cooperate on a task, the participants and confederates were to provide their opinion on a number of political statements. Participants in the depersonalised condition reported significantly more negative outgroup stereotypes and significantly higher outgroup homogeneity compared to participants in the individuated condition. This was despite the fact that participants in the depersonalised condition reported significantly higher group salience than participants in the individuated condition. However, this may be due to the fact that the outgroup members did not challenge stereotypes about their group – the authors specifically had them provide opinions that were stereotypical of their group, in which case the higher group salience may have facilitated individual-to-group generalisation that was negative. These divergent results in regard to the role of anonymity and depersonalisation during the interaction provide fertile ground for future research. It may be that there is an optimal level of individuation during CMC that maintains group salience as well as the quality of the interaction in order for prejudice-reduction to occur.

One further factor that has been examined in relation to E-contact is the timing of group membership disclosure. Within intergroup contact encounters and E-contact in particular, there is evidence that early disclosure of homosexuality, compared to late disclosure, is beneficial. MacInnis and Hodson (2015) had heterosexual university students interact via text-based E-contact with a gender-matched pre-programmed confederate who the participants learned, either before or after the interaction to be same-sex attracted from a profile ostensibly completed by their interacting partner. Compared to participants in the later disclosure condition, participants in the earlier disclosure condition reported the encounter as being more positive and reported more positive attitudes towards and a closer bond with their interacting partner. Similarly, across three studies, Dane et al. (2015) found that earlier, compared to later, disclosure of a confederate's minority sexual orientation via a pre-recorded video lead to more positive perceptions of the confederate. In Dane et al. (2015), researchers did not assess attitudes towards the entire outgroup, and MacInnis and Hodson (2015) found no difference in prejudice towards lesbian women and gay men in general between their early and late disclosure conditions. Nevertheless, we believe that earlier disclosure of a stigmatised identity during text-based E-contact could be beneficial for intergroup bias. Early disclosure is likely to raise the extent to which an interaction is intergroup compared to interpersonal, and for attitudes towards one outgroup member to generalise to positive attitudes towards the entire outgroups, impressions of the contacted outgroup member should be as positive as possible.

Limitations and future directions for E-contact

We have now described evidence for the main effect of text-based E-contact on intergroup bias, as well as potential mediators and moderators of the effect. We have also discussed the strengths of E-contact over other forms of intergroup contact, such as the incorporation of Allport's (1954) optimal contact conditions, the synchronicity of the interaction, and the anonymity and increased psychological control over the interaction which may engender lower levels of anxiety, increase engagement, and facilitate individual-to-group generalisation. We have also demonstrated how, similar to indirect contact interventions, E-contact is able to overcome barriers to direct contact including segregation and avoidance. Now, we consider the limitations of the empirical E-contact studies we have reviewed here to make further suggestions for future research.

Differences between the E-contact interventions

First, we acknowledge that the operationalisation of the live and pre-programmed versions of E-contact differ from one another in several ways. Most obviously, the studies conducted by White and Abu-Rayya (2012), (2014), Abu-Rayya (2017), Cao and Lin (2017), Mustafa and Poh (2019), and Schumann et al. (2017) enabled interaction between real group members compared to the pre-programmed outgroup members utilised by White, Turner et al. (2019), White, Verrelli et al. (2019), Maunder et al. (2019), Berry and White (2016), and Boccanfuso et al. (under review), and Römpke et al. (Römpke et al., 2019, Study, p. 1). The use of pre-programmed out-group members renders the E-contact intervention more practical to administer and affords researchers strict control over the content of the interaction, but it also presents some issues that should be addressed going forward. For example, as illustrated in Figure 1, it necessitates the use of a pre-programmed moderator to guide the interaction. This is designed to prevent the participant from asking questions of the confederate which they have not been programmed to answer. The supervised nature of the interaction may cause it to be perceived as somewhat superficial and less natural in flow than the unmoderated version of text-based E-contact. Moreover, despite efforts to disguise the pre-programmed nature of the confederate, some participants nevertheless identify the interacting partner to not be real; this was as many as 13.6% of participants in Maunder et al., (2019). The effect of the interaction on these participants' prejudice is unknown, as they have typically been excluded from our studies. One possibility is that the deception causes a rebound in prejudice, increasing prejudice as a backlash against the deception. However, prejudice may also be reduced despite knowing the interacting partner to be pre-programmed. Imagined contact reduces prejudice in spite of participants' awareness of the outgroup member being a figment of their imagination, so this is not inconceivable. In fact, the E-contact intervention administered by Römpke et al. (Römpke et al., 2019, Study 1) successfully improved intergroup relations despite participants' being informed that their interacting partner was a pre-programmed confederate responding in a pre-determined manner. As well, new analyses conducted on data from Maunder et al. (2019) yielded no significant interaction between E-contact condition (intergroup, intragroup, or no contact) and participants' suspicion of the pre-programmed nature of the interaction on any of the outcome variables ($ps > .478$), with the exception of pity towards people with schizophrenia ($p = .043$). On this variable, the difference between the intergroup E-contact condition and the two control conditions was larger for the suspicious participants than the non-suspicious participants. It should be noted that the number of suspicious participants was very small ($n = 14$), but the possibility of socially desirable responding or even demand characteristics should not be ruled out. Comparing the effect of intergroup E-contact on participants who are aware and unaware of the confederate being pre-programmed is an important avenue for future research, as is comparing the highly structured form of E-contact necessitated by the use of a pre-programmed confederate to the less structured form used with live outgroup members.

Second, the participants in some studies engaged in multiple sessions of E-contact, which were also substantially longer in duration compared to others. In accordance with the importance of time in intergroup contact (see Davies et al., 2011; Pettigrew, 1998), White, Harvey, Abu-Rayya et al.'s

(2015) best practice framework for E-contact recommends that participants engage in multiple sessions. This component of the best practice framework has yet to be investigated empirically. In fact, the significant reductions in intergroup bias observed in the truncated interventions suggests such a design, which is also less practical for researchers to administer, may not be necessary. However, these studies only measured bias immediately after the intervention. It is possible that the effect of these interventions may not endure as long as the studies utilising multiple, extended sessions of text-based E-contact. Therefore, future research should compare multiple sessions of contact with a single session as well as systematically varying the length of the session. Further, longer intervals between the intervention and bias measures would be preferable to better gauge the temporal efficacy of text-based E-contact (White, Harvey, Abu-Rayya et al., 2015).

Finally, in contrast to the differences noted across the E-contact studies reviewed here (see Table 2), one common aspect of many of the studies is that they have been conducted on relatively small sample sizes. Future researchers will need to address this limitation, especially when one considers that a significant benefit of E-contact, particularly with computer-programmed partners, is the "scalability" of the intervention to be successfully tested amongst larger samples.

Comparisons with other contact strategies

Just as the specific qualities that characterise the different implementations of text-based E-contact have yet to be compared, few studies to date have compared the effectiveness of E-contact to the effectiveness of other direct and indirect contact interventions (but see Mustafa & Poh, 2019). Our meta-analysis found text-based E-contact to have an average effect size on cognitive measures of prejudice numerically similar to the overall effect of true experiments manipulating face-to-face contact (Pettigrew & Tropp, 2006) and the effect of extended contact on cognitive variables (Zhou et al., 2019) and numerically larger than the average effect of imagined contact on cognitive measures (Miles & Crisp, 2014). The average effect size on the affective and behavioural intentions measures were numerically smaller than the overall effect of rue experiments manipulating face-to-face contact, but similar to that of imagined contact and extended contact. However, differences in inclusion criteria, outcome variables, and outgroups makes it inappropriate to directly compare the size of these effects. As the number of studies utilising intergroup E-contact increases, researchers must directly compare the effect of these interventions on prejudice in a single meta-analysis, or in individual studies in which factors such as adherence to Allport's (1954) optimal contact conditions and the duration of the intervention are matched.

Other outcome variables and moderators

Although E-contact has been found to be effective in improving prejudice captured by multiple cognitive and affective measures as well as proxy measures of behaviour such as behavioural intentions, the effectiveness of E-contact for improving other pertinent outcomes such as implicit bias, actual behaviour, and collective action have yet to be thoroughly assessed. There is evidence that intergroup contact may compromise collective action intentions, being participants' willingness to engage in action for social change (Dovidio et al., 2017). Whether the same is true of text-based E-contact must be determined. As well, determining whether E-contact is capable of reducing prejudice against other outgroups not involved in the interaction, as per the secondary transfer effect (Pettigrew, 2009), is a worthwhile endeavour.

Factors that might moderate the effectiveness of E-contact, other than those related to the participants, should also be investigated in future studies. The text-only nature of E-contact, particularly the pre-programmed version, makes it highly suited to adaptation and further experimentation to ascertain the key features of the online contact situation. To this end, future E-contact research could examine new moderators, such as the nature of disclosure of outgroup status, group salience and prototypicality, and the relative effectiveness of Allport's (1954) optimal conditions, as well as further evaluating the impact of anonymity and the timing of disclosure on intergroup bias.

Expanding text-based E-contact to other forms of Internet-based communication

The majority of E-contact research to date has employed a text-only interaction and we argued above that text-based communication may have advantages over other forms of online contact such as those involving audio and video. Nevertheless, White, Harvey, Abu-Rayya et al. (2015) and Maunder et al. (2019) argue that E-contact could expanded to incorporate other forms of frequently-used online interaction such as audio and video calls, as well as emerging technologies such as augmented and virtual reality. As well as being potentially effective on their own, these interventions could also be utilised as intermediate E-contact stages between indirect and direct contact interventions in a contact continuum. In the continuum of contact (e.g., Crisp & Turner, 2009), individuals with low previous contact with the outgroup first engage in more distal, indirect forms of contact (e.g., imagined contact) prior to face-to-face contact. Amichai-Hamburger and Furnham (2007) propose participants first interact via the Internet through text, then text accompanied with live image, followed by video and audio interaction, then face-to-face contact. E-contact interactions with pre-programmed outgroup members may be also be useful as an antecedent to interactions with real outgroup members via E-contact (White, Verrelli, et al., 2019). This sequential exposure to the outgroup is predicted to prepare individuals for more proximal forms of contact by reducing anxiety and increasing contact self-efficacy.

There is some evidence already that less intensive outgroup exposure such as text-only communication, may prepare participants for direct intergroup contact. For example, Hoter et al. (2009) evaluated the acceptability of an IT course in which Arabic orthodox and secular Jewish students collaborated together on a number of assigned tasks such as the development of an educational video game. The participants spent the first few months communicating asynchronously in text-based forums then synchronously via audio prior to meeting face-to-face via video or in person. In a survey administered at the conclusion of the course, the participants highlighted the importance of the progressive exposure to the outgroup members, with specific reference to lessened feelings of threat and heightened self-disclosure. Corroborating these results, O'Donnell et al. (2019) found a significantly stronger negative relationship between intergroup anxiety and willingness to engage in virtual reality intergroup contact compared to face-to-face contact, suggesting that virtual reality intergroup contact may provide a less aversive contact-choice for highly anxious participants. Further research is needed to validate the effectiveness of a continuum of contact approach, particularly in regard to text-based E-contact.

Conclusion

Since the early days of the Internet, social psychology researchers have made strides to incorporate this technology into existing theories such as Allport's (1954) intergroup contact hypothesis (e.g., Amichai-Hamburger & Furnham, 2007). Researchers have been encouraged to harness the positive elements of the Internet to establish contact between conflicting groups as a means of reducing harmful intergroup bias. One form of Internet-based contact, formulated specifically to accommodate Allport's optimal contact conditions while also comprising other qualities relevant to prejudice reduction, is E-contact.

In this review paper, we have summarised the growing theoretical and empirical evidence base, the latter of which predominantly supports the notion that text-based intergroup E-contact significantly reduces prejudice. Importantly, this reduction in prejudice has been observed against a range of stigmatised groups, including those defined by religion, ethnicity, sexuality, mental health, and gender identity. These beneficial effects are apparent immediately after the intervention and in the short- and long-term, and across a variety of outcome variables, including attitudes and beliefs, emotions, intergroup anxiety, expectations for future contact, behavioural intentions, and actual outgroup knowledge. Moreover, by employing rigorous experimental designs such as random allocation of participants, controlled before and after studies, with no contact and intragroup contact control conditions, alternative explanations for the intergroup E-contact effect can be eliminated, such as self-selection biases and contact with ingroup members increasing prejudice.

Text-based E-contact represents the first Internet-based contact paradigm involving an intergroup interaction specifically designed to accommodate Allport's optimal contact conditions and recategorisation processes. As well as being more practical to administer than direct contact interventions, E-contact overcomes shortcomings of indirect contact interventions and comprises other features pertinent to prejudice-reduction. In particular, the synchronous, text-only nature of E-contact provides individuals with a comfortable intergroup context in which their initial intolerant and stereotypical outgroup attitudes are challenged through getting to know and working cooperatively with an outgroup member. The empirical evidence base for E-contact is still in its infancy, but the findings reviewed here are promising, suggesting E-contact may be capable of reducing prejudice across a diverse range of intergroup contexts where " ... formerly only barriers may have existed" (Allport, 1954, p. 454).

Funding

This work was supported by the Australian Research Council (AU) [DP0985598].

ORCID

Fiona A. White (iD) http://orcid.org/0000-0002-3040-7130
Rachel Maunder (iD) http://orcid.org/0000-0002-8436-691X
Stefano Verrelli (iD) http://orcid.org/0000-0002-4268-7061

References

Abu-Rayya, H. M. (2017). Majority members' endorsement of the acculturation integrationist orientation improves their outgroup attitudes toward ethnic minority members: An electronic-contact experiment. *Computers in Human Behavior, 75*, 660–666. https://doi.org/10.1016/j.chb.2017.06.010
Allport, G. W. (1954). *The nature of prejudice*. Addison Wesley.
Alvídrez, S., Piñeiro-Naval, V., Marcos-Ramos, M., & Rojas-Solís, J. L. (2015). Intergroup contact in computer-mediated communication: The interplay of a stereotype-disconfirming behavior and a lasting group identity on reduced prejudiced perceptions. *Computers in Human Behavior, 52*, 533–540. https://doi.org/10.1016/j.chb.2014.09.006
Amichai-Hamburger, Y., & Furnham, A. (2007). The positive net. *Computers in Human Behavior, 23*, 1033–1045. https://doi.org/10.1016/j.chb.2005.08

Amichai-Hamburger, Y., Hasler, B. S., & Shani-Sherman, T. (2015). Structured and unstructured intergroup contact in the digital age. *Computers in Human Behavior*, *52*, 515–522. https://doi.org/10.1016/j.chb.2015.02.022

Amichai-Hamburger, Y., & McKenna, K. Y. A. (2006). The contact hypothesis reconsidered: Interacting via the Internet. *Journal of Computer-Mediated Communication*, *11*(3), 825–843. https://doi.org/10.1111/j.1083-6101.2006.00037.x

Berry, S. A., & White, F. A. (2016). E-contact as a strategy for improving attitudes towards Indigenous Australians (Unpublished honours thesis). The University of Sydney.

Boccanfuso, E., Maunder, R. D., & White, F. A. (under review). Reducing transgender stigma via an E-contact intervention. Manuscript submitted for publication.

Brown, R., & Paterson, J. (2016). Indirect contact and prejudice reduction: Limits and possibilities. *Current Opinion in Psychology*, *11*, 20–24. https://doi.org/10.1016/j.copsyc.2016.03.005

Cao, B., & Lin, W.-Y. (2017). Revisiting the contact hypothesis: Effects of different modes of computer-mediated communication on intergroup relationships. *International Journal of Intercultural Relations*, *58*, 23–30. https://doi.org/10.1016/j.ijintrel.2017.03.003

Crisp, R. J., & Turner, R. N. (2009). Can imagined interactions produce positive perceptions?: Reducing prejudice through simulated social contact. *American Psychologist*, *64*(4), 231–240. https://doi.org/10.1037/a0014718

Dane, S. K., Masser, B. M., MacDonald, G., Duck, J. M., & Dominguez, J. M. (2015). When "in your face" is not out of place: The effect of timing of disclosure of a same-sex dating partner under conditions of contact. *PloS One*, *10*(8), e0135023. https://doi.org/10.1371/journal.pone.0135023

Davies, K., Tropp, L. R., Aron, A., Pettigrew, T. F., & Wright, S. C. (2011). Cross-group friendships and intergroup attitudes: A meta-analytic review. *Personality and Social Psychology Review*, *15*(4), 332–351. https://doi.org/10.1177/1088868311411103

Dixon, J., & Durrheim, K. (2003). Contact and the ecology of racial division: Some varieties of informal segregation. *British Journal of Social Psychology*, *42*(1), 1–23. https://doi.org/10.1348/014466603763276090

Dovidio, J. F., Gaertner, S. L., Pearson, A. R., & Riek, B. M. (2005). Social identities and social context: Attitudes and personal well-being. In S. R. Thye & E. J. Lawler (Eds.), *Advances in group processes: Social identification processes in groups* (pp. 231–260). Elsevier.

Dovidio, J. F., Eller, A., & Hewstone, M. (2011). Improving intergroup relations through direct, extended and other forms of indirect contact. *Group Processes & Intergroup Relations*, *14*(2), 147–160. https://doi.org/10.1177/1368430210390555

Dovidio, J. F., Gaertner, S. L., & Kawakami, K. (2003). Intergroup contact: The past, present, and the future. *Group Processes & Intergroup Relations*, *6*(1), 5–21. https://doi.org/10.1177/1368430203006001009

Dovidio, J. F., Gaertner, S. L., & Saguy, T. (2009). Commonality and the complexity of "we". Social Attitudes and Social Change. *Personality and Social Psychology Review*, *13*, 3–20. https://doi.org/10.1177/1088868308326751

Dovidio, J. F., Love, A., Schellhaas, F. M., & Hewstone, M. (2017). Reducing intergroup bias through intergroup contact: Twenty years of progress and future directions. *Group Processes & Intergroup Relations*, *20*(5), 606–620. https://doi.org/10.1177/1368430217712052

Dubrovsky, V. J., Kiesler, S., & Sethna, B. N. (1991). The equalization phenomenon: Status effects in computer-mediated and face-to-face decision-making groups. *Human-Computer Interaction*, 6(2), 119–146. https://doi.org/10.1207/s15327051hci0602_2

Funder, D. C., & Ozer, D. J. (2019). Evaluating effect size in psychological research: Sense and nonsense. *Advances in Methods and Practices in Psychological Science*, 2(2), 156–168. https://doi.org/10.1177/2515245919847202

Halualani, R. T., Chitgopekar, A. S., Morrison, J. H. T. A., & Dodge, P. S. W. (2004). Diverse in name only? Intercultural interaction at a multicultural university. *Journal of Communication*, 54(2), 270–286. https://doi.org/10.1111/j.1460-2466.2004.tb02628.x

Henry, P. J. (2008). College sophomores in the laboratory redux: Influences of a narrow data base on social psychology's view of the nature of prejudice. *Psychological Inquiry*, 19(2), 49–71. https://doi.org/10.1080/10478400802049936

Hewstone, M., & Swart, H. (2011). Fifty-odd years of inter-group contact: From hypothesis to integrated theory. *British Journal of Social Psychology*, 50(3), 374–386. https://doi.org/10.1111/j.2044-8309.2011.02047.x

Hodson, G. (2011). Do ideologically intolerant people benefit from intergroup contact? *Current Directions in Psychological Science*, 20(3), 154–159. https://doi.org/10.1177/0963721411409025

Hodson, G., Harry, H., & Mitchell, A. (2009). Independent benefits of contact and friendship on attitudes toward homosexuals among authoritarians and highly identified heterosexuals. *European Journal of Social Psychology*, 39(4), 509–529. https://doi.org/10.1002/ejsp.558

Hoter, E., Shonfeld, M., & Ganayim, A. (2009). Information and communication technology (ICT) in the service of multiculturalism. *The International Review of Research in Open and Distributed Learning*, 10(2). http://www.irrodl.org/index.php/irrodl/article/view/601/1207.

Hrastinski, S. (2008). The potential of synchronous communication to enhance participation in online discussions: A case study of two e-learning courses. *Information & Management*, 45(7), 499–506. https://doi.org/10.1016/j.im.2008.07.005

International Telecommunication Union (2018). *Statistics*. Switzerland: International Telecommunication Union (ITU). Retrieved from https://www.itu.int/en/ITU-D/Statistics/Pages/stat/default.aspx

Kemp, S. (2019). *Digital 2019: Global Internet use accelerates*. We are social. https://wearesocial.com/blog/2019/01/digital-2019-global-internet-use-accelerates

Kite, M. E., & Whitley Jr, B. E. (1996). Sex differences in attitudes toward homosexual persons, behaviors, and civil rights a meta-analysis. *Personality and Social Psychology Bulletin*, 22(4), 336–353. https://doi.org/10.1177/0146167296224002

MacInnis, C. C., & Hodson, G. (2015). The development of online cross-group relationships among university students. *Journal of Social and Personal Relationships*, 32(6), 788–809. https://doi.org/10.1177/0265407514548394

Maunder, R. D., White, F. A., & Verrelli, S. (2019). Modern avenues for intergroup contact: Using E-contact and intergroup emotions to reduce stereotyping and social distancing against people with schizophrenia. *Group Processes & Intergroup Relations*, 22(7), 947–963. https://doi.org/10.1177/1368430218794873

Mazziotta, A., Mummendey, A., & Wright, S. C. (2011). Vicarious intergroup contact effects: Applying social-cognitive theory to intergroup contact research. *Group*

Processes & Intergroup Relations, 14(2), 255–274. https://doi.org/10.1177/1368430210390533
McKenna, K. Y., Green, A. S., & Gleason, M. E. (2002). Relationship formation on the Internet: What's the big attraction? Journal of Social Issues, 58(1), 9–31. https://doi.org/10.1111/1540-4560.00246
McKeown, S. (2013). Identity, segregation and peace-building in Northern Ireland: A social psychological perspective. Palgrave Macmillan.
Miles, E., & Crisp, R. J. (2014). A meta-analytic test of the imagined contact hypothesis. Group Processes & Intergroup Relations, 17(1), 3–26. https://doi.org/10.1177/1368430213510573
Mustafa, H., Hamid, H. A., Ahmad, J., & Siarap, K. (2012). Intercultural relationship, prejudice and ethnocentrism in a Computer-Mediated Communication (CMC): A time-series experiment. Asian Social Science, 8(3), 34–48. https://doi.org/10.5539/ass.v8n3p34
Mustafa, H., & Poh, S. K. C. (2019). Increasing intercultural contact in cyberspace: How does it affect the level of prejudice among Malaysians? Pertanika Journal of Social Sciences & Humanities, 27(1), 601-620.
O'Donnell, A. W., Neumann, D. L., & Duffy, A. L. (2019). Virtual reality intergroup contact: An examination of intergroup anxiety and willingness to approach a modern contact choice. Talk Presented at SPSSI-SASP Group Meeting on Intergroup Contact, Newcastle, Australia.
Paolini, S., Harwood, J., Hewstone, M., & Neumann, D. L. (2018). Seeking and avoiding intergroup contact: Future frontiers of research on building social integration. Social and Personality Psychology Compass, 12(12), e12422. https://doi.org/10.1111/spc3.12422
Paolini, S., Hewstone, M., Cairns, E., & Voci, A. (2004). Effects of direct and indirect cross-group friendships on judgments of Catholics and Protestants in Northern Ireland: The mediating role of an anxiety-reduction mechanism. Personality and Social Psychology Bulletin, 30(6), 770–786. https://doi.org/10.1177/0146167203262848
Pearson, A. R, West, T. V, Dovidio, J. F, Powers, S. R, Buck, R, & Henning, R. (2008). The fragility of intergroup relations: Divergent effects of delayed audiovisual feedback in intergroup and intragroup interaction. Psychological Science, 19 (12), 1272–1279. doi: 10.1111/j.1467-9280.2008.02236.x
Pennebaker, J. W., Booth, R. J., Boyd, R. L., & Francis, M. E. (2015). Linguistic Inquiry and Word Count: LIWC 2015. Pennebaker Conglomerates.
Pettigrew, T. F. (1998). Intergroup contact theory. Annual Review of Psychology, 49 (1), 65–85. https://doi.org/10.1146/annurev.psych.49.1.65
Pettigrew, T. F. (2009). Secondary transfer effect of contact: Do intergroup contact effects spread to noncontacted outgroups? Social Psychology, 40(2), 55–65. https://doi.org/10.1027/1864-9335.40.2.55
Pettigrew, T. F., & Tropp, L. R. (2006). A meta-analytic test of intergroup contact theory. Journal of Personality and Social Psychology, 90(5), 751–783. https://doi.org/10.1037/00223514.90.5.751
Pettigrew, T. F., & Tropp, L. R. (2008). How does intergroup contact reduce prejudice? Meta-analytic tests of three mediators. European Journal of Social Psychology, 38(6), 922–934. https://doi.org/10.1002/ejsp.504
Pettigrew, T. F., & Tropp, L. R. (2011). When groups meet: The dynamics of intergroup contact. Psychology Press.

Plant, E. A., & Devine, P. (2003). The antecedents and implications of interracial anxiety. *Personality and Social Psychology Bulletin*, *29*(6), 790–801. https://doi.org/10.1177/0146167203029006011

Postmes, T, Spears, R, & Lea, M. (2002). Intergroup differentiation in computer-mediated communication: effects of depersonalization. *Group Dynamics*, *6*, 3 – 16.

Riek, B. M., Mania, E. W., & Gaertner, S. L. (2006). Intergroup threat and outgroup attitudes: A meta-analytic review. *Personality and Social Psychology Review*, *10*(4), 336–353. https://doi.org/10.1207/s15327957pspr1004_4

Riggs, D. W., Webber, K., & Fell, G. R. (2012). Australian undergraduate psychology students' attitudes towards, trans people. *Gay and Lesbian Issues in Psychology Review*, *8*(1), 52–62.

Römpke, A.-K., Fritsche, I., & Reese, G. (2019). Get together, feel together, act together: International personal contact increases identification with humanity and global collective action. *Journal of Theoretical Social Psychology*, *3*(1), 35–48. https://doi.org/10.1002/jts5.34

Schumann, S., Klein, O., Douglas, K., & Hewstone, M. (2017). When is computer-mediated intergroup contact most promising? Examining the effect of out-group members' anonymity on prejudice. *Computers in Human Behavior*, *77*, 198–210. https://doi.org/10.1016/j.chb.2017.08.006

Schwier, R., & Balbar, S. (2002). The interplay of content and community in synchronous and asynchronous communication: Virtual communication in a graduate seminar. *Canadian Journal of Learning and Technology*, *28*, 2. https://doi.org/10.21432/T20K64

Statista (2019). *Mobile Internet & apps: Statistics and market data on mobile Internet & apps*. Retrieved from https://www.statista.com/markets/424/topic/538/mobile-internet-apps/

Stephan, W. G. (2014). Intergroup anxiety: Theory, research, and practice. *Personality and Social Psychology Review*, *18*(3), 239–255. https://doi.org/10.1177/1088868314530518

Tausch, N., & Hewstone, M. (2010). Intergroup contact and prejudice. In J. F. Dovidio, M. Hewstone, P. Glick, & V. M. Esses (Eds.), *The SAGE handbook of prejudice, stereotyping, and discrimination*. SAGE Publications Inc.

Trawalter, S., Richeson, J. A., & Shelton, J. N. (2009). Predicting behavior during interracial interactions: A stress and coping approach. *Personality and Social Psychology Review*, *13*(4), 243–268. https://doi.org/10.1177/1088868309345850

Vezzali, L., Hewstone, M., Capozza, D., Giovannini, D., & Wölfer, R. (2014). Improving intergroup relations with extended and vicarious forms of indirect contact. *European Review of Social Psychology*, *25*(1), 314–389. https://doi.org/10.1080/10463283.2014.982948

Walther, J. B. (1996). Computer-mediated communication: Impersonal, interpersonal, and hyperpersonal interaction. *Communication Research*, *23*(1), 3–43. https://doi.org/10.1177/009365096023001001

Walther, J. B. (2009). In point of practice: Computer-mediated communication and virtual groups: Applications to interethnic conflict. *Journal of Applied Communication Research*, *37*(3), 225–238. https://doi.org/10.1080/00909880903025937

White, F. A., & Abu-Rayya, H. M. (2012). A dual identity-electronic contact (DIEC) experiment promoting short- and long-term intergroup harmony. *Journal of Experimental Social Psychology*, *48*(3), 597–608. https://doi.org/10.1016/j.jesp.2012.01.007

White, F. A., Abu-Rayya, H. M., & Weitzel, C. (2014). Achieving twelve-months of intergroup bias reduction: The dual identity-electronic contact (DIEC) experiment. *International Journal of Intercultural Relations*, *38*, 158–163. https://doi.org/10.1016/j.ijintrel.2013.08.002

White, F. A, Harvey, L, & Abu-Rayya, H. M. (2015). Improving intergroup relations in the internet age: a critical review. *Review Of General Psychology*, *19*(2), 129–139. doi: 10.1037/gpr0000036

White, F. A., Harvey, L., & Abu-Rayya, H. M. (2015). Improving intergroup relations in the Internet age: A critical review. *Review of General Psychology*, *19*(2), 129–139. https://doi.org/10.1037/gpr0000036

White, F. A., Harvey, L., & Verrelli, S. (2015). Including both voices: A new bidirectional framework for understanding and improving intergroup relations. *Australian Psychologist*, *50*(6), 421–433. https://doi.org/10.1111/ap.12108

White, F. A., Turner, R. N., Verrelli, S., Harvey, L. J., & Hanna, J. R. (2019). Improving intergroup relations between Catholics and Protestants in Northern Ireland via E-Contact. *European Journal of Social Psychology*, *49*(2), 429–438. https://doi.org/10.1002/ejsp.2515

White, F. A., Verrelli, S., Maunder, R. D., & Kervinen, A. (2019). Using electronic contact to reduce homonegative attitudes, emotions, and behavioral intentions among heterosexual women and men: A contemporary extension of the contact hypothesis. *The Journal of Sex Research*, *56*(9), 1179–1191. https://doi.org/10.1080/00224499.2018.1491943

Wright, S. C., Aron, A., McLaughlin-Volpe, T., & Ropp, S. A. (1997). The extended contact effect: Knowledge of cross-group friendships and prejudice. *Journal of Personality and Social Psychology*, *73*(1), 73–90. https://doi.org/10.1037/0022-3514.73.173

Zhou, S., Page-Gould, E., Aron, A., Moyer, A., & Hewstone, M. (2019). The extended contact hypothesis: A meta-analysis on 20 years of research. *Personality and Social Psychology Review*, *23*(2), 132–160. https://doi.org/10.1177/1088868318762647

ARTICLE

How static facial cues relate to real-world leaders' success: a review and meta-analysis

Miranda Giacomin[a] and Nicholas O. Rule [b]

[a]MacEwan University, Edmonton, AB, Canada; [b]University of Toronto (Sidney Smith Hall, Toronto, ON, Canada

ABSTRACT
People use facial information to infer others' leadership potential across numerous domains; but what forms the basis of these judgements and how much do they matter? Here, we quantitatively reviewed the literature on perceptions of leaders from facial cues to better understand the association between physical appearance and leader outcomes. We used standard random-effects meta-analytic techniques to determine how appearance cues relate to leader perceptions and associated constructs. Appearance cues suggesting the presence of qualities often desired in leaders correlated with leader selection and success (M_{Z-r} =.26, 95% CI [.21,.31]). Larger effect sizes emerged for popularity outcomes (i.e., those based on perceptions) than for performance outcomes (i.e., those based on external measures). These data help to explain how people envision leaders and their characteristics, providing potential insights to why they select and follow particular individuals over others.

ARTICLE HISTORY Received 1 February 2019; Accepted 18 May 2020

KEYWORDS Leader; person perception; facial appearance; ceo; attractiveness

There is a reason why election posters and campaign materials feature a candidate's face, and why real estate agents' business cards and lawn signs often prominently display their headshots: faces are a rich source of social information (Perrett, 2010; Zebrowitz, 1997; Zebrowitz & Montepare, 2008). People quickly judge others' traits from their faces based on minimal information (e.g., Borkenau et al., 2009). More striking, these judgements sometimes predict real-world events. For example, people use shallow decision heuristics (i.e., impressions of political candidates' personality traits from their faces) when casting their ballots in democratic elections across the globe (e.g., Antonakis & Eubanks, 2017; Olivola & Todorov, 2010; Todorov et al., 2015). Indeed, perceptions of a variety of traits (e.g., attractiveness, dominance, competence) predict leader outcomes in both politics and business (Hall et al., 2005; N. Rule & Ambady, 2010; Van Vugt & Grabo,

CONTACT Miranda Giacomin ✉ miranda.giacomin@macewan.ca ➔ University of Toronto (Sidney Smith Hall, 100 St. George Street, Toronto, Canada

© 2020 European Association of Social Psychology

2015). Yet the specific traits that correlate with leaders' success depend on context (e.g., time, place) and the outcome measured (e.g., CEOs' personal compensation vs. their companies' profits). Such variability has led to disparate findings in the literature about how particular facial cues relate to leaders' success. To harmonise this information, we reviewed the existing literature and systematically examined studies on the role of facial appearance in leader selection and performance by quantitatively aggregating their results via meta-analysis.

Why do people make inferences from leaders' faces?

Few other domains rely on individuals' opinions of others as much as leader selection. Here, we define leaders as those who have higher status or power over others (e.g., CEOs, elected legislators, presidents). Not only do people in most of the world enjoy the privilege of freely electing their political leaders, individuals routinely decide whom to follow, support, ignore, or oppose in even the most rigidly organised societies. Leaders' facial appearance plays a role in these selection decisions.

People often decide who should be a leader based on their beliefs about who *looks* like a leader (Berger & Wagner, 2007; Lenz & Lawson, 2011). This tendency may have developed over the course of human evolution. Biosocial models, for example, suggest that people judge leaders based on the masculinity of a person's facial features because masculine features have become associated with dominant, leader-like behaviour over time (Spisak et al., 2012). Leaders' physical appearance may precipitate individuals' lay beliefs about the behaviours and characteristics of leaders (i.e., leader prototypes; Eden & Leviathan, 1975; Tskhay et al., 2020). For example, the prototypical leader is usually conceptualised as white, male, attractive, and dominant (Eagly & Karau, 2002; Rosette et al., 2008). Reciprocally, the extent to which a person seems leader-like often depends on a predetermined set of beliefs about what a leader looks like and how well a candidate leader matches those beliefs (e.g., Kenney et al., 1996). Thus, people use their leader prototypes when hiring or electing leaders.

Indeed, people rely on stereotypes about the traits and appearance that leaders should have when choosing whom to follow. Leadership categorisation theory suggests that leaders will be evaluated favourably when they seem to possess qualities prototypical of a leader (Lord & Maher, 1991). Similarly, expectation states theory suggests that a group's expectations about how an individual will perform influences status hierarchies (Berger & Wagner, 2007; for a review, see Correll & Ridgeway, 2006). That is, individuals whose characteristics best match the evaluator's leader prototype garner the most favourable reception as leaders (e.g., Eagly & Karau, 2002; Ensari & Murphy, 2003; Rosette et al., 2008). Importantly, the attributions that people make about others' traits often determine how they vote in elections, and whom they hire and promote in organisations (Dipboye et al., 1977; Little et al., 2007). For example, competent-looking candidates were more likely to win the 2010 British general election (Mattes & Milazzo, 2014). Thus, the outcomes of these decisions can affect a wide cast of individuals, particularly when they determine who will lead a group, company, or government entity.

Researchers have considered potential explanations for why perceptions of leader-like qualities in others predict their selection and success. Facial appearance may relate to leader selection through self-fulfiling prophecies such that those who "look like a leader" are treated like a leader and, in turn, rise to actual leadership roles faster (Calder, 1977). Likewise, people with leader-like behavioural characteristics may believe in their ability to be a good leader and subsequently act more leader-like, perhaps because others regularly encouraged them and expected them to lead. This could create a feedback loop in which appearance and behaviour eventually converge; for example, dominant-looking people may be treated like leaders and thus become leaders (Re & Rule, 2015; Haselhuhn et al., 2013; McArthur & Baron, 1983). Similarly, people with dominant faces might act more leader-like because of predetermined personality characteristics (e.g., traits that motivate them to subjugate others to achieve higher ranks). Alternatively, people who engage in leadership may come to look dominant because their leadership role requires them to express themselves in dominant ways (see Malatesta et al., 1987). Another possibility is that the same core underlies both facial features and leadership effectiveness. For instance, both facial width-to-height ratio (fWHR; the vertical distance between the lower eyebrow and top lip divided by the distance between the two cheekbones) and leadership success have shown associations with testosterone levels (Lefevre et al., 2013; Lewis et al., 2012; though see Bird et al., 2016). Given that people compulsively employ facial appearance to form impressions of others (e.g., N. O. Rule et al., 2014), researchers have endeavoured to understand how the physical features of people's faces predict trait attributions, inform leader selection, and how (if at all) they then relate to measures of leaders' actual performance.

How do researchers measure perceptions of leaders' success?

Past studies have showcased a variety of methods for investigating how people infer leadership from faces. Here, we focus on the most typical example in which naïve participants view facial photographs of real-world leaders and then cast hypothetical votes, rate their perceived leadership ability or various traits (e.g., attractiveness, competence), or make a binary choice between two faces (e.g., selecting the leader or more competent-looking person). Researchers use these responses to statistically predict popularity and performance on leader outcomes (e.g., election results, company profits). In addition, several studies have measured aspects of leaders' physical facial structure and related these measurements either to participants' impressions of the leaders' traits or to measures of their success (e.g., Alrajih & Ward, 2014; D. E. Re & Rule, 2016b; Wong et al., 2011). Across these various methods, researchers have generally found that people reliably agree about others' leader-like ability when looking at their faces and that these consensual judgements sometimes predict important phenomena, such as election outcomes and companies' performance.

An important consideration when examining perceptions of leaders is the criterion for assessing leader selection or success. When studying political leaders, researchers often use leader selection or popularity as an outcome variable (e.g., who receives the most votes in a public election). Being voted into power may not necessarily reflect one's future success as a lawmaker, however, as election outcomes are often subjective and based on the candidate's popularity; that is, leader selection does not equate with leader success. Quantifying political success is difficult, as different political beliefs may lead to different opinions about what constitutes success. In some cases, a politician who fails to meet a particular campaign goal might be seen as a failure. Yet that failure may have occurred as a diplomatic concession in the service of a longer-term or alternate goal, which may thus represent a success. Although some opportunity exists to quantify how well a politician advances his or her political agenda, success in politics may therefore be more sensitive to opinions compared to other domains (e.g., profits in business). Here, we refer to leader selection of this type as a *popularity* leader outcome.

In contrast to popularity leader outcomes, researchers also employ readily available statistics and performance measures to quantify business leaders' performance. For example, companies' annual gross revenues and net profits are typically publicly accessible through their tax filings, especially for large Fortune 500 companies. Studies have accordingly examined the association between corporate financial performance and CEOs' facial appearance (for a review, see D. E. Re & Rule, 2015). Law firms similarly reveal their yearly earnings to the public, and researchers have used this information to relate firm success to their Managing Partners' facial appearance (Rule & Ambady, 2011a, 2011b). Estimates of a company's performance therefore provide a more objective measure of leadership success than does popularity among voters. Measures of success that comprise measures of leaders' performance have no apparent relation to opinions about appearance. For instance, given that people do not typically decide whether to pump Chevron's gas based on what the company's Chief Executive Officer (CEO) looks like, research participants' opinions about CEOs' faces has no bearing on the profits that their companies earn (Rule & Ambady, 2008). We therefore refer to leader effectiveness or an organisation's performance as a *performance* leader outcome here.

How much facial appearance influences leader selection and success may vary, however. Stoker et al. (2016) found that the faces of CEOs of US Fortune 500 firms differ from regular citizens and university professors. This suggests that CEOs look objectively different and that facial appearance may enhance their hireability as leaders, though a comparison of the top and bottom 100 CEOs suggested that their faces do not differ. Thus, the outcome type (i.e., measure of success) may affect whether leaders' facial appearance influences leader selection and performance. We investigate this discrepancy in the current meta-analysis.

What facial feature predicts leader success?

Researchers have examined a variety of personality characteristics and facial features to investigate what leads people to perceive leaders as successful. Though comprehensive, this plurality has stirred some confusion as to which facial feature best relates to perceptions of leader success. Below, we review research examining how perceptions of different characteristics relate to leader popularity and performance, including attractiveness, competence, dominance, warmth, and affect.

Attractiveness. Good-looking people benefit by receiving more leader-like attributions (Dion et al., 1972; Higgle et al., 1997; Rosenberg et al., 1991). Given its broad positive halo, attractive candidates are more likely to be ascribed qualities associated with successful politicians. These inferences not only influence impressions of their efficacy but can also affect the outcomes of elections (Banducci et al., 2008; Berggren et al., 2010; Martin, 1978; Sigelman et al., 1987). Indeed, facial attractiveness correlated with the percentage of votes electoral candidates obtained across several studies (Budesheim & Depaola, 1994; King & Leigh, 2009). Many studies on leaders' facial cues therefore statistically control for facial attractiveness, lest its blockbuster effects overwhelm researchers' capacity to observe the contributions of other traits.

Power. Leaders hold power and authority over others by definition. Beyond pronounced physiognomic cues like attractiveness, researchers have examined how perceptions of power from facial appearance relate to leader selection and success. Often, "power" serves as an umbrella term representing various agentic traits. Here, we focus on two that have largely commanded the attention of researchers examining perceptions of leadership: competence and dominance.

Competence. Researchers have extensively examined the importance of competence judgements in predicting leader outcomes (Castelli et al., 2009;

Poutvaara et al., 2009; Sussman et al., 2013; Todorov, 2005). Studies of American electoral candidates have reported a strong association between how competent candidates appear in their campaign photographs and their likelihood of winning an election (e.g., Ballew & Todorov, 2007; Praino et al., 2014; Todorov, 2005). Examining the Democratic and Republican candidates in the 2006 US gubernatorial elections, Ballew and Todorov (2007) found that participants rated the winners as more competent when seeing their faces as briefly as 100 milliseconds, suggesting that the evaluations occurred reflexively.

Studies of business CEOs have likewise found associations with perceived competence. Graham et al. (2016) found that CEOs' faces look more competent than non-CEOs' faces, that CEOs from large firms look more competent than CEOs from small firms, and that competence perceptions related to the total sales of the CEOs' firms and to their individual compensation but not to their companies' return on assets (a measure of management efficiency). Competence plays a role in the evaluation of both male and female CEOs. Rule and Ambady (2009), for instance, found that perceived leadership ability and competence statistically predicted company profits among the 20 female CEOs from the 2006 Fortune 1,000. However, Pillemer et al. (2014) found that agentic traits (competence, dominance, facial maturity, leadership, and powerfulness) did not predict company profits for female CEOs. Thus, perceptions of political and business leaders' competence from their facial appearance may statistically predict leader selection and, in some cases, their success.

Dominance. Facial dominance, facial maturity, and masculinity relate closely to competence and also play critical roles in leader selection (Riggio & Riggio, 2010). For instance, studies have shown that a collection of dominance-related inferences statistically predicts election outcomes, the rise of attorneys within law firms, and the financial success of CEOs (e.g., Livingston & Pearce, 2009; Rule & Ambady, 2008, 2011a; Rule, Ambady, et al., 2010). Moreover, judgements of military cadets' facial dominance statistically predicted rank promotions late into their career, nearly 20 years after the photographs were taken (Mueller & Mazur, 1996).

Facial cues to dominance and physical stature also portend leader selection. CEOs' facial structure significantly differs from that of ordinary people (Stoker et al., 2016). Specifically, both mouth width and fWHR show links to dominant behaviour, and people attend to these cues when forming impressions of leadership that, in some cases, correspond to leaders' popularity and success (Alrajih & Ward, 2014; Carré & McCormick, 2008; D. E. Re & Rule, 2016a; Geniole et al., 2015; Wong et al., 2011). Mouth width relates to both CEOs' perceived leadership ability and actual financial performance (i.e., the profitability of their companies; Alrajih & Ward, 2014; D. E. Re & Rule, 2016a). In addition, men with higher fWHR are accurately perceived as less trustworthy, more likely to cheat, and more aggressive and ambitious (Carré et al., 2009; Haselhuhn & Wong, 2011). Moreover, the fWHR of male Fortune 500 CEOs relates to both their perceived and actual leader performance (if they work in companies that allow these behaviours to thrive; Wong et al., 2011), though fWHR may not relate to occupational hierarchy (Linke et al., 2016). People also tend to act more selfishly when engaging with men who have higher fWHR, eliciting more selfish behaviour in return (Haselhuhn et al., 2013). Although fWHR has been considered a distinct marker of leaders and leader-like behaviour, a recent study found that fWHR did not relate to self-reported behavioural tendencies in a large-scale study (e.g., personality traits, impulsiveness, intelligence, impression management; Kosinski, 2017). Thus, investigating whether physical facial cues influence leader selection and performance seems warranted.

Warmth. In contrast to agentic traits (e.g., dominance, power), communal traits like warmth and trustworthiness often do not relate to leaders' success (Hogan, 1995). For example, unlike power-related traits, perceptions of warmth (i.e., likeability and trustworthiness) from the faces of Managing Partners of America's top 100 law firms did not statistically predict their firms' success (e.g., profit margin, profitability index; Rule & Ambady, 2011a). Yet some studies have found that communal traits (e.g., warmth) do relate to the perceived and actual success of leaders in some contexts (e.g., collectivist cultures). For example, perceptions of warmth statistically predicted election outcomes in Japan (Rule, Ambady, et al., 2010) and facial trustworthiness related to managers' position within an occupational hierarchy (the difference in the number of subordinates and superiors) in the Czech Republic when controlling for how attractive they looked (Linke et al., 2016). Warmth may also benefit female CEOs more than male CEOs, and the CEOs of non-profit organisations more than the CEOs of profit-motivated companies (D. E. Re & Rule, 2016b; Pillemer et al., 2014).

Closely related to warmth, baby-faced adults appear more trustworthy and innocent (but less competent) than mature-faced adults (Zebrowitz, 1997). For instance, baby-faced politicians looked less competent than mature-faced politicians in one study but this did not relate to election outcomes (Poutvaara et al., 2009). Whereas a babyish face may hinder adults striving to attain high positions of leadership, some leaders do reap benefits from looking warm. Specifically, warm-looking Black men tend to fare better in terms of leader selection because their apparent warmth counteracts and disarms negative stereotypes of Black men as aggressive and dominant (Livingston & Pearce, 2009; see also Wilson et al., 2017). Looking exceptional for one's group can thus facilitate leader emergence (see D. E. Re & Rule, 2017). Perceptions of leaders' warmth or communal qualities therefore show mixed associations with leader selection and success, and often depend on the context.

Affect. Related to warmth, researchers have also considered how emotional expression may influence leader perceptions. In one study, participants rated CEOs with more positive emotional expressions as better leaders, though affect did not relate to their actual performance (Harms et al., 2012). Similarly, Pillemer et al. (2014) found that ratings of positive affect from male and female CEOs' headshots correlated with how warm they seemed but did not predict their actual performance. Most researchers have controlled for perceived affect (and attractiveness) in their studies, however, still finding significant associations between impressions based on facial appearance and popularity and performance measures of leadership when ablating its influence (e.g., Pillemer et al., 2014; Rule & Ambady, 2008).

Despite the wide trait-specific variability reviewed above, judgements of leader-related attributes from faces show high levels of consensus. This has led to some apparent inconsistencies in the literature on how facial appearance relates to leadership, obscuring the magnitude of the association. We therefore conducted a meta-analysis to determine the strength of the association between perceptions of facial appearance and leaders' status, and to explore potential domain-related moderators of that association.

The current research

Zanna and Fazio (1982) noted that research questions develop as an area of research grows. First-generation questions ask whether associations between variables exist (i.e., Does facial appearance relate to leader selection and performance?). Second-generation questions address the boundary conditions of the associations established in the first-generation (e.g., In what political climate does facial appearance relate to leader selection?). As the study of leaders' facial appearance moves towards second-generation questions, scholars must first pause to synthesise the nature and strength of the first-generation questions. Many studies have demonstrated that trait judgements from facial appearance predict leader selection, an association that spans leaders' identities, cultures, and domains of influence. In the same vein, other studies have criticised these findings and found limited evidence for the association between facial judgements and leader success (e.g., Stoker et al., 2016).

Here, we conducted a meta-analysis to quantitatively summarise the relation between leaders' facial appearance and their subsequent selection and success. Meta-analysis allows researchers to review past literature, synthesise findings, and quantitatively assess the robustness of the extant effects. Because results vary between studies, estimating an overall mean effect size provides important information about the average weight of phenomena in a particular research area. We aimed to determine how strongly impressions from facial cues relate to leaders' outcomes and to examine how differences between studies may influence the magnitude of that association (e.g., types of face-based trait perceptions, popularity and performance outcomes).

Method

Search strategies

Three research assistants conducted a literature search to find published, empirical studies examining perceptions of leaders based on facial appearance through popular databases (e.g., Google Scholar, PsycInfo, Web of Science) using the keywords *leader, leaders, leadership*, and *face, face perception, facial appearance, facial cues*, with *accuracy, attractiveness, business, CEO, corporations, Democrats, education, elections, electoral outcomes, governor, law firms, military, nonverbal behaviour, organisations, peace, person perception, personality, politicians, president, profits, Republicans, senator, social perception, sports*, and *war*, locating 231 relevant published articles. To reduce publication bias, the authors subsequently requested unpublished data via the electronic mailing lists of the Society for Personality and Social Psychology and Academy of Management, individually contacted prominent researchers in the field asking for additional data, and examined unpublished dissertations available online, finding four additional sources of unpublished relevant data.

Inclusion and exclusion criteria. A research assistant reviewed all 231 articles to ensure inclusion of only those that correlated impressions formed from real-world leaders' facial appearance with some form of leader outcome (e.g., perceived leadership ability, electoral vote share, organisational performance). We focused the meta-analysis on perceptions of real-world leaders' faces rather than on studies that used nonleaders (e.g., undergraduate students, standardised laboratory or computerised photographs). We concentrate on studies examining real-world leaders because hypothetical leaders (e.g., undergraduate students) may look different than real leaders. People may arbitrarily give more weight to unimportant cues when rating such photographs, which would mask the important facial cues that predict real leader success. Thus, research examining real-world leaders' faces offers more external validity and provides a stringent test of whether facial cues predict leaders' success.

We included studies in which researchers used perceivers' inferences of leaders' traits (e.g., attractiveness, competence, dominance, and trustworthiness), specific features (e.g., babyfacedness, affect), or leadership ability (e.g., which leader will win an election) to predict either performance indices of leader success (e.g., company profits during the leader's tenure) or popular perceptions of leadership ability (e.g., electoral votes). All of the analysed studies tested static facial photographs of real-world leaders and did not include live behaviour or videos. Excluding verbal or dynamic nonverbal cues provides a more stringent test of the effect of leaders' facial appearance on their popularity and performance.

We excluded studies that focused on leader perceptions and peripheral target information (e.g., age, ballot position, race, religion, sex, sexual orientation, verbal behaviour), studies that did not use a popularity or performance outcome, studies that related leader judgements to neural correlates, and studies in which the available statistical information did not suffice for calculating effect sizes ($n = 2$). In total, this yielded a final sample of 91 articles published from 1990–2019, consisting of 122 studies and 1,258 effect sizes.[1] In addition, we collected data from three unpublished articles, containing four studies and 60 effect sizes. Thus, we analysed 94 articles, 126 studies, and 1,318 effect sizes in total.

Coding Procedure The coding protocol for extracting relevant information from each article included the authors, journal of publication, year of publication, experiment number (where applicable), leadership context (e.g., politics, business), number of perceiving participants, number of perceived targets, target demographic features (i.e., gender), outcome and predictor variables (indicated below), type of statistical analysis (e.g., correlation, test of independence), test statistics and associated significance levels, effect size r (if available), and unit of analysis (i.e., the level at which researchers conducted their analyses – typically either the targets or perceivers). One research assistant did the initial coding and a second checked a random subset of 200 statistics (approximately 15% of total sample). The original research assistant corrected any errors (21/200, roughly 10%) by revisiting the respective experiment and a third research assistant verified the remaining effect sizes.

Subcategories. Prior to analysis, we separated leader outcomes from appearance-related cues (or predictor variables). Although we use the term "outcome," note that we do not necessarily mean to suggest causality; rather, in many cases, "outcome" represents a simple correlate. We divided outcomes into those that the leader's face might directly influence the outcomes (which we termed "popularity outcomes;" e.g., voters have probably seen the faces of political candidates at a rally, in the news, or on a yard sign) versus outcomes in which the leader's face would not likely influence the outcomes (which we termed "performance outcomes;" e.g., people pumping gas at a Chevron station likely do not know what the CEO looks like). We thus coded employee satisfaction, fundraising revenue, leader salary, number of promotions, organisation gross profit, organisation net profit, organisation profit margin, organisation profitability index, organisation rank, organisation return on assets, organisation sales, and organisation size as "performance" leader outcomes;

---

[1]We did not include tests of interactions between multiple variables.

and coded election win versus loss, hypothetical votes, leader margin of victory, leader vote share, perceived leadership ability, perceived leader salary, and perceived leader success as "popularity" leader outcomes.

We also categorised the predictor variables (i.e., type of judgement made from the face): attractiveness, perceived leadership ability (i.e., general leadership ratings, hypothetical vote judgements, and expected success as a leader), positive affect (i.e., negative [reverse coded], positive), power (i.e., ratings of aggression, competence, determination, dominance, intelligence, power, and threat level), physical features (i.e., babyfacedness [reverse coded], body-mass index, face shape, facial elongation, facial hair, femininity [reverse coded], fWHR, gender typicality, glasses, masculinity, maturity, mouth width, perceived age, perceived health, regional prototypicality – the typicality of facial traits for a given area, and skin tone), and warmth (i.e., agreeableness, approachability, creativity, honesty, morality, openness, pleasantness, sociability, social competence, supportiveness, and trustworthiness).

Notably, whether perceived leadership ability functions as a predictor or outcome variable sometimes depends on the nature of the study. In some cases, participants rated the perceived leadership ability of actual leaders (e.g., CEOS), so their perceptions served as a predictor variable predicting another measure or outcome (e.g., company net profits). In other cases, appearance-related qualities (e.g., fWHR) correlated with perceptions of leaders' ability, and thus leadership ability served as an ostensible outcome itself.

We also coded properties of the articles, including publication status, leadership domain (i.e., business, politics, or other), and target gender (i.e., all female, all male, or heterogeneous).

Analytic strategy

Our goal was to estimate the overall effect size representing the association between various facial cues and leader-related outcomes. We used the correlation coefficient, r, as our effect size estimate, applying Fisher's r-to-Z transformation for analysis (see Corey et al., 1998). All the studies we included thus reported either a correlation coefficient (75%) or sufficient statistical results to calculate a correlation coefficient effect size (25%). We transformed the results of t tests, unstandardised regression coefficients (bs), F tests, and χ^2 test statistics to rs using standard formulas (Cohen et al., 2003); converted logistic regression coefficients to odds ratios and then to rs (Borenstein et al., 2009); and transformed the proportion index π to r following the formula provided by Rosnow and Rosenthal (2003). We used standardised regression coefficients (βs) as the effect size when reported. Finally, we conservatively imputed any statistically nonsignificant effects reported without statistics as $r = 0$ ($n = 8$).

We used Comprehensive Meta-Analysis Version 3 (CMA) to analyse the data (Borenstein et al., 2009). Using a random-effects model (Cheung, 2015; Hunter & Schmidt, 2004), we pooled effect sizes based on participant samples (most typically labelled as separate studies) within manuscripts. We assessed effect size heterogeneity using Cochran's (1964) Q statistic, which represents observed dispersion, and report I^2, which quantifies how much the proportion of variability in effect size estimates in a meta-analysis is due to interstudy heterogeneity (rather than simply sampling error within the studies; Higgins, 2003).

We similarly examined publication bias using multiple statistical tools. We examined a funnel plot, which visually depicts bias among reported effect sizes (i.e., a majority of the reported effect sizes falling above the mean), and tested for asymmetry in the distribution of our effect sizes in the plot as an indication of publication bias using Egger's Regression (Egger et al., 1997; Sterne & Egger, 2001; Sterne et al., 2001). We employed Duval and Tweedie (2000) "Trim and Fill" to determine where missing studies are likely to fall in reference to the mean (i.e., above or below) by adding hypothetical effect sizes to the analysis and then recomputing the effect size with these adjustments. We also conducted a "file-drawer analysis" by calculating the fail-safe N to estimate how many unretrieved studies with effect sizes averaging zero would be needed to render a particular result nonsignificant (Rosenthal, 1979). Last, we compared aggregate effect sizes for published and unpublished research, such that significant differences would indicate distortions in the published literature due to systematic suppression of small or nonsignificant effect sizes. To interpret effect sizes, we adopt the standards recommended by Funder and Ozer (2019) where an effect size r of .10 is small, .20 is moderate, and .30 is large.

Results

We aggregated the effect sizes based on the 126 participant samples (equivalent to the total number of studies reported in the articles). Using a random-effects model, the omnibus analysis revealed a moderate-large positive association between aspects of facial appearance and leader outcomes ($M_{Z\text{-}r} = .26$, 95% CI [.21, .31]; Table 1).[2] The sample was heterogeneous, with roughly 96% of the observed variance between studies due to differences between the effect sizes (as opposed to error in measuring them). Thus, aspects of facial appearance significantly relate to perceptions of leadership ability and to leader outcomes, and seem to vary depending on characteristics of the studies measuring their association; we therefore proceeded to better understand the sources of this variability by examining the moderator variables.

---

[2]A fixed-effects analysis alternatively showed a positive but smaller effect size: $M_{Z\text{-}r} = .16$, *SE* =.004, 95% CI [.14,.16].

Moderator analyses

Study characteristics. We computed separate aggregate effect sizes for the subgroups of studies (see Table 1). Notably, effect sizes should be interpreted cautiously in cases where a limited number of studies fit the criteria. We compared effect sizes between study characteristics by conducting a series of moderator analyses that nested the Fisher-transformed effect sizes within each study for similar study characteristics (e.g., traits judged). However, comparisons made across characteristics within the same study are treated as independent. Doing so leads to effect size estimates that are more conservative (i.e., lower Type 1 error); however, the test comparing effect sizes across comparisons is less conservative (i.e., high Type 2 error; Borenstein et al., 2009). Thus, comparisons of effect sizes between moderators should be interpreted cautiously.

Leader outcome. We first examined the aggregate effect sizes for performance (e.g., leader salary, organisation profit) and popularity leader outcomes (e.g., ratings of perceived leadership ability, election outcomes) (see Table 1).

Table 1. Descriptive Statistics and Heterogeneity Test Results for Each Coded Subcategory by Sample.

Variable	k	M_{Z-r} (SE)	95% CI	Q	I^2
Overall	126	.26 (.03)	[.21, .31]	3755.33***	96.67
Leader Outcome					
Performance	52	.15 (.04)	[.07, .24]	317.75***	83.95
Popularity	93	.33 (.03)	[.27, .39]	3594.00***	97.44
Leader Domain					
Business	25	.21 (.06)	[.09, .33]	133.90***	82.08
Politics	76	.28 (.03)	[.22, .35]	3475.97***	97.84
Other	25	.21 (.06)	[.10, .32]	118.54***	79.75
Target Gender					
Men only	79	.22 (.04)	[.15, .29]	2299.58***	96.61
Women only	10	.02 (.10)	[−.17, .22]	329.15***	97.27
Men and women	41	.35 (.05)	[.25, .44]	1546.51***	97.41
Facial Feature					
Attractiveness	53	.22 (.04)	[14, .29]	832.34***	93.75
Leadership ability	35	.33 (.05)	[.23, .42]	211.62***	83.93
Physical features	34	.12 (.05)	[.03, .21]	229.93***	85.65
Facial Maturity	8	.06 (.08)	[−.09, .21]	88.64***	92.10
fWHR	9	.09 (.07)	[−.05, .24]	61.81***	87.07
Masculinity	4	.01 (.12)	[−.23, .26]	4.00	25.01
Positive Affect	17	.05 (.07)	[−.09, .18]	25.10	36.27
Power	81	.30 (.03)	[.24, .36]	1447.80***	94.47
Warmth	58	.21 (.04)	[.14, .28]	1776.60***	96.79
Publication Status					
Published data	122	.26 (.03)	[.21, .31]	3752.46***	96.77
Unpublished data	4	.19 (.14)	[−.09, .47]	2.71	0.00

Note. k = number of effect sizes in sample, M_{Z-r} = mean Fisher's Z-transformed standardised effect size r, SE = standard error of the mean Fisher's Z-transformed standardised effect size r, CI = confidence interval.
Significant Q values indicate heterogeneity within the samples.
I^2 values refer to the proportion of variance within the sample not due to sampling error.
* $p < .05$, *** $p < .001$.

Both showed moderate positive effects, though aspects of facial appearance unsurprisingly related to popularity outcomes to a greater extent than it did to performance outcomes, $Q(1) = 10.95$, $p < .001$.

Leader domain. We observed moderate effect sizes for the association between inferences from facial appearance and leader outcomes for studies that focused on different leadership domains (i.e., political, business, other). None of the effect sizes between domains statistically differed from one another (all $|Q|$s ≤ 1.03, all $ps \geq .31$).

Target gender. Comparing studies based on the gender of the targets used showed that the magnitude of the effect size was similar for studies that used only female targets as for studies that used only male targets, $Q(1) = 3.18$, $p = .07$. The effect size for studies that used targets of both genders differed from studies that used only male targets, $Q(1) = 4.39$, $p = .04$, and differed from studies that used only female targets (of which there were very few), $Q(1) = 9.51$, $p = .002$.

Leader Facial Feature. Grouping effect sizes based on the types of judgements that the participants made revealed moderate effect sizes that did not statistically differ from one another for ratings of attractiveness, power, perceptions of targets' leadership ability and warmth (all $|Q|$s ≤ 3.83, all $ps \geq .05$), though ratings of warmth did not significantly differ from perceived leadership, $Q(1) = 2.19$, $p = .14$. Ratings of physical features demonstrated a small effect size, which significantly differed from ratings of attractiveness, power, and perceptions of targets' leadership ability, all $|Q|$s ≥ 4.91, all $ps \leq .03$, but did not differ from ratings of warmth, $Q(1) = 1.50$, $p = .22$. Specific facial features such as facial maturity, fWHR, and masculinity produced small effect sizes and did not significantly predict leader outcomes.

A limited number of studies assessed perceptions of targets' positive affect, which did not significantly predict leader outcomes (see Table 1). Accordingly, the effect sizes for ratings of attractiveness, power, warmth, and perceptions of leadership ability significantly exceeded that for ratings of positive affect, all $|Q|$s ≥ 6.94, all $ps \leq .008$, but the effect size for ratings of physical facial features did not significantly exceed it, $Q(1) = 1.26$, $p = .26$.

We also calculated effect sizes for each facial feature separately for performance and popularity leader outcomes (see Table 2). Small-to-moderate positive effects emerged for each predictor of popularity leader outcomes. Attractiveness, perceived leadership, and power all related to performance leader outcomes, but positive affect, physical features, and warmth did not. Effect sizes were larger for popularity compared to performance leader outcomes for warmth, $Q(1) = 6.02$, $p = .01$, but not for affect, attractiveness, perceived leadership, physical features, or power, all $|Q|$s ≤ 2.41, all $ps \geq .12$.

Publication Bias. Although we could only identify a limited number of unpublished studies ($k = 4$), their effect sizes did not differ from those of the

Table 2. Effect Sizes for Each Facial Feature by Leader Outcome.

	Performance Leader Outcomes			Popularity Leader Outcomes		
Facial Feature	k	M_{Z-r} (SE)	95% CI	k	M_{Z-r} (SE)	95% CI
Attractiveness	20	.16 (.06)	[.03, .28]	44	.24 (.04)	[.16, .32]
Perceived leadership	18	.26 (.06)	[.14, .38]	20	.37 (.06)	[.26, .49]
Physical features	19	.09 (.05)	[−.04, .20]	24	.18 (.04)	[.10, .27]
Positive Affect	15	.05 (.05)	[−.05, .15]	10	.13 (.06)	[.01, .25]
Power	33	.24 (.05)	[.15, .33]	60	.33 (.03)	[.26, .39]
Warmth	28	.08 (.08)	[−.08, .23]	41	.33 (.06)	[.20, .45]

Note. k = number of effect sizes in sample, M_{Z-r} = mean Fisher's Z-transformed standardised effect size r, SE = standard error of the mean Fisher's Z-transformed standardised effect size r, CI = confidence interval.

published work, $Q(1) = 0.22$, $p = .64$. The funnel plot showed evidence of asymmetry in the effect size distribution, however, which the results of Egger's Regression signalled may be due to publication bias, bias = 2.03, SE = 0.68, $t(124) = 2.98$, $p = .003$ (Figure 1). Indeed, Duval and Tweedie (2000) "Trim and Fill" procedure suggested an additional 48 studies to the left side of the mean, which would decrease the mean effect size to Fisher's $Z = .09$, 95% CI [.03, .14].

Results of the two-tailed fail-safe N analysis indicated that it would take an additional 4,886 studies whose effect sizes average zero to reduce the aggregate effect size to nonsignificant ($p = .05$; Rosenthal, 1979). Because this quantity greatly exceeds our tolerance level of 640 studies, which represents the number

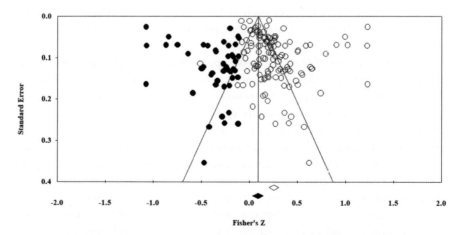

Figure 1. Funnel plot displaying the mean effect sizes for the 126 studies in the meta-analysis.

Note. Effect size estimates along the x-axis expressed as Fisher Z-transformed correlation coefficients and corresponding standard errors of the estimates along the y-axis represent the sample sizes (calculated from the inverse of the degrees of freedom based on the sample size used in the given study). Filled circles represent imputed "missing" studies suggested by the Trim-and-Fill procedure.

of studies that might already exist whose effect size averages zero (calculated using the 5 k + 10 formula, where k = 126 for the number of samples examined here), it is highly unlikely that sufficient unpublished studies exist to nullify the association between aspects of facial appearance and leader outcomes.

Discussion

People hold implicit leadership prototypes that guide who they think looks like a good leader (Kenney et al., 1996). Variability in people's opinions about the traits a leader should have (and how a leader with those traits would look) has led to contrasting findings on how facial cues relate to leader success. Here, we qualitatively review and quantitatively assess the association between various facial cues that predict leader selection and success.

Using random-effects meta-analysis, we found that judgements of physical features, behavioural attributes, and leadership ability from leaders' faces significantly positively relate to leader outcomes across multiple indices to a moderate extent. The effect sizes remained positive and moderate in size despite the outcome type (i.e., performance vs. popularity leader outcomes), leader domain (i.e., business vs. political vs. other types of leaders), or targets' gender (i.e., all men vs. all women vs. both men and women), though the number of studies in each category influenced the respective effect sizes. Notably, the medium effect size found here is comparable to the average effect size in social psychology and personality (Fraley & Marks, 2007; Richard et al., 2003). According to Funder and Ozer (2019), a medium effect size has explanatory and practical use. For example, in the short run, people typically have stereotypes about who looks like a leader (which develop early in life) that they use when deciding whether to elect or promote leaders, which reinforces those initial leader prototypes. In the long run, these decisions influence the state of our countries (e.g., how democratic, autocratic) and the profitability of companies all over the world.

Facial cues related to leader outcomes that were also based on popular perceptions (e.g., perceived leadership ability, hypothetical voting decisions) more than outcomes not directly determined by perceptions (e.g., companies' financial performance). Interestingly, whereas a host of perceptions predicted popularity leader outcomes, only attractiveness, perceived leadership, and power predicted performance leader outcomes. Thus, studies with higher external validity may observe smaller effect sizes because of the greater distance between the judgements made and the outcomes measured; researchers may therefore require larger target samples to have the statistical power needed to obtain reliable results when examining objective performance outcomes. Reciprocally, researchers studying popularity leader outcomes should take caution that judgements by the same perceivers (or around the same time as the outcomes become determined – e.g., during elections or political campaigns) may inflate the size of the association due to common method variance and item covariation (Markus & Borsboom, 2013; Williams & Brown, 1994).

The specific judgements related to these outcomes may also introduce variance. To date, researchers have examined how various trait inferences and physical features relate to perceptions of who makes a good leader. Here, we have provided estimates of the typical size of these associations. Every judgement except positive affect positively related to leader outcomes: attractiveness, power, warmth, perceived leadership ability, and physical measurements of several facial features. Yet, despite their consistently positive associations, these characteristics may relate to leadership differently. Although perceptions of power and warmth (both broadly defined) positively related to popularity and performance leader outcomes, traits associated with power (e.g., competence and dominance) generally relate to leader success in individual studies, whereas traits related to warmth usually do not – particularly when a performance outcome is used (e.g., trustworthiness; Rule & Ambady, 2011a; Todorov, 2005). Indeed, the association between warmth and leader outcomes may heavily depend on context. For example, people in Western cultures may prefer trustworthy leaders during times of peace but not war (Little et al., 2012), people living in collectivistic (vs. individualistic) cultures seem to prefer more trustworthy or socially competent leaders (e.g., F. F. Chen et al., 2012, 2016), and perceptions of warmth may relate to the company rank and profits earned for female CEOs but not for male CEOs (Pillemer et al., 2014). The present meta-analysis did not account for these distinctions because the limited number of studies in each category would undermine the reliability of the results. As researchers continue to study these traits and related second-generation questions, however, sufficient data may accumulate to allow for a deeper investigation of the distinction between traits.

Notably, the effect sizes are only as good as the data that produce them (Funder & Ozer, 2019). Meta-analyses can amplify biases produced through publication bias, which tends to censor small effect sizes as significant results are published more often than nonsignificant results (e.g., Franco et al., 2016; Lipsey & Wilson, 2001; Schooler, 2011; Sterling et al., 1995). The asymmetry in our funnel plot and corresponding trim-and-fill analysis indicates that the mean effect size should be smaller than what we found here, suggesting that some null effects have gone unreported, skewing the findings towards positive results. With publication norms changing (i.e., greater acceptance for reporting null results), we hope that a clearer picture of the association between aspects of leaders' facial appearance and related outcomes will emerge as the body of research continues to grow.

Future research

In the future, researchers should seek to develop greater understanding of the specific paths that connect various facial cues to leader selection and success. Voting decisions, for example, involve considerations of candidates' platforms, political orientation, speeches, and social appearances (e.g., Carpinella & Johnson, 2016). Moreover, the financial performance of a company ought not to rely on consumers' impressions of its CEO's face. Preliminary gains on the topic suggest that voters' level of information processing (e.g., Lenz & Lawson, 2011), employees' appetite for success (Wong et al., 2011), and how the brain responds to particular leaders (Rule, Moran, et al., 2011) might help to clarify the mechanisms linking facial appearance to the outcomes examined here. Much more work remains outstanding to grasp a full understanding of the association, however. Along these lines, although we focused only on research investigating how facial appearance influences leader selection and success, much additional research focuses more broadly on how other aspects of appearance, nonverbal behaviour, and verbal behaviour also influence leader selection (e.g., Hall et al., 2005; Tskhay et al., 2014). Considering and integrating these additional dimensions may prove productive in future research.

Last, this meta-analysis cannot contribute towards clarifying the direction of the association between appearance and leader outcomes. For instance, do companies promote more attractive employees into leadership positions, or do more attractive leaders shepherd companies to greater success? Although the results of some studies might suggest the former (e.g., Graham et al., 2016), others offer evidence in favour of the latter (e.g., Wong et al., 2011). More research should experimentally investigate this important question to gain sharper insight about the causes underlying the association between aspects of facial appearance and leader success.

Conclusion

People spend billions of dollars annually to advertise themselves and persuade others of their suitability for leadership positions (Pinto-Duschinsky, 2002). Yet this review, and the research that it summarises, demonstrates that one significant factor gating the efficacy of those efforts begins with the individual's face. Given the importance of leader selection, it may come as a surprise that perceptions of facial cues contribute so consistently to the impressions that people form about a person's ability to lead (e.g., Zebrowitz & Montepare, 2008). The robust associations found in this meta-analysis encourage confidence about the observation that facial appearance cues and leadership do correlate, and that the topic merits further inquiry. This research therefore helps to clarify how people decide who looks like a leader, who gets elected to powerful public offices, and who ascends to the top levels of organisations. Indeed, the results of this meta-analysis may serve as a reference for researchers designing studies investigating elements of facial appearance and leader outcomes, helping to supply guideposts for statistical power, sample size estimation, and a sense of the strength of the links between appearance, perception, and behaviour. To that end, our results provide researchers with an overall effect size for the association between appearance cues suggesting the presence of qualities often desired in leaders and leader outcomes, and with effect size estimates for a broad range of specific trait judgements and other moderating variables. We hope this review and meta-analysis will prove useful to researchers planning and designing high-quality, well-powered studies investigating the facial appearance of leaders, and that it will encourage further insights towards better understanding this curious but critical phenomenon.

ORCID

Nicholas O. Rule (iD) http://orcid.org/0000-0002-2332-9058

References

* indicates article included in meta-analysis

Ahler, D. J., Citrin, J., Dougal, M. C., & Lenz, G. S. 2017. Face value? Experimental evidence that candidate appearance influences electoral choice. *Political Behavior*, 39(1), 77–102. https://doi.org/10.1007/s11109-016-9348-6.*

Ahmed, S., Sihvonen, J., & Vähämaa, S. 2019. CEO facial masculinity and bank risk-taking. *Personality and Individual Differences*, 138, 133–139. https://doi.org/10.1016/j.paid.2018.09.029.*

Alrajih, S., & Ward, J. 2014. Increased facial width-to-height ratio and perceived dominance in the faces of the UK's leading business leaders. *British Journal of Psychology*, 105(2), 153–161. https://doi.org/10.1111/bjop.12035.*

Antonakis, J., & Dalgas, O. 2009. Predicting elections: Child's play!. *Science*, 323 (5918), 1183. https://doi.org/10.1126/science.1167748.*

Antonakis, J., & Eubanks, D. L. (2017). Looking leadership in the face. *Current Directions in Psychological Science*, 26(3), 270–275. https://doi.org/10.1177/0963721417705888

Atkinson, M. D., Enos, R. D., & Hill, S. J. 2009. Candidate faces and election outcomes: Is the face–vote correlation caused by candidate selection?. *Quarterly Journal of Political Science*, 4(3), 229–249. https://doi.org/10.1561/100.00008062_supp.*

Ballew, C. C., & Todorov, A. (2007). Predicting political elections from rapid and unreflective face judgments. *Proceedings of the National Academy of Sciences*, 104, 17948–17953. https://doi.org/10.1073/pnas.0705435104.*

Banducci, S. A., Karp, J. A., Thrasher, M., & Rallings, C. 2008. Ballot photographs as cues in low-information elections. *Political Psychology*, 29(6), 903–917. https://doi.org/10.1111/j.1467-9221.2008.00672.x.*

Barrett, A. W., & Barrington, L. W. (2005). Bias in newspaper photograph selection. *Political Research Quarterly*, 58(4), 609–618. https://doi.org/10.2307/3595646.*

Barrett, A. W., & Barrington, L. W. 2005. Is a picture worth a thousand words? Newspaper photographs and voter evaluations of political candidates. *Harvard International Journal of Press/Politics*, 10(4), 98–113. https://doi.org/10.1177/1081180X05281392.*

Battaglini, A., Tian, L., Alaei, R., & Rule, N. O. 2020. *Do you have brains or brawn?*.*

Bean, C. 1993. The electoral influence of party leader images in Australia and New Zealand. *Comparative Political Studies*, 26(1), 111–132. https://doi.org/10.1177/0010414093026001005.*

Berger, J., & Wagner, D. G. (2007). Expectation states theory. *The Blackwell Encyclopedia of Sociology*, 1–5. https://doi.org/10.1002/9781405165518.wbeose084.pub2

Berggren, N., Jordahl, H., & Poutvaara, P. 2010. The looks of a winner: Beauty and electoral success. *Journal of Public Economics*, 94(1–2), 8–15. https://doi.org/10.1016/j.jpubeco.2009.11.002.*

Berggren, N., Jordahl, H., & Poutvaara, P. 2017. The right look: Conservative politicians look better and voters reward it. *Journal of Public Economics*, 146, 79–86. https://doi.org/10.1016/j.jpubeco.2016.12.008.*

Berinsky, A. J., Chatfield, S., & Lenz, G. 2019. Facial dominance and electoral success in times of war and peace. *The Journal of Politics*, 81(3), 1096–1100. https://doi.org/10.1086/703384.*

Biddle, J. E., & Hamermesh, D. S. 1998. Beauty, productivity, and discrimination: Lawyers' looks and lucre. *Journal of Labor Economics*, 323(1), 172–201. https://doi.org/10.1086/209886.*

Bird, B. M., Jofré, V. S. C., Geniole, S. N., Welker, K. M., Zilioli, S., Maestripieri, D., ... Carre, J. M. (2016). Does the facial width-to-height ratio map onto variability in men's testosterone concentrations?. *Evolution and Human Behavior*, 37(5), 392–398. https://doi.org/10.1016/j.evolhumbehav.2016.03.004

Borenstein, M., Hedges, L. V., Higgins, J. P. T., & Rothstein, H. R. (2009). Introduction to Meta-Analysis. In *Chichester*. Wiley.

Borkenau, P., Brecke, S., Möttig, C., & Paelecke, M. (2009). Extraversion is accurately perceived after a 50-ms exposure to a face. *Journal of Research in Personality*, 43(4), 703–706. https://doi.org/10.1016/j.jrp.2009.03.007

Brizi, A., & Mannetti, L. 2016. How competence and trustworthiness inferences made by voters in the centre of Italy predicts the North Italian political elections: The impact of the city size. *Rassegna di Psicologia*, 33(2), 5–12. https://doi.org/10.4558/8043-01.*

Budesheim, T. L., & Depaola, S. J. (1994). Beauty or the beast? The effects of appearance, personality, and issue information on evaluations of political candidates. *Personality & Social Psychology Bulletin*, 20(4), 339–348. https://doi.org/10.1177/0146167294204001

Calder, B. J. (1977). An attribution theory of leadership. In B. M. Staw & G. R. Salanick (Eds.), *New Directions in Organizational Behavior* (pp. 179–204). St. Clair Press.

Carpinella, C. M., Hehman, E., Freeman, J. B., & Johnson, K. L. 2016. The gendered face of partisan politics: Consequences of facial sex typicality for vote choice. *Political Communication*, 33(1), 21–38. https://doi.org/10.1080/10584609.2014.958260.*

Carpinella, C. M., & Johnson, K. L. (2016). Visual political communication: The impact of facial cues from social constituencies to personal pocketbooks. *Social and Personality Psychology Compass*, *10*(5), 281–297. https://doi.org/10.1111/spc3.12249

Carré, J. M., & McCormick, C. M. (2008). In your face: Facial metrics predict aggressive behaviour in the laboratory and in varsity and professional hockey players. Proceedings of the Royal Society B: Biological Sciences, 275(1651), 2651–2656. https://doi.org/10.1098/rspb.2008.0873

Carré, J. M., McCormick, C. M., & Mondloch, C. J. (2009). Facial structure is a reliable cue of aggressive behavior. *Psychological Science*, *20*(10), 1194–1198. https://doi.org/10.1111/j.1467-9280.2009.02423.x

Castelli, L., Carraro, L., Ghitti, C., & Pastore, M. 2009. The effects of perceived competence and sociability on electoral outcomes. *Journal of Experimental Social Psychology*, *45*(5), 1152–1155. https://doi.org/10.1016/j.jesp.2009.06.018.*

Chang, C. T., Lee, Y. K., & Cheng, Z. H. 2017. Baby face wins? Examining election success based on candidate election bulletin via multilevel modeling. *Asian Journal of Social Psychology*, *20*(2), 97–112. https://doi.org/10.1111/ajsp.12172.*

Chen, F. F., Jing, Y., & Lee, J. M. 2012. "I" value competence but "we" value social competence: The moderating role of voters' individualistic and collectivistic orientation in political elections. *Journal of Experimental Social Psychology*, *48*(6), 1350–1355. https://doi.org/10.1016/j.jesp.2012.07.006.*

Chen, F. F., Jing, Y., & Lee, J. M. 2014. The looks of a leader: Competent and trustworthy, but not dominant. *Journal of Experimental Social Psychology*, *51*, 27–33. https://doi.org/10.1016/j.jesp.2013.10.008.*

Chen, F. F., Jing, Y., Lee, J. M., & Bai, L. 2016. Culture matters: The looks of a leader are not all the same. *Social Psychological and Personality Science*, *7*(6), 570–578. https://doi.org/10.1177/1948550616644962.*

Cherulnik, P. D., Turns, L. C., & Wilderman, S. K. 1990. Physical appearance and leadership Exploring the role of appearance-based attribution in leader emergence. *Journal of Applied Social Psychology*, *20*(18), 1530–1539. https://doi.org/10.1111/j.1559-1816.1990.tb01491.x.*

Cheung, M. W. L. (2015). *Meta-analysis: A structural equation modeling approach*. John Wiley & Sons.

Chiao, J. Y., Bowman, N. E., & Gill, H. 2008. The political gender gap: Gender bias in facial inferences that predict voting behavior. *PloS One*, *3*(10), e3666. https://doi.org/10.1371/journal.pone.0003666.*

Cochran, W. G. (1964). Comparison of two methods of handling covariates in discriminatory analysis. *Annals of the Institute of Statistical Mathematics*, *16*(1), 43–53. https://doi.org/10.1007/BF02868561

Cohen, J., Cohen, P., West, S. G., & Aiken, L. S. (2003). *Applied Multiple*. Routledge.

Corey, D. M., Dunlap, W. P., & Burke, M. J. (1998). Averaging correlations: Expected values and bias in combined pearsonrs and fisher'sz transformations. *The Journal of General Psychology*, *125*(3), 245–261. https://doi.org/10.1080/00221309809595548

Correll, S. J., & Ridgeway, C. L. (2006). Expectation states theory. In *Handbook of social psychology* (pp. 29–51). Springer.

Dietl, E., & Rule, N. O. (under review). *It's in your face! People infer leader-follower status and occupation type from faces better than chance*.*

Dietl, E., Rule, N. O., & Blickle, G. 2018. Core self-evaluations mediate the association between leaders' facial appearance and their professional success: Adults' and children's perceptions. *The Leadership Quarterly*, *29*(4), 476–488. https://doi.org/10.1016/j.leaqua.2018.01.002.*

Dilger, A., Lütkenhöner, L., & Müller, H. 2015. Scholars' physical appearance, research performance, and feelings of happiness. *Scientometrics*, *104*(2), 555–573. https://doi.org/10.1007/s11192-015-1623-5.*

Dion, K., Berscheid, E., & Walster, E. (1972). What is beautiful is good. *Journal of Personality and Social Psychology*, *24*(3), 285–290. https://doi.org/10.1037/h0033731

Dipboye, R. L., Arvey, R. D., & Terpstra, D. E. (1977). Sex and physical attractiveness of raters and applicants as determinants of resumé evaluations. *Journal of Applied Psychology*, *62*(3), 288–294. https://doi.org/10.1037/0021-9010.62.3.288

Duval, S., & Tweedie, R. (2000). Trim and fill: A simple funnel-plot–based method of testing and adjusting for publication bias in meta-analysis. *Biometrics*, *56*(2), 455–463. https://doi.org/10.1111/j.0006-341X.2000.00455.x

Eagly, A. H., & Karau, S. J. (2002). Role congruity theory of prejudice toward female leaders. *Psychological Review*, *109*(3), 573–598. https://doi.org/10.1037/0033-295X.109.3.573

Eden, D., & Leviathan, U. (1975). Implicit leadership theory as a determinant of the factor structure underlying supervisory behavior scales. *Journal of Applied Psychology*, *60*(6), 736–741. https://doi.org/10.1037/0021-9010.60.6.736

Efrain, M. G., & Patterson, E. W. J. 1974. Voters vote beautiful: The effect of physical appearance on a national election. *Canadian Journal of Behavioural Science*, *6*(4). 352–356. https://doi.org/10.1037/h0081881.*

Egger, M., Smith, G. D., Schneider, M., & Minder, C. (1997). Bias in meta-analysis detected by a simple, graphical test. *Bmj*, *315*(7109), 629–634. https://doi.org/10.1136/bmj.315.7109.629

Ensari, N., & Murphy, S. E. (2003). Cross-cultural variations in leadership perceptions and attribution of charisma to the leader. *Organizational Behavior and Human Decision Processes*, *92*(1–2), 52–66. https://doi.org/10.1016/S0749-5978(03)00066-9

Fleischmann, A., Lammers, J., Stoker, J. I., & Garretsen, H. 2018. You can leave your glasses on. *Social Psychology*, *50*(1). 38–52. https://doi.org/10.1027/1864-9335-a000359.*

Fraley, R. C., & Marks, M. J. (2007). The null hypothesis significance testing debate and its implications for personality research. In R. W. Robins, R. C. Fraley, & R. F. Krueger (Eds.), *Handbook of research methods in personality psychology* (pp. 149–169). Guilford Press.

Franco, A., Malhotra, N., & Simonovits, G. (2016). Underreporting in psychology experiments: Evidence from a study registry. *Social Psychological and Personality Science*, *7*(1), 8–12. https://doi.org/10.1177/1948550615598377

Franklin, J. R. G., & Zebrowitz, L. A. 2016. The influence of political candidates' facial appearance on older and younger adults' voting choices and actual electoral success. *Cogent Psychology*, *3*(1), 1151602. https://doi.org/10.1080/23311908.2016.1151602.*

Funder, D. C., & Ozer, D. J. (2019). Evaluating effect size in psychological research: Sense and nonsense. *Advances in Methods and Practices in Psychological Science*, *2*(2), 156–168. https://doi.org/10.1177/2515245919847202

Funk, C. L. 1999. Bringing the candidate into models of candidate evaluation. *The Journal of Politics*, *61*(3), 700–720. https://doi.org/10.2307/2647824.*

Garretsen, H., Stoker, J., Alessie, R. J., & Lammers, J. (2014). Simply a matter of luck & looks? predicting elections when both the world economy and the psychology of faces count. CESifo Working paper, No. 4857.*

Geniole, S. N., Denson, T. F., Dixson, B. J., Carré, J. M., & McCormick, C. M. (2015). Evidence from meta-analyses of the facial width-to-height ratio as an evolved cue of threat. *PloS One, 10*(7), e0132726. https://doi.org/10.1371/journal.pone.0132726

Gheorghiu, A. I., Callan, M. J., & Skylark, W. J. 2017. Facial appearance affects science communication. *Proceedings of the National Academy of Sciences, 114* (23), 5970–5975. https://doi.org/10.1073/pnas.1620542114.*

Giacomin, M., Mulligan, A., & Rule, N. O. (under review). *Warmth differentiate dictators from democrats. Unpublished data.*

Gomulya, D., Wong, E. M., Ormiston, M. E., & Boeker, W. 2017. The role of facial appearance on CEO selection after firm misconduct. *Journal of Applied Psychology, 102*(4), 617–635. https://doi.org/10.1037/apl0000172.*

Graham, J. R., Harvey, C. R., & Puri, M. 2016. A corporate beauty contest. *Management Science, 63*(9). 3044–3056. https://doi.org/10.1287/mnsc.2016.2484.*

Hahn, T., Winter, N. R., Anderl, C., Notebaert, K., Wuttke, A. M., Clément, C. C., & Windmann, S. 2017. Facial width-to-height ratio differs by social rank across organizations, countries, and value systems. *PloS One, 12*(11), e0187957. https://doi.org/10.1371/journal.pone.0187957.*

Hall, J. A., Coats, E. J., & LeBeau, L. S. (2005). Nonverbal behaviour and the vertical dimension of social relations: A meta-analysis. *Psychological Bulletin, 131*(6), 898–924. https://doi.org/10.1037/0033-2909.131.6.898

Harms, P. D., Han, G., & Chen, H. 2012. Recognizing leadership at a distance: A study of leader effectiveness across cultures. *Journal of Leadership & Organizational Studies, 19*(2). 164–172. https://doi.org/10.1177/1548051812436812.*

Haselhuhn, M. P., & Wong, E. M. (2011). Bad to the bone: Facial structure predicts unethical behaviour. *Proceedings of the Royal Society of London B: Biological Sciences, 279*(1728), rspb20111193. https://doi.org/10.1098/rspb.2011.1193

Haselhuhn, M. P., Wong, E. M., & Ormiston, M. E. (2013). Self-fulfilling prophecies as a link between men's facial width-to-height ratio and behavior. *PloS One, 8*(8), e72259. https://doi.org/10.1371/journal.pone.0072259

Hehman, E., Carpinella, C. M., Johnson, K. L., Leitner, J. B., & Freeman, J. B. 2014. Early processing of gendered facial cues predicts the electoral success of female politicians. *Social Psychological and Personality Science, 5*(7). 815–824. https://doi.org/10.1177/1948550614534701.*

Higgins, J. P. (2003). Measuring inconsistency in meta-analyses. *BMJ: British Medical Journal, 327*(7414), 557–560. https://doi.org/10.1136/bmj.327.7414.557

Higgle, E. D. B., Miller, P. M., Shields, T. G., & Johnson, M. M. S. (1997). Gender stereotypes and decision context in the evaluation of political candidates. *Women & Politics, 17*(3), 69–88. https://doi.org/10.1300/J014v17n03_04

Hochschild, J. T. R., & Borch, C. 2011. About face: The association between facial appearance and status attainment among military personnel. *Sociological Spectrum, 31*(3), 369–395. https://doi.org/10.1080/02732173.2011.557132.*

Hogan, R. (1995). *Hogan personality inventory.* Hogan Assessment Systems.

Hunter, J. E., & Schmidt, F. L. (2004). *Methods of meta-analysis: Correcting error and bias in research findings.* Sage.

Jäckle, S., & Metz, T. 2017. Beauty contest revisited: The effects of perceived attractiveness, competence, and likability on the electoral success of German MPs. *Politics & Policy*, *45*(4). 495–534. https://doi.org/10.1111/polp.12209.*

Jaeger, B., Evans, A., & van Beest, I. 2019. Facial appearances and electoral success: Does regional corruption moderate preferences for trustworthy-looking politicians?. doi: 10.31234/osf.io/btcxm
*

Johns, R., & Shephard, M. 2007. Gender, candidate image and electoral preference. *The British Journal of Politics and International Relations*, *9*(3). 434–460. https://doi.org/10.1111/j.1467-856x.2006.00263.x.*

Kamiya, S., Kim, Y. H., & Park, S. 2019. The face of risk: CEO facial masculinity and firm risk. *European Financial Management*, *25*(2). 239–270. https://doi.org/10.1111/eufm.12175.*

Kenney, R. A., Schwartz-Kenney, B. M., & Blascovich, J. (1996). Implicit leadership theories: Defining leaders described as worthy of influence. *Personality & Social Psychology Bulletin*, *22*(11), 1128–1143. https://doi.org/10.1177/01461672962211004

King, A., & Leigh, A. 2009. Beautiful Politicians. *KYKLOS*, *62*(4), 579–593. https://doi.org/10.1111/j.1467-6435.2009.00452.x.*

Klofstad, C. A. 2017. Looks and sounds like a winner: Perceptions of competence in candidates' faces and voices influences vote choice. *Journal of Experimental Political Science*, *4*(3). 229–240. https://doi.org/10.1017/XPS.2017.19.*

Kocoglu, I., & Mithani, M. A. 2019. Does an attractive partner make you a better leader? Only if you are a male!. *The Leadership Quarterly*, *31*(2), 101339. https://doi.org/10.1016/j.leaqua.2019.101339.*

Kosinski, M. (2017). Facial width-to-height ratio does not predict self-reported behavioral tendencies. *Psychological Science*, *28*(11), 1675–1682. https://doi.org/10.1177/0956797617716929

Laustsen, L. 2014. Decomposing the relationship between candidates' facial appearance and electoral success. *Political Behavior*, *36*(4). 777–791. https://doi.org/10.1007/s11109-013-9253-1.*

Laustsen, L., & Petersen, M. B. 2018. When the party decides: The effects of facial competence and dominance on internal nominations of political candidates. *Evolutionary Psychology*, *16*(2). 1–13. https://doi.org/10.1177/1474704917732005.*

Lawson, C., Lenz, G. S., Baker, A., & Myers, M. 2010. Looking like a winner: Candidate appearance and electoral success in new democracies. *World Politics*, *62*(4). 561–593. https://doi.org/10.1017/S0043887110000195.*

Lefevre, C. E., Lewis, G. J., Perrett, D. I., & Penke, L. (2013). Telling facial metrics: Facial width is associated with testosterone levels in men. *Evolution and Human Behavior*, *34*(4), 273–279. https://doi.org/10.1016/j.evolhumbehav.2013.03.005

Leigh, A. 2009. Does the world economy swing national elections?. *Oxford Bulletin of Economics and Statistics*, *71*(2), 163–181. https://doi.org/10.1111/j.1468-0084.2008.00545.x.*

Leigh, A., & Susilo, T. 2009. Is voting skin-deep? Estimating the effect of candidate ballot photographs on election outcomes. *Journal Of Economic Psychology*, *30*(1). 61–70. https://doi.org/10.1016/j.joep.2008.07.008.*

Lenz, G. S., & Lawson, C. 2011. Looking the part: Television leads less informed citizens to vote based on candidates' appearance. *American Journal of Political Science*, *55*(3). 574–589. https://doi.org/10.1111/j.1540-5907.2011.00511.x.*

Lewis, G. J., Lefevre, C. E., & Bates, T. C. (2012). Facial width-to-height ratio predicts achievement drive in US presidents. *Personality and Individual Differences*, 52(7), 855–857. https://doi.org/10.1016/j.paid.2011.12.030

Lin, C., Adolphs, R., & Alvarez, R. M. 2017. Cultural effects on the association between election outcomes and face-based trait inferences. *PloS One*, 12(7), e0180837. https://doi.org/10.1371/journal.pone.0180837.*

Lin, C., Adolphs, R., & Alvarez, R. M. 2018. Inferring whether officials are corruptible from looking at their faces. *Psychological Science*, 29(11). 1807–1823. https://doi.org/10.1177/0956797618788882.*

Linke, L., Saribay, S. A., & Kleisner, K. 2016. Perceived trustworthiness is associated with position in a corporate hierarchy. *Personality and Individual Differences*, 99, 22–27. https://doi.org/10.1016/j.paid.2016.04.076.*

Lipsey, M. W., & Wilson, D. B. (2001). *Applied social research methods series; Vol. 49. Practical meta-analysis*. Thousand Oaks. US: Sage Publications, Inc.

Little, A. C., Burriss, R. P., Jones, B. C., & Roberts, S. C. 2007. Facial appearance affects voting decisions. *Evolution and Human Behavior*, 28(1). 18–27. https://doi.org/10.1016/j.evolhumbehav.2006.09.002.*

Little, A. C., Roberts, S. C., Jones, B. C., & DeBruine, L. M. (2012). The perception of attractiveness and trustworthiness in male faces affects hypothetical voting decisions differently in wartime and peacetime scenarios. *The Quarterly Journal of Experimental Psychology*, 65(10), 2018–2032. https://doi.org/10.1080/17470218.2012.677048

Livingston, R. W., & Pearce, N. A. 2009. The teddy-bear effect: Does having a baby face benefit black Chief Executive Officers?. *Psychological Science*, 20(10). 1229–1236. https://doi.org/10.1111/j.1467-9280.2009.02431.x.*

Loehr, J., & O'Hara, R. B. 2013. Facial morphology predicts male fitness and rank but not survival in Second World War Finnish soldiers. *Biology Letters*, 9(4), 20130049. https://doi.org/10.1098/rsbl.2013.0049.*

Lord, R. G., & Maher, K. J. (1991). *Leadership and information processing: Linking perceptions and performance*. Routledge.

Lutz, G. 2010. The electoral success of beauties and beasts. *Swiss Political Science Review*, 16(3). 457–480. https://doi.org/10.1002/j.1662-6370.2010.tb00437.x.*

Malatesta, C. Z., Fiore, M. J., & Messina, J. J. (1987). Affect, personality, and facial expressive characteristics of older people. *Psychology and Aging*, 2(1), 64–69. https://doi.org/10.1037/0882-7974.2.1.64

Mannetti, L., Brizi, A., Belanger, J., & Bufalari, I. 2016. All we need is the candidate's face: The irrelevance of information about political coalition affiliation and campaign promises. *Cogent Psychology*, 3(1), 1268365. https://doi.org/10.1080/23311908.2016.1268365.*

Markus, K. A., & Borsboom, D. (2013). *Frontiers of test validity theory: Measurement, causation, and meaning*. Routledge.

Martin, D. S. 1978. Person perception and real-life electoral behaviour. *Australian Journal of Psychology*, 30(3). 255–262. https://doi.org/10.1080/00049537808256378.*

Mattes, K., & Milazzo, C. 2014. Pretty faces, marginal races: Predicting election outcomes using trait assessments of British parliamentary candidates. *Electoral Studies*, 34, 177–189. https://doi.org/10.1016/j.electstud.2013.11.004.*

Mattes, K., Spezio, M., Kim, H., Todorov, A., Adolphs, R., & Alvarez, R. M. 2010. Predicting election outcomes from positive and negative trait assessments of candidate images. *Political Psychology*, 31(1). 41–58. https://doi.org/10.1111/j.1467-9221.2009.00745.x.*

Mazur, A., Mazur, J., & Keating, C. 1984. Military Rank Attainment of a West Point Class: Effects of Cadets' Physical Features. *American Journal of Sociology*, 90(1). 125–150. https://doi.org/10.1086/228050.*

McArthur, L. Z., & Baron, R. M. (1983). Toward an ecological theory of social perception. *Psychological Review*, 90(3), 215–238. https://doi.org/10.1037/0033-295X.90.3.215

Milazzo, C., & Mattes, K. 2016. Looking good for election day: Does attractiveness predict electoral success in Britain?. *The British Journal of Politics and International Relations*, 18(1). 161–178. https://doi.org/10.1111/1467-856X.12074.*

Mueller, U., & Mazur, A. 1996. Facial dominance of West Point cadets as a predictor of later military rank. *Social Forces*, 74(3). 823–850. https://doi.org/10.2307/2580383.*

Myers, C. P., Kopelman, C. G., & Garcia, S. M. 2012. The hierarchical face: Higher rankings lead to less cooperative looks. *Journal of Applied Psychology*, 97(2). 479–486. https://doi.org/10.1037/a0026308.*

Na, J., Kim, S., Oh, H., Choi, I., & O'Toole, A. 2015. Competence judgments based on facial appearance are better predictors of American elections than of Korean elections. *Psychological Science*, 26(7). 1107–1113. https://doi.org/10.1177/0956797615576489.*

Nana, E., Jackson, B., & St. J. Burch, G. 2010. Attributing leadership personality and effectiveness from the leader's face: An exploratory study. *Leadership & Organization Development Journal*, 31(8). 720–742. https://doi.org/10.1108/01437731011094775.*

Olivola, C. Y., Eubanks, D. L., & Lovelace, J. B. 2014. The many (distinctive) faces of leadership: Inferring leadership domain from facial appearance. *The Leadership Quarterly*, 25(5). 817–834. https://doi.org/10.1016/j.leaqua.2014.06.002.*

Olivola, C. Y., & Todorov, A. (2010). Elected in 100 milliseconds: Appearance-based trait inferences and voting. *Journal of Nonverbal Behavior*, 34(2), 83–110. https://doi.org/10.1007/s10919-009-0082-1

Perrett, D. (2010). *In your face: The new science of human attraction*. Palgrave Macmillan.

Pfann, G. A., Biddle, J. E., Hamermesh, D. S., & Bosman, C. M. 2000. Business success and businesses' beauty capital. *Economics Letters*, 67(2), 201–207. https://doi.org/10.1016/S0165-1765(99)00255-4.*

Pillemer, J., Graham, E. R., & Burke, D. M. 2014. The face says it all: CEOs, gender, and predicting corporate performance. *The Leadership Quarterly*, 25(5), 855–864. https://doi.org/10.1016/j.leaqua.2014.07.002.*

Pinto-Duschinsky, M. (2002). Financing politics: A global view. *Journal of Democracy*, 13(4), 69–86. https://doi.org/10.1353/jod.2002.0074

Poutvaara, P., Jordahl, H., & Berggren, N. 2009. Faces of politicians: Babyfacedness predicts inferred competence but not electoral success. *Journal of Experimental Social Psychology*, 45(5). 1132–1135. https://doi.org/10.1016/j.jesp.2009.06.007.*

Praino, R., Stockemer, D., & Ratis, J. 2014. Looking good or looking competent? Physical appearance and electoral success in the 2008 congressional elections. *American Politics Research*, 42(6). 1096–1117. https://doi.org/10.1177/1532673X14532825.*

Re, D. E., & Rule, N. O. (2015). Appearance and physiognomy. In D. Matsumoto, H. Hwang, & M. Frank (Eds..), *APA Handbook of Nonverbal Communication* (pp. 221–256). American Psychological Association. https://doi.org/10.1037/14669-009

Re, D. E., & Rule, N. O. 2016a. The big man has a big mouth: Mouth width correlates with perceived leadership ability and actual leadership performance. *Journal of Experimental Social Psychology, 63*, 86–92. https://doi.org/0.1016/j.jesp.2015.12.005.*

Re, D. E., & Rule, N. O. 2016b. Predicting firm success from the facial appearance of Chief Executive Officers of Non-Profit Organizations. *Perception, 45*(10). 1137–1150. https://doi.org/10.1177/0301006616652043.*

Re, D. E., & Rule, N. O. 2016c. Making a (false) impression: The role of business expertise in first impressions of CEO leadership ability. *Journal of Nonverbal Behavior, 40*(3). 235–245. https://doi.org/10.1007/s10919-016-0231-2.*

Re, D. E., & Rule, N. O. 2017. Distinctive facial cues predict leadership rank and selection. *Personality & Social Psychology Bulletin, 43*(9). 1311–1322. https://doi.org/10.1177/0146167217712989.*

Richard, F. D., Bond, C. F., & Stokes-Zoota, J. J. (2003). One hundred years of social psychology quantitatively described. *Review of General Psychology, 7*(4), 331–363. https://doi.org/10.1037/1089-2680.7.4.331

Riggio, H. R., & Riggio, R. E. (2010). Appearance-based trait inferences and voting: Evolutionary roots and implications for leadership. *Journal of Nonverbal Behavior, 34*(2), 119–125. https://doi.org/10.1007/s10919-009-0083-0

Rosenberg, S. W., Kahn, S., & Tran, T. (1991). Creating a political image: Shaping appearance and manipulating the vote. *Political Behavior, 13*(4), 345–367. https://doi.org/10.1007/BF00992868

Rosenthal, R. (1979). The file drawer problem and tolerance for null results. *Psychological Bulletin, 86*(3), 638–641. https://doi.org/10.1037/0033-2909.86.3.638

Rosette, A. S., Leonardelli, G. J., & Phillips, K. W. (2008). The White standard: Racial bias in leader categorization. *Journal of Applied Psychology, 93*(4), 758–777. https://doi.org/10.1037/0021-9010.93.4.758

Rosnow, R. L., & Rosenthal, R. (2003). Effect sizes for experimenting psychologists. *Canadian Journal of Experimental Psychology/Revue Canadienne De Psychologie Expérimentale, 57*(3), 221–237. https://doi.org/10.1037/h0087427

Rule, N., & Ambady, N. (2010). First impressions of the face: Predicting success. *Social and Personality Psychology Compass, 4*(8), 506–516. https://doi.org/10.1111/j.1751-9004.2010.00282.x

Rule, N. O., & Ambady, N. 2008. The face of success inferences from chief executive officers' appearance predict company profits. *Psychological Science, 19*(2). 109–111. https://doi.org/10.1111/j.1467-9280.2008.02054.x.*

Rule, N. O., & Ambady, N. 2009. She's got the look: Inferences from female chief executive officers' faces predict their success. *Sex Roles, 61*(9–10). 644–652. https://doi.org/10.1007/s11199-009-9658-9.*

Rule, N. O., & Ambady, N. 2011a. Face and fortune: Inferences of personality from Managing Partners' faces predict their law firms' financial success. *The Leadership Quarterly, 22*(4). 690–696. https://doi.org/10.1016/j.leaqua.2011.05.009.*

Rule, N. O., & Ambady, N. 2011b. Judgments of power from college yearbook photos and later career success. *Social Psychological and Personality Science, 2*(2). 154–158. https://doi.org/10.1177/1948550610385473.*

Rule, N. O., Ambady, N., Adams, J. R., Ozono, B., Nakashima, H., Yoshikawa, S., & Watabe, M. 2010. Polling the face: Prediction and consensus across cultures. *Journal of Personality and Social Psychology, 98*(1). 1–15. https://doi.org/10.1037/a0017673.*

Rule, N. O., Freeman, J. B., Moran, J. M., Gabrieli, J. D. E., Adams, R. B., Jr., & Ambady, N. (2010). Voting behavior is reflected in amygdala response across cultures. *Social Cognitive and Affective Neuroscience*, *98*(2-3), 349–355. https://doi.org/10.1093/scan/nsp046

Rule, N. O., Ishii, K., & Ambady, N. 2011. Cross-cultural impressions of leaders' faces: Consensus and predictive validity. *International Journal of Intercultural Relations*, *35*(6). 833–841. https://doi.org/10.1016/j.ijintrel.2011.06.001.*

Rule, N. O., Moran, J. M., Freeman, J. B., Whitfield-Gabrieli, S., Gabrieli, J. D., & Ambady, N. (2011). Face value: Amygdala response reflects the validity of first impressions. *NeuroImage*, *54*(1), 734–741. https://doi.org/10.1016/j.neuroimage.2010.07.007

Rule, N. O., & Tskhay, K. O. 2014. The influence of economic context on the relationship between chief executive officer facial appearance and company profits. *The Leadership Quarterly*, *25*(5). 846–854. https://doi.org/10.1016/j.leaqua.2014.01.001.*

Rule, N. O., Tskhay, K. O., Freeman, J., & Ambady, N. (2014). On the interactive influence of facial appearance and explicit knowledge in social categorization. *European Journal of Social Psychology*, *44*(6), 529–535. https://doi.org/10.1002/ejsp.2043

Schooler, J. (2011). Unpublished results hide the decline effect. *Nature*, *470*, 437.

Sigelman, L., Sigelman, C. K., & Fowler, C. (1987). A bird of a different feather? An experimental investigation of physical attractiveness and the electability of female candidates. *Social Psychology Quarterly*, *50*(1), 32–43. https://doi.org/10.2307/2786888

Spezio, M., Loesch, L., Gosselin, F., Mattes, K., & Alvarez, R. M. 2012. Thin-slice decisions do not need faces to be predictive of election outcomes. *Political Psychology*, *33*(3). 331–341. https://doi.org/10.1111/j.1467-9221.2012.00897.x.*

Spisak, B. R. 2012. The general age of leadership: Older-looking presidential candidates win elections during war. *PloS One*, *7*(5). e36945. https://doi.org/10.1371/journal.pone.0036945.*

Spisak, B. R., Dekker, P. H., Krüger, M., & Van Vugt, M. (2012). Warriors and peacekeepers: Testing a biosocial implicit leadership hypothesis of intergroup relations using masculine and feminine faces. *PloS One*, *7*(1), e30399. https://doi.org/10.1371/journal.pone.0030399

Sterling, T. D., Rosenbaum, W. L., & Weinkam, J. J. (1995). Publication decisions revisited: The effect of the outcome of statistical tests on the decision to publish and vice versa. *The American Statistician*, *49*, 108–112. https://doi.org/10.1080/00031305.1995.10476125

Sterne, J. A., & Egger, M. (2001). Funnel plots for detecting bias in meta-analysis: Guidelines on choice of axis. *Journal of Clinical Epidemiology*, *54*(10), 1046–1055. https://doi.org/10.1016/S0895-4356(01)00377-8

Sterne, J. A., Egger, M., & Smith, G. D. (2001). Investigating and dealing with publication and other biases in meta-analysis. *BMJ: British Medical Journal*, *323* (7304), 101–105. https://doi.org/10.1002/9780470693926.ch11

Stoker, J. I., Garretsen, H., & Spreeuwers, L. J. (2016). The facial appearance of CEOs: Faces signal selection but not performance. *PloS One*, *11*(7), e0159950. https://doi.org/10.1371/journal.pone.0159950

Sussman, A. B., Petkova, K., & Todorov, A. 2013. Competence ratings in US predict presidential election outcomes in Bulgaria. *Journal of Experimental Social Psychology*, *49*(4). 771–775. https://doi.org/10.1016/j.jesp.2013.02.003.*

Todorov, A. 2005. Inferences of competence from faces predict election outcomes. *Science*, *308*(5728). 1623–1626. https://doi.org/10.1126/science.1110589.

Todorov, A., Olivola, C. Y., Dotsch, R., & Mende-Siedlecki, P. (2015). Social attributions from faces: Determinants, consequences, accuracy, and functional significance. *Annual Review of Psychology*, 66(1), 519–545. https://doi.org/10.1146/annurev-psych-113011-143831

Tskhay, K. O., Giacomin, M., & Rule, N. O. (2020). *Gender stereotypes explain different mental prototypes of male and female leaders*. Manuscript under review.

Tskhay, K. O., Xu, H., & Rule, N. O. (2014). Perceptions of leadership success from nonverbal cues communicated by orchestra conductors. *The Leadership Quarterly*, 25(5), 901–911. https://doi.org/10.1016/j.leaqua.2014.07.001

Van Vugt, M., & Grabo, A. E. (2015). The many faces of leadership: An evolutionary-psychology approach. *Current Directions in Psychological Science*, 24(6), 484–489. https://doi.org/10.1177/0963721415601971

Wang, X., Guinote, A., & Krumhuber, E. G. 2018. Dominance biases in the perception and memory for the faces of powerholders, with consequences for social inferences. *Journal of Experimental Social Psychology*, 78, 23–33. https://doi.org/10.1016/j.jesp.2018.05.003.*

White, A. E., Kenrick, D. T., & Neuberg, S. L. 2013. Beauty at the ballot box: Disease threats predict preferences for physically attractive leaders. *Psychological Science*, 24(12). 2429–2436. https://doi.org/10.1177/0956797613493642.*

Williams, L. J., & Brown, B. K. (1994). Method variance in organizational behavior and human resources research: Effects on correlations, path coefficients, and hypothesis testing. *Organizational Behavior and Human Decision Processes*, 57(2), 185–209. https://doi.org/10.1006/obhd.1994.1011

Wilson, J. P., Remedios, J. D., & Rule, N. O. (2017). Interactive effects of obvious and ambiguous social categories on perceptions of leadership: When double-minority status may be beneficial. *Personality & Social Psychology Bulletin*, 43(6), 888–900. https://doi.org/10.1177/0146167217702373

Wong, E. M., Ormiston, M. E., & Haselhuhn, M. P. 2011. A face only an investor could love CEOs' facial structure predicts their Firms' financial performance. *Psychological Science*, 22(12). 1478–1483. https://doi.org/10.1177/0956797611418838.*

Wong, S. H. W., & Zeng, Y. 2017. Do inferences of competence from faces predict political selection in authoritarian regimes? Evidence from China. *Social Science Research*, 66, 248–263. https://doi.org/10.1016/j.ssresearch.2016.11.002.*

Zanna, M. P., & Fazio, R. H. (1982). The attitude-behavior relation: Moving toward a third generation of research. *In Consistency in social behavior: The Ontario symposium* (Vol.2, pp. 283–301).x`

Zebrowitz, L. A. (1997). *Reading faces: Window to the soul?*. Westview Press.

Zebrowitz, L. A., & Montepare, J. M. (2008). Social psychological face perception: Why appearance matters. *Social and personality psychology compass*, 2(3), 1497–1517. https://doi.org/10.1111/j.1751-9004.2008.00109.x

ARTICLE

Bystanders' reactions to intimate partner violence: an experimental approach

Stefano Pagliaro [a], Maria Giuseppina Pacilli [b] and Anna Costanza Baldry [c]

[a]Università degli Studi di Chieti-Pescara, Dipartimento di Neuroscienze, Imaging e Scienze Cliniche, Chieti, Italy; [b]Università degli Studi di Perugia, Dipartimento di Scienze Politiche, Perugia, 106123, Italy; [c]Università degli Studi della Campania "Luigi Vanvitelli", Dipartimento di Psicologia, Caserta, Italy

ABSTRACT

Intimate Partner Violence (IPV) is a widespread phenomenon. Despite the prevalence of IPV in Western societies, most cases remain unnoticed or at least unreported to authorities. Social psychologists have been investigating bystanders' reactions to IPV, to understand which factors may influence the willingness to intervene in support of a female victim of violence. We review a research programme that directly investigated personal and situational factors that make potential bystanders believe a woman victim of IPV deserves and needs (their) help and support, and what, on the contrary, makes them deny any such willingness to help. We present evidence about the *situational antecedents* of bystander's reaction, the *underlying mechanisms* of this intervention, and an extension of such evidence to *non-prototypical cases*, i.e., to an IPV episode occurring within a same-sex couple. We conclude by discussing future directions, and by highlighting the theoretical and practical contributions of this programme of research to the understanding of IPV for both researchers and practitioners.

ARTICLE HISTORY Received 6 April 2019; Accepted 27 May 2020

KEYWORDS Intimate Partner Violence; Bystander Intervention; Extra-legal factors

Bystanders' reactions to intimate partner violence: an experimental approach

Intimate Partner Violence (IPV) – that is, physical, psychological, and sexual violence perpetrated by a victim's current or former partner – is a widespread phenomenon affecting one out of four women at least once in life, with a wide range of negative physical and psychological consequences for the victims, even death (WHO, 2013). This phenomenon has reached such alarming proportions that, more than 20 years ago, the Forty-Nine World Health

CONTACT Stefano Pagliaro s.pagliaro@unich.it Università Degli Studi Di Chieti, Dipartimento Di Neuroscienze, Imaging E Scienze Cliniche; Group Processes and Morality – GPM-Lab, 66100, Chieti, ITALY.

© 2020 European Association of Social Psychology

Assembly definitively defined violence (against women and children in particular) as a "leading worldwide public health problem" (Resolution WHA49.25; see also Hart, 2008). Given its prominence in the societal agenda, in the last decades, there has been a growing interest among researchers and practitioners on this topic. Nevertheless, despite the prevalence of IPV in Western societies, most cases remain unnoticed or at least unreported to authorities (e.g., Gracia et al., 2009; WHO, 2013). For these reasons, social psychologists have been investigating bystanders' reaction to IPV, suggesting (and ascertaining) that multiple factors may influence willingness to intervene in support of a (female) victim of violence (e.g., Flood & Pease, 2009). Although most studies focus attention on specific antecedents of bystanders' intervention, what has become apparent to scholars and practitioners is that this phenomenon requires a holistic, ecological approach. Thus, starting from the classical "individualistic" approach of Latané and Darley (1970), scholars have tried to integrate these predictive factors into an ecological model (e.g., Baldry et al., 2015; Baldry & Winkel, 2008; Banyard, 2008, 2015), in order to trace a conceptual framework for the prevention of sexual violence, examining the crucial role of bystander intervention.

In the present paper, we review a programme of research in which we aimed at deepening our understanding of the antecedents and underlying mechanisms of bystanders' reaction to IPV. This research programme directly investigated personal and situational factors that make a woman victim[1] of IPV worthy of help, support, and protection in the eye of bystanders. Although this research line dates back to the early work of Baldry and Winkel (1998, 2008), recently we adopted experimental paradigms to disentangle the causal links between some of the so-called *extra-legal factors* – meaning those characteristics that are independent of the actual crime, such as for instance, alleged victim's infidelity, victim's perceived humanness, or referential group norms – and bystanders' willingness to support the victim. In the studies reviewed in the paper, situational elements and features relative to the victim and the perpetrator were systematically varied employing fictitious newspaper articles describing episodes of IPV with participants being asked to identify with potential bystanders of the described victims. In the studies, we manipulated the content of these articles in relation to different elements – of the situation, the victim, and the perpetrator – in order to investigate whether and how the reactions of potential bystanders could change accordingly. Moreover, this research programme has systematically analysed the mediators of helping intentions, trying to understand what drives the bystander to intervene or not in favour of the victim.

This contribution is structured as follows: First, we introduce the topic of IPV and present the classical bystander approach (Latané & Darley, 1970), together with the subsequent and more recent ecological approach proposed about the related situation of sexual assault (e.g., Burn, 2009; Banyard, 2008,

2015). We then review our research programme (see Table 1 for an overview) by presenting evidence about (a) the *antecedents* of bystander's reaction (i.e., victim's infidelity and sexualised appearance, aggressor alcohol abuse, and group norms; Baldry & Pagliaro, 2014; Baldry et al., 2013; Baldry et al., 2015; Cinquegrana et al., 2018; Gramazio, Cadinu, Pagliaro, & Pacilli, 2018; Pacilli et al., 2017; Pagliaro et al., 2018), and (b) the *underlying mechanisms* (i.e., honour-related beliefs, moral evaluation of the victim, perceived humanness of the victim, and attribution of responsibility to her; Baldry et al., 2013; Baldry et al., 2015; Gramazio et al., 2019; Pacilli et al., 2017; Pagliaro et al., 2018, 2019). We then (c) present evidence that extends such an understanding of IPV to *non-prototypical cases*, that is, to an IPV episode occurring within a same-sex couple (Pagliaro et al., 2019; Paolini et al., 2020). We focused attention on this under-investigated issue and provided evidence that responses to the violence do not depend upon the victim's sexual orientation. However, we highlighted some boundary conditions that exacerbate the willingness (not) to intervene in the case of a gay/lesbian victim (e.g., high level of Right-Wing Authoritarianism). We conclude by discussing limitations of the research programme and future directions, and by highlighting the theoretical and practical contributions of this programme of research to the understanding of IPV for both researchers and practitioners.

Intimate partner violence and bystanders behaviour

According to the WHO (2010, 2013), IPV refers to a wide range of violent behaviours – including sexual assaults, physical and emotional abuse, and controlling behaviours – by a current or a former partner, which occur all over the world, among all the socioeconomic, religious, and cultural groups. In the research literature, IPV, Violence Against Women (VAW), and Domestic Violence (DV) are often used as synonyms. Nevertheless, although the common matrix of these phenomena is violence, some relevant differences need to be considered. For instance, even though the great bulk of research on IPV focused on the prototypical male-against-female case, as also the most robust part of our own research programme did, men can be the victims of IPV as well: Thus, IPV cannot be equated with VAW. In a similar vein, DM may refer both to IPV and to child or elder abuse as well. Considering these differences, in the present paper we will refer to IPV as to "behaviour within an intimate relationship that causes physical, sexual or psychological harm" (WHO, 2010, p. 11), regardless of the gender of the perpetrator and of the victim, and without any restriction in terms of sexual orientation of the partners (e.g., Ali et al., 2016).

IPV is a complex phenomenon with serious (and sometimes fatal) consequences for the victims (see also, Buzawa & Buzawa, 2013; Matjasko et al., 2012; Saltzman et al., 2002). Nevertheless, although it represents such a widespread threat, the data show that a worrying number of cases of violence are not

Table 1. Overview of the research programme describing sample(s), antecedents, and mediators of helping behaviour towards the victim considered in each specific study. Studies marked with * are relative to non-prototypical cases of IPV. Study marked with + is relative to the investigation of workplace sexual harassment.

Study	Sample(s)	Antecedent(s) of the helping behaviour	Mediators Examined
Baldry et al., 2013	Afghan police officers	Admission of infidelity	Attitude towards violence against women
Baldry & Pagliaro, 2014	Lay people (St 1) Italian police officers (St 2)	Group norms Ingroup Identification	–
Baldry et al., 2015	Lay people	Admission of infidelity	Perceived humaness
Pagliaro, Pacilli, Giannella, Giovannelli, Spaccatini, & Baldry (in press)	Lay people	Admission of infidelity	Moral valuation of the victim Attribution of responsibility to the victim
Pacilli et al. (2017)	Lay people	Sexualisation (St 1 and St 2) Admission of infidelity (St 2)	Victim's moral patiency
Cinquegrana et al. (2018)	Lay people and professionals (social workers, teachers, psychologists, police officers)	Admission of infidelity and perpetrator's alcohol abuse	–
*Pagliaro et al. (2018)	Heterosexual lay people (St 1) Gay and lesbian lay people (St 2)	Admission of infidelity Right-Wing Authoritarianism	Moral evaluation of the victim Attribution of responsibility to the victim
*Paolini et al. (2020)	Heterosexual lay people	Admission of infidelity Gender-role expression	Moral evaluation of the victim Attribution of responsibility to the victim
+Gramazio et al. (2018)	Female lay people (St 1) Lay people (St 2)	Victim's sexualisation	Moral evaluation of the victim Victim blaming

reported to the authorities, remaining confined within the domestic walls (e.g., Gracia et al., 2009; WHO, 2013). The reasons why victims choose to remain silent can be multiple and act at different levels: For example, victims may feel ashamed of what happened and feel somewhat responsible or fail to leave the violent partner for fear of retaliation (Baldry & Winkel, 2008). When the victims are women, a decisive role in persevering violence is played by the culture of honour (Baldry et al., 2013; Nisbett & Cohen, 1996), which considers masculine honour a positive moral standard, related to one's perception of worth and to other people's respect, or more generally, by the so-called "lad culture", documented in sociological research (e.g., Fenton & Mott, 2017; Phipps & Young, 2015).

For all these reasons, social psychologists have focused on bystanders as a source of both prevention and intervention in the cases of violence in general, and IPV in particular. Bystanders are meant as individuals who are not directly involved in the emergency situation, but "by their very presence, have the potential to do nothing, to step in and diffuse a high-risk situation, to help and make it better, or to make the situation worse by condoning a perpetrator's behaviour [...] or being unsupportive in responding to a victim [...]" (Banyard, 2011, p. 216). According to the classical approach by Latané and Darley (1970), the process that leads potential bystanders to intervene in a threatening situation or emergency goes through five sequential phases. First, a bystander should (1) notice the event, and (2) interpret the situation as unequivocally requiring an intervention. Then, they should (3) take personal responsibility in reaction to this interpretation of the situation and (4) decide which is the best strategy to help. Finally, the bystander should (5) translate this intention into an actual behaviour. Barriers to intervention are present at each step of this model (for a review, see Burn, 2009). For instance, bystanders may fail to note the situation because of distraction or may fail to recognise the situation as a threatening one. Moreover, they may fail to take personal responsibility because of the well-known diffusion of responsibility effect, or they may not have the proper skills to intervene, or even decide not to intervene for personal (individual characteristics) or social (e.g., group norms) reasons. Four decades after Latané and Darley (1970) seminal work, Banyard (2011; McMahon & Banyard, 2012; see also, Banyard 2008) proposed an ecological model of bystander intervention which considers several levels of possible intervention. Although Banyard's studies focused specifically on violence occurring on college campuses, her model relies on the ecological approach developed by Bronfenbrenner (1977) and Kelly (2006), and it traces a conceptual framework for the prevention of sexual violence examining the role of bystander intervention. Interestingly, the model considers bystanders' intervention opportunities as distributed on a continuum, according to multiple levels of prevention (McMahon & Banyard, 2012), such as primary prevention (e.g., proactive prevention before an assault occurs), secondary prevention (e.g., responses in a high-risk situation), and tertiary prevention (e.g., responding after an assault occurs). Recently, Banyard further elaborated on the effects that bystander behaviour may have on subsequent reactions and proposed the Action Coils model (Banyard, 2015). Interestingly, this model suggests that bystander behaviour is not as linear as it was previously hypothesised, rather it "operates like a feedback loop, where the consequences of taking action have repercussions for future action" (Banyard et al., 2019). In this way, the model not only considers the antecedents of actionism, but also what happens after the bystander action, which could be highly relevant for those involved (that is, the engaged bystander, the victim, the perpetrator, and the potential additional bystanders). The Action Coils model predicts that bystander intervention may thus influence perceived efficacy and subsequent intention to help.

To sum up, IPV is a dangerous phenomenon, and bystanders may represent a valuable resource to stop it. Research has shown that helping behaviour is the result of the interaction between personal and situational factors, including for instance, how the situation is interpreted (Harada, 1985; Shotland & Straw, 1976) or whether one has witnessed others intervening in past, analogous situations (Carlo & Randall, 2001Banyard, 2008). As regards bystander's support to female victims of violence, for instance, scholars suggested that respondents' age and gender matter, with women and younger people being more prone to help the victim than men and older people (Bryant & Spencer, 2003). Or again, cultural misogynistic beliefs (Baldry et al., 2013; Leone & Parrott, 2019; Leone et al., 2016; Nisbett & Cohen, 1996) and violence-condoning beliefs (Vandello & Cohen, 2003) may inhibit intervention, justifying IPV to re-establish the jeopardised masculine-based honour (Baldry & Winkel, 2008; Vandello & Cohen, 2003; for a review, see Flood & Pease, 2009).

In the research programme reviewed here, we decided to adopt an experimental approach to deepen our understanding of what makes bystanders believe a victim of IPV is deserving (or not) of help and support. Thus, even though in each study we investigated a specific aspect of a more complex situation, at the same time this parcelisation allowed us to disentangle the causal relation between extra-legal antecedents of bystanders' intervention, their interpretation of the situation, and their willingness to support (or not) the victim.

The role of masculine honour in inhibiting intervention

We started our research programme by taking advantage of the important opportunity to collect data on a sample of Afghan police officers (Baldry et al., 2013). Anna Baldry, the third author of the present paper, was in charge of training Afghan police officers and police trainers on gender-based violence for NATO Training Mission in Afghanistan, International Security

Assistance Force (NTM-A, ISAF). Thus, we had a unique opportunity to investigate the role of a well-established correlate of IPV, masculine honour (Rodriguez Mosquera et al., 2002a;b), in a setting that was highly relevant to test our hypotheses considering its cultural climate. In this country, many people act towards women more in the name of honour, rather than in the name of the law: As a result, most Afghan women are victims of violent behaviours such as, for instance, forced marriages, rape, educational deprivation, and IPV (Brodsky, 2003). According to the *Global Database on Violence against Women* of the UN, 51% of Afghan women are victim at least once in the lifetime of physical and/or sexual IPV[2]. Research on honour has defined it as a two-side construct (Stewart, 1994). On the one hand, honour may be viewed as virtue referring to altruism and pride (Pitt-Rivers, 1966). On the other hand, in a negative way, honour is related to status and/ or reputation, and it is based on an individual's (typically, a man's) power to enforce his will on others (Vandello & Cohen, 2003). Some cultures – for instance, in Mediterranean regions, Arabic, and Latin American countries (Caro Baroja, 1966; Rodriguez Mosquera et al., 2002a; Nisbett & Cohen, 1996; Pitt-Rivers, 1966) – embrace this second view of honour more than others do, to the extent that in some of them, honour codes may be even formal and codified. In such cultures, women's divergence from role expectancies can be seen as a threat to men's reputations, and consequently, women can be punished *in the name of honour* (Nisbett & Cohen, 1996; Vandello & Cohen, 2003).

Masculine honour refers to a specific form of honour related to the regulation of male and female roles, and it is usually created (or threatened) by female (in)fidelity (Vandello & Cohen, 2003). Research so far consistently showed that masculine beliefs – e.g., misogynistic peer norms and adherence to hegemonic male norms that celebrate antifemininity and toughness – may decrease the likelihood of bystander intervention in support of a victim of aggression (e.g., Leone & Parrott, 2019; Leone et al., 2016). In countries characterised by honour cultures, such as Afghanistan, female infidelity represents a severe threat to male honour, and it is even considered a crime and punishable by law. In masculine honour cultures, honour beliefs permeate reactions of the criminal justice system, of law enforcement in general, and of public opinion as well (Baldry, 2001; Kilpatrick, 2004). As a result, IPV is justified or even accepted when it is committed to maintain or re-establish the status quo of traditional gender roles (Baldry & Winkel, 2008; Vandello & Cohen, 2003).

In the first study of the research programme described here, we sampled Afghan police officers (N = 108), with the aim to investigate the role that masculine honour plays when police officers make decisions with regard to help and support the victims of IPV (Baldry et al., 2013). We were interested in understanding whether their reactions towards a victim of IPV would have been not only guided by the rule of law, but also biased by masculine-based attitudes. To this end, we asked participants to read an extract of a police intervention in an IPV case. This extract was actually a modified version of a real Afghan police case of "family disputes" dealt with by the Family Response Unit (FRU). Participants read about a phone call the police received by the mother of an alleged victim asking for help because her son-in-law was severely beating her daughter. Arriving at the home, the police officers witnessed the victim crying, with clear signs of severe physical abuse. The extract described the alleged perpetrator as minimising what had been going on and as telling the police those were private matters. After that, the police interviewed the woman in a separate room. She reported that her husband was furious because she came back home later than usual. He was accusing her of having dishonoured him by committing adultery, and also threatening to kill her in order to restore his honour. At this stage, we manipulated the victim's behaviour (see, Viki & Abrams, 2002): In one condition, participants read that the victim then admitted to the police that she had an affair with another man (i.e., admitting infidelity condition) while in the other condition participants did not receive this additional information (i.e., not admitting infidelity condition). After that, participants completed a measure of justification of VAW – as a proxy of adherence to masculine honour beliefs – and an ad hoc scale of willingness to intervene in support of the victim. Interestingly, in the admission of infidelity condition police officers reported more lenient attitudes towards VAW ($M_{admission}$ = 6.89, $SD_{admission}$ = 1.52 vs. $M_{no\text{-}admission}$ = 6.20, $SD_{no\text{-}admission}$ = 1.85) and a lower intention to intervene in support of the victim ($M_{admission}$ = 2.51, $SD_{admission}$ = 1.66 vs. $M_{no\text{-}admission}$ = 3.38, $SD_{no\text{-}admission}$ = 2.22). Moreover, the effect of the extra-legal factor (that is, infidelity) on the willingness to support the victim was mediated by adherence to masculine honour beliefs, in the form of more lenient attitudes towards VAW (see Figure 1), as attested by a reliable Sobel test (p <.05).

This first study provided evidence that the IPV can be considered by perpetrators a way to restore the threatened honour. Moreover, it represented an experimental test to the idea that extra-legal factors, such as adultery, may elicit the co-existence of an informal rule of masculine honour, going side by side the rule of law, and this co-existence may trigger a biased evaluation even among police officers in those countries characterised by honour culture. The examination of (suspected) infidelity as a key extra-legal factor in the dynamics and interpretation of IPV was followed up in a series of research conducted in Italy, together with a closer investigation of the cognitive mechanisms driving this effect.

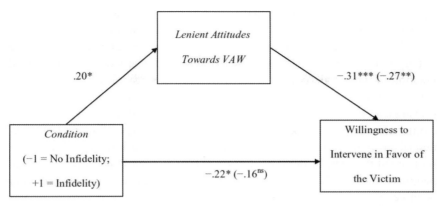

Figure 1. The effect of infidelity (vs. no infidelity) on police officers' willingness to intervene in favour of the victim, through adherence to masculine honour beliefs (Baldry et al., 2013).

Infidelity as a driver of bystanders' interpretation of IPV: its effects and underlying mechanisms

Victim's infra-humanisation. Although the study described above provided evidence about the role of honour beliefs in reacting to IPV, it was carried out in a cultural context in which adultery is still considered as a crime and punished by law. Nonetheless, it spoke about the role that traditional, misogynistic, and sexually hostile gender role attitudes and beliefs may play in driving the interpretation of an IPV event (Flood & Pease, 2009; Heise, 1998; Murnen et al., 2002). This is why we then investigated how such gender role attitudes and beliefs together with attribution of responsibility to the victim co-operate when the victim's behaviour violates such implicit norms.

In a first follow up, Baldry et al. (2015) examined the association between a victim's perceived humanness and bystanders' willingness to provide help and support to her. Previous literature has highlighted that attribution of blame, credibility, and responsibility to the victim represent powerful predictors of the social perception people have about IPV events (Pavlou & Knowles, 2001; Pierce & Harris, 1993; Witte et al., 2006). Thus, attitudes play a leading role in the comprehension of, and reaction to, episode of violence (for a review, see Flood & Pease, 2009), in particular when referring to gender-role prejudice and role-expectancies violation. For instance, researchers ascertained that individuals who endorse a violence-supporting/condoning set of attitudes are more likely to blame the victim and be more lenient with offenders (Pavlou & Knowles, 2001; Spaccatini et al., 2019; West & Wandrei, 2002). Based on these insights, Baldry et al. (2015) examined the role of a specific prejudicial attitude on people's willingness to report and condemn an IPV episode, that is, victim's infra-humanisation (Leyens et al., 2001; Paladino et al., 2002; see also Costello & Hodson, 2010, 2011).

Although infra-humanisation does not overlap entirely with prejudice (Kteily et al., 2016), it is still possible to consider it a very distinct prejudicial reaction (Wilde et al., 2014). This reaction relies on the distinction between primary and secondary emotions, according to which the former (e.g., anger, joy) are experienced by both humans and animals, while the latter (e.g., guilt, compassionate, nostalgia) are unique to human beings (Ekman, 1992). As described in the intergroup relations literature, infra-humanisation represents a subtle form of dehumanisation (Haslam, 2006) according to which people tend to ascribe to a target person fewer secondary emotions – whether positive or negative – which are usually considered typically human (Leyens et al., 2001). Dating back to Bandura et al.'s (1975) findings, which showed that people who were divested of human qualities were treated particularly harshly, we investigated whether willingness not to help and support a victim of IPV may be driven by less humanness attributed to her.

We asked undergraduate students (N = 303) to complete a paper-and-pencil questionnaire that included an extract from a fictitious article, taken from a local newspaper describing an IPV episode. The article described an episode of IPV, in which her husband had beaten up a woman because he suspected a betrayal. According to the experimental condition, participants read either that the victim admitted or denied any such adultery. We then asked them to complete a measure of victim infra-humanisation (Albarello & Rubini, 2012), by indicating to what extent she felt each of 16 emotions, 8 primary (e.g., surprise, pain) and 8 secondary (e.g., optimism, sorrow). Then, participants completed an ad hoc measure of willingness to report the IPV episode and support the victim: we asked them to imagine themselves as neighbours of the victim and to indicate to what extent they would themselves engage in each of three specific reporting behaviours (e.g., "Reporting the case to the police", "Offering support to the victim"). We found evidence that a victim admitting a betrayal (vs. a victim denying such accuse) was perceived as less human ($M_{admission}$ = 3.39, $SD_{admission}$ = 0.84 vs. $M_{no\text{-}admission}$ = 3.67, $SD_{no\text{-}admission}$ = 0.79), that is, participants attributed to her less secondary emotions, regardless of the gender of respondents, and supported to a less extent ($M_{admission}$ = 5.51, $SD_{admission}$ = 2.03 vs. $M_{no\text{-}admission}$ = 6.21, $SD_{no\text{-}admission}$ = 2.14). Moreover, reduced perceived humanness further elicited less willingness to help and support the victim.

This study deepened our understanding of the mechanisms underlying bystanders' reactions towards the victim, investigating such reactions in the light of bystanders' social perception, and considering a subtle form of prejudice towards the victim (i.e., infra-humanisation) as a plausible driver of such perception. Even in this case, as with masculine honour, prejudiced, gender-based beliefs about the victim had a stronger effect on the social perception of IPV than the possible shame related to hitting a wife when respondents could make attributions, based on the context or situation, that she was deserving of the treatment. Once again, our study witnessed a re-victimisation phenomenon, according to which a victim of IPV not only suffers this violence, but she is also blamed for what had happened.

Evaluation of morality and attribution of responsibility. The research presented so far has confirmed that extra-legal features, such as the victim's infidelity, lead bystanders to a biased and prejudiced interpretation of the situation, which in turn prevents the helping of the IPV victim. In an effort to further deepen our understanding of the social perception of IPV, we tried to connect the evidence presented above with the more general topics of attribution and social perception. According to attribution theory (Heider, 1958), individuals' reaction to what they witness relates to the identification of the cause of what is going on. With regards to IPV cases, researchers focused on victim-blaming and attribution of responsibility as crucial factors in comprehending bystanders' reactions (Langhinrichsen-Rohling et al., 2004; Lerner, 1970; Pavlou & Knowles, 2001; Witte et al., 2006). In other words, the more the victim is deemed responsible for what had happened, the less bystanders should be willing to help and support her (Penone & Spaccatini, 2019). This is why Pagliaro and colleagues (2018) examined what leads bystanders to attribute responsibility to the victim of IPV, or more precisely, they examined the process by which internal causal attributions for IPV victims are formed (Stewart et al., 2012).

As already described, Baldry et al. (2013) have suggested that one of the possible mechanisms driving this effect was victim's infrahumanisation, a form of subtle prejudice that has been often associated in the literature with immoral evaluations of the target. In fact, morality and humanness are distinct but related concepts, and individuals are often considered to deserve moral treatment by virtue of being human (Pacilli et al., 2016). Connecting this evidence with Baldry et al. (2013) findings, we focused on the (im)moral evaluation of a victim of IPV as a fundamental driver for the subsequent attribution of responsibility and intention not to help her. Morality, in fact, emerged as a leading evaluative dimension in impression formation about an unknown target and subsequent behavioural reactions (Brambilla & Leach, 2014; Pagliaro et al., 2013). The prominence of morality over other evaluative dimensions such as competence or sociability in social perception and behaviour (Leach et al., 2007) is likely to occur because morality-based (vs. competence or sociability) evaluations are more stable over time and better predictors of future behaviour as they mirror the true nature of a person (Pagliaro et al., 2016). Therefore, we proposed that moral evaluation would most likely lead to internal attribution of responsibility to the victim, in particular when extra-legal factors such as infidelity suggest such an explanation. In our reasoning, a causal chain would connect the victim infidelity to the bystanders' willingness not to intervene in support of the female victim *via* moral evaluations of the victim and attribution of responsibility to her for what had happened (Pagliaro et al., 2019).

In order to provide evidence to this idea, we asked a sample of undergraduates ($N = 121$) to complete a paper-and-pencil questionnaire that included an extract from a fictitious article, similar to Baldry et al.'s (2013) procedure. We again manipulated the victim's infidelity between participants. According to condition, participants read either that the victim admitted or denied having committed the claimed adultery. After reading the IPV event, participants evaluated the victim on the three fundamental dimensions of evaluation, that is, morality, competence, and sociability (Leach et al., 2007). We assessed competence and sociability evaluations side by side with morality evaluation in order to disentangle whether bystanders' reactions in IPV cases are affected by moral rather than more general positive/negative evaluations. Then, participants indicated the extent to which they considered the victim responsible for the episode, and indicated to what extent they would engage in each of eight possible helping behaviours (e.g., "Reporting the case to the police"; "Refer the victim to a shelter"; "Face directly the victim's partner, asking explanations for his violent behaviour"). A victim admitting a betrayal was evaluated as less moral ($M = 4.49$, $SD = 1.76$) in comparison to a victim denying the betrayal ($M = 6.59$, $SD = 1.62$), while the victim's evaluations in terms of competence and sociability seemed unrelated to her behaviour. Moreover, when the victim admitted a betrayal, she was deemed more responsible for what had happened ($M_{admission} = 3.41$, $SD_{admission} = 1.83$ vs. $M_{no-admission} = 2.49$, $SD_{no-admission} = 1.21$). The victim's infidelity then influenced bystanders' willingness to help and support her through the (reduced) moral evaluation of the victim and (increased) attribution of responsibility to her, as we predicted, as the indirect effect confirmed.

In a subsequent investigation, Cinquegrana et al. (2018) interviewed a more heterogeneous sample ($N = 464$) comprising both lay members of the general public and professionals (social workers, psychologists, teachers, police officers). Cinquegrana and colleagues compared the effect of the admission of infidelity on attribution of responsibility and willingness to help the victim with that of a different contextual feature, that is, the perpetrator's alcohol abuse (plus a third, control condition in which no additional contextual information were provided to participants). That is, in the infidelity condition the woman was reported admitting having had an affair with another man; in the alcohol condition, the aggressor was reported as abusing alcohol; in the control condition, no additional information was provided. In this case, participants attributed slight more responsibility to the victim when she admitted infidelity ($M = 2.49$, $SD = 1.61$), controlling for gender role norms and sexism, compared to both the other two conditions ($M_{alcohol} = 2.16$, $SD_{alcohol} = 1.53$; $M_{control} = 1.99$, $SD_{control} = 1.32$). Willingness to intervene in favour of the victim was significantly lower both in the infidelity ($M = 5.62$, $SD = 0.11$) and in the alcohol conditions ($M = 5.51$, $SD = 0.08$), compared to the control condition ($M = 5.83$, $SD = 0.09$). Attribution of responsibility ($\beta = -.33$, $p <.01$) and attitudes towards the male gender role – measured through the Male Role Norm Inventory ($\beta = -.25$, $p <.01$) and the Ambivalent Sexism Inventory ($\beta = -.11$, $p <.05$) – were significantly associated with less willingness to help the victim. The more participants attributed responsibility to the victim and endorsed gender role attitudes, the less they were willing to help and support the victim herself.

Thus, the research described until now provided evidence about the role that infidelity may play in driving bystanders' interpretation of the IPV situation, and the following behavioural intention to support the victim against the perpetrator. In the following section, the focus will be on a further predictor of misattribution and behaviour in the context of IPV: That is, victim's sexualisation.

Sexualisation and helping intentions: when the victim falls outside our moral concern

The social perception of IPV – meaning the perception of the perpetrator, the victim, and the situation as a whole – drives bystanders' reactions. In many cases, such a perception is influenced by the way others represent the situation. For instance, how a victim is represented in the public opinion seems to be crucial in guiding individual's evaluation of, and reaction to her. In the last decades, the portrayal of women and girls by western media has become increasingly sexualised (e.g., American Psychological Association, 2007; Zurbriggen & Roberts, 2013). Female sexualisation is virtually visible in all fields, from advertising (e.g., Gill, 2008; Pacilli et al., 2016) to politics (e.g., Carlin & Winfrey, 2009; Funk & Coker, 2016) to academic and working settings (Fasoli et al., 2018). In this vein, IPV appears an emblematic case in which female sexualisation is at stake, because IPV news is often accompanied with sexualised images of women partially undressed or with sexy clothing or postures.

Sexualisation reflects a complex of interlocking factors – e.g., the extent of nudity, revealing, or suggestive attire, and poses suggestive of sexual activity or availability – that contribute to depict someone in a sexually suggestive manner (Hatton & Trautner, 2011). Researchers described perceivers' cognitive processing of sexualised women, showing that they are basically reduced to their parts akin to objects (for a recent review, see Bernard et al., 2018). Most relevant to our purpose, sexualisation is also related to humanness (Vaes et al., 2011). Sexualised women are considered less than fully human, since they are denied human nature (Heflick & Goldenberg, 2009) and mental states (Gray et al., 2011; Holland & Haslam, 2013; Loughnan et al., 2010, 2013). Whether or not people are deemed morally relevant is associated with whether or not they are or not considered human

(Bastian et al., 2011) and having a mind (Gray & Wegner, 2009; Waytz et al., 2010). According to Gray and colleagues, one crucial component of an individual's moral status is *moral patiency*, the ability to experience psychological or physical pleasure and pain (e.g., Gray & Wegner, 2009; see also Bentham, 1789/2011). Importantly, when such perception of individuals' moral status is at stake, if they fall outside the moral circle, they are not morally relevant, and therefore actions towards them carry no moral weigh with the result that people are more willing to hurt them (Majdandzic et al., 2012). Researchers have so far highlighted that sexualised women are typically considered as lacking moral patiency, or at least as less patient than non-sexualised women (Loughnan et al., 2010, 2013). And, relevant for the present purpose, even women behave more aggressively towards a sexualised woman, with this effect being driven by lower ratings of the target's humanness (Arnocky et al., 2019).

Building on these premises, Pacilli et al. (2017) examined whether the sexualisation of women may be tied to withdrawal of help in cases of IPV, indicative of a lack of moral concern for women. In particular, they hypothesised that the victim's sexualisation would reduce her moral patiency with the distal consequence of reduced willingness to help and support her. These hypotheses were tested in two experimental studies. In Study 1 ($N = 109$ university students), participants read the already presented fictitious article from a local newspaper, describing an IPV incident provoked by suspected infidelity. Pacilli and colleagues then presented participants with a picture of the victim, ostensibly taken from her Facebook profile. According to condition, this picture differed in the degree of woman's sexiness, as emerged in a pilot test (see Figure 2a, 2b). In particular, in the sexualised condition the picture depicted a woman wearing sexy clothing, lying on a sofa. In the non-sexualised condition, the picture depicted the same woman sitting in a pub wearing casual clothing. Participants then evaluated the victim's moral patiency, moral virtue, and provided their willingness to help and support her in several ways. Results showed that in the sexualised condition (vs. non-sexualised condition) participants ascribed less moral patiency to the victim ($M_{sexualised} = 7.28$, $SD_{sexualised} = 1.46$; $M_{non-sexualised} = 7.83$, $SD_{non-sexualised} = 1.27$), and this attribution mediated the relationship between sexualisation and willingness to help the victim. In Study 2 ($N = 150$ members of the general public), we elaborated on this pattern by testing whether the victim's infidelity triggered attribution of moral patiency. In this case, the picture accompanying the description of IPV in the non-sexualised condition was slightly modified by cropping the alcoholic drink from the scene, in order to avoid a possible confounding effect of alcohol (see Figure 2c). Once again, the IPV victim was significantly less likely to receive help from bystanders because she was viewed as a lesser moral patient ($M_{sexualised} = 7.51$, $SD_{sexualised} = 1.59$; $M_{non-sexualised} = 8.15$, $SD_{non-sexualised} = 1.21$). In both

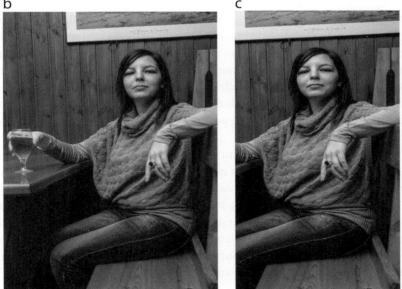

Figure 2. (a) Sexualised condition, Study 1, Study 2 (Pacilli et al., 2017). (b) non-sexualised condition, Study 1 (Pacilli et al., 2017). (c) non-sexualised condition, Study 2 (Pacilli et al., 2017).

studies, we tested the indirect effect of the victim's sexualisation on participants' willingness to help her *through* attribution of moral patiency, and a bootstrapping procedure confirmed this indirect effect was significant.

In a follow up of this research, Gramazio et al. (2018) examined the effect of sexualisation in a peculiar situation of women's mistreatment, that is, Sexual Harassment (SH) in a workplace. This time two samples of undergraduate students (Study 1: $N = 151$, only female participants; Study 2: $N = 160$, 80 males, 80 females) were faced with a situation in which a woman reported being sexually harassed by her boss in the workplace: The victim's sexualisation was manipulated similarly to Pacilli et al.'s (2017) studies, that is, we presented participants with a picture allegedly taken from the victim's Facebook profile. The two pictures show the same woman in an identical pose, wearing the same makeup, but different clothing. In the sexualised condition the victim she is scantily dressed and wears sexy clothes and high-heeled shoes (see Figure 3a), while in the nonsexualised condition she wears jeans and sweater (see Figure 3b). In both the studies reported by Gramazio and colleagues, sexualisation reduced the perception of the victim's morality (Study 1: $M_{sexualised} = 5.85$, $SD_{sexualised} = 1.25$ vs. $M_{non-sexualised} = 6.39$, $SD_{non-sexualised} = 1.24$; Study 2: $M_{sexualised} = 6.06$, $SD_{sexualised} = 1.21$ vs. $M_{non-sexualised} = 6.71$, $SD_{non-sexualised} = 1.34$) and increased blaming attributions to the victim (Study 1: $M_{sexualised} = 3.81$, $SD_{sexualised} = 1.94$ vs. $M_{non-sexualised} = 2.84$, $SD_{non-sexualised} = 1.70$; Study 2: $M_{sexualised} = 4.11$, $SD_{sexualised} = 2.40$ vs. $M_{non-sexualised} = 3.06$, $SD_{non-sexualised} = 2.10$), which in turn reduced the willingness to help her. Importantly, in the second study the authors further reported that sexualisation reduced perception of morality especially when individuals endorse traditional masculine norms about sex. Further research has confirmed that the effects of sexualisation regards also preadolescent children who were victims of bullying, showing that a sexualised appearance is associated with a dehumanising perception and withdrawal of help (Pacilli et al., 2019).

These studies highlight the negative consequences of sexualisation in relatively unexplored fields, such as IPV and SH. Interestingly, the mechanisms subsuming the effect of sexualisation on bystanders' willingness (not) to intervene calls into question an evaluation of the victim humanness and morality, and an evaluation of her deservingness and worthiness. Once again, a victim not only suffers the violence itself, but she also suffers a secondary re-victimisation that brings her outside the moral circle. She does not deserve bystanders' moral consideration and help.

The role of group norms on bystanders' reactions

A further extra-legal factor that may influence bystanders' reaction towards IPV, and that has been relatively under-investigated at least in an experimental vein, is represented by referential group norms, defined as an "accepted way of thinking, feeling or behaving that is endorsed and expected because it is perceived as the right and proper thing to do" (Turner, 1991, p. 3). As anticipated above, recent ecological models of prevention of violence focus

Figure 3. (a) Sexualised condition (Gramazio et al., 2018). (b) non-sexualised condition (Gramazio et al., 2018).

on the importance that community-based norms may play in driving the definition of, and reaction towards, violence. And indeed, with regard to violence against women, research provided support for this contention: For example, informal norms about IPV seem to affect the evaluation of a victim in terms of fault and responsibility (Taylor & Sorenson, 2005). Or again, Fabiano and colleagues reported that a social norm approach to prevent sexual assault could help men becoming better allies (Fabiano et al., 2003). According to them, men's own willingness to intervene by providing help was significantly and strongly associated with socially shared norms (ibidem, pp. 109–110). Nevertheless, even though literature had shown that referential group norms exert a strong influence on group members' behaviour (Tajfel & Turner, 1979), in particular when they are defined in terms of moral concerns (Ellemers et al., 2013, 2008; Pagliaro et al., 2011), direct evidence about their effect on the willingness to intervene and provide help in a case of IPV was still scant. Thus, although the relevance of group norms appears to be self-evident, Baldry and Pagliaro (2014) attempted to provide experimental evidence showing their impact on bystanders' reactions in IPV cases and on police decision to arrest an alleged perpetrator of such crime.

In order to deal with this topic, Baldry and Pagliaro (2014) relied on the social identity framework (Tajfel & Turner, 1979) and carried out two experimental studies in which the content of referential group norms was systematically varied. In the first study ($N = 218$ undergraduates), the authors examined the role of group norms on the intention to provide help by potential bystanders (i.e., neighbours) witnessing an IPV case. At the beginning of the study, participants filled in a measure of social identification with the national group (in this case, Italians). Then, as in much of the research described in this paper, they read a fictitious article from a local newspaper, describing an IPV episode, taking place in an apartment between a husband and a wife. Participants provided their willingness to help the victim (T1) on a 9-point Likert scale, and after that, Baldry and Pagliaro manipulated the content of a (moral) group norm, and provided participants with a bogus feedback on what other people (i.e., Italians) taking part in a study conducted by the National Statistical Institute said they would have done in a similar situation. According to condition, they were told either that the majority of previously interviewed Italians (i.e., ingroup members) considered that same episode as serious and morally condemnable, and as a consequence would be willing to help the victim by calling the police and providing her some form of help because it is morally correct to do so (helping condition); or, they were told that the majority of previously interviewed Italians (i.e., ingroup members) stated that, even though such an episode is not good, they would not be willing to seek help and intrude in the victim's live (or call the police, or help the victim) because it is morally inconvenient to violate the privacy of an intimate relationship (not helping condition). A third, control condition was added in which participants were not provided with additional information. Then, willingness to help the victim was assessed again (T2). Results showed the predicted 3-way interaction (Time X Condition X Identification). Post-hoc comparisons showed that, in the helping condition, participants were more willing to help the victim after exposure to the helping norm ($M = 7.43$, $SD = 1.03$) than in the pre-test assessment ($M = 6.42$, $SD = 1.03$). This effect was qualified by the Time X Identification, showing than high identifiers expressed a higher willingness to help the IPV victim after exposure to the helping norm than did low identifiers, whereas no differences emerged before the manipulation of the ingroup norm. In the not-helping condition, instead, only the main effect of willingness to help was significant, showing that participants exhibited a lower willingness to help the IPV victim after exposure to the not-helping norm ($M = 5.98$, $SD = 1.54$) than in the pre-test assessment ($M = 6.23$, $SD = 1.40$). Finally, no significant effect emerged in the control condition. To sum up, results showed that participants' willingness to report the IPV episode and provide support to the victim varied from T1 to T2 according to condition. In particular, participants' willingness to help the IPV victim decreased after the exposure to the non-helping norm; by contrast, it increased after the exposure to the helping moral norm, in particular among high identifiers.

In the second study ($N = 216$), Baldry and Pagliaro (2014) sampled Italian police officers and examined the effect of group norm on their intention to arrest the perpetrator when intervening in a case of alleged IPV. According to the Italian legal system, police officers' decision to arrest the perpetrator in such cases is not mandatory and should be made under the following condition: severity of the action, danger of the person assumed by his/her personality or the circumstances under which the crime took place (see art. 381 of the criminal procedure code). Participants, in this case, were asked to read a real case extracted from police files regarding the intervention of the police following a so-called "home dispute". In the case, the police officers saw a woman in tears with bruises and blood over her leg in her own apartment, with the husband telling them to leave because they had a personal confrontation provoked by his wife's cheating. Police officers were then asked to imagine how they would manage such a case if they were on duty and had to intervene. As in Study 1, group norms were manipulated by providing bogus information about what then happened in the scenario they were presented. According to condition, they read either that another patrol car with two further police officers decided together with the third police officer to arrest the aggressor because it was a high-risk situation and it was the right thing to do (*arrest condition*); or, that the other police officers decided not to arrest the offender given that these were mainly private matters that they could solve by themselves (*no arrest condition*). In the *control* condition, no additional information was provided to participants.

Police officers were asked then to indicate their willingness to engage in intervening behaviours. Even in this case, participants' behaviour was (at least partially) modified by referential group norms. In fact, results showed that in the arrest condition, high (vs low) identifiers with the police officers showed a higher tendency to act on the perpetrator by arresting him and call for reinforcement (M_{high} = 6.92; SD_{high} = 2.53 vs M_{low} = 4.73; SD_{low} = 2.84). No differences emerged in no arrest (M_{high} = 5.72; SD_{high} = 3.27 vs M_{low} = 6.33; SD_{low} = 2.81) and the control condition (M_{high} = 5.80; SD_{high} = 3.16 vs M_{low} = 6.40; SD_{low} = 2.64).

To sum up, helping a victim of IPV seems to be influenced also by social norms people share with their reference group: Both lay bystanders and police officers relied on what is deemed by the referential group as morally correct (see also Ellemers et al., 2013). This is particularly relevant in projecting prevention strategies at a community level: it suggests that specific strategies should be directed to make people aware of norms that condone violence as well as to increase awareness about how to deal with biased perceptions of violence and consequent loafing behaviour.

IPV is not only a matter of violence against women. The case of same-sex violence

In recent years, we have tried to complement the research programme presented in the present paper by looking at the so-called non-prototypical cases of IPV, that is, those cases that do not refer to the widely investigated male-against-female IPV (Hellemans et al., 2015). We reasoned in fact that this is a worth noting field of investigation because, even though by definition IPV-label refers to any possible close or romantic relationship, the vast majority of the studies conducted on the topic focused on the classical male-against-female violence (Alexander, 2008; Seelau & Seelau, 2005; WHO, 2013). Whereas it is imperative to investigate violence against women, this substantially totalising focus has led to underestimating the presence of such forms of violence within different contexts, such as the one represented by same-sex couples. In turn, this can lead to believing that IPV that occurred in same-sex couples is less widespread and common, thus less worthy of attention. Nevertheless, some researchers have been investigating these non-prototypical cases. Seelau and Seelau (2005), for instance, reported that the pattern of prevalence, recurrence, and escalation of violence within same-sex couples mirrors that occurring within male-against-female IPV case (see also, Brand & Kidd, 1986; Seelau et al., 2003; Turell, 2000). The authors further advanced that, when evaluating IPV, bystanders' reactions are guided by gender-role stereotypes rather than homophobic prejudice: In their study, regardless of male-against-female or same-sex cases, participants judged more severely violence perpetrated by men or against women was judged more severely than violence perpetrated by women or against men. Aligning with this, female victims are considered as needing more help and support than male victims, regardless of whether they are a same-sex or opposite-sex couple (Poorman et al., 2003; Seelau et al., 2003).

When considering IPV involving same-sex couples in comparison with male-against-female IPV cases some differences may emerge – for example, in the rates, because of the ways gay-men and lesbian-women define violence and are willing to report it (Crittenden et al., 2017). Nevertheless, the few studies that have examined whether and how attitudes vary when considering the same and opposite-sex cases suggest little differences in attitudes towards violence in these different relations (Sorenson & Thomas, 2009). Based on these premises, Pagliaro et al. (2019) extended the examination of bystanders' reaction to IPV to non-prototypical cases, in particular to same-sex cases. In particular, in two studies (N = 195 and 120, respectively) the authors attempted to understand whether the key mechanisms identified in response to male-against-female violence – that is, moral evaluation of the victim and attribution of responsibility to her (Pagliaro et al., 2018) – are at work even when evaluating a victim in the context of same-sex IPV. The experimental paradigm of both studies resembled the one adopted in the research described above (Pagliaro et al., 2018), but, this time, participants were faced with either a male-against-male or female-against-female IPV case. Study 1 was carried out with a sample of heterosexual undergraduates, while Study 2 sampled gay/lesbian participants recruited among the general public through a snowball sampling procedure. In both studies, the pattern of bystanders' reactions was similar to the one reported by Pagliaro et al. (2018): Regardless of the victim's gender, when they admitted infidelity they were judged as less moral (Study 1: $M_{infidelity}$ = 3.77, $SD_{infidelity}$ = 1.75 vs. $M_{no-infidelity}$ = 5.75, $SD_{no-infidelity}$ = 1.93; Study 2: $M_{infidelity}$ = 3.28, $SD_{infidelity}$ = 1.56 vs. $M_{no-infidelity}$ = 5.83, $SD_{no-infidelity}$ = 1.97) and more responsible for what had happened (Study 1: $M_{infidelity}$ = 4.91, $SD_{infidelity}$ = 1.80 vs. $M_{no-infidelity}$ = 2.87, $SD_{no-infidelity}$ = 1.57; Study 2: $M_{infidelity}$ = 4.29, $SD_{infidelity}$ = 1.78 vs. $M_{no-infidelity}$ = 3.07, $SD_{no-infidelity}$ = 1.75), and this diminished bystanders' willingness to help them. Moreover, in Study 1 heterosexual bystanders' reactions were further moderated by Right-Wing Authoritarianism (RWA): That is, the more they embraced a RWA ideology, the more they were sensitive to extra-legal factors (i.e., admission of infidelity) when they decided whether to intervene to support the victim. Such a moderation effect did not emerge in Study 2, that is, when we sampled gay/lesbian participants. In a subsequent follow up of this research, Paolini et al. (2020) confirmed this pattern among a sample of 128 undergraduates, and showed that the stereotypical characterisation of a gay man victim of

IPV – in terms of masculine vs. feminine traits – did not affect bystanders' willingness to provide help and support to the victim.

This last set of studies highlighted that IPV is not equal to VAW. Interestingly, we were able to show that the underlying mechanisms subsuming bystanders' interpretation of, and reaction to, IPV does not depend upon the gender and the sexual orientation of the victim. In particular, extralegal factors – such as for instance, admission of betrayal – seem to guide biased perception of the episode regardless of whether it occurs in a prototypical male-against-female case or in same-sex case. In this latter case, heterosexual bystanders' perceptions are biased further by endorsement of conservative ideologies.

General discussion

Summary of the main findings

IPV is a widespread, perverse, dangerous phenomenon that has significant consequences on the physical and psychological health of the victims. The scientific literature has long investigated the individual, social, and cultural factors that explain the phenomenon of violence. However, less attention has been devoted to the analysis of how bystanders perceive this phenomenon and how these perceptions then determine their helping behaviour. Nevertheless, since attitudes and beliefs represent strong drivers for individual's behaviour, such knowledge could be very useful in empowering potential witnesses and making them violence prevention agents at all levels. For this reason, we have considered necessary in recent years to investigate the reasons why bystanders decide not to intervene in support of a victim, reasons that can be manifold and bound to both individual and contextual aspects. In the research programme reviewed here, we have systematically examined some of the extra-legal factors that impact on bystanders' behavioural intentions, as well as the underlying cognitive mechanisms that connect these factors with the intention not to intervene in support of a victim. Starting from our research evidence, we are able to enrich the Latané and Darley's model (1970) providing consistent evidence that group norms, contextual features, and cognitive processes of evaluation and attribution affect both the identification of the episode as an emergency (step 2) and the consequent decision to take responsibility to act (step 3). Our research showed that admission of infidelity and victim's sexualisation have a detrimental effect on bystanders' perception of, and reaction to, IPV. In particular, summing up evidence, they seem to inhibit intentions to intervene because a victim admitting infidelity or depicted in a sexualised manner is perceived as less honest and moral patient, and more responsible for what happened. Honour-related beliefs and group norms play a role as well in this process, by enhancing individual's adherence to gender-based interpretation of the situation and to what the other ingroup members would do in the same situation (for a similar argument, Leone & Parrott, 2019; Leone et al., 2016). Our research programme further shows that interpretation of, and reaction to, IPV is similar even when the episode occurs within a same-sex couple: In this case, conservative ideologies (i.e., RWA) moderate the effect of admission of infidelity on helping intentions, that is, people endorsing right-wing authoritarianism are more sensitive to extra-legal factors when reacting to IPV: in particular, the more they endorse a RWA ideology, the stronger the negative effect of admission of infidelity on their intention to support the victim.

Limitations of the research programme and future directions

Whereas the research programme we reviewed above provides consistent findings about the effect of extra-legal factors on bystander behavioural intentions, as well as on the biased perception driving their actionism, two main and interconnected limitations are worth noting and should be considered in future ad hoc research. These two limitations are relative to the fact that our experimental manipulations relied on simulations that evoke bystanders' imagined reactions, and our main dependent variables are behavioural intentions rather than actual behaviours. Despite these not being true behaviours, this represents one the most common way to study helping behaviours in laboratory context, which allows researchers to minimise the possible confounds by means of controlled procedures. Moreover, if behavioural intentions do not represent actual behaviours, at the same time it is true that they represent significant antecedents of the course of action (Ajzen, 1991; Sheeran, 2002; but for a different perspective, see Kawakami et al., 2009). This of course opens the road for future studies that directly assess participants' actual behaviour as well, which would attest the ecological validity of our experimental approach.

Two other peculiar aspects of our research programme that may be interpreted as a limitation are the following. The first one pertains to the sample size of our studies. Although we acknowledge that the numerosity of our samples can be an issue in terms of statistical power, the consistency of the main results hypothesised and found across the different studies we conducted is worth note in terms of the strength of our conclusions. The second one pertains the fact that, for experimental constraints, in each study, we investigated a specific aspect of a broader and more complex situation. We are fully aware of the complexity of the phenomenon, and how it does not end with the bystander decision to intervene or not in favour of the victim (e.g., Banyard, 2015). Nevertheless, reproducing some specific features of the situation time by time in the lab allowed us to disentangle the causal relation between extra-legal antecedents of bystanders' intervention, their interpretation of the situation, and their willingness to support (or not) the victim.

Nevertheless, in line with Banyard et al. (2019), future studies should test whether the bystander intervention – not inhibited by the extra-legal factors we tested – may increase a subsequent intention to help when encountering a new episode of violence like the previous one. A further aspect that is worth noting is the fact that the studies reviewed above focused on adult relationships. A separate line of research showed indeed that teen dating violence is highly prevalent and is associated with internalising and externalising problems (for a review, Van Camp et al., 2014). Future ad hoc research may be directed therefore to understand whether what we have shown regarding adult relationship may be extended to the context of teen dating violence as well, which can be considered a form of IPV. In this specific case, peers are often considered as the crucial bystanders, so it seems worth to examine which factors may lead them to become engaged individuals and intervene in support of a potential victim.

Finally, our research programme focussed mainly on the characteristics of the victim. As we have argued in the introduction, the bystander model and its subsequent evolutions, such as the Action Coils model, consider bystander behaviour as potentially determined by the interaction between multiple actors (the victim, the perpetrator, and the bystander) and the situation. Thus, future ad hoc studies may be directed to investigate the factors that we did not consider in the present research programme.

Practical implications

The research programme reviewed in the present paper contributes to the understanding of the role of extra-legal factors on people's intention to provide help and support to victims of IPV. Based on this theoretical advancement, our studies may have important practical implications for researchers and practitioners as well.

First of all, our findings may inform awareness campaigns towards better prevention of and intervention against intimate partner violence (see also, Baldry & Sebire, 2016). In fact, theoretical advance in this field may guide policy agenda as well, building evidence-based recommendations that further inform future decision-makers. In this regard, a fundamental insight that policy-makers and practitioners should take into account is that an ecological approach to the problem is the more comprehensive and effective one in both preventing violence and reacting to it. Research showed that bystanders' interpretation of IPV is biased by a plethora of cognitive and social factors – including, for instance, honour-related and gender-related beliefs, group norms, conservative ideologies. Thus, we must act in order to disjoint these false beliefs and disengage them from the reality of things. A potentially effective strategy to make bystanders aware of their biased interpretations could be to have them adopt the victim's perspective. This could make them understand that such distorted perceptions produce a secondary victimisation through which the victim, in addition to suffering violence, is also held in some way responsible for the incident. One possible distal consequence of this secondary victimisation is the victim ostracism: Future studies could be directed to investigate whether this is the case. Learning about what can increase the sense of responsibility of potential bystanders in cases of IPV is crucial. Such knowledge could inform the developing campaigns to increase social awareness, for instance, by addressing the issue of "breaking the silence" and that it is morally right to "interfere" with what may be considered in a wrong way a private issue. Thus, such an awareness campaign may help to make people allies of victims, instead of external judges.

The studies described here can provide useful indications also for police, and in particular for those who provide police offers with specific training on the domestic disturbances and domestic violence. Training should focus on the fact that police officers can decide on intervention in IPV cases not only according to the law (as they should do) but also according to biased cultural beliefs and group rules that could lead to a wrong decision.

Another important practical implication of our research programme is related to the role of mass media in sustaining a cultural model that legitimates and tolerates gender violence and discourages helping victims. Being aware that a sexualised image activates an objectification of the person portrayed is highly relevant, particularly when the person reported is the victim of a crime.

IPV is not a private issue; it is a serious matter and a crime. Approaches to reducing IPV should be multifactorial, involving assisting the victims, legislating against the perpetrators, and raising awareness and support in the community (for a review, see Whitaker & Lutzker, 2009). We attempted to contribute to this comprehensive orientation adopting an experimental approach that allowed us to investigate the causal link between extra-legal factors and bystanders' (un)willingness to support the victim.

In the feminist literature, the word "survivor" is sometimes preferred to the word "victim" since it recognises an agentic status to the person who has been harmed and has started a healing process (Kelly, 2013). Although we agree with the importance of avoiding one-dimensional representations of human beings harmed by violence, within the context of the examination of bystander intervention, we believe that the term "victim" is more apt than survivor because it describes the stage in which the person has been harmed and is still in need of help.

Source: Central Statistics Organisation (CSO), Ministry of Public Health (MoPH), and ICF. 2017. Afghanistan Demographic and Health Survey 2015. Kabul, Afghanistan: Central Statistics Organisation.

Authors' note

The authors conceived together this contribution. Anna Costanza Baldry, who was at the head of the research line, left us prematurely in March 2019. Stefano Pagliaro and Maria Giuseppina Pacilli equally contributed to the writing. This work is dedicated to the loving memory of Anna Costanza Baldry who has dedicated her entire professional life to fight against gender violence as well as to support women victims of violence with extraordinary determination and courage.

ORCID

Stefano Pagliaro 🆔 http://orcid.org/0000-0003-0573-0937
Maria Giuseppina Pacilli 🆔 http://orcid.org/0000-0001-6875-6961
Anna Costanza Baldry 🆔 http://orcid.org/0000-0003-3520-0048

References

Ajzen, I. (1991). The theory of planned behavior. *Organanizational Behavior and Human Decision Processes, 50*(2), 179–211. https://doi.org/10.1016/0749-5978(91)90020-T

Albarello, F., & Rubini, M. (2012). Reducing dehumanisation outcomes towards Blacks: The role of multiple categorisation and human identity. *European Journal of Social Psychology, 42*(7), 875–882. https://doi.org/10.1002/ejsp.1902.

Alexander, C. J. (2008). Violence in gay and lesbian relationships. *Journal of Gay & Lesbian Social Services, 14*(1), 95–98. https://doi.org/10.1300/J041v14n01_06.

Ali, P. A., Dhingra, K., & McGarry, J. (2016). A literature review of intimate partner violence and its classifications. *Aggression and Violent Behavior, 31*, 16–25. https://doi.org/10.1016/j.avb.2016.06.008.

American Psychological Association. (2007). *Report of the APA task force on the sexualisation of girls.* Author.

Arnocky, S., Proietti, V., Ruddick, E. L., Côté, T. R., Ortiz, T. L., Hodson, G., & Carré, J. M. (2019). Aggression toward sexualized women is mediated by decreased perceptions of humanness. *Psychological Science, 30*(5), 748–756. https://doi.org/10.1177/0956797619836106

Baldry, A. C., & Winkel, F. W. (1998). Perception of the credibility and evidential value of victim an suspect statements in interviews. In J. Boros, I. Munnich, & M. Szegedi (Eds.), *Psychology and Criminal justice* (pp. pp. 74–81). de Gruyter.

Baldry, A. C. (2001). Italy. In R. Summers & A. Hoffman (Eds.), *Domestic violence: Global perspective* (pp. pp. 55–68). Greenwood.

Baldry, A. C., Pacilli, M. G., & Pagliaro, S. (2015). She's not a person ... She's just a woman! Infra-humanization and intimate partner violence. *Journal of Interpersonal Violence, 30*(9), 1567–1582. https://doi.org/10.1177/0886260514540801.

Baldry, A. C., & Pagliaro, S. (2014). Helping victims of intimate partner violence: The influence of group norms among lay people and the police. *Psychology of Violence*, 4(3), 334–347. https://doi.org/10.1037/a0034844.

Baldry, A. C., Pagliaro, S., & Porcaro, C. (2013). The rule of law in a time of masculine honor: Afghan police attitudes on intimate partner violence. *Group Processes & Intergroup Relations*, 16(3), 363–374. https://doi.org/10.1177/1368430212462492.

Baldry, A. C., & Sebire, J. (2016). Policing and domestic abuse: Challenges and ways to go. *Policing: A Journal of Policy and Practice*, 10(4), 323–327. https://doi.org/10.1093/police/paw038.

Baldry, A. C., & Winkel, F. W. (2008). *Intimate partner violence prevention and intervention: The risk assessment and management approach*. Nova Science.

Bandura, A., Underwood, B., & Fromson, M. E. (1975). Disinhibition of aggression through diffusion of responsibility and dehumanization of victims. *Journal of Research in Personality*, 9(4), 253–269. https://doi.org/10.1016/0092-6566(75)90001-X.

Banyard, V. L. (2008). Measurement and correlates of prosocial bystander behavior: The case of interpersonal violence. *Violence and Victims*, 23(1), 83–97. https://doi.org/10.1891/0886-6708.23.1.83

Banyard, V. L. (2011). Who will help prevent sexual violence: Creating an ecological model of bystander intervention. *Psychology of Violence*, 1(3), 216–229. https://doi.org/10.1037/a0023739

Banyard, V. L. (2015). *Toward the next generation of bystander prevention of sexual and relationship violence: Action coils to engage communities*. Springer Briefs in Criminology.

Banyard, V. L., Moschella, E., Jouriles, E., & Grych, J. (2019). Exploring action coils for bystander intervention: Modeling bystander consequences. *Journal of American College Health*, 1–7. https://doi.org/10.1080/07448481.2019.1665052. Online ahead of print.

Bastian, B., Laham, S., Wilson, S., Haslam, N., & Koval, P. (2011). Blaming, praising, and protecting our humanity: The implications of everyday dehumanization for judgments of moral status. *British Journal of Social Psychology*, 50(3), 469–483. https://doi.org/10.1348/014466610X521383.

Bentham, J. (1789/2011). *An introduction to the principles of morals and legislation*. British Library.

Bernard, P., Gervais, S. J., & Klein, O. (2018). Objectifying objectification: When and why people are cognitively reduced to their parts akin to objects. *European Review of Social Psychology*, 29(1), 82–121. https://doi.org/10.1080/10463283.2018.1471949.

Brambilla, M., & Leach, C. W. (2014). On the importance of being moral: The distinctive role of morality in social judgment. *Social Cognition*, 32(4), 397–408. https://doi.org/10.1521/soco.2014.32.4.397.

Brand, P. A., & Kidd, A. H. (1986). Frequency of physical aggression in heterosexual and female homosexual dyads. *Psychological Reports*, 59(3), 1307–1313. https://doi.org/10.2466/pr0.1986.59.3.1307.

Brodsky, A. E. (2003). *With all our strength: The revolutionary association of the women of Afghanistan*. Routledge.

Bronfenbrenner, U. (1977). Toward an experimental ecology of human development. *American Psychologist*, 32(7), 513–531. https://doi.org/10.1037/0003-066X.32.7.513.

Bryant, S. A., & Spencer, G. A. (2003). University students' attitudes about attributing blame in domestic violence. *Journal of Family Violence, 18*(6), 369–376. https://doi.org/10.1023/A:1026205817132

Burn, S. M. (2009). A situational model of sexual assault prevention through bystander intervention. *Sex Roles, 60*(11–12), 779–792. https://doi.org/10.1007/s11199-008-9581-5.

Buzawa, E. S., & Buzawa, G. G. (2013). What does research suggest are the primary risk and protective factors for intimate partner violence (IPV) and what is the role of economic factors? *Journal of Policy Analysis and Management, 32*(1), 128–137. https://doi.org/10.1002/pam.21668

Carlin, D. B., & Winfrey, K. L. (2009). Have you come a long way, baby? Hillary Clinton, Sarah Palin, and sexism in 2008 campaign coverage. *Communication Studies, 60*(4), 326–343. https://doi.org/10.1080/10510970903109904.

Carlo, G., & Randall, B. A. (2001). Are all prosocial behaviors equal? A socioecological developmental conception of prosocial behavior. In F. Columbus (Ed.), *Advances in psychology research, Volume II* (pp. pp. 151–170). Nova Science.

Caro Baroja, J. (1966). Honour and shame: A historical account of several conflicts. In J. G. Peristiany (Ed.), *Honour and shame: The values of Mediterranean society* (pp. pp. 80–137). Weidenfeld and Nicolson.

Cinquegrana, V., Baldry, A. C., & Pagliaro, S. (2018). Intimate partner violence and bystanders' helping behaviour: An experimental study. *Journal of Aggression, Conflict and Peace Research, 10*(1), 24–35. https://doi.org/10.1108/JACPR-08-2016-0243.

Costello, K., & Hodson, G. (2010). Exploring the roots of dehumanization: The role of animal-human similarity in promoting immigrant humanization. *Group Processes and Intergroup Relations, 13*(1), 3–22. https://doi.org/10.1177/1368430209347725

Costello, K., & Hodson, G. (2011). Social dominance-based threat reactions to immigrants in need of assistance. *European Journal of Social Psychology, 41*(2), 220–231. https://doi.org/10.1002/ejsp.769

Crittenden, C. A., Policastro, C., & Eigenberg, H. M. (2017). Attitudes toward dating violence: How does sexual identity influence perceptions among college students? *Journal of Aggression, Maltreatment & Trauma, 26*(7), 804–824. https://doi.org/10.1080/10926771.2017.1328473.

Ekman, P. (1992). An argument for basic emotions. *Cognition & Emotion, 6*(3–4), 169–200. https://doi.org/10.1080/02699939208411068.

Ellemers, N., Pagliaro, S., & Barreto, M. (2013). Morality and behavioural regulation in groups: A social identity approach. *European Review of Social Psychology, 24*(1), 160–193. https://doi.org/10.1080/10463283.2013.841490.

Ellemers, N., Pagliaro, S., Barreto, M., & Leach, C. W. (2008). Is it better to be moral than smart? The effects of morality and competence norms on the decision to work at group status improvement. *Journal of Personality and Social Psychology, 95* (6), 1397–1410. https://doi.org/10.1037/a0012628.

Fabiano, P. M., Perkins, H. W., Berkowitz, A., Linkenbach, J., & Stark, C. (2003). Engaging men as social justice allies in ending violence against women: Evidence for a social norms approach. *Journal of American College Health, 52*(3), 105–112. https://doi.org/10.1080/07448480309595732.

Fasoli, F., Maass, A., Volpato, C., & Pacilli, M. G. (2018). The (female) graduate: Choice and consequences of women's clothing. *Frontiers in Psychology, 9*, 2401. https://doi.org/10.3389/fpsyg.2018.02401

Fenton, R. A., & Mott, H. (2017). The bystander approach to violence prevention: Considerations for implementation in Europe. *Psychology of Violence*, *7*(3), 450–458. https://doi.org/10.1037/vio0000104.

Flood, M., & Pease, B. (2009). Factors influencing attitudes to violence against women. *Trauma, Violence & Abuse*, *10*(2), 125–142. https://doi.org/10.1177/1524838009334131.

Funk, M. E., & Coker, C. R. (2016). She's hot, for a politician: The impact of objectifying commentary on perceived credibility of female candidates. *Communication Studies*, *67*(4), 1–19. https://doi.org/10.1080/10510974.2016.1196380.

Gill, R. (2008). Empowerment/sexism: Figuring female sexual agency in contemporary advertising. *Feminism & Psychology*, *18*(1), 35–60. https://doi.org/10.1177/0959353507084950

Gracia, E., García, F., & Lila, M. (2009). Public responses to intimate partner violence against women: The influence of perceived severity and personal responsibility. *The Spanish Journal of Psychology*, *12*(2), 648–656. https://doi.org/10.1017/S1138741600002018.

Gramazio, S., Cadinu, M., Pagliaro, S., & Pacilli, M. G. (2018). Sexualisation of sexual harassment victims reduces bystanders' help: The mediating role of attribution of immorality and blame. *Journal of Interpersonal Violence*. https://doi.org/10.1177/0886260518816326. Online ahead of print.

Gray, K., Knobe, J., Sheskin, M., Bloom, P., & Barrett, L. F. (2011). More than a body: Mind perception and the nature of objectification. *Journal of Personality and Social Psychology*, *101*(6), 1207–1220. https://doi.org/10.1037/a0025883.

Gray, K., & Wegner, D. M. (2009). Moral typecasting: Divergent perceptions of moral agents and moral patients. *Journal of Personality and Social Psychology*, *96*(3), 505–520. https://doi.org/10.1037/a0013748.

Harada, J. (1985). Bystander intervention: The effect of ambiguity of the helping situation and the interpersonal relationship between bystanders. *Japanese Psychological Research*, *27*(4), 177–184. https://doi.org/10.4992/psycholres1954.27.177

Hart, S. D. (2008). Preventing violence: The role of risk assessment and management. In A. C. Baldry & F. W. Winkel (Eds.), *Intimate partner violence prevention and intervention: The risk assessment and management approach* (pp. pp. 7–18). Nova Science.

Haslam, N. (2006). Dehumanization: An integrative review. *Personality and Social Psychology Review*, *10*(3), 252–264. https://doi.org/10.1207/s15327957pspr1003_4.

Hatton, E., & Trautner, M. N. (2011). Equal opportunity objectification? The sexualization of men and women on the cover of Rolling Stone. *Sexuality & Culture*, *15*(3), 256–278. https://doi.org/10.1007/s12119-011-9093-2.

Heflick, N., & Goldenberg, J. (2009). Objectifying Sarah Palin: Evidence that objectification causes women to be perceived as less competent and less fully human. *Journal of Experimental Social Psychology*, *45*(3), 598–601. https://doi.org/10.1016/j.jesp.2009.02.008.

Heider, F. (1958). *The psychology of interpersonal relations*. Wiley.

Heise, L. L. (1998). Violence against women: An integrated, ecological framework. *Violence against Women*, *4*(3), 262–290. https://doi.org/10.1177/1077801298004003002.

Hellemans, S., Loeys, T., Buysse, A., Dewaele, A., & De Smet, O. (2015). Intimate partner violence victimization among non-heterosexuals: Prevalence and associations with mental and sexual well-being. *Journal of Family Violence*, 30(2), 171–188. https://doi.org/10.1007/s10896-015-9669-y.

Holland, E., & Haslam, N. (2013). Worth the weight: The objectification of overweight versus thin targets. *Psychology of Women Quarterly*, 37(4), 572–581. https://doi.org/10.1177/0361684312474800.

Kawakami, K., Dunn, E., Karmali, F., & Dovidio, J. F. (2009). Mispredicting affective and behavioral responses to racism. *Science*, 323(5911), 276–278. https://doi.org/10.1126/science.1164951

Kelly, J. G. (Ed). (2006). *Becoming ecological: An expedition into community psychology*. Oxford University Press.

Kelly, L. (2013). *Surviving sexual violence*. John Wiley & Sons.

Kilpatrick, D. G. (2004). What is violence against women? Defining and measuring the problem. *Journal of Interpersonal Violence*, 19(11), 1209–1234. https://doi.org/10.1177/0886260504269679.

Kteily, N., Hodson, G., & Bruneau, E. (2016). They see us as less than human: Metadehumanization predicts intergroup conflict via reciprocal dehumanization. *Journal of Personality and Social Psychology*, 110(3), 343–370. https://doi.org/10.1037/pspa0000044

Langhinrichsen-Rohling, J., Shlien-Dellinger, R. K., Huss, M. T., & Kramer, V. L. (2004). Attributions about perpetrators and victims of interpersonal abuse: Results from an analogue study. *Journal of Interpersonal Violence*, 19(4), 484–498. https://doi.org/10.1177/0886260503262084.

Latané, B., & Darley, J. M. (1970). *The unresponsive bystander: Why doesn't he help?* Appleton Century Crofts.

Leach, C. W., Ellemers, N., & Barreto, M. (2007). Group virtue: The importance of morality (vs. competence and sociability) in the positive evaluation of in-groups. *Journal of Personality and Social Psychology*, 93(2), 234–249. https://doi.org/10.1037/0022-3514.93.2.234.

Leone, R. M., & Parrott, D. J. (2019). Misogynistic peers, masculinity, and bystander intervention for sexual aggression: Is it really just "locker-room talk?". *Aggressive Behavior*, 45(1), 42–51. https://doi.org/10.1002/ab.21795

Leone, R. M., Parrott, D. J., Swartout, K. M., & Tharp, A. T. (2016). Masculinity and bystander attitudes: Moderating effects of masculine gender role stress. *Psychology of Violence*, 6(1), 82–90. https://doi.org/10.1037/a0038926.

Lerner, M. J. (1970). The desire for justice and reactions to victims. In J. Macaulay & L. Berkowitz (Eds.), *Altruism and helping behavior* (pp. pp. 205–229). Academic Press.

Leyens,, J. P., Rodriguez, A. P., Rodriguez, R. T., Gaunt, R., Paladino, M. P., Vaes, J., & Demoulin, S. (2001). Psychological essentialism and the differential attribution of uniquely human emotions to ingroups and outgroups. *European Journal of Social Psychology*, 31(4), 395–411. https://doi.org/10.1002/ejsp.50

Loughnan, S., Haslam, N., Murnane, T., Vaes, J., Reynolds, C., & Suitner, C. (2010). Objectification leads to depersonalization: The denial of mind and moral concern to objectified others. *European Journal of Social Psychology*, 40(5), 709–717. https://doi.org/10.1002/ejsp.755.

Loughnan, S., Pina, A., Vasquez, E. A., & Puvia, E. (2013). Sexual objectification increases rape victim blame and decreases perceived suffering. *Psychology of Women Quarterly*, 37(4), 455–461. https://doi.org/10.1177/0361684313485718.

Majdandzic, J., Bauer, H., Windischberger, C., Moser, E., Engl, E., & Lamm, C. (2012). The human factor: Behavioral and neural correlates of humanized

perception in moral decision making. *PloS One, 7*(10), e47698. https://doi.org/10. 1371/journal.pone.0047698.
Matjasko, J. L., Holditch Niolon, P., & Valle, L. A. (2012). The role of economic factors and economic support in preventing and escaping from intimate partner violence. *Journal of Policy Analysis and Management, 32*(1), 122–128. https://doi. org/10.1002/pam.21666.
McMahon, S., & Banyard, V. L. (2012). When can I help? A conceptual framework for the prevention of sexual violence through bystander. *Trauma, Violence & Abuse, 13*(1), 3–14. https://doi.org/10.1177/1524838011426015.
Murnen, S. K., Wright, C., & Kaluzny, G. (2002). If "boys will be boys," then girls will be victims? A meta-analytic review of the research that relates masculine ideology to sexual aggression. *Sex Roles, 46*(11/12), 359–375. https://doi.org/0360-0025/02/ 0600-0359/0.
Nisbett, R. E., & Cohen, D. (1996). *Culture of honor: The psychology of violence in the south.* Westview.
Pacilli, M. G., Pagliaro, S., Loughnan, S., Gramazio, S., Spaccatini, F., & Baldry, A. C. (2017). Sexualization reduces helping intentions towards female victims of intimate partner violence through mediation of moral patiency. *British Journal of Social Psychology, 56*(2), 293–313. https://doi.org/10.1111/bjso.12169.
Pacilli, M. G., Roccato, M., Pagliaro, S., & Russo, S. (2016). From political opponents to enemies? The role of perceived moral distance in the animalistic dehumanization of the political outgroup. *Group Processes & Intergroup Relations, 19*(3), 360– 373. https://doi.org/10.1177/1368430215590490.
Pacilli, M. G., Spaccatini, F., Barresi, C., & Tomasetto, C. (2019). Less human and help-worthy: Sexualization affects children's perceptions of and intentions toward bullied peers. *International Journal of Behavioral Development, 43*(6), 481–491. https://doi.org/10.1177/0165025419873040
Pacilli, M. G., Tomasetto, C., & Cadinu, M. (2016). Exposure to sexualized advertisements disrupts children's math performance by reducing working memory. *Sex Roles, 74*(9–10), 389–398. https://doi.org/Doi:10.1007/s11199-016-0581-6
Pagliaro, S., Brambilla, M., Sacchi, S., D'Angelo, M., & Ellemers, N. (2013). Initial impressions determine behaviours: Morality predicts the willingness to help newcomers. *Journal of Business Ethics, 117*(1), 37–44. https://doi.org/10.1007/s10551- 012-1508-y.
Pagliaro, S., Ellemers, N., & Barreto, M. (2011). Sharing moral values: Anticipated ingroup respect as a determinant of adherence to morality-based (but not competence-based) group norms. *Personality & Social Psychology Bulletin, 37*(8), 1117– 1129. https://doi.org/10.1177/0146167211406906.
Pagliaro, S., Ellemers, N., Barreto, M., & Di Cesare, C. (2016). The impact of perceived pervasiveness of moral evaluations of the self on motivation to restore a moral reputation. *Frontiers in Psychology, 7*, 586. https://doi.org/10.3389/fpsyg. 2016.00586.
Pagliaro, S., Pacilli, M. G., Giannella, V. A., Giovannelli, I., Spaccatini, F., & Baldry, A. C. (2018). Legitimizing intimate partner violence: Moral evaluations, attribution of responsibility, and (reduced) helping intentions. *Journal of Interpersonal Violence.* https://doi.org/10.1177/0886260518760611.Online ahead of print.
Pagliaro, S., Pacilli, M. G., & Paolini, D. (2019). Intimate partner violence and same-sex couples: Examining the antecedents of bystanders' helping intentions. *Journal of Interpersonal Violence.* https://doi.org/10.1177/0886260519888530. Online ahead of print.

Paladino, P. M., Leyens, J.-P., Rodriguez, R. T., Rodriguez, A. P., Gaunt, R., & Demoulin, S. (2002). Differential association of uniquely and non uniquely human emotions to the ingroup and the outgroups. *Group Processes & Intergroup Relations*, 5(2), 105–117. https://doi.org/10.1177/1368430202005002539.

Paolini, D., Pagliaro, S., & Pacilli, M. G. (2020). Bystanders' reactions to intimate partner violence within gay men couples: The role of infidelity and stereotypes. *Psicologia Sociale*, 1, 67–79. https://doi.org/10.1482/96295.

Pavlou, M., & Knowles, A. (2001). Domestic violence: Attribution, recommended punishments by the victim. *Psychiatry, Psychology and Law*, 8(1), 6–85. https://doi.org/10.1080/13218710109525006.

Penone, G., & Spaccatini, F. (2019). Attribution of blame to gender violence victims: A literature review of antecedents, consequences and measures of victim blame. *Psicologia Sociale*, 2, 133–164. https://doi.org/10.1482/94264

Phipps, A., & Young, I. (2015). 'Lad culture' in higher education: Agency in the sexualization debates. *Sexualities*, 18(4), 459–479. https://doi.org/10.1177/1363460714550909

Pierce, M. C., & Harris, R. J. (1993). The effect of provocation, race, and injury description on men's and women's perception of a wife-battering incident. *Journal of Applied Social Psychology*, 23(10), 767–790. https://doi.org/10.1111/j.1559-1816.1993.tb01006.x.

Pitt-Rivers, J. (1966). Honor and social status. In J. G. Peristiany (Ed.), *Honor and shame: The values of Mediterranean society* (pp. pp. 19–78). University of Chicago Press.

Poorman, P. B., Seelau, E. P., & Seelau, S. M. (2003). Perceptions of domestic abuse in same-sex relationships and implications for criminal justice and mental health responses. *Violence and Victims*, 18(6), 659–669. https://doi.org/10.1891/088667003780928026.

Rodriguez Mosquera, P. M., Manstead, A. S. R., & Fischer, A. H. (2000). The role of honor-related values in the elicitation, experience and communication of pride, shame and anger: Spain and the Netherlands compared. *Personality & Social Psychology Bulletin*, 26(7), 833–844. https://doi.org/10.1177/0146167200269008.

Rodriguez Mosquera, P. M., Manstead, A. S. R., & Fischer, A. H. (2002a). Honor in the Mediterranean and in the North Europe. *Journal of Cross-cultural Psychology*, 33(1), 16–36. https://doi.org/10.1080/02699930143000167.

Rodriguez Mosquera, P. M., Manstead, A. S. R., & Fischer, A. H. (2002b). The role of honor concerns in emotional reactions to offences. *Cognition & Emotion*, 16(1), 143–163. https://doi.org/10.1177/0022022102033001002.

Saltzman, L. E., Fanslow, J., McMahon, P., & Shelley, G. (2002). *Intimate partner violence surveillance: Uniform definitions and recommended data elements (version 1.0)*. National Center for Injury Prevention and Control, Atlanta.

Seelau, E. P., Seelau, S. M., & Poorman, P. B. (2003). Gender and role-based perceptions of domestic abuse: Does sexual orientation matter? *Behavioral Sciences & the Law*, 21(2), 199–214. https://doi.org/10.1002/bsl.524.

Seelau, S. M., & Seelau, E. P. (2005). Gender-role stereotypes and perceptions of heterosexual, gay and lesbian domestic violence. *Journal of Family Violence*, 20(6), 363–371. https://doi.org/10.1007/s10896-005-7798-4.

Sheeran, P. (2002). Intention—behavior relations: A conceptual and empirical review. *European Review of Social Psychology*, 12(1), 1–36. https://doi.org/10.1080/14792772143000003

Shotland, R. L., & Straw, M. K. (1976). Bystander response to an assault: When a man attacks a woman. *Journal of Personality and Social Psychology*, *34*(5), 990–999. https://doi.org/10.1037/0022-3514.34.5.990

Sorenson, S. B., & Thomas, K. A. (2009). Views of intimate partner violence in same- and opposite-sex relationships. *Journal of Marriage and Family*, *71*(2), 337–352. https://doi.org/10.1111/j.1741-3737.2009.00602.x.

Spaccatini, F., Pacilli, M. G., Giovannelli, I., Roccato, M., & Penone, G. (2019). Sexualized victims of stranger harassment and victim blaming: The moderating role of right-wing authoritarianism. *Sexuality & Culture*, *3*, 1–15. https://doi.org/10.1007/s12119-019-09592-9

Stewart, C., Moore, T., Crone, T., Craft DeFreitas, S., & Rhatigan, D. (2012). Who gets blamed for intimate partner violence? The relative contributions of perpetrator sex category, victim confrontation, and observer attitudes. *Journal of Interpersonal Violence*, *27*(18), 3739–3754. https://doi.org/10.1177/0886260512447571.

Stewart, F. H. (1994). *Honor*. Chicago University Press.

Tajfel, H., & Turner, J. C. (1979). An integrative theory of intergroup conflict. In W. G. Austin & S. Worchel (Eds.), *The social psychology of intergroup relations* (pp. pp. 33–47). Brooks Cole.

Taylor, C. A., & Sorenson, S. B. (2005). Community-based norms about intimate partner violence: Putting attributions of fault and responsibility into context. *Sex Roles*, *53*(7–8), 573–589. https://doi.org/10.1007/s11199-005-7143-7

Turell, S. C. (2000). A descriptive analysis of same-sex relationship violence for a diverse sample. *Journal of Family Violence*, *15*(3), 281–293. https://doi.org/10.1023/A:1007505619577

Turner, J. C. (1991). *Social influence*. Open University Press.

Vaes, J., Paladino, P., & Puvia, E. (2011). Are sexualized women complete human beings? Why men and women dehumanize sexually objectified women. *European Journal of Social Psychology*, *41*(6), 774–785. https://doi.org/10.1002/ejsp.824.

Van Camp, T., Hébert, M., Guidi, E., Lavoie, F., & Blais, M. (2014). Teens' self-efficacy to deal with dating violence as victim, perpetrator or bystander. *International Review of Victimology*, *20*(3), 289–303. https://doi.org/10.1177/0269758014521741.

Vandello, J. A., & Cohen, D. (2003). Male honor and female fidelity: Implicit cultural scripts that perpetuate domestic violence. *Journal of Personality and Social Psychology*, *84*(5), 997–1010. https://doi.org/10.1037/00223514.84.5.997.

Viki, G. T., & Abrams, D. (2002). But she was unfaithful: Benevolent sexism and reactions to rape victims who violate traditional gender role expectations. *Sex Roles*, *47*(5/6), 289–293. https://doi.org/10.1023/A:1021342912248

Waytz, A., Gray, K., Epley, N., & Wegner, D. (2010). Causes and consequences of mind perception. *Trends in Cognitive Science*, *14*(8), 383–388. https://doi.org/10.1016/j.tics.2010.05.006.

West, A., & Wandrei, M. L. (2002). Intimate partner violence: A model for predicting interventions by informal helpers. *Journal of Interpersonal Violence*, *17*(9), 972–986. https://doi.org/10.1177/0886260502017009004.

Whitaker, D. J., & Lutzker, J. R. (2009). *Preventing partner violence: Research and evidence-based intervention strategies*. American Psychological Association.

WHO. (2010). *Preventing intimate partner and sexual violence against women: Taking action and generating evidence*. World Health Organisation and London School of Hygiene and Tropical Medicine.

WHO. (2013). *Global and regional estimates of violence against women: Prevalence and health effects of intimate partner violence and non partner sexual violence.* World Health Organization.

Wilde, V. K., Martin, K. D., & Goff, P. A. (2014). Dehumanization as a distinct form of prejudice. *TPM: Testing, Psychometrics, Methodology in Applied Psychology, 21 (3)*, 1–7. http://www.tpmap.org/wp-content/uploads/2015/11/21.3.5.pdf

Witte, T. H., Schroeder, D., & Lohr, J. (2006). Blame for intimate partner violence: An attributional analysis. *Journal of Social and Clinical Psychology, 25(6)*, 647-668. https://doi.org/10.1521/jscp.2006.25.6.647.

Zurbriggen, E. L., & Roberts, T. A. (2013). *The sexualization of girls and girlhood: Causes, consequences, and resistance.* Oxford University Press.

ARTICLE

A meta-analytic integration of research on the relationship between right-wing ideological attitudes and aggressive tendencies

Alain Van Hiel, Emma Onraet, Dries H. Bostyn, Jonas Stadeus, Tessa Haesevoets, Jasper Van Assche and Arne Roets

Department of Developmental, Personality, and Social Psychology, Ghent University, Ghent, Belgium

ABSTRACT
Many studies have investigated the relationship between ideological attitudes and aggressive tendencies. The present meta-analytic integration of research on this relationship included data of 177 samples (total $N = 47{,}933$ participants). The results revealed that this relationship was substantial, $r = .31$, 95% CI [.27 to .35], $p < .001$. Such a relationship emerged for both attitudes towards violence and behavioural indicators, although the former relationship was stronger. Moreover, with respect to the different types of attitudes towards violence, we obtained equally strong relationships for attitudes towards war and military action, intergroup hostility and aggression, punitive attitudes, and intimate violence. Among the behavioural measures, context-specific aggression bore out a stronger effect size than chronic aggressive behaviour. Finally, type of right-wing attitude did not moderate the relationship under study. In the discussion, we argue that the pattern of results indicates that the greater aggressive tendencies among right-wing individuals are manifested both attitudinally and behaviourally.

ARTICLE HISTORY Received 24 May 2019; Accepted 29 May 2020

KEYWORDS Interpersonal aggression; attitudes towards violence; right-wing ideological attitudes; authoritarianism

About 70 years ago, Adorno et al. (1950) published their book "The Authoritarian Personality". This work advanced a host of hypotheses that have inspired much follow-up research until today. In the present contribution, we specifically focus on the relationship between right-wing ideological attitudes and aggressive tendencies. We do so by collecting all available studies that relate right-wing attitudes to aggression, and by calculating effect sizes to estimate the magnitude of this relationship.

CONTACT Alain Van Hiel ✉ Alain.VanHiel@UGent.be · Department of Developmental, Personality, and Social Psychology, Ghent University, Ghent, Belgium
 Supplemental data for this article can be accessed here.
© 2020 European Association of Social Psychology

In the recent past, our research team has already conducted several meta-analytic integrations of findings in order to verify whether or not the original hypotheses of Adorno et al. (1950) hold true and can be further specified. For instance, as can be anticipated from the work of Adorno et al., a relationship between cognitive style variables such as rigidity and intolerance of ambiguity, and right-wing attitudes was confirmed (Van Hiel et al., 2010, based on 124 samples and a total of 29,209 participants), although this relationship proved to be considerably stronger for self-report studies than for studies that derive cognitive style from problem solving behaviour in a test setting (Van Hiel et al., 2016, 103 samples, 12,714 participants). Partially in line with expectations, threat and right-wing attitudes also yielded a substantial effect size, although this turned out to be especially the case for external threats from the environment, and less so for internal threats and fears from within the person (Onraet, Van Hiel, Dhont et al., 2013, 109 samples, 22,086 participants). However, somewhat unexpected because it was hardly given attention by Adorno et al., the relationship between cognitive abilities and right-wing attitudes yielded a significantly negative effect-size (Onraet et al., 2015, 90 samples, 111,028 participants). Finally, whereas the reading of Adorno et al. would certainly lead one to conclude that right-wing adherents are unhappy, the empirical relationship between right-wing attitudes and well-being turned out to be trivial and even non-significant for most indicators (Onraet, Van Hiel, Dhont et al., 2013, 97 samples, 69,221 participants). With the present contribution, our aim was to further provide a meta-analytic empirical test of key assumptions made in the seminal work of Adorno and colleagues.

Introduction

Over the last seven decades, scholars have hypothesised that there is a relationship between right-wing attitudes and aggressive tendencies (e.g. Altemeyer, 1981; Adorno et al., 1950). Ample empirical evidence has accumulated showing a relationship between right-wing attitudes and multiple indicators of ideology-based aggression, such as support for hostile actions against outgroups (e.g. A. Golecde Zavala et al., 2010; Thomsen et al., 2008) and military actions against adversary nations (Crowson, 2009a, 2009b; Crowson et al., 2005). However, and this is the more puzzling observation, right-wing attitudes have also been reported to relate to indicators of aggression tendencies that are not straightforwardly tied to any ideology, such as interpersonal aggression (e.g. Epstein, 1965, 1966).

The many studies in this domain have merely aimed to demonstrate a significant relationship between right-wing attitudes and specific aggressive tendencies. To the best of our knowledge, however, no integration of these piecemeal findings has yet been attempted; as a result, the relative strength of these relationships is unclear. However, to understand right-wing-based aggression, one should have a view of exactly which attitudes favouring violence and which aggressive behaviours are implied, as well as of the extent to which their relationship with right-wing attitudes is similar in magnitude. In addition to this lack of empirical integration, theory development has lagged far behind. The present meta-analytic integration of studies therefore aims to contribute to the literature by investigating the relative weight of the relationships between right-wing attitudes and various aggressive tendencies. A more comprehensive insight into how different right-wing attitudes relate to various forms of aggressive tendencies should provide a necessary first step and will, hopefully, form the basis of what can become a theory of right-wing aggression.

In the present Study, we distinguished between several right-wing attitudes and we used a comprehensive view on aggression. Specifically, there is a broad consensus that ideological attitudes constitute two broad dimensions (see Duckitt, 2001; Lipset, 1981; Middendorp, 1978). The first dimension––social-cultural attitudes––relates to social conservatism and traditionalism at one pole versus openness, autonomy, liberalism, and personal freedom at the other pole. According to Duckitt (2001), Right-Wing Authoritarianism (RWA) is a typical indicator of this pattern of broad social attitudes. The second dimension––the economic-hierarchical dimension––relates to power, belief in hierarchy and inequality at one pole versus egalitarianism, humanitarianism, and concern with social welfare at the other pole. Scales such as Toughmindedness (Eysenck, 1954) and Social Dominance Orientation (SDO; Pratto et al., 1994; Sidanius & Pratto, 2001) are typical indicators of the latter broad social attitude (Duckitt, 2001). Importantly, previous studies have shown that both social-cultural and economic-hierarchical attitudes relate to indicators of aggressive tendencies (e.g. Cohrs, Moschner et al., 2005; Eysenck, 1954; Sibley et al., 2007), but their effect sizes are still unclear.

Moreover, we also advanced a comprehensive perspective on aggressive tendencies. Aggression is defined as behaviour intended to harm others (Harré & Lamb, 1983), but we do not limit ourselves to this behavioural component. Specifically, in the present meta-analysis we also include attitudes and beliefs that indicate a favourable orientation towards aggression and violence. Such attitudes may promote behavioural aggression, and it has been argued that they can be considered to be part of an aggressive personality structure that "includes a well-developed network of aggression-related knowledge structures (e.g. schemas and scripts), affect, and reflexive motor responses" (Anderson et al., 2006, p. 122; see also Anderson & Bushman, 2002a; Dodge & Crick, 1990). Moreover, such attitudes not only allow the person him- or herself to aggress, they may also facilitate other persons or societal actors to behave aggressively, thereby indirectly promoting aggression. That being said, it should be acknowledged that the majority of studies on right-wing aggressive tendencies included attitudes that favour aggression rather than behavioural indicators of aggression. Moreover, the latter type of studies often included behavioural measures based on self-reports, and only a few studies used observational measures of actual behaviour.

An important limitation that we should mention before presenting the literature on the relationship between right-wing attitudes and aggression pertains to the scientific case of left-wing aggression (see Van Hiel et al., 2006). History proves that any ideology––political, religious, or philosophi-cal––which is (too) strongly adhered to can be a source of aggression.[1] However, to the very best of our knowledge, we are not aware of any empirical study that has investigated typical targets of left-wing aggression, such as police officers, bankers, rich people, conservatives, etc. (for a similar rationale, see Brandt et al., 2014). It is possible that high-scoring left-wingers are more aggressively inclined towards members of such groups, but because of the lack of relevant studies we are not able to test this assumption.

The relationship between right-wing attitudes and aggressive tendencies

Right-wing policies typically involve a more forceful stance towards other countries and other groups. The imposition of brute force or violence is considered to be a valid way of managing international relationships. For instance, on the right-wing side of the political spectrum, "Hawks" who advocate an aggressive foreign policy based on strong military power typi-cally outnumber "Doves" who try to more peacefully resolve international disputes. Conversely, on the left-wing side, the "Doves" outnumber the "Hawks" (Holsti, 1996; Hurwitz & Peffley, 1990). Not surprisingly, then, theorising has considered support for aggressive policies––especially in the context of international conflicts––to be a typical characteristic of those on the right-wing side of the political spectrum.

Right-wing adherents not only tend to show more support for aggression in international disputes, but scholars have even considered such aggressive tendencies to constitute a core aspect in the psychology of right-wing attitudes. Authoritarianism theory constitutes the clearest example of this perspective (Altemeyer, 1981; Adorno et al., 1950). From the early days of authoritarianism research, a facet called "authoritarian aggression" has been

---

[1]Stalin, Mao, or Pol Pot were communist leaders who have been accountable for millions of deaths. These horrific examples of what might be called "left-wing" aggression, however, are probably more akin to right-wing aggression, in the sense that the persons who supported those regimes most strongly seem to be psychologically similar to right-wing persons living in Western democracies (Altemeyer & Kamenshikov, 1991; McFarland et al., 1996; Van Hiel et al., 2006).

included in the broad authoritarianism concept. According to Adorno et al., authoritarian aggression refers to "the tendency to be on the lookout for, and to condemn, reject, and punish people who violate conventional values" (p. 255). Authoritarian aggression items refer to a hostile orientation to "radicals", "deviants", "troublemakers", "criminals", "homosexuals", and so on, which may possibly spill over to the aggression attitudes we investigate in the present study. In more recent theorising about authoritarianism, the role of aggression as one of the most important components has been reiterated repeatedly, and it has also been explicitly included as an important facet scale in more recent measurements of the concept (e.g. Stellmacher & Petzel, 2005; Van Hiel et al., 2007). In case of authoritarianism, it is therefore important to check for the presence of possible predictor-criterion overlap (as presently has been done in our pilot study, see below).

Although Adorno et al. (1950), and many scholars after them, conceptualised authoritarian aggression in terms of aggression towards norm-violating people and outgroups, their work also contains references to interpersonal aggression. For instance, according to Adorno and colleagues, responses to projective questions showed that authoritarian people demonstrated "concrete, impersonal, aggressive acts, usually directed against 'irritating' people" (p. 557). Moreover, in their well-known case study of Mack, it is mentioned that "the aggression appears to be out of touch with the rest of the personality; it is something which is entirely disclaimed, but which might suddenly explode in a blindly impulsive way" (p. 814). According to Altemeyer (2006), "while on the surface high RWAs [i.e. those scoring high on Right-Wing Authoritarianism] can be pleasant, sociable, and friendly, they seemingly have a lot of hostility boiling away inside them" (p. 52). As these citations clarify, aggression in right-wing people was hypothesised to be directed not only towards norm-violating people and outgroup members but can also manifest itself in interpersonal aggression. In the remainder of this literature review section, we address the relationship between right-wing attitudes and attitudes favouring violence on the one hand, and aggressive behaviour on the other hand.

The relationship between right-wing attitudes and attitudes favouring violence

As already mentioned, right-wing aggression has been primarily studied in relation to people who do not conform to conventional societal norms, as well as members of outgroups. Not surprisingly, the types of aggression measures that are typically studied in the domain of ideological attitudes, and which have been found to reveal strong correlations, include, among others, hostile attitudes against outgroups (e.g. Golecde Zavala et al., 2010) and violence against minority groups. We will refer to this type of aggression with the term "intergroup aggression". Other types of violence related attitudes have been discerned in the literature as well, and some of them have also been related to right-wing attitudes. For instance, Anderson et al. (2006) distinguished four dimensions of violence related attitudes: violence in war, penal code violence, corporal punishment of children, and intimate violence. Below, we elaborate in more detail on these four types of violence related attitudes.

Regarding the first type, pro-attitudes towards war have been frequently studied in relationship with right-wing attitudes and include support for military programmes (e.g. Pratto et al., 1994), for going to war in Iraq (e.g. McFarland., 2005), for militarism and for taking military actions in Afghanistan (Bonanno & Jost, 2006), and for military aggression as part of the war on terror (e.g. Crowson, 2009a, 2009b; Van Hiel & Kossowska, 2007).

With respect to the second type of violence related attitudes, right-wing attitudes are also typical of a "law-and-order mentality". In line with this, previous studies have generally revealed a positive relationship between right-wing attitudes and penal code violence, as indicated, among others, by a pro-attitude towards capital punishment (e.g. Feather & Souter, 2002; McKee & Feather, 2008; Moran & Comfort, 1986) and corporal punishment (e.g. Benjamin, 2006), as well as harsh punishment goals (e.g. Colémont et al., 2011; Tam et al., 2008) and desire for retribution (e.g. Feather & Souter, 2002; McKee & Feather, 2008).

The third dimension of violence related attitudes––corporal punishment of children––has hardly been studied in the context of right-wing attitudes. This is rather surprising because theoretical accounts of right-wing attitudes often stress child-rearing (see Altemeyer, 1981; 2006; Feldman & Stenner, 1997, Stenner 2005), but focused on the fundamental values conveyed by childrearing in terms of parental authority versus autonomy, not on harsh, punitive childrearing behaviours in themselves as, for example, the use of corporal punishment.

The fourth dimension of violence related attitudes, intimate violence and woman-unfriendly attitudes, has also been repeatedly documented in the literature to correlate with right-wing attitudes. These aggressive tendencies prevail in the form of, for example, greater acceptance of rape myths (e.g. Walker et al., 1993).

The relationship between right-wing attitudes and aggressive behaviour

Right-wing attitudes have not only been related to attitudes favouring violence, but to aggressive behaviour as well. We distinguish between two types of aggressive behaviours, which we call "chronic" and "context-specific", respectively. "Chronic aggression" is based on so-called measures of trait aggression, which probe into self-reported aggressive behaviour in general, across situations. A number of studies have investigated the relationship between right-wing attitudes and measures of trait aggression, most notably Buss and Durkee (1957) Hostility Inventory and Buss and Perry (1992) Aggression Questionnaire, which are considered to be gold standards in aggression research (Gerevich et al., 2007). These measures include a number of statements about the occurrence of aggressive acts, such as "I get into fights a little more than the average person," and the experience of anger, such as expressed in the item "Some of my friends think I'm a hothead." These items do not refer to a specific context or situation, but rather probe into the frequency of aggression elicited across multiple contexts.

The context-specific aggression component refers to aggressive behaviours that are mobilised within a specific context. Some of the studies that include such an aggression measure are based on the registration of actual behaviours, which often takes the form of delivering electroshocks to another participant in a lab context (e.g. Dambrun & Vatiné, 2010; Epstein, 1965, 1966). Other instances of context-specific interpersonal aggression associated with right-wing attitudes include bullying behaviour (Parkins et al., 2006), and maltreatment behaviour enacted by officers (Barron & Ogle, 2014).

Besides the investigation of the realm of interpersonal contexts, some context-specific aggression studies have been conducted in the context of intimate, intergroup and war. With respect to intimate violence, these behavioural indicators are based on self-reports of behaviours enacted in the past, or on intentions and future plans in real or in hypothetical situations (e.g. Hogben et al., 2001; Kelly et al., 2015; LeeChai & Bargh, 2001). In the latter category, individuals indicate whether or not they would enact intimate violence in situations in which they cannot get punished for such acts. With respect to intergroup aggression, a number of behavioural studies has been conducted as well, among these Altemeyer's (1988) "posse studies" in which participants expressed their agreement with actions against outgroups if these would be outlawed in the future (see also Thomsen et al., 2008). Finally, some studies have investigated participants' willingness to go to war (Besta et al., 2015; Bizumic et al., 2013).

The studies that included interpersonal and intimate aggressive behaviours are typically "non-ideological", as the target of aggression has no relationship whatsoever with any political outgroup or politically relevant group. Conversely, intergroup aggression and going to war target "ideological" relevant groups, that is, groups which are often explicitly targeted by right-wing propaganda, politics and politicians.

Right-wing aggressive tendencies: four specific comparisons

The comparison of the magnitude of the relationships between right-wing attitudes, on the one hand, and the specific aggression types on the other hand, is important as it allows us to move forward in terms of theory. At least four possible comparisons are interesting and can help to solve the scientific puzzle of whether right-wing attitudes relate to aggression, as well as the contexts and targets that elicit such aggression.

Attitudes versus behaviour

First, we compare the magnitude of the relationship between right-wing ideological attitudes and attitudes favouring violence on the one hand, versus aggressive behaviours on the other hand, across all included samples in our meta-analysis. A possible outcome of the present meta-analysis could be that the effect sizes for all attitudinal and behavioural aggression types are substantial, which would imply that right-wing adherents possess the inherent characteristic to aggress. In other words, right-wing attitudes could coincide with a general, deeply rooted inclination towards aggression at large. However, other outcomes may also be possible. For instance, it is possible that the relationships for attitudes favouring violence is strong, whereas it is weak for behaviour, which would indicate that such a relationship is merely about "beliefs" and less about enacted aggression in daily life.

On the basis of these theoretical considerations, the following Research Question 1 has been formulated: Does the magnitude of the relationship between right-wing attitudes and aggressive tendencies depend on type of measurement, i.e. attitudes versus behaviour?

Variation in terms of type of attitude favouring violence

A second important comparison is among the different attitudinal indicators of aggression (intergroup aggression, intimate violence, punitive attitudes, and support of war and the military). As we already stated above, violence related attitudes are often "ideological". Specifically, a tough stance in the international arena and support of the military is often advocated by right-wing politicians and are part of the political programme of such parties. This can also be said about the harsh treatment of criminals, and the rather negative stance towards groups that do not abide to the conventional norms. The case of intimate violence, however, is not easy to classify in terms of ideologically-driven aggression. On the one hand, we agree that right-wing politics often favour traditional gender roles, which in turn may be related to intimate violence. On the other hand, such roles do not necessitate nor imply, of course, the enactment of intimate violence. Right-wing politicians do not call for any such violence, neither does it constitute a part of any political party program. It is therefore an interesting question if attitudes towards intimate violence yields relationships of different magnitude with right wing ideology, compared to relationships with aggression attitudes towards more ideologically inspired targets.

Hence, Research Question 2 has been formulated: Does the magnitude of the relationship between right-wing attitudes and attitudes favouring aggressive tendencies depend on target group?

Variation in terms of type of behaviour

A third interesting comparison is among the behavioural indicators (chronic aggression and context-specific aggression in the interpersonal, intimate violence, intergroup and war domains). An intriguing possibility is that chronic aggression is poorly related to right-wing attitudes, whereas context-specific aggression invariably yields the stronger effect sizes. Such a result would indicate that high scores on right-wing attitudes do *not* correlate with a greater inherent, trait-wise tendency, as expressed in the chronic occurrence of aggression, anger and hostility-related thoughts. Conversely, the increased levels of specific aggressive tendencies would then be suggestive of the operation of general processes that increase the readiness of right-wing adherents to perceive specific contexts as aggression-eliciting.

We therefore formulate Research Question 3: Does the magnitude of the relationship between right-wing attitudes and aggressive behaviour depend on chronic versus context-specific aggression?

Variation in terms of type of right-wing attitude

A fourth and final issue, that is highly relevant in terms of theory, is the extent to which all right-wing attitudes are similarly related to different types of aggressive tendencies. If these relationships were to emerge for only one dimension of right-wing attitudes, then the basis of right-wing aggression is much more specific; only processes related to this one dimension of right-wing attitudes should then be considered relevant. Conversely, if all right-wing attitudes were to show a relationship with aggressive tendencies, only processes that apply to all right-wing attitudes could be at the basis of such tendencies.

Finally, Research Question 4 has been formulated as follows: Does the magnitude of the relationship between right-wing attitudes and aggressive behaviour depend on type of ideological attitude?

The present studies

As demonstrated in the previous sections, scholars have related right-wing attitudes to various types of aggressive tendencies. However, it remains unclear whether the relationship between right-wing attitudes and aggression is significant for various aggression types and, if this were the case, whether differences in the magnitude of this relationship would arise. Before proceeding to the meta-analysis, we wanted to ascertain that the right-wing ideological measures are truly distinctive from aggressive tendencies. In a pilot study reported in the Online Appendix, we therefore investigated the potential predictor-criterion overlap between the ideological variables and several aggression variables. To the best of our knowledge, and somewhat surprisingly, no such study has been conducted before. It is, however, necessary to ascertain that overlap is not an issue here. Authoritarianism scales especially may fall short in terms of predictor-criterion overlap because of the presence of some items that describe authoritarian aggression, which may lead to tautological relationships. Indeed, it is possible that authoritarianism and aggression show strong correlations not because of their true relationship, but merely because of sheer item overlap. Or put otherwise, one cannot use aggression (included in authoritarianism) as a predictor of aggression (as the criterion variable), unless one is able to show that these two aggression concepts do not overlap (see Lemery et al., 2002; Lengua et al., 1998). As can be seen in the Online Appendix, the mild levels of predictor-criterion overlap allowed us to proceed with the meta-analysis.

As such, we subsequently conducted our planned meta-analysis, based on relevant studies, which were classified in the broad categories of attitudes favouring violence, and aggressive behaviours. These categories were further divided in more fine-grained classes. Specifically, the attitudes favouring violence category has been further divided into attitudes towards war and military aggression, intergroup hostility and aggression, punitive attitudes, and intimate violence. The behavioural category was further divided into chronic and context-specific aggressive behaviour, and the context-specific category could include interpersonal, intimate, intergroup and war aggression. We thus computed an overall effect size across all studies and investigated whether the aggression types yield relationships of different magnitude with right-wing attitudes. Moreover, we investigated the impact of possible moderator variables, such as the type of scale measuring right-wing attitudes, and of study and publication characteristics. Publication bias was investigated as well.

Method

Selection and coding of studies

We searched for studies for this meta-analysis in different ways. Specifically, we searched for studies using a variety of keywords in various combinations in the databases of ISI Web of Knowledge, Google Scholar, and ProQuest. Keywords for aggression were: aggression, violence, anger, hostility, revenge, punitive attitudes, punishment, penal code, war, military, rape, harassing/harassment. Keywords for right-wing ideological attitudes were: authoritarianism, conservatism/conservative, liberal, social dominance orientation, left/right-wing, Democrat and Republican. We also checked reference lists of the obtained studies to look for additional studies of relevance. Besides looking for published studies, we also contacted researchers in the field to share relevant unpublished data. We contacted individual researchers who previously did research on aggression and right-wing ideological attitudes and we also distributed a call for unpublished data via the websites or mailing lists of the International Society of Political Psychology, European Association of Social Psychology and Social Psychology Network. Twelve unpublished samples were obtained. We ended our search for studies in July 2017.

To be included in the meta-analysis, studies had to administer at least one measure of right-wing ideological attitudes and at least one measure of aggression. Studies meeting these criteria were coded for several design, sample, and publication characteristics. First, we coded according to the specific type right-wing ideological attitudes: authoritarianism, social dominance orientation, conservatism, and political self-placement (measured with a conservative-liberal, or democrat-republican self-placement item). We also coded for the type of aggression, based on the following types: attitudes favouring aggression and aggressive behaviour, chronic and context-specific aggressive behaviour, attitudes favouring intergroup aggression, support for war and military action, punitive attitudes, and intimate violence (see Anderson et al., 2006). Because coding the samples into type of aggression was not always straightforward, in a limited number of cases, the two first authors separately coded each study, and the final coding was decided after deliberation between the two authors.[2]

We also coded some sample characteristics. First, we coded for type of sample, that is, in which group of individuals was the study conducted? The different types of samples were: adolescents, students, adults, and a "mixed" category in the case that different groups were combined. We also coded for

---

[2]The ideology and aggression classifications were cross-validated by the third author. We selected 25 samples. Twenty three classifications of the ideology measure were correct (two self-placement scales with "conservative" as an anchor were incorrectly assigned to the conservatism category). All aggression classifications were correct.

the geographic location of the sample: United States/Canada, Europe, Middle East & North-Africa, South-America, Australia & New Zealand, and International (one study included participants from all over the world). As an indicator of publication characteristics, the year of data acquisition was coded into three categories: before 1990, 1990–2009, 2010-present.

Because samples included in a meta-analysis have to be statistically independent (Mullen, 1989), a sample can only be included once in the meta-analysis. Because many of the obtained samples included several indicators of ideological attitudes or aggression, we constructed several "selection rules" to select a single data point for each sample (see also, Onraet et al., 2015; Van Hiel et al., 2010). When multiple indicators of a single type of right-wing ideological attitudes (e.g. two authoritarianism scales) or aggression (e.g. two indicators of interpersonal aggression) were administered, the mean correlation was calculated and used for further analyses. In the case that multiple indicators of aggression were administered in the same sample, we selected the type least prevalent across the other samples. The same rule was applied in the case that multiple indicators of ideological attitudes were included in the same sample, except when a sample included a measure of authoritarianism and social dominance orientation. Although we had more samples including authoritarianism ($N = 96$ compared to social dominance orientation ($N = 47$), we alternated between selecting the data point with authoritarianism and the one with social dominance orientation, because many samples ($N = 60$) included both at the same time. After this selection of studies, we obtained a final collection of 177 samples with a total of 47,933 participants. All studies are displayed in the online Appendix.

Statistical analyses

For the statistical meta-analyses, we used the metafor package in R (R Core Team, 2013; Viechtbauer, 2010). Because effect sizes are expected to vary across studies and in order to produce results that can be generalised to future studies with different designs (Hedges & Vevea, 1998), we used a random effects model with a Hunter-Schmidt estimator to model heterogeneity of the true effect sizes. The data and statistical code for all reported meta-analyses are available on https://osf.io/wjy94/.

Pearson product-moment correlation coefficients (rs) were used as effect size estimates. For studies that did not report correlation coefficients, but mean differences in scores on aggression across groups with low or high right-wing ideological attitudes, we used the reported test statistics (F-, t- or p-values) and/or the means and standard deviations for each group to calculate the effect sizes (Borenstein et al., 2005). First, Fisher-Z coefficients were calculated to permit an unbiased comparison of effect sizes. Next, mean weighted effect sizes and 95% confidence intervals around the point estimate of the combined estimates were computed. Next, the effect size estimates were transformed back to correlations.

We also examined the role of potential moderator variables. Therefore, we conducted homogeneity analyses to test whether the sets of effect sizes were heterogeneous, and moderation analyses using categorical testing procedures (Lipsey & Wilson, 2001). A significant within-groups Q (Q_w) estimate indicates that the effect sizes within each moderator category are heterogeneous. A significant between-groups Q (Q_b) estimate indicates that the effect sizes of the moderator subgroups are significantly different. I2 indices (Higgins & Thompson, 2002) indicate the percentage of variability in point estimates due to between-study heterogeneity, rather than sampling error (I2-values in the order of 25, 50, and 75 represent low, moderate, and high between-study heterogeneity).

Finally, we also checked for publication bias. Publication bias refers to the increased likelihood that a study gets published because of the presence of statistically significant results. Because non-significant results are less likely to get published (and hence unlikely to be included in a meta-analysis), publication bias can potentially jeopardise the representativeness of a meta-analytical sample set and might overestimate the meta-analytical effect sizes (Kepes et al., 2012, 2013). In the current manuscript, we checked for publication bias in three ways. First, we used a trim-and-fill approach to impute the effect sizes for "missing" studies (Duval & Tweedie, 2000). Secondly, we explicitly tested if the effect size for published studies differed significantly from those of the unpublished studies. Finally, we used the p-uniform method to test for the possibility of publication bias (Van Assen et al., 2015). The p-uniform method uses only the statistically significant findings in a set of studies and is based on the rationale that the distribution of p-values should be uniform conditional on the population effect size. As such, the method tests if the distribution of significant p-values within a set of studies deviates from the uniform distribution, hereby assuming that the population level effect equals the meta-analytic effect estimate of a fixed-effects model. Research by Van Aert et al. (2016) suggests that when the check for publication bias through the p-uniform method turns out to be non-significant, one can subsequently run a fixed or random-effects meta-analysis.

Results

Overall meta-analysis: right-wing ideological attitudes and aggressive tendencies

First, we performed a meta-analysis of the overall relationship between right-wing ideological attitudes and aggressive tendencies. Twelve samples

A. VAN HIEL ET AL.

Table 1. Moderators of effect sizes for studies on the relationship between right-wing ideological attitudes and aggression.

Moderator	N	k	r		95%CI	Q_b		Q_w		l2
Type of Aggression						8.73	**			89.78
Behavioural	13,578	67	.24	***	.19 to.29			472.32	***	85.69
Attitudinal	34,355	110	.34	***	.29 to.38			1274.70	***	91.29
Attitudinal subcategory						7.02				89.47
Intergroup Aggression	5495	16	.33	***	.25 to.41			101.41	***	83.64
Intimate Violence	2328	11	.38	***	.31 to.46			46.10	***	75.46
Attitudes towards Penal Code	12,268	38	.27	***	.19 to.34			292.06	***	86.51
Attitudes towards War/Military Action	14,264	45	.40	***	.33 to.47			634.34	***	92.74
Behaviour subcategory						18.48	***			79.36
Chronic	5614	30	.13	***	.07 to.20			138.70	***	78.03
Context-specific	7964	37	.31	***	.26 to.36			190.87	***	80.31
Type of Ideological Attitude						1.20				90.08
Authoritarianism	22,162	96	.32	***	.27 to.37			989.58	***	90.17
Social Dominance Orientation	12,734	47	.33	***	.27 to.39			524.02	***	90.91
Conservatism	3623	12	.32	***	.21 to.43			121.05	***	89.57
Political self-placement	9414	22	.26	***	.17 to.35			196.86	***	88.14
Sample Type						3.21				90.07
Adolescents	572	2	.14	*	.02 to.27			4.59	*	54.83
Students	23,558	104	.29	***	.25 to.34			790.84	***	86.71
Adults	20,586	64	.32	***	.26 to.39			1018.68	***	93.63
Mixed	3217	7	.39	***	.33 to.45			17.73	**	54.21
Location						12.99	*			89.98
USA/Canada	32,892	124	.31	***	.27 to.36			1235.89	***	89.88
Europe	11,455	35	.34	***	.27 to.40			320.79	***	88.69
Australia/New Zealand	1550	8	.25	***	.11 to.39			69.11	***	88.16
Middle East/North Africa	1214	7	.18		−.07 to.43			164.12	***	95.58
South America	397	2	−.04		−.15 to.07			2.57		22.14
International	425	1	.40	***	.32 to.48			0.00		0.00
Time of publication						0.66				90.48
Before 1990	7353	33	.34	***	.27 to.40			205.02	***	83.53
1990–2009	14,415	60	.30	***	.23 to.36			611.81	***	90.00
2010-present	26,165	84	.31	***	.25 to.37			1072.79	***	92.07
Total Set	47,933	177	.31	***	.27 to.35			1897.26	***	90.61

Note. N = number of participants; k = number of studies; CI = confidence interval; Q_b = homogeneity statistic between classes; Q_w = homogeneity statistic within classes. l2 = homogeneity statistic (percentage of heterogeneity).
* p <.05; ** p <.01; *** p <.001

revealed negative relations, a single sample showed a correlation of approximately 0, and 164 samples showed positive relations. The meta-analysis (for all results see Table 1) revealed an overall strong positive relation, $r = .31$, 95% CI [.27 to .35], $p < .001$. In other words, right-wing ideological attitudes were associated with higher scores on aggression.

We then tested for publication bias. Trim-and-fill suggests that 2 studies were missing on the left side of the effect size distribution. Importantly, including these studies did not impact the estimate for the effect, $r = .31$, 95% CI [.27 to .34], $p < .001$. A comparison of published versus non-published studies did not reveal significant differences, $Q(1) = 1.35$, $p = .25$. Finally, the p-uniform method did not suggest the presence of publication bias, $p = 1$.

The overall effect size was heterogeneous, $Q(176) = 1897.26$, $p < .001$, $I^2 = 90.61$, which allowed us to test the influence of potential moderators. We first looked into the results in terms of our Research Questions. Pertaining to Research Question 1, type of aggression (attitudinal vs. behavioural), Q $(1) = 8.73$, $p = .003$, yielded a significant moderator effect. More specifically, the effect size of attitudes favouring aggression, $r = .34$, $p < .001$, 95% CI [.29 to .38], was stronger compared to the effect size for behavioural aggression, $r = .24$, $p < .001$, 95% CI [.19 to .29]. With respect to Research Question 2, the moderator effect of type of violence attitude was non-significant, $Q(3) = 7.02$, $p = .071$. In answer of Research Question 3, the moderator effect of type of aggressive behaviour (chronic versus context-specific), $Q(1) = 18.48$, $p < .001$. was significant, with a smaller effect size for chronic aggressive behaviour, $r = .13$, $p < .001$, 95% CI [.07 to .20], than for context-specific aggressive behaviour, $r = .31$, $p < .001$, 95% CI [.26 to .36]. Finally, in answer of Research Question 4, type of ideological attitude did not reveal a significant moderator effect, $Q(3) = 1.20$, $p = .754$. Next, we analysed the impact of 3 additional moderators: sample type, location of the sample, and time of publication. Only location of sample yielded a significant effect, but this was due to the few South-American samples that showed a negative effect.

We performed an additional meta-analysis solely including samples containing attitudes favouring violence, and an additional meta-analysis including solely samples using a measure of behavioural aggression. Our aim was to further test the moderator effect of type of ideology (Research Question 4) for attitudes and behaviour separately. Moreover, we wanted to further check whether the various types of context-specific aggressive behaviour yielded effect sizes of different magnitude.

Separate meta-analysis: right-wing attitudes and attitudes favouring violence

The meta-analysis of violence favouring attitudes (for all results see Table 2) was based on 110 samples.[1] Only five samples showed negative relations, whereas 104 showed positive relations. Again, in answer of Research Question 4, type of right-wing attitudes was not a significant moderator of the effect, $Q(3) = 3.56$, $p = .313$. Specifically, there were no significant differences between the effect sizes for authoritarianism, $r = .36$, $p = <.001$, 95% CI [.30 to .43]), social dominance orientation, $r = .38$, $p < .001$, 95% CI [.30 to .46], conservatism, $r = .35$, $p = <.001$, 95% CI [.23 to .46], and political self-placement, $r = .26$, $p < .001$, 95% CI [.17 to .35].

198 A. VAN HIEL ET AL.

Table 2. Moderators of effect sizes for studies on the relationship between right-wing ideological attitudes and attitudes favouring violence.

Moderator	N	k	r		95%CI	Q_b	Q_w		I2
Type of Ideological Attitude						3.56			90.04
Authoritarianism	14,232	53	.36	***	.30 to.43		497.76	***	89.09
Social Dominance Orientation	7880	28	.38	***	.30 to.46		366.87	***	92.18
Conservatism	3069	9	.35	***	.23 to.46		88.83	***	89.32
Political self-placement	9174	20	.26	***	.17 to.35		192.47	***	88.96
Total Set	34,355	110	.34	***	.29 to.38		1247.70	***	91.29

Note. N = number of participants; k = number of studies; CI = confidence interval; Q_b = homogeneity statistic between classes; Q_w = homogeneity statistic within classes. I2 = homogeneity statistic (percentage of heterogeneity).
*** p <.001

Table 3. Moderators of effect sizes for studies on the relationship between right-wing ideological attitudes and behavioural indices of interpersonal aggression.

Moderator	N	k	r		95%CI	Q_b	Q_w		I2
Type of Aggression						26.22 ***			75.75
Trait	5614	30	.13	***	.07 to.20		138.70	***	78.03
Context-specific Intimate	1903	9	.25	***	.16 to.33		30.70	***	69.70
Context-specific Interpersonal	1183	10	.21	**	.08 to.34		43.12	***	76.17
Context-specific Intergroup	3893	13	.38	***	.32 to.44		58.46	***	77.18
Going to War	985	5	.30	***	.17 to.43		15.43	**	60.93
Ideology						1.19			85.04
Authoritarianism	7930	43	.24	***	.17 to.32		388.71	***	88.75
Social Dominance Orientation	4854	19	.24	***	.19 to.30		66.60	***	70.92
Conservatism	554	3	.14	**	.06 to.22		0.79		0.00
Political self-placement	240	2	.15	*	.03 to.27		0.08		0.00
Total Set	13,578	67	.24	***	.19 to.29		472.32	***	85.69

Note. N = number of participants; k = number of studies; CI = confidence interval; Q_b = homogeneity statistic between classes; Q_w = homogeneity statistic within classes. I2 = homogeneity statistic (percentage of heterogeneity).
* p <.05; ** p <.01; *** p <.001

Separate meta-analyses: right-wing attitudes and aggressive behaviour

The separate meta-analysis of aggressive behaviour (for all results see Table 3) was based on 67 samples. Seven samples revealed negative relations, 61 showed positive relations. The moderator effect for type of aggression was significant, $Q(4) = 26.22$, $p < .001$, further illuminating Research Question 3. The effect size for context-specific aggression was strong for intergroup aggression, $r = .38$, $p < .001$, 95% CI [.31 to .44]), and going to war, $r = .30$, $p < .001$, 95% CI [.17 to .43], whereas it was moderate for interpersonal, $r = .21$, $p = .001$, 95% CI [.08 to .34], and intimate behaviour, $r = .25$, $p < .001$, 95% CI [.16 to .33], as well as rather small for chronic aggression, $r = .13$, $p < .001$, 95% CI [.07 to .20].

Again, in answer of Research Question 4, type of right-wing attitudes did not yield a significant moderator effect, $Q(3) = 1.19$, $p = .756$. Specifically, there were no significant differences between the effect sizes for authoritarianism, $r = .24$, $p < .001$, 95% CI [.17 to .32]), social dominance orientation, $r = .24$, $p < .001$, 95% CI [.19 to .30], conservatism, $r = .14$, $p = <.001$, 95% CI [.06 to .22], and political self-placement, $r = .15$, $p = .018$, 95% CI [.03 to .27]).

Subsidiary analysis: comparison of attitude and behaviour within aggression domains

Finally, we have conducted three meta-analyses which compared studies that administered attitudinal measures with those which used behavioural indicators within the domains of war, intergroup aggression, and intimate violence (for all results see Table 4). We were not able to conduct such direct comparisons for studies in the punitive and interpersonal domains as the former category only includes studies with attitudinal measures of aggression, and the latter category only studies with behavioural indicators.

The meta-analysis of war was based on 50 samples. Three samples revealed negative relations, 47 showed positive relations. The moderator effect for type of measure (attitudinal versus behavioural) was not significant, $Q(1) = .73$, $p = .394$. The effect sizes for the attitudinal measures, $r = .40$,

Table 4. Moderation by behaviour versus attitudes of effect sizes for studies in the domain of war aggression, intergroup aggression, and intimate aggression.

War Aggression								
Moderator	N	k	r		95%CI	Q_b	Q_w	I2
Behaviour versus Attitudes						0.73		92.12
Behaviour	985	5	.30	***	.17 to.43		15.43 ***	60.93
Attitudes	14,264	45	.40	***	.33 to.47		634.34 ***	92.74
Total Set	15,249	50	.39	***	.32 to.46		666.04 ***	92.33

Intergroup Aggression								
Moderator	N	k	r		95%CI	Q_b	Q_w	I2
Behaviour versus Attitudes						0.83		81.28
Behaviour	3893	13	.38	***	.31 to.44		58.46 ***	77.18
Attitudes	5495	16	.33	***	.25 to.41		101.41 ***	83.64
Total Set	9388	29	.35	***	.30 to.40		165.12 ***	82.15

Intimate Aggression								
Moderator	N	k	r		95%CI	Q_b	Q_w	I2
Behaviour versus Attitudes						5.36 *		73.19
Behaviour	1903	9	.25	***	.16 to.33		30.70 ***	69.70
Attitudes	2328	11	.38	***	.31 to.46		46.10 ***	75.46
Total Set	4231	20	.32	***	.26 to.39		103.88 ***	80.43

Note. N = number of participants; k = number of studies; CI = confidence interval; Q_b = homogeneity statistic between classes; Q_w = homogeneity statistic within classes. I2 = homogeneity statistic (percentage of heterogeneity).
* $p <.05$; ** $p <.01$; *** $p <.001$

$p < .001$, 95% CI [.33 to .47]) and going to war, $r = .30$, $p < .001$, 95% CI [.17 to .43] did not differ significantly. The meta-analysis of intergroup aggression based on 29 samples (all showing positive relations) neither showed a significant moderator effect for type of measure, $Q(1) = .83$, $p = .364$. The effect sizes for the attitudinal measures, $r = .33$, $p < .001$, 95% CI [.25 to .41]) and the behavioural measures, $r = .38$, $p < .001$, 95% CI [.31 to .44] did not differ significantly. Finally, the meta-analysis based on 20 samples (one sample revealed a negative relation, 19 showed positive relations) revealed a significant moderation effect of type of measurement for intimate violence, $Q(1) = 5.36$, $p = .021$. The effect size for the attitudinal measures, $r = .38$, $p < .001$, 95% CI [.31 to .46]) was stronger than for the behavioural measures, $r = .25$, $p < .001$, 95% CI [.16 to .33].

General discussion

To the best of our knowledge, a meta-analytic integration of research on the relationship between right-wing attitudes and aggressive tendencies has not been conducted yet. An important but unanswered question, therefore, pertained to the general relationship between right-wing attitudes and aggressive tendencies, as well as the more specific relationships for the various aggression types. The present study sought to establish the importance of all these relationships in terms of their effect size.

Main conclusions

In the pilot study reported in the online Appendix, we first have investigated possible item overlap between the right-wing attitudes and the aggression indicators. The resulting negligible levels of item overlap allowed us to proceed with the meta-analysis, which yielded at least five important results. First, the present effect size across all included samples, $r = .31$, revealed a substantial link between right-wing attitudes and aggressive tendencies. Since the classic work of Adorno et al. (1950) such a relationship has been hypothesised and then substantiated by a host of empirical studies (e.g. Altemeyer, 1981; Epstein, 1965, 1966; Crowson, 2009a; Thomsen et al., 2008). Moreover, because of the resurgence of interest in the relationship between right-wing attitudes and aggression, many studies included in the present meta-analysis have been published very recently, that is, after 2010. According to the guidelines of Funder and Ozer (2019) and Gignac and Szodorai (2016) for meta-analytic effects sizes in psychological research, effect sizes of about .10, .20, and .30 should be considered small, moderate, and large effects, respectively. The relationship between right-wing attitudes and aggressive tendencies thus qualifies to be labelled large. Also, compared to other effect sizes in the broad literature on aggressive behaviour, the present effect size cannot be said to be trivial. For instance, smaller effect sizes have been obtained for antecedents of aggression which have rightfully been considered as problematic, such as in case of the consumption of media violence (r between .17 and .23 across different methodologies, see Anderson & Bushman, 2002b).

Attitudes favouring aggression versus aggressive behaviour

A second important result pertains to the difference between attitudes favouring aggression and aggressive behaviours, which was referred to as Research Question 1. Samples that included attitudes favouring violence yielded a considerably stronger effect size than studies which included behavioural aggression indices. Specifically, the relationship between right-wing attitudes and violence attitudes, $r = .34$, should be considered large, whereas the relationship with aggressive behaviour, $r = .24$, should be considered moderate. This result thus clarifies that right-wing individuals particularly adhere to various attitudes that support violence. It is not very surprising that, if a relationship between right-wing attitudes and aggression exists, it should primarily manifest itself in the aggression types of violence related attitudes towards war and military action, intergroup hostility and aggression, and punitive attitudes and the like. All these aggressions have a clear link to ideology. The relationship in terms of enacted behaviour is less pronounced, but this is mainly caused by the studies that included chronic aggression. In other words, in their personal life, right-wing individuals are less chronically aggressive than suggested by their attitudes and beliefs.

Nevertheless, subsidiary analyses revealed that in terms of the context specific aggression measures, the relationship under study is about equally strong for the attitudes favouring violence than for the corresponding behavioural indices, at least for the categories war and intergroup aggression. A significant difference was obtained for intimate violence, with studies including attitudinal measures yielding the stronger effect size as compared to the behavioural studies. But, even in the case of intimate violence, the relationships for the behavioural measure were still significant and by no means trivial.

The curious case of intimate violence

A third interesting finding pertains to Research Question 2, that is, the magnitudes of the relationships between right-wing attitudes and the various attitudes favouring aggression. The moderator effect for these different aggression types did not yield a significant difference. Especially, the comparison between intimate violence on the one hand, and the other attitudes favouring aggression towards ideological groups on the other hand elicited our interest. The observation that the effect size of the relationship between right-wing attitudes and intimate violence was almost at the same level is surprising. The severity and harshness of the kinds of aggressive imagery included in these measures is worthy of further reflection. Indeed, some of the measures for intimate violence probe the acceptance of very serious transgressions, such as acceptance of interpersonal violence and rape myth acceptance (e.g. Walker et al., 1993). These are indeed among the boldest manifestations of sexual aggression. One could have hoped that the tendency to accept such fierce expressions of intimate violence would not be tied to any ideological attitude, but our results instead testify that the acceptance of such severe forms of sexual aggression tend to go along with right-wing attitudes.

Particularly troublesome in this respect is that the studies which included a behavioural measure of intimate violence also yielded a significant, albeit weaker relationship. This finding thus indicates that right-wing adherents may also show less restraint in enacting such aggressive behaviours. These behavioural indicators are based on self-reports of behaviours enacted in the past, or of intentions and future plans in real life or in hypothetical situations where they cannot get caught.

Aggressive behaviour: chronic versus context-specific

A fourth interesting finding concerns Research Question 3 and pertains to the effect-size for chronic aggressive behaviour, $r = .13$, as compared to the context-specific aggressive behaviours, $r = .31$. Subsequent analyses of the context-specific aggressive behaviours also yielded a significant effect, with the intergroup aggression and the going to war variables as the strongest ones, $r = .38$ and $.30$, respectively, whereas the interpersonal and intimate aggression types yielded moderate effect sizes, $r = .21$ and $.25$, respectively. These results suggest that when a "good reason" is present, people scoring high on right-wing attitudes may behave aggressively, and this to a larger extent than the level suggested by their trait-wise chronic aggressive tendencies. This finding also attunes well with the writings of Altemeyer (1996) who stated that: "Right-wing authoritarianism is an individual difference variable, a personality trait if you like, developed on the premise that some individuals need little situational pressure to … attack others, while others require significantly more" (p. 8).

It should also be noted that there is a lot of heterogeneity in the magnitude of relationships among the context-specific aggression studies, which vary in the interpersonal domain between .06 (Parkins et al., 2006) and .58. (Epstein, 1965) and in the intimate domain between .06 (Hogben et al., 2001) and .40 (Tang & Fox, 2016). A closer look at some of these studies is therefore warranted. Specifically, those studies that investigated situations in which participants delivered shocks to another student (Berke & Zeichner, 2016; Epstein, 1965, 1966; Lipetz & Ossorio,

1967), often in the context of unprovoked aggression, yielded substantial effects. In these studies, the experimenter proclaimed that he or she was interested in the effects of electroshocks on learning processes. Two other included shock studies have been conducted in the context of obedience using a Milgram-like paradigm (Altemeyer, 1981; Dambrun & Vatiné, 2010). From these behavioural studies, it can thus be inferred that people scoring higher on right-wing attitudes are more inclined to deliver shocks to another person and that this effect occurs both in situations where an authority is present as well as when such an authority is lacking.

The perpetrators of interpersonal aggressions might explain their aggressive behaviours in many ways and may even think of such behaviours as being non-aggressive. For instance, high scorers on right-wing attitudes may have considered the deliverance of electroshocks to be "the necessary thing to do" for the success of the study in which they participated. They might have been surprised were they to have been told that such shocks were, in fact, a measure of aggression, as in their eyes, they only did what was expected from them. High scorers might say that harassment behaviour in video games is something that people normally do in such a situation, and they may discredit this behaviour as aggression because it occurred in a game context, not the real world. They may also consider the use of aggression for self-protection to be legitimate and much needed. Regardless of all these rationalisations, which, in fact, closely mirror the observations of Adorno et al. (1950); see also Altemeyer, 1981, 1996, 2006, the suggestion here is that high scorers on right-wing attitudes typically seem to easily "find a reason" to react aggressively when situations--in their eyes--calls for such a reaction.

Different right-wing attitudes

A final important finding, in answer of Research Question 4, is that type of right-wing measure did not moderate the effect, meaning that the relationship between right-wing attitudes and aggressive tendencies occurred for both the social-cultural and economic-hierarchical domains.[3] This result is important in terms of theory development, because it clarifies that any theory of right-wing aggression should

---

[3]It should be noted that our results do not reveal significant differences between RWA and SDO in relationship with aggressive tendencies. Such differential relationships have been obtained for some other constructs that broadly fall into the cluster of prosocial versus antiscocial tendencies. For instance, in a meta-analysis conducted by Sibley and Duckitt (2008), SDO was clearly the stronger correlate of the Five-Factor Model dimension Agreeableness, although part of this effect can be attributed to self-presentation (Ludeke et al., 2016). However, in other domains, like in social dilemma research, RWA and SDO have been found to bear relationships of more or less similar magnitude (e.g. Haesevoets et al., 2015).

incorporate processes that can be linked to both social-cultural and economic-hierarchical attitudes. Many previous studies building on the Dual Process Model (Duckitt, 2001; Duckitt et al., 2010) have shown that social-cultural and economic-hierarchical right-wing attitudes have different sources and distinctive effects, but aggressive tendencies seems to represent an exception to this.

Towards the development of a theoretical framework

How can we best explain the present findings? What processes should play a role in a general model of right-wing aggression? Such processes should fulfill at least three criteria. A first and quite obvious criterion is that potential candidates on the list are variables that have been related in the literature to *both* right-wing attitudes and to aggressive tendencies. Given that our meta-analysis reveals that aggressive tendencies are directed to a whole range of targets, a second criterion is that relevant processes should apply to a similar diversity in contexts as well. Specifically, well-known aggression cues such as the presence of weapons or increased temperatures only apply to well-defined situations and do not occur across a range of contexts, which makes them unlikely candidates as possible sources of right-wing aggression. A third criterion relates to the present finding that the aggression relationships were replicated across various right-wing attitudes. Hence, variables that are typical to one type of right-wing attitude but not to other right-wing attitudes are not the ideal candidates to explain right-wing aggression. With these three criteria in mind, we looked for variables included in integrative models of aggression (e.g. Anderson et al., 1996; Denson et al., 2012; DeWall et al., 2011) that may contribute to right-wing aggression.

As an illustration, we consider a variable that is considered to be very important in both aggression models and right-wing attitudes but is nevertheless unlikely to explain right-wing aggression because it does not fit the third criterion. Specifically, aggression models include higher-order cognition and self-control as important inhibitory mechanisms that counteract the expression of aggression. Impaired cognitive resources, such as being intoxicated (Laplace et al., 1994) or fatigued (Denson et al., 2010), have been related to increased aggression. Chronic levels of lower cognitive abilities have also been related to social-cultural ideology (for meta-analytic evidence, see Onraet et al., 2015; Van Hiel et al., 2010). However, and this is problematic in light of the present evidence that all right-wing attitudes relate alike to aggression, there is increasing evidence that the relationship between right-wing attitudes and intelligence does not hold for economic-hierarchical right-wing attitudes (e.g. Carl, 2014). Hence, cognitive capacity variables are unlikely bases of general right-wing aggression, precisely because the capacity to process information is not consistently related to all right-wing attitudes.

Variables to be included in the study of right-wing aggression

As we explained above, to be a viable candidate as a relevant variable to explain right-wing aggression, at least three criteria must be fulfilled. Lower levels of emotional intelligence and high provocation proneness fulfill all criteria and are thus very likely to be important in this respect, whereas the status of negative affect is more uncertain and should be further investigated. Finally, we assume that a variable that curbs the relationship between right-wing attitudes and aggression is also relevant in this particular domain of study. In this respect, we advance the tendency of those higher on right-wing attitudes to avoid aggression-eliciting situations or to psychologically distance themselves from aggressive tendencies as a variable to be included in the study of right-wing aggression. In the remainder of the discussion, we go into depth into each of these potentially interesting variables.

Emotional intelligence

People higher in emotional intelligence are typically better able to manage, understand, interpret, use, and deal with emotions (Petrides, 2009) and are more able to identify and describe them (Bagby et al., 1994). They show higher levels of empathy as well. Emotional intelligence relates negatively to aggression (García-Sancho et al., 2014; Richardson et al., 1994) and negatively to indicators of both social-cultural and economic-hierarchical attitudes (Onraet, Van Hiel, De keersmaecker, & Fontaine, 2017; Van Hiel et al., 2019). Hence, based on their low scores on emotional intelligence, right-wing adherents may show increased aggressive tendencies.

Provocation proneness

Another potential interesting variable resides in one's personal life history. According to the social learning perspective, people scoring high on right-wing attitudes are more likely to have experienced a punitive parental style as a child (Altemeyer, 1981, 2006). It has been argued that a punitive instead of a permissive parental style may lead to the perception of one's environment as unsafe (Duriez et al., 2007), which may result in heightened levels of threat proneness and an increased probability to chronically interpret cues as aggressive (Coccaro et al., 2007). An important contribution made in the aggression literature involves the distinction between reactive and proactive aggression (Dodge & Coie, 1987). Reactive aggressive behaviours occur in response to perceived provocation or threat, whereas proactive aggression is enacted to achieve particular benefits. We thus argue that right-wing aggression is a form of reactive aggression, not proactive aggression. Another important aspect of punitive parenting that has not granted much attention among scholars investigating ideological attitudes is the effect of corporal punishment in itself. The literature mentions many examples of "copycat" aggression: Those who witnessed aggression themselves at an early age, are more prone to use aggression themselves later on in life (see Kemme et al., 2014).

Regulation of negative affect

A third potentially interesting variable involved in right-wing aggression might reside in negative affect, which has been considered an important input factor of aggression (Berkowitz, 1989, 1993). Right-wing attitudes are hypothesised to go together with negativity bias, or the tendency to react with greater physiological responses to negative stimuli and to devote more psychological resources to them (Hibbing et al., 2014). People with right-wing attitudes are also more likely to believe that negative life events will happen to them (Lambert et al., 1999). However, the role of negative affect in right-wing attitudes is not yet well understood. It is still debated whether high scorers on right-wing attitudes are better able to cope with negative events (Van Hiel & De Clercq, 2009) or not (Duriez et al., 2012). Emotion regulation––especially in case of negative emotions––has been considered to lie at the basis of aggressive behaviour (Burt & Donellan, 2008), and therefore certainly needs to be addressed in greater detail in future research on right-wing aggression.

Avoidance

An integrated model of right-wing aggression should include a mechanism that explains why context-specific aggression yields the stronger relationships whereas the relationship with chronic aggression is curbed. Avoidance can be taken literally in terms of attempting not to confront aggression-eliciting social contexts, but it can also be understood in terms of psychological distancing, that is, minimising one's own contribution in aggression. Such additional avoidance mechanisms are necessary because they explain why the effect size of the relationship between right-wing attitudes and trait aggression is curbed, whereas it is often strong in the form of aggression in specific contexts.

Avoidance has been used to describe right-wing ideology in general, that is, the focus on preventing harm and negative outcomes in general has been conceived as the hallmark of right-wing ideology (Janoff-Bulman, 2009). High scorers on right-wing attitudes also avoid new, possibly other-minded people, which may reduce the likeability of conflicts. Specifically, they prefer familiar individuals in their social network (Altemeyer, 1981, 2006; Oesterreich, 2005; Pettigrew, 2016). They also tend to avoid contact with people of other ethnicities (Allport, 1954), a relationship that has been found to be valid for both social-cultural and economic-hierarchical attitudes (Dhont & Van Hiel, 2009). Hence, despite their increased reactivity in aggression-eliciting situations, avoidance tendencies may explain why high-scoring people on right-wing attitudes do not report higher levels of physical and verbal aggression in general.

Another avoidance mechanism might reside in psychological distancing. According to Adorno et al. (1950), right-wing adherents typically attribute aggression episodes to external sources, a phenomenon that these authors labelled scapegoating. They thus externalise blame for negative outcomes that would otherwise incriminate themselves; therefore, their self-image remains unaffected and intact (Rothschild et al., 2012). In other situations, people or institutions behaving badly are considered to have total responsibility and can therefore be blamed themselves for being treated harshly (Feather, 1996). Right-wing adherents are thus more "likely to blame victims of misfortune for the calamities that befall them" (Altemeyer, 2006, p. 52) than to consider themselves as causing the inflicted aggression. Any action inflicted on targets of aggression can be seen as legitimate and rightful (see Altemeyer, 2006) and is therefore ascribed not to the self but to the target, thus leaving the self-concept in terms of aggression unchanged.

Future studies

The present study draws attention to a number of processes that have hardly been studied empirically in the literature about right-wing aggression, and which are nevertheless worthwhile to investigate. The role of the four above-mentioned variables—emotional abilities, provocation proneness, regulation of negative affect, and avoidance—certainly merits further scholarly attention. The lack of theoretically guided studies in the investigation of the dynamics of right-wing aggression is remarkable and unfortunate. We hope that the present meta-analysis helps investigators to select variables that may explain right-wing aggression. The present list of potentially interesting process variables is not meant to be limitative, but instead we hope to have illustrated how such variables can be selected.

Another call for future studies is based on the observation that there is an underrepresentation of studies that administer behavioural measures of aggression, and this pertains to both self-reported indicators of aggression well as the observation of actual aggressive behaviour. This relative lack of research attention is also clearly present in the domain of intimate and interpersonal aggression. Especially the studies using electroshocks in a lab context (e.g. Dambrun & Vatiné, 2010; Epstein, 1965, 1966) represent a very useful paradigm to implement.

A final important issue pertains to left-wing aggression. As mentioned in the Introduction, left-wing aggression has not yet been investigated empirically. But, do the present results imply that left-wing aggression does not exist? This is certainly not the message we want to convey. It is definitely possible that typical targets of left-wing negativity, like police officers, rich people, and Evangelical Christians, elicit aggression among high scoring left-wingers. However, and this is an important point, people scoring higher on left-wing attitudes (or, put otherwise, those scoring low on right-wing attitudes) are expected to demonstrate less aggressive tendencies towards non-ideological groups, such as in interpersonal contexts and in case of intimate aggression. The fundamental distinction between right-wing and left-wing aggression thus does not reside in the fact that one of these two ideological groups were to show no aggression whatsoever whereas the other would, but instead in the observation that right-wing aggression (but not left-wing aggression) is also manifested towards non-ideological groups. Left-wing aggression is, however, an understudied phenomenon that deserves more scholarly attention.

Conclusion

From the review of accumulated evidence from 177 samples collected in different countries over a time period of six decades, we are inclined to conclude that right-wing attitudes are indeed related to aggressive tendencies. Right-wing adherents tend to agree with aggression that targets adversary countries and particular social groups and categories, and even seem to accept and enact aggression, some of which is only loosely connected to any ideology. Having said this, it should be acknowledged that more research is needed to understand why these aggressive tendencies occur. Moreover, more scholarly attention is needed to identify the aggression potential of left-wing ideologies towards typical right-wing targets.

ORCID

Dries H. Bostyn (iD) http://orcid.org/0000-0001-9994-4615
Jasper Van Assche (iD) http://orcid.org/0000-0002-2570-2928

References

References preceded by " † have been included in the meta-analysis.
Adorno, T. W., Frenkel-Brunswik, E., Levinson, D. J., & Sanford, R. N. (1950). *The authoritarian personality*. Harper and Row.
Allport, G. W. (1954). *The nature of prejudice*. Addison-Wesley.
†Altemeyer, R. A. (1981) *Right-wing authoritarianism*. University of Manitoba Press.
†Altemeyer, R. A. (1988). *Enemies of Freedom*. Jossey Bass.
†Altemeyer, R. A. (1996). *The authoritarian specter*. Harvard University Press.

†Altemeyer, R. A. (2006). *The authoritarians.* University of Manitoba. http://theauthoritarians.org/Downloads/TheAuthoritarians.pdf

†Altemeyer, R. A., & Kamenshikov, A. (1991). Impressions of American and Soviet behaviour: RWA changes in a mirror. *South African Journal of Psychology, 21* (4), 255–260. https://doi.org/10.1177/008124639102100409

Anderson, C. A., Anderson, K. B., & Deuser, W. E. (1996). Examining an affective aggression framework weapon and temperature effects on aggressive thoughts, affect, and attitudes. *Personality and Social Psychology Bulletin, 22*(4), 366–376. https://doi.org/10.1177/0146167296224004

Anderson, C. A., Benjamin, A. J., Jr., Wood, P. K., & Bonacci, A. M. (2006). Development and testing of the velicer attitudes toward violence scale: Evidence for a four-factor model. *Aggressive Behavior, 32,* 122–136. 2 https://doi.org/10.1002/ab.20112

Anderson, C. A., & Bushman, B. (2002b). The effect of media violence on society. *Science, 295*(5564), 2377–2379. https://doi.org/10.1126/science.1070765

Anderson, C. A., & Bushman, B. J. (2002a). Human aggression. *Annual Review of Psychology, 53,* 27–51. 1 https://doi.org/10.1146/annurev.psych.53.100901.135231

†Anisfeld, M., Munoz, S. R., & Lambert, W. E. (1963). The structure and dynamics of the ethnic attitudes of jewish adolescents. *The Journal of Abnormal and Social Psychology, 66*(1), 31–36. https://doi.org/10.1037/h0040287

Bagby, R. M., Parker, J. D., & Taylor, G. J. (1994). The twenty-item toronto alexithymia scale—I. Item selection and cross-validation of the factor structure. *Journal of Psychosomatic Research, 38*(1), 23–32. https://doi.org/10.1016/0022-3999(94)90005-1

†Barnes, C. D., Brown, R. P., & Osterman, L. L. (2012). Don't tread on me: Masculine honor ideology in the US and militant responses to terrorism. *Personality and Social Psychology Bulletin, 38*(8), 1018–1029. https://doi.org/10.1177/0146167212443383

†Barnes, T. N., Smith, S. W., & Miller, M. D. (2014). School-based cognitive-behavioral interventions in the treatment of aggression in the United States: A meta-analysis. *Aggression and Violent Behavior, 19*(4), 311–321. https://doi.org/10.1016/j.avb.2014.04.013

†Barron, L. G., & Ogle, A. D. (2014). Individual differences in instructor attitudes underlying maltreatment and effective mentoring in basic military training. *Military Psychology, 26*(5–6), 386–396. https://doi.org/10.1037/mil0000053

†Begany, J. J., & Milburn, M. A. (2002). Psychological predictors of sexual harassment: Authoritarianism, hostile sexism, and rape myths. *Psychology of Men and Masculinity 3*(2), 119–126. https://doi.org/10.1037/1524-9220.3.2.119

†Benjamin, A. J., Jr. (2006). The relationship between right-wing authoritarianism and attitudes toward violence: Further validation of the attitudes toward violence scale. *Journal of Social Behavior and Personality, 11*(6), 625–632. doi: 10.2224/sbp.2016.44.6.881

†Benjamin, A. J., Jr. (2016). Right-wing authoritarianism and attitudes toward torture. *Social Behavior and Personality: An International Journal, 44*(6), 881–887. https://doi.org/10.2224/sbp.2016.44.6.881

†Berke, D. S., & Zeichner, A. (2016). Testing a dual process model of gender-based violence: A laboratory examination. *Violence and Victims, 31*(2), 200–214. https://doi.org/10.1891/0886-6708.VV-D-14-00060

Berkowitz, L. (1989). Frustration-aggression hypothesis: Examination and reformulation. *Psychological Bulletin*, *106*(1), 59–73. https://doi.org/10.1037/0033-2909.106.1.59

Berkowitz, L. (1993). *Aggression: Its causes, consequences, and control*. Mcgraw-Hill Book Company.

†Besta, T., Szulc, M., & Jaśkiewicz, M. (2015). Political extremism, group membership and personality traits: Who accepts violence?/Extremismo político, pertenencia al grupo y rasgos de personalidad:¿ Quién acepta la violencia? *Revista de Psicología Social*, *30*(3), 563–585. https://doi.org/10.1080/02134748.2015.1065085

†Bizumic, B., Stubager, R., Mellon, S., Van der Linden, N., Iyer, R., & Jones, B. M. (2013). On the (in) compatibility of attitudes toward peace and war. *Political Psychology*, *34*(5), 673–693. doi: 10.1111/pops.12032

†Blumberg, H. H., Zeligman, R., Appel, L., & Tibon-Czopp, S. (2017). Personality dimensions and attitudes towards peace and war. *Journal of Aggression, Conflict and Peace Research*, *9*(1), 13–23. https://doi.org/10.1108/JACPR-05-2016-0231

Bonanno, G. A., & Jost, J. T. (2006). Conservative shift among high-exposure survivors of the September 11th terrorist attacks. *Basic and Applied Social Psychology*, *28*(4), 311–323. https://doi.org/10.1207/s15324834basp2804_4

Borenstein, M., Hedges, L. V., Higgins, J., & Rothstein, H. (2005). *Comprehensive meta-analysis version 2*. Biostat.

Brandt, M. J., Reyna, C., Chambers, J. R., Crawford, J., & Wetherell, G. (2014). The ideological conflict hypothesis: Intolerance among both liberals and conservatives. *Current Directions in Psychological Science*, *23*, 27–34. doi: 10.1177/0963721413510932

Burt, M. (1980). Cultural myths and supports for rape. *Journal of Personality and Social Psychology*, *38*(2), 217–230. doi: 10.1037/0022-3514.38.2.217

Burt, S. A., & Donellan, M. B. (2008). Personality correlates of aggressive and non-aggressive antisocial behavior. *Personality and Individual Differences*, *44*(1), 53–63. https://doi.org/10.1016/j.paid.2007.07.022

Buss, A. H., & Durkee, A. (1957). An Inventory for assessing different kinds of hostility. *Journal of Consulting Psychology*, *21*, 343–349. 4 https://doi.org/10.1037/h0046900

Buss, A. H., & Perry, M. (1992) The aggression questionnaire. *Journal of Personality and Social Psychology*, *63*, 452–459. 3 https://doi.org/10.1037/0022-3514.63.3.452

†Çamaş, G. G., & Mese, G. (2016). *Sosyal Hiyerarşi*: Cinsel Şiddet Mitlerini Anlamak. [Social hierarchy: Understanding the myths of sexual violence] *Türk Psikoloji Dergisi, Aralık 2016*, *31*, 62–74.

†Campbell, M. (2015). *The complex role of religious beliefs in supporting peaceful or violent policies: A multi-method study in the U.S. Christian context* [Unpublished doctoral dissertation]. Clark University

†Campbell, M., & Vollhardt, J. R. (2014). Fighting the good fight: The relationship between belief in evil and support for violent policies. *Personality and Social Psychology Bulletin*, *40*(1), 16–33. https://doi.org/10.1177/0146167213500997

†Canto, J. M., Perles, F., & Martín, J. S. (2014). The role of right-wing authoritarianism, sexism and culture of honour in rape myths acceptance/El papel del autoritarismo de derechas, del sexismo y de la cultura del honor en la aceptación de los mitos sobre la violación. *Revista de Psicología Social*, *29*(2), 296–318. https://doi.org/10.1080/02134748.2014.918822

Capps, J. S. (2010). *Collateral damage in Iraq and capital punishment in the USA: How the public makes sense of extreme violence and death* [Doctoral dissertation]. University of Kansas.

Carl, N. (2014). Verbal intelligence is correlated with socially and economically liberal beliefs. *Intelligence, 44*, 142–148. https://doi.org/10.1016/j.intell.2014.03.005

†Carnahan, T., & McFarland, S. (2007). Revisiting the stanford prison experiment: Could participant self-selection have led to the cruelty? *Personality and Social Psychology Bulletin, 33*(5), 603–614. https://doi.org/10.1177/0146167206292689

Coccaro, E. F., McCloskey, M. S., Fitzgerald, D. A., & Phan, K. L. (2007). Amygdala and orbitofrontal reactivity to social threat in individuals with impulsive aggression. *Biological Psychiatry, 62*(2), 168–178. https://doi.org/10.1016/j.biopsych.2006.08.024

†Cohrs, J. C., Kielmann, S., Maes, J., & Moschner, B. (2005). Effects of right-wing authoritarianism and threat from terrorism on restriction of civil liberties. *Analysis of Social Issues and Public Policy, 5*, 263–276. 1 https://doi.org/10.1111/j.1530-2415.2005.00071.x

Cohrs, J. C., Moschner, B., Maes, J., & Kielmann, S. (2005). The motivational bases of right-wing authoritarianism and social dominance orientation: Relations to values and attitudes in the aftermath of September 11, 2001. *Personality and Social Psychology Bulletin, 31*(10), 1425–1434. https://doi.org/10.1177/0146167205275614

†Colémont, A., Van Hiel, A., & Cornelis, I. (2011). Five-Factor Model personality dimensions and right-wing attitudes: Psychological bases of punitive attitudes? *Personality and Individual Differences, 50*, 486–491. 4 https://doi.org/10.1016/j.paid.2010.10.032

†Crawford, J. T., Wiley, S., & Ventresco, N. (2014). Examining Americans' attitudes toward drone strikes on the eve of the 2012 presidential election. *Analyses of Social Issues and Public Policy, 14*(1), 46–60. https://doi.org/10.1111/asap.12030

†Crowson, H. M., DeBacker, T. K., & Thoma, S. J. (2005). Does authoritarianism predict post-9/11 attitudes? *Personality and Individual Differences, 39*, 1273–1283. 7 https://doi.org/10.1016/j.paid.2005.06.005

†Crowson, M. H. (2009a). Right-wing authoritarianism and social dominance orientation as mediators of worldviews beliefs on attitudes related to the war on terror. *Social Psychology, 40*, 93–103. 2 https://doi.org/10.1027/1864-9335.40.2.93

†Crowson, M. H. (2009b). Nationalism, Internationalism, and perceived un irrelevance: Mediators of relationships between authoritarianism and support for military aggression as part of the war on terror. *Journal of Applied Social Psychology, 39*, 1137–1162. 5 https://doi.org/10.1111/j.1559-1816.2009.00475.x

†Crowson, M. H. (2009c). Are all conservatives alike? A study of the psychological correlates of cultural and economic conservatism. *Journal of Psychology, 143*(5), 449–463. doi: 10.3200/JRL.143.5.449-463

†Dambrun, M., & Vatiné, E. (2010). Reopening the study of extreme social behaviors obedience to authority within an immersive video environment. *European Journal of Social Psychology, 40*(5), 760–773. https://doi.org/10.1002/ejsp.646

Denson, T. F., DeWall, C. N., & Finkel, E. J. (2012). Self-control and aggression. *Current Directions in Psychological Science, 21*(1), 20–25. https://doi.org/10.1177/0963721411429451

Denson, T. F., von Hippel, W., Kemp, R. I., & Teo, L. S. (2010). Glucose consumption decreases impulsive aggression in response to provocation in aggressive individuals. *Journal of Experimental Social Psychology, 46*(6), 1023–1028. https://doi.org/10.1016/j.jesp.2010.05.023

DeWall, C. N., Anderson, C. A., & Bushman, B. J. (2011). The general aggression model: Theoretical extensions to violence. *Psychology of Violence, 1*(3), 245. https://doi.org/10.1037/a0023842

Dhont, K., & Van Hiel, A. (2009). We must not be enemies: Interracial contact and the reduction of prejudice among authoritarians. *Personality and Individual Differences 46*, 172–177. 2 https://doi.org/10.1016/j.paid.2008.09.022

†Djeriouat, H., & Mullet, E. (2013). Public perception of the motives that lead political leaders to launch interstate armed conflicts: A structural and cross-cultural study. *Universitas Psychologica, 12*(2), 327–346.

Dodge, K. A., & Coie, J. D. (1987). Social information processing factors in reactive and proactive aggression in children's peer groups. *Journal of Personality and Social Psychology, 53*, 1146–1158. 6 https://doi.org/10.1037/0022-3514.53.6.1146

Dodge, K. A., & Crick, N. R. (1990). Social information-processing bases of aggressive behavior in children. *Personality and Social Psychology Bulletin, 16*(1), 8–22. https://doi.org/10.1177/0146167290161002

Duckitt, J. (2001). A dual-process cognitive-motivational theory of ideology and prejudice. *Advances in Experimental Social Psychology, 33*, 41–113. doi: 10.1016/S0065-2601(01)80004-6

†Duckitt, J., Bizumic, B., Krauss, S. W., & Heled, E. (2010). A tripartite approach to right-wing authoritarianism: The authoritarianism-conservatism-traditionalism model. *Political Psychology, 31*(5), 685–715. https://doi.org/10.1111/j.1467-9221.2010.00781.x

Duriez, B., Klimstra, T. A., Luyckx, K., Beyers, W., & Soenens, B. (2012). Right-wing authoritarianism: protective factor against or risk factor for depression? *European Journal of Personality, 26*(5), 536–549. https://doi.org/10.1002/per.853

Duriez, B., Vansteenkiste, M., Soenens, B., & De Witte, H. (2007). The social costs of extrinsic relative to intrinsic goal pursuits: Their relation with social dominance and racial and ethnic prejudice. *Journal of Personality, 75*(4), 757–782. https://doi.org/10.1111/j.1467-6494.2007.00456.x

Duval, S., & Tweedie, R. (2000). A non-parametric "trim and fill" method of accounting for publication bias in meta-analysis. *Journal of the American Statistical Association, 95*(449), 89–98. https://doi.org/10.1080/01621459.2000.10473905

†Egan, V. (1989) Links between personality, ability and attitudes in a low-IQ sample. *Personality and Individual Differences, 10*, 997–1001. 9 https://doi.org/10.1016/0191-8869(89)90065-2

†Ensz, S., & Jankowski, P. J. (2017). Religiousness and rape myth acceptance: Risk and protective effects. *Journal of Interpersonal Violence*, 7-8. doi: 10.1177/0886260517698281

†Epstein, R. (1965). Authoritarianism, displaced aggression, and social status of the target. *Journal of Personality and Social Psychology, 2*, 585–589. 4 https://doi.org/10.1037/h0022494

†Epstein, R. (1966). Aggression toward outgroups as a function of authoritarianism and imitation of aggressive models. *Journal of Personality and Social Psychology, 3*, 574–579. 5 https://doi.org/10.1037/h0023290

Eysenck, H. J. (1954). *The psychology of politics.* Routledge & Kegan Paul.

†Feather, N. T. (1996). Reactions to penalties for an offense in relation to authoritarianism, values, perceived responsibility, perceived seriousness, and deservingness. *Journal of Personality and Social Psychology*, 71, 571–587. 3 https://doi.org/10.1037/0022-3514.71.3.571

†Feather, N. T., & Souter, J. (2002). Reactions to mandatory sentences in relation to the ethnic identity and criminal history of the offender. *Law and Human Behavior*, 26, 417–438. 4 https://doi.org/10.1023/A:1016331221797

Feldman, S., & Stenner, K. (1997). Perceived threat and authoritarianism. *Political Psychology*, 18, 741–770. 4 https://doi.org/10.1111/0162-895X.00077

†Fetchenhauer, D., & Bierhoff, H. W. (2004). Attitudes toward a military enforcement of human rights. *Social Justice Research*, 17, 75–92. 1 https://doi.org/10.1023/B:SORE.0000018093.23790.0d

Funder, D. C., & Ozer, D. J. (2019). Evaluating effect size in psychological research: Sense and nonsense. *Advances in Methods and Practices in Psychological Science*, 1(2), 259–269. https://doi.org/10.1177/2515245919847202

†Garcia, L. T., & Griffitt, W. (1978). Authoritarianism-situation interactions in the determination of punitiveness: Engaging authoritarian ideology. *Journal of Research in Personality*, 12(4), 469–478. https://doi.org/10.1016/0092-6566(78)90072-7

García-Sancho, E., Salguero, J. M., & Fernández-Berrocal, P. (2014). Relationship between emotional intelligence and aggression: A systematic review. *Aggression and Violent Behavior*, 19(5), 584–591. https://doi.org/10.1016/j.avb.2014.07.007

†Gehrke, R. C. (2016). *Get tough on juvenile criminals: An assessment of punitiveness and punitive attitudes* [Unpublished Master Thesis]. Minnesota State University.

†Gerber, M. M., & Jackson, J. (2013). Retribution as revenge and retribution as just deserts. *Social Justice Research*, 26, 61–80. 1 https://doi.org/10.1007/s11211-012-0174-7

†Gerber, M. M., & Jackson, J. (2016). Authority and punishment: On the ideological basis of punitive attitudes towards criminals. *Psychiatry, Psychology and Law*, 23(1), 113–134. https://doi.org/10.1080/13218719.2015.1034060

†Gerber, M. M., & Jackson, J. (2017). Justifying violence: Legitimacy, ideology and public support for police use of force. *Psychology, Crime & Law*, 23(1), 79–95. https://doi.org/10.1080/1068316X.2016.1220556

Gerevich, J., Bácskai, E., & Czobor, P. (2007). The generalizability of the buss–perry aggression questionnaire. *International Journal of Methods in Psychiatric Research*, 16(3), 124–136. https://doi.org/10.1002/mpr.221

Gignac, G. E., & Szodorai, E. T. (2016). Effect size guidelines for individual differences researchers. *Personality and Individual Differences*, 102, 74–78. https://doi.org/10.1016/j.paid.2016.06.069

†Golec de Zavala, A., Cichocka, A., Eidelson, R., & Jayawickreme, N. (2009). Collective narcissism as and its social consequences. *Journal of Personality and Social Psychology*, 97, 1074–1096. https://doi.org/10.1037/a0016904

†Golecde Zavala, A., Cichocka, A., & Iskra-Golec, I. (2013). Collective narcissism moderates the effect of in-group image threat on intergroup hostility. *Journal of Personality and Social Psychology*, 104, 1019–1039. 6 https://doi.org/10.1037/a0032215

Golecde Zavala, A., Cisłak, A., & Wesołowska, E. (2010) Political conservatism, need for cognitive closure and intergroup hostility. *Political Psychology*, 31, 521–541. 4 https://doi.org/10.1111/j.1467-9221.2010.00767.x

†Golecde Zavala, A., & Kossowska, M. (2011). Correspondence between images of terrorists and preferred approaches to counterterrorism: The moderating role of the ideological orientations. *European. Journal of Social Psychology, 41*, 538–549. 4 https://doi.org/10.1002/ejsp.810

†Golecde Zavala, A., Peker, M., Guerra, R., & Baran, T. (2016) Collective narcissism predicts hypersensitivity to in-group insult and direct and indirect retaliatory intergroup hostility. *European Journal of Personality, 30*, 532–551. 6 https://doi.org/10.1002/per.2067

†Gonzalez, J. B. (2013). *The relationship between aggression and authoritarianism* [Unpublished Master Thesis]. Texas A & M University.

†Goodnight, B. L., Cook, S. L., Parrott, D. J., & Peterson, J. L. (2014). Effects of masculinity, authoritarianism, and prejudice on antigay aggression: A path analysis of gender-role enforcement. *Psychology of Men & Masculinity, 15*, 437–444. 4 https://doi.org/10.1037/a0034565

†Guimond, S., De Oliveira, P., Kamiesjki, R., & Sidanius, J. (2010). The trouble with assimilation: Social dominance and the emergence of hostility against immigrants. *International Journal of Intercultural Relations, 34*, 642–650. 6 https://doi.org/10.1016/j.ijintrel.2010.01.002

†Gulevich, O., Sarieva, I., Nevruev, A., & Yagiyayev, I. (2017). How do social beliefs affect political action motivation? The cases of Russia and Ukraine. *Group Processes & Intergroup Relations, 20*(3), 382–395. https://doi.org/10.1177/1368430216683531

Haesevoets, T., Reinders-Folmer, C., & Van Hiel, A. (2015). Cooperation in mixed-motive games: The role of individual differences in selfish and prosocial orientation. *European Journal of Personality, 29*, 445–458. 4 https://doi.org/10.1002/per.1992

†Hantzi, A., Lampridis, E., Tsantila, K., & Bohner, G. (2015). Validation of the greek acceptance of modern myths about sexual aggression (AMMSA) scale: Examining its relationships with sexist and conservative political beliefs. *International Journal of Conflict and Violence, 9*(1), 122–133. https://doi.org/10.4119/ijcv-3072

Harré, R., & Lamb, R. (1983). *The encyclopedic dictionary of psychology*. The MIT Press.

†Hart, V. (2013). *Justice and the nature of human nature: What, why, and how beliefs and values matter* [Unpublished Doctoral Thesis]. James Madison University.

†Hastings, B. M., & Shaffer, B. A. (2005). Authoritarianism and sociopolitical attitudes in response to threats of terror. *Psychological Reports, 97*, 623–630. 6 https://doi.org/10.2466/PR0.97.6.623-630

†Heaven, P. C. L., Organ, L., Supavadeeprasit, S., & Leeson, P. R. (2006). War and prejudice: A study of social values, right-wing authoritarianism, and social dominance orientation. *Personality and Individual Differences, 40*, 599–608. 3 https://doi.org/10.1016/j.paid.2005.08.005

Hedges, L. V., & Vevea, J. L. (1998). Fixed- and random-effects models in meta-analysis. *Psychological Methods, 3*, 486–504. 4 https://doi.org/10.1037/1082-989X.3.4.486

Hemphill, J. F. (2003). Interpreting the magnitudes of correlation coefficients. *American Psychologist, 58*(1), 78–80. https://doi.org/10.1037/0003-066X.58.1.78

†Henry, P. J., Sidanius, J., Levin, S., & Pratto, F. (2005). Social dominance orientation, authoritarianism, and support for intergroup violence between the Middle East

and America. *Political Psychology, 26,* 569–583. 4 https://doi.org/10.1111/j.1467-9221.2005.00432.x

†Hetherington, M., & Suhay, E. (2011). Authoritarianism, threat, and Americans' support for the war on terror. *American Journal of Political Science, 55*(3), 546–560. https://doi.org/10.1111/j.1540-5907.2011.00514.x

Hibbing, J. R., Smith, K. B., & Alford, J. R. (2014). Differences in negativity bias underlie variations in political ideology. *Behavioral and Brain Sciences, 37*(3), 297–307. https://doi.org/10.1017/S0140525X13001192

Higgins, J., & Thompson, S. G. (2002). Quantifying heterogeneity in a meta-analysis. *Statistics in Medicine, 21*(11), 1539–1558. https://doi.org/10.1002/sim.1186

†Hockett, J. M., Saucier, D. A., Hoffman, B. H., Smith, S. J., & Craig, A. W. (2009). Oppression through acceptance? Predicting rape myth acceptance and attitudes toward rape victims. *Violence Against Women, 15*(8), 877–897. https://doi.org/10.1177/1077801209335489

†Hogben, M., Byrne, D., Hamburger, M. E., & Osland, J. (2001). Legitimized aggression and sexual coercion: Individual differences in cultural spillover. *Aggressive Behavior, 27*(1), 26–43. https://doi.org/10.1002/1098-2337(20010101/31)27:1<26::AID-AB3>3.0.CO;2-V

Holsti, O. P. 1996. *Public opinion and american foreign policy.* University of Michigan Press.

Hurwitz, J., & Peffley, M. (1990). Public images of the Soviet Union: The impact on foreign policy attitudes. *The Journal of Politics, 52*(1), 3–28. https://doi.org/10.2307/2131417

†Jackson, L. E., & Gaertner, L. (2010) Mechanisms of moral disengagement and their differential use by right-wing authoritarianism and social dominance orientation in support of war. *Aggressive Behavior 36,* 238–250. 4 https://doi.org/10.1002/ab.20344

Janoff-Bulman, R. (2009). To provide or protect: Motivational bases of political liberalism and conservatism. *Psychological Inquiry, 20,* 120–128. 2–3 https://doi.org/10.1080/10478400903028581

†Johnson, D., McDermott, R., Cowden, J., & Tingley, D. (2012). Dead certain: Confidence and conservatism predict aggression in simulated international crisis decision-making. *Human Nature, 23,* 98–126. 1 https://doi.org/10.1007/s12110-012-9134-z

†Kelly, A. J., Dubbs, S. L., & Barlow, F. K. (2015). Social dominance orientation predicts heterosexual men's adverse reactions to romantic rejection. *Archives of Sexual Behavior, 44*(4), 903–919. https://doi.org/10.1007/s10508-014-0348-5

Kemme, S., Hanslmaier, M., & Pfeiffer, C. (2014). Experience of parental corporal punishment in childhood and adolescence and it effect on punitiveness. *Journal of Family Violence, 29,* 129–142. 2 https://doi.org/10.1007/s10896-013-9564-3

Kepes, S., Banks, G. C., McDaniel, M., & Whetzel, D. L. (2012). Publication bias in the organizational sciences. *Organizational Research Methods, 15*(4), 624–662. https://doi.org/10.1177/1094428112452760

Kepes, S., McDaniel, M. A., Brannick, M. T., & Banks, G. C. (2013). Meta-analytic reviews in the organizational sciences: Two meta-analytic schools on the way to MARS (the meta-analytic reporting standards). *Journal of Business and Psychology, 28*(2), 123–143. https://doi.org/10.1007/s10869-013-9300-2

†Kossowska, M., Bukowski, M., & Van Hiel, A. (2008). The impact of submissive versus dominant authoritarianism and negative emotions on prejudice.

Personality and Individual Differences, 45(8), 744–749. https://doi.org/10.1016/j. paid.2008.07.022

†Kteily, N., Hodson, G., & Bruneau, E. (2016). They see us as less than human: Metadehumanization predicts intergroup conflict via reciprocal dehumanization. *Journal of Personality and Social Psychology, 110*(3), 343–370. https://doi.org/10. 1037/pspa0000044

Lambert, A. J., Burroughs, T., & Nguyen, T. (1999). Perceptions of risk and the buffering hypothesis: The role of just world beliefs and right-wing authoritarianism. *Personality and Social Psychology Bulletin, 25*(6), 643–656. https://doi.org/10.1177/0146167299025006001

Laplace, A. C., Chermack, S. T., & Taylor, S. P. (1994). Effects of alcohol and drinking experience on human physical aggression. *Personality and Social Psychology Bulletin, 20*(4), 439–444. https://doi.org/10.1177/0146167294204011

†Larsson, M. R., Björklund, F., & Bäckström, M. (2012). Right-wing authoritarianism is a risk factor of torture-like abuse, but so is social dominance orientation. *Personality and Individual Differences, 53*, 927–929. 7 https://doi.org/10.1016/j. paid.2012.06.015

†LeeChai, A. Y., & Bargh, J. A. (Eds.). (2001). *The use and abuse of power: Multiple perspectives on the causes of corruption*. Psychology Press.

Lemery, K. S., Essex, M. J., & Smider, N. A. (2002). Revealing the relation between temperament and behavior problem symptoms by eliminating measurement confounding: Expert ratings and factor analyses. *Child Development, 73*, 867–882. 3 https://doi.org/10.1111/1467-8624.00444

Lengua, L. J., West, S. G., & Sandler, I. N. (1998). Temperament as a predictor of symptomatology in children: Addressing contamination of measures. *Child Development, 69*, 164–181. 1 https://doi.org/10.1111/j.1467-8624. 1998.tb06141.x

Levin, S., Roccas, S., Sidanius, J., & Pratto, F. (2015). Personal values and intergroup outcomes of concern for group honor. *Personality and Individual Differences, 86*, 374–384. https://doi.org/10.1016/j.paid.2015.06.047

†Lindén, M., Björklund, F., & Bäckström, M. (2016). What makes authoritarian and socially dominant people more positive to using torture in the war on terrorism? *Personality and Individual Differences, 91*, 98–101. https://doi.org/10.1016/j.paid. 2015.11.058

†Lipetz, M. E., & Ossorio, P. G. (1967). Authoritarianism, aggression, and status. *Journal of Personality and Social Psychology, 5*, 468–472. 4 https://doi.org/10.1037/ h0021214

†Lippa, R., & Arad, S. (1999). Gender, personality,and prejudice: The display of authoritarianism and social dominance in interviews with college men and women. *Journal of Research in Personality 33*, 463–493. 33 4 https://doi.org/10. 1006/jrpe.1999.2266

Lipset, S. (1981). *Political man: The social basis of politics*. The John Hopkins University Press.

Lipsey, M. W., & Wilson, D. B. (2001). *Practical meta-analysis*. Sage Publications, Inc.

†Ljubin, T., & Grubišić-Ilić, M. (2002). Some factors related to police cadets' perceptions of deviant police behavior. In *Policing in Central and Eastern Europe: Deviance, Violence and Victimization: Conference Proceedings* (pp. 387–394), Ljubljana.

Ludeke, S., Tagar, M. R., & De Young, C. G. (2016). Not as different as we want to be: Attitudinally consistent trait desirability leads to exaggerated associations between personality and sociopolitical attitudes. *Political Psychology, 37*, 125–135. 1 https://doi.org/10.1111/pops.12221

†Lyall, H. C., & Thorsteinsson, E. B. (2007). Attitudes to the Iraq war and mandatory detention of asylum seekers: Associations with authoritarianism, social dominance, and mortality salience. *Australian Journal of Psychology, 59*(2), 70–77. https://doi.org/10.1080/00049530601148421

†Malka, A., & Soto, C. J. (2011). The conflicting influences of religiosity on attitude toward torture. *Personality and Social Psychology Bulletin, 37*(8), 1091–1103. https://doi.org/10.1177/0146167211406508

†Mayeux, L. (2014). Understanding popularity *and* relational aggression in adolescence: The role of social dominance orientation. *Social Development, 23*, 502–517. 3 https://doi.org/10.1111/sode.12054

†McFarland, S. G. (1998). *Toward a typology of prejudiced persons*. Paper presented at the annual convention of the International Society for Political Psychology, Montreal, Canada, July.

†McFarland, S. G. (1999, July). *Personality, values, and latent prejudice: A test of a causal model*. Paper presented at the annual convention of the International Society for Political Psychology, Amsterdam, the Netherlands.

†McFarland, S. G., & Adelson, S. (1996). *An omnibus study of personality, values and prejudices*. Paper presented at the Annual Convention of the International Society for Political Psychology, Vancouver, British Columbia.

†McFarland, S. G., Ageyev, V. S., & Djintcharadze, N. (1996). Russian authoritarianism two years after communism. *Personality and Social Psychology Bulletin, 22*, 210–217. 2 https://doi.org/10.1177/0146167296222010

†McFarland. S. G. (2005). On the eve of war: Authoritarianism, social dominance, and american students' attitudes toward attacking Iraq. *Personality and Social Psychology Bulletin, 31*, 360–367. 3 https://doi.org/10.1177/0146167204271596

†McKee, I. R., & Feather, N. T. (2008). Revenge, retribution, and values: Social attitudes and punitive sentencing. *Social Justice Research, 21*, 138–163. 2 https://doi.org/10.1007/s11211-008-0066-z

†Međedović, J., & Petrović, B. (2016). The militant extremist mind-set as a conservative ideology mediated by ethos of conflict. *Peace and Conflict: Journal of Peace Psychology, 22*(4), 404–408. https://doi.org/10.1037/pac0000175

†Melikian, L. H. (1956). Some correlates of authoritarianism in two cultural groups. *The Journal of Psychology, 42*(2), 237–248. https://doi.org/10.1080/00223980.1956.9713037

†Messick, S., & Frederikson, N. (1958). Ability, acquiescence, and "authoritarianism." *Psychological Reports, 4*, 687–697. https://doi.org/10.2466/PR0.4.7.687-697

Middendorp, C. (1978). *Progressiveness and conservatism. the fundamental dimensions of ideological controversy and their relationship to social class.* Mouton.

†Milburn, M. A., Niwa, M., & Patterson, M. D. (2014). Authoritarianism, anger, and hostile attribution bias: A test of affect displacement. *Political Psychology, 35*(2), 225–243. https://doi.org/10.1111/pops.12061

†Mitchell, H. E., & Byrne, D. (1973). The defendant's dilemma: Effects of jurors' attitudes and authoritarianism on judicial decisions. *Journal of Personality and Social Psychology, 25*, 123–129. 1 https://doi.org/10.1037/h0034263

Moran, G., & Comfort, J. C. (1986). Neither" tentative" nor" fragmentary": Verdict preference of impaneled felony jurors as a function of attitude toward capital punishment. *Journal of Applied Psychology, 71*(1), 146. https://doi.org/10.1037/0021-9010.71.1.146

†Motyl, M., Hart, J., & Pyszczysnki, T. (2010). When animals attack: The effects of mortality salience, infrahumanization of violence, and authoritarianism on support for war. *Journal of Experimental Social Psychology, 46*, 200–203. 1 https://doi.org/10.1016/j.jesp.2009.08.012

Mullen, B. (1989). *Advanced BASIC meta-analysis.* Lawrence Erlbaum Associates.

†Navarrete, C. D., McDonald, M. M., Molina, L. E., & Sidanius, J. (2010). Prejudice at the nexus of race and gender: An outgroup male target hypothesis. *Journal of Personality and Social Psychology, 98*, 933–945. 6 https://doi.org/10.1037/a0017931

†Nofziger, H. A. (2013). *The psychology of genocide and the perpetration of extreme violence (PEV) model* [Unpublished doctoral dissertation]. The State University of New Jersey.

Oesterreich, D. (2005). Flight into security: A new approach and measure of the authoritarian personality. *Political Psychology, 26*(2), 275–298. https://doi.org/10.1111/j.1467-9221.2005.00418.x

Onraet, E., Van Hiel, A., De Keersmaecker, J., & Fontaine, J. R. J. (2017). The relationship of trait emotional intelligence with right-wing attitudes and subtle racial prejudice. *Personality and Individual Differences, 110*, 27–30. https://doi.org/10.1016/j.paid.2017.01.017

Onraet, E., Van Hiel, A., & Dhont, K. (2013). The relationship between right-wing ideological attitudes and psychological well-being. *Personality and Social Psychology Bulletin, 39*, 509–522. 4 https://doi.org/10.1177/0146167213478199

Onraet, E., Van Hiel, A., Dhont, K., Hodson, G., Schittekatte, M., & De Pauw, S. (2015). The association of cognitive ability with right-wing ideological attitudes and prejudice: A meta-analytic review. *European Journal of Personality 29*, 599–621. 6 https://doi.org/10.1002/per.2027

Onraet, E., Van Hiel, A., Dhont, K., & Pattyn, S. (2013). Internal and external threat in relationship with right-wing attitudes. *Journal of Personality, 83*, 233–248. 3 https://doi.org/10.1111/jopy.12011

†Palasinski, M., & Shortland, N. (2016). Individual determinants of punitive attitudes towards sexual and domestic abuse offenders. *Safer Communities, 15*(3), 125–133. https://doi.org/10.1108/SC-03-2016-0007

†Parkins, I. S., Fishbein, H. D., & Ritchey, P. N. (2006). The influence of personality on workplace bullying and discrimination. *Journal of Applied Social Psychology, 36*, 2554–2577. 10 https://doi.org/10.1111/j.0021-9029.2006.00117.x

†Peterson, B. E., Doty, R. M., & Winter, D. G. (1993). Authoritarianism and attitudes toward contemporary social issues. *Personality and Social Psychology Bulletin, 19* (2), 174–184. https://doi.org/10.1177/0146167293192006

†Peterson, B. E., Pratt, M. W., Olsen, J. R., & Alisat, S. (2016). The authoritarian personality in emerging adulthood: Longitudinal analysis using standardized scales, observer ratings, and content coding of the life story. *Journal of Personality, 84*, 225–236. 2 https://doi.org/10.1111/jopy.12154

Petrides, K. V. (2009). Psychometric properties of the trait emotional intelligence questionnaire (TEIQue). In *Assessing Emotional Intelligence,* C. Stough, D. H. Saklofske, & J. D. A. Parker (Eds.) (pp. 85–101). Springer US.

Pettigrew, T. F. (2016). In pursuit of three theories: Authoritarianism, relative deprivation, and intergroup contact. *Annual Review of Psychology, 67,* 1–21. 1 https://doi.org/10.1146/annurev-psych-122414-033327

†Pratto, F., Sidanius, J., Stallworth, L., & Malle, B. (1994). Social dominance orientation: A personality variable predicting social and political attitudes. *Journal of Personality and Social Psychology, 67,* 741–763. 4 https://doi.org/10.1037/0022-3514.67.4.741

R Core Team (2013). *R: A language and environment for statistical computing.*

Richardson, D. R., Hammock, G. S., Smith, S. M., Gardner, W., & Signo, M. (1994). Empathy as a cognitive inhibitor of interpersonal aggression. *Aggressive Behavior, 20*(4), 275–289. https://doi.org/10.1002/1098-2337(1994)20:4<275::AID-AB2480200402>3.0.CO;2-4

†Roberts, A. H., & Jessor, R. (1958). Authoritarianism, punitiveness, and perceived social status. *The Journal of Abnormal and Social Psychology, 56,* 311–314. 3 https://doi.org/10.1037/h0040779

†Rothschild, Z. K., Abdollahi, A., & Pyszczynski, T. (2009). Does peace have a prayer? The effect of mortality salience, compassionate values, and religious fundamentalism on hostility toward out-groups. *Journal of Experimental Social Psychology, 45* (4), 816–827. https://doi.org/10.1016/j.jesp.2009.05.016

Rothschild, Z. K., Landau, M. J., Sullivan, D., & Keefer, L. A. (2012). A dual-motive model of scapegoating: Displacing blame to reduce guilt or increase control. *Journal of Personality and Social Psychology, 102*(6), 1148. https://doi.org/10.1037/a0027413

†Russell, B. L., & Trigg, K. Y. (2004). Tolerance of sexual harassment: An examination of gender differences, ambivalent sexism, social dominance, and gender roles. *Sex Roles, 50,* 565–573. 7/8 https://doi.org/10.1023/B:SERS.0000023075.32252.fd

†Saucier, D. A., Stanford, A. J., Miller, S. S., Martens, A. L., Miller, A. K., Jones, T. L., ... Burns, M. D. (2016). Masculine honor beliefs: Measurement and correlates. *Personality and Individual Differences, 94,* 7–15. https://doi.org/10.1016/j.paid.2015.12.049

†Schlachter, A., & Duckitt, J. (2002). Psychopathology, authoritarian attitudes, and prejudice. *South African Journal of Psychology, 32*(2), 1–8. https://doi.org/10.1177/008124630203200201

†Schulz, W., & Weiss, H. (1993). Conservatism and the political views of young men in Austria. *European Sociological Review, 9,* 79–93. 1 https://doi.org/10.1093/oxfordjournals.esr.a036662

Sibley, C. G., & Duckitt, J. (2008). Personality and prejudice: A meta-analysis and theoretical review. *Personality and Social Psychology Review, 12,* 248–279. 3 https://doi.org/10.1177/1088868308319226

Sibley, C. G., Wilson, M. S., & Duckitt, J. (2007). Antecedents of men's hostile and benevolent sexism: The dual roles of social dominance orientation and right-wing authoritarianism. *Personality and Social Psychology Bulletin, 33*(2), 160–172. https://doi.org/10.1177/0146167206294745

†Sidanius, J., & Liu, J. H. (1992) The gulf war and the rodney king beating: Implications of the general conservatism and social dominance perspectives.

Journal of Social Psychology, 136, 685–700. 6 https://doi.org/10.1080/00224545.1992.9712099

Sidanius, J., & Pratto, F. (2001). *Social dominance: An intergroup theory of social hierarchy and oppression*. Cambridge University Press.

†Siegel, S. M. (1956). The relationship of hostility to authoritarianism. *Journal of Abnormal and Social Psychology*, 52, 368–372. 3 https://doi.org/10.1037/h0046038

†Singer, R. D., & Feshbach, S. (1959). Some relationships between manifest anxiety, authoritarian tendencies, and modes of reaction to frustration. *Journal of Abnormal and Social Psychology*, 59, 404–408. 3 https://doi.org/10.1037/h0044511

†Snortum, J. R., & Ashear, V. H. (1972). Prejudice, punitiveness, and personality. *Journal of Personality Assessment*, 36, 291–296. 3 https://doi.org/10.1080/00223891.1972.10119759

Stellmacher, J., & Petzel, T. (2005). Authoritarianism as a group phenomenon. *Political Psychology*, 26, 245–274. 2 https://doi.org/10.1111/j.1467-9221.2005.00417.x

Stenner, K. (2005). *The authoritarian dynamic*. Cambridge University Press.

Süssenbach, P., & Bohner, G. (2011). Acceptance of sexual aggression myths in a representative sample of German residents. *Aggressive Behavior*, 37, 374–385. 4 https://doi.org/10.1002/ab.20390

†Tam, K. P., Leung, K. Y., & Chiu, C. Y. (2008). On being a mindful authoritarian: Is need for cognition always associated with less punitiveness? *Political Psychology*, 29, 77–91. 1 https://doi.org/10.1111/j.1467-9221.2007.00613.x

†Tang, W. Y., & Fox, J. (2016). Men's harassment behavior in online video games: Personality traits and game factors. *Aggressive Behavior*, 42(6), 513–521. https://doi.org/10.1002/ab.21646

†Thomsen, L., Green, E. G. T., & Sidanius, J. (2008). We will hunt them down: How social dominance orientation and right-wing authoritarianism fuel ethnic persecution of immigrants in fundamentally different ways. *Journal of Experimental Social Psychology*, 44, 1455–1464. 6 https://doi.org/10.1016/j.jesp.2008.06.011

†Torabian, S., & Abalakina, M. (2012). Attitudes toward war in the United States and Iran. *Iranian Studies*, 45(4), 463–478. https://doi.org/10.1080/00210862.2012.673825

†VailIII, K. E., Arndt, J., Motyl, M., & Pyszczynski, T. (2012). The aftermath of destruction: Images of destroyed buildings increase support for war, dogmatism, and death thought accessibility. *Journal of Experimental Social Psychology*, 48(5), 1069–1081. https://doi.org/10.1016/j.jesp.2012.05.004

van Aert, R. C., Wicherts, J. M., & van Assen, M. A. (2016). Conducting meta-analyses based on p values. *Perspectives on Psychological Science*, 11, 713–729. 5 https://doi.org/10.1177/1745691616650874

van Assen, M. A. L. M., van Aert, R. C. M., & Wicherts, J. M. (2015). Meta-analysis using effect size distributions of only statistically significant studies. *Psychological Methods*, 20, 293–309. 3 https://doi.org/10.1037/met0000025

Van Hiel, A., Cornelis, I., Roets, A., & De Clercq, B. (2007). A comparison of various authoritarianism scales in Belgian Flanders. *European Journal of Personality* 21, 149–168. 2 https://doi.org/10.1002/per.617

Van Hiel, A., & De Clercq, B. (2009). Authoritarianism is good for you: Right-wing authoritarianism as a buffering factor for mental distress. *European Journal of Personality, 23*, 33–50. 1 https://doi.org/10.1002/per.702

Van Hiel, A., De Keersmaecker, J., Onraet, E., Haesevoets, T., Roets, A., & Fontaine, J. R. J. (2019). The relationship between emotional abilities and right-wing and prejudiced attitudes. *Emotion, 19*(5), 917–922. https://doi.org/10.1037/emo0000497

Van Hiel, A., Duriez, B., & Kossowska, M. (2006). The presence of left-wing authoritarianism in Western Europe and its relationship with conservative ideology. *Political Psychology 27*, 769–793. 5 https://doi.org/10.1111/j.1467-9221.2006.00532.x

Van Hiel, A., & Kossowska, M. (2007). Contemporary attitudes and their ideological representation in Flanders (Belgium), Poland, and the Ukraine. *International Journal of Psychology 42*, 16–26. 1 https://doi.org/10.1080/00207590500411443

Van Hiel, A., Onraet, E., Crowson, H. M., & Roets, A. (2016). The relationship between right-wing attitudes and cognitive style: A comparison of self-report and behavioral measures of rigidity and intolerance of ambiguity. *European Journal of Personality, 30*, 523–531. 6 https://doi.org/10.1002/per.2082

Van Hiel, A., Onraet, E., & De Pauw, S. (2010). The relationship between social-cultural attitudes and behavioral measures of cognitive style: A meta-analytic integration of studies. *Journal of Personality, 78*, 1765–1799. 6 https://doi.org/10.1111/j.1467-6494.2010.00669.x

†Vidmar, N. (1974). Retributive and utilitarian motives and other correlates of Canadian attitudes toward the death penalty. *Canadian Psychologist/Psychologie Canadienne, 15*, 337–356. 4 https://doi.org/10.1037/h0081769

Viechtbauer, W. (2010). Conducting meta-analyses in R with the metafor package. *Journal of Statistical Software, 36*(3), 1–48. https://doi.org/10.18637/jss.v036.i03

†Walker, W. D., Rowe, R. C., & Quinsey, V. L. (1993). Authoritarianism and sexual aggression. *Journal of Personality and Social Psychology, 65*, 1036–1045. 5 https://doi.org/10.1037/0022-3514.65.5.1036

†Washburn, A. N., & Skitka, L. J. (2015). Motivated and displaced revenge: Remembering 9/11 suppresses opposition to military intervention in Syria (for some). *Analyses of Social Issues and Public Policy, 15*(1), 89–104. https://doi.org/10.1111/asap.12062

†Webster, R. J., & Saucier, D. A. (2013). Angels and demons are among us: Assessing individual differences in belief in pure evil and belief in pure good. *Personality and Social Psychology Bulletin, 39*(11), 1455–1470. https://doi.org/10.1177/0146167213496282

ARTICLE

Social game theory: Preferences, perceptions, and choices

Joachim I. Krueger[a], Patrick R. Heck [b], Anthony M. Evans [c] and Theresa E. DiDonato[d]

[a]Department of Cognitive, Linguistic & Psychological Sciences, Brown University, Providence, RI, USA; [b]Geisinger Health System, Lewisburg, PA, USA; [c]Department of Social Psychology, Tilburg University, Tilburg, Netherlands; [d]Psychology Department, Loyola University Maryland, Baltimore, MD, USA

ABSTRACT
Building on classic game theory, psychologists have explored the effects of social preferences and expectations on strategic behaviour. Ordinary social perceivers are sensitive to additional contextual factors not addressed by game theory and its recent psychological extensions. We review the results of a research programme exploring how observers judge "players" (i.e., individuals making strategic decisions in social dilemmas) on the dimensions of competence and morality. We explore social perception in several well-known dilemmas, including the prisoner's dilemma, the volunteer's dilemma, and the trust dilemma. We also introduce a novel self-presentational dilemma. In research conducted over a decade and a half, we have found that judgements of competence are sensitive to both players' choices and the dilemma's (expected and actual) outcomes. In contrast, judgements of morality respond strongly to players' behaviour and little else. We discuss how these social-perceptual patterns might affect expectations, preferences, and strategic choices.

ARTICLE HISTORY Received 16 December 2019; Accepted 1 June 2020

KEYWORDS Social dilemmas; social perception; reputation; cooperation; moral judgement

It is just as foolish to complain that people are selfish and treacherous as it is to complain that the magnetic field does not increase unless [it] has a curl. Both are laws of nature. – John von Neumann, as quoted by E. Wigner (1967, p. 261)

When John von Neumann (1928) introduced his ideas about parlour games, or *Gesellschaftsspiele*, few anticipated that his mathematical approach to strategic behaviour would take the social sciences by storm. This storm still rages today, continually reshaping science and public discourse (Brams, 2004). The main impact of game theory has been to show how rational and self-interested agents operate in uncertain environments populated by other rational and self-interested agents. The theory assumes that people play to

CONTACT Joachim I. Krueger joachim_krueger@brown.edu Department of Cognitive, Linguistic & Psychological Sciences, Brown University., Providence, RI 02912, USA
© 2020 European Association of Social Psychology

win, that is, that they seek to maximise their own expected value. It soon became apparent, however, that many of these games yield no winners if all players act rationally. The object of game-theoretically rational player then reduces to the more modest goal of not being exploited. When all manage to do this, there are no longer any losers either. For symmetrical games, social interaction turns into a fair affair. Everyone does as well as is mathematically possible.

Game theory predicts equilibrium outcomes, but it does not guarantee collective riches. The outcome can be a lose-lose affair – as in the prisoner's dilemma – where pairs of irrational players could have done better. Individual players can win only if others err because they are, for instance, distracted or stupid. Game theory allows naïve players to leave an advantage to savvy players, but this advantage should decline as the former learn from experience. One might say that the theory treats equilibria as attractors. Like the *Logos* of Greek tragedy, they draw human choice to what is mathematically necessary (Binmore, 2007; Hardin, 1968).

Within two decades after its first sketch, game theory received its full formal expression, and within a few years after the publication of the master-work (von Neumann & Morgenstern, 1944), many of its crucial elements had been worked out (Luce & Raiffa, 1957; Rapoport, 1966). It took another two decades for psychology and other social sciences to incorporate game theory into their study of human behaviour, document its limitations as a descriptive theory, and propose modifications and extensions (Kelley & Thibaut, 1978; Pruitt & Kimmel, 1977; Rapoport, 1966). Theories of behavioural (Camerer, 2003) or psychological game theory (Colman, 2003) sprang up, and the term "social dilemma" slowly replaced the term "game" (Dawes, 1980; Murnighan & Wang, 2016; van Lange et al., 2017). This semantic shift signalled the rise of a new paradigm. The thinking and feeling player began to be recognised as a person who brings more to the table than a set of coherent preferences. This player experiences, beliefs, and expectations, as well as cognitive capacities of varying depth and sophistication (Usher et al., 2019). Being socially intelligent, this player wonders what others will do, and why (Rabin, 1993), and use the results of such "mentalizing" to make his or her own decisions. Ultimately, this psychologically engaged person may be playing a game that is different from the one intended by the game theorist (Halevy et al., 2012).

Classic game theory does not tap the richness of the psychological world. Although the theory is elegant and coherent, it fails to predict human cooperation in many settings. One pragmatic approach to this descriptive shortfall is to retain game theory's analytical arsenal and to evaluate human behaviour against a background of idealised rationality. When researchers find surprisingly high rates of cooperation (Sally, 1995), for example, they can search for the psychological processes that account for the difference.

People's choices – and their associated beliefs, expectations, and perceptions – are psychologically rich and interdependent. In this review, we summarise the results of research that asks how people judge decisions made by others in several social dilemmas. The study of third-party social perception is of theoretical interest because strategically acting humans seek to manage their self-images and social reputations (Jordan & Rand, 2020). Decisions made when interacting with others, or merely in the presence of others, are necessarily social. As reflected appraisals, social perceptions and judgements can become co-determinants of social choice.

We focus on two-person one-shot games, played among strangers whose preferences are not perfectly aligned. Each game offers a choice between two strategies, conveniently labelled cooperation and defection, resulting in four possible combinations of outcomes. Many different games are possible (Rapoport & Guyer, 1966), but only a few have captured the imaginations of both researchers and the public. We begin with a review of the "the big three" (Kollock, 1998), namely the prisoner's dilemma, the assurance game (or stag hunt), and the game of chicken (or hawk-dove or snowdrift game). Then, we describe findings from a research program exploring how third-party observers perceive and judge players along the dimensions of competence and morality. Of the big three, we focus on the prisoner's dilemma. We then move on to the volunteer's dilemma, which is related to the game of chicken, the sequential game of trust, which is related to the assurance game, and finally a dilemma of self-enhancement obtained from a recasting of social comparisons in game-theoretic lights. We conclude with some thoughts about how the presented concepts and findings might serve as building blocks for a more comprehensive and social psychological variant of game theory.

The big three games

The prisoner's dilemma

The prisoner's dilemma takes its name from a scenario used by Professor Albert Tucker to introduce his students to the conflict and its theory. In his scenario, two suspects are held in separate cells. The prosecutor offers each the following terms if they confess: "If the other does not confess, you go free; if the other also confesses, you each receive a 10-year sentence. If you do not confess, you receive a 5-year sentence for a lesser crime if the other also refuses to confess; but if the other confesses, your refusal will earn you 20 years in prison." This scenario is a bit roundabout because it frames the consequences as losses. At any rate, it is clear that confession amounts to defection from the other suspect and that a refusal to confess amounts to cooperation (with the other suspect, not the prosecutor!). This is a dilemma because mutual cooperation (refusals to confess) results in a lesser sentence (5 years) than mutual defection (confessing) does (10 years). Yet, each suspect is better off confessing regardless of what the other does (see Poundstone, 1992, for an excellent and accessible introduction to the prisoner's dilemma and other essential games).

One horn of the dilemma is that an individual player obtains a better outcome from defection, no matter what the other one does; the other horn is that players collectively prefer mutual cooperation over mutual defection. Rapoport's (1967) notation offers a convenient way to describe games in an abstract and general way. This notation uses positive numbers, where larger values are preferred. Specifically, the payoffs are labelled T ("Temptation" = 4) for unilateral defection; R ("Reward" = 3) for mutual cooperation; P ("Penalty" = 2) for mutual defection; and S ("Sucker" = 1) for unilateral cooperation. The preference ranking of $T > R > P > S$ constitutes a prisoner's dilemma (see Appendix A).[1] Game theory holds that rational players defect, and thus a pair of defectors does worse than a pair of cooperators ($2P < 2R$). Though appealing, mutual cooperation is not an equilibrium state. If both players cooperated, each would have an incentive to defect. Thinking only about their own transition from cooperation to defection, players might seek the improvement offered by T over R. As game theory does not consider a temporary state of mutual cooperation, it does not conceptualise one player's defection from a state that should have never occurred in the first place. The theory recognises defection as the dominating strategy (Savage, 1954). It's a sure thing; whatever the other player does, the defector is better off than the cooperator (Shafir & Tversky, 1992). As a Nash equilibrium, mutual defection is a state of poverty. It can't be helped, according to the theory.[2]

The assurance game

This game at first resembles the prisoner's dilemma. Again, players prefer mutual cooperation over mutual defection, but defection is not a dominating strategy (Skyrms, 2003). Rousseau (1754/1984) described a "stag hunt" to illustrate the problem. Two hunters do well if they cooperate and slay a stag ($R = 4$). If one defects from this joint project by stalking a small deer instead, he will have less meat ($T = 3$), while the other hunter returns home empty-handed ($S = 1$). If both defect, each can at least snare a hare for a modest supper ($P = 2$). This preference ranking of $R > T > P > S$ shows that the critical difference to the prisoner's dilemma lies in the inversion of the top

---

[1] An efficiency constraint of $2R > (T + S)$ ensures that two cooperators do collectively better than a cooperator-defector pair.

[2] Appendix B shows payoff matrices for the prisoner's dilemma and other games studied in this research, but not for the assurance game or the game of chicken.

two preferences. Individual rationality does not demand defection, but neither does it guarantee cooperation.

The puzzle is why a player would not cooperate in such a benign game. If mutual cooperation is achieved, neither player has an incentive to defect. Alas, mutual cooperation is not guaranteed because cooperation is not a dominating strategy. If the other's choice is not known, a player *might* defect, especially if this player fears, for whatever reason, that the other might defect. This player would love to have an assurance of the other's cooperation. Then, cooperation would be the best response. If the trigger of defection is the fear that the other player might defect, where does this fear originate? There is no unique point of origin. A player may worry that the other player is fearful, perhaps because that player fears the first player is fearful, a sentiment which quickly devolves into an infinite regress (Klein, 1999).

Game theory provides a circuit breaker with a strategy of probabilistic cooperation. The goal is to cooperate with that probability, which makes the other player indifferent between cooperation and defection. If one player cooperates with this particular probability, then the expected values of cooperation and defection are the same for the other player. If one treats the ranked payoffs as interval scaled, the equilibrium probability of cooperation is $p = (S - P)/(S + T - R - P)$ (Krueger, Evans et al., 2017). For preference values running from 1 to 4, $p = .5$. When both players use this strategy, they protect themselves from exploitation, but they do worse than they would if they both cooperated. As in the prisoner's dilemma, the game theoretic solution is still a lose-lose proposition.

The game of chicken

If the reassurance game is "nicer" than the prisoner's dilemma, the game of chicken is "nastier." The dilemma derives its name from legends of reckless competition between dominance-seeking youths equipped with fast cars. As two drivers speed towards each other, each must choose between the cooperative move of swerving right and the competitive strategy of staying the course, which amounts to defection. The most desirable outcome is to get the other to swerve. If this happens, the defector wins ($T = 4$), while the cooperator is the chicken ($S = 2$). If both swerve ($R = 3$), they live to compete another day. If both count on the other to swerve, both find that this was their last race ($P = 1$).

Compared with the prisoner's dilemma, the game of chicken reverses the order of the two lowest preferences such that $T > R > S > P$ (Rapoport & Chammah, 1966). Mutual defection is catastrophic, and it is no longer a Nash equilibrium. Neither defection nor cooperation are dominating strategies. Ideally, a player would counter the other's strategy by doing the opposite. Not knowing the opponent's choice, the player can only resort to a probabilistic strategy, which is the same as in the assurance game. Assuming self-interest, the only psychological motive is to avoid exploitation.

The big three games in review

This sketch of the three most prominent games shows that game theory prepares fertile ground for the study of social behaviour, but that it shortcuts much of the psychological complexity. Game theory makes no room for social interest or social intelligence. In the prisoner's dilemma, a rational player only needs to be able to rank the payoffs to recognise defection as the dominating strategy. In contrast, a rational player needs a calculator in the games of stag and chicken in order to avoid exploitation. What is missing from game theory is that real players worry about some properties of the social situation that are not represented in the payoff matrices. We now consider some traditional behavioural theories, which are concerned with social preferences and predictions.

Social preferences and predictions

Psychology enters the picture when people find themselves in real-world dilemmas. Many spontaneously ask with whom or against whom they are playing. Ordinary people often imagine a known partner about whom they care. The closer they assume that person to be to them in social or psychological terms, the more optimistic they are that this person will cooperate and the more they consider that person's payoffs when making their own choice.

A known person resides at a shorter social-psychological distance[3] than a stranger, and if the game offers the highest collective payoff for mutual cooperation, cooperation is more attractive than classic game theory predicts (Krueger et al., 2016). The cooperation-inducing properties of social preferences, that is, the willingness to assign a positive weight to the other person's payoffs, and expectations of cooperation are aligned over social distance (Bogaert et al., 2008). A prosocial person values a friend's payoffs and transforms the objective values into subjective ones by adding the friend's values – with a positive weight – to his or her own (Bohnet & Frey, 1999). This prosocial person also expects the friend to do the same, and to cooperate with a high probability. This expected high probability becomes part of the prosocial person's strategic calculation and further increases the probability of cooperating.

---

[3]Use of the term "psychological distance" or "social distance" is a convenient if imprecise terminological shortcut to capture a multiplicity of ways in which individuals are separated from one another. A low distance may, for example, indicate frequent exposure to and high familiarity with one another, or it may refer to the degree of genetic relatedness or the degree of interdependence in one's outcomes.

In the game of chicken, the joint effects of social preferences and expectations are more complex. A prosocial player may transform objective payoffs into subjective ones in the same way he or she would in a prisoner's dilemma or a stag hunt. Assuming a positive weight of .5 assigned to the friend's payoffs, and using given payoff values from 4 (best) down to 1 (worst), the subjectively transformed values are $T = 5$, $R = 4.5$, $S = 4$, and $P = 1.5$. The resulting equilibrium strategy is to cooperate with $p = .833$. There is little room for expectations to undo the drift towards mutual cooperation. Only a player who is nearly certain that the other will cooperate might consider defection for a small extra gain. But this would probably not be the kind of person who made the prosocial value transformation in the first place. Conversely, a player who retains the untransformed values will defect if expecting the other to cooperate, and will cooperate if expecting defection. In short, both social preferences and social expectations can impact behaviour in the game of chicken, but they point the player in opposite directions.

The expected probability of the other's cooperation is one of two kinds of probability with psychological relevance. The other kind of probabilistic expectation is the strength of the belief that the other person will choose whatever strategy the self is choosing (Krueger, 2013). This probability should be greater than .5 because whichever strategy a player selects is by necessity likely the strategy of the majority. This rationale works inasmuch as there is high uncertainty about the behaviour of others. Players who have good knowledge or strong prior beliefs about how others will choose have less room to use their own choice as a diagnostic sign to predict the other's choice.

Some orthodox game theorists dismiss this argument as magical thinking (Binmore, 2007). Granted, a player cannot *make* another person cooperate by cooperating him- or herself in a one-shot, simultaneous-choice came. A player *can*, however, choose cooperation on the assumption that neither the self's nor the other's choice is free in the libertarian sense. Rather, players will more likely converge than diverge in their choices because both have the same structural information, and because both share the same basic psychological make-up. The expected similarity of one's own and the other's choice then emerges as a non-causal correlation. Choices end up being aligned because they stem from a common cause (see Krueger et al., 2012, for formal arguments, simulations, and empirical evidence).

Classic game theory assumes that the preferences shown in a formal description of a game are faithful representations of the preferences in the player's head. This view precludes expectations regarding the opponent's strategy from having any relevance for strategic choice. Classic game theorists consider the distinction between objective (i.e., conveyed) preferences and subjective (i.e., experienced) preferences (Kelley & Thibaut, 1978), to be spurious. For a taste of the misunderstandings between game theorists and other social scientists, consider again the prisoner's dilemma. A social psychologist, working in the tradition of interdependence theory (Kelley et al., 2003), might say that half of her research participants have been identified as prosocials who weight the other person's payoffs as much as they weight their own (van Lange, 1999). The "objective", or given, payoffs of $T = 4$, $R = 3$, $P = 2$, and $S = 1$ turn into the "subjective", or effective, payoffs of $T = 5$ $(4 + 1)$, $R = 6$ $(3 + 3)$, $P = 4$ $(2 + 2)$, and $S = 5$ $(1 + 4)$. Having made these transformations, this prosocial player will likely cooperate. Game theorists might object that the prosocial player is playing a different game, one in which cooperation is the dominating strategy.

Preferences and expectations in review

We have given a brief description of the role of social preferences and expectations regarding the choices of others as the main contributions of psychological or behavioural revisions of game theory. Social preferences and expectations redefine what it means to be rational in a social dilemma. The door to a fully social-psychological consideration of interdependent play is now thrust open. Yet, players are still not seen as agents who are concerned about how they come across in the court of social judgement. Expanding analysis to incorporate social perceptions requires a conceptual shift. Whereas classic game theory ignores the moral dimension of choice, theories of social preference and expectation point to a convergence of competence and morality (e.g., prosocials are typically portrayed as both rational and morally good). In the research we review next, we show that perceptions of competence and morality show distinctive patterns. Perceived morality is neither irrelevant, nor is it reducible to perceived rationality. The distinctiveness of these patterns poses new challenges to the social player who is sensitive to reputation, and new opportunities for the researchers who study them.

Social perception, reputation, and the reflected self

The controversies over preferences and expectations neglect other matters of psychological interest, namely concerns with self-image, reflected appraisals, and reputation (Barclay, 2015). We have asked third-party observers to evaluate individuals, or players, engaged in various social dilemmas. The minimum input provided was the target player's strategic choice, be it cooperation or defection. Some experiments conveyed additional information, such as the opponent's strategic choice – and thus the resulting payoffs for the player and the opponent – or the player's expectation regarding the opponent's choice. The findings provide a basis for further inquiry into how these observed patterns of perception and judgement may contribute to a player's choice process (Barclay, 2016).

The rating dimensions we used reflect current theory in social perception and judgement, which favours a two-dimensional space of competence and morality (Abele, Hauke, Peters, Louvet, Szymkow & Duan, 2016; Fiske, 2018). There are many available models, which are held together by the bonds of family resemblance. We settled for the terminology recommended by Wojciszke (2005). The dimension called *competence* relates to notions of intelligence, skill, rationality, as well as power and agency. The dimension called *morality* relates to notions of warmth, trustworthiness, honesty, and communion more generally. We used short adjective scales in our studies and leave it to future research to replicate and extend the findings with a broader item base.[4]

The two-dimensional model suggests that behavioural explanations and predictions can advance once we know how people perceive themselves and others along the dimensions of competence and morality. Previous research showed that perceptions of morality are closely aligned with generic, or content-free, conceptions of "goodness" (Goodwin et al., 2014; Ray et al., in press; Wojciszke et al., 1998). When differences emerge between individuals or groups, the differences in perceived morality are larger than the differences in perceived competence (Prati et al., 2018) – a finding we replicated. Relatedly, morality is always considered good, but competence is considered good only if it is deployed in the service of moral aims (Landy et al., 2016). Conceptually, the dimensions of competence and morality are orthogonal, but empirical correlations vary. One way to see how competence and morality are related is to consider their requirements and ingredients. Do they overlap? If the overlap is complete, the larger set subsumes the smaller. There is no agreement on this point. Many philosophers, from Plato and Kant, have argued that morality can be derived from rationality (i.e., a type of competence), whereas others have taken the opposite view (cf. Gauthier, 1986). The claim that rationality emerges from morality is appealing to those who consider – presumably for moral reasons – the primacy of morality to be essential.

Researchers not only value conceptual clarity; they also study the correlations between measures of morality and competence. A study designer may wish to create two independent scales in order to maximise the explained variance. The social psychological research tradition has a good record of mapping the big two dimensions into an orthogonal space, although important exceptions have been observed. Whereas early work showed a positive

---

[4]Some of the samples used in the earlier studies are rather small and limited in terms of the diversity of the subject pool. Yet, positive replications within the research program were achieved for all effects of interest. There are no unpublished studies in our file drawers.

alignment of judgements of morality with judgements of competence (Rosenberg et al., 1968), Kervyn et al. (2010) have found a negative relation when perceivers were given information relevant to one dimension and asked to infer a target's standing on the other. Such findings suggest that a highly moral person is not perceived as fully rational.

For classic game theory, the question of social perception and its funda-mental dimensions does not arise. The theory addresses the question of which strategy a self-interested and rational player will select. This strategy might incidentally have moral appeal, or it may be repugnant, but such reactions lie outside the theory's domain. Theories of social preferences and expectations lean towards predicting a positive, halo-like, association of competence and morality. As we will show, neither theory hits the mark perfectly. This is so, in our view, because these theories fail to see that reflected appraisals also matter. In what follows, we review the findings of a series of studies conducted over the course of a decade and a half. With one exception, we follow the chronological order of the work as it shows the incremental depth of the research and its theoretical implications. As we review the findings, we note sample sizes and selected effect sizes (d or r).

Choice and outcome bias in the prisoner's dilemma

Our first objective was to test the hypothesis that observers view cooperators as more moral and less competent than defectors. This hypothesis was supported in an experiment by Krueger and Acevedo (2007, total $N = 405$) where participants were introduced to the prisoner's dilemma and asked to rate a player with regard to the trait adjectives *intelligent, rational*, and *naïve* (reverse-scored), which captured the idea of competence, and with regard to the adjectives *generous, trustworthy, ethical, egocentric* (reverse-scored), and *deceitful* (reverse-scored), which captured the idea of morality. The two short scales had acceptable reliability, and the correlation between them was slightly negative ($r = -.15$). As expected, when the other player's choice was unknown, cooperators were seen as far more moral ($d = 1.93$) and slightly less competent ($d = .29$)[5] than defectors.

The second objective was to test the presence of an *outcome bias*. An outcome bias is said to occur if the quality of a decision is judged in light of consequences that were not foreseeable (Baron & Hershey, 1988). Respondents were informed of the other player's strategic choice, thereby revealing the payoff outcomes falling to both players. Here, we found an important dissociation between the dimensions of competence and morality. Only perceptions of competence, but not perceptions of morality, showed an outcome bias. The cooperator was perceived as less competent than the

---

[5]This effect was marginally significant, $p = .09$.

defector only if the other player defected ($d = .70$). In other words, observers imposed a "sucker's penalty" upon the cooperator. By contrast, no matter what the other player chose, and thus regardless of the target player's payoff, the cooperator was seen as more moral than the defector.

A critical feature of decisions under uncertainty is that the decision-maker seeks to make the best choice combining potential consequences with the objective or the perceived probabilities with which they will occur. Any evaluation of a decision must therefore be limited to a consideration of what the decision-maker knew or believed to be probable at the time of making the choice (Dawes, 1988). A prisoner's dilemma among strangers is a situation of decision-making under uncertainty *par excellence*. A cooperative player may hope or even believe that the other player will cooperate, but he or she cannot know this. The prospect of being suckered is a calculated risk. When observers fault the cooperator's competence after the fact, that is, when the observers are privileged to know the outcome but fail to ignore it, they are demonstrating an outcome bias.

The second study in Krueger and Acevedo (2007) focused on the conditions in which the other player's choice was known. Again, observers perceived the defector as less moral ($d = 1.91$) than the cooperator regardless of the other's choice, and again, the other's choice moderated perceptions of competence. A cooperator who met with defection was rated as less competent than a defector who met with defection ($d = 1.09$). When the other player cooperated, there was no difference. Three additional findings corroborated the outcome bias. First, observers thought that players would expect others to select the same strategy that they themselves selected ($d = .49$). They thereby attributed processes of social projection to the target player, granting that cooperators did not expect to be suckered. Second, observers themselves had little insight into their own use of outcome information – or they denied having it. The correlation between self-reported use of outcome information and competence ratings was low ($r = -.19$). Third, the outcome bias reduced observers' trust in a suckered player's decision-making ability. When asked whether they would yield a group decision (where the group comprised them and the judged player) to the player in a new game against a different opponent, observers were less likely to let a previously suckered player than a non-suckered player decide for the group ($d = .67$). In short, the outcome bias was robust because observers attributed reasonable, and projective, expectations to the player, because they did not attribute foreknowledge of being suckered to him (the target person was described as a male), and because they assumed that an unforeseen and unforeseeable adverse consequence would foreshadow negative outcomes in a future but independent dilemma of the same kind.

The third study replicated the competence-morality differential. In addition, we considered the roles of observers' own social-perceptual biases of self-enhancement and social projection. To assess these biases, we asked respondents to rate themselves and the average student on the traits relevant to competence and morality. We computed an index of self-enhancement as the difference between self- and other ratings after coding the ratings such that higher numbers reflected a more positive evaluation. We computed an index of social projection as the within-rater correlation between self- and other ratings. That is to say, we assessed self-enhancement as a mean-level or elevation effect, and we assessed social projection as a profile-similarity effect (Krueger, 2002). We found that individual differences in projection were weakly predictive of observers' own inclination to cooperate ($r = .15$), but that self-enhancement had no effect (see also Tappin & McKay, 2019). Neither of these two observer biases moderated the social evaluations of the target players.

Expectations and reputation in the prisoner's dilemma

In the next stage of this project, we manipulated the apparent strength and direction of target players' expectations regarding their opponents' strategy (Krueger & DiDonato, 2010, total $N = 161$). In the first study, we described players who had either cooperated or defected and who either thought it likely (an 80% chance) or unlikely (a 20% chance) that the other player would cooperate. We reasoned that a defector who believes that the other person will cooperate will seem like a calculating exploiter who ought to be judged low on morality. Conversely, a cooperator who believes that the other person will defect seems like a pure altruist (Batson & Ahmad, 2001) or someone who willingly accepts exploitation. In the latter case, this cooperator will likely be judged low on competence.

The findings showed this low-morality ascription for the strategic exploiter ($d = 2.40$)[6] and the low-competence effect for the willingly exploited ($d = .70$). There was no extra altruism credit as observers perceived cooperators as equally moral regardless of what they expected from the other player. These findings show that observers do not judge targets' behaviour only in light of choices and outcomes, but also in light of the outcomes the target person expects. Letting these expectations affect judgement and evaluation is rationally defensible as these expectations reveal the decision maker's motives and intentions.

Interestingly, the findings suggest that social projection can provide some reputational self-protection. A player who has decided to defect would not want to express the belief that the opponent will cooperate, lest being perceived as a heartless exploiter. A player who has decided to cooperate

---

[6]The effect sizes in Krueger and DiDonato (2010) were reported as partial η^2. Using a formula recommended by Cohen (1988, pp. 279–280), we converted these indices to the more familiar d metric.

would not want to express the belief that the opponent will defect, lest being perceived as an incompetent sucker. Although the patterns of social projection typically found in the prisoner's dilemma (e.g., Dawes et al., 1977) can be modelled as rational inductive inferences (Krueger, 2013), they need not be. Concerns about reputation maintenance steer expectations in the same direction.

In the second study, we found that the expectancy effects are specific to situations of interdependence such as social dilemmas. Observers judged target persons who either agreed to or declined to help an experimenter in a research study. These decisions were riskless and not strategic. Target individuals were said to believe that either few (20%) or many others (80%) were willing to comply. Although, as we shall see, this request-compliance scenario can be modelled as a volunteer's dilemma, we considered its dilemmatic press to be low. Indeed, we found that observers judged compliant targets as more moral ($d = 1.92$) and less competent ($d = 1.15$) than declining targets, and the target's expectations about the decisions of others did not moderate this pattern. There was only a main effect on competence judgements such that those targets who expected more non-compliance were seen as more competent ($d = 1.12$).

In the third study, we used two versions of a multi-person give-some scenario (Dawes, 1980), presenting one as a classical dilemma and another as a modified "charity game." Targets, assembled in groups of four, were said to have an endowment of \$30. They could donate the money, and if at least three of them did, the multiplied proceeds would go to a food bank; otherwise, they would keep the endowment. In this version of the game, cooperators could not be exploited; they could not lose anything beyond what they were willing to give. Targets were then said to either have high or low expectations of others donating. As predicted, the dilemma version replicated the finding that defectors expecting cooperation are seen as comparatively immoral ($d = .84$) and that cooperators expecting defection are seen as comparatively incompetent ($d = 1.66$). In the charity version, however, where exploitation was not a concern, a cooperator expecting cooperation was seen as more moral ($d = 1.44$) and equally competent as a cooperator expecting defection.

Taken together, these studies show that choices, outcomes, and expectations are relevant inputs into observers' perceptions and judgements in the prisoner's dilemma. It is noteworthy that the evaluative dimensions of competence and morality yield distinctive patterns of evaluation. While judgements of morality depend on whether the chosen strategy benefits others, there is no bonus for self-sacrificial altruism. Cooperators who expect others to defect are seen as no more moral than those who do not. Defectors are, however, penalised if they expect to exploit cooperators. The findings for judged competence were more complex but smaller in magnitude. Defectors face reputational hazards if they expect others to cooperate, and cooperators risk being seen as incompetent if they are suckered.

Choices, outcomes, and expectations in the volunteer's dilemma

The volunteer's dilemma resembles the game of chicken in that a rational player will reason that it is best to defect against a volunteer and to volunteer for a defector (Krueger, 2019). In this game, however, the payoff for volunteering (i.e., the prosocial strategy) does not vary with the other player's choice. The payoff ranking is therefore T > [R = S] > P (see Appendix A). Diekmann (1985) wryly referred to the volunteer's dilemma as a "degenerate game of chicken" (p. 606). Classic game theory again holds that a rational player volunteers with the probability that finds the Nash equilibrium. As in the game of chicken, it should be noted that if loss aversion is accepted as a rational orientation, a player might volunteer simply to ensure that the awful outcome of mutual defection will not occur (Rabin & Thaler, 2001).

We conducted three studies (Heck & Krueger, 2017; total $N = 352$) using the observer paradigm developed for the prisoner's dilemma. As expected, observers considered volunteers more moral than defectors (tested in studies 1 and 2 with $d = .87$ and 1.09). They also considered volunteers more competent ($d = .76$ and .85), a finding that contrasts with the prisoner's dilemma. In the volunteer's dilemma, defection is not a dominating strategy, and therefore not necessarily the smart choice. Given the parallel effects of volunteering on judgements of competence and morality, it might seem that the two dimensions are confounded in this setting. Critically, however, we found again that outcomes and expectations only moderated judgements of competence. There was a robust outcome bias when the other player's choice was revealed. Observers saw a defector as less competent when the other defected instead of volunteered ($d = .79$). The commonality with the prisoner's dilemma is that only competence judgements show an outcome bias in the form of a penalty for the player who ends up with the worst outcome. The difference is where it occurs. In the prisoner's dilemma, the unilateral cooperator does worst, whereas in the volunteer's dilemma it is the mutual defectors.

We then expanded the design by also providing the player's expectations regarding the other's choice. Observers judged volunteers as highly competent regardless of whether they expected the other player to volunteer or to defect. This is a remarkable departure from game-theoretic logic, which suggests that a volunteer who expects defection can claim to choose rationally, whereas a volunteer who expects volunteering appears to willingly accept an inefficient outcome. Given an expectation of volunteering, observers rated a volunteer as more competent than a defector ($d = .45$), although the latter maximised the personal and the collective payoff.

We also found that observers rewarded accurate predictions. They judged those players who expected volunteering and got it, or who expected defection and got it, as more competent than players who predicted one strategy but got another, $d = .41$. This pattern implies an *observer bias*: opponents' strategies are not predictable in a one-shot anonymous dilemma. Accuracy requires luck. Recall, however, that the perspective of social prediction allows for some accuracy by assuming that players may consider it likely that others choose as they themselves do. Yet, the design of the experiment reported here eliminated this possibility because expectations and outcomes were varied independently. In a naturalistic context, where expectations can be positively correlated with outcomes, observers can reward accuracy with perceptions of competence without being biased. In the three-dimensional space of choice, expectation, and outcome, the target player's own strategic choice adds the final flourish. If it is bad to expect and to receive defection, it is worse to also have defected oneself. Observers sanctioned this triple layer of defection with the lowest competence ratings.

Across studies, judgements of morality arise from a simpler set of inputs than judgements of competence, but when morality judgements do differ, the effects are large. This difference between the two main dimensions of social judgement suggests that global correlations can only be a first pass in explorations of their (mis)alignment. Finally, we have seen that social perception departs from the simple predictions of classic game theory. These departures offer input for models of strategic choice that incorporate elements of signalling, self-image management, and reputation.

In a final set of analyses, we considered the role of observers' self-images in an approach similar to the one taken in Krueger and DiDonato (2010). We found consistent evidence for self-enhancement and social projection. Observers claimed that they themselves would be more likely to volunteer than the average person (*enhancement, $d = .42$ and .53*), and across observers, the correlation between intended volunteering and the volunteering expected from others was positive (*projection, $r = .32$ and .46*). Besides replicating these well-known egocentric biases, we found an additional kind of egocentrism in judgements of the target persons. The more willing observers were to volunteer, the greater was the difference in their evaluations of the volunteer and the defector. Observers ready to volunteer judged another volunteer to be far moral ($r = .47$ and .49, after converting from standardised β in a multiple regression, Peterson & Brown, 2005) and more competent ($r = .46$ and .40) than a defector, whereas observers ready to defect made no such distinctions. It was only the observers' self-judgements that predicted these discriminatory evaluations; observers' judgements of the average person had no effect. Social perception in social dilemmas appears to be closely linked to self-perception. People praise others who act as they themselves would. This is one of the reasons for the conclusion that individuals are acting reasonably when allowing their strategic choices to be informed by the anticipated evaluations from the outside.

Social perception in a sequential game: the trust dilemma

Challenges of interpersonal trust arise in many social dilemmas. In the prisoner's dilemma and the assurance game, players might wonder if they can trust each other to cooperate. In these games, trust is given or withheld and it is rewarded or punished at the same time. In the game of chicken and the volunteer's dilemma, by contrast, players might hope that the other picks the strategy opposite to their own. Here, the standard psychological meaning of trust as the expectation to not be harmed does not apply. A would-be cooperator might hope that the other player will defect so that he or she can maximise the other's payoff and prevent catastrophe for the self.

The trust game proper was introduced as a sequential interaction to conceptually and empirically separate trust and trustworthiness (Berg et al., 1995; Evans & Krueger, 2009; 2014). In the canonical game, the first mover, or trustor, decides what proportion of an endowment (e.g., $10) to transfer to the second mover, or trustee. The trustee receives a multiple of this invest-ment (e.g., to a maximum of $30) and decides what proportion of it, if any, to return to the trustor. On average, trustors transfer about half of their endowment, and trustees return just enough for trustors not to do worse than they would have had they not trusted (Johnson & Mislin, 2011).

Classic game theory applies the logic of backward induction (Aumann, 1995) to assert that trustors should know that trustees have no financial incentive to return anything, and therefore, trustors should transfer nothing to begin with. Attempts to explain the empirically observed trust in rational terms have included references to social preferences, social expectations, and social norms. People may trust if they care about the well-being of the other, if they expect the other to reciprocate, or if they consider trust a normative obligation.

We first review some properties of these earlier revisions of game theory. For the trustees, we find that they must either return nothing or return that amount that establishes payoff equality (Krueger, Massey et al., 2008). This finding follows from the assumption that trustees put a positive weight on trustors' payoffs or a negative weight on the difference between their own and the trustors' payoffs, and the assumption that trustees value money linearly. Trustees with other-regarding preferences or an aversion to inequal-ity should seek equality if these prosocial preferences surpass a certain derivable threshold. Otherwise, they should keep the money. Intermediate returns of the type typically seen among research participants can be math-ematically recovered only if the trustees feel that the money they return is worth less to themselves than to the trustee, a condition requiring a concave value function. Trustors' investments can be modelled nonlinearly, but only if complex assumptions about their expectations regarding the probability of reciprocity are allowed (Krueger, Massey, et al., 2008).

The social-normative approach makes a clear prediction for the trustee. Reciprocity is a universal moral imperative (Gouldner, 1960), grounded in social evolution (Axelrod, 1984; Trivers, 1971), extendable to indirect social exchanges (Nowak & Sigmund, 2005), and projectible into the future (Luhmann, 1979). When exchanges continue and past exchanges are remembered, positive reciprocity is rational in that it maximises both individual and collective gains, at least as long as neither player knows how many exchanges are still to come (Ely & Välimäki, 2002). The weakness of the norm-based explanation of trustworthiness is that returns are highly variable empirically. Flat distributions are common. If a norm is meant to standardise human behaviour, the norm of reciprocity fails in the trust game.

The normative approach makes no clear prediction for the trustor. There is no universal norm demanding that "thou shalt trust a stranger." Indeed, much of socialisation is dedicated to teaching the young to treat trust as a fragile resource and to learn when and whom to grant it. Bicchieri et al. (2011) rejected the idea that trust is normative because people are willing to punish those who fail to reciprocate, but are not willing to punish those who fail to trust. Nonetheless, many people do feel an obligation to trust when the opportunity arises (Dunning et al., 2019). They may see trust as a moral good because it is necessary for joint success in contexts of interdependence (Evans & van de Calseyde, 2018). In some situations, this sense of moral obligation is particularly strong, as when not trusting harms the trustee (Evans & van Beest, 2017).

Much like cooperation in other dilemmas, trust is not an act of pure altruism. Few trustors transfer money without hoping for a positive return. When trustees are barred from reciprocating and trustors know it, the trust game reduces to a dictator game, and transfers are small (Cox, 2004), even among young children (Evans et al., 2013). In other words, both trust and trustworthiness raise questions of competence and morality. We conducted a scenario study presenting respondents with descriptions of trustors and trustees who transferred no money, an intermediate amount, or the maximum amount (Krueger, Massey, et al., 2008, $N = 138$). For the trustor, the maximum was the entire endowment; for the trustee, the maximum was the amount needed to equalise the final accounts of the two players. Observers rated these target persons on short adjective scales as in the studies reported above.

Strikingly, variation in the transfers did not affect perceptions of competence, but massively affected perceptions of morality ($d = 2.35$). Competence ratings hugged the middle of the scale, suggesting that trusting and reciprocating are not seen as matters of rationality. This is surprising because both classic and revised game theories make different predictions. According to classic game theory, a total lack of trust and a total lack of reciprocity (if an irrational trustor had sent money) are the marks of rationality. The social-value variant of social preference theory (van Lange, 1999) predicts that high and low transfers by the trustee can be rational, but intermediate transfers cannot.

While observers credited both trustors and trustees with greater morality the more money they sent, they regarded trustors as more moral overall ($d = .35$). There may be two reasons for this. First, trustees may lose moral credit because they obey a moral imperative. Unlike Kant, ordinary observers may discount the force of a social norm when judging moral character (Kelley, 1972). They may see trustors as more moral because these trustors *did not have to trust*. Second, trustors, unlike trustees, make decisions under uncertainty. Whereas trustees only need to consider their social preferences or their willingness to honour the norm of reciprocity, trustors must engage in perspective-taking, theory of mind, and social prediction. These forecasting tasks are difficult. Observers may have granted trustors moral credit for engaging in this task regardless of whether they did it well. Indeed, there was no information about whether they did it well, which is why observers may not have used morality judgements to signal approval or disapproval.

These results echo recent work showing that many respondents show more trust than their own expectations of reciprocity would suggest (Dunning et al., 2014; Evans & Krueger, 2017). Still, the concept of moral obligation does not offer a sufficient explanation. We submit that inter-personal trust helps to support a positive self-image as a moral person. Trusting behaviour sends a positive signal to the self, as it does to others (Sliwka, 2007), much like moralistic punishment does (Jordan & Rand, 2020). Trustors can broadcast their morality by choosing the strategy that benefits others while also cultivating the prospect of receiving the greatest financial payoff for themselves. Because reciprocated trust is good for both players, the trustor's signal of morality is somewhat jammed. Likewise, trustees cannot easily signal morality because they have to contend with the just-doing-one's-duty discount. Unlike trustors, however, trustees know that their transfers are lost to them for sure, which makes their behaviour morally significant.

Social comparison as a social dilemma

We have assumed that observers' judgements convey a kind of social consensus that is relevant for self-perception. This assumption is supported by high inter-rater agreement. When, for example, we find that cooperation, volunteering, and trust reap moral approval, we can predict that the individuals contributing to this social consensus will also apply it to themselves.

They will cooperate, volunteer, and trust in part because they value the reflection of these acts on the self.

The motive to gain and maintain a positive self-image and social reputation is a staple in most people's motivational lives (Alicke & Sedikides, 2011). How do people satisfy this motive, and why do they often find it difficult to do so? We propose that self-esteem and self-enhancement have the characteristics of social dilemmas, and we report the findings of a study where observers evaluated individuals who self-enhanced or self-effaced. Consider self-esteem first. Social approval, praise, respect, and inclusion are important sources of self-esteem. Some argue that they are the only sources (Leary, 2005). The self then reduces to the socially reflected self, an idea pioneered by Cooley's (1902) metaphor of the looking-glass self. Respect must be given before it can be received, and, according to sociometer theory, you can't give it to yourself. Praising oneself, like tickling oneself, doesn't do the trick. The mind realises that it cannot be an independent judge of itself. We need others before we can enjoy the warm glow of approval. Persons within a group or community are interdependent. When giving respect amounts to an act of cooperation and withholding respect amounts to an act of defection, there is a prisoner's dilemma (Krueger, Vohs et al., 2008). Again, classic game theory projects a society of losers. Luckily, many people cooperate. Extrapolating from the work reviewed above, we predict that giving respect is seen as moral and withholding it as smart. The sucker's penalty falls on those who give respect without receiving any.

In its interpersonal form, self-enhancement is the belief in one's own superiority (Alicke & Govorun, 2005; Heck et al., 2018). Imagine a group in which these beliefs are common knowledge. Claiming to be better than others amounts to an act of defection ("You think you're better than me?"), whereas seeing oneself on a par with others, or as being below, is an act of cooperation. As with self-esteem – with which self-enhancement is confounded (Krueger, Heck et al., 2017) – the winner is the person whose self-enhancing beliefs are confirmed by others, that is, by the very persons the self-enhancers regard as inferior. This sort of victory is hard to achieve because it requires unrequited love. Social-comparative self-enhancement can thus be modelled as a prisoner's dilemma.

Although we have not studied observer judgements in the full context of the self-enhancement dilemma, we conducted two studies asking how observers judge self-enhancers and self-effacers (Heck & Krueger, 2016, total $N = 396$). In this work, we made a critical distinction between *bias* and *error* (Heck & Krueger, 2015). Whereas self-enhancement bias comprises all better-than-average claims, self-enhancement errors are limited to those individuals who perform worse than average while believing they did better. Likewise, we distinguished between a general bias of self-effacement and the specific error of self-effacement, that is, cases of individuals who think their performance is below average when it is not.

In the first study, we provided information about the four possible types of person who had either taken a test of intelligence or morality. The intersection of their comparative self-judgements and their test scores classified them into those who correctly believed to be above average (Hits), those who falsely believed to be above average (False Alarms), those who falsely believed to not be above average (Misses), and those who correctly believed to not be above average (Correct Rejections). Observers then evaluated these targets along the dimensions of competence and morality.

In the context of the intelligence test, observers rewarded Hits (H) and punished False Alarms (FA) respectively with high and low competence ratings ($d = 2.36$ for the difference between the two). Ratings for Misses (M) and Correct Rejections (CR) were intermediate and their means were not different from each other. Thus, self-enhancement can benefit one's social reputation if it turns out to be justified. A self-enhancement error is sanctioned because it entails two failures: the failure to do well and the failure to understand one's own performance. Observers penalised those who are unskilled and unaware of it (Krueger & Mueller, 2002; Kruger & Dunning, 1999). Observers also penalised FA targets with low morality judgements ($d = 1.10$ for the difference between FA and H). Self-enhancement errors thus not only signal low competence, but also unethicality. In the context of the morality test, the pattern for competence judgements mirrored the pattern seen after an intelligence test. Again, observers ascribed the highest and lowest competence respectively to H and FA ($d = 2.05$). The pattern for morality judgements was different, however, as, perhaps not surprisingly, test performance dominated social perception. H and M, who had scored high, were seen as more moral than FA and CR ($d = 1.93$).

These findings were replicated in a second study focused on intelligence tests. One additional question was whether observers would rate self-enhancers differently in the absence of outcome knowledge. Indeed, they viewed self-enhancers as more competent ($d = .59$) and less moral than self-effacers ($d = .38$). One might have expected that since self-enhancers comprise both competent (H) and incompetent (FA) individuals as much as self-effacers comprise both competent (M) and incompetent (CR) individuals, any perceived differences might wash out. Perhaps observers gave self-enhancers the benefit of the doubt, assuming that they might be truly superior until proven otherwise. Recent research suggests, however, that people assume self-enhancement to be more likely associated with error than with accuracy (Heck & Krueger, in press). The difference in the direction of the competence and the morality effect poses a dilemma for the self-presenter. Should one self-enhance with a view towards receiving a competence credit, or should one self-efface hoping to receive a humility bonus? Personal preferences and the context of the task might moderate this choice. Yet, some bold and possibly overconfident individuals try to have it both ways with the awkward and generally failing tactic of humble-bragging (Sezer et al., 2018). It should be difficult to get both types of credit as competence and morality considerations compete in the eyes of the observers.

Review across games and dilemmas

Our research programme has evolved over a decade and a half. Stable and informative patterns of social perception have emerged, pointing to promising directions for the study of classic social dilemmas as well as prominent social perceptual biases that can be modelled as social dilemmas. One pervasive finding is that moral judgements dominate observers' judgements. Judgements of competence matter too, but their effects are smaller and context dependent. Judgements of morality and competence show distinctive patterns, which linear measures of association will miss. It is now clear that competence judgements respond uniquely to the consequences of strategic choice, even when these consequences are unforeseen or unforeseeable.

For perceptions of morality, the broadest common denominator is that observers reward targets for behaviour benefiting others. As we have seen, cooperators and volunteers are perceived as equally moral regardless of whether the other person cooperates or volunteers. The intent to benefit others appears to be critical, and the size of the sacrifice is a relevant cue. In the trust game, making larger investments is seen as more moral, although it opens the door to receiving a larger return for the self. In the volunteer's dilemma, observers grant moral credit even though the volunteer's decision might be driven by the desire to avoid the catastrophe of mutual defection. Again, the intent to make it possible for others to benefit is critical. The findings suggest the operation of a simple imperative. Act to make it possible for the other to benefit! How much these others will receive then depends on their own choice. For the prisoner's dilemma and the trust game, a utilitarian perspective is compatible with the moral appeal of cooperation because only cooperation and trust can maximise joint outcomes. In a volunteer's dilemma, however, collective cooperation is still seen as moral, although it is inefficient (Krueger et al., 2016). In the context of comparative self-evaluation, moral judgement favours self-effacement. A modesty heuristic may be at play here, with observers censuring self-enhancers because of the inferiority they attribute to others.

We speculate that social perceptions and judgements enter a person's strategic considerations, but we have presented no direct evidence for this. It is well known that people use their impressions of others' morality and competence as input for their own strategic choices (van Lange & Kuhlman, 1994; see also De Bruin & van Lange, 1999). The present research builds on this work by suggesting that these choices depend, in part, on the kinds of impressions players wish to project. In social life and in social games, people play to audiences (Goffman, 1959), even to internal ones (Leary, 1996). Many ingenious studies in behavioural economics have shown that decisions are driven by the desire to appear fair and ethical, rather than to *be* fair and ethical (e.g., Dana et al., 2006, 2007; Gino & Ariely, 2016). The desire to build and maintain a moral reputation and self-image can help establish the collective well-being of mutual cooperation (Milinski et al., 2002), but the conflict with the maximum obtainable material interests remains. The player must ask if the moral credit is worth more than the material benefit of unilateral defection.

Recent theories of belief utility point to a possible integration of this work within a general theory of strategic choice (Loewenstein & Molnar, 2018). Until such an integration is achieved, research should continue to replicate and extend the evidentiary foundation laid here. Many social dilemmas and other forms of interdependence are ripe for study. Selecting research contexts randomly is not efficient. A heuristic sampling strategy might begin with contexts of interdependence that have already received much attention but that are not derivatives of the dilemmas reviewed here. Another possibility is to look to more exotic games. One aspect of morality is retribution. In our work, moral credit was aligned with benevolence. In other contexts, such as the ultimatum game (Güth, 1995), moral reputations do not come from allowing others to take the lion's share of available resources – which would be benevolence – but from punishing greedy others at a cost to the self. Again, moral credit seems to grow best on the soil of personal sacrifice (Krueger, unpublished).

A lone ego in a social world

We have argued that economic game theory and the psychology of social dilemmas can profit from greater attention to the impressions that observers and the players themselves form on the basis of available information about behaviour, motives, and expectations. Perhaps John von Neumann (see epigraph) misjudged the nature of egocentrism. Although it provides a myopic lens to view the social world, egocentrism does not amount to egoism. Egocentric perceptions of the outcomes available in a social dilemma do not eliminate cooperation (Krueger et al., 2018; Krueger, 2013, 2019). As social animals, human beings seek to make sense of their social word (Chater & Loewenstein, 2016), and this search for meaning requires an interest in the beliefs of others (Baumeister et al., 2018). A concern about the perceptions of others is thus baked into an egocentric worldview. A person cannot afford to ignore what others think about him or her, and especially if these others are future interaction partners (Krasnow et al., 2012). Social perception guides social communication, and communication is a powerful tool for creating (Griskevicius et al., 2010) and destroying reputations (Feinberg et al., 2012).

The sensitivity to social reputation is documented most clearly by the finding that people act more prosocially when they are observed (Bradley et al., 2018). Social pressure can be so powerful that eventually many individuals internalise its demands. They act prosocially even when no one is watching (from the outside) (Jordan & Rand, 2020). Over time, reputation can become self-image and personality. A person who began with attempts to fool others or curry favour can turn into the projected image. In an essay praising Dostoevsky's biographer Joseph Frank, the writer David Foster Wallace put the process (and the dilemma) thus: "Am I a good person? Deep down, do I even really want to be a good person, or do I only want to *seem* like a good person so that people (including myself) will approve of me? Is there a difference? How do I ever actually know whether I'm bullshitting myself, morally speaking?" (Wallace, 2005, p. 257).

The desire to attain and maintain a positive social reputation emerges as a critical ingredient to decision-making that models of rational choice or social preferences have neglected. Yet, a sensitivity to one's social reputation need not result in a unidirectional drive towards greater cooperation and morality. Although concerns about moral reputations loom large (Hartley et al., 2016), competence and rationality are far from irrelevant. Barclay (2015) argues that conflicting reputational concerns create a higher-order dilemma. To be viable, the social animal cannot bet exclusively on being seen as cooperative (i.e., moral) or as being competitive (i.e., competent [in most dilemmas]). The former case opens the door to being exploited, whereas the latter case threatens abandonment and isolation (Raihani & Barclay, 2016). Perhaps the inescapability of this trade-off is John von Neumann's last laugh. "I told you so," he might say. "It's a dilemma all right!".

Acknowledgments

We thank Pat Barclay and Max Krasnow for comments on a draft of this manuscript.

ORCID

Patrick R. Heck (iD) http://orcid.org/0000-0003-0819-3890
Anthony M. Evans (iD) http://orcid.org/0000-0003-3345-5282

References

Abele, A. E., Hauke, N., Peters, K., Louvet, E., Szymkow, A., & Duan, Y. (2016). Facets of the fundamental content dimensions: Agency with competence and assertiveness-communion with warmth and morality. *Frontiers in Psychology, 7*. Article 1810. https://doi.org/10.3389/fpsyg.2016.01810

Alicke, M. D., & Govorun, O. (2005). The better-than-average effect. In M. D. Alicke, D. D. Dunning, & J. I. Krueger (Eds.), *The self in social judgment* (pp. 85–106). Psychology.

Alicke, M. D., & Sedikides, C. (2011). *Handbook of self-enhancement and self-protection.* Guilford.

Aumann, R. (1995). Backward induction and common knowledge of rationality. *Games and Economic Behavior, 8*(1), 6–19. https://doi.org/10.1016/S0899-8256(05)80015-6

Axelrod, R. (1984). *The evolution of cooperation.* Basic Books.

Barclay, P. (2015). Reputation. In D. Buss (Ed.), *Handbook of Evolutionary Psychology* (2nd ed., pp. 810–828). J. Wiley & Sons.

Barclay, P. (2016). Biological markets and the effects of partner choice on cooperation and friendship. *Current Opinion in Psychology, 7*, 33–38. https://doi.org/10.1016/j.copsyc.2015.07.012

Baron, J., & Hershey, J. C. (1988). Outcome bias in decision evaluation. *Journal of Personality and Social Psychology, 54*(4), 569–579. https://doi.org/10.1037//0022-3514.54.4.569

Batson, C. D., & Ahmad, N. (2001). Empathy-induced altruism in a prisoner's dilemma II: What if the target of empathy has defected? *European Journal of Social Psychology, 31*(1), 25–36. https://doi.org/10.1002/ejsp.26

Baumeister, R. F., Maranges, H. M., & Vohs, K. D. (2018). Human self as information agent: Functioning in a social environment based on shared meanings. *Review of General Psychology, 22*(1), 36–47. https://doi.org/10.1037/gpr0000114

Berg, J., Dickhaut, J., & McCabe, K. (1995). Trust, reciprocity, and social-history. *Games and Economic Behavior, 10*(1), 122–142. https://doi.org/10.1006/game.1995.1027

Bicchieri, C., Xiao, E., & Muldoon, R. (2011). Trustworthiness is a social norm, but trusting is not. *Politics, Philosophy & Economics, 10*(2), 170–187. https://doi.org/10.1177/1470594X10387260

Binmore, K. (2007). *Game theory: A very short introduction.* Oxford University Press.

Bogaert, S., Boone, C., & Declerck, C. (2008). Social value orientation and cooperation in social dilemmas: A review and conceptual model. *British Journal of Social Psychology, 47*(3), 453–480. https://doi.org/10.1348/014466607X244970

Bohnet, I., & Frey, B. S. (1999). Social distance and other-regarding behavior in dictator games: Comment. *American Economic Review, 89*(1), 335–339. https://doi.org/10.1257/aer.89.1.335

Bradley, A., Lawrence, C., & Ferguson, E. (2018). Does observability affect prosociality? *Proceedings of the Royal Society B: Biological Sciences, 285*:20180116. https://doi.10.1098/rspb.2018.0116

Brams, S. J. (2004). Game Theory. In C. K. Rowley & F. Schneider (Eds.), *The encyclopedia of public choice* (pp. 581–582). Springer.

Camerer, C. F. (2003). *Behavioral game theory.* Princeton University Press.

Chater, N., & Loewenstein, G. (2016). The under-appreciated drive for sense-making. *Journal of Economic Behavior & Organization*, *126*, Part B, 137–154. https://doi.org/10.1016/j.jebo.2015.10.016

Cohen, J. (1988). *Statistical power analysis for the behavioral sciences* (2nd ed.). Lawrence Erlbaum.

Colman, A. (2003). Cooperation, psychological game theory, and limitations of rationality in social interaction. *Behavioral and Brain Sciences*, *26*(2), 139–153. https://doi.org/10.1017/S0140525X03000050

Cooley, C. H. (1902). The looking-glass self. In *Human nature and the social order*. New York, NY: . Scribner's.

Cox, J. C. (2004). How to identify trust and reciprocity. *Games and Economic Behavior*, *46*(2), 260–281. https://doi.org/10.1016/S0899-8256(03)00119-2

Dana, J., Cain, D. M., & Dawes, R. M. (2006). What you don't know won't hurt me: Costly (but quiet) exit in a dictator game. *Organizational Behavior and Human Decision Processes*, *100*(2), 193–201. https://doi.org/10.1016/j.obhdp.2005.10.001

Dana, J., Weber, R., & Kuang, J. X. (2007). Exploiting moral wriggle room: Behavior inconsistent with a preference for fair outcomes. *Economic Theory*, *33*(1), 67–80. https://doi.org/10.2139/ssrn.400900

Dawes, R. M. (1980). Social dilemmas. *Annual Review of Psychology*, *31*(1), 169–193. https://doi.org/10.1146/annurev.ps.31.020180.001125

Dawes, R. M. (1988). *Rational choice in an uncertain world*. Harcourt Brace Jovanovich.

Dawes, R. M., McTavish, J., & Shaklee, H. (1977). Behavior, communication, and assumptions about other people's behavior in a commons dilemma situation. *Journal of Personality and Social Psychology*, *35*(1), 1–11. https://doi.org/10.1037/0022-3514.35.1.1

De Bruin, E. N. M., & van Lange, P. A. M. (1999). Impression formation and cooperative behavior. *European Journal of Social Psychology*, *29*(2–3), 305–328. https://doi.org/10.1002/

Diekmann, A. (1985). Volunteer's dilemma. *Journal of Conflict Resolution*, *29*(4), 605–610. https://doi.org/10.1177/0022002785029004003

Dunning, D., Anderson, J. E., Schlösser, T., Ehlebracht, D., & Fetchenhauer, D. (2014). Trust at zero acquaintance: More a matter of respect than expectation of reward. *Journal of Personality and Social Psychology*, *107*(1), 122–141. https://doi.org/10.1037/a0036673

Dunning, D., Fetchenhauer, D., & Schlösser, T. (2019). Why people trust: Solved puzzled and open mysteries. *Current Directions in Psychological Science*, *28*(4), 366–371. https://doi.org/10.1177/0963721419838255

Ely, J. C., & Välimäki, J. (2002). A robust folk theorem for the Prisoner's Dilemma. *Journal of Economic Theory*, *102*(1), 84–105. https://doi.org/10.1006/jeth.2000.2774

Evans, A. M., Athenstaedt, U., & Krueger, J. I. (2013). The development of trust and altruism during childhood. *Journal Of Economic Psychology*, *36*, 82–95. https://doi.org/10.1016/j.joep.2013.02.010

Evans, A. M., & Krueger, J. I. (2009). The psychology (and economics) of trust. *Social and Personality Psychology Compass: Intrapersonal Processes*, *3*(6), 1003-1017. doi: 10.1111/spco.2009.3.issue-6

Evans, A. M., & Krueger, J. I. (2014). Outcomes and expectations in dilemmas of trust. *Judgment and Decision Making*, *9*(2), 90–103. http://journal.sjdm.org/13/13502/jdm13502.pdf

Evans, A. M., & Krueger, J. I. (2016). Bounded prospection in dilemmas of trust and reciprocity. *Review of General Psychology*, *20*(1), 17–28. https://doi.org/10.1037/gpr0000063

Evans, A. M., & Krueger, J. K. (2017). Ambiguity and expectation-neglect in dilemmas of trust. *Judgment and Decision Making*, *12*(6) 584–595. http://journal.sjdm.org/17/17131/jdm17131.pdf

Evans, A. M., & van Beest, I. (2017). Gain-loss framing effects in dilemmas of trust and reciprocity. *Journal of Experimental Social Psychology*, *73*, 151–163. https://doi.org/10.1016/j.jesp.2017.06.012

Evans, A. M., & van de Calseyde, P. F. M. (2018). The reputational consequences of generalized trust. *Personality & Social Psychology Bulletin*, *44*(4), 492–507. https://doi.org/10.1177/0146167217742886

Feinberg, M., Willer, R., Stellar, J., & Keltner, D. (2012). The virtues of gossip: Reputational information sharing as prosocial behavior. *Journal of Personality and Social Psychology*, *102*(5), 1015–1030. https://doi.org/10.1037/a0026650

Fiske, S. T. (2018). Stereotype content: Warmth and competence endure. *Current Directions in Psychological Science*, *27*(2), 67–73. https://doi.org/10.1177/0963721417738825

Gauthier, D. (1986). *Morals by agreement*. Oxford University Press.

Gino, F., & Ariely, D. (2016). Dishonesty explained: What leads moral people to act immorally. In A. G. Miller (Ed.), *The social psychology of good and evil* (2nd ed., pp. 322–344). The Guilford Press.

Goffman, E. (1959). *The presentation of self in everyday life*. Anchor Books.

Goodwin, G. P., Piazza, J., & Rozin, P. (2014). Moral character predominates inre person perception and evaluation. *Journal of Personality and Social Psychology*, *106*(1), 1–21. https://doi.org/10.1037/a0034726

Gouldner, A. W. (1960). the norm of reciprocity: A preliminary statement. *American Sociological Review*, *25*(2), 161–179. https://doi.org/10.2307/2092623

Griskevicius, V., Tybur, J. M., & Van den Bergh, B. (2010). Going green to be seen: Status, reputation, and conspicuous consumption. *Journal of Personality and Social Psychology*, *98*(3), 392–404. https://doi.org/10.1037/a0017346

Güth, W. (1995). On ultimatum bargaining experiments—A personal review. *Journal of Economic Behavior & Organization*, *27*(3), 329–344. https://doi.org/10.1016/0167-2681(94)00071-L

Halevy, N., Chou, E. Y., & Murnighan, J. K. (2012). Mind games: The mental representation of conflict. *Journal of Personality and Social Psychology*, *102*(1), 132–148. https://doi.org/10.1037/a0025389

Hardin, G. (1968). The tragedy of the commons. *Science*, *162*(3859), 1243–1248. https://doi.org/10.1126/science.162.3859.1243

Hartley, A. G., Furr, R. M., Helzer, E. G., Jayawickreme, E., Velasquez, K. R., & Fleeson, W. (2016). Morality's centrality to liking, respecting, and understanding others. *Social Psychological and Personality Science*, *7*(7), 648–657. https://doi.org/10.1177/1948550616655359

Heck, P. R., & Krueger, J. I. (2015). Self-enhancement diminished. *Journal of Experimental Psychology. General*, *144*(5), 1003–1020. https://doi.org/10.1037/xge0000105

Heck, P. R., & Krueger, J. I. (2016). Social perception of self-enhancement bias and error. *Social Psychology*, *47*(6), 327–339. https://doi.org/10.1027/1864-9335/a000287

Heck, P. R., & Krueger, J. I. (2017). Social perception in the volunteer's dilemma: Role of choice, outcome, and expectation. *Social Cognition*, 35(5), 497–519. https://doi.org/10.1521/soco.2017.35.5.497

Heck, P. R., & Krueger, J. I. (in press). Self-enhancement error increases social projection. *Social Cognition*. https://psyarxiv.com/k3xuv

Heck, P. R., Simons, D. J., & Chabris, C. F. (2018). 65% of Americans believe they are above average in intelligence: Results of two nationally representative surveys. *PloS One*, 13(7), e0200103. https://doi.org/10.1371/journal.pone.0200103

Johnson, N. D., & Mislin, A. A. (2011). Trust games: A meta-analysis. *Journal Of Economic Psychology*, 32(5), 865–889. https://doi.org/10.1016/j.joep.2011.05.007

Jordan, J. J., & Rand, D. G. (2020). Signaling when no one is watching: A reputation heuristics account of outrage and punishment in one-shot anonymous interactions. *Journal of Personality and Social Psychology*, 118(1), 57–88. https://doi.org/10.1037/pspi0000186

Kelley, H. H. (1972). Causal schemata and the attribution process. In E. E. Jones, D. E. Kanouse, H. H. Kelley, R. S. Nisbett, S. Valins, & B. Weiner (Eds.), *Attribution: Perceiving the causes of behavior* (pp. 151–174). General Learning Press.

Kelley, H. H., Holmes, J. G., Kerr, N. L., Reis, H. T., Rusbult, C. E., & Van Lange, P. A. M. (2003). *An atlas of interpersonal situations*. Cambridge University Press.

Kelley, H. H., & Thibaut, J. W. (1978). *Interpersonal relations*. Wiley.

Kervyn, K., Yzerbyt, V., & Judd, C. M. (2010). Compensation between warmth and competence: Antecedents and consequences of a negative relation between the two fundamental dimensions of social perception. *European Review of Social Psychology*, 21(1), 155–187. https://doi.org/10.1080/13546805.2010.517997

Klein, P. D. (1999). Human knowledge and the infinite regress of reasons. *Philosophical Perspectives*, 13, 297–325. https://www.jstor.org/stable/2676107

Kollock, P. (1998). Social dilemmas: The anatomy of human cooperation. *Annual Review of Sociology*, 24(1), 183–214. https://doi.org/10.1146/annurev.soc.24.1.183

Krasnow, M. M., Cosmides, L., Pedersen, E. J., & Tooby, J. (2012). What are punishment and reputation for? *PloS One*, 7(9), e45662. https://doi.org/10.1371/journal.pone.0045662

Krueger, J. (2002). On the reduction of self-other asymmetries: Benefits, pitfalls, and other correlates of social projection. *Psychologica Belgica*, 42, 23–41.

Krueger, J., & Mueller, R. A. (2002). Unskilled, unaware, or both? The contribution of social-perceptual skills and statistical regression to self-enhancement biases. *Journal of Personality and Social Psychology*, 82(2), 180–188. https://doi.org/10.1037/0022-3514.82.2.180

Krueger, J. I. (2013). Social projection as a source of cooperation. *Current Directions in Psychological Science*, 22(4), 289–294. https://doi.org/10.1177/0963721413481352

Krueger, J. I., Evans, A. M., & Heck, P. R. (2017). Let me help you help me: Trust between profit and prosociality. In P. A. M. Van Lange, B. Rockenbach, & T. Yamagishi (Eds.), *Social dilemmas: New perspectives on trust* (pp. 121–138). Oxford University Press.

Krueger, J. I. (2019). The vexing volunteer's dilemma. *Current Directions in Psychological Science*, 28(1), 53–58. https://doi.org//10.1177/0963721418807709

Krueger, J. I. (unpublished). *Social perception in the ultimatum game.* Working paper. Brown University.

Krueger, J. I., & Acevedo, M. (2007). Perceptions of self and other in the prisoner's dilemma: Outcome bias and evidential reasoning. *American Journal of Psychology, 120*(4), 593–618.

Krueger, J. I., & DiDonato, T. E. (2010). Person perception in (non)interdependent games. *Acta psychologica, 134*(1), 85–93. https://doi.org/10.1016/j.actpsy.2009.12.010

Krueger, J. I., DiDonato, T. E., & Freestone, D. (2012). Social projection can solve social dilemmas. *Psychological Inquiry, 23*(1), 1–27. (target article, published with 9 peer commentaries). https://doi.org/10.1080/1047840X.2012.641167

Krueger, J. I., Heck, P. R., & Asendorpf, J. B. (2017). Self-enhancement: Conceptualization and assessment. *Collabra: Psychology, 3*(1), 28. https://doi.org/10.1525/collabra.91

Krueger, J. I., Heck, P. R., & Wagner, D. (2018). Egocentrism in the volunteer's dilemma. *American Journal of Psychology, 131*(4), 403–415. https://doi.org/10.5406/amerjpsyc.131.4.0403

Krueger, J. I., Massey, A. L., & DiDonato, T. E. (2008). A matter of trust: From social preferences to the strategic adherence to social norms. *Negotiation & Conflict Management Research, 1*(1), 31–52. https://doi.org/10.1111/j.1750-4716.2007.00003.x

Krueger, J. I., Ullrich, J., & Chen, L. J. (2016). Expectations and decisions in the volunteer's dilemma: Effects of social distance and social projection. *Frontiers in Psychology: Cognition, 7.* article 1909. https://doi.org/10.3389/fpsyg.2016.01909

Krueger, J. I., Vohs, K. D., & Baumeister, R. F. (2008). Is the allure of self-esteem a mirage after all? *American Psychologist, 63*(1), 64–65. https://doi.org/10.1037/0003-066X.63.1.64

Kruger, J., & Dunning, D. (1999). Unskilled and unaware of it: How difficulties in recognizing one's own incompetence lead to inflated self-assessments. *Journal of Personality and Social Psychology, 77*(6), 1121–1134. https://doi.org/10.1037/0022-3514.77.6.1121

Landy, J. F., Piazza, J., & Goodwin, G. P. (2016). When it's bad to be friendly and smart: The desirability of sociability and competence depends on morality. *Personality & Social Psychology Bulletin, 42*(9), 1272–1290. https://doi.org/10.1177/0146167216655984

Leary, M. R. (1996). *Self-presentation: Impression management and interpersonal behavior.* Routledge.

Leary, M. R. (2005). Sociometer theory and the pursuit of relational value: Getting to the root of self-esteem. *European Review of Social Psychology, 16*(1), 75–111. https://doi.org/10.1080/10463280540000007

Loewenstein, G., & Molnar, A. (2018). The renaissance of belief-based utility in economics. *Nature Human Behaviour, 2*(3), 166–167. https://doi.org/10.1038/s41562-018-0301-z

Luce, R. D., & Raiffa, H. (1957). *Games and decisions.* Wiley.

Luhmann, N. (1979). *Trust and power.* Wiley.

Milinski, M., Semmann, D., & Krambeck, H.-J. (2002). Reputation helps solve the 'tragedy of the commons'. *Nature, 415*(6870), 424–426. https://doi.org/10.1038/415424a

Murnighan, J. K., & Wang, L. (2016). The social world as an experimental game. *Organizational Behavior and Human Decision Processes*, *136*, 80–94. https://doi.org/10.1016/j.obhdp.2016.02.003

Nowak, M. A., & Sigmund, K. (2005). Evolution of indirect reciprocity. *Nature*, *437*(7063), 1291–1298. https://doi.org/10.1038/nature04131

Peterson, R. A., & Brown, S. P. (2005). On the use of beta coefficients in meta-analysis. *Journal of Applied Psychology*, *90*(1), 175–181. https://doi.org/10.1037/0021-9010.90.1.175

Poundstone, W. (1992). *Prisoner's dilemma*. Anchor Books.

Prati, F., Moscatelli, S., van Lange, P. A. M., van Doesum, N. J., & Rubini, M. (2018). The central role of morality in perceived humanness and unselfish behavior. *Social Psychology*, *49*(6), 330–343. https://doi.org/10.1027/1864-9335/a000352

Pruitt, D. G., & Kimmel, M. J. (1977). Twenty years of experimental gaming: Critique, synthesis, and suggestions for the future. *Annual Review of Psychology*, *28*(1), 363–392. https://doi.org/10.1146/annurev.ps.28.020177.002051

Rabin, M. (1993). Incorporating fairness into game theory and economics. *The American Economic Review*, *83*(5), 1281–1302. https://www.jstor.org/stable/2117561

Rabin, M., & Thaler, R. H. (2001). Anomalies: Risk aversion. *Journal of Economic Perspectives*, *15*(1), 219–232. https://doi.org/10.1257/jep.15.1.219

Raihani, N., & Barclay, P. (2016). Exploring the trade-off between quality and fairness in human partner choice. *Royal Society Open Science*, *3*(11), 160510. https://doi.org/10.1098/rsos.160510

Rapoport, A. (1966). *Two-person game theory: The essential ideas*. University of Michigan Press.

Rapoport, A. (1967). A note on the index of cooperation for prisoner's dilemma. *Journal of Conflict Resolution*, *11*(1), 101–103. https://doi.org/10.1177/002200276701100108

Rapoport, A., & Chammah, A. M. (1966). The game of chicken. *American Behavioral Scientist*, *10*(3), 10–28. https://doi.org/10.1177/000276426601000303

Rapoport, A., & Guyer, M. (1966). A taxonomy of two by two games. *General Systems*, *11*, 205.

Ray, J. L., Mende-Siedlecki, P., Gantman, A. P., & Van Bavel, J. J. (in press). The role of morality in social cognition. In K. Ochsner & M. Gilead (Eds.), *The neural bases of mentalizing*. Springer. Retrieved from https://psyarxiv.com/yzqtj

Rosenberg, S., Nelson, C., & Vivekananthan, P. (1968). A multidimensional approach to the structure of personality impressions. *Journal of Personality and Social Psychology*, *9*(4), 283–294. https://doi.org/10.1037/h0026086

Rousseau, -J.-J. (1754/1984). *A discourse on inequality*. Penguin.

Sally, D. (1995). Conversation and cooperation in social dilemmas. *Rationality and Society*, *7*(1), 58–92. https://doi.org/10.1177/1043463195007001004

Savage, L. J. (1954). *The foundations of statistics*. Wiley.

Sezer, O., Gino, F., & Norton, M. I. (2018). Humblebragging: A distinct – And ineffective – Self-presentation strategy. *Journal of Personality and Social Psychology*, *114*(1), 52–74. https://doi.org/10.1037/pspi0000108

Skyrms, B. (2003). *Stag-hunt game and the evolution of social structure*. Cambridge University Press.

Sliwka, D. (2007). Trust as a signal of a social norm and the hidden costs of incentive schemes. *American Economic Review*, *97*(3), 999–1012. https://doi.org/10.1257/aer.97.3.999

Tappin, B. M., & McKay, R. T. (2019). Investigating the relationship between self-perceived moral superiority and moral behavior using economic games. *Social Psychological and Personality Science, 10*(2), 135–143. https://doi.org/10.1177/1948550617750736

Trivers, R. L. (1971). The evolution of reciprocal altruism. *The Quarterly Review of Biology, 46*(1), 35–47. https://doi.org/10.1086/406755

Tversky, A., & Tversky, A. (1992). The disjunction effect in choice under uncertainty. *Psychological Science, 3*(5), 305–309. https://doi.org/10.1111/j.1467-9280.1992.tb00678.x

Usher, M., Tsetsos, K., Glickman, M., & Chater, N. (2019). Selective integration: An attentional theory of choice biases and adaptive choice. *Current Directions in Psychological Science, 28*(6), 552–559. https://doi.org/10.1177/0963721419862277

van Lange, P. A. M. (1999). The pursuit of joint outcomes and equality in outcomes: An integrative model of social value orientation. *Journal of Personality and Social Psychology, 77*(2), 337–349. https://doi.org/10.1037/0022-3514.77.2.337

Van Lange, P. A. M., & Kuhlman, D. M. (1994). Social value orientations and impressions of partner's honesty and intelligence: A test of the might versus morality effect. *Journal of Personality and Social Psychology, 67*(1), 126–141. https://doi.org/10.1037/0022-3514.67.1.126

van Lange, P. A. M., Rockenbach, B., & Yamagishi, T. (2017). *Social dilemmas: New perspectives on trust*. Oxford University Press.

von Neumann, J., & Morgenstern, O. (1944). *Theory of games and economic behavior*. Princeton University Press.

von Neunann, J. (1928). Zur Theorie der Gesellschaftsspiele [On the theory of parlor games]. *Matbematishe Annalen, 100*(1), 295–320. https://doi.org/10.1007/BF01448847

Wallace, D. F. (2005). *Consider the lobster and other essays*. Little, Brown and Co.

Wigner, E. (1967). *Symmetries and reflections*. Cambridge, MA: MIT Press.

Wojciszke, B. (2005). Morality and competence in person- and self-perception. *European Review of Social Psychology, 16*(1), 155–188. https://doi.org/10.1080/10463280500229619

Wojciszke, B., Bazinska, R., & Jaworski, M. (1998). On the dominance of moral categories in impression formation. *Personality & Social Psychology Bulletin, 24*(12), 1245–1257. https://doi.org/10.1177/01461672982412001

Appendix A. Payoff Matrices and Player Preferences

Payoff notation used throughout paper

		Player 2 Decision	
		Cooperate	Defect
Player 1 Decision	Cooperate	**R**eward	**S**ucker
	Defect	**T**emptation	**P**enalty

Summary of preferences

Table A1. Summary of Player 1 Preferences

Game	Player 1 Payoff Preference
Prisoner's Dilemma	T > R > P > S
Assurance (Stag Hunt)	R > T > P > S
Chicken	T > R > S > P
Trust	???
Volunteer's Dilemma	T > [R = S] > P
Social Comparison (Self-enhancement)	T > R > P > S

Appendix B. Illustrative payoff matrices for a suite of games

Prisoner's Dilemma

		Player 2 Decision	
		Cooperate	Defect
Player 1 Decision	Cooperate	3,3	1,4
	Defect	4,1	2,2

Assurance Game

		Player 2 Decision	
		Cooperate	Defect
Player 1 Decision	Cooperate	4,4	1,3
	Defect	3,1	2,2

Game of Chicken

		Player 2 Decision	
		Cooperate	Defect
Player 1 Decision	Cooperate	3,3	2,4
	Defect	4,2	1,1

Volunteer's Dilemma

		Player 2 Decision	
		Cooperate	Defect
Player 1 Decision	Cooperate	2,2	2,3
	Defect	3,2	1,1

Trust Game		Player 2 Decision	
		Cooperate	Defect
Player 1 Decision	Cooperate	3,3	1,4
	Defect	2,1	

Social Comparison		Reality	
		Actually above average	Actually not above average
Decision	Claim to be above average	2	0
	Claim not to be above average	1	1

ARTICLE

Harm inflation: Making sense of concept creep

Nick Haslam[a], Brodie C. Dakin[a], Fabian Fabiano[a], Melanie J. McGrath[a], Joshua Rhee[a], Ekaterina Vylomova[a], Morgan Weaving[a] and Melissa A. Wheeler[b]

[a]Melbourne School of Psychological Sciences, University of Melbourne, Melbourne, Australia; [b]Department of Management and Marketing, Swinburne University of Technology, Melbourne, Australia

ABSTRACT
"Concept creep" is the gradual semantic expansion of harm-related concepts such as bullying, mental disorder, prejudice, and trauma. This review presents a synopsis of relevant theoretical advances and empirical research findings on the phenomenon. It addresses three fundamental questions. First, it clarifies the characterisation of concept creep by refining its theoretical and historical dimensions and presenting studies investigating the change in harm-related concepts using computational linguistics. Second, it examines factors that have caused concept creep, including cultural shifts in sensitivity to harm, societal changes in the prevalence of harm, and intentional meaning changes engineered for political ends. Third, the paper develops an account of the consequences of concept creep, including social conflict, political polarisation, speech restrictions, victim identities, and progressive social change. This extended analysis of concept creep helps to understand its mixed implications and sets a multi-pronged agenda for future research on the topic.

ARTICLE HISTORY Received 20 September 2019; Accepted 10 July 2020

KEYWORDS Concept creep; conflict; harm; identity; morality

The idea of "concept creep" was introduced by N. Haslam (2016a) to describe a pattern of semantic inflation in some of the psychology's key concepts. Haslam argued that a set of related concepts had broadened their meanings over the past half-century, so that they now referred to a much wider range of phenomena than they did in earlier times. He noted that the meanings of academic concepts would not be expected to sit still, evolving in response to new evidence and changing theoretical fashions, but that it was important for psychologists to recognise and understand these historical changes.

As a case in point, Haslam examined the concept of "bullying". As initially defined in the developmental psychology literature in the 1970s, the term was

CONTACT Nick Haslam nhaslam@unimelb.edu.au Melbourne School of Psychological Sciences, University of Melbourne, Parkville VIC 3010 Melbourne, Australia

© 2020 European Association of Social Psychology

explicitly distinguished from general peer aggression and referred to direct aggressive behaviour that was intentional, repeated, and carried out in the context of power imbalance, where the perpetrator was more powerful than the victim in age, stature, or number. Over time, every one of these criteria was relaxed in the field of bullying research and theory. Increasingly it was recognised among adults in workplaces in addition to children in schoolyards, the requirements of intentionality and repetition were abandoned, and behaviour targeting those of equal or greater power was also commonly defined as bullying. Indirect, digitally mediated forms of aggression were acknowledged as "cyber-bullying", and increased acts of omission such as shunning were counted as bullying alongside acts of commission.

N. Haslam (2016a) presented several additional case studies of conceptual expansion. "Trauma" progressively broadened to include adverse life events of decreasing severity and those experienced vicariously rather than directly. "Mental disorder" came to include a wider range of conditions, so that new forms of psychopathology were added in each revision of diagnostic manuals and the threshold for diagnosing some existing forms was lowered (Fabiano & Haslam, in press;N. Haslam, 2016b). "Abuse" extended from physical acts to verbal and emotional slights, and incorporated forms of passive neglect in addition to active aggression. In the mid-20th century, "prejudice" referred to blatant antagonism to particular racial or ethnic groups, but in subsequent decades grew to include aversive, modern, benign, implicit, and unconscious attitudes towards an expanding set of disadvantaged and marginal identities.

After presenting these case studies of creeping concepts, N. Haslam (2016a) advanced four propositions. First, he distinguished two forms of semantic broadening. "Horizontal creep" occurs when a concept extends outward to refer to qualitatively new phenomena (e.g., "mental disorder" encompassing entirely new forms of behaviour and experience; "abuse" coming to include neglect), whereas "vertical creep" occurs when a concept's meaning extends downwards to refer to quantitatively less severe phenomena (e.g., "trauma" referring to vicarious or non-life-threatening experiences (N. Haslam & McGrath, in press); "prejudice" referring to subtle and ambiguous micro-aggressions (Lilienfeld, 2017)). The two forms of creep are not mutually exclusive but represent distinct dimensions – a concept might expand to refer to qualitatively new phenomena that are also less severe – and it may be difficult to determine whether a particular conceptual change is best described as vertical, horizontal, or both. Second, he argued that the case studies were all examples of a general pattern of conceptual expansion. Although it might be tempting to explain each concept's semantic shifts separately – the spread of mental disorder as evidence of "medicalisation" and the spread of prejudice as "political correctness", for example, a generalised explanation would be more parsimonious and might open up new ways of understanding the nature and drivers of conceptual change across the disparate conceptual domains. For example, a unified explanation might identify factors beyond the rise of medical discourse that accounts for why the concept of mental disorder has inflated, or point to factors that identify new ways of thinking about that rise as part of a broader pattern. Third, Haslam proposed that the common thread among the identified creeping concepts was *harm* – they all represented forms of harmful behaviour and experience or ways of being harmed – and any generalised explanation of concept creep therefore had to address the enlargement of specifically harm-related concepts. Finally, he suggested that concept creep was driven by a rising sensitivity to harm within at least some Western cultures, such that previously innocuous or unremarked phenomena were increasingly identified as harmful, and that this rising sensitivity reflected a politically liberal moral agenda.

In the years following the publication of the initial paper in 2016, "concept creep" has been widely deployed in political discourse, especially in the North American context (e.g., Campbell & Manning, 2018; Lukianoff & Haidt, 2018). N. Haslam (2016a) was at pains to emphasise that "concept creep" was a descriptive rather than critical term, intended to characterise a pattern of conceptual change rather than condemn it, and that the expansion of harm-related concepts was sure to have benefits as well as costs. However, it has come to be understood by some as a conservative or even reactionary idea. For example, it has occasionally been enlisted by combatants in the so-called "culture wars", highly politicised debates on social justice, oppression, and the limits on expression primarily centred on American college campuses, into narratives involving "fragility", "snowflakes", and the supposed decline of Western civilisation (Glancy, 2018).

In this context, it is timely to review the substantial programme of research on concept creep that we have been undertaking. Our review addresses three primary questions. First, we examine the characterisation of concept creep, presenting some theoretical refinements that update the original understanding of the phenomenon and a body of research that rigorously assesses historical semantic expansion in putative creeping concepts using the tools of computational linguistics. Second, we investigate the factors that may be causally responsible for concept creep, proposing several cultural, societal, and intentional or motivated sources of conceptual change, and review evidence for the proposition that sensitivity to harm has risen in recent decades. Third, we address the potential consequences of concept creep, both negative and positive. We then present an integrative model of concept creep and lay out an agenda for future research.

Characterising concept creep

Clarifying the boundaries of creep

The original presentation of concept creep (N. Haslam, 2016a) exemplified the phenomenon using case studies of six concepts drawn from the fields of clinical (addiction, mental disorder, trauma), developmental (abuse, bullying), and social psychology (prejudice). It argued that the common thematic element in these concepts was harm and noted that all of the concepts referred in some fashion to the negative or undesirable side of human experience. It further proposed that the semantic inflation that the concepts underwent had taken place "in recent decades" and illustrated accompanying rises in their relative frequency of use within the Google Books corpus from 1960 to 2005 to illustrate. This initial characterisation of concept creep was ambiguous or inaccurate in three respects, and subsequent evidence has clarified it.

First, it has sometimes been inferred that "concept creep" refers only to the six concepts that were first used to exemplify it. Instead, it should be made explicit that concept creep can refer to the semantic broadening of *any* harm-related concept in psychology or beyond. For example, we have examined a semantic change in "harassment" (Vylomova et al., 2019) and "hate" (N. Haslam & Murphy, 2020), and concept creep could also be explored in relation to such varied concepts as aggression, bipolar disorder, disability, misogyny, pain, racism, sexual assault, and violence, among many others. Harm-related concepts are semantically central to psychology, given its traditional foci on suffering, social conflict, and their amelioration. The primary claim of the theory of concept creep is not that every harm-related concept in psychology has demonstrated a semantic expansion in recent decades, but that there is a general tendency for this to be the case to a greater degree than for other concepts. It does not challenge the concept creep hypothesis if certain non-harm-related concepts expand their meanings, or if certain harm-related concepts do not. Determining whether there is indeed a general tendency for harm-related concepts to broaden semantically more than non-harm-related concepts is a focus of ongoing research.

Second, Haslam's (2016a) analysis of concept creep at times blurred the boundary between harm-relatedness and negativity. Harm is of course normally undesirable, and the six exemplary creeping concepts were all negative in this sense, but harm-related concepts as a semantic domain are not invariably undesirable. Within moral foundations theory (Graham et al., 2011), Harm is just one of five registers in which moral goodness as well as badness can be apprehended, and encompasses values and virtues involving Care. A dictionary of Harm foundation-related words contains positive terms such as compassion, empathy, protection, and safety, which are desirable because they shield against or otherwise mitigate harm. As concept creep is theorised to involve the semantic broadening of harm-related concepts, positive or negative, we might expect some or all of these desirable concepts to show evidence of expanded meanings, or to treat evidence against such expansion as grounds for qualifying the concept creep hypothesis. There is certainly anecdotal evidence that "safety" has extended its meaning in recent years to encompass protection from verbal and ideological as well as physical dangers (Campbell & Manning, 2018). In sum, "harm", not "negativity", is the central conceptual element when making sense of concept creep, a claim that is also supported by the finding, discussed at greater length later in the review, that people who endorse a harm-based morality tend to hold broad definitions of creeping concepts (McGrath et al., 2019).

Third, N. Haslam (2016a) was non-specific about when concept creep has occurred. As a process understood to be gradual it may be challenging to delimit when creep begins or ends, and it is highly unlikely that all harm-related concepts would display identically timed semantic expansions. Nevertheless, specifying more precisely when concept creep has occurred is important both to characterise it and to identify the concurrent historical trends that might be driving it. For example, one reading of concept creep, drawn from the work of Pinker (2011) on the decline of violence in the West, is that it is linked to the rights revolutions of the 1960s and 1970s. By this account, concepts of harm broadened as the result of a "civilising offensive": that is, previously tolerated forms of aggressive, domineering, and discriminatory behaviour became less socially acceptable at this time, and expanding concepts of what is harmful helped to define them as intolerable. If concept creep was a direct outgrowth of the rights revolutions, we would expect to see it accelerating when they were at the height of their influence and perhaps slowing again following their retreat in the 1980s.

Although definitive evidence is lacking, recent findings challenge this timeline. An analysis of semantic change in five harm-related concepts within a massive corpus of psychology articles (Vylomova et al., 2019), also discussed later in this review, found that change was greatest in every concept between the 1980s and the 1990s. Inspection of changes in the cultural salience of creeping concepts from 1960 to 2005 in N. Haslam (2016a) also consistently shows the steepest increases in the 1980s and 1990s, and Wheeler et al. (2019) similarly found the steepest rises in harm-related concepts in these decades. When characterising concept creep, it therefore now seems warranted to refer not to "recent decades" but to a process that has been particularly active in the 1980s and since, albeit not in lockstep for every concept. For example, N. Haslam and McGrath (in press) documented changes in the relative frequency of trauma-related concepts in the massive Google Books corpus from 1960 to 2008 as an index of their shifting cultural prominence. They found that "trauma" as a general concept rose most steeply in frequency during the 1980s but that specifically "psychological trauma" increased most sharply in the 1990s, and an ensemble of shared forms of trauma (i.e., "collective", "cultural" and "intergenerational" trauma) accelerated upwards in the 2000s. Thus, although concept creep and its cultural drivers may have been most evident from around 1980, specific concepts have distinctive creep trajectories during this period.

Explaining why concept creep may have gathered force since the 1980s remains extremely challenging, as many correlated historical changes took place around this time. Politically, the rise of neoliberal regimes across much of the Anglosphere (e.g., Reagan in the USA, Thatcher in the UK) may have led to a backlash focus on marginalised groups among traditionally liberal university researchers. Intellectually, the growing influence of critical theories originating in continental Europe may have driven attention to subtle forms of oppression. Culturally, the rise of post-materialist values favouring quality of life over materialist values of physical and economic security, which may have underpinned a growing concern with harm, was especially steep in the 1980s (Inglehart, 2008). Disentangling this skein of potential influences, and demonstrating how political, intellectual, and cultural factors produce semantic changes in concepts, is enormously difficult. However complex these factors may be, by locating an apparent historical inflexion point in the 1980s our recent work should help to resolve them.

Methods for assessing historical semantic change

The original analysis of creeping concepts presented in N. Haslam (2016a) was qualitative, based on a close reading of changes in the meaning of specific concepts within the psychological literature. This analysis was supported by quantitative analyses of changes in the relative frequency of related words in the Google Books corpus, a demonstration of "culturomics" (Michel et al., 2011). However, such frequency-based analyses do not assess changes in semantic breadth and thus cannot index concept creep directly. Evaluating semantic change in harm-related concepts in a systematic and quantitative manner is, therefore, an important task. Several computational methods for doing so have been developed in recent years, all based on changes in how language is used (Bybee, 2010).

Early computational attempts to evaluate semantic change examined large historical text corpora for evidence of changes between predefined periods in a word's frequency and in the words with which it is collocated. These approaches rested on the assumption that such changes in frequency and collocations reflect changes in word meanings and have been employed in numerous investigations (e.g., Heyer et al., 2009; Hilpert & Gries, 2016; Juola, 2003). Some have investigated n-grams (strings of words of length n) rather than single words. For example, Gulordava and Baroni (2011) used an n-gram corpus to compare language usage in the 1960s and 1990s by applying a distributional semantics approach that estimates the similarity between word meanings as a similarity of contexts in which they are used. Each word was represented as a high-dimensional sparse vector of its collocations with other (contextual) words, and historical change was estimated as cosine similarity between the corresponding word vectors from the two periods. The authors showed this similarity-based method to be superior to frequency-based methods for automatic detection of semantic change.

Although such quantitative analysis was prominent in corpus linguistics for many years, its limitations – primarily problems of generalisation – led to the development of models for language change that rely on dense representations of words (embeddings) that are obtained either from word co-occurrence statistics (count-based) or by training a model to predict a word from its context or vice versa (prediction-based). Prediction-based models, which are now dominant and have been shown to outperform count-based approaches (Kulkarni et al., 2015; Schlechtweg et al., 2019), involve training language models (such as word2vec, SGNS; Mikolov et al., 2013) incrementally for each subsequent time period ("epoch") and assessing cosine similarity between word vector representations in each epoch to track semantic changes so that the timing of changes can be located. Epoch-specific models can also be aligned post hoc using linear matrix transformations to evaluate the degree of change (Hamilton et al., 2016a). Hamilton et al. (2016b) further demonstrated the value of systematically examining nearest neighbours of a target word to evaluate semantic changes that are due to cultural shifts. One outcome of these technical advances has been the formulation and testing of laws of semantic change (e.g., Dubossarsky et al., 2017; Winter et al., 2014; Xu & Kemp, 2015), such as the relationship between rate of change and word frequency.

Applying computation methods to study concept creep

Inspired by these developments in lexical semantic change detection, Vylomova et al. (2019) applied some of the successful models to evaluate changes of five putatively creeping concepts: "bullying", "prejudice", "trauma", "harassment", and "addiction". Because concept creep is argued to originate in the recent academic literature of psychology and cognate fields, the analysis was carried out using a new corpus of abstracts from more than 800,000 articles published in 875 psychology journals between 1970 and 2019. Abstracts were chosen as the source of text because they provide a compact summary of the main contributions and intellectual context of the research reported in the articles.

Vylomova et al. (2019) first evaluated the change in semantic breadth of the five terms using a count-based method developed by Sagi et al. (2011) that employs latent semantic analysis. Semantic breadth was estimated as average cosine similarity between vector representations of the contextual usage of each word in each decade from the 1980s to the 2010s, where higher similarity represents lower semantic breadth (i.e., less disparate semantic vectors). The five concepts showed differing temporal trajectories over the four decades, although there was ample evidence of semantic broadening. "Addiction", for example, showed a consistency if there is a gentle increase in semantic breadth, whereas "harassment" broadened substantially from the 1990s onwards after narrowing from the 1980 to the 1990s.

Vylomova et al. then conducted a more detailed analysis, using the model proposed by Hamilton et al. (2016a). For each decade they first trained a prediction-based language model and then aligned the trained epoch-specific models using Procrustes. For each word, they extracted its most common collocation in each period of time and evaluated the dynamics of cosine similarity (i.e., how similarity between the word and its collocations changes over time). This analysis affords a finely detailed quantitative description of the shifting associations between a putatively creeping concept and its most common semantic contexts.

Figures 1 and 2 illustrate these analyses for "addiction" and "bullying", respectively. As Figure 1 shows, in the 1980s "addiction" had the highest similarity to terms related to substances such as "drug", "alcohol" and "heroin". In later decades, those similarities decline as the concept's strongest similarities shift towards behavioural terms such as "internet", "gaming" and "sexual", consistent with N. Haslam's (2016a) argument that addiction had inflated its meanings to encompass non-consummatory activities, as in so-called "behavioural addictions". Figure 2 shows that the meaning of "bullying" underwent a pattern of differentiated broadening. Its traditional associations with children and schooling remain relatively stable, but there is

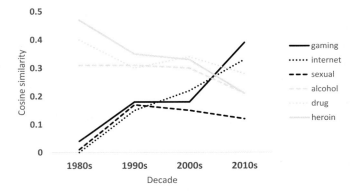

Figure 1. Changes in the semantic association of "addiction" with its most common nearest neighbours in psychology article abstracts by decade, 1980–2017, fromVylomova et al. (2019)

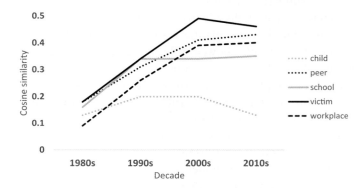

Figure 2. Changes in the semantic association of "bullying" with its most common nearest neighbours in psychology article abstracts by decade, 1980–2017, from Vylomova et al. (2019)

a growing emphasis on victimisation and on more adult- and organisation-focused meanings embodied by "workplace" and "peer". These trends are again in accordance with the argument that harm-related concepts are progressively acquiring new, broadened meanings in the academic discourse of psychology.

Further linguistic dimensions of concept creep

Findings such as those of Vylomova and colleagues support the general concept creep hypothesis that a variety of harm-related concepts have increased their semantic breadth over time. Further analyses are required to examine semantic changes in specific concepts in greater detail, and to explore new text corpora. The challenges involved in demonstrating historical semantic change computationally should not be under-estimated. However, computational analyses such as these do not exhaust the ways in which concept creep might be understood as a linguistic as well as a psychological phenomenon. Language, being a dynamic system, constantly changes in many ways: phonologically, morphologically, syntactically, and semantically, and linguists have a long history of studying language evolution and change. Some of these might shine a new light on concept creep.

Linguistic studies of diachronic (temporal) change processes have examined how words transform grammatically (grammaticalisation; Lehmann, 1985), how new words form, how other words become obsolete and fall out of use, and how existing words acquire new meanings or how they lose part of their meaning. The latter two changes are associated with semantic shifts – and are most relevant to the understanding of concept creep.

Bloomfield (1933) conducted the first comprehensive study of semantic shifts, defined as "innovations which change the lexical meaning rather than the grammatical function of a form" (p. 425), and developed a typology of nine forms or mechanisms of semantic change that is still used by researchers. Several of these may be particularly relevant to concept creep. First, Bloomfield distinguished narrowing (e.g., the Old English "mete", meaning food, becoming "meat", meaning edible flesh, a subset of food) and widening (e.g., the Middle English "bridde", meaning young birdling, coming to refer, as "bird", to birds of all ages). Second, Bloomfield presented litotes as a shift from a weaker to a stronger meaning (e.g., the pro-English "*kwalljan" [to torment] becoming the Old English "cwellan" [to kill]), whereas hyperbole is a shift in the opposite direction (e.g., the pre-French "*extonare" [to strike with thunder] becoming "astonish"). Finally, metaphor is a process whereby a word's meaning may extend to new, analogically linked meanings (e.g., the Germanic "biting" engendering "bitter", meaning harsh of taste).

Bloomfield's typology affords several ways to understand concept creep that might be explored in the future linguistic research. As a form of semantic expansion, some instances of creep might be interpreted as an expression of widening, hyperbole, or metaphoric extension. It could be argued that some instances of horizontal creep, in which a concept's meaning extends into qualitatively new phenomena (e.g., active "abuse" coming to refer also to passive neglect) might be viewed as examples of widening, and other instances of horizontal creep, where the new meaning is more clearly analogous to the original meaning (e.g., "cyber-bullying" vis-à-vis unmediated "bullying"), might be ascribed to metaphor. Hyperbole, in contrast, appears to be more germane to vertical creep, where a concept's meaning stretches to include less severe or intense phenomena (e.g., "trauma" being used to refer to relatively mild or vicariously experienced adversities).

The linguistic notion of "semantic bleaching" may also illuminate concept creep. This phenomenon occurs when concepts gradually lose semantic content (i.e., intensional features). For example, in earlier times "awesome" referred to events that induced awe, whereas it has come to refer to events that are merely positive, "awe" having been washed from the meaning. Although bleaching is generally understood as a form of semantic loss, the increased vagueness of bleached concepts creates a gain in the range of phenomena to which they may refer. Semantic bleaching can, therefore, be seen as a shift or change in the distribution of meaning rather than a simple loss (Hopper & Traugott, 1993). Arguably the relaxation of the original repetition criterion in recent definitions of bullying is an example of semantic bleaching that illustrates this point: if the concept of bullying loses this semantic feature, coming to refer to any antagonistic interpersonal behaviour directed towards someone of relatively low power, then bullying broadens to encompass single episodes of antagonism.

Linguistic concepts such as these should help to make sense of concept creep, as it is ultimately a claim about shifts in concept meanings. There is ample evidence from sociolinguistics that language change commonly reflects societal and cultural shifts of the sort implicated in concept creep (Blank & Koch, 2013; Kutuzov et al., 2018). Future research must examine which of the forms of semantic change best capture examples of concept creep, and also whether creep is best understood to involve gradual changes in a word's core meaning or more rapid changes in its nearest neighbours. This distinction, sometimes described as between linguistic drifts and cultural shifts, has been supported by the recent work of Hamilton et al. (2016b) and is amenable to computational linguistic study.

Causes of concept creep

The previous section introduced a sharpened analysis of the boundaries of concept creep by clarifying the domain of concepts proposed to have crept. In addition to this conceptual refinement, it presented evidence that harm-related concepts in psychology have indeed tended to undergo semantic inflation in the past half-century when semantic change is evaluated using methods drawn from computational linguistics. The section also suggests that the semantic changes involved may have been especially marked in the 1980s and since, and that in certain respects they resemble forms of semantic widening identified in the linguistic literature. These theoretical and empirical advances help to refine the characterisation of concept creep first sketched in N. Haslam (2016a), taking the evidence for concept creep well beyond its qualitative interpretation of conceptual change and quantitative analysis of word frequencies.

Improving how concept creep is characterised is an important basis for future research, but it is only a preliminary step towards explaining concept creep. If harm-related concepts have tended to broaden their meanings within psychology in the 1980s and since, especially if it can be shown that this broadening is at least somewhat distinctive to these concepts; then, we must ask what factors are responsible for that semantic inflation. No simple or definitive answer can be provided at present, and clarifying the complex, correlated, and multi-level factors involved in studying historical change processes is notoriously difficult. However, several candidates' causal influences can be sought in cultural shifts, societal changes, and intentional changes brought about by motivated political actors. In addition, we argue that cross-sectional evidence about the sorts of people who hold broader harm-related concepts may point to factors driving historical conceptual change.

Cultural causes

One of the most plausible explanations for concept creep is a growing sensitivity to harm in Western cultures, manifest in a rise in harm-based morality. If people have collectively become more sensitive to harm in their environments, we might expect them to identify a wider variety of phenomena as harmful. Expanded concepts of harm would serve this end. Evidence for this claim comes from a recent study by Wheeler et al. (2019), who examined trends in the use of moral language across the 20th century through the lens of the five domains of moral concerns proposed by Moral Foundations Theory (MFT; Graham et al., 2011). MFT, designed to categorise the automatic and intuitive emotional reactions that commonly occur in moral evaluation across cultures, identified five psychological systems (or foundations): Harm, Fairness, Ingroup, Authority, and Purity.

Each of the moral foundations is distinct, in that each embodies a separate set of associated concerns, virtues, and vices. The Harm foundation refers to issues of cruelty, the suffering of others, and the virtues of compassion, caring, and kindness. Fairness includes concerns of injustice, unfair treatment, reciprocity, equality, cheating, and individual rights. The Ingroup foundation covers loyalty and obligations for group membership, self-sacrifice, and betrayal. Authority is concerned with social order, an obligation to conform to hierarchical relationships, and obedience and respect for authority and tradition. The Purity foundation refers to contagion, both physical and spiritual, and encompasses concerns of sanctity, self-control, and the virtues of innocence and wholesomeness (Haidt & Graham, 2007; Haidt & Kesebir, 2010).

Using Google NGram Viewer, which allows users to gather relative word frequencies from the vast Google Books corpus of digitised books, we measured the proportion of moral foundation-related words within the corpus for the years 1900–2007. Foundation-specific terms were drawn from the Moral Foundations Dictionary (Graham et al., 2009), which was designed to include both positive "virtue" terms and negative "vice" terms, reflecting the valued and disvalued concepts of each of the five moral foundations. The dictionaries for each of the five moral foundations contained an average of 55 words and with one exception demonstrated excellent internal consistency. Trends in the relative frequency of each term in each year were standardised and then summed to generate average trajectories for each moral foundation, conceptualised as indices of its shifting cultural salience. We anticipated that the Harm foundation would show rising salience in recent decades, a requirement if rising cultural salience of harm underpins concept creep.

Figure 3 presents the trajectories for the five moral foundations, highlighting Harm, which shows a gentle decline until about 1960, punctuated by noticeable short-term rises around the two World Wars, and then rises steeply from about 1980. No other moral foundation demonstrates

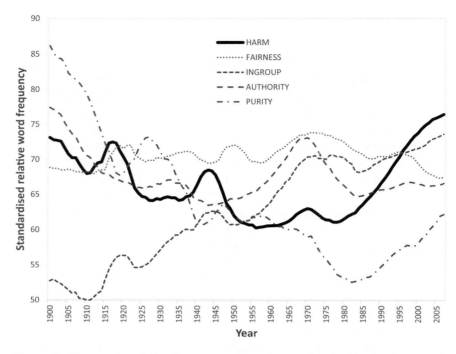

Figure 3. Changes in relative frequency of words associated with the five moral foundations in the Google Books corpus, 1900–2007, fromWheeler et al. (2019)

a similar rising trajectory in this period, suggesting that the upswing is specific to Harm. This sharp but steady increase in the late 20th century is consistent with N. Haslam's (2016a) proposition regarding concept creep and with the evidence of the computational analyses conducted by Vylomova et al. (2019) which identified the 1980s and 1990s as the period of greatest conceptual change. It is worth noting that positive and negative terms (i.e., virtues and vices) were highly correlated within the foundation of Harm, indicating that the late increase in harm sensitivity was not restricted to only negative terms (e.g., endanger, hurt, suffer) but also included terms relating to a morality of care (e.g., compassion, protect, peace). Although this analysis falls well short of demonstrating that large-scale cultural changes in the cultural salience of or sensitivity to harm are causally responsible for concept creep, it raises the plausibility of that proposition.

Societal causes

Broadening concepts of harm might reflect shifts in cultural values and preoccupations, but they could also spring from objective changes in social conditions. In particular, they might be due to decreases in the rates of harmful phenomena that people are exposed to in everyday life. It has been argued that rates of violence (e.g., homicide, war deaths) and other kinds of harm have been steadily declining for centuries (Pinker, 2011). While there are a variety of factors contributing to this decline, Pinker highlights that a central contributor is increased in empathy, self-control, and rationality in the modern era. The prevalence of severe harm is in decline because violence is becoming increasingly reprehensible to people worldwide.

However, despite the apparent decline in almost all kinds of violence, Pinker (2018) argues that people are if anything more focused on the prevalence of harm than in earlier times. Although he attributes some of this intensifying focus to the saturation and sensationalist coverage of contemporary media, psychological factors also contribute to it. We suggest that one reason why people continue to perceive harm as undiminished or even rising despite its reducing prevalence is because notions of what counts as "harm" inflate in response to that decreasing prevalence. In other words, as the rates of objective harm reduce, concepts of harm may expand to encompass new and previously innocuous phenomena, making harm appear as widespread as it ever was.

This possible mechanism linking reductions in the objective prevalence of harm to the semantic inflation of harm-related concepts has recently been investigated experimentally. In seven studies, Levari et al. (2018) found evidence of "prevalence-induced concept change", wherein people expanded their concepts in response to decreasing exposure to instances of those concepts. This was first demonstrated using simple perceptual phenomena. Participants were exposed to a long series of coloured dots on a screen that ranged from very purple to very blue and asked to categorise each dot as "blue" or "not blue". Participants in a condition which gradually decreased the proportion of blue dots began to classify dots as blue that they previously identified as purple, suggesting they adaptively expanded their concept of "blue" in response to seeing fewer blue dots. In subsequent studies, this same effect was replicated using more complex social phenomena. Participants who were exposed to decreasing prevalence of threatening faces on a screen grew more likely to categorise ambiguous faces as "threatening" and others asked to review the ethicality of research proposals were more likely to reject ethically neutral research proposals as unethical when the proportion of unethical proposals they read decreased.

Levari et al.'s (2018) findings imply that concept creep could be caused distally by the decreasing prevalence of the phenomena relevant to that concept. If crime and automobile accident rates decline, concepts of trauma may tend to broaden to include less serious harms, and if blatant expressions of bigotry recede the concepts of prejudice may extend to subtler manifestations. The implications of such conceptual changes may often be minor. However, both Pinker (2018) and Levari et al. (2018) point out that an unfortunate implication of this tendency to creep harm-related concepts in response to vanishing prevalence is that it can prevent us from acknowledging how much the prevalence of harms has declined. Determining whether concept creep is causally connected to downward shifts in the objective rate of harm in society, outside artificial experimental conditions, is therefore an important task for future research.

Concept creep as a motivated process

The preceding sections proposed that concept creep might be an unintended consequence of deeper cultural or societal changes. However, as several commentators have convincingly argued (Furedi, 2016; Sunstein, 2018), some examples of concept creep are surely the work of deliberate actors who might be called "expansion entrepreneurs". These actors actively seek the expansion of concepts to serve specific goals. In this section, we systematically explore the idea of concept creep as a motivated phenomenon by identifying some of the potential goals and incentives. We identify two broad domains of motivation that may drive expansion entrepreneurs: amplifying social problems; and importing moral, political or legal responses from already legitimised social issues.

The most well-established body of academic research on motivated concept creep appears in the context of collective action, where concept expansion can be used as a tactic to amplify the perceived seriousness of a movement's chosen social problem (Best, 1990; Charmaz et al., 2019). Movements for social change generally arise out of the group's identification of a social problem that the collective actors are driven to address (Van Zomeren, 2013; Wright et al., 1990). However, the definitions of these social problems rarely remain static as a social movement unfolds (Jenness, 1995), and groups may be motivated to expand or reframe the social problem in order to meet their strategic ends (Charmaz et al., 2019).

The process by which a social problem expands to cover a broader range of issues has been extensively documented within the context of real-world social movements by sociologists who describe the phenomenon as "domain expansion" (Best, 1990; Jenness, 1995). Such expansion can be effective means of enhancing the perceived seriousness of a social problem or threat by increasing the perceived prevalence of both "victims" and "perpetrators" (Jenness, 1995; see also Haidt, 2016). In one analysis, for example, Jenness (1995) analysed 32 campaigns against anti-gay/lesbian violence starting in the late 1980s, and found that the movement encouraged individuals affected by violence to share experiences that they may have otherwise considered too trivial or non-problematic; enabled the documentation of instances of anti-gay/lesbian violence that would not be classified as illegal; and garnered greater visibility to anti-gay/lesbian violence by proliferating reports on the high prevalence of the issue. Arguably, a similar strategic dynamic appears in recent activism that seeks to eradicate sexual harassment and promote gender equality. Where once sexual harassment referred to the use of threats or bribes to extort sex from employees (Best, 1999), in the age of #MeToo it commonly includes verbal and online behaviours. By this expanded definition, the prevalence of victims of sexual harassment was found to be 81% of American women in 2019 (Center on Gender Equity and Health, 2019), almost double the 43.6% rate reported by the Centres for Disease Controls and Prevention in 2015 (Smith et al., 2018) using a less expansive definition.

Another form of motivated concept creep, identified recently by Sunstein (2018), involves deliberately enlarging a concept so as to import the existing (negative) social or legal responses from its original narrower meaning into the new conceptual territory. This re-drawing of conceptual boundaries features in Sunstein's (2018) account of "opprobrium entrepreneurs", who seek to extend the opprobrium associated with an existing concept (e.g., bullying, prejudice) to the specific cases that they wish to condemn. Even if such extensions do not directly give rise to institutional remedies that apply to the narrower meaning, the stigma attached to the term may publicly tarnish the perpetrator. According to Sunstein (2018), the ultimate goal of opprobrium entrepreneurs is to trigger informational and reputational cascades against people holding views they oppose. If an opposed belief or expression can be labelled a form of "violence" or "hate", even if it does not rise to the level of legal definitions of those concepts, it may provoke the intensely moralised reaction normally recruited against other forms of violence or hate.

We have proposed that deliberate actors may expand concepts of harm either to amplify the perceived seriousness of social problems or to extend social, political or legal responses from already legitimated harms to new ones. It is uncertain how great such motivated processes play a role in concept creep and how they relate to the broader cultural and societal factors discussed previously (e.g., whether expansion entrepreneurs lead or merely capitalise on cultural trends favouring increased sensitivity to harm). However, we strongly suspect that concept creep is driven at least in part by motivated processes.

Individual differences in concept breadth

Concept creep is a historical phenomenon, and efforts to clarify its causes must, therefore, explore longitudinal dynamics. However, examining cross-sectional differences between people in concepts of harm may inform our understanding of concept creep in two ways. First, if harm-related concepts are expanding over time, people may adopt the broadened meanings to different extents as a function of their differing exposure to concept creep.

Second, the individual differences in political attitudes, personality traits, or demographic characteristics that are associated with holding broader concepts of harm may have implications for the historical drivers of concept broadening. With this rationale, we have carried out two studies of the individual difference correlates of harm-related concept breadth (HCB), defined as variations in the inclusiveness of concepts harm.

McGrath et al. (2019) developed a measure of HCB in which participants judged on a 1–6 scale whether abuse, bullying, prejudice, and trauma were present in vignettes that presented ambiguous or marginal examples of these concepts (five vignettes per concept). Against the possibility that concept breadth would be concept-specific, and for the proposition that they all share a common theme of harm (N. Haslam, 2016a), the subscales of the HCB measure were all positively correlated (mean rs =.33 and .35 in the two studies). Participants holding inclusive concepts of trauma also tended to hold inclusive concepts of prejudice, for example. The new scale had good reliability (α = .78 & .79 in Studies 1 & 2) as a measure of general HCB.

The two studies reported in McGrath et al. (2019) examined several potential correlates of the new HCB scale. In both studies, the strongest correlates of holding expansive concepts of harm were compassion-related trait values, left-liberal political attitudes, and forms of morality associated with both. However, several other distinctive associations were also found. In the first study of 276 American Amazon Mechanical Turk (MTurk) Workers, HCB was associated with affective and cognitive empathy, assessed by the Interpersonal Reactivity Index (Davis, 1983), a liberal political orientation, and most strongly of all with endorsement of harm- and fairness-based morality (rs = .44 & .40), as assessed by the Moral Foundations Questionnaire (Graham et al., 2011). Although endorsement of the harm-based morality covaried with liberalism and affective empathy, these three associations were the three independent predictors of HCB in a multiple regression analysis. Subsequent work (Jones & McNally, 2020) has replicated the association between liberalism and holding broader concepts of trauma, using a different measure of concept breadth, suggesting that this association is robust.

In the second study of 309 American MTurk Workers, constructs reflecting emotional concern for others and liberalism again emerged as strong correlates of holding broader concepts of harm (McGrath et al., 2019), which were also associated with sensitivity to perceiving injustice towards others, assessed by the Justice Sensitivity Inventory (Schmitt et al., 2010). However, in this study HCB was additionally associated with several variables that are less straightforwardly prosocial or political. HCB was found to correlate modestly with a tendency to see oneself as the victim of injustice ("victim sensitivity") and to greater feelings of personal vulnerability (a facet of Neuroticism), and a sense of personal entitlement (Brummel & Parker, 2015). The study also demonstrated that most of these individual difference variables were associated with HCB even after statistically controlling for a generalised tendency to hold more inclusive concepts. Interestingly, holding broader concepts of harm was not consistently associated with younger age in the two studies (Study 1 $r = -.02$, $p > .05$; Study 2 $r = -.21$, $p < .01$). Given that concept creep has been occurring gradually over recent decades, it might be expected that older individuals would tend to hold the relatively narrow concepts of harm that prevailed when they were growing up, but a weak negative correlation between HCB and age was only obtained in one study. Evidently, a simple generation-based interpretation of variations in the expansiveness of concepts of harm is untenable. More generally, although the samples in the two studies had substantial age ranges, their cross-sectional nature means they cannot directly inform us about processes of historical change, and their exclusively American composition further qualifies any general statements about how age is associated with HCB.

Our examinations of the correlates of harm concept breath to date have implications for popular narratives of concept creep. On one narrative, the expansion of concepts of harm represents a welcome and politically progressive increase in concern for the welfare of others, and especially the most vulnerable (e.g., Cikara, 2016). According to another narrative, concept creep is associated with "fragility" and "victimhood" and is most evident among younger people (e.g., Lukianoff & Haidt, 2018). Although both narratives find a degree of support in this work, our findings suggest that people who hold broader concepts of harm tend to demonstrate a strong concern for others and are not disproportionately young.

Consequences of concept creep

It is a truism that how we classify and interpret our experience is socially shaped, and that it influences how we behave and interact. It is also obvious that changes in the concepts we use to make sense of our experience are likely to induce changes in behaviour and social relations. This point has been made most forcefully by the philosopher Ian Hacking (1995), whose work on "looping effects" demonstrates how new concepts and classifications give rise to new social realities as people recognise themselves and others in new ways and form new identities and attitudes. Conceptual changes loop back to engender changed realities. It is therefore timely to ask what the effects of concept creep might be.

Social conflict

One probable effect of concept creep is widespread disagreement among people who hold harm-related concepts of differing breadth. If concepts of abuse, bullying, prejudice and the like are undergoing gradual expansion then people whose formative experiences are closer to and farther from recent shifts – whether as a function of age or social location (e.g., education) – may have discrepant thresholds for identifying harm, notwithstanding the evidence from McGrath et al. (2019) that age is only modestly associated with harm-related concept breadth. In effect, concept creep may stretch not only the definition of harm-related concepts but also the distribution of variants of those definitions within the population. The result of this stretching may be an increasing lack of consensus on moral issues and a widening penumbra of cases that are morally ambiguous or contestable.

The fact that people tend to understand harm so differently may therefore help to explain some yet to be determined proportion of public disagreement on morally charged social issues. Although moral disagreement is often attributed to differences in values, motives, or ideologies, some of it may be due to differences in the breadth of harm-related concepts. It is no wonder that people disagree fiercely if they are perceiving an ambiguous moral situation as either a heinous transgression (broad concepts of harm) or a minor peccadillo (narrow concepts of harm), or if childrearing practices considered normative by members of one generation are viewed as abusive by the next. These disagreements are likely to lead to conflicting opinions about whether problematic behaviour has occurred, how severe it is, what if anything should be done to punish "perpetrators", whether "victims" have legitimate standing as such, and whether institutional intervention is required to ensure justice for them. The fact that concept creep has taken place widens the range of social disagreements that arise. These conflicts may be especially challenging and intractable because, being based ultimately on understandings of "harm", they are intimately associated with moral and political commitments.

Moral typecasting and polarisation

As a result of its intimate connection to harm, concept creep and individual differences in harm-related concept breadth have the potential to contribute to social and political polarisation. One lens through which to understand this contribution is the theory of dyadic morality (Schein & Gray, 2016). This theory argues that the dyad of moral agent (the perpetrator of moral or immoral actions) and moral patient (the recipient of those actions) is central to morality and proposes that perceived harm is the basis for all moral judgement. When concepts creep, new and less severe forms of suffering or maltreatment come to be considered harmful. In this way, concept creep increases the range of actions and experiences that have moral relevance and thereby increases the number of people identified as moral agents and patients. We note in passing here that in identifying some experiences as less severe than others we are referring primarily to their subtlety and lack of intensity as single events rather than to the lack of severity of their effects. We do not deny that subtle events (e.g., ambiguous and deniable examples of racist behaviour) or repeated experiences (e.g., "death by thousand cuts" of street harassment) may have destructive outcomes.

Research in dyadic morality has identified the phenomenon of "moral typecasting" (Gray & Wegner, 2009). It demonstrates that moral patients are perceived as having a greater capacity for experience and sensitivity to pain, that moral agents are perceived as having a greater capacity for intention and responsibility, and that these agencies and patiency perceptions are inversely related. Being identified as a perpetrator of a harm results in diminished perception of patient-like qualities and amplification of agentic qualities. Inversely, for identified victims of harm, perceived agency is diminished, and perceived suffering is augmented. The upshot is that moral typecasting tends to generate polarised perceptions of cold and villainous perpetrators and deeply wounded and passive victims.

The dynamics of moral typecasting may thus contribute to aggravated punishment of moral transgressors because they are seen as being less sensitive to pain, and increased calls for third party protection of victims of moral harms because of their diminished capacity for personal responsibility. As concepts creep and individuals increasingly differ in the range of actions they believe are harmful, discrepant views regarding appropriate responses to these behaviours and experiences may further fuel polarisation. In essence, by broadening the range of situations in which harm is perceived, concept creep is likely to promote polarised views of perpetrators and victims, and by increasing differences between people in moral judgements of complex or ambiguous situations it is likely to deepen moral divisions.

In an illustrative study, Chan and Haslam (2019) examined the correlates of individual differences in the expansiveness of concepts of sexism. A sample of 201 MTurk workers rated whether 20 vignettes describing ambiguous potential instances of sexual harassment and gender discrimination were examples of these concepts. These ratings formed reliable scales for assessing the breadth of the two concepts. Participants then read another vignette describing a female employee encountering sexist behaviour perpetrated by male co-workers and rated her moral patiency (e.g., how upsetting the events were, how much she deserved compensation, whether a third party should intervene) and their moral agency (e.g., how responsible they were for their behaviour, how severe it was, how much they deserved punishment). They also completed the Moral Foundations Questionnaire (Graham et al., 2011) to assess endorsement of the five moral foundations and measures of political orientation and religiosity.

Chan and Haslam (2019) found that people holding broader concepts of sexual harassment and gender discrimination were more likely to endorse harm-based morality (rs = .27 & .39, ps <.01), consistent with our theoretical claim about the centrality of harm to concept creep and the findings of

McGrath et al. (2019) presented earlier. They were also somewhat more likely to have a liberal political orientation and to be female. In addition, participants holding broader concepts of sexism were more likely to see the woman and her male co-workers in the workplace sexism vignette in morally typecast ways (Gray et al., 2012). They saw the female victim as especially high in moral patiency (rs = .43 & .63, ps <.01) and the male perpetrators as especially high in moral agency (rs = .41 & .67, ps <.01). Importantly, the breadth of participants' concepts of sexism predicted these polarised judgements much more strongly (βs = .55 & .58, ps < .001) than their political orientation or gender, although more liberal participants also made significantly more sympathetic judgements of the woman (β = .16, p = .01) and nonsignificantly harsher judgements of the men (β = .09, p = .16). By implication, the breadth of people's concepts of harm may be a pre-eminent determinant of their moral judgements, potentially more influential than their political ideology or identity-based interests in some cases. Although this correlational study does not licence causal inferences, it is consistent with the view that concept creep leads ideas of harm to inflate, and that inflation may contribute to polarised moral judgements and resulting social conflict.

Speech codes and hate

The expansion of harm-related concepts has implications for acceptable self-expression and free speech. Creeping concepts enlarge the range of expressions judged to be unacceptably harmful, thereby increasing calls for speech restrictions. Expansion of the harm-related concepts of "hate" and "hate speech" exemplifies this possibility. N. Haslam and Murphy (2020) present evidence that the word "hate" has risen steeply in frequency of use both within the culture at large and in academic psychology. In the Google Books corpus, the relative frequency of the word dropped from 1920 to around 1980 then rapidly rose about 70% to the end of the corpus in 2008. In a corpus of over 500,000 psychology article abstracts from 1970 to 2018 the relative frequency of "hate" rose even more steeply, increasingly roughly threefold from the 1970s and 1980s to the 2010s. As was seen in the earlier findings of Vylomova et al. (2019) and Wheeler et al. (2019), both rises are steepest in the 1980s and since, as is true of other harm-related terms. This increase in the frequency of use commonly co-occurs with semantic broadening. In legal and political scholarship, "hate speech" has also changed its meaning in relation to harm in the recently proposed view that hate speech *constitutes* harm itself (Waldron, 2012) rather than it only *causing* harm to occur (Barendt, 2019). An obvious consequence for speech that is labelled "hateful" is that it usually becomes legally or socially disallowed from public discourse (Barendt, 2019). While we support the need for social and legal regulation on unmitigated free expression, we also note the inevitable trade-off between increasing speech prohibitions and people's autonomy for self-expression. A probable consequence of an expanding "hate speech" concept is increasing prohibitions on what is deemed acceptable belief expression and exchanging of ideas.

A second plausible consequence of creep in the concept of "hate" is the divisions it may sow in society. Concept creep does not occur uniformly or concurrently across the population but may be adopted more quickly by some individuals and groups than others, perhaps as a partial function of its social or political benefits to them or its alignment with their existing sympathies. A recent report on attitudes to free speech in the USA. (Ekins, 2017) revealed very large differences between people in concepts of "hate speech", with much of this variance being associated with differences in race, gender, age, and political ideology. Non-white, female, young, and politically liberal people were generally more likely to identify as hateful phenomena that others judged to be merely offensive or innocuous. There was also a tendency for more conservative people to identify "hate" more often in negative statement towards the USA, White people, and the police, implying that the link between concept creep and liberalism may not be invariant, but this tendency was weak relative to the more general pattern. This evidence of more conservative people holding a relatively low threshold for identifying "hate" when entities they value are targeted raises the possibility that there might be concepts where conservatism rather than liberalism is associated with greater concept breadth, contrary to the general pattern observed by McGrath et al. (2019).

Differing definitions of "hate", such as those documented by Ekins (2017), not only fuel disagreement about how specific episodes of controversial expression should be classified but also about their causes and remedies. Ekins found that groups who held more expansive concepts of "hate" were more likely to believe that problematic expressions sprang from the speaker's bad intentions, that they constituted acts of violence, and that there should be laws against them. Concept creep, and associated differences in the breadth of concepts of harm, may therefore have substantial implications for political disagreement over the limits of expression and may foster hostile and restrictive responses.

Concept creep and identity

A fourth domain in which concept creep is likely to have significant effects is its effects on identities. As Hacking's (1995) writings on looping effects and what he calls "dynamic nominalism" show, new concepts create new human kinds by altering the identities we ascribe to ourselves and others. As concept creep expands the range of phenomena that are perceived as harmful, it expands the range of people who are touched by harm and who may thereby come to identify as harmed or harmful.

The implications of concept creep for identity are particularly obvious in the field of mental disorder. Concepts of disorder have broadened considerably in recent decades, both through horizontal creep ("disease mongering") and vertical creep ("threshold lowering"). These enlargements of the field of psychopathology, sometimes referred to as diagnostic expansion or inflation (Frances, 2013; N. Haslam, 2016b), have taken place steadily over successive editions of the Diagnostic and Statistical Manual of Mental Disorders (DSM), and increase the prevalence of diagnosable mental disorder in the population. As more people receive diagnoses, they are apt to adopt the disorder as part of their self-concept and to have their selfhood perceived through that lens by others who are aware of their diagnosis. Adopting a disorder identity may have mixed blessings for the person who receives a diagnosis. On the positive side of the ledger, it may offer clarity about previously confusing experiences, the hope of suitable treatment and recovery, and a community of fellow sufferers. On the negative side, however, this identity may foster a view that their problems are fixed rather than mutable, that they are damaged or broken, and that they cannot control their fate (N. Haslam & Kvaale, 2015).

The increasing prevalence of diagnoses may also lead to increases in the tendency for individuals to assume social identities that are defined in terms of their relevant disorder. While the adoption of social identities is generally thought to be beneficial for individual well-being (C. Haslam et al., 2012), a growing body of evidence suggests that increased identification may, in fact, be detrimental in the case of identification with mental illness (see Cruwys & Gunaseelan, 2016; Klik et al., 2019). For example, Cruwys and Gunaseelan (2016) demonstrate that diagnosed individuals who perceive depression to be a central part of their identity were more likely to internalise the symptom norms related to depression (e.g., "keep thinking negative and unhelpful thoughts"), in turn leading to lower psychological well-being. Thus, for some individuals, a disorder diagnosis may, in fact, become a self-fulfiling prophecy, where the resultant assumption of a disorder-based identity may lead to the internalisation and manifestation of group norms dictating the way that those with the disorder should think and behave. In addition to any such effects on identity, broadened concepts of mental disorder may have other consequences such as unnecessary treatment via over-diagnosis, and exposure to the stigma and discrimination that face many people with mental health conditions. Rapid apparent rises in the prevalence of particular conditions, which actually reflect broadened diagnostic criteria, may also prompt mistaken searches for new causal agents to account for the change. This dynamic may underpin the spurious attribution of rising rates of autism to vaccination, as well as other spurious explanations of questionable "epidemics" (e.g., anxiety, attention deficit hyperactivity disorder). Concept creep in the psychiatric arena therefore potentially has substantial implications.

Concept creep may also have implications for identity outside that arena. Mental disorder is just one form of creeping harm, and broadening concepts of abuse, bullying, prejudice, and trauma might also lead an increasing number of people not only to label their experiences in these terms but also to self-identify as victims of them (Branscombe et al. 1999; Ellemers & Barreto, 2006). As these concepts come to refer to new and less extreme phenomena than they did in earlier times, they become available to a wider range of people as ways to make sense of their experience. As with mental disorder concepts, the implications of identifying oneself as a victim of one of these experiences may be mixed, but it is credible that some implications may be negative. For example, as people tend to infer that "traumas" have severe and enduring effects that require professional intervention, identifying oneself as a victim of trauma – perhaps especially in the case of marginal examples of this creeping concept – may be detrimental. Seeing oneself as a permanently wounded victim of a trauma may be less conducive to resilience than interpreting the experience in less catastrophic terms. Recently, Jones and McNally (2020) provided experimental evidence consistent with this possibility. Participants exposed to a gruesome video clip were more likely to define it as a trauma and report negative emotions and subsequent post-traumatic symptoms if they held broader concepts of trauma.

It is debatable whether there has been a marked increase in the adoption of victim identities as some commentators have argued (Campbell & Manning, 2018). It can also be debated whether victim identities have adverse implications, such as promoting passivity, self-exculpation, moral grandstanding, and entitlement, or are primarily empowering (Cikara, 2016). However, concept creep would be a plausible partial explanation of these cultural shifts if they have even a germ of truth. It remains to be determined how changes in concepts of harm have altered how people make sense of their experiences with adversity, or how many people have incorporated those experiences in an identity as a harmed person.

Positive consequences of concept creep

Sometimes concept creep is presented in an exclusively negative frame, on the assumption that its effects are invariably damaging or the belief that concepts should remain static. However, a balanced evaluation of concept creep requires an exploration of its both negative and positive implications. To that end, we offer three positive consequences of the phenomenon. First, concept creep creates labels that can be useful in drawing attention to harms previously overlooked. Consider the vertical expansion of abuse to include "emotional abuse". Prior to this development, society lacked a conceptual framework to interpret the behaviour as harmful; it was "just part of life" – a problem without a name. The invention of the label resulted in a collective appreciation of maltreatment of intimates as abuse. It alerted the collective conscience to the harms associated with emotional abuse, delivering an essential tool for observers and victims to interpret, identify, and protest it. Similarly, although the broadening of the concept of mental disorder by the accretion of newly labelled conditions is often criticised as disease mongering, it enables people whose difficulties were previously ignored to seek support.

Second, concept creep can prevent harmful practices by modifying social norms. Social norms emerge, in part, due to normative expectations: the belief that behaviour is typically condemned or endorsed by one's community (Bicchieri, 2016). As psychological concepts of bullying, prejudice, and abuse hold normative weight, marking new phenomena with these labels indicates that they are norm violations. For example, the collective labelling of child neglect as "abuse" signals that the behaviour is communally rejected, establishing a social norm that child neglect is wrong. Because social norms are powerful determinants of behaviour, the conceptual extension of negative psychological concepts should prompt a decrease in newly problematised behaviours. Changing definitions of bullying that include social exclusion and antagonistic acts expressed horizontally rather than only downwards in organisational hierarchies may also entrench norms against the commission of destructive behaviour.

Finally, the expansion of psychology's negative concepts can motivate interventions aimed at preventing or reducing the harms associated with the newly categorised behaviours. For instance, the conceptual expansion of addiction to include "behavioural" addictions (e.g., gambling and internet addictions) has prompted a flurry of research into treatment options, which has found that a range of psychosocial treatments can be successfully used to treat gambling, internet, and sexual addictions (Yau & Potenza, 2015). If these interventions are successfully implemented, their introduction constitutes a cause for celebration, and concept creep can be credited with creating the label that motivated the response.

An integrative model

Figure 4 synthesises the links we have proposed between concept creep as a historical phenomenon and its causes, correlates, and consequences. Concept creep itself is understood to take two primary forms that may be conceptualised linguistically through mechanisms such as metaphor, semantic widening, hyperbole, and semantic bleaching. It is hypothesised to be driven by a combination of cultural changes reflected in rising sensitivity to harm, operating primarily from the 1980s and since; societal changes reflected in gradually declining rates of adversity and risk in Western nations; and motivated conceptual expansions in the service of social or political ends. Concept creep is hypothesised to be associated with systematic individual differences in tendencies to inflate harm, which research shows to involve a combination of prosocial tendencies, political liberalism, and personal vulnerability and sensitivity to threat. Creep is hypothesised to be in part responsible for an assortment of consequences, including the promotion of social disagreements and polarised moral judgements, drives to restrict expression, personal identities based on harm and victimisation, but also progressive social change.

Agenda for future research

Research on concept creep is in its early stages and substantial work is required to fill in many of the gaps and speculations identified in this review. Future studies must address a variety of lingering issues related to the characterisation, causes, and consequences of this phenomenon.

In regard to characterisation, considerable work is needed to refine computational linguistic analyses of the time course of semantic inflation of harm-related concepts, and to determine whether such inflation is indeed somewhat distinctive to harm-related concepts relative to others. Research is also needed to answer whether concept creep is primarily about harm as a thematic domain rather than negativity as a conceptual valence, and to clarify the relationship between rises in the use frequency (i.e., cultural salience) of concepts and rises in their semantic breadth. Studies must also examine semantic inflation in text corpora beyond psychology articles to clarify whether the same broadening has occurred in other academic disciplines and in the culture at large, and to explore how changes in academic discourse have disseminated into that culture. Research should examine broad trends across multiple creeping concepts as well as explore the historical trajectories of specific concepts (e.g., trauma, prejudice). In addition, researchers should examine possible semantic broadening of harm-related concepts in languages other than English. Finally, linguistic analyses should investigate how well examples of concept creep can be understood in terms of known forms of semantic change such as widening and hyperbole.

Future research on the causes of concept creep must specify more precisely the cultural changes that have contributed to the phenomenon, clarifying whether, where, and how any rising sensitivity to harm has manifested in our societies, and in the process attempt to locate when semantic broadening accelerated, noting lines of evidence pointing to the 1980s as a critical decade. Research should also ask whether the link between the reduced prevalence of a phenomenon and widening concepts of it demonstrated experimentally by Levari et al. (2018) is plausible as a mechanism for explaining widening concepts of harm. Finally, studies must resolve the extent to which concept creep reflects deliberate expansion entrepreneurship by politically or otherwise motivated actors.

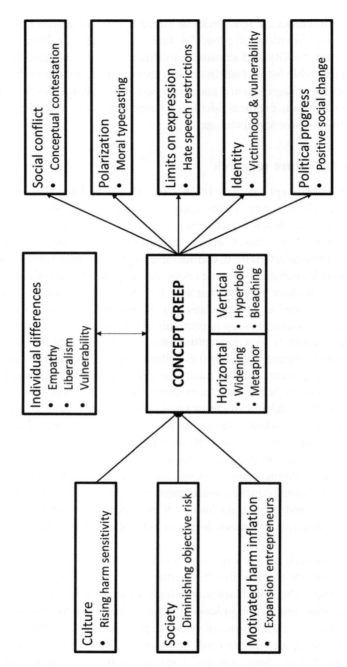

Figure 4. Integrative model of concept creep's proposed causes, correlates, and consequences.

In relation to the consequences of concept creep, further research should examine the extent to which the historical broadening of harm-related concepts does indeed contribute to social and political polarisation and disagreements about the interpretation of problematic events, such as whether or not they represent bullying, prejudice, or trauma. Studies are also urgently needed to clarify how inflating concepts of harm influence people's identities, whether victim-based identities are indeed on the rise as a result of such inflation, and whether such identities primarily engender vulnerability or empowerment in people who adopt them. More basically, it will be crucial to determine whether the legacy of concept creep is, on balance, predominantly positive or negative, and whether that question can even be answered in a neutral and unbiased way.

Many of these future research directions, especially in relation to concept creep's causes and consequences, are exploratory. The theory of concept creep does not make strong claims about which of several possible causal influences is most central or whether the consequences are primarily desirable or undesirable. However, some questions imply more stringent tests of the theory. If semantic broadening over the past half-century has not been greater among harm-related concepts than among other concepts on average, the theory is challenged. It is similarly challenged if close examination of concepts that have and have not broadened points to systematic exceptions to the prediction (i.e., groups of harm-related concepts that have not inflated or groups of harm-adjacent concepts [e.g., fairness-related] that have inflated), which might suggest that "harm" is too broad or narrow a concept to account for observed patterns of semantic expansion. The theory of concept creep would also be called into question if observed patterns of semantic broadening were found to be mere artefacts of increasing word frequency or if it was confined to academic discourse and not present in public discourse. A systematic investigation of semantic changes within psychology and beyond might enable more searching tests of concept creep theory, and serious consideration of exceptions to its claims might assist in refining it.

Conclusions

Concept creep is a phenomenon that has wide-ranging social and cultural ramifications. It is implicated in several of the most timely and contentious social issues in contemporary Western societies, and places psychology at the forefront of them as a source of many of our dominant concepts for making sense of harm. We believe that social psychology has a special role to play in accounting for the benefits, costs, and causes of creeping concepts. In taking on that role, however, social psychologists will have to engage deeply with theories, findings, methodologies, and scholars from other disciplines in overcoming the challenges of understanding historical, cultural, and linguistic change.

Funding

This work was supported by the Australian Research Council [DP170104948].

ORCID

Nick Haslam (iD) http://orcid.org/0000-0002-1913-2340
Melanie J. McGrath (iD) http://orcid.org/0000-0001-8632-218X
Joshua Rhee (iD) http://orcid.org/0000-0002-6245-7060
Ekaterina Vylomova (iD) http://orcid.org/0000-0002-4058-5459
Morgan Weaving (iD) http://orcid.org/0000-0002-8519-868X
Melissa A. Wheeler (iD) http://orcid.org/0000-0002-0319-1987

References

Barendt, E. (2019). What is the harm of hate speech? *Ethical Theory and Moral Practice, 22*(3), 539–553. https://doi.org/10.1007/s10677-019-10002-0

Best, J. (1990). *Threatened children: Rhetoric and concern about child-victims.* University of Chicago Press.

Best, J. (1999). *Random violence: How we talk about new crimes and new victims.* University of California Press.

Bicchieri, C. (2016). *Norms in the wild.* Oxford University Press.

Blank, A., & Koch, P. (Eds.). (2013). *Historical semantics and cognition* (Vol. 13). Walter de Gruyter.

Bloomfield, L. (1933). *Language.* Rinehart and Winston.

Brummel, B. J., & Parker, K. N. (2015). Obligation and entitlement in society and the workplace. *Applied Psychology, 64*(1), 127–160. https://doi.org/10.1111/apps.12023

Bybee, J. (2010). *Language, usage and cognition.* Cambridge University Press.

Campbell, B., & Manning, J. (2018). *The rise of victimhood: Microaggressions, safe spaces, and the new culture wars.* Palgrave Macmillan.

Center on Gender Equity and Health. (2019). *Measuring #MeToo: A national study on sexual harassment and assault.* University of California.

Chan, J., & Haslam, N. (2019). Broad concepts of sexism predict polarized moral judgments of victims and perpetrators. *Personality and Individual Differences, 150,* 109488. https://doi.org/10.1016/j.paid.2019.06.031

Charmaz, K., Harris, S. R., & Irvine, L. (2019). *The social self and everyday life: Understanding the world through symbolic interactionism.* John Wiley & Sons.

Cikara, M. (2016). Concept expansion as a source of empowerment. *Psychological Inquiry, 27*(1), 29–33. https://doi.org/10.1080/1047840X.2016.1111830

Cruwys, T., & Gunaseelan, S. (2016). "Depression is who I am": Mental illness identity, stigma and wellbeing. *Journal of Affective Disorders, 189,* 36–42. https://doi.org/10.1016/j.jad.2015.09.012

Davis, M. H. (1983). Measuring individual differences in empathy: Evidence for a multidimensional approach. *Journal of Personality and Social Psychology, 44* (1), 113–126. https://doi.org/10.1037/0022-3514.44.1.113

Dubossarsky, H., Weinshall, D., & Grossman, E. (2017). Outta control: Laws of semantic change and inherent biases in word representation models. In

EUROPEAN REVIEW OF SOCIAL PSYCHOLOGY 283

Proceedings of the 2017 conference on empirical methods in natural language processing (pp. 1136–1145), Copenhagen, Denmark.

Ekins, E. (2017). *The state of free speech and tolerance in America: Attitudes about free speech, campus speech, religious liberty, and tolerance of political expression*. Cato Institute.

Ellemers, N., & Barreto, M. (2006). Social identity and self-presentation at work: How attempts to hide a stigmatised identity affect emotional well-being, social inclusion and performance. *Netherlands Journal of Psychology*, *62*(1), 51–57. https://doi.org/10.1007/BF03061051

Fabiano, F., & Haslam, N. (in press). Diagnostic inflation in the DSM: A meta-analysis of changes in the stringency of psychiatric diagnosis from DSM-III to DSM-5. Clinical Psychology Review. http://doi.org/10.1016/j.cpr.2020.101889

Frances, A. (2013). *Saving normal: An insider's revolt against out-of- control psychiatric diagnosis, DSM-5, big pharma, and the medicalization of ordinary life*. William Morrow.

Furedi, F. (2016). The cultural underpinning of concept creep. *Psychological Inquiry*, *27*(1), 34–39. https://doi.org/10.1080/1047840X.2016.1111120

Glancy, J. (2018 September 2). Generation snowflake: Meet the professors who blame helicopter parents for coddling the minds of today's students. *The Sunday Times*. https://www.thetimes.co.uk/article/generation-snowflake-meet-the-professors-who-blame-helicopter-parents-for-coddling-the-minds-of-todays-students-mjwdxftx9

Graham, J., Haidt, J., & Nosek, B. A. (2009). Liberals and conservatives rely on different sets of moral foundations. *Journal of Personality and Social Psychology*, *96*(5), 1029–1046. https://doi.org/10.1037/a0015141

Graham, J., Nosek, B. A., Haidt, J., Iyer, R., Koleva, S., & Ditto, P. H. (2011). Mapping the moral domain. *Journal of Personality and Social Psychology*, *101*(2), 366–385. https://doi.org/10.1037/a0021847

Gray, K., & Wegner, D. M. (2009). Moral typecasting: Divergent perceptions of moral agents and moral patients. *Journal of Personality and Social Psychology*, *96*(3), 505–520. https://doi.org/10.1037/a0013748

Gray, K., Young, L., & Young, L. (2012). Mind perception is the essence of morality. *Psychological Inquiry*, *23*(2), 101–124. https://doi.org/10.1080/1047840X.2012.651387

Gulordava, K., & Baroni, M. (2011). A distributional similarity approach to the detection of semantic change in the Google Books Ngram corpus. In *Proceedings of the GEMS 2011 workshop on geometrical models of natural language semantics* (pp. 67–71). Edinburgh.

Hacking, I. (1995). The looping effect of human kinds. In D. Sperber, D. Premack, & A. J. Premack (Eds.), *Causal cognition: A multidisciplinary debate* (pp. 351–383). Oxford University Press.

Haidt, J., & Kesebir, S. (2010). Morality. In S. T. Fiske, D. T. Gilbert, & G. Lindzey (Eds.), *Handbook of social psychology* (Vol. 5, pp. 797–832). Wiley.

Haidt, J. (2016). Why concepts creep to the left. *Psychological Inquiry*, *27*(1), 40–45. https://doi.org/10.1080/1047840X.2016.1115713

Haidt, J., & Graham, J. (2007). When morality opposes justice: Conservatives have moral intuitions that liberals may not recognize. *Social Justice Research*, *20*(1), 98–116. https://doi.org/10.1007/s11211-007-0034-z

Hamilton, W. L., Leskovec, J., & Jurafsky, D. (2016a). Diachronic word embeddings reveal statistical laws of semantic change. In *Proceedings of the 54th annual meeting of the association for computational linguistics (Volume 1: Long Papers)* (pp. 1489–1501), Berlin, Germany.

Hamilton, W. L., Leskovec, J., & Jurafsky, D. (2016b). Cultural shift or linguistic drift? Comparing two computational measures of semantic change. In *Proceedings of the conference on empirical methods in natural language processing. conference on empirical methods in natural language processing* (Vol. 2016, p. 2116), Austin, Texas, USA.

Haslam, C., Jetten, J., & Haslam, S. A. (2012). *The social cure: Identity, health and well-being.* Psychology press.

Haslam, N. (2016a). Concept creep: Psychology's expanding concepts of harm and pathology. *Psychological Inquiry, 27*(1), 1–17. https://doi.org/10.1080/1047840X.2016.1082418

Haslam, N. (2016b). Looping effects and the expanding concept of mental disorder. *Journal of Psychopathology, 22,* 4–9.

Haslam, N., & Murphy, S. C. (2020). Hate, dehumanization, and "hate". In R. J. Sternberg (Ed.), *Perspectives on hate: How it originates, develops, manifests, and spreads* (pp. 27–41). American Psychological Association.

Haslam, N., & Kvaale, E. (2015). Biogenetic explanations of mental disorder: The mixed blessings model. *Current Directions in Psychological Science, 24*(5), 399–404. https://doi.org/10.1177/0963721415588082

Haslam, N., & McGrath, M. J. (in press). The concept creep of trauma. *Social Research.*

Heyer, G., Holz, F., & Teresniak, S. (2009). Change of topics over time-tracking topics by their change of meaning. *KDIR, 9,* 223–228.

Hilpert, M., & Gries, S. T. (2016). Quantitative approaches to diachronic corpus linguistics. In M. Kytö & P. Pahta (Eds.), *The Cambridge handbook of English historical linguistics* (pp. 36–53). Cambridge University Press.

Hopper, P. J., & Traugott, E. (1993). *Grammaticalization.* Cambridge University Press.

Inglehart, R. F. (2008). Changing values among Western publics from 1970 to 2006. *West European Politics, 31*(1–2), 130–146. https://doi.org/10.1080/01402380701834747

Jenness, V. (1995). Social movement growth, domain expansion, and framing processes: The gay/lesbian movement and violence against gays and lesbians as a social problem. *Social Problems, 42*(1), 145–170. https://doi.org/10.2307/3097009

Jones, P. J., & McNally, R. J. (2020, May 11). *Does broadening one's concept of trauma undermine resilience?* https://doi.org/10.31234/osf.io/5ureb

Juola, P. (2003). The time course of language change. *Computers and the Humanities, 37*(1), 77–96. https://doi.org/10.1023/A:1021839220474

Klik, K. A., Williams, S. L., & Reynolds, K. J. (2019). Toward understanding mental illness stigma and help-seeking: A social identity perspective. *Social Science & Medicine, 222,* 35–43. https://doi.org/10.1016/j.socscimed.2018.12.001

Kulkarni, V., Al-Rfou, R., Perozzi, B., & Skiena, S. (2015). Statistically significant detection of linguistic change. In *Proceedings of the 24th international conference on world wide web* (pp. 625–635). International World Wide Web Conferences Steering Committee.

Kutuzov, A., Øvrelid, L., Szymanski, T., & Velldal, E. (2018). Diachronic word embeddings and semantic shifts: A survey. In *Proceedings of the 27th international conference on computational linguistics* (pp. 1384–1397). Association for Computational Linguistics, Santa Fe, New Mexico, USA.

Lehmann, C. (1985). *Grammaticalization: Synchronic variation and diachronic change* (Vol. 20). Na.

Levari, D. E., Gilbert, D. T., Wilson, T. D., Sievers, B., Amodio, D. M., & Wheatley, T. (2018). Prevalence-induced concept change in human judgment. *Science, 360* (6396), 1465–1467. https://doi.org/10.1126/science.aap8731

Lilienfeld, S. O. (2017). Microaggressions: Strong claims, inadequate evidence. *Perspectives on Psychological Science, 12*(1), 138–169. https://doi.org/10.1177/1745691616659391

Lukianoff, G., & Haidt, J. (2018). *The coddling of the American mind: How good intentions and bad ideas are setting up a generation for failure.* Penguin.

McGrath, M. J., Randall-Dzerdz, K., Wheeler, M. A., Murphy, S., & Haslam, N. (2019). Concept creepers: Individual differences in harm-related concepts and their correlates. *Personality and Individual Differences, 147*, 79–84. https://doi.org/10.1016/j.paid.2019.04.015

Michel, J. B., Shen, Y. K., Aiden, A. P., Veres, A., Gray, M. K., Pickett, J. P., Hoiberg, D., Clancy, D., Norvig, P., Orwant, J., & Pinker, S. (2011). Quantitative analysis of culture using millions of digitized books. *Science, 331*(6014), 176–182. https://doi.org/10.1126/science.1199644

Mikolov, T., Chen, K., Corrado, G., & Dean, J. (2013). Efficient estimation of word representations in vector space. *arXiv Preprint arXiv:1301.3781.*

Pinker, S. (2011). *The better angels of our nature: Why violence has declined.* Viking.

Pinker, S. (2018). *Enlightenment now: The case for reason, science, humanism, and progress.* Penguin.

Sagi, E., Kaufmann, S., & Clark, B. (2011). Tracing semantic change with latent semantic analysis. In K. Allen & J. A. Robinson (Eds.), *Current Methods in Historical Semantics* (pp. 161–183).De Gruyter Mouton.

Schein, C., & Gray, K. (2016). Moralization and harmification: The dyadic loop explains how the innocuous becomes harmful and wrong. *Psychological Inquiry, 27*(1), 62–65. https://doi.org/10.1080/1047840X.2016.1111121

Schlechtweg, D., Hätty, A., Del Tredici, M., & Walde, S. S. I. (2019). A wind of change: Detecting and evaluating lexical semantic change across times and domains. In *Proceedings of the 57th annual meeting of the association for computational linguistics* (pp. 732–746). Association for Computational Linguistics, Florence, Italy.

Schmitt, M., Baumert, A., Gollwitzer, M., & Maes, J. (2010). The justice sensitivity inventory: Factorial validity, location in the personality facet space, demographic pattern, and normative data. *Social Justice Research, 23*(2–3), 211–238. https://doi.org/10.1007/s11211-010-0115-2

Smith, S. G., Zhang, X., Basile, K. C., Merrick, M. T., Wang, J., Kresnow, M., & Chen, J. (2018). *The National intimate partner and sexual violence survey (NISVS): 2015 data brief – updated release.* Centers for Disease Control and Prevention.

Sunstein, C. R. (2018). *The power of the normal.* Available at SSRN https://ssrn.com/abstract=3239204

Van Zomeren, M. (2013). Four core social-psychological motivations to undertake collective action. *Social and Personality Psychology Compass, 7*(6), 378–388. https://doi.org/10.1111/spc3.12031

Vylomova, E., Murphy, S., & Haslam, N. (2019). Evaluation of semantic change of harm-related concepts in psychology. In *Proceedings of the 1st International Workshop on Computational Approaches to Historical Language Change* (pp. 29–34). Association for Computational Linguistics, Florence, Italy.

Waldron, J. (2012). *The harm in hate speech*. Harvard University Press.
Wheeler, M. A., McGrath, M. J., & Haslam, N. (2019). Twentieth century morality: The rise and fall of moral concepts from 1900 to 2007. *PLoS ONE, 14*(2), e0212267. https://doi.org/10.1371/journal.pone.0212267
Winter, B., Thompson, G., & Urban, M. (2014). Cognitive factors motivating the evolution of word meanings: Evidence from corpora, behavioral data and encyclopedic network structure. In E. A. Cartmill, S. Roberts, H. Lyn & H. Cornish (Eds.), *The Evolution of Language* (pp. 353–360).World Scientific.
Wright, S. C., Taylor, D. M., & Moghaddam, F. M. (1990). Responding to membership in a disadvantaged group: From acceptance to collective protest. *Journal of Personality and Social Psychology, 58*(6), 994–1003. https://doi.org/10.1037/0022-3514.58.6.994
Xu, Y., & Kemp, C. (2015). A computational evaluation of two laws of semantic change. In *Proceedings of the 37th Annual Conference of the Cognitive Science Society*, Pasadena, California, USA.
Yau, Y. H. C., & Potenza, M. N. (2015). Gambling disorder and other behavioral addictions. *Harvard Review of Psychiatry, 23*(2), 134–146. https://doi.org/10.1097/HRP.0000000000000051

ARTICLE

A communal approach to sexual need responsiveness in romantic relationships

Emily A. Impett[a], James J. Kim[b] and Amy Muise[c]

[a]Department of Psychology, University of Toronto Mississauga, Toronto, Canada; [b]Department of Psychology, Western University, London, Canada; [c]Department of Psychology, York University, Toronto, Canada

ABSTRACT
Sex is a crucial factor that impacts the quality and stability of relationships, yet many couples report recurrent sexual issues – such as discrepancies in their desired sexual frequency or levels of sexual desire – that detract from their relationship quality. This article describes how applying the theory of communal motivation from relationship science to the sexual domain of relationships can shed light onto understanding how couples can maintain desire over time, remain satisfied in the face of conflicting sexual interests, and decline one another's sexual advances in ways that protect their relationship. We integrate a decade of research on communal motivation, sexual rejection, and responses to sexual rejection to provide a better, and more holistic, understanding of how partners can successfully balance their sexual needs to ultimately reap the powerful rewards of a fulfiling sexual connection.

ARTICLE HISTORY Received 4 July 2019; Accepted 11 July 2020

KEYWORDS Relationships; sexuality; communal motivation; rejection; need fulfilment

Romantic relationships profoundly shape physical health (Holt-Lunstad et al., 2010) and psychological well-being (Diener & Seligman, 2002) by providing people with intimacy, support and companionship. Even with these powerful benefits, satisfying romantic relationships are difficult to maintain, with 40–50% of marriages in Europe (Eurostat, 2019), the United States (Pew Research Center, 2017) and Canada (Kelly, 2015) ending in divorce. Sexual intimacy is a core ingredient of happy, stable relationships (e.g., Birnbaum & Finkel, 2015; Sprecher, 2002), yet many couples find it challenging to maintain feelings of passion and desire over the course of a long-term relationship (see reviews by Impett et al., 2014; Carswell & Impett, under review). Sexual desire tends to decline with increased relationship duration (Baumeister & Bratslavsky, 1999; Schmiedeberg & Schröder, 2016), particularly when couples transition to parenthood

CONTACT Emily A. Impett emily.impett@utoronto.ca University of Toronto Mississauga, Toronto, Canada

© 2020 European Association of Social Psychology

(Ahlborg et al., 2005; Woolhouse et al., 2012) and older adulthood (DeLamater, 2012; Syme, 2014). More than one-third (38%) of partners in long-term relationships report experiencing a sexual issue (e.g., low desire, disagreements about preferred sexual frequency; Miller et al., 2003), and, in the majority of long-term, heterosexual relationships, one partner has chronically lower sexual desire than the other (Davies et al., 1999; Mark, 2015). Conflicts about sexual issues fuel interpersonal vulnerability (Rehman et al., 2019, 2017), are more impactful than non-sexual conflicts in predicting relationship quality (Rehman et al., 2017), and are one of the most difficult types of conflict to resolve (Geiss & O'Leary, 1981; Sanford, 2003).

To better understand how couples can successfully manage situations in which their sexual interests diverge, the bulk of previous research has examined factors that boost or reignite sexual desire to increase couples' sexual frequency and satisfaction (Impett et al., 2015). It is certainly important for romantic couples to prioritise sex since sexual frequency is robustly linked with increased life and relationship satisfaction (Kashdan et al., 2018; Muise et al., 2016). However, because it is not always possible or optimal for partners to engage in sex, especially when they have low desire (Impett & Peplau, 2003), they may frequently be in the position of needing to decline one another's sexual advances. Indeed, married and cohabiting couples report that sexual rejection occurs about once a week (Byers & Heinlein, 1989; Dobson et al., 2020), which is the same frequency with which couples in long-term relationships report engaging in sexual activity (Muise et al., 2016). Given this, another critical way to help couples successfully navigate differences in their sexual interests – one that has received much less attention by relationship and sexuality researchers – is to understand how people can sensitively decline a partner's sexual advances and respond to sexual rejection.

In this article, we provide a synthesis of the empirical studies we have conducted over the past decade that have taken a *communal approach to the study of sexuality* (see reviews by Impett et al., 2015; Muise & Impett, 2016). This perspective provides insight into how some couples are able to maintain desire over time and remain satisfied during times when partners experience differing sexual interests, as well as more successfully balance their sexual needs. At the core of this perspective is the idea that romantic partners are dependent on one another to meet their sexual needs given that the majority of long-term couples are monogamous (Blanchflower & Oswald, 2004) and partners rely on one another exclusively for sexual fulfilment. This sets the sexual realm apart from other relationship domains in which partners are able to get their emotional and social needs (e.g., engaging in leisure activities, providing or receiving emotional support) met by people outside the relationship (Rubin et al., 2014).

We organise this article on a communal approach to sexual need responsiveness in four parts. First, we introduce the theory of communal motivation (Clark & Mills, 2011), apply this theory to the study of sexuality, and discuss distinctions between sexual communal motivation and other relevant theories in relationship science. Second, we review research demonstrating the relationship rewards of having a strong communal motivation to meet a partner's sexual needs, even when partners have conflicting interests, unmet sexual ideals, or diagnosed clinical issues, as well as boundary conditions of these effects. Third, we discuss the navigation of situations in which one partner is *not* interested in sex, specifically examining how partners can most responsively decline one another's advances and respond to sexual rejection to preserve the quality of their connection. Fourth, we integrate our work on sexual communal motivation and sexual rejection to understand how partners can most effectively balance their sexual needs, concluding with some considerations for future research.

At the outset, we would like to define the scope of our article. First, the research that we review focuses primarily on heterosexual individuals and couples, and future research with more diverse samples is certainly needed to provide evidence for the generalisability of the effects. Second, most of the research focuses on convenience samples of couples drawn from the community, although when relevant, we discuss recent studies of couples with diagnosed clinical sexual issues. Third, many of the processes we cover apply to both women and men in romantic relationships, but at the end of the article, we discuss any relevant gender differences in the effects.

Applying the theory of communal motivation to the sexual domain

In romantic relationships, partners inevitably face situations in which their interests or preferences conflict, termed interdependence dilemmas (see review by Rusbult & Van Lange, 2008). In these dilemmas, partners have to decide whether they will behave in a communal fashion in which they will try to satisfy the other person's needs or desires (Clark & Aragón, 2013; Mills et al., 2004), even if incurring costs for the self, or whether they will behave in a more individualistic fashion and prioritise their own needs and desires. According to interdependence theory, as two people in a relationship become increasingly interdependent, a transformation of motivation occurs in which individualistic preferences give way to communal preferences (Thibaut & Kelley, 1959). To the extent that two partners' preferences are interwoven, they are each more likely to adopt goals to maintain the other person's well-being in addition to their own well-being.

Building on interdependence theory, the theory of communal motivation suggests that in communal relationships – such as those we have with family members, romantic partners, and close friends – people provide care non-contingently; that is, they give care to each other with little concern for what they will receive in return. In contrast, in exchange relationships, benefits are given with the expectation of direct reciprocation, with partners tracking benefits to keep things even (Clark & Mills, 2011). Romantic partners indicate that following communal norms as opposed to exchange norms is ideal in long-term relationships as doing so creates opportunities for couples to engage in mutually enjoyable activities that meet both partners' needs (Clark et al., 2010). Although initial research has documented broad differences between communal and exchange relationships, more recent work has shown that across close relationships, people vary in the extent to which they feel responsible for meeting a partner's needs. Individual differences in the motivation to respond non-contingently to a specific partner's needs are referred to as *communal strength* (Mills et al., 2004). People high in communal strength report feeling more authentic and satisfied with their relationships on days when they sacrifice for the good or their partner or their relationship (Kogan et al., 2010). In addition, people high in communal strength give to their partner insofar as the personal costs incurred in meeting their partner's needs are reasonable, and they trust that their partner will be responsive to their own needs when they arise (Mills et al., 2004). Thus, rather than trying to make sure a partner's caring acts are reciprocated in a tit-for-tat fashion, highly communal people are guided by norms in which partners provide more balanced care in the relationship.

Individual differences in strength of sexual communal motivation

Interdependence dilemmas can take place in any domain in which partners are dependent on one another. Perhaps no other specific relationship domain involves more dependence between partners than the domain of sexuality, given that the majority of couples rely on one another almost exclusively for sexual need fulfilment. Over the past decade, we have conducted a body of research applying the theory of communal motivation to understand how couples resolve common interdependence dilemmas in the sexual domain. In particular, in situations in which partners experience conflicting sexual interests (e.g., discrepant levels of sexual desire), partners can transform their motivation to be more communal than individualistic in several key ways that are the focus of this article. In situations in which one partner is not interested in engaging in sex but their partner's desire is high, they could consent to engage in sex to please their partner or keep harmony in the relationship (Impett & Peplau, 2003), or alternatively, they could sensitively decline their partner's advances by reassuring their partner of their continued love and attraction (J. J. Kim et al., 2018). In situations in which one partner is interested in engaging in sex but the other is "not in the mood," they could accept their partner's disinterest and refrain from initiating sex (Muise, Kim et al., 2017), or alternatively, if they do initiate sex and have their advances rejected, they could respond with care and understanding rather than resentment and hostility (Kim et al., 2019).

A common thread underlying the resolution of these different sexual interdependence dilemmas is that when romantic partners experience differing sexual needs, they aim to respond to these needs in ways that enhance a partner's well-being, but without the expectation that their partner will directly reciprocate their actions. People who are high in *sexual communal strength* are motivated to do just that: to be noncontingently responsive to their partner's sexual needs (Muise et al., 2013). In eight studies comprising a total of 2,421 individuals (Muise & Impett, 2019), we developed a reliable and valid self-report measure capturing individual differences in the strength of people's motivation to meet their partner's sexual needs (e.g., "How far would you be willing to go to meet your partner's sexual needs?" and "How likely are you to sacrifice your own sexual needs to meet the sexual needs of your partner?" (*Mean* = 5.56; *SD* =.94; 7-point scale[1]). Our qualitative research has shown that people high in sexual communal strength report that they sometimes engage in sex with their partner when they are not entirely in the mood, keep an open mind about their partner's preferences, communicate with their partner about their sexual likes and dislikes, and try to ensure that *both* partner's needs are met in sexual interactions (Muise & Impett, 2015). We have shown that it crucial to measure people's sexual communal strength independent of their more general communal strength given that these measures are only moderately correlated (r = .45; Muise & Impett, 2015) and that all of the effects of sexual communal strength that we have documented exist above and beyond any influence of people's more general tendencies to be communally oriented in their relationships (e.g., Muise & Impett, 2015; Muise et al., 2013).

Distinctions from other relational theories

In defining sexual communal strength, it is important to discuss distinctions between the motivation to meet a partner's sexual needs and other relevant relational theories, including interdependence theory (Thibaut & Kelley, 1959), social exchange theory (see Sprecher & Sprecher, 1998 for a review) and the broad, organising theoretical framework of perceived partner responsiveness (Reis, 2007).

Interdependence theory fittingly highlights why situations in which partners' interests diverge are commonplace and central to relationships and their successful maintenance. However, it is less specific in prescribing the

---

[1]Mean and standard deviation are from Study 2 reported in Muise and Impett (2019).

ways partners may be able to best go about managing these situations. A communal approach may be uniquely poised to understand sexual need fulfilment between romantic partners as it is grounded in a need-based perspective. As such, it is particularly relevant for understanding specific situations of how people feel about and resolve interdependence dilemmas in which meeting the needs of a specific relationship partner is often at the forefront. A communal perspective suggests that decision-making should be based on whosever need is the strongest, and that this can vary across people and situations.

In theory on communal motivation more broadly, communal relationships have been contrasted with exchange relationships in which benefits are given with the expectation of receiving a comparable benefit in return (or in response to benefits received in the past) (Clark & Mills, 2011). Therefore, communal approaches involve need-based giving whereas exchange approaches are focused on keeping things even between partners to maintain a sense of "fairness." Although previous work guided by the Interpersonal Exchange Model of Sexual Satisfaction (IEMSS; see review by Byers & Wang, 2004) has shown that people tend to be most sexually satisfied when they perceive that both partners are relatively equal in sexual rewards and costs (Lawrance & Byers, 1995), in our recent work we have found that endorsing sexual exchange norms in relationships – aiming to keep things even sexually between partners – is associated with lower sexual and relationship satisfaction (Raposo et al., in press). It is possible that a focus on keeping things even makes sex feel more transactional and less intimate, whereas being communal and focusing on being responsive to a partner's specific sexual needs fosters closeness.

Perhaps the relational construct with the most seeming overlap with communal strength is responsiveness, defined as expressing understanding, validation, and caring for a partner's needs (Reis et al., 2004). Communal strength refers to one's motivation to be attuned to and motivated to meet a partner's needs (Mills et al., 2004), whereas responsiveness (most of the relevant work in this area has looked at perceived partner responsiveness) reflects the extent to which individuals believe their relationship partners understand, validate, and care for them (Reis, 2007). In the domain of sexuality, people higher in sexual communal strength are perceived as more responsive to their partner's needs during sex (Muise & Impett, 2015), but there is a distinction between trait level sexual communal strength and perceived partner responsiveness. More specifically, one key reason why having a partner who is high in sexual communal strength might be beneficial for relationships is because partners higher in sexual communal strength are perceived as more responsive in general (Muise et al., 2013) and to the person's needs during sex specifically, and in turn, perceived partner responsiveness is associated with higher sexual and relationship quality (Muise & Impett, 2015). That said, one of the key differences between sexual communal strength and responsiveness (generally and specifically for sex) is that sexual communal strength is the motivation to meet a partner's need without the expectation of direction reciprocation. Whereas responsiveness is enacted or perceived care provided to a partner, sexual communal strength is more of a motivation to meet a partner's sexual needs and is less about, although linked to, actual responsive behaviours.

Rewards of sexual communal motivation

The growing body of research on communal approaches to sexuality documents the personal and relationship rewards of sexual communal motivation, even when partners' sexual interests conflict and sexual ideals are unmet, as well as the importance of not losing sight of one's own sexual needs in romantic relationships. Given the highly interdependent nature of sexual interactions in relationships, situations in which romantic partners are tasked with fulfilling one another's sexual needs are particularly important to study using a dyadic approach. As such, this work is often guided by the Actor-Partner Interdependence Model (Kenny et al., 2006) which utilises a dyadic framework to account for the interdependence inherent in romantic partners' sexual lives, and provides greater understanding of the ways in which partners can influence one other in their sexual motivations and behaviours. The Actor-Partner Interdependence Model allows researchers to simultaneously determine the effect of a person's own independent variable on their own outcomes (known as an actor effect) as well as the effect on their partner's outcomes (known as a partner effect). Approaching the benefits of sexual communal motivation through a dyadic analytical lens is especially valuable as it contributes to an understanding of couples' sexual interactions as a product of their dyadic environment rather than a sum of individual experiences.

Across a wide body of studies (see Table 1), we find consistent evidence that sexual communal strength is associated with benefits for both partners in a relationship. Perhaps the most intuitive finding from our research, demonstrated in a sample of 118 couples with a 3-week follow-up and a 21-day experience sampling study of 44 couples, is that people with communally motivated partners do, in fact, report that their partners are more responsive to their sexual needs, and in turn, report greater satisfaction and commitment (Muise & Impett, 2015). In another 21-day study of 101 couples, the partners of people higher in sexual communal strength also reported high subjective feelings of sexual satisfaction (Day et al., 2015). Additional evidence from related research on sexual transformations (i.e., changes made to one's own sexual habits such as increasing sexual frequency) suggests that when one person makes a sexual transformation, their partner reports higher

Table 1. Actor and partner effects of sexual communal strength on relationship and sexual outcomes in eight published papers.

Article	Sample	Method	Actor Effects	Partner Effects
Muise et al. (2013)	Community sample (N = 44 couples)	21-day daily experience study with 4-month longitudinal follow-up	Greater daily sexual desire (b =.90) Sustained sexual desire over four months (b =.53)	*No significant partner effect on sexual desire
Muise and Impett (2015)	Study 1: Community sample (N = 118 couples)	Three-week longitudinal study	Greater baseline(b =.32) and daily relationship satisfaction (b =.18) Greater baseline (b =.26) and daily commitment (b =.24)	Greater partner relationship satisfaction at baseline (b =.24), daily (b =.20) and marginal increases in partner satisfaction three weeks later (b =.13) Greater partner commitment at baseline (b =.12), daily (b =.27) and increases in partner commitment three weeks later (b =.14)
Muise and Impett (2015)	Study 2: Community sample (N = 44 couples)	21-day daily experience study	Greater daily relationship quality (aggregate of satisfaction and commitment; b =.43)	Greater partner daily relationship quality (aggregate of satisfaction and commitment; b =.31)
Day et al. (2015)	Study 1: Individuals from Amazon's Mechanical Turk (N = 456)	Experimental study	Greater relationship satisfaction (t = 2.58) Greater sexual satisfaction (t = 2.05)	[data was not dyadic]
Day et al. (2015)	Study 2: Individuals from Amazon's Mechanical Turk (N = 371)	Cross-sectional study	Greater willingness to engage in undesired sex (b =.39) Greater relationship satisfaction (b =.49) Greater sexual satisfaction (b =.50)	[data was not dyadic]
Day et al. (2015)	Study 3: Community sample (N = 101 couples)	21-day daily diary	Increased daily likelihood of engaging in sex (b =.18) Greater daily relationship satisfaction (b =.20) Greater daily sexual satisfaction (b =.37)	Greater partner daily relationship satisfaction (b =.16) Greater partner daily sexual satisfaction b =.16)

(Continued)

Table 1. (Continued).

Article	Sample	Method	Actor Effects	Partner Effects
Muise, Bergeron et al. (2017)	Women diagnosed with vulvodynia and their partners (N = 95 couples)	52- day daily diary study	Greater daily sexual satisfaction (women's b =.20; partner's b =.22) Greater daily sexual functioning (women's b = 1.53; partner's b =.93)	Greater partner daily relationship satisfaction (partner's SCS → women b =.10; women's SCS → partner b =.110) Greater partner daily sexual satisfaction (partner SCS → women b =.18; women's SCS → partner b =.17) Greater partner daily sexual functioning (partner SCS → women b = 1.47; women's SCS → partner b = 2.44)
Muise et al. (2018)	Women diagnosed with vulvodynia and their partners (95 couples)	52- day daily diary study	Lower daily sexual pain (only for women, b = −.24) Lower daily anxiety (only for women, b = −.12)	No significant partner effects
Muise et al. (2019) [Study 2]	Individuals in consensually nonmonogamous (CNM) relationships (N = 649; N = 410 from community websites, 239 from Amazon's Mechanical Turk)	Cross-sectional study	Greater relationship satisfaction Greater sexual satisfaction	[data was not dyadic]
Impett et al. (2019)	Community sample (N = 122 couples)	21-day daily diary study	Greater daily relationship satisfaction (b =.10) Greater daily sexual satisfaction (b =.11) Greater daily sexual desire (b =.15)	Higher partner daily sexual desire (b =.11)
Hogue et al. (2019)	Women diagnosed with Female Sexual Interest/Arousal Disorder and their partners (N = 97 couples)	Cross-sectional study	Greater sexual desire (women's b = 3.73, partner's b = 5.63) Greater sexual satisfaction (only for women, b = 3.68)	No significant partner effects

Note: Actor effects refer to effects of a person's own sexual communal strength on their own outcomes, controlling for the influence of their partner's sexual communal strength; partner effects refer to effects of a person's sexual communal strength on their partner's outcomes, controlling for their partner's own sexual communal strength; all of the coefficients are taken from the original articles; b coefficients represent unstandardised MLM coefficients; all coefficients are significant at $p < .05$ unless otherwise noted; * denotes effects not tested and reported in the original paper, but effects we tested for the purposes of inclusion in this table.

relationship quality (Burke & Young, 2012). Our qualitative research confirms these findings by showing that one way that people demonstrate their communal responsiveness is by talking about likes and dislikes with their partners so that they can be more in tune with their partner's preferences (Muise & Impett, 2015). Further, responsiveness to a partner's sexual needs is especially beneficial for people high in attachment anxiety (i.e., individuals who crave intimacy and fear rejection; Mikulincer & Shaver, 2016). In a 21-day daily experience study of 121 couples, on days when people high in attachment anxiety perceived their partner as more communally motivated to meet their sexual needs, they maintained higher levels of relationship satisfaction than on days when they perceived their partner as less communal (Raposo & Muise, 2019).

The associations between sexual communal strength and sexual and relationship satisfaction also extend to people in consensually nonmonogamous (CNM) relationships (Muise, Laughton et al., 2019). Specifically, across both their primary and secondary relationships, people in CNM relationships who perceived their partner as more sexually communal reported higher sexual and relationship satisfaction in that same relationship. In some cases, there were carry-over effects to the other relationship; when people perceived their primary partner as more sexually communal, they reported higher sexual and relationship satisfaction with a secondary partner. Our research on people in CNM relationships includes the most diverse samples in terms of gender and sexual orientation across all of the studies we have conducted on sexual communal strength. Given that we did not find differences across gender or sexual orientation, this works provides some preliminary evidence that associations between sexual communal strength and satisfaction may generalise to more diverse populations.

In addition to providing benefits for the partner, focusing on meeting a partner's sexual needs is also linked to increased benefits for the *self*. In a sample of long-term couples, sexual communal strength was positively associated with a person's own sexual desire and satisfaction (Muise & Impett, 2015; Muise et al., 2013). In a 4-month longitudinal study of 44 long-term couples who had been together for an average of 11 years, whereas people lower in sexual communal strength experienced declines in sexual desire, people high in sexual strength began the study with slightly higher desire and were able to maintain sexual desire over time (Muise et al., 2013). One key reason why individuals high in sexual communal strength experience these benefits is because they are genuinely motivated to promote positive outcomes in their relationships (i.e., approach goals) such as intimacy and connection, and not because they are motivated to avoid negative outcomes (i.e., avoidance goals) such as conflict, a partner's disappointment, or feelings of guilt (Muise et al., 2013). This research suggests that people high in sexual communal strength engage in sex out of a genuine desire to promote their partner's enjoyment rather than out of a sense of duty or obligation, and this is one reason why they experience relationship and sexual benefits.

When sexual interests conflict or ideals are not met

The picture painted by existing research demonstrates clear benefits of sexual communal motivation for both partners. A particularly stringent test of the potential benefits of sexual communal strength is whether communal people are also willing to meet their partner's needs in situations in which partners have different sexual interests. In a 21-day daily experience study of 101 community couples, people high in sexual communal strength indicated that they would be more willing to engage in sex and reported increased sexual and relationship satisfaction, even on days when they reported having lower sexual desire than their partner, relative to less communal people (Day et al., 2015). In addition and as shown in Figure 1, whereas less communal people experienced lower sexual satisfaction on days when they engaged in sex but were not in the mood compared with days when both partners experienced similarly high levels of sexual desire, strikingly, however, people high in sexual communal strength felt equally sexually satisfied on days when their desire was similar to their partner's desire and on days when they were less sexually enthused than their partner (Day et al., 2015). These results suggest that communal people also benefit from responding to their partner's sexual needs in more challenging situations, such as when partners experience a significant desire discrepancy.

The motivation to meet a partner's sexual needs can also be beneficial when couples have more chronic sexual differences or unfulfilled needs. Across four studies using dyadic, daily experience, longitudinal and experimental methods ($N = 1,532$), when a person reported or was made to believe that their sexual ideals (i.e., characteristics or traits that they desire in a sexual partner) were unmet, they reported feeling less satisfied with their sex life and relationship, as well as less committed to maintaining their relationship over time. However, people who had partners who were higher in sexual communal strength were buffered against the lower satisfaction and commitment associated with having unmet sexual ideals (Balzarini et al., in press). In other words, people whose partners were low in sexual communal strength reported lower sexual satisfaction and relationship quality when they had unmet sexual ideals in the relationship, whereas people with partners high in sexual communal strength were able to maintain sexual and relationship quality even when they had unmet sexual ideals (see Figure 2 for the findings for sexual satisfaction; the pattern of results was the same for relationship satisfaction and commitment). The benefits of sexual communal strength in a relationship are not attributed to communal people engaging in more

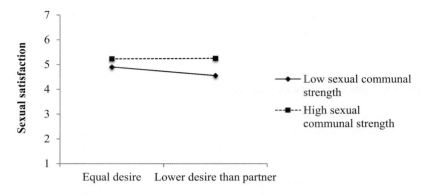

Figure 1. The buffering effect of sexual communal strength on the association between desire discrepancy and sexual satisfaction (adapted from Day et al., 2015, Study 3).

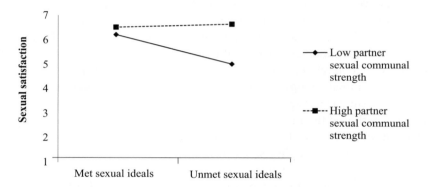

Figure 2. The buffering effect of a partner's sexual communal strength on the association between unmet sexual ideals and sexual satisfaction (adapted from Balzarini et al., in press, Study, 1).

frequent sex. In fact, sexual communal strength is often not associated with sexual frequency, but instead, people high in sexual communal strength tend to be responsive and understanding about their partner's sexual needs and, in turn, sex is more enjoyable for both partners.

Couples also face times in their relationships when partners are more likely to experience differences in their sexual interests. During the transition to parenthood, both partners, but especially women who give birth, report changes in their sexual desire (McBride & Kwee, 2017). In one study, in the year after the birth of their first baby, women reported lower sexual desire compared to women who did not transition to parenthood, and compared to their own partner (Schwenk et al., 2020). Importantly, however, in a sample of 279 new parent couples, we found that new parents who were higher in sexual communal strength reported greater satisfaction with their sex lives and relationships, as did their romantic partners (Muise, Kim et al., 2017).

The benefits of sexual communal strength also extend to couples who are coping with clinical sexual issues. In an intensive 56-day daily experience study of 95 couples, on days when women diagnosed with vulvodynia (i.e., pain during sex; Rosen & Bergeron, 2019) and their partners reported higher sexual communal strength, both partners reported greater sexual and relationship satisfaction and better sexual functioning (Muise, Bergeron et al., 2017), and women reported less pain (Muise et al., 2018). Similarly, in a sample of 97 women (and their partners) diagnosed with Sexual Interest Arousal Disorder (i.e., low sexual desire or arousal accompanied by distress), both women and their partners reported greater sexual satisfaction when the woman was higher in sexual communal strength, and the woman herself reported higher sexual desire (Hogue et al., 2019). Because this clinical research focused solely on women, future research is needed to determine if men who are more sexually communal (or have partners who are more sexually communal) may also be better able to cope with their own sexual challenges (e.g., erectile dysfunction).

The importance of attending to one's own sexual needs

Of course, there are situations in which it is not possible or preferred to meet a partner's sexual needs (Impett & Peplau, 2003; Katz & Tirone, 2009). People who are communally motivated not only strive to meet their partner's needs, but also expect that their partner will be similarly motivated to meet their own needs when they arise (Mills et al., 2004). Although the motivation to meet a partner's sexual needs can be beneficial for both partners, doing so to the exclusion of one's own needs is unlikely to be beneficial for either partner in the relationship. Indeed, research has shown that individuals high in *unmitigated communion* (i.e., the tendency to give to others without concern for one's own needs; Fritz & Helgeson, 1998) experience more negative affect and less positive affect in situations of interpersonal conflict than those whose communal motivation is mitigated by their own sense of agency (Nagurney, 2007). In essence, people higher in unmitigated communion take the value of interpersonal connectedness to an unhealthy extreme, prioritising the needs of others while neglecting their own psychological and physical well-being (Fritz & Helgeson, 1998).

Applied to the domain of sexuality, we have found that although the motivation to meet a partner's sexual needs can be beneficial for both partners, these benefits begin to unravel when people strive to meet their partner's sexual needs to the exclusion of their own needs. People who are high in *unmitigated sexual communion* indicate that they focus solely on their partner's sexual needs, placing those needs over their own (e.g., "I put my partner's sexual needs ahead of my own" and "It is impossible for me to satisfy by own sexual needs if they conflict with my partner's sexual needs"). In a 21-day daily experience study of 122 couples, on days when people reported higher sexual communal strength ($M = 5.33$; $SD = 1.36$; 7-point scale), they attended more to positive sexual cues (e.g., partner responsiveness) and in turn, both partners experienced greater daily sexual and relationship satisfaction. In contrast, on days when people reported higher unmitigated sexual communion ($M = 3.51$, $SD = 1.47$; 7-point scale), they reported greater attention to negative sexual cues (e.g., feelings of distraction, detachment, or boredom), and in turn, experienced lower relationship and sexual satisfaction (Impett et al., 2019). Similarly, in both community samples and clinical samples of couples coping with a sexual dysfunction, sexual communal strength is associated with higher approach goals for sex, but not higher avoidance goals (Hogue et al., 2019; Muise et al., 2013) suggesting that, in general, being communally motivated to meet a partner's sexual needs is focused on the pursuit of positive relational outcomes and not to avoid conflict or a partner's disappointment. In contrast, people higher in unmitigated sexual communion do not report being more approach motivated to engage in sex (Hogue et al., 2019), and instead, may do so out of feelings of insecurity or obligation.

Whereas sexual communal strength may help couples more successfully navigate a clinical sexual issue, unmitigated sexual communion may exacerbate the challenges. In a 56-day study of 95 women diagnosed with vulvodynia (and their partners), on days when women reported higher sexual communal strength, they reported lower levels of anxiety and less pain during sex, whereas on days when women reported higher unmitigated sexual communion, they experienced greater pain during sex and more sexual distress and both partners reported lower satisfaction, more depressive symptoms, and poorer sexual functioning (Muise et al., 2018; Muise, Bergeron et al., 2017). Taken together, these findings suggest that even though people high in unmitigated sexual communion report being solely focused on meeting their partner's sexual needs, their partners do not benefit from this hypervigilance and, in some cases, report personal and interpersonal costs. These findings point to the importance of striking the right balance between being responsive to a partner's sexual needs and asserting one's own needs.

The importance of balancing needs in a relationship is consistent with other theoretical and clinical approaches in psychology. For example, differentiation is a process by which people manage their needs for both autonomy and connection with a partner (Schnarch & Regas, 2012). We suspect that people higher in sexual communal strength would be more differentiated in terms of having the capacity for connection with a partner alongside a having solid sense of their own needs, whereas people high in unmitigated communion would be low in differentiation since they are challenged to express their own needs, although we do not yet have data to test this assertion. In thinking about potential application to clinical practice, clinicians could consider whether partners are struggling to understand or meet each other's needs or if they are overly focused on their partner and not asserting their own needs. Low responsiveness to a partner's sexual needs or responsiveness that involves self-neglect could be problematic for relationships and thinking about imbalances in relationships through a communal lens could provide novel insights into therapeutic intervention.

When the need is to *not* have sex

Almost all of the existing research that has taken a communal approach to sexuality has focused on people's motivation to meet a partner's needs *for* sex. In contrast, very little research has examined the other side of the coin – what happens when people *do not want to have sex* – and if there are communal ways to buffer a partner against the emotional sting of sexual rejection and ways to respond to rejection that help couples preserve intimacy. The lack of research on sexual rejection is surprising given its prevalence in romantic relationships (about once a week, on average; Byers & Heinlein, 1989; Dobson et al., 2020). Many psychological theories indicate that human beings have a fundamental need to belong and feel accepted by others (e.g., Baumeister & Leary, 1995; Ryan & Deci, 2000), but experiencing interpersonal rejection – the refusal of desired social connectedness – directly violates this need (Blackhart et al., 2009). People report that rejection by a romantic partner is one of life's most painful experiences (Leary et al., 1998), and the more an individual feels valued by and close to a person who rejects them, the more the rejection tends to hurt (Leary, 2001).

Sexual rejection involves the communication – subtle or explicit – to one's partner the desire or need to not have sex. Compared to other types of rejection, sexual rejection may be more emotionally painful and especially detrimental to well-being. In a pilot, cross-sectional study of 190 individuals in relationships, we found that people expected to feel more rejected, insecure, and dissatisfied when their partner rejected their advances for sex compared to when their partner declined their request to engage in a non-sexual activity such as going to dinner or attending a work function (Impett & Sisson, 2020). The private and often sensitive nature of sexual interactions tends to exacerbate emotional vulnerability when sexual conflicts arise (Rehman et al., 2019, 2017). Indeed, experiencing sexual rejection from a partner may lead individuals to doubt their self-worth and question their partner's interest in the relationship (Metts et al., 1992). People in both cohabitating and married relationships report feeling lower relationship and sexual satisfaction when their sexual initiations are met with refusal, as opposed to acceptance, by their partner (Byers & Heinlein, 1989), and these effects can linger up to two days after rejection occurs (Dobson et al., 2020). Given the substantial impact that sexual rejection can have in romantic relationships, our work has sought to understand if there are specific ways that people can decline a partner's sexual advances and communicate sexual rejection, as well as respond to sexual rejection that can help couples sustain relationship and sexual satisfaction.

Communicating sexual rejection

Existing research on the communication of sexual rejection has been primarily examined in interactions among strangers, acquaintances, or potential romantic partners (e.g., Goodboy & Brann, 2010; Jouriles et al., 2014; Metts et al., 1992). One early study which focused on romantic relationships and relied on hypothetical scenarios showed that people expected to feel less discomfort and threat when sexual rejection was delivered with moderate, compared to very high or low, levels of directness, as it communicated rejection effectively, while also buffering the rejected person against embarrassment and shame (Metts et al., 1992).

In six studies comprising a total of 1,949 total participants, we developed the Sexual Rejection Scale (SRS; J. J. Kim et al., 2019) to extend the research on sexual rejection, identifying four distinct ways that people reject their partner's interest for sex. These included *reassuring rejection* (affirming attraction towards a partner or offering other forms of affection, e.g., "I reassure my partner that I love them"; Means = 2.78–3.51; SDs = .74–1.23; 5-point scale), as well as assertive rejection (stating clearly the reason for rejection; e.g., "I am clear and direct about the reason why I don't want to have sex"; Means = 2.85–3.35; SDs = .73–1.26), hostile rejection (expressing anger or criticising a partner; e.g., "I display frustration toward my partner"; Means = 1.4–2.4; SDs = .62 – .95), and deflecting behaviours (diverting attention away from the situation; e.g., "I pretend not to notice that my partner is interested in sex"; Means = 1.74–2.46; SDs = .79 – .96). In a 28-day experience sampling study of 98 couples, we then found that when people perceived their partner reject their advances in a reassuring manner, they maintained higher relationship and sexual satisfaction; however, when they perceived their partner reject their sexual advances in a hostile manner, they reported lower relationship satisfaction (Kim et al., 2020). Further, we found that perceptions of a partner's responsiveness (i.e., the extent to which their partner understands, validates, and cares about their needs) accounted for both of these links. Specifically, high perceived partner responsiveness accounted for the link between perceived reassuring behaviours and higher relationship and sexual satisfaction, whereas low perceived partner responsiveness explained why perceptions of a partner's hostile rejection were associated with lower satisfaction (Kim et al., 2020). We have also shown that people who score high on our trait measure of sexual communal strength are the ones most likely to engage in reassuring rejection behaviours (Kim, Muise et al., 2019), suggesting that communally motivated people do not invariably engage in sex at their partner's behest and they remain responsive even when declining their partner's advances. Thus, reassuring rejection is an example of how communal care can be enacted.

Given that couples typically report higher satisfaction on days when they engage in sex compared to days when they do not (Muise et al., 2013), one interesting question concerns whether reassuring rejection is a viable alternative to engaging in sex when people find themselves more motivated to engage in sex for avoidance as opposed to approach-based reasons. In the daily experience study described above, in combination with two experimental studies (between- and within-person) of 642 individuals, we found that when people engaged in reassuring rejection, both they and their partner reported equivalent levels of relationship satisfaction compared to days when they engaged in sex for avoidance goals (see Figure 3 for the findings for the actor effect from Study 3; the pattern of results was the same for the partner effect). In contrast and as shown in Figure 4, sexual satisfaction was always higher on days when couples engaged in sex, regardless of their levels of avoidance motivation, suggesting that sexual satisfaction might be more dependent than relationship satisfaction on people getting their physical needs met (Kim et al., 2018). These finding suggest that when people find themselves in situations in which they need to decide whether to accept or decline a partner's sexual advances, they might need to weigh different factors depending on whether they are concerned with maintaining relationship as opposed to sexual satisfaction.

Responding to sexual rejection

An equally important and complementary aspect of understanding how couples can maintain their connection in the absence of sexual activity concerns how people respond to sexual rejection. Common emotions elicited in the context of more general interpersonal rejection include hurt, jealousy, loneliness, guilt, shame, embarrassment, anger, and sadness (Leary, 2001; Leary et al., 2001). The few studies that focus on responses to sexual rejection, just like the studies on how people reject a partner's sexual advances, have been conducted in the context of sexual encounters with strangers or casual sex partners (e.g., Struckman-Johnson & Struckman-Johnson, 1991; Wright et al., 2010) rather than with romantic partners. In our work, we sought to expand upon this work to examine people's emotional and behavioural responses to sexual rejection in the context of romantic relationships. In doing so, we developed and validated the Responses to Sexual Rejection

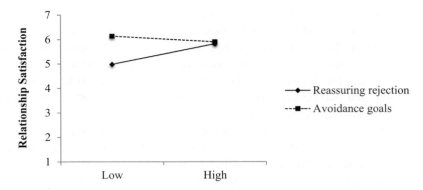

Figure 3. Actor effects of reassuring rejection (on sex days) and avoidance sexual goals (on non-sex days) at various degrees on daily relationship satisfaction (adapted from Kim et al., 2018, Study 2). Note: Low = one standard deviation below the mean on either reassuring rejection or avoidance goals; High = one standard deviation above the mean in either reassuring rejection or avoidance goals.

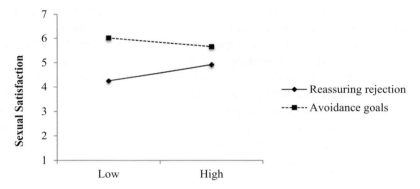

Figure 4. Actor effects of reassuring rejection (on sex days) and avoidance sexual goals (on non-sex days) at various degrees on daily sexual satisfaction (adapted from Kim et al., 2018, Study 2). Note: Low = one standard deviation below the mean on either reassuring rejection or avoidance goals; High = one standard deviation above the mean on either reassuring rejection or avoidance goals.

Scale (RSRS; Kim, Horne et al., 2019) with data from a total of 1,051 individuals in relationships. This work has uncovered four distinct responses to sexual rejection. Two of these – resentment responses (acting with anger and resentment, e.g., "I express anger at my partner"; $Mean = 1.59$; $SD = .76$, measured on a 5-point scale[2]) and insecure responses (expressing sadness and insecurity, e.g., "I think something is wrong in the relationship"; $Mean = 2.15$; $SD = .99$) – closely map onto responses identified in the

---

[2]The means and standard deviations are from Study 2 reported in Kim, Horne et al. (2019).

prior literature on sexual refusals in the context of stranger or casual sex encounters (Wright et al., 2010). However, two of these were more unique to the context of romantic relationships, including enticing responses (trying to entice a partner and continuing to pursue sex; e.g., "I ask if there is anything I can do to get my partner in the mood"; *Mean* = 2.31; *SD* = 1.03), as well as, most commonly and of particular interest in this article, *understanding responses* (showing acceptance and understanding when a partner does want to engage in sex; e.g., "I am understanding and accepting"; *Mean* = 3.27; *SD* = 1.06).

Consistent with our communal perspective on sexuality, we have found that people who scored high on our trait measure of sexual communal strength were the ones most likely to respond to rejection with understanding and the least likely to respond with hostility or insecurity (Kim, Horne et al., 2019), suggesting that communal people also show responsiveness to a partner's needs when sex does not occur. In addition, we found that, in the context of the transition to parenthood in which new mothers often report lower sexual desire than their partners, new mothers who were higher in sexual communal strength had partners who expressed greater understanding about mothers' lower interest sex (Muise, Kim et al., 2017). Insofar as communal motivated individuals are models for maintaining sexual intimacy in relationships (e.g., Muise et al., 2013) and being responsive to a partner's sexual needs both when they engage in sex and do not engage in sex, this emerging evidence suggests that expressing understanding in response to sexual rejection may be integral for buffering partners from the negative experiences associated with sexual rejection, although this possibility needs to be tested in future research.

Balancing sexual needs in relationships

Our article thus far has focused on how partners can express care and understanding in situations in which they desire, as well as do not desire, to engage in sex. However, we do not view these as isolated processes, and instead, think that the ways that people pursue sexual intimacy as well as deliver and respond to sexual rejection are intricately interwoven. In this final part of our article, we synthesise and integrate what we have learned from research on sexual communal motivation and sexual rejection to discuss how partners can better *balance their sexual needs* in romantic relationships and conclude this section with future research directions.

Risk regulation theory

A prominent theoretical perspective in relationship science, risk regulation theory (Murray et al., 2006), is uniquely positioned to inform how couples can balance their simultaneous need to experience intimacy with their need to avoid experiencing the pain of rejection. Risk regulation theory highlights the importance of perceptions of a partner's responsiveness – that is, feeling that a partner understands, validates, and cares about one's needs (Reis et al., 2004) – in determining how people respond to rejection. Specifically, people who perceive low partner responsiveness seek to guard against the pain of rejection by minimising closeness and dependence on their partner, whereas those who perceive high responsiveness are able to use these perceptions as a resource to buffer them against the sting of rejection and, instead, prioritise their needs for intimacy and connection to ultimately bolster the relationship (Murray et al., 2006).

It is possible that either of these two core needs – the need to approach intimacy and the need to avoid rejection – could be heightened in the context of sexual interactions in romantic relationships. On the one hand, the need to avoid the pain of rejection may be especially strong since people could easily interpret a partner's sexual rejection as a sign of their waning interest in the relationship. At the same time, given the powerful emotional and physical rewards of sexual activity in romantic relationships (Debrot et al., 2017; Diamond & Huebner, 2012), the need to pursue connection may also be heightened in this context. Risk regulation theory suggests that the way people balance these two needs is based, at least in part, on their confidence in a partner's regard, as can be demonstrated through perceptions of their partner's responsiveness. Applying risk regulation theory to the context of sexual rejection, when people are unsure of their partner's regard or responsiveness to their sexual needs (e.g., when sexual advances made towards a partner have been frequently declined in the past), they may be motivated to guard against the pain of sexual rejection by withdrawing from situations that could afford intimacy and avoiding future sexual interactions with their partner. In contrast, the receipt and experience of high levels of responsiveness from a partner may lead people to prioritise and continue to pursue their needs for intimacy and connection, even when their sexual advances are declined.

Recent empirical evidence

Our own recent research provides initial support for these broad theoretical ideas. In a 28-day experience sampling study of 98 couples (Debrot et al., 2019), people who perceived their partner reject their interest in sex in a reassuring manner reported increased understanding of sexual rejection and in turn, enhanced approach motives to engage in sex, such as pursuing intimacy or pleasing a partner. In contrast, people who perceived their partner reject them in a hostile manner were more likely to respond with anger, which was associated with dampened approach motives. In addition, perceptions of hostile rejection were associated with increased insecurity in the rejected partner, which were in turn associated with increased motivation to avoid negative outcomes such as conflict and a partner's disappointment when engaging in sex. This work is the first in the literature to demonstrate the usefulness of risk regulation theory in strengthening our understanding of sexual rejection dynamics in ongoing romantic relationships.

There are also certain ways of rejecting a partner's sexual advances that promote the motivation to engage in non-sexual affectionate behaviours which might allow for sexual need fulfilment to occur in other ways. In the same daily experience study of 98 couples described above, on days when people rejected their partner's interest in sex in a more reassuring manner, they engaged in more frequent non-sexual affectionate behaviours (e.g., hugging, kissing, cuddling), and reported doing so for more partner-focused reasons, such as to promote intimacy in the relationship. This new empirical data linking reassuring rejection to approach sexual motivation as well as affectionate touch is important because it shows that even in the context of sexual rejection, there is still a path to intimacy and connection through affectionate behaviours and the pursuit of positive sexual experiences in the future. The findings from this emerging line of research indicate the importance of demonstrating responsiveness, even in the absence of sex, in helping couples to express and sustain interest in sex and affection.

Gender differences

Given the extensive literature on gender differences in sexuality in relationships (see review by Peplau, 2003), a natural point of interest across this body of research concerns the extent to which the findings are influenced by gender. Broadly, the patterns and effects of sexual responsiveness in relationships outlined in this article tend be largely consistent across gender. However, certain differences do emerge. For example, we find in multiple samples that men tend to have higher mean levels of sexual communal strength than women, for example, in Study 1 (men = 5.69 and women = 5.42 on 7-point scale) and Study 2 (men = 3.12 and women = 2.83 on 0–4 point scale) in Muise et al. (2013). While this contrasts with previous work showing that women are generally more communally motivated than men in line with their social role (Le et al., 2018), this finding is likely due to men's tendency to have greater sexual desire and interest (Baumeister et al., 2001). Indeed, once accounting for men's higher sexual desire, men and women did not differ in sexual communal strength in any of our studies. Additionally, few consistent gender effects emerge in terms of the role of sexual communal motivation in shaping relationship and sexual outcomes.

We do, however, observe select gender differences in how men and women engage in and experience sexual rejection. For example, one consistent finding from this work is that women tend to reject their partner's sexual advances more frequently than do men, in line with traditional sexual scripts depicting men as the initiators and women as the gatekeepers in sexual situations (Byers, 1996). For example, in our study of 98 couples' daily sexual experiences, women reported engaging in sexual rejection on a greater number of days (17%) compared to men (9%), $\chi^2(1) = 68.27$, $p < .001$. However, when examining the specific ways that men and women reject their partner's advances, men tended to be more hostile (men: $M = 2.10$, $SD = 1.46$; women: $M = 1.63$, $SD = 1.13$) and deflecting (men: $M = 2.18$, $SD = 1.38$; women: $M = 1.70$, $SD = 1.10$) in their communication of sexual disinterest than women. Thus, women may engage in more sexual rejection on average, but when men do engage in sexual rejection, they do so in more hostile and deflecting ways, perhaps because they are challenging stereotypes that men do not decline sex.

Sexual script theory also appears to inform a gender difference in how people respond to sexual rejection from their partner. More specifically, we have found that men are more likely to respond to sexual rejection by engaging in greater sexual persistence (i.e., enticing responses) whereas women tend to exhibit greater insecure responses (such as feeling hurt or sad). This finding is again consistent with sexual scripts which cast men as always wanting to have sex and describe how women may be more likely to feel surprised and interpret rejection as a reflection of their own shortcomings if their sexual advances are declined (de Graaf & Sandfort, 2004; O'Sullivan & Byers, 1996). On the whole, however, we have found that the effects of sexual responsiveness on relationship and sexual satisfaction during situations of rejection are robust to and largely unaffected by differences in gender.

Future research directions

The underlying focus of the body of research covered in this article has been to examine how efforts to provide sexual need responsiveness to a partner can directly promote higher quality sexual relationships. However, this is not to suggest that these effects operate exclusively in this direction. To address questions of causality and rule out alternative explanations, many of the studies we have presented incorporate different types of methods, such as lagged analyses in longitudinal designs, or experimental manipulations of sexual communal motivation or perceived sexually responsive behaviours (e.g., Day et al., 2015; Kim et al., 2018). Yet, an important point of consideration is that the processes by which relationship and sexual outcomes are shaped by sexual communal motives and behaviours likely operate in the reverse direction as well. Individuals who are more satisfied or have higher desire may be inclined to report (or have their partners report) higher sexual communal strength or reassuring rejection behaviours as a direct result. Indeed, a meta-analytic review on general communal motivation and well-being suggests that these links are likely bidirectional (Le et al., 2018). Thus, a key avenue for future work consists of mapping the precise ways in which positive sexual experiences and sexual communal motivation shape and are shaped by one another.

Our recent research on balancing partners' sexual needs in a relationship highlights the importance of including both partners in research and examining dyadic sexual processes over time. In particular, one person's responses to rejection might be informed by how their partner declined their sexual advances, and sexual rejection (and responses to sexual rejection) on a - particular day might influence future sexual interactions and motivations. One notable direction for future research is to understand how sexual rejection unfolds between partners in the moment – how sex is initiated, declined and responded to – as well as how the accumulation of rejection behaviours and responses influences the quality of couples' relationship and sexual connection over time. Future behavioural observation research in which couples discuss an experience of sexual rejection could provide insight into how communally motivated partners communicate about and respond to sexual rejection. The ways that people communicate rejection to a partner in the moment might also influence the quality and nature of their sexual experiences over time, perhaps with more reassuring ways of rejecting a partner's sexual advances leading to greater approach motivation to pursue sex in the future.

Another important future direction that requires a dyadic approach involves examining the attributions that people make for their partner's sexual rejection. It is possible that people higher in sexual communal strength might make more benevolent attributions (i.e., attribute the cause of the rejection to external rather than internal factors; see review by Bradbury & Fincham, 1990) for their partner's rejection. Although not in the context of sexual rejection, recent research has shown that new mothers who reported more stable, partner-focused attributions for postpartum sexual concerns reported feeling less sexually satisfied (Vannier et al., 2018). Applied to the domain of sexual rejection, it is possible that communal people might be more likely to attribute their partner declining their sexual advances to something external (e.g., stress from a long day at work) as opposed to something internal (e.g., a lack of desire or interest in them), and these attributions may be a key driver of how people feel about their sex lives and relationships.

Another important future direction is to examine the relational functions and the underlying relational dynamics of sexual rejection. We have shown that reassuring sexual rejection – and not more assertive, direct forms of rejection in which people clearly communicate their reason for rejecting a partner's advances – communicates responsiveness to a partner's needs and protects the partner's satisfaction (Kim et al., 2020). However, it is likely not functional for people to chronically reassure a partner when rejecting their sexual advances, demonstrate acceptance of a partner's low sexual desire, or respond to sexual rejection with understanding. Indeed, engaging in some of these behaviours habitually, especially in the face of chronic desire discrepancies between partners, may prevent couples from overcoming important challenges or obstacles in their sexual relationships. For example, in the case in which a person rejects their partner's sexual advances because they are "turned off" by how the partner initiates sex, it is likely more functional for partners to openly discuss their sexual likes and dislikes than to continually reassure a partner and express understanding. That is, reassuring rejection behaviours or understanding responses could prevent couples from making important changes to their sexual behaviours that could ultimately improve the quality of their sexual connection. These ideas are consistent with findings from the literature on partner regulation in which greater levels of directness, even if combined with negativity, may be more effective in promoting a partner to change undesired behaviours or characteristics underlying important relationship issues (McNulty & Russell, 2010; Overall et al., 2009).

In our work we have focused on how both partners' levels of sexual communal motivation are associated with sexual and relationship satisfaction, but future work should also consider whether correspondence between partners' sexual communal strength is associated with satisfaction and if, specifically, there might be additional benefits of "matching" between partners in sexual communal strength. In our research, we have tested statistical interactions between both partners' levels of sexual communal strength to test questions such as whether relational and sexual outcomes are even better when both partners are highly communal. While tests of these interactions have yielded null or inconsistent results, interactions are not the ideal approach for testing matching effects (e.g., Edwards, 2001). Recent advances in statistical analyses, such as response surface analysis (RSA; Humberg et al., 2018; Schönbrodt, 2016) can provide a powerful approach to testing matching effects and can enable researchers to determine whether and under what conditions correspondence between partners in sexual communal strength is associated with sexual and relationship satisfaction. It is possible that above and beyond associations between partners' sexual communal strength and sexual and relationship quality, matching on sexual communal strength between partners might also predict satisfaction. Although we typically find that lower sexual communal strength is associated with lower satisfaction, if both partners are low on sexual communal strength and perhaps both take an exchange perspective, they may be able to maintain relationship satisfaction. However, our recent work shows that greater matching between partners on sexual desire is not specifically associated with satisfaction above and beyond the effects of both partner's level of desire (Kim et al., 2020), so perhaps matching on sexual communal strength would not be associated with satisfaction and, instead, is an important factor that helps couples to maintain satisfaction even when they are mismatched in desire. Exploring the extent to which satisfaction in couples is impacted by discrepant patterns in partners' self-reported – as well as perceived – communal and exchange motives in the sexual domain remains a promising avenue for future work.

Conclusions

Although couples certainly face many challenges to maintaining their sexual connection over time, our research suggests that a communal approach to sexual need responsiveness can inform how couples can keep the spark alive, even during times when their sexual connection may be wavering, as well as how partners can most sensitively decline each other's advances and respond to sexual rejection. Maintaining desire and satisfaction, especially during challenging times in a relationship, can be far from easy, and likely requires partners to put in effort and work to be successful (Maxwell et al., 2017). Several ways that couples can put in this effort – reviewed in this article – involve trying to meet a partner's sexual needs even when those needs are different than one's own, declining a partner's advances with love and responsiveness, communicating understanding in the face of rejection, and accepting that there will be times when a partner is not in the mood for sex. A communal approach to sexuality highlights that when people are willing to put in this work, they are more likely to experience the rich rewards of a fulfiling, intimate sexual relationship.

Funding

This work is supported by Insight Grants from the Social Sciences and Humanities Research Council (SSHRC) awarded to Emily A. Impett and Amy Muise, a SSHRC Insight Development Grant awarded to Emily A. Impett, and a SSHRC CGS Doctoral Scholarship awarded to James J. Kim. Please address correspondence to: Emily Impett, Department of Psychology, 3359 Mississauga Road, Mississauga, ON L5L 1C6, Canada

References

Ahlborg, T., Dahlöf, L. G., & Hallberg, L. R. M. (2005). Quality of the intimate and sexual relationship in first-time parents six months after delivery. *Journal of Sex Research*, *42*(2), 167–174. http://doi.10.1080/00224490509552270

Balzarini, R. N., Muise, A., Dobson, K., Kohut, T., Raposo, S., & Campbell, L. (in press). The dilemma of discrepant sexual ideals and buffering effect of sexual communal strength. *Journal of Personality and Social Psychology*.

Baumeister, R. F., & Bratslavsky, E. (1999). Passion, Intimacy, and Time: Passionate Love as a Function of Change in Intimacy. *Personality and Social Psychology Review*, 3, 49-67. doi:10.1207/s15327957pspr0301_3 1

Baumeister, R. F., Catanese, K. R., & Vohs, K. D. (2001). Is there a gender difference in strength of sex drive? Theoretical views, conceptual distinctions, and a review of relevant evidence. *Personality and Social Psychology Review*, 5(3), 242–273. https://doi.org/10.1207/S15327957PSPR0503_5

Baumeister, R. F., & Leary, M. R. (1995). The need to belong: Desire for interpersonal attachments as a fundamental human motivation. *Psychological Bulletin*, 117(3), 497–529. https://doi.org/10.1037/0033-2909.117.3.497

Birnbaum, G. E., & Finkel, E. J. (2015). The magnetism that holds us together: Sexuality and relationship maintenance across relationship development. *Current Opinion in Psychology*, 1, 29–33. https://doi.org/10.1016/j.copsyc.2014.11.009

Blackhart, G. C., Nelson, B. C., Knowles, M. L., & Baumeister, R. F. (2009). Rejection elicits emotional reactions but neither causes immediate distress nor lowers self-esteem: A meta-analytic review of 192 studies on social exclusion. *Personality and Social Psychology Review*, 13(4), 269–309. https://doi.org/10.1177/1088868309346065

Blanchflower, D. G., & Oswald, A. J. (2004). Money, sex and happiness: An empirical study. *Scandinavian Journal of Economics*, 106(3), 393–415. https://doi.org/10.1111/j.1467-9442.2004.00369.x

Bradbury, T. N., & Fincham, F. D. (1990). Attributions in marriage: Review and critique. *Psychological Bulletin*, 107(1), 3–33. https://doi.org/10.1037/0033-2909.107.1.3

Burke, T. J., & Young, V. J. (2012). Sexual transformations and intimate behaviors in romantic relationships. *Journal of Sex Research*, 49(5), 454–463. https://doi.org/10.1080/00224499.2011.569977

Byers, E. S. (1996). How well does the traditional sexual script explain sexual coercion? Review of a program of research. *Journal of Psychology & Human Sexuality*, 8(1–2), 7–25. https://doi.org/10.1300/J056v08n01_02

Byers, E. S., & Wang, A. (2004). Understanding sexuality in close relationship from the social exchange perspective. In A. W. J. H. Harvey & S. Sprecher (Eds.), *The handbook of sexuality in close relationships* (pp. 183–201). Lawrence Erlbaum.

Byers, E. S., & Heinlein, L. H. (1989). Predicting initiations and refusals of sexual activities in married and cohabiting heterosexual couples. *The Journal of Sex Research*, 26(2), 210–231. http://doi.10.1080/00224498909551507

Carswell, K., & Impett, E. A. (under review). What fuels passion: An integrative review of competing theories of romantic passion. *Social and Personality Psychology Compass*.

Clark, M. S., & Mills, J. R. (2011). A theory of communal (and exchange) relationships. In P. A. M. Van Lange & A. W. Kruglanski (Eds.), *Handbook of theories of social psychology* (Vol. 2, pp. 232–250). Sage.

Clark, M. S., & Aragón, O. R. (2013). Communal (and other) relationships: History, theory development, recent findings, and future directions. In J. A. Simpson & L. Campbell (Eds.), Oxford library of psychology. *The Oxford handbook of close relationships* (p. 255–280). Oxford University Press.

Clark, M. S., Lemay, E. P., Graham, S. M., Pataki, S. P., & Finkel, E. J. (2010). Ways of giving benefits in marriage: Norm use, relationship satisfaction, and attachment-related variability. *Psychological Science*, *21*(7), 944–951. http://doi.10. 1177/0956797610373882

Davies, S., Katz, J., & Jackson, J. L. (1999). Sexual desire discrepancies: Effects on sexual and relationship satisfaction in heterosexual dating couples. *Archives of Sexual Behavior*, *28*(6), 553–567. https://doi.org/10.1023/a:1018721417683

Day, L., Muise, A., Joel, S., & Impett, E. A. (2015). To do it or not to do it? How communally motivated people navigate sexual interdependence dilemmas. *Personality and Social Psychology Bulletin*, *41*(6), 791–804. https://doi.org/10. 1177/0146167215580129

de Graaf, H., & Sandfort, T. G. (2004). Gender differences in affective responses to sexual rejection. *Archives of Sexual Behavior*, *33*(4), 395–403. https://doi.org/10. 1023/B:ASEB.0000028892.63150.be

Debrot, A., Impett, E. A., Muise, A., & Kim, J. (2019). *Sex and touch dyadic daily diary study* [Unpublished data]. UNC Dataverse, V1. https://doi.org/10.15139/S3/ TAI2FI

Debrot, A., Meuwly, N., Muise, A., Impett, E. A., & Schoebi, D. (2017). More than just sex: Affection mediates the association between sexual activity and well-being. *Personality and Social Psychology Bulletin*, *43*(3), 287–299. https://doi.org/10.1177/ 0146167216684124

DeLamater, J. (2012). Sexual expression in later life: A review and synthesis. *Journal of Sex Research*, *49*(2–3), 125–141. https://doi.org/10.1080/00224499.2011. 603168

Diamond, L. M., & Huebner, D. M. (2012). Is good sex good for you? Rethinking sexuality and health. *Social and Personality Psychology Compass*, *6*(1), 54–69. https://doi.org/10.1111/j.1751-9004.2011.00408.x

Diener, E., & Seligman, M. E. P. (2002). Very happy people. *Psychological Science*, *13* (1), 81–84. http://doi.10.1111/1467-9280.00415

Dobson, K., Zhu, J., Balzarini, R., & Campbell, L. (2020). Responses to sexual advances and satisfaction in romantic relationships: Is yes good and no bad? *Social Psychological and Personality Science*. Advance online publication, *11* (6), 801–811. https://doi.org/10.1177/1948550619888884

Edwards, J. R. (2001). Ten difference score myths. *Organizational Research Methods*, *4*(3), 265–287. https://doi.org/10.1177/109442810143005

Eurostat. (2019). Retrieved July 4, 2019, from https://ec.europa.eu/eurostat/statistics-explained/index.php?title=Marriage_and_divorce_statistics&oldid=73274

Fritz, H. L., & Helgeson, V. S. (1998). Distinctions of unmitigated communion from communion: Self-neglect and overinvolvement with others. *Journal of Personality and Social Psychology*, *75*(1), 121–140. https://doi.org/10.1037/0022-3514.75.1.121

Geiss, S. K., & O'Leary, K. D. (1981). Therapist ratings of frequency and severity of marital problems: Implications for research. *Journal of Marital and Family Therapy*, *7*(4), 515–520. http://doi.10.1111/j.1752-0606.1981.tb01407.x

Goodboy, A. K., & Brann, M. (2010). Flirtation rejection strategies: Toward an understanding of communicative disinterest in flirting. *The Qualitative Report*, *15*(2), 268–278. https://nsuworks.nova.edu/tqr/vol15/iss2/3

Haupert, M. L., Gesselman, A. N., Moors, A. C., Fisher, H. E., & Garcia, J. R. (2017). Prevalence of experiences with consensual nonmonogamous relationships: Findings from two national samples of single Americans. *Journal of Sex & Marital Therapy*, *43*(5), 424–440. https://doi.org/10.1080/0092623X.2016.1178675

Hogue, J. V., Rosen, N. O., Bockaj, A., Impett, E. A., & Muise, A. (2019). Sexual communal motivation in couples coping with low sexual interest/arousal:

Associations with sexual well-being and sexual goals. *PLoS ONE, 14*(7), e0219768. https://doi.org/10.1371/journal.pone.0219768

Holt-Lunstad, J., Smith, T. B., & Layton, J. B. (2010). Social relationships and mortality risk: A meta-analytic review. *PLoS Medicine, 7*(7), e1000316. https://doi.org/http://doi.10.1371/journal.pmed.1000316

Humberg, S., Nestler, S., & Back, M. D. (2018). Response surface analysis in personality and social psychology: Checklist and clarifications for the case of congruence hypotheses. *Social Psychological and Personality Science, 10*(3), 409–419. https://doi.org/10.1177/1948550618757600

Impett, E. A., Muise, A., & Peragine, D. (2014). Sexuality in the context of relationships. In D. L. Tolman, L. M. Diamond, J. A. Bauermeister, W. H. George, J. G. Pfaus, & L. M. Ward (Eds.), *APA handbook of sexuality and psychology* (Vol. 1, pp. 269–315). American Psychological Association. http://doi.org/101037/14193-010

Impett, E. A., Muise, A., & Harasymchuk, C. (2019). Giving in the bedroom: The costs and benefits of responding to a partner's sexual needs in daily life. *Journal of Social and Personal Relationships, 36*(8), 2455–2473. https://doi.org/10.1177/0265407518787349

Impett, E. A., Muise, A., & Rosen, N. O. (2015). Is it good to be giving in the bedroom? A prosocial perspective on sexual health and well-being in romantic relationships. *Current Sexual Health Reports, 7*(3), 180–190. https://doi.org/10.1007/s11930-015-0055-9

Impett, E. A., & Peplau, L. A. (2003). Sexual compliance: Gender, motivational, and relationship perspectives. *Journal of Sex Research, 40*(1), 87–100. http://doi.10.1080/00224490309552169

Impett, E. A., & Sisson, N. (2020). *Sexuality and partner change* [Unpublished raw data]. University of Toronto Mississauga.

Jouriles, E. N., Simpson Rowe, L., McDonald, R., & Kleinsasser, A. L. (2014). Women's expression of anger in response to unwanted sexual advances: Associations with sexual victimization. *Psychology of Violence, 4*(2), 170–183. https://doi.org/10.1037/a0033191

Kashdan, T. B., Goodman, F. R., Stiksma, M., Milius, C. R., & McKnight, P. E. (2018). Sexuality leads to boosts in mood and meaning in life with no evidence for the reverse direction: A daily diary investigation. *Emotion, 18*(4), 563–576. http://doi.10.1037/emo0000324

Katz, J., & Tirone, V. (2009). Women's sexual compliance with male dating partners: Associations with investment in ideal womanhood and romantic well-being. *Sex Roles, 60*(5–6), 347–356. https://doi.org/10.1007/s11199-008-9566-4

Kelly, M. B. (2015). Divorce cases in civil course, 2010/2011. Juristat. Statistics Canada catalogue no. 85-002-X. http://bit.ly/18tCSOo.

Kenny, D. A., Kashy, D. A., & Cook, W. L. (2006). *Dyadic data analysis*. Guilford Press.

Kim, J., Horne, R., Muise, A., & Impett, E. A. (2019). Development and validation of the responses to sexual rejection scale. *Personality and Individual Differences, 144*, 88–93. https://doi.org/10.1016/j.paid.2019.02.039

Kim, J., Muise, A., Barranti, M., Mark, K., Rosen, N., Harasymchuk, C., & Impett, E. A. (2020). Are couples more satisfied when they match in sexual desire? New insights from response surface analyses. *Social Psychological and Personality Science*. Advance online publication. doi: 10.1177/1948550620926770.

Kim, J. J., Muise, A., Sakaluk, J. K., & Impett, E. A. (2019). Sexual rejection scale. In R. Milhausen, J. K. Sakaluk, T. Fisher, C. Davis, & W. Yarber (Eds.), *Handbook of sexuality-related measures* (pp. 441–443). Taylor & Francis.

Kim, J. J., Muise, A., & Impett, E. A. (2018). The relationship implications of rejecting a partner for sex kindly versus having sex reluctantly. *Journal of Social and Personal Relationships*, 35(4), 485–508. https://doi.org/10.1177/0265407517743084

Kim, J. J., Muise, A., Sakaluk, J., Rosen, N., & Impett, E. A. (2020). When tonight is not the night: Sexual rejection and satisfaction in romantic relationships. *Personality and Social Psychology Bulletin*. Advance online publication. https://doi.org/10.1177/0146167220907469

Kogan, A., Impett, E. A., Oveis, C., Hui, B., Gordon, A., & Keltner, D. (2010). When giving feels good: The intrinsic benefits of sacrifice in romantic relationships for the communally motivated. *Psychological Science*, 21(12), 1918–1924. https://doi.org/10.1177/0956797610388815

Lawrance, K., & Byers, E. S. (1995). Sexual satisfaction in long-term heterosexual relationships: The interpersonal exchange model of sexual satisfaction. *Personal Relationships*, 2(4), 267-285. https://doi.org/10.1111/j.1475-6811.1995.tb00092.x

Le, B. M., Impett, E. A., Lemay, E. P., Muise, A., & Tskhay, K. O. (2018). Communal motivation and subjective well-being in interpersonal relationships: An integrative review and meta-analysis. Psychological Bulletin, 144, 1-25. doi: 10.1037/bul0000133.

Leary, M. R., Koch, E. J., & Hechenbleikner, N. R. (2001). Emotional responses to interpersonal rejection. In M. R. Leary (Ed.), *Interpersonal rejection* (pp. 145–166). Oxford University Press.

Leary, M. R. (2001). Responses to social exclusion: Social anxiety, jealousy, loneliness, depression, and low self-esteem. *Journal of Social and Clinical Psychology*, 9(2), 221–229. https://doi.org/10.1521/jscp.1990.9.2.221

Leary, M. R., Springer, C., Negel, L., Ansell, E., & Evans, K. (1998). The causes, phenomenology, and consequences of hurt feelings. *Journal of Personality and Social Psychology*, 74(5), 1225–1237. http://doi.10.1037/0022-3514.74.5.1225

Mark, K. P. (2015). Sexual desire discrepancy. *Current Sexual Health Reports*, 7(3), 198–202. https://doi.org/10.1007/s11930-015-0057-7

Maxwell, J. A., Muise, A., MacDonald, G., Day, L. C., Rosen, N. O., & Impett, E. A. (2017). How implicit theories of sexuality shape sexual and relationship well-being. *Journal of Personality and Social Psychology*, 112(2), 238–279. https://doi.org/10.1037/pspi0000078

McBride, H. L., & Kwee, J. L. (2017). Sex after baby: Women's sexual function in the postpartum period. *Current Sexual Health Reports*, 9(3), 142–149. https://doi.org/10.1007/s11930-017-0116-3

McNulty, J. K., & Russell, V. M. (2010). When "negative" behaviors are positive: A contextual analysis of the long-term effects of problem-solving behaviors on changes in relationship satisfaction. *Journal of Personality and Social Psychology*, 98(4), 587–604. https://doi.org/10.1037/a0017479

Metts, S., Cupach, W. R., & Imahori, T. T. (1992). Perceptions of sexual compliance-resisting messages in three types of cross-sex relationships. *Western Journal of Communication*, 56(1), 1–17. https://doi.org/10.1080/10570319209374398

Mikulincer, M., & Shaver, P. R. (2016). *Attachment in adulthood: Structure, dynamics, and change* (2nd ed.). Guilford Press.

Miller, R. B., Yorgason, J. B., Sandberg, J. G., & White, M. B. (2003). Problems that couples bring to therapy: A view across the family life cycle. *American Journal of Family Therapy, 31*(5), 395–407. http://doi.10.1080/01926180390223950

Mills, J., Clark, M. S., Ford, T. E., & Johnson, M. (2004). Measurement of communal strength. *Personal Relationships, 11*(2), 213–230. https://doi.org/10.1111/j.1475-6811.2004.00079.x

Muise, A., & Impett, E. A. (2019). Sexual communal strength scale. In R. Milhausen, J. K. Sakaluk, T. Fisher, C. Davis, & W. Yarber (Eds.), *Handbook of sexuality-related measures* (pp. 443–445). Taylor & Francis.

Muise, A., Bergeron, S., Impett, E. A., Delisle, I., & Rosen, N. O. (2018). Communal motivation in couples coping with vulvodynia: Sexual distress mediates associations with pain, depression, and anxiety. *Journal of Psychosomatic Research, 106,* 34–40. https://doi.org/10.1016/j.jpsychores.2018.01.006

Muise, A., Bergeron, S., Impett, E. A., & Rosen, N. O. (2017). The costs and benefits of sexual communal motivation for couples coping with vulvodynia. *Health Psychology, 36*(8), 819–827. https://doi.org/10.1037/hea0000470

Muise, A., & Impett, E. A. (2015). Good, giving and game: The relationship benefits of communal sexual responsiveness. *Social Psychological and Personality Science, 6*(2), 164–172. https://doi.org/10.1177/1948550614553641

Muise, A., & Impett, E. A. (2016). Applying theories of communal motivation to sexuality. *Social and Personality Psychology Compass, 10*(8), 455–467. https://doi.org/10.1111/spc3.12261

Muise, A., Impett, E. A., Kogan, A., & Desmarais, S. (2013). Keeping the spark alive: Being motivated to meet a partner's sexual needs sustains sexual desire in long-term romantic relationships. *Social Psychological and Personality Science, 4*(3), 267–273. https://doi.org/10.1177/1948550612457185

Muise, A., Kim, J. J., Impett, E. A., & Rosen, N. O. (2017). Understanding when a partner is not in the mood: Sexual communal motivation in couples transitioning to parenthood. *Archives of Sexual Behavior, 46*(7), 1993–2006. https://doi.org/10.1007/s10508-016-0920-2

Muise, A., Laughton, A., Moors, A., & Impett, E. A. (2019). Sexual communal motivation and relationship satisfaction in consensually non-monogamous relationships. *Journal of Social and Personal Relationships, 36*(7), 1917–1938. https://doi.org/10.1177/0265407518774638

Muise, A., Laughton, A., Moors, A., & Impett, E. A. (2019). Sexual communal motivation and relationship satisfaction in consensually non-monogamous relationships. Journal of Social and Personal Relationships, 36 (7), 1917-1938. https://doi.org/10.1177/0265407518774638

Muise, A., Schimmack, U., & Impett, E. A. (2016). Sexual frequency predicts greater well-being, but more is not always better. *Social Psychological and Personality Science, 7*(4), 295–302. http://doi.10.1177/1948550615616462

Murray, S. L., Holmes, J. G., & Collins, N. L. (2006). Optimizing assurance: The risk regulation system in relationships. *Psychological Bulletin, 132*(5), 641–666. https://doi.org/10.1037/0033-2909.132.5.641

Nagurney, A. J. (2007). The effects of relationship stress and unmitigated communion on physical and mental health outcomes. *Stress and Health, 23*(4), 267–273. https://doi.org/10.1002/smi.1146

O'Sullivan, L. F., & Byers, E. S. (1996). Gender differences in responses to discrepancies in desired level of sexual intimacy. *Journal of Psychology & Human Sexuality, 8*(1–2), 49–67. https://doi.org/10.1300/J056v08n01_04

Overall, N. C., Fletcher, G. J. O., Simpson, J. A., & Sibley, C. G. (2009). Regulating partners in intimate relationships: The costs and benefits of different communication strategies. *Journal of Personality and Social Psychology, 96*(3), 620–639. https://doi.org/10.1037/a0012961

Peplau, L. A. (2003). Human sexuality: How do men and women differ? *Current Directions in Psychological Science, 12*(2), 37–40. https://doi.org/10.1111/1467-8721.01221

Pew Research Center. (2017). Retrieved July 4, 2019, from https://www.pewresearch.org/fact-tank/2017/09/14/as-u-s-marriage-rate-hovers-at-50-education-gap-in-marital-status-widens/

Raposo, S., Impett, E. A., & Muise, A. (in press). Keeping things even in the bedroom: Attachment avoidance is associated with being more sexually exchange-oriented and less sexually communal. *Archives of Sexual Behavior.*

Raposo, S., & Muise, A. (2019). *Perceived partner sexual responsiveness buffers anxiously attached individuals from lower relationship and sexual quality in daily life* [Manuscript submitted for publication].

Rehman, U. S., Balan, D., Sutherland, S., & McNeil, J. (2019). Understanding barriers to sexual communication. *Journal of Social and Personal Relationships, 36*(9), 2605–2623. https://doi.org/10.1177/0265407518794900

Rehman, U. S., Lizdek, I., Fallis, E. E., Sutherland, S., & Goodnight, J. A. (2017). How is sexual communication different from nonsexual communication? A moment-by-moment analysis of discussions between romantic partners. *Archives of Sexual Behavior, 46*(8), 2339–2352. http://doi.10.1007/s10508-017-1006-5

Reis, H. T., Clark, M. S., & Holmes, J. G. (2004). Perceived partner responsiveness as an organizing construct in the study of intimacy and closeness. In D. J. Mashek & A. Aron (Eds.), *Handbook of closeness and intimacy* (pp. 201–225). Erlbaum. http://doi.10.1037/13486-002

Reis, H. T. (2007). Steps toward the ripening of relationship science. *Personal Relationships, 14*(1), 1–23. https://doi.org/1350-4126=07

Rosen, N. O., & Bergeron, S. (2019). Genito-pelvic pain through a dyadic lens: Moving toward an interpersonal emotion regulation model of women's sexual dysfunction. *Annual Review of Sex Research, 56 (4-5),* 440–461. https://doi.org/10.1080/00224499.2018.1513987

Rubin, J. D., Moors, A., Matsick, J. L., Ziegler, A., & Conley, T. D. (2014). On the margins: Consideing diversity among consensually non-monogamous relationships. *Journal Fur Psychologie, 22* (1).

Rusbult, C. E., & Van Lange, P. A. M. (2008). Why we need interdependence theory. *Social and Personality Psychology Compass, 2*(5), 2049–2070. https://doi.org/10.1111/j.1751-9004.2008.00147.x

Ryan, R. M., & Deci, E. L. (2000). Self-determination theory and the facilitation of intrinsic motivation, social development, and well-being. *American Psychologist, 55*(1), 68–78. https://doi.org/10.1037/0003-066X.55.1.68

Sanford, K. (2003). Problem-solving conversations in marriage: Does it matter what topics couples discuss? *Personal Relationships, 10*(1), 97–112. http://doi.10.1111/1475-6811.00038

Schmiedeberg, C., & Schröder, J. (2016). Does sexual satisfaction change with relationship duration? *Archives of Sexual Behavior, 45*(1), 99–107. http://doi.10.1007/s10508-015-0587-0

Schnarch, D., & Regas, S. (2012). The crucible differentiation scale: Assessing differentiation in human relationships. *Journal of Marital and Family Therapy, 38*(4), 639–652. https://doi.org/10.1111/j.1752-0606.2011.00259.x

Schönbrodt, F. D. (2016). *RSA: An R package for response surface analysis (version 0.9.10)*. https://cran.r-project.org/package=RSA

Schwenk, G. C., Dawson, S. J., Muise, A., & Rosen, N. O. (2020). *It's not us, it's parenthood. Comparing sexual well-being in new parents and community couples.* Manuscript submitted for publication.

Sprecher, S., & Sprecher. (1998). Social exchange theories and sexuality. *Journal of Sex Research, 35*(1), 32–43. https://doi.org/10.1080/00224499809551915

Sprecher, S. (2002). Sexual satisfaction in premarital relationships: Associations with satisfaction, love, commitment, and stability. *Journal of Sex Research, 39*(3), 190–196. https://doi.org/10.1080/00224490209552141

Struckman-Johnson, D., & Struckman-Johnson, C. (1991). Men's and women's acceptance of coercive sexual strategies varied by initiator gender and couple intimacy. *Sex Roles, 25*(11–12), 661–676. https://doi.org/10.1007/bf00289570

Syme, M. L. (2014). The evolving concept of older adult sexual behavior and its benefits. *Generations – Journal of the American Society on Aging, 38 (1)*, 35–41.

Thibaut, J. W., & Kelley, H. H. (1959). *The social psychology of groups*. Wiley.

Vannier, S. A., Adare, K. E., & Rosen, N. O. (2018). Is it me or you? First-time mothers' attributions for postpartum sexual concerns are associated with sexual and relationship satisfaction in the transition to parenthood. *Journal of Social and Personal Relationships, 35*(4), 577–599. https://doi.org/10.1177/0265407517743086

Woolhouse, H., McDonald, E., & Brown, S. (2012). Women's experiences of sex and intimacy after childbirth: Making the adjustment to motherhood. *Journal of Psychosomatic Obstetrics and Gynecology, 33*(4), 185–190. http://doi.10.3109/0167482X.2012.720314

Wright, N. O., Norton, D. L., & Matusek, J. A. (2010). Predicting verbal coercion following sexual refusal during a hookup: Diverging gender patterns. *Sex Roles, 62* (9–10), 647–660. https://doi.org/10.1007/s11199-010-9763-9

ARTICLE

Ideological differences in attitude and belief similarity: distinguishing perception and reality

Chadly Stern

Department of Psychology, University of Illinois, Urbana-Champaign, USA

ABSTRACT
Attitude and belief similarity have long stood as topics of inquiry for social psychology. Recent research suggests that there might be meaningful differences across people in the extent to which they perceive and actually share others' attitudes and beliefs. I outline research examining the relationship between political ideology and the perception and reality of attitude similarity. Specifically, I review research documenting that (a) conservatives *perceive* greater ingroup similarity than do liberals, (b) conservatives *overestimate* and liberals *underestimate* ingroup similarity, (c) liberals and conservatives both *underestimate* similarity to outgroup members, and (d) liberals possess more *actual* ingroup similarity than do conservatives on a national level. Collectively, this review contributes to understanding how political ideology relates to (perceived) attitude similarity.

ARTICLE HISTORY Received 2 July 2019; Accepted 14 July 2020

KEYWORDS Political ideology; perceived similarity; actual similarity

Possessing shared attitudes and beliefs about the world, such as that the colour of the sky is called "blue" and that money can be used to purchase food at a grocery store, allows people to effectively communicate and engage in everyday social interactions (Higgins, 2019). It should not be surprising then that attitude and belief similarity have long stood as topics of study for social psychology. For example, during social interactions people change their beliefs to align with those of others (Sherif, 1935), even when they report a response that is objectively and obviously inaccurate (Asch, 1956). Additionally, when people are asked to estimate others' attitudes, they reliably assume that others share their attitudes and beliefs (Ross et al., 1977). Thus, people generally form attitudes and beliefs about the world that reflect those that others possess.

Shared attitudes and beliefs are not only important for seemingly mundane communication and decision-making (e.g., determining how much a dot is moving or how long a line is), but are also central to navigating

---

CONTACT Chadly Stern chadly@illinois.edu Champaign, IL 61820
© 2020 European Association of Social Psychology

and engaging with the political world (Stern & Ondish, 2018). For example, people who perceive others as having attitudes and beliefs that are similar to their own are more likely to engage in political decision-making in their community (Festinger et al., 1950). Thus, determining the extent to which people possess (or at least think they possess) agreement in their attitudes and beliefs with others has implications for understanding important social and political phenomena.

Recent research suggests that there might be systematic differences between people who are politically liberal and conservative that could impact the extent to which they perceive and actually possess attitude similarity in their political groups. For example, liberals and conservatives differ in the strength of certain psychological motivations (Feldman, 2003; Graham et al., 2009; Jost, Sterling et al., 2018), and diverge in the informational environments with which they engage (Rodriguez et al., 2017; Stroud, 2008). However, the question of whether and when there are ideological differences in perceived and actual attitude similarity has remained relatively unaddressed. Specifically, there is not currently a theoretically informed picture of whether liberals and conservatives differ in the extent to which they (a) perceive that their attitudes and beliefs are similar to those of like-minded others and (b) possess actual agreement with like-minded others.

Both the *perception* and *actual degree* of attitude similarity within a group can impact a group's ability to mobilise and achieve goals. Specifically, perceiving that group members share one's beliefs on an issue or experiencing that they actually do fosters confidence that a goal can be achieved (Festinger et al., 1950; Van Zomeren et al., 2004). This feeling in turn promotes coordination among group members, which translates into individual and collective behaviour (e.g., donating to a cause, engaging in protest; Bandura, 2000; Gibson et al., 2000; Van Zomeren et al., 2004). As such, understanding whether there are liberal-conservative differences in perceived and actual attitude similarity sheds light on the interface of social cognition with political psychology and holds implications for determining how ideology corresponds to interpersonal (e.g., close relationship maintenance) and collective outcomes (e.g., social change).

In this review, I describe research investigating whether and when conservatives perceive like-minded others (i.e., ingroup members) as sharing their attitudes and beliefs to a greater extent than liberals do. However, I also highlight how these perceptions might not translate into accurate reflections of reality. To situate the broader discussion, I first describe previous research examining perceptions of attitude similarity and the role of ideology in social judgement. I then turn to the main focus of this review and discuss research that examines ideological differences in (a) the *perception* of how similar one's attitude and beliefs are to those of ingroup members, (b) the *accuracy* of perceived similarity to ingroup members, (c) the *accuracy* of perceived similarity to outgroup members, and (d) how similar people's attitudes and beliefs *actually* are to ingroup members. In the general discussion, I outline potential explanations for ideological differences in perceived and actual attitude similarity, and highlight meaning directions for future research. Throughout this review, I develop a broad picture of the way in which political ideology relates to perceptions and actual degrees of similarity.

Perceptions of attitude and belief similarity

The idea that people perceive others as sharing their beliefs and attitudes harkens back to the inception of psychology. Freud (1936) argued that people assume others share their views and attributes, which he called "projection", because it allows them to ascribe attributes onto others that they personally wish to repress (e.g., unwanted sexual urges and emotions). Horney (1945, p. 116) similarly described this process as consisting of "shifting the blame and responsibility to someone else for subjectively rejected trends or qualities, such as suspecting others of one's own tendencies toward betrayal, ambition, domination, self-righteousness, meekness, and so on." Although perceived similarity initially received a relatively negative framing within psychodynamic descriptions, object relations theorists also argued that assuming similarity with others could be a mechanism through which people identify, strengthen emotional bonds, and develop intimacy with loved ones (Klein, 1940).

Over time, psychodynamic approaches became predominantly rejected within most empirical areas of psychology. Nevertheless, the idea that people might view others as sharing their beliefs and attitudes became a pervasive topic of interest for researchers. This phenomenon has been given a wide variety of names throughout the history of psychology, such as "social projection" (Allport, 1924), "supplementary apperceptive projection" (Murray, 1933), "NIPE" (naïve inferences based on limited personal experience; Cattell, 1944), "assimilative projection" (Cameron & Margaret, 1951), "naïve projection" (Murstein, 1957), "attributive projection" (Holmes, 1968), "looking glass perceptions" (Fields & Schuman, 1976), the "false consensus effect" (Ross et al., 1977), "assumed similarity" (Marks & Miller, 1982), and "perceived consensus" (Hoch, 1987). It is important to point out that while researchers who used these different terms often employed slightly different methodological approaches, they all converged in the overarching conclusion that people assume others share their attitudes and beliefs. To maintain consistency with the most commonly employed terminology, I use the terms *perceived similarity* or *assumed similarity* when discussing people's tendency to think that others' share their beliefs and attitudes.

Previous research has documented that people assume others are similar to them in a variety of different ways. For example, people perceive others as sharing their political views and behaviours (Koudenburg et al., 2011). They also perceive similarity in more trivial domains, such as thinking others share their food preferences and likelihood of wearing a sign in public with the phrase "Eat at Joes" (Mullen et al., 1989; Ross et al., 1977). A general tendency for people, on average, to assume that others share their beliefs and attitudes appears to be highly robust and replicable (Klein et al., 2018). However, there is also considerable variability across people in the tendency to assume that others share their views (Mullen et al., 1985; Robbins & Krueger, 2005). Understanding the source of this variability has remained a constant point of debate within psychology (Davis, 2017; Holmes, 1978; Mullen & Hu, 1988). Thus, shedding light on when perceptions of attitude similarity vary across people stands as an important question for psychological science.

Political ideology and social judgement

Differences between people who adopt politically liberal and conservative views potentially serve as one source of variability in assumptions and constructions of attitude similarity. Generally speaking, conservative and right-wing worldviews support the status quo or (in some situations) advocate for reactive forms of change, whereas liberal and left-wing worldviews support novel change (Jost et al., 2009, 2003). Researchers have long held an interest in understanding whether and when political beliefs correspond to the way that people perceive and engage with the world (e.g., Adorno et al., 1950; Onraet et al., 2013; Jost et al., 2003). These perspectives galvanised decades of theoretical debates and empirical inquiries into understanding liberal-conservative differences.

Some researchers have documented ways in which political ideology is related to overtly political outcomes, such as electoral choices and support for governmental leaders (e.g., Morisi et al., 2019). However, scholars have also argued that characteristics of an individual can modulate more basic social judgement and perception processes (e.g., Brunswik, 1955; West & Kenny, 2011). Consistent with this perspective, researchers have provided generative insights into the ways that political ideology is associated with basic perceptions and experiences, often in non-political domains. For example, researchers have highlighted ideological differences in affective reactions to disgusting stimuli (Smith et al., 2011), detection of deviance in shapes (Okimoto & Gromet, 2016), and the construction of attitudes towards novel and mundane stimuli (e.g., beans; Shook & Fazio, 2009). Here, I further contribute to understanding the role of ideology in social judgement through reviewing findings concerning whether and when liberals and conservatives diverge in the perception and reality of attitude similarity.

Ideological differences in perceived similarity

Stern, West, Jost et al. (2014) examined whether liberals and conservatives would diverge in how strongly they perceived similarity with liked-minded others (i.e., political ingroup members). Specifically, across three studies (Study 1: N = 107, 67% women, M_{age} = 34.66 years; Study 2: N = 150, 63% women, M_{age} = 34.03 years; Study 3: N = 311, 68% women, M_{age} = 32.89 years), they examined whether conservatives would be more likely than liberals to perceive politically like-minded others as sharing their judgements about the world. To test this question, the researchers showed participants photographs of the faces of White men. Participants made a judgement for each face. They were randomly assigned to either make a judgement about each target person's sexual orientation (gay-straight; Study 1: n = 54; Study 2: n = 51; Study 3: n = 101), month of birth (November-December; Study 1: n = 53; Study 2: n = 49; Study 3: n = 106), or food preferences (fruits-vegetables; Study 2: n = 50; Study 3: n = 104).

After making the judgements, participants estimated what percentage of people sharing their political beliefs in the study had made similar judgements as they had. In other words, they estimated how similar political ingroup members' judgements were to their own. Participants reported their political ideology using a scale ranging from 1 (*extremely liberal*) to 9 (*extremely conservative*). A single item measure is commonly used to gauge political ideology (e.g., Graham et al., 2009; McAdams et al., 2008; Prusaczyk & Hodson, 2019). Overall, people who reported being more conservative (versus liberal) estimated that a greater percentage of political ingroup members had made similar judgements as they did. This ideological difference did not vary across the specific judgement that participants made.

These findings suggest that conservatives perceive greater similarity with ingroup members than do liberals. However, this research did not address when liberals and conservatives would differ in their assumptions of similarity. In other words, when do liberals' and conservatives' judgement processes result in greater perceived similarity among conservatives? There are at least two perspectives that could help address this question. The first perspective is that there are differences between liberals and conservatives in their initial inferences about ingroup similarity. People's initial assessments of whether others share their attitudes and beliefs tend to be relatively automatic (Epley et al., 2004; Tamir & Mitchell, 2013). In other words, people "anchor" on their own attitudes and beliefs to gauge where others stand on an issue and will initially do so without much thought into their inference. Some findings also suggest that various factors (e.g., motivations, previous experiences) can shape automatic processes, including snap inferences that people make (Gawronski & Cesario, 2013). Thus, it is possible that liberals and conservatives diverge in their assumptions of similarity during the process of rendering initial judgements, such that conservatives automatically assume that ingroup members share their attitudes and beliefs to a greater degree than liberals do.

The second perspective is that there are differences between liberals and conservatives in the extent to which they engage in effortful and deliberative adjustment of their initial inferences of ingroup similarity. Directly relevant to this possibility, Skitka et al. (2002) proposed that when a person's initial inference clashes with their expectations or active goals and they have time to deliberate on their judgement, they would be more likely to engage in a "two stage" process whereby they adjust their initial inference. Skitka et al. (2002) argued that this process could lead liberals *or* conservatives to engage in adjustment. However, given that liberals (versus conservatives) tend to report a chronically stronger goal to deliberate and score slightly higher on measures of cognitive reflection (Jost, Sterling et al., 2018), liberals might be more inclined to adjust their initial inferences. Consistent with this perspective, liberals were often more likely than conservatives to change their initial attributions for the source of a person's behaviour (Skitka et al., 2002) and also adjusted their snap impressions of others' group memberships when the judgement was made from limited information (Stern et al., 2013). Importantly, however, this adjustment process is effortful and requires both time and cognitive resources to complete (Epley et al., 2004; Tamir & Mitchell, 2013). In turn, liberals were only more likely to adjust their initial judgements when they had sufficient cognitive resources to do so (Skitka et al., 2002; Stern et al., 2013). Thus, it is possible that liberals and conservatives diverge in their assumptions of similarity during the process of adjusting initial judgements, such that liberals will assume less ingroup similarity than conservatives when they can deliberate on their judgements.

Stern and West (2016) examined whether liberals and conservatives diverged in their assumptions of ingroup similarity during automatic (anchoring) or effortful (adjustment) judgement processes. To test this question, the authors borrowed a commonly employed paradigm for assessing how strongly people assume that others share their attitudes (e.g., Arndt et al., 1999; Krueger & Clement, 1994). The paradigm includes two steps. The first step consists of participants reporting their attitudes towards a variety of issues in a binary agree-disagree manner. In this case, participants reported attitudes towards twenty statements. Some statements were political (e.g., "Gun control laws are not nearly strict enough", "Racial profiling is okay if it makes the country safer") and some were non-political (e.g., "My hardest battles are with myself", "I enjoy coffee").

The second step consists of participants estimating the percentage of people who would agree with each statement. In this case, participants estimated the percentage of politically like-minded others who would agree with each statement. For example, a conservative participant would estimate the percentage of conservatives who agree with the statement "Gun control laws are not nearly strict enough". A single score can then be calculated reflecting the degree of perceived attitude similarity with ingroup members. Specifically, an ideographic correlation is calculated for each participant between their own binary attitudes (Column A in Table 1) and their estimates of what percentage of ingroup members would agree with each statement (Column B in Table 1). A participant indicating that a higher percentage of ingroup members agree to statements with which they personally agree (and that a lower percentage agree to statements with which they personally disagree) would receive a higher perceived ingroup similarity score.

To test when ideological differences emerged in the process of generating inferences, the researchers also experimentally manipulated the amount of time that participants could deliberate on their judgements of others' attitudes. Participants ($N = 259$, 47% women, $M_{age} = 36.28$ years) were randomly assigned to either estimate ingroup members' attitudes on each topic within 6 seconds (i.e., under time pressure; $n = 132$) or were given an unlimited amount of time to render judgements ($n = 127$). This procedure is commonly used to alter how much participants can engage in effortful thought about their judgements (Epley et al., 2004; Woltin & Yzerbyt, in press). Judgements that emerge under time pressure were expected to more strongly capture automatic inferences, whereas judgements made when time was unlimited were expected to reflect more effortful and deliberate inferences.

Results indicated that when participants had an unlimited amount of time to estimate ingroup members' attitudes, conservatives perceived more similarity between their own attitudes and those of ingroup members than did liberals (Figure 1). In other words, conservatives perceived more ingroup similarity. However, when participants were required to quickly determine ingroup members' attitudes (i.e., were under time pressure), liberals and conservatives did not differ in their perceptions of ingroup similarity. Importantly, the time pressure manipulation differentially affected liberals and conservatives. Liberals were less likely to assume that politically like-minded others shared their attitudes when they could deliberate on their

Table 1. Information for calculating example perceived similarity and accuracy scores. Values are hypothetical. For Participant Attitude, 1 = Agreed with the Statement, −1 = Disagreed with the Statement.

Statement	Participant Attitude (A)	Perceived Ingroup/Outgroup Agreement (B)	Actual Ingroup/Outgroup Agreement (C)	Perceived Ingroup/Outgroup Agreement − Actual Ingroup/Outgroup Agreement (D)
1	1	45	60	−15
2	1	60	85	−25
3	−1	25	30	−5
4	1	70	50	20
5	−1	55	70	−15

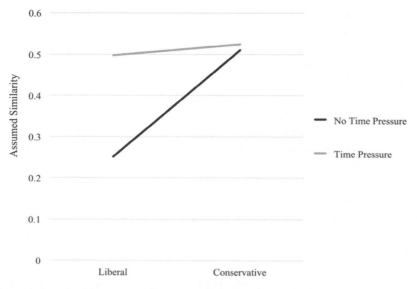

Figure 1. Perceived ingroup similarity among liberals and conservatives (1 SD below and above the ideology mean) as a function of experimental condition reported in Study 1 of Stern and West (2016). Figure reproduced with permission from SAGE.

judgements compared to when they made judgements under time pressure. In contrast, conservatives were just as likely to assume that other conservatives shared their attitudes when they had limited or unlimited amounts of time to make judgements. These findings suggest that liberals were more likely than conservatives to effortfully adjust their initial inferences of similarity when they had the time do so.

These findings provide support for the perspective that ideological differences in perceived ingroup similarity emerge during the stage of judgement adjustment. Specifically, liberals and conservatives appear to make comparable initial judgements of how similar their attitudes are to those of like-minded others. When given adequate time to deliberate on their initial judgements, however, liberals were more likely than conservatives to engage in a subsequent process of "adjustment" and to change their estimates of others' attitudes to be farther away from their own attitude. It is important to highlight that both liberals and conservatives assumed that political ingroup members' attitudes were, overall, more similar than different from their own. In other words, liberals were not assuming that their attitudes and beliefs were highly dissimilar from those that other liberals hold. Instead, there was simply variation in the degree to which liberals and conservatives perceived similarity with ingroup members, such that conservatives perceived more similarity than did liberals.

Assessing the (In)accuracy of perceived *Ingroup* similarity

The findings reviewed thus far suggest that conservatives perceive greater ingroup similarity than do liberals, and that these differences are more likely to emerge when liberals possess sufficient time to adjust their initial judgements. To what degree do these perceptions reflect reality? This question is important to consider given that some commonly referenced findings about perceived similarity invoke ideas about accuracy. For example, some researchers have described people's tendency to assume that others share their attitudes and beliefs as the "false consensus effect" (Coleman, 2018; Mullen et al., 1985; Ross et al., 1977). This terminology suggests that perceiving others as sharing one's beliefs leads to erroneous conclusions. However, assuming similarity can increase the chance of making an accurate judgement of others' attitudes when there is a strong degree of general similarity with others (Hoch, 1987; Kenny & Acitelli, 2001). People tend to sort into ideologically homogeneous communities and primary interact with politically like-minded others (Bishop, 2009). In turn, the attitudes that people observe others in their social networks as espousing could inform their assessments of how similar they are to others, and perceptions of similarity to politically like-minded others could be relatively accurate. To determine the accuracy of people's perceptions of similarity, perceptions of others' attitudes must be compared to the reality of others' attitudes (i.e., the "truth"; West & Kenny, 2011). Through doing so, researchers can more strongly determine the degree to which perceptions of similarity reflect or diverge from reality.

Stern, West, and Schmitt (2014) sought to address this point and examined the degree to which liberals and conservatives generated (in)accurate perceptions of ingroup similarity. To do so, in two studies (Study 1: $N = 292$, 59% women, $M_{age} = 35.89$ years; Study 2: $N = 287$, 56% women, $M_{age} = 35.36$ years) participants reported whether they agreed with forty-one different statements (e.g., "America should strive to strengthen its military") and indicated the percentage of politically like-minded others whom they believed would also agree with each statement. Participants reported their political ideology in a categorical manner as liberal (Study 1: $n = 137$; Study 2: $n = 125$), moderate (Study 1: $n = 93$; Study 2: $n = 96$), or conservative (Study 1: $n = 62$; Study 2: $n = 66$).

The authors then calculated a score reflecting how accurate each participant's perceptions of ingroup similarity were. To do so, they first computed the percentage of people in each political group who actually agreed with each statement (e.g., the percentage of liberals who agreed with the statement "America should strive to strengthen its military"; Column C in Table 1). Next, they computed a difference score between participant's estimate of what percentage of political ingroup members agreed with a statement and the percentage that actually did (Column D in Table 1). Lastly, they correlated each participant's self-reported attitudes with these difference scores (the correlation between Columns A and D in Table 1). A positive score indicates that the participant consistently overestimated the extent to which ingroup members shared their attitudes, a negative score indicates that the participant consistently underestimated the extent to which ingroup members shared their attitudes, and a score of zero indicates that the participant did not systematically overestimate or underestimate how much ingroup members shared their attitudes.

Overall, results of both studies indicated that conservatives *overestimated* how similar their attitudes were to those of political ingroup members. Conservatives thought that their attitudes were more similar to those of other conservatives than they actually were. In contrast, liberals *underestimated* how similar their attitudes were to those of political ingroup members. Liberals thought that their attitudes were more different from those of other liberals than they actually were. Thus, both liberals and conservatives rendered inaccurate judgements of how similar their attitudes were to those of like-minded others, but they were inaccurate in divergent ways (Table 2). These finding highlight that both liberals and conservatives generate perceptions that are not simply reflections of reality. Liberals and conservatives both hold a distorted understanding of precisely how much common ground they stand on with like-minded others.

One interesting question that arises from these findings is whether the differential number of people who identify as liberal and conservative plays a role in the accuracy of similarity perceptions. While there is some fluctuation in group sizes over time, there are consistently more people who identify as conservative than liberal in the United States (Saad, 2019). Previous research indicates that when group size is a salient factor that contributes to perceptions of similarity, those with a smaller group size are more motivated to perceive support for their worldview than are those with a larger group size. For example, in the context of minority-majority relations, Wetzel and Walton (1985, p. 1357) point out that people in the minority are "highly motivated to misperceive their own uniqueness" in order to normalise their attitudes. Indeed, people who hold a minority

Table 2. Mean accuracy scores as a function of participant ideology, as reported in Stern, West, and Schmitt (2014). Calculation of these scores also adjusted for the perceived social desirability of endorsing each item (Studies 1 and 2) and the personal importance of the topic in each item (Study 2). Within a row, scores with different subscripts are significantly different ($p < .05$). Table reproduced with permission from SAGE.

Study	Liberal	Moderate	Conservative
1	$-.09_a$	$.05_b$	$.09_b$
2	$-.09_a$	$.07_b$	$.22_c$

perspective tend to *overestimate* the extent to which others share their attitude, whereas those who hold a majority perspective *underestimate* the amount of social support for their perspective (Krueger & Clement, 1997; Sanders & Mullen, 1983). If group size were strongly contributing to ideological differences in the accuracy of perceived similarity, liberals would be expected to overestimate similarity to a greater degree than conservatives. Importantly, however, the exact opposite pattern was observed, which suggests that group size is not a primary factor contributing to conservatives' and liberals' perceptions.

Assessing the (In)accuracy of perceived *outgroup* similarity

The findings discussed above indicate that conservatives overestimate and liberals underestimate their degree of ingroup similarity. Do these patterns also extend to perceptions of outgroup similarity? In other words, are conservatives more likely to overestimate (and liberals more likely to underestimate) how similar their attitudes and beliefs are to those of other people in general, or are these differences specific to perceptions of the ingroup? Liberals and conservatives appear to be similarly inclined to avoid aspects of the world that might challenge their political beliefs. For example, liberals and conservatives report comparable degrees of dislike towards ideological outgroup members (Brandt et al., 2014; Crawford, 2014) and express similarly strong desires to avoid outgroup members' political viewpoints (Frimer et al., 2017). When generating perceptions of outgroup members, both liberals and conservatives also rely on stereotypes that exaggerate ideological differences (Graham et al., 2012; Scherer et al., 2015). Further, people tend to perceive the political landscape as being highly polarised, and often more so than it actually is (Robinson et al., 1995; Van Boven et al., 2012; Westfall et al., 2015). Thus, liberals and conservatives might be similarly likely to overestimate the degree to which outgroup members' attitudes diverge from their own.

To address this question, Stern and Kleiman (2015; $N = 230$, 59% women, $M_{age} = 32.37$ years) asked liberals (measured as Democrats; $n = 166$) and conservatives (measured as Republicans; $n = 64$) to provide their political attitudes through indicating a binary position on eight different issues. For example, participants indicated whether they supported or opposed the death penalty for a person convicted of murder. All political attitude questions were drawn from Gallup polls – a widely cited source of public opinion – that were conducted either the year the research was carried out or one year before.

To examine when people were most likely to generate inaccurate perceptions of outgroup (dis)similarity, participants were next randomly assigned to one of two conditions. In the experimental condition ($n = 114$), participants completed a task that would prompt a mindset of deliberation.

Participants wrote about two goals that they wanted to achieve and that were important to them, but that also conflicted with one another. For example, one participant in the study wrote about how their goal to enhance their physical fitness conflicted with their goal of advancing their career. Effortful thought and deliberation generally decrease reliance on stereotypes (Kleiman et al., 2014; Schaller et al., 1995). To the extent that partisan stereotypes (e.g., thinking all Republican oppose same-sex marriage) were contributing to overestimates of outgroup dissimilarity, participants assigned to this condition were expected to make more accurate judgements. Participants in a control condition ($n = 116$) wrote several sentences about their morning.

After completing their assigned task, participants reported perceptions of outgroup members attitudes. They indicated the percentage of political outgroup members who would report one of the response options for each political attitude. For example, Democratic [Republican] participants estimated the percentage of Republicans [Democrats] who favoured the death penalty. The specific attitudinal positions being estimated among the outgroup were selected such that half were stances that Democrats were more likely to endorse (e.g., being pro-choice on abortion) and half were stances that Republicans were more likely to endorse (e.g., opposing the legalisation of marijuana use). Because the attitude items were taken from Gallup, the authors were able to obtain representative information about the percentage of Republicans and Democrats who *actually* held each political attitude based on Gallup's reporting. They then used this information to calculate a score reflecting the extent to which people systematically underestimated or overestimated how similar their attitudes were to those of political outgroup members. This score was calculated using the same procedure as described above for Stern, West, and Schmitt (2014).

Results indicated that both liberals and conservatives *underestimated* how similar their attitudes were to those of political *outgroup* members. In other words, liberals and conservatives both perceived outgroup members' attitudes as being more different from their own attitudes than they actually were. Additionally, participants were less likely to overestimate dissimilarity when they were prompted (versus not prompted) to deliberate on their judgement (Figure 2). The manipulation impacted judgements among liberals and conservatives to a comparable degree, suggesting that both liberals and conservatives overrode their initial and exaggerated judgements of outgroup dissimilarity.

These findings are especially informative when considered in concert with those regarding the accuracy of perceived ingroup similarity. Specifically, these results suggest that conservatives do not systemically overestimate how similar their attitudes are to those of other people *in general*. Rather, conservatives' overestimation of similarity is constrained to ingroup members. In contrast, liberals show a comparable pattern of underestimating similarity towards both

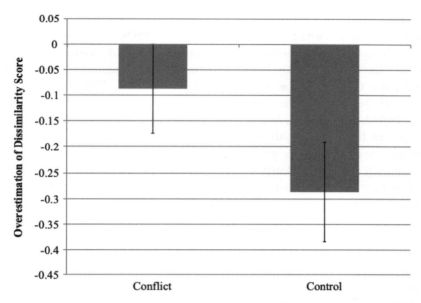

Figure 2. Overestimation of outgroup dissimilarity as a function of experimental condition reported in Study 1 of Stern and Kleiman (2015). Bars represent 95% confidence intervals. Figure reproduced with permission from SAGE.

ingroup and outgroup members. Rabinowitz et al. (2016; $N = 367$, 64% women, $M_{age} = 34.92$ years) found further support for this distinction in the context of attitudes about vaccines. They found that conservatives overestimated attitude similarity to ingroup members and underestimated similarity to outgroup members. Liberals, on the other hand, underestimated how much their vaccine attitudes were shared with both ingroup and outgroup members. Relatedly, Howell and O'Mara (2020) found that people who supported Donald Trump in the 2016 U.S. presidential election (i.e., those who were more conservative) overestimated their attitude similarity to Trump (the more conservative candidate) and underestimated similarity to Hillary Clinton (the more liberal candidate). In contrast, people who supported Clinton (i.e., those who were more liberal) underestimated similarity to *both* Clinton and Trump. Thus, a divergence in the direction of perceived similarity accuracy towards ingroup and outgroup members among conservatives (but not liberals) appears relatively consistent.

Ideological differences in actual attitude agreement

Both liberals and conservatives appear to have distorted perceptions of how similar their attitudes and beliefs are to those of like-minded others. In turn, an important question arises of what the reality of attitude similarity is when gauged broadly on a national level. Do liberals or conservatives *actually* have more ingroup attitude agreement, or are there no actual differences?

To investigate this question, Ondish and Stern (2018) analysed approximately forty years (1970s-2010s) of nationally representative survey data using the General Social Survey (GSS; N = 53,081, 55% women, M_{age} = 45.93 years) and the American National Election Studies (ANES; N = 29,042, 52% women, M_{age} = 45.62 years). These surveys include attitude responses from individuals throughout the United Stated on a variety of political topics, such as gun control, abortion, and same-sex marriage. Examining attitude similarity over an extended period of time and substantial number of issues provided greater confidence that any observed ideological differences were not attributable to a specific point in time or issue.

Both the GSS and ANES measured political ideology using a continuous scale ranging from 1 (*extremely liberal*) to 7 (*extremely conservative*). Participants were also able to indicate a "don't know" response. Individuals who did so were not included in analyses. Examining the degree of agreement within a group necessitates developing a clear definition of who belongs to what group (Kenny, 1994). To this end, in both data sets the authors categorised people who responded 1–3 as "liberal" (GSS: n = 14,550; ANES: n = 7,491), 4 as "moderate" (GSS: n = 20,515; ANES: n = 9,873) and 5–7 as "conservative" (GSS: n = 18,016; ANES: n = 11,678).

To examine the degree of attitude similarity within political groups, the authors employed a decomposition approach that estimated sources of variance in attitude responses (Back & Kenny, 2010). The approach estimated three sources of variance in attitude responses: systematic patterns in how individuals responded to a political issue (i.e., attitude similarity), systematic patterns of responses within an individual (i.e., response bias), and any remaining error variance. This approach circumvented issues of other measures that could be used to estimate attitude similarity within a collection of individuals (e.g., standard deviations of attitude responses) because it partitioned out response biases in attitude responding (Flink & Park, 1991; Kenny, 1994). The final score that is used from this approach indexed the percentage of variance in responses within a group (e.g., liberals) that was uniquely attributable to attitude similarity.

Results revealed a relatively consistent pattern (Figure 3). Over the course of approximately forty years, liberals tended to possess a greater degree of similarity in their attitudes than did conservatives. In other words, liberals were more homogeneous in their political attitudes when gauged on a national level. Additionally, this pattern persisted when statistically adjusting for demographic characteristics that are often associated with political ideology, such as education, gender, and race. Interestingly, these findings contrast with conservatives' greater *perceptions* of ingroup similarity (Stern & West, 2016; Stern, West, Jost et al., 2014), which further suggests that

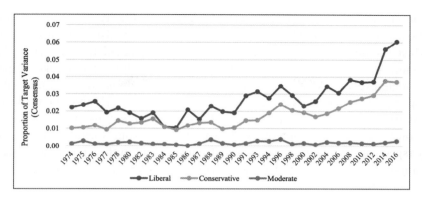

Figure 3. Ingroup attitude similarity among liberals, conservatives, and moderates in the General Social Survey, as reported in Study 1 of Ondish and Stern (2018). Figure reproduced with permission from SAGE.

perceptions of ingroup similarity are not entirely grounded in (and sometimes strongly diverge from) reality.

General discussion

In this article, I reviewed research examining how political ideology corresponds to perceived and actual attitude similarity. The research that I reviewed documents that (a) conservatives *perceive* greater ingroup similarity than do liberals, (b) conservatives *overestimate* and liberals *underestimate* ingroup similarity, (c) liberals and conservatives both *underestimate* similarity to outgroup members, and (d) liberals possess more *actual* ingroup similarity than do conservatives on a national level. These findings support the perspective that liberal-conservative differences in perceptions of ingroup similarity are not simply mirror reflections of reality. This review contributes to integrating social cognition and political psychology research through outlining a broad picture of how political ideology relates to attitude similarity. Moving forward, this research also raises several important questions that relate to emerging debates in psychology. In this section, I discuss some of the most theoretically relevant points.

Potential explanations for ideological differences

The findings reviewed here provide insight into *whether* and *when* liberals and conservatives differ in the perception and reality of attitude similarity. However, they do not clearly indicate *why* these differences emerge. In other words, what processes help to collectively explain why liberals and conservative differ in perceptions of ingroup similarity, the accuracy of those perceptions, and how much agreement actually exists in their groups? Most (if not all) psychological outcomes are explained through multiple factors that operate in tandem (Higgins, 1998). Thus, it is unlikely that a single explanation accounts for the reviewed findings. Instead, multiple aspects of a person (e.g., goals, previous experiences) and their social environment (e.g., characteristics of a situation) are likely to simultaneously guide these outcomes. Below, I draw from various theoretical perspectives to integrate the reviewed findings and outline potential explanations concerning why there are ideological differences in perceived and actual similarity.

Relational motivations

One possible factor that contributes to ideological differences are relational motivations to connect and affiliate with other people. Attitudes and beliefs that cannot be physically tested (e.g., whether abortion is moral or whether pizza is delicious) are infused with legitimacy to the extent that other people share those views (Festinger, 1950). Put another way, groups act as "epistemic providers" that verify socially constructed attitudes and beliefs (Bar-Tal, 2000; Hardin & Higgins, 1996; Kruglanski et al., 2006; Sherif, 1936). However, Festinger et al. (1950, p. 168, emphasis added) also noted it is quite common that "the 'social reality' upon which an opinion or attitude rests for its justification is the degree to which the individual *perceives* that the opinion or attitude is shared by others". In other words, people are *motivated* to perceive that others share their attitudes and, when possible, develop actual attitude similarity (Festinger & Bramel, 1962; Holtz, 2004; Holtz & Miller, 1985).

Some evidence suggests that relational motivations contribute to ideological differences in perceived similarity. Stern, West, Jost et al. (2014) found that conservatives reported a greater motivation to "share reality", in the sense that it was important to see the world in a similar way as people who generally shared their beliefs. Accounting for ideological differences in the motivation to share reality significantly reduced the relationship between conservatism and perceived ingroup similarity (Figure 4). Relatedly, Stern, West, and Schmitt (2014) assessed participants' motivation to be unique and stand out from others (e.g., "It is better to break rules than always to conform with an impersonal society"; Snyder & Fromkin, 1977). Liberals reported a stronger motivation to be unique. Accounting for ideological differences in this motivation significantly reduced differences between ideological groups in the accuracy of their perceptions of similarity (Figure 5). Together, these findings suggest that relational motivations could in part contribute to ideological differences in perceived ingroup similarity, as well as the accuracy of those perceptions. However, it is important to point out that measures of

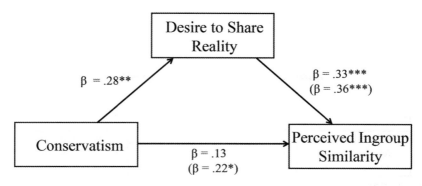

Figure 4. Mediation model in which conservatism and perceived ingroup similarity are linked through the desire to share reality, as reported in Study 1 of Stern, West, Jost et al. (2014). All values are standardised beta coefficients and represent relationships in which gender is included as a covariate. Values in parentheses represent direct relationships; values without parentheses represent relationships after including all variables in the model. Figure adapted with permission from SAGE. Note: *p <.05, **p <.01, ***p <.001.

motivation accounted for only some degree of the observed ideological differences. Additionally, the research primarily employed correlation designs and could not directly infer causation. It would be generative for future research to employ experimental paradigms that directly manipulate the strength of motivations.

Relational motivations might also contribute to why liberals underestimate similarity to both ingroup and outgroup members, whereas conservatives overestimate ingroup similarity and underestimate outgroup similarity. Differentiating oneself from both the ingroup and the outgroup can satisfy a uniqueness goal (Leonardelli et al., 2010; Snyder & Fromkin, 1980). In contrast, ingroup members best fulfil a desire to share reality (i.e., to affiliate and verify one's attitudes), whereas outgroup members can subvert this goal (Abrams et al., 1990; Echterhoff et al., 2005). As a result, liberals' stronger uniqueness goal might orient them towards underestimating similarity to others in general, whereas conservatives' stronger shared reality goal might more readily differentiate to whom they overestimate and underestimate similarity.

Lastly, relational motivations could help account for liberals' greater agreement on a national level (Ondish & Stern, 2018). Conservatives appear to develop social connections within a more restricted network, such as their romantic partners, friends, and immediate community (Jost et al., 2008; Waytz et al., 2019). In other words, conservatives are more motivated to build connections and psychological bonds with others who are physically and psychologically close (Janoff-Bulman & Carnes, 2013; Waytz et al., 2016). As similarities increase within a local group, differences tend to increase on

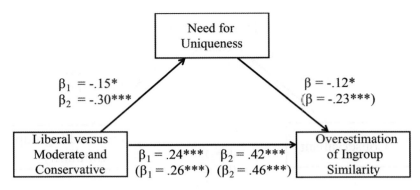

Figure 5. Mediation model in which ideology and overestimation of ingroup similarity are linked through the need for uniqueness, as reported in Study 2 of Stern, West, and Schmitt (2014). Path symbols indicate the comparison between liberals and moderates (β_1), and between liberals and conservatives (β_2). All values are standardised beta coefficients. Values in parentheses represent direct relationships; values without parentheses represent relationships after all variables were included in the model. Figure adapted with permission from SAGE. Note: *p <.05, ***p <.001.

a more expansive scale (Henrich & Boyd, 1998). In turn, conservatives' desire to connect with close others could contribute to the formation of more attitude *differences* than liberals possess on a national level.

Information ecosystems

The informational networks or "ecosystems" with which liberals and conservatives engage could also meaningfully contribute to differences in perceived similarity. For example, Republicans (people who are more conservative) place the majority of their trust in one news source (Fox News) whereas Democrats (people who are more liberal) place their trust in a larger number of news sources (Jurkowitz et al., 2020; Mitchell et al., 2014). Additionally, while both liberals and conservatives share information from political ingroup members on social media, conservatives are less likely than liberals to share information that originated from political outgroup members (Barberá et al., 2015). As a result, conservatives are more likely than liberals to receive an ideologically consistent perspective about political topics. Liberals might also be more likely to publicly voice dissent than conservatives (Feldman, 2003; Jost, van der Linden et al., 2018), something which both liberals and conservatives could observe. Collectively, these differences could (reasonably) lead conservatives to be more likely than liberals to assume that like-minded others share their attitudes.

Engagement with varying information ecosystems could also contribute to ideological differences in actual agreement on a national level. Conservatives are more likely to reference local media (e.g., radio, newspapers, television stations) for information about political issues whereas liberals focus on sources that are aired and distributed nationally (e.g., CNN, the New York Times; Mitchell et al., 2014). In turn, liberals might adopt attitudes that are being widely discussed and held by other liberals throughout the United States whereas conservatives more readily assimilate to the attitudes within their local community.

Framing of political issues

Another possible contributor to ideological differences in actual attitude similarity is the moral framing of some topics. Strimling et al. (2019) found that issue positions that directly invoke harm and fairness (e.g., support for gay rights) possess more immediate interest among liberals and become increasingly appealing to both liberals and conservatives over time. It is possible that when issues are discussed in terms of harm and fairness, liberals will readily adopt these positions whereas conservatives will be more dispersed in when they come to hold the perspective. In turn, liberals would be expected to possess greater agreement than conservatives. For example, a recent global attitudes survey indicated that acceptance of homosexuality has substantially increased over the past fifteen years and has generally done so throughout the world (Poushter & Kent, 2020). However, there are ideological divides. Liberals and people on the left are generally in agreement of holding more positive attitudes towards sexual minorities. In contrast, conservatives and people on the right are more divided: some have adopted more positive attitudes, whereas others have resisted changing their attitudes. Future research could examine whether the framing of issues contributes to ideological differences in actual similarity, at least on some topics.

Will there be cross-cultural and contextual variability in ideological differences?

The findings reviewed here relied on participant samples in the United States. A core component of social psychological theorising concerns the impact of context on human judgement and behaviour, and recent scholarship has begun to address whether the strength and direction of ideological differences might vary across contexts (e.g., Federico & Malka, 2018; Malka et al., 2014). Some research conducted outside of the United States has observed findings that mirror those reviewed here. For example, people who reported more right-wing (versus left-wing) attitudes in Israel were more likely to overestimate the prevalence of their political viewpoints (S. Dvir-Gvirsman, 2015a; 2015b). Israeli culture, on average, is less individualistic than the cultural backdrop of the United States (Kurman, 2003), and so it is possible that ideological differences in the accuracy of perceived similarity are not constrained to highly individualist cultures like the United

States. Further research examining ideological differences in perceived similarity outside of the United States would be fruitful.

Different patterns from those reviewed here might emerge when a context prompts liberals to adjust their motivational orientation and, at least temporary, more strongly prioritise the ingroup. For example, liberals might be more inclined to perceive and possibly overestimate similarity to the ingroup when they encounter strong physical and psychological threats that the ingroup can help address (e.g., a global pandemic; Correll & Park, 2005) or when they are repeatedly immersed in an environment that promotes dependence on the ingroup (e.g., kibbutzim in Israel). Examining the possibility for cross-cultural and contextual variability in the finding reviewed here would be a generative direction for future research.

Perceived and actual similarity among political moderates

Throughout this review, I have focused on comparing perceived and actual similarity between people who are more liberal or conservative, without attention to political moderates. The scientific literature both past and present has focused on understanding the psychological factors that draw people more towards the left or right of the political spectrum (e.g., Jost et al., 2003; Jost, Sterling et al., 2018), with a general neglect of the centre. Due to this focus in past research, the studies reviewed here did not have strong (or any) a priori theoretical predictions about what patterns would emerge among moderates. Thus, at the current time it is challenging to directly situate moderates into broader discussions of ideological differences. Nevertheless, because some of the studies reviewed here categorised participants into distinct ideological groups that included moderates, it is possible to speculate about the factors that might drive perceived and actual similarity among moderates.

In terms of the accuracy of perceived similarity, moderates overestimated attitude similarity to ingroup members (Table 2; Stern, West, and Schmitt 2014). In this way, moderates were more similar to conservatives than to liberals, although moderates overestimated ingroup similarity to a less strong degree than conservatives did. People are motivated to perceive similarity for their attitudes and beliefs unless they have a strong countervailing goal to do otherwise (Suls & Wan, 1987). At the same time, some research suggests that people who are more moderate tend to be less cognitively rigid than people on the extremes of the left and the right (Van Prooijen & Krouwel, 2019). Thus, moderates might be inclined to overestimate similarity to ingroup members, but also engage in some degree of reflection and deliberation that ultimately tempers their degree of inaccuracy.

In terms of actual similarity to ingroup members, moderates possessed lower levels of similarity than both liberals and conservatives (Figure 3;

Ondish & Stern, 2018). A person who states that they are moderate might be expected to consistently adopt political attitudes that fall between those of liberals and conservatives (e.g., neither strongly favouring nor opposing legalised abortion access). However, moderates do not seem to be consistently centrist in their political attitudes (Drutman, 2019). Instead, people who state that they are moderate might do so because they are motivated to explicitly reject polarised ideological labels (Hawkins & Nosek, 2012), while simultaneously preferring a particular ideological perspective on an implicit level (Arcuri et al., 2008; Choma & Hafer, 2009). Implicit ideological orientations predict non-centrist political stances (Hawkins & Nosek, 2012). Thus, to the degree that some moderates are implicitly oriented to liberalism and some to conservatism, low attitude agreement on political topics will ultimately emerge.

Implications for ideological differences

What are the implications of ideological differences in perceived and actual similarity? Previous research suggests that similarity (both perceived and actual) tends to be a meaningful contributor to important outcomes, such as relationship development, feelings of group efficacy, and political participation (e.g., Festinger et al., 1950; Tidwell et al., 2013; West et al., 2014). As such, it is possible that liberal-conservative differences in perceived and actual similarity with like-minded others could contribute to outcomes on individual and collective levels.

Perceptions of similarity could play a distinctive role in shaping the policy attitudes that people hold, especially when perceptions are oriented towards people in power. Individuals often adopt political views that align with those of political parties and leadership (Cohen, 2003), possibly as a means of feeling that their views as valid (Stern & Ondish, 2018). Perceived similarity could function in a similar way. For example, conservatives' greater opposition to abortion was explained in part by their stronger beliefs that Neil Gorsuch (a conservative member of the US Supreme Court) shared their stance on abortion (Prusaczyk & Hodson, 2019). To the degree that conservatives (versus liberals) more readily assume that political ingroup leaders share their views on specific issues (Howell & O'Mara, 2020), these perceptions might contribute to explaining a source of conservatives' attitudes and even the certainty with which they hold their views (Jost & Krochik, 2014; Ruisch & Stern, in press).

Perceived similarity could also foster different relationship structures among liberals and conservatives. Perceiving that others share one's views on both political and non-political topics is associated with lower levels of emotional responses that impair interactions (e.g., anxiety, nervousness) and greater interest in prolonged contact (Stern & Crawford, in press; West et al.,

2014). Thus, conservatives' greater perceptions of similarity could reinforce close and positive bonds with important others (e.g., friends, family, political ingroup members). In contrast, liberals' weaker perceptions of similarity could forge a broader network of social relationships that are less tightly connected and in which they maintain a stronger sense of individuality.

This process could also help to explain the apparent disconnect between ideological differences in attitude similarity on national and local levels. Given that conservatives consistently possess lower levels of attitude agreement on a national level (Ondish & Stern, 2018), in novel social contexts conservatives should be more likely than liberals to encounter political ingroup members who differ in their views on specific political topics (e.g., abortion, taxation). Even with this lower similarity on a national level, however, conservatives (relative to liberals) still appear to more readily create homogeneous groups when they encounter new social networks (Barberá et al., 2015; Boutyline & Willer, 2017). It is possible that when conservatives encounter a situation with fellow conservatives whom they have not previously met, they initially perceive similarity and assume that shared viewpoints exist. When points of disagreement eventually become known, the lower anxiety and greater desire for prolonged contact that results from initially perceiving similarity might facilitate attitude conformity or persuasion as a means to achieving actual similarity. Liberals, on the other hand, should be more likely to encounter political ingroup members who echo their viewpoints. In turn, they might respond through perceiving less similarity and grasping onto salient points of disagreement as a compensatory process of fulfiling their greater uniqueness goal.

The disconnect of conservatives perceiving greater ingroup similarity but liberals possessing greater actual ingroup similarity might also create a divergence in the advantages that each possesses in achieving collective goals. Perceptions of ingroup similarity foster a sense of collective efficacy, which can motivate action on issues of relevance to the group (Festinger et al., 1950; Van Zomeren et al., 2004). However, achieving an outcome that requires mass support (e.g., electing a leader) also necessitates actual agreement among members of a group. For conservatives, this requires turning overestimates of ingroup similarity into actual agreement. The more positive feelings towards others that are linked to perceptions of similarity potentially facilitate smoothing out areas of remaining disagreement during interactions and ultimately promoting greater coordination and mobilisation among conservatives. In contrast, liberals already possess greater agreement on a national level, but their weaker perceptions (and underestimation) of similarity might undermine their ability to capitalise on that agreement. For example, when liberal supporters of Hillary Clinton underestimated similarity to her in the 2016 US presidential election (Howell & O'Mara, 2020), this potentially decreased their interest in voting for or canvassing on behalf of Clinton. Overall, perceived and actual similarity hold a variety of potential implications for understanding ideological differences in interpersonal and collective outcomes.

Concluding remarks

Examining when people perceive that others share their attitudes and beliefs has long been a topic of study for psychology. For a comparable period of time, psychologists have also attempted to build insight into how political beliefs correspond to the way in which people perceive and engage with the world. In this review, I have outlined how political ideology corresponds to perceptions of ingroup similarity, the accuracy of perceived similarity to ingroup and outgroup members, and actual degrees of ingroup similarity. Through doing so, this review provides a picture of when liberals and conservatives construct different perceptions of the world and in what manner these perceptions might diverge from reality.

References

Abrams, D., Wetherell, M., Cochrane, S., Hogg, M. A., & Turner, J. C. (1990). Knowing what to think by knowing who you are: Self-categorization and the nature of norm formation, conformity and group polarization. *British Journal of Social Psychology*, *29*(2), 97–119. https://doi.org/10.1111/j.2044-8309.1990. tb00892.x

Adorno, T. W., Frenkel-Brunswik, E., Levinson, D. J., & Sanford, R. N. (1950). *The authoritarian personality*. Harper.

Allport, F. H. (1924). *Social psychology*. Houghton Mifflin.

Arcuri, L., Castelli, L., Galdi, S., Zogmaister, C., & Amadori, A. (2008). Predicting the vote: Implicit attitudes as predictors of the future behaviour of decided and undecided voters. *Political Psychology*, *29*(3), 369–387. https://doi.org/10.1111/j. 1467-9221.2008.00635.x

Arndt, J., Greenberg, J., Solomon, S., Pyszczynski, T., & Schimel, J. (1999). Creativity and terror management: Evidence that creative activity increases guilt and social projection following mortality salience. *Journal of Personality and Social Psychology*, *77*(1), 19. https://doi.org/10.1037/0022-3514.77.1.19

Asch, S. E. (1956). Studies of independence and conformity: I. A minority of one against a unanimous majority. *Psychological Monographs: General and Applied*, *70*(9), 1–70. https://doi.org/10.1037/h0093718

Back, M. D., & Kenny, D. A. (2010). The social relations model: How to understand dyadic processes. *Social and Personality Psychology Compass*, *4*(10), 855–870. https://doi.org/10.1111/j.1751-9004.2010.00303.x

Bandura, A. (2000). Exercise of human agency through collective efficacy. *Current Directions in Psychological Science*, 9(3), 75–78. https://doi.org/10.1111/1467-8721.00064

Barberá, P., Jost, J. T., Nagler, J., Tucker, J. A., & Bonneau, R. (2015). Tweeting from left to right: Is online political communication more than an echo chamber? *Psychological Science*, 26(10), 1531–1542. https://doi.org/10.1177/0956797615594620

Bar-Tal, D. (2000). *Shared beliefs in a society: Social psychological analysis*. Sage.

Bishop, B. (2009). *The big sort: Why the clustering of like-minded America is tearing us apart*. Houghton Mifflin Harcourt.

Boutyline, A., & Willer, R. (2017). The social structure of political echo chambers: Variation in ideological homophily in online networks. *Political Psychology*, 38(3), 551–569. https://doi.org/10.1111/pops.12337

Brandt, M. J., Reyna, C., Chambers, J. R., Crawford, J. T., & Wetherell, G. (2014). The ideological-conflict hypothesis: Intolerance among both liberals and conservatives. *Current Directions in Psychological Science*, 23(1), 27–34. https://doi.org/10.1177/0963721413510932

Brunswik, E. (1955). Representative design and probabilistic theory in a functional psychology. *Psychological Review*, 62(3), 193. https://doi.org/10.1037/h0047470

Cameron, N., & Margaret, A. (1951). *Behaviour pathology*. Houghton Mifflin.

Cattell, R. B. (1944). Projection and the design of projective tests of personality. *Journal of Personality*, 12(3), 177–194. https://doi.org/10.1111/j.1467-6494.1944.tb01956.x

Choma, B. L., & Hafer, C. L. (2009). Understanding the relation between explicitly and implicitly measured political orientation: The moderating role of political sophistication. *Personality and Individual Differences*, 47(8), 964–967. https://doi.org/10.1016/j.paid.2009.07.024

Cohen, G. L. (2003). Party over policy: The dominating impact of group influence on political beliefs. *Journal of Personality and Social Psychology*, 85(5), 808. https://doi.org/10.1037/0022-3514.85.5.808

Coleman, M. D. (2018). Emotion and the false consensus effect. *Current Psychology*, 37(1), 58–64. https://doi.org/10.1007/s12144-016-9489-0

Correll, J., & Park, B. (2005). A model of the ingroup as a social resource. *Personality and Social Psychology Review*, 9(4), 341–359. https://doi.org/10.1207/s15327957pspr0904_4

Crawford, J. T. (2014). Ideological symmetries and asymmetries in political intolerance and prejudice toward political activist groups. *Journal of Experimental Social Psychology*, 55, 284–298. https://doi.org/10.1016/j.jesp.2014.08.002

Davis, M. H. (2017). Social projection to liked and disliked targets: The role of perceived similarity. *Journal of Experimental Social Psychology*, 70, 286–293. https://doi.org/10.1016/j.jesp.2016.11.012

Drutman, L. (2019). *The moderate middle is a myth*. FiveThirtyEight. https://fivethirtyeight.com/features/the-moderate-middle-is-a-myth/

Dvir-Gvirsman, S. (2015a). Size matters: The effects of political orientation, majority status, and majority size on misperceptions of public opinion. *Public Opinion Quarterly*, 79(1), 1–27. https://doi.org/10.1093/poq/nfu061

Dvir-Gvirsman, S. (2015b). Testing our quasi-statistical sense: News use, political knowledge, and false projection. *Political Psychology*, 36(6), 729–747. https://doi.org/10.1111/pops.12203

Echterhoff, G., Higgins, E. T., & Groll, S. (2005). Audience-tuning effects on memory: The role of shared reality. *Journal of Personality and Social Psychology*, 89(3), 257. https://doi.org/10.1037/0022-3514.89.3.257

Epley, N., Keysar, B., Van Boven, L., & Gilovich, T. (2004). Perspective taking as egocentric anchoring and adjustment. *Journal of Personality and Social Psychology*, 87(3), 327. https://doi.org/10.1037/0022-3514.87.3.327

Federico, C. M., & Malka, A. (2018). The contingent, contextual nature of the relationship between needs for security and certainty and political preferences: Evidence and implications. *Political Psychology*, 39, 3–48. https://doi.org/10.1111/pops.12477

Feldman, S. (2003). Enforcing social conformity: A theory of authoritarianism. *Political Psychology*, 24(1), 41–74. https://doi.org/10.1111/0162-895X.00316

Festinger, L. (1950). Informal social communication. *Psychological Review*, 57(5), 271–282. https://doi.org/10.1037/h0056932

Festinger, L., & Bramel, D. (1962). The reactions of humans to cognitive dissonance. In A. J. Bachrach (Ed.), *Experimental foundations of clinical psychology* (pp. 244–280). Basic Books.

Festinger, L., Schachter, S., & Black, K. (1950). *Social pressures in informal groups*. Stanford University Press.

Fields, J. M., & Schuman, H. (1976). Public beliefs about the beliefs of the public. *Public Opinion Quarterly*, 40(4), 427–448. https://doi.org/10.1086/268330

Flink, C., & Park, B. (1991). Increasing consensus in trait judgments through outcome dependency. *Journal of Experimental Social Psychology*, 27(5), 453–467. https://doi.org/10.1016/0022-1031(91)90003-O

Freud, A. (1936). *The ego and the mechanisms of defence*. Karnac Books.

Frimer, J. A., Skitka, L. J., & Motyl, M. (2017). Liberals and conservatives are similarly motivated to avoid exposure to one another's opinions. *Journal of Experimental Social Psychology*, 72, 1–12. https://doi.org/10.1016/j.jesp.2017.04.003

Gawronski, B., & Cesario, J. (2013). Of mice and men: What animal research can tell us about context effects on automatic responses in humans. *Personality and Social Psychology Review*, 17(2), 187–215. https://doi.org/10.1177/1088868313480096

Gibson, C. B., Randel, A. E., & Earley, P. C. (2000). Understanding group efficacy: An empirical test of multiple assessment methods. *Group & Organization Management*, 25(1), 67–97. https://doi.org/10.1177/1059601100251005

Graham, J., Haidt, J., & Nosek, B. A. (2009). Liberals and conservatives rely on different sets of moral foundations. *Journal of Personality and Social Psychology*, 96(5), 1029–1046. https://doi.org/10.1037/a0015141

Graham, J., Nosek, B. A., & Haidt, J. (2012). The moral stereotypes of liberals and conservatives: Exaggeration of differences across the political spectrum. *PloS One*, 7(12), 12. https://doi.org/10.1371/journal.pone.0050092

Hardin, C. D., & Higgins, E. T. (1996). Shared reality: How social verification makes the subjective objective. In R. M. Sorrentino & E. T. Higgins (Eds.), *Handbook of motivation and cognition: The interpersonal context* (Vol. 3, pp. 28–84). Guilford Press.

Hawkins, C. B., & Nosek, B. A. (2012). Motivated independence? Implicit party identity predicts political judgments among self-proclaimed independents. *Personality & Social Psychology Bulletin*, 38(11), 1437–1452. https://doi.org/10.1177/0146167212452313

Henrich, J., & Boyd, R. (1998). The evolution of conformist transmission and the emergence of between-group differences. *Evolution and Human Behaviour, 19*(4), 215–241. https://doi.org/10.1016/S1090-5138(98)00018-X

Higgins, E. T. (1998). The aboutness principle: A pervasive influence on human inference. *Social Cognition, 16*(1), 173–198. https://doi.org/10.1521/soco.1998.16.1.173

Higgins, E. T. (2019). *Shared reality: What makes us strong and tears us apart.* Oxford University Press.

Hoch, S. J. (1987). Perceived consensus and predictive accuracy: The pros and cons of projection. *Journal of Personality and Social Psychology, 53*(2), 221. https://doi.org/10.1037/0022-3514.53.2.221

Holmes, D. S. (1968). Dimensions of projection. *Psychological Bulletin, 69*(4), 248–268. https://doi.org/10.1037/h0025725

Holmes, D. S. (1978). Projection as a defense mechanism. *Psychological Bulletin, 85*(4), 677. https://doi.org/10.1037/0033-2909.85.4.677

Holtz, R. (2004). Group Cohesion, Attitude Projection, and Opinion Certainty: Beyond Interaction. *Group Dynamics: Theory, Research, and Practice, 8*(2), 112. https://doi.org/10.1037/1089-2699.8.2.112

Holtz, R., & Miller, N. (1985). Assumed similarity and opinion certainty. *Journal of Personality and Social Psychology, 48*(4), 890. https://doi.org/10.1037/0022-3514.48.4.890

Horney, K. (1945). *Our inner conflicts: A constructive theory of neurosis.* Routledge.

Howell, J. L., & O'Mara, E. M. (2020). Political behaviour, perceived similarity to the candidates, and defensiveness: The curious case of a group of first-time voters in a bellwether-swing-state in 2016. *Self and Identity, 19*(2), 164–180. https://doi.org/10.1080/15298868.2018.1546225

Janoff-Bulman, R., & Carnes, N. C. (2013). Surveying the moral landscape: Moral motives and group-based moralities. *Personality and Social Psychology Review, 17*(3), 219–236. https://doi.org/10.1177/1088868313480274

Jost, J. T., Federico, C. M., & Napier, J. L. (2009). Political ideology: Its structure, functions, and elective affinities. *Annual Review of Psychology, 60*(1), 307–337. https://doi.org/10.1146/annurev.psych.60.110707.163600

Jost, J. T., Glaser, J., Kruglanski, A. W., & Sulloway, F. J. (2003). Political conservatism as motivated social cognition. *Psychological Bulletin, 129*(3), 339. https://doi.org/10.1037/0033-2909.129.3.339

Jost, J. T., & Krochik, M. (2014). Ideological differences in epistemic motivation: Implications for attitude structure, depth of information processing, susceptibility to persuasion, and stereotyping. In A. J. Elliot (Eds.), *Advances in motivation science* (Vol. 1, pp. 181–231). Elsevier.

Jost, J. T., Ledgerwood, A., & Hardin, C. D. (2008). Shared reality, system justification, and the relational basis of ideological beliefs. *Social and Personality Psychology Compass, 2*(1), 171–186. https://doi.org/10.1111/j.1751-9004.2007.00056.x

Jost, J. T., Sterling, J., & Stern, C. (2018). Getting closure on conservatism, or the politics of epistemic and existential motivation. In C. Kopetz & A. Fishbach (Eds.), *The Motivation-Cognition Interface, From the Lab to the Real World: A Festschrift in Honor of Arie W. Kruglanski* (Vol. I, pp. 56–87). Routledge.

Jost, J. T., van der Linden, S., Panagopoulos, C., & Hardin, C. D. (2018). Ideological asymmetries in conformity, desire for shared reality, and the spread of misinformation. *Current Opinion in Psychology*, 23, 77–83. https://doi.org/10.1016/j.copsyc.2018.01.003

Jurkowitz, M., Mitchell, A., Shearer, E., & Walker, M. (2020). *U.S. Media Polarization and the 2020 Election: A Nation Divided*. Pew Research Center. https://www.journalism.org/2020/01/24/u-s-media-polarization-and-the-2020-election-a-nation-divided/

Kenny, D. A. (1994). *Interpersonal perception: A social relations analysis*. Guilford Press.

Kenny, D. A., & Acitelli, L. K. (2001). Accuracy and bias in the perception of the partner in a close relationship. *Journal of Personality and Social Psychology*, 80(3), 439. https://doi.org/10.1037/0022-3514.80.3.439

Kleiman, T., Hassin, R. R., & Trope, Y. (2014). The control-freak mind: Stereotypical biases are eliminated following conflict-activated cognitive control. *Journal of Experimental Psychology. General*, 143(2), 498. https://doi.org/10.1037/a0033047

Klein, M. (1940). Mourning and its relationship with manic-depressive states. *International Journal of Psychoanalysis*, 21, 47–82.

Klein, R. A., Vianello, M., Hasselman, F., Adams, B. G., Adams, R. B., Jr, Alper, S., Batra, R., Babalola, M. T., Bahník, Š., Batra, R., Berkics, M., Bernstein, M. J., Berry, D. R., Bialobrzeska, O., Binan, E. D., Bocian, K., Brandt, M. J., Busching, R., Rédei, A. C., Nosek, B. A., & Aveyard, M. (2018). Many Labs 2: Investigating variation in replicability across samples and settings. *Advances in Methods and Practices in Psychological Science*, 1(4), 443–490. https://doi.org/10.1177/2515245918810225

Koudenburg, N., Postmes, T., & Gordijn, E. H. (2011). If they were to vote, they would vote for us. *Psychological Science*, 22(12), 1506–1510. https://doi.org/10.1177/0956797611420164

Krueger, J., & Clement, R. W. (1994). The truly false consensus effect: An ineradicable and egocentric bias in social perception. *Journal of Personality and Social Psychology*, 67(4), 596. https://doi.org/10.1037/0022-3514.67.4.596

Krueger, J., & Clement, R. W. (1997). Estimates of social consensus by majorities and minorities: The case for social projection. *Personality and Social Psychology Review*, 1(4), 299–313. https://doi.org/10.1207/s15327957pspr0104_2

Kruglanski, A. W., Pierro, A., Mannetti, L., & De Grada, E. (2006). Groups as epistemic providers: Need for closure and the unfolding of group-centrism. *Psychological Review*, 113(1), 84–100. https://doi.org/10.1037/0033-295X.113.1.84

Kurman, J. (2003). Why is self-enhancement low in certain collectivist cultures? An investigation of two competing explanations. *Journal of Cross-cultural Psychology*, 34(5), 496–510. https://doi.org/10.1177/0022022103256474

Leonardelli, G. J., Pickett, C. L., & Brewer, M. B. (2010). Optimal distinctiveness theory: A framework for social identity, social cognition, and intergroup relations. In M.P. Zanna (Eds.), *Advances in experimental social psychology* (Vol. 43, pp. 63–113). Academic Press.

Malka, A., Soto, C. J., Inzlicht, M., & Lelkes, Y. (2014). Do needs for security and certainty predict cultural and economic conservatism? A cross-national analysis. *Journal of Personality and Social Psychology*, 106(6), 1031. https://doi.org/10.1037/a0036170

Marks, G., & Miller, N. (1982). Target attractiveness as a mediator of assumed attitude similarity. *Personality & Social Psychology Bulletin*, 8(4), 728–735. https://doi.org/10.1177/0146167282084020

McAdams, D. P., Albaugh, M., Farber, E., Daniels, J., Logan, R. L., & Olson, B. (2008). Family metaphors and moral intuitions: How conservatives and liberals narrate their lives. *Journal of Personality and Social Psychology, 95*(4), 978. https://doi.org/10.1037/a0012650

Mitchell, A., Gottfried, J., Kiley, J., & Matsa, K. A. (2014). *Political polarization & media habits.* Pew Research Center. https://www.journalism.org/2014/10/21/political-polarization-media-habits/

Morisi, D., Jost, J. T., & Singh, V. (2019). An asymmetrical "president-in-power" effect. *American Political Science Review, 113*(2), 614–620. https://doi.org/10.1017/S0003055418000850

Mullen, B., Atkins, J. L., Champion, D. S., Edwards, C., Hardy, D., Story, J. E., & Vanderklok, M. (1985). The false consensus effect: A meta-analysis of 115 hypothesis tests. *Journal of Experimental Social Psychology, 21*(3), 262–283. https://doi.org/10.1016/0022-1031(85)90020-4

Mullen, B., Driskell, J. E., & Smith, C. (1989). Availability and social projection: The effects of sequence of measurement and wording of question on estimates of consensus. *Personality & Social Psychology Bulletin, 15*(1), 84–90. https://doi.org/10.1177/0146167289151008

Mullen, B., & Hu, L. T. (1988). Social projection as a function of cognitive mechanisms: Two meta-analytic integrations. *British Journal of Social Psychology, 27*(4), 333–356. https://doi.org/10.1111/j.2044-8309.1988.tb00836.x

Murray, H. A., Jr. (1933). The effect of fear upon estimates of the maliciousness of other personalities. *The Journal of Social Psychology, 4*(3), 310–329. https://doi.org/10.1080/00224545.1933.9919325

Murstein, B. I. (1957). Studies in projection: A critique. *Journal of Projective Techniques, 21*(2), 129–136. https://doi.org/10.1080/08853126.1957.10380760

Okimoto, T. G., & Gromet, D. M. (2016). Differences in sensitivity to deviance partly explain ideological divides in social policy support. *Journal of Personality and Social Psychology, 111*(1), 98. https://doi.org/10.1037/pspp0000080

Ondish, P., & Stern, C. (2018). Liberals possess more national consensus on political attitudes in the United States: An examination across 40 years. *Social Psychological and Personality Science, 8*(8), 935–943. https://doi.org/10.1177/1948550617729410

Onraet, E., Van Hiel, A., Dhont, K., & Pattyn, S. (2013). Internal and external threat in relationship with right-wing attitudes. *Journal of Personality, 81*(3), 233–248. https://doi.org/10.1111/jopy.12011

Poushter, J., & Kent, N. (2020). *The global divide on homosexuality persists.* Pew Research Center. https://www.pewresearch.org/global/2020/06/25/global-divide-on-homosexuality-persists/

Prusaczyk, E., & Hodson, G. (2019). Re-examining left-right differences in abortion opposition: The roles of sexism and shared reality. *Testing, Psychometrics, Methodology in Applied Psychology, 26*(3), 431–445. doi:10.4473/TPM26.3.8

Rabinowitz, M., Latella, L., Stern, C., & Jost, J. T. (2016). Beliefs about childhood vaccination in the United States: Political ideology, false consensus, and the illusion of uniqueness. *PloS One, 11*(7), 7. https://doi.org/10.1371/journal.pone.0158382

Robbins, J. M., & Krueger, J. I. (2005). Social projection to ingroups and outgroups: A review and meta-analysis. *Personality and Social Psychology Review, 9*(1), 32–47. https://doi.org/10.1207/s15327957pspr0901_3

Robinson, R. J., Keltner, D., Ward, A., & Ross, L. (1995). Actual versus assumed differences in construal: "Naive realism" in intergroup perception and conflict.

Journal of Personality and Social Psychology, 68(3), 404. https://doi.org/10.1037/0022-3514.68.3.404

Rodriguez, C. G., Moskowitz, J. P., Salem, R. M., & Ditto, P. H. (2017). Partisan selective exposure: The role of party, ideology and ideological extremity over time. *Translational Issues in Psychological Science, 3*(3), 254. https://doi.org/10.1037/tps0000121

Ross, L., Greene, D., & House, P. (1977). The "false consensus effect": An egocentric bias in social perception and attribution processes. *Journal of Experimental Social Psychology, 13*(3), 279–301. https://doi.org/10.1016/0022-1031(77)90049-X

Ruisch, B., & Stern, C. (in press). The confident conservative: Ideological differences in judgment and decision-making confidence. *Journal of Experimental Psychology. General.*

Saad, L. (2019). *U.S. still leans conservative, but liberals keep recent gains.* In Gallup. https://news.gallup.com/poll/245813/leans-conservative-liberals-keep-recent-gains.aspx

Sanders, G. S., & Mullen, B. (1983). Accuracy in perceptions of consensus: Differential tendencies of people with majority and minority positions. *European Journal of Social Psychology, 13*(1), 57–70. https://doi.org/10.1002/ejsp.2420130104

Schaller, M., Boyd, C., Yohannes, J., & O'Brien, M. (1995). The prejudiced personality revisited: Personal need for structure and formation of erroneous group stereotypes. *Journal of Personality and Social Psychology, 68*(3), 544. https://doi.org/10.1037/0022-3514.68.3.544

Scherer, A. M., Windschitl, P. D., & Graham, J. (2015). An ideological house of mirrors: Political stereotypes as exaggerations of motivated social cognition differences. *Social Psychological and Personality Science, 6*(2), 201–209. https://doi.org/10.1177/1948550614549385

Sherif, M. (1935). A study of some social factors in perception. *Archives of Psychology, 27 (187)*, 1–60. https://psycnet.apa.org/record/1936-01332-001

Sherif, M. (1936). *The psychology of social norms.* Harper.

Shook, N. J., & Fazio, R. H. (2009). Political ideology, exploration of novel stimuli, and attitude formation. *Journal of Experimental Social Psychology, 45*(4), 995–998. https://doi.org/10.1016/j.jesp.2009.04.003

Skitka, L. J., Mullen, E., Griffin, T., Hutchinson, S., & Chamberlin, B. (2002). Dispositions, scripts, or motivated correction? Understanding ideological differences in explanations for social problems. *Journal of Personality and Social Psychology, 83*(2), 470. https://doi.org/10.1037/0022-3514.83.2.470

Smith, K. B., Oxley, D., Hibbing, M. V., Alford, J. R., & Hibbing, J. R. (2011). Disgust sensitivity and the neurophysiology of left-right political orientations. *PloS One, 6* (10), e25552. https://doi.org/10.1371/journal.pone.0025552

Snyder, C. R., & Fromkin, H. L. (1977). Abnormality as a positive characteristic: The development and validation of a scale measuring need for uniqueness. *Journal of Abnormal Psychology, 86*(5), 518. https://doi.org/10.1037/0021-843X.86.5.518

Snyder, C. R., & Fromkin, H. L. (1980). *Uniqueness: The pursuit of human difference.* New York: Plenum.

Stern, C., & Crawford, J. (in press). Ideological conflict and prejudice: An adversarial collaboration examining correlates and ideological (a)symmetries. *Social Psychological and Personality Science.* https://doi.org/10.1177/1948550620904275

Stern, C., & Kleiman, T. (2015). Know thy outgroup: Promoting accurate judgments of political attitude differences through a conflict mindset. *Social Psychological and Personality Science, 6*(8), 950–958. https://doi.org/10.1177/1948550615596209

Stern, C., & Ondish, P. (2018). Political aspects of shared reality. *Current Opinion in Psychology, 23*, 11–14. https://doi.org/10.1016/j.copsyc.2017.11.004

Stern, C., & West, T. V. (2016). Ideological differences in anchoring and adjustment during social inferences. *Personality & Social Psychology Bulletin, 42*(11), 1466–1479. https://doi.org/10.1177/0146167216664058

Stern, C., West, T. V., Jost, J. T., & Rule, N. O. (2013). The politics of gaydar: Ideological differences in the use of gendered cues in categorizing sexual orientation. *Journal of Personality and Social Psychology, 104*(3), 520. https://doi.org/10.1037/a0031187

Stern, C., West, T. V., Jost, J. T., & Rule, N. O. (2014). "Ditto Heads": Do conservatives perceive greater consensus within their ranks than liberals? *Personality & Social Psychology Bulletin, 40*(9), 1162–1177. https://doi.org/10.1177/0146167214537834

Stern, C., West, T. V., & Schmitt, P. G. (2014). The liberal illusion of uniqueness. *Psychological Science, 25*(1), 137–144. https://doi.org/10.1177/0956797613500796

Strimling, P., Vartanova, I., Jansson, F., & Eriksson, K. (2019). The connection between moral positions and moral arguments drives opinion change. *Nature Human Behaviour, 3*(9), 922–930. https://doi.org/10.1038/s41562-019-0647-x

Stroud, N. J. (2008). Media use and political predispositions: Revisiting the concept of selective exposure. *Political Behaviour, 30*(3), 341–366. https://doi.org/10.1007/s11109-007-9050-9

Suls, J., & Wan, C. K. (1987). In search of the false-uniqueness phenomenon: Fear and estimates of social consensus. *Journal of Personality and Social Psychology, 52*(1), 211. https://doi.org/10.1037/0022-3514.52.1.211

Tamir, D. I., & Mitchell, J. P. (2013). Anchoring and adjustment during social inferences. *Journal of Experimental Psychology. General, 142*(1), 151. https://doi.org/10.1037/a0028232

Tidwell, N. D., Eastwick, P. W., & Finkel, E. J. (2013). Perceived, not actual, similarity predicts initial attraction in a live romantic context: Evidence from the speed-dating paradigm. *Personal Relationships, 20*(2), 199–215. https://doi.org/10.1111/j.1475-6811.2012.01405.x

Van Boven, L., Judd, C. M., & Sherman, D. K. (2012). Political polarization projection: Social projection of partisan attitude extremity and attitudinal processes. *Journal of Personality and Social Psychology, 103*(1), 84. https://doi.org/10.1037/a0028145

van Prooijen, J. W., & Krouwel, A. P. (2019). Psychological features of extreme political ideologies. *Current Directions in Psychological Science, 28*(2), 159–163. https://doi.org/10.1177/0963721418817755

van Zomeren, M., Spears, R., Fischer, A. H., & Leach, C. W. (2004). Put your money where your mouth is! Explaining collective action tendencies through group-based anger and group efficacy. *Journal of Personality and Social Psychology, 87*(5), 649. https://doi.org/10.1037/0022-3514.87.5.649

Waytz, A., Iyer, R., Young, L., & Graham, J. (2016). Ideological differences in the expanse of empathy. In P. Valdesolo & J. Graham (Eds.), *Social psychology of political polarization* (pp. 61–77). New York, NY: Routledge.

Waytz, A., Iyer, R., Young, L., Haidt, J., & Graham, J. (2019). Ideological differences in the expanse of the moral circle. *Nature Communications, 10*(1), 1–12. https://doi.org/10.1038/s41467-019-12227-0

West, T. V., & Kenny, D. A. (2011). The truth and bias model of judgment. *Psychological Review, 118*(2), 357. https://doi.org/10.1037/a0022936

West, T. V., Magee, J. C., Gordon, S. H., & Gullett, L. (2014). A little similarity goes a long way: The effects of peripheral but self-revealing similarities on improving and sustaining interracial relationships. *Journal of Personality and Social Psychology*, *107*(1), 81. https://doi.org/10.1037/a0036556

Westfall, J., Van Boven, L., Chambers, J. R., & Judd, C. M. (2015). Perceiving political polarization in the United States: Party identity strength and attitude extremity exacerbate the perceived partisan divide. *Perspectives on Psychological Science*, *10*(2), 145–158. https://doi.org/10.1177/1745691615569849

Wetzel, C. G., & Walton, M. D. (1985). Developing biased social judgments: The false-consensus effect. *Journal of Personality and Social Psychology*, *49*(5), 1352. https://doi.org/10.1037/0022-3514.49.5.1352

Woltin, K. A., & Yzerbyt, V. Y. (in press). From regulation to projection: Reliance on regulatory mode in predictions about others. *European Journal of Social Psychology*. https://doi.org/10.1002/ejsp.2660

ARTICLE

Changing prejudiced attitudes, promoting egalitarianism, and enhancing diversity through fundamental processes of persuasion

Pablo Briñol[a] and Richard E. Petty[b]

[a]Facultad de Psicología, Universidad Autónoma de Madrid, Campus de Cantoblanco, Madrid, Spain; [b]Distinguished University Professor, Department of Psychology, The Ohio State University, Columbus, OH, USA

ABSTRACT
We review work from persuasion science relevant to reducing prejudiced attitudes. We begin by introducing the idea that the thoughts people generate – their number and valence – are critical for understanding when responding to persuasive attempts will result in egalitarian attitudes. A focus on thinking highlights the importance of understanding short and long-term attitude change in promoting diversity. How much people think is also consequential for spreading of initial change to more distal attitudes and generalization of change to other judgments. The second section describes a process of thought validation that emphasizes the importance of considering what people think and feel about their own thoughts. This meta-cognitive process is shown to make a difference in producing consequential changes in reducing prejudiced attitudes toward African Americans, immigrants, refugees, individuals with disabilities, and beyond. The conditions under which variables such as minority status and stigmatized sources affect elaboration and validation are also specified. The fourth section explores how these two processes are relevant for understanding explicit and implicit ambivalence and change in the domain of prejudiced attitudes. We highlight the utility of a process-oriented approach for designing future research and promoting more inclusive attitudes and actions.

ARTICLE HISTORY Received 29 May 2019; Accepted 14 July 2020

KEYWORDS Attitudes; prejudice; stereotype; persuasion; elaboration; validation

The public policy of many governments as well as that of private institutions and businesses typically has a goal of encouraging the inclusion of members of under-represented groups into all levels of society and the organisation. Addressing this challenge depends in part on the extent to which messages, campaigns, and interventions are effective in changing people's prejudiced

CONTACT Pablo Briñol ✉ pablo.brinnol@uam.es; www.pablobrinol.com Facultad de Psicología, Universidad Autónoma de Madrid, Campus de Cantoblanco, Carretera Colmenar, Km. 15, Madrid, 28049, Spain

European Review of Social Psychology 2019-0018 R4
This article has been corrected with minor changes. These changes do not impact the academic content of the article.

© 2020 European Association of Social Psychology

attitudes. Developments in the science of persuasion over the past few decades have provided guidance on this matter by focusing on the fundamental processes underlying attitude change (e.g. G. R. Maio et al., 2019). Although prejudice reduction is a complex phenomenon shaped by multiple factors (Dixon et al., 2012; Pettigrew & Tropp, 2006), changing prejudiced attitudes plays a critical role in undermining discrimination (J. E. Dovidio et al., 2019; Paluck & Green, 2009). The present review contributes to this domain by focusing on the basic processes of persuasion as a foundation so that researchers and practitioners can understand and improve the efficacy of their influence attempts.

This article focuses mostly on two of the fundamental processes of persuasion that have proven to be particularly useful in producing consequential attitude changes in the domain of prejudiced attitudes: *elaboration* and *validation*. We review work on reducing prejudiced attitudes and increasing diversity which allows us to introduce a series of discoveries in regard to the fundamental processes underlying these phenomena, therefore advancing both basic and applied research.

Overview, Goal, and Scope

We begin our review by introducing the role of *elaboration* processes in changing prejudiced attitudes. A focus on elaboration highlights the importance of considering the amount and valence of people's thoughts in response to persuasive attempts (e.g. advocating the hiring of South American immigrants), the importance of understanding the short and long-term consequences of those changes, and also the consequences for the spreading and generalisation of change. The second section describes the role of thought *validation* processes in reducing prejudiced attitudes towards individuals with disabilities, African Americans, and others. The process of validation highlights the distinction between primary and secondary cognition, and emphasises the importance of considering what people think and feel about their own thoughts, and the thoughts and meta-cognitions that others are perceived to have.

In the third section, we specify the conditions under which elaboration and validation processes are more likely to operate using examples from research on prejudice-relevant variables such as minority status sources and stigmatised sources. The fourth section describes how elaboration and validation processes are also relevant for understanding changes on both explicit and implicit measures of attitudes as well as the implications for both explicit and implicit ambivalence regarding prejudiced attitudes. The firth section focuses on practical tips that researchers, practitioners, and institutions can take in making more effective diversity interventions. The closing section describes how our process approach can be useful for designing future research.

Before beginning our analysis of these two core persuasion processes, it should be noted that the studies reviewed were systematically selected based on whether (1) the attitude object, or any of the elements of the persuasive context were relevant to the domains of stereotyping, group identity, or prejudice, (2) a persuasive attempt or treatment was attempted, (3) the process underlying observed changes in prejudiced attitudes was related to the two mechanism highlighted, elaboration and validation, and (4) whether there were any consequences associated with those psychological processes in terms of attitude change or attitude strength.

Definitions and Conceptual Framework

Attitudes refer to general evaluations (e.g. good-bad, like-dislike) people have regarding people, groups, and issues. Attitudes serve a number of important functions such as guiding choices (e.g. being more likely to hire people from positively evaluated minority groups) and actions (e.g. discrimination, keeping social distance from members of disliked minority groups). In addition to their function in guiding behaviour, attitudes can also serve the functions of giving people a sense of identity, belonging, and self-esteem (e.g. Katz, 1960; Allport, 1954). For example, a person might develop a prejudiced attitude towards a minority group because this negative evaluation of the out-group makes the person feel better about the in-group and about the self.

Attitudes can differ in their strength, with some attitudes being more impactful and predictive of behaviour than others (R. E. Petty & Krosnick, 1995). As will be illustrated in this article, some indicators of holding a strong attitude have been viewed as relatively objective in nature (e.g. their stability, resistance, spreading) whereas others are more subjective in nature (e.g. their perceived stability, subjective knowledge about them, felt ambivalence). Attitudes can also differ in the extent to which they are based on affect, cognition, and behaviour. Thus, prejudiced attitudes can stem from emotional feelings (e.g. how much fear or disgust a group makes people feel), cognitions (e.g. stereotypical beliefs about the work habits of an out-group), or a combination of the two (e.g. Crites et al., 1994; Ashton-James et al; 2012). Beyond affect and cognition, prejudiced attitudes can also be influenced by a person's behaviours, as illustrated by work on self-perception theory (Bem, 1972) and embodied evaluation (P. Briñol et al., 2009).

The accumulated work on prejudice reduction has suggested that a variety of low deliberation processes can produce attitude change towards minority groups, such as mere exposure (Pettigrew & Tropp, 2006), classical conditioning (J. F. Dovidio et al., 2003; Phills et al., 2011), and simple inferences and heuristics (e.g. *"if I am sitting next to her, I must like her,"* Bem, 1972; Chaiken, 1987; Pinel & Long, 2012). Although relevant, low-thinking processes are not the only means of attitude change towards stigmatised others.

According to dual-process models such as the Elaboration Likelihood Model (ELM, R. E. Petty & Briñol, 2012; R. E. Petty & Cacioppo, 1986), attitude formation and change can also be produced by thoughtful processes.

Persuasion research demonstrates that an individual's idiosyncratic reactions to a proposal (or to a seminar, or to a contact-based initiative) are more important than learning the specific campaign content. That is, in contrast to the traditional learning model of persuasion (e.g. Hovland et al., 1953) in which the efficacy of educational campaigns was presumed to depend upon learning and remembering the message content, the cognitive response approach maintains that individuals play an active role in the persuasion process by relating the proposal to the recipients' own knowledge (Greenwald, 1968; Petty, Ostrom et al, 1981). According to this paradigm, the extent of persuasion is determined by the person's thoughts in response to this information rather than learning the information per se. In general, more favourable thoughts towards a message lead to more persuasion. More unfavourable thoughts leads to less persuasion, or can even change the recipient's attitude in a direction opposite to the advocacy.[1]

Following the cognitive response approach, the ELM proposed that to understand attitude change, it was important to consider not only the valence of thoughts but also the amount of thinking done by the message recipient. The ELM is an early example of what became an explosion of dual process and system theories that distinguished thoughtful (deliberative) from non-thoughtful (gut, experiential, snap) judgements (R. E. Petty & Briñol, 2008; Forscher & Devine, 2014; see Sherman et al., 2012, for reviews). As will be illustrated shortly, the extent of thinking is important not only because it determines the process by which a variable affects attitudes, but also because in the ELM, more thoughtful persuasion is postulated to be more consequential than is persuasion produced by lower thought processes (R. E. Petty et al., 1995).

The variables relevant to persuasion settings are traditionally categorised into those that are part of the communication *source* (e.g. majority status, race of the source), the *message* itself (e.g. complexity), the *recipient* of influence (e.g. one's group identity, stereotypes) or the *context* in which persuasion occurs (e.g. noisy auditorium or at home). The ELM specifies five fundamental processes by which these variables can affect attitudes. That is, these variables can affect: (1) the amount of thinking that takes place, (2) the valence (favourable or unfavourable) of the thinking, (3) the structural properties of the thoughts generated such as the confidence one has in them, or variables can serve as (4) persuasive arguments for the merits of a proposal, or (5) as simple cues to the desirability of the proposal. Although the ELM identifies these five core psychological processes by which variables such as minority sources, one's

---

[1]Learning about others can reduce prejudice not only by changing cognitions about out-group members, but also by changing emotions (Brown & Hewstone, 2005; Turner & Crisp, 2010).

group identity, and so forth can influence evaluation, and proposes that these processes operate in different circumstances (e.g. variables are more likely to serve as simple cues when the likelihood of thinking is low), here the focus here is primarily on two of the relatively high elaboration processes that have proven particularly useful in producing consequential judgements relevant to prejudice.

Changing Prejudiced Attitudes with Elaboration

One of the most important ways in which variables can influence attitudes is by affecting the amount of thinking in which people engage when making an evaluation. A variable is most likely to have this effect when thinking is not already constrained to be high or low by other variables. As noted earlier, persuasion variables are often classified as whether they belong to the source, the message, the recipient or the context. They also can be classified as to whether they affect motivation (e.g. personal relevance) or ability (e.g. distraction) to think.[2] In this section we chose personal responsibility (e.g. Petty et al., 1980), as an illustrative example of a variable that affects a person's motivation to process a message (R. E. Petty & Cacioppo, 1990). However, the same predictions apply to other variables capable of affecting motivation and ability to think.

Specifically, Gandarillas et al. (2014) examined the effect of organisational responsibility on the extent to which eighty employees within a variety of professional organisations processed persuasive messages in favour of incorporating more people with disabilities into their companies. Attitudes towards hiring people with disabilities are becoming critical for promoting diversity and egalitarianism within organisations (Rohmer & Louvet, 2018; Vornholt et al., 2013).[3] The messages contained either strong or weak arguments advocating in favour of hiring people with disabilities. As illustrated in Figure 1, the results indicated that having responsibility over other employees led to more information processing as indicated by greater argument quality effects. That is, individuals having (vs. not having) responsibility over other employees were better able to discriminate between persuasive messages that contained strong arguments vs. weak arguments. Therefore, having responsibility increased persuasion for strong arguments but reduced persuasion for weak arguments.[4]

---

[2]For some variables, a combination of motivational and ability factors could be at work. For example, being in a positive mood might make it easier for positive thoughts to come to mind (an ability bias), but might also motivate people to want to stay in that positive state by generating positive thoughts (motivational bias).

[3]In the ELM, the same persuasion processes that are relevant for changing a relatively specific attitude that might have been biased by prejudice (e.g. attitudes towards hiring individuals with mental challenges in organisations) are useful for changing more general prejudiced attitudes (e.g. attitudes towards out-groups) and for changing the level of agreement with statements that promote equality (e.g. being in favour of incorporating people from more diverse backgrounds within institutions).

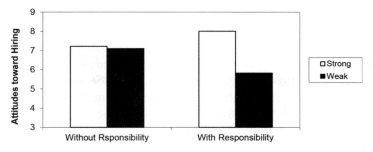

Figure 1. Attitudes towards hiring people with disabilities as a function of organisational responsibility and argument quality. Adopted from.Gandarillas et al. (2014)

This initial example illustrates that by focusing on the process underlying attitude change (i.e. extent of elaboration), the very same variable (responsibility) can either be good for persuasion (e.g. when arguments are strong) or bad (e.g. when arguments are weak). Although this is just a single example, this research tentatively suggests that both the valence and the extent of thinking are important factors in determining the extent and direction of attitude change towards proposals that promote the hiring of people with disabilities in organisations. Importantly, other research provides convergent evidence showing that messages promoting egalitarian attitudes can backfire when the content and valence of the thoughts are different than intended by the persuasive attempt (Dixon et al., 2010; Kim et al., 2018; Major et al., 2014; Saguy et al., 2009). Similarly, anti-prejudice messages have been found to produce ironic effects (increasing rather than decreasing prejudice) depending on the thoughts generated by recipients (Legault et al., 2011; Schultz & Maddox, 2013). In sum, an initial conclusion is that the thoughts people generate in response to persuasive attempts can play a role in producing change in the desired direction or not.

Long Term Consequences of Changes in Prejudiced Attitudes

How much recipients think about information and experiences promoting egalitarianism plays a critical role in determining not only the discrimination between strong and weak arguments and thus the direction of influence, but also whether the resulting attitudes are consequential. Specifically, in accord with the ELM, we argue that there are important benefits associated with high thinking change. First, when thinking is high, people tend to access their

---

[4]People generally find arguments to be more compelling the more they point to desirable and likely consequences of adopting the position advocated (R. E. Petty & Wegener, 1991). Manipulating argument quality and measuring the differential impact of strong vs. weak messages on subsequent attitudes towards the proposal is a methodological tool to assess how different variables affect the extent of thinking (see R. E. Petty et al., 1976; see Carpenter, 2015, for a review of studies using argument quality as a tool to gauge message processing).

attitudes as they update them with each new argument processed. This updating leads high thought attitudes to be more readily accessible when the attitude object is encountered (Tormala & Petty, 2001). The more likely attitudes are to come to mind quickly and spontaneously, the more people can use them to guide their behaviour (Fazio, 1990). Second, attitudes based on high thought are held with more confidence than those based on little thought (Barden & Petty, 2008). When people are deciding what to do, they are more likely to act on an attitude if they are sure it is correct than if they are not (Rucker et al., 2014).

One illustration that provides evidence that differential consequences are associated with attitudes changed by different degrees of elaboration comes from work on prejudice reduction. In one study, Cárdaba et al. (2013) presented seventy- six undergraduates with a persuasive message composed of compelling arguments in favour of a minority group or with a control message. Participants received a message composed of strong arguments and positive cues in favour of South American immigrants in Spain.[5] The extent of thinking was studied by examining people who differed in their chronic motivation to think as assessed with the need for cognition scale (Cacioppo & Petty, 1982). As shown in Figure 2, although both high and low thinkers showed reduced prejudice following the message, the newly changed attitudes were more predictive of participants' attitudes two days later when motivation to think about the initial message was relatively high rather than low. The degree of attitude stability is an important feature to consider since the goal of most prejudice-reduction interventions is to create attitudes that will last over time (Lick et al., 2017).

In a second study, Cárdaba et al. (2014) presented one hundred and three undergraduates with a message in favour of South American immigrants in

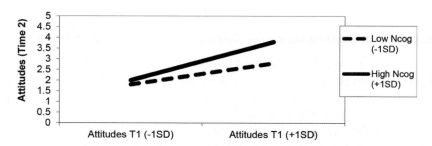

Figure 2. Attitudes (time 1 and time 2) towards South American immigrants in Spain as a function of elaboration (measured by need for cognition). Adopted from.Cárdaba et al. (2013)

---

[5]An attitude towards a stigmatised or minority group (e.g. South American immigrants in Spain) is considered prejudiced when it is less favourable than the attitude towards another non-stigmatised or majority group (e.g. Spaniards in Spain), although it can be positive in absolute terms.

Spain. This time, the amount of thinking about the proposal was manipulated by varying the targets' ability (via different levels of distraction) and motivation (via differences in activation of the self-concept) to think about the message. The results showed that even when the obtained attitude change in favour of the minority group was equivalent under low and high thinking conditions, the reductions in prejudice produced by high thinking processes were more resistant to subsequent attacks than equivalent changes produced by less thoughtful mechanisms (see also, Haugtvedt & Petty, 1992). As these studies demonstrate, understanding the nature of the processes by which attitudes change is essential because the future persistence and resistance of the induced change.

In sum, whether attitude change occurs as the result of relatively high or low amounts of thinking matters not only for determining what attitude is formed but also how consequential or strong that attitude is over time. The more a judgement is based on thinking, the more persist over time, resist attempts at change, and as described in the next section, even to have consequences for other judgements and behaviour.

Elaboration: Spreading Change

An important matter is whether attitudes might show some additional properties associated with strength beyond stability and resistance when changed through high elaboration processes. This section shows that high elaboration attitude change is also associated with spreading to other relevant attitude objects, producing indirect change.

The mental activities characterising elaboration involve people adding something of their own to the information available and are likely to lead to the integration of information into the underlying structure for the attitude object. For example, attitude change processes which require thinking deeply about the attitude object are likely to result in attitude representations that are well integrated and connected with other material in memory (McGuire, 1981; Tesser, 1978). Because of the strong linkage among constructs associated with high thinking, activating one mental representation should activate related ones relatively easily (R. E. Petty et al., 2008).

Recent research examined the extent to which this argument holds for attitudes regarding stigmatised groups. Specifically, in a series of studies, the effect of elaboration on attitude spreading was tested (Moreno et al., 2020). For example, one study examined whether changing attitudes towards a healthy (or unhealthy) diet through high elaboration processes would increase (or reduce) prejudiced attitudes towards overweight people. In this study, three hundred thirty eight undergraduates were first asked to generate positive thoughts either about a healthy or an unhealthy diet (see also, Rudolph & Hilbert, 2017). After listing their thoughts, participants reported their attitudes towards the assigned diet as the focal attitude measure. Elaboration was assessed in this study merely by counting the number of thoughts listed by each participant. In addition to manipulating attitudes towards diets and measuring elaboration, participants were also asked to rate a number of social groups as part of an unrelated study. The key group of interest embedded in this list was people who were overweight. Thus, attitudes towards obese people were the distal (indirect) attitudes.

First, it was predicted and found that the manipulation of attitudes towards diets was successful. That is, participants asked to generate positive thoughts towards healthy diets reported higher liking for eating healthier than those assigned to generate positive thoughts towards unhealthy diets. Most importantly, those focal attitudes (towards diets) were more related to distal attitudes (towards overweight people) for individuals who were higher in the number of thoughts they generated. Higher thinking participants with positive attitudes towards healthy eating reported significantly more negative attitudes towards obese people than those with lower thinking. Also, higher thinking participants induced to like unhealthy foods reported more favourable attitudes towards obese people than those with lower thinking. These findings were replicated in other studies in which elaboration was measured differently (e.g. by assessing reading time) and when elaboration was manipulated rather than measured.

In another study, Moreno et al. (2020) examined whether focal attitudes (thinking about the legalisation of doping in sports) would be more predictive of distal attitudes (towards drug addicts) under relatively high (vs. low) thinking conditions. This study began by randomly assigning undergraduates to read a message either in favour of or against doping legalisation and then attitudes towards this topic (i.e. doping legalisation) were assessed. These messages were pretested in previous research designed to change doping attitudes (J. Horcajo et al., 2019). As in some previous research (Cárdaba et al., 2013; R. E. Petty et al., 2008), in this study participant's need for cognition (NC) was measured to classify participants based on their reported enjoyment of thinking. Finally, as part of an unrelated study, participants were asked to rate a number of social groups, including attitudes towards drug addicts (distal attitudes). As predicted, NC moderated the relationship between attitudes towards doping legalisation (i.e. focal attitudes) and prejudiced attitudes towards drug addicts (i.e. distal attitudes), such that greater correspondence between focal and distal attitudes emerged in higher (vs. lower) thinking participants.

In sum, this research revealed that attitudes unrelated to prejudice (e.g. healthy eating, doping) can spread and generalise leading to changes in prejudiced attitudes towards stigmatised others (e.g. towards obese people, drug addicts). As demonstrated, this indirect change depends, at least in part, on high thinking processes with respect to the focal message. Of course, there are other factors that can contribute to spreading beyond elaboration (e.g. Blankenship et al., 2015; Brannon et al., 2019; Cvencek et al., 2020; Glaser et al., 2015; Leippe & Eisenstadt, 1994; G. R. Maio et al., 2009; Walther, 2002). However, the research we reviewed focused on elaboration because it has received relatively less attention with regard to this particular consequence.

In accord with previous research on secondary transfer effects (Pettigrew, 2009; Tausch et al., 2010), one of the key implications of this idea might be that programmes requiring high thinking for reducing prejudice towards one particular stigmatised group might also be helpful in making people more egalitarian with regard to other groups (Bergh et al., 2016; Ehrke et al., 2014; Meleady et al., 2019; Scroggins et al., 2016). Furthermore, generalising change from a single individual or exemplar to the whole social category is more likely to occur when elaboration is high rather than low (Strark et al., 2013). Indeed, consistent with this elaboration-spreading notion, other research has shown that variables associated with elaboration such as accountability moderate member-to-group generalisation (Paolini et al., 2009).

Summary and Implications for Stereotypes

The first part of our review illustrated how changing prejudiced attitudes towards diverse groups such as people with disabilities in organisations, South American immigrants, and people with obesity can vary in the extent of thought on which the new attitudes are based. Furthermore, the extent of thought relates to how consequential the resulting attitudes are. That is, prejudiced attitudes that came about through relatively thoughtful processes were shown to be more stable and resistant as well as being particularly likely to generalise to other distally related attitudes compared to those induced through less thoughtful means. After showing how elaboration determines both the extent of attitude change and attitude strength, this section closes by outlining some key implications of our process approach for understanding the use of stereotypes.

As noted, stereotypes are important in this domain because they can be considered the cognitive component at the base of many prejudiced attitudes. Each of the components of prejudiced attitudes (beliefs, stereotypes, and emotions) can play multiple roles in persuasion, and therefore elaboration processes can be applied to stereotypes as they apply to attitudes. The studies covered so far demonstrated that the elaboration-strength link is important for changing prejudiced attitudes. The elaboration-strength link is also important when considering the use of stereotypes.

In one illustration Wegener et al. (2006) demonstrated that group stereotypes can influence judgements about individual people in both thoughtful and non-thoughtful ways. Although all the participants in these studies relied upon stereotypes in making explicit judgements about target individuals, and the judgements appeared to be the same (i.e. they were equally extreme) across high and low elaboration conditions, the consequences of the stereotype-based judgements differed depending on the amount of processing of the target information presented. Judgements about the target individual that were based on thoughtful use of the stereotype were less likely to change in reaction to a challenge than were judgements based on less thoughtful use of the stereotype (i.e. using the stereotype as a simple cue). Thus, when the activation of stereotypes influenced judgement by biasing the valence of the thoughts that came to mind, prejudiced responses were more resistant to change than when that same stereotype influenced the judgement through low thinking processes.

Changing Prejudiced Attitudes by Meta-Cognitive Processes of Validation

The previous section described that one way in which researchers and practitioners can reduce prejudiced attitudes is by creating strong attitudes through high elaboration of compelling messages. This section introduces another way of creating strong attitudes based on producing confident thoughts via validation.

Unlike elaboration, which focuses on first-order or primary cognition (e.g. Men are good at maths), validation emphasises secondary or meta-cognition which refers to people's thoughts about their thoughts (e.g. I am sure that men are good at maths; It feels good to believe that men are good at maths). Given its meta-cognitive nature, validation requires relatively high thinking conditions. In an initial study, R. E. Petty et al. (2002) demonstrated that self-validation is more likely to operate when people have the motivation and ability to think about their thoughts (e.g. if participants are high in need for cognition, Cacioppo & Petty, 1982; when there is high personal relevance of the persuasion topic; R. E. Petty & Cacioppo, 1979). Thus, for validation processes to matter, people need to have some thoughts to validate, and also to be motivated and able to consider whether their thoughts are correct (cognitive validation) and/or whether they feel good about them (affective validation). As outlined in this section, another boundary condition on the operation of validation processes is that confidence from the validating variable should be salient during or following thought generation rather than prior to it.

Recent research used this meta-cognitive approach to change prejudiced attitudes towards a group for which thoughtful processes are often overlooked or denied. Specifically, this work evaluated the role that thought confidence can play in attitude change towards a proposal that advocates hiring individuals with mental challenges in organisations. Among other reasons, attitudes towards people with disabilities were studied because this group is often subject to a dehumanisation process through which individual members are perceived as less competent and unable to have sophisticated mental processes (Bogdan & Taylor, 1989; O'Brien, 2003).

In an initial study (Requero, Santos et al., 2020b), one hundred sixty four undergraduates were asked to generate either positive or negative thoughts about hiring people with disabilities (figure 3). Specifically, in the positive thoughts condition, participants were told to write the positive aspects and some potentially beneficial consequences that could result from the implementation of this egalitarian initiative. In the negative thoughts condition, participants were told to write about the negative aspects and potentially damaging consequences of it. Next, participants were asked to indicate the extent to which they were confident in the thoughts they had listed, and their attitudes towards the proposal. Results indicated that thoughts were a significantly better predictor of attitudes when thought confidence was reported to be relatively high vs. low. As depicted in Figure 3, higher levels of confidence were associated with more persuasion for positive thoughts but less persuasion for negative thoughts. Put differently, to the extent that confidence in thoughts was lacking, persuasion was less dependent on thought valence.

A second study moved to a full experimental approach. In this study, two hundred sixty-four undergraduates were first asked to carefully read a proposal in which a company advocated hiring individuals with disabilities. As in the first study, participants were randomly assigned to list either positive thoughts or negative thoughts about this proposal. Then, participants were asked to think about past situations in which they experienced confidence or doubt. Participants who recalled past instances of confidence reported more certainty in the validity of their thoughts about the proposal compared to those who recalled instances of doubt. Similar to the study just described, confidence increased the impact of thought valence on attitudes compared to doubt. As a consequence, when thoughts were mostly positive, increased confidence enhanced persuasion, but when thoughts were

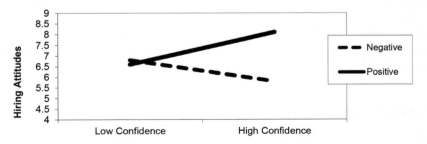

Figure 3. Attitudes towards the hiring proposal as a function of thought valence and thought confidence measured. Adopted Requero, Santos et al., 2020b.

negative, increased confidence reduced persuasion. In sum, meta-cognitive confidence polarised the effects of both positive and negative thoughts on attitudes. A final study revealed that confidence regarding one's prejudice-related thoughts can also be manipulated through more subtle ways, such as revealing the credibility of the source following the message (see also, Tormala et al., 2007).

Other studies on validation have shown that the perceived validity of prejudice-relevant thoughts can be manipulated by having participants engage in confident (vs. doubtful) actions such as head nodding (P. Briñol et al., 2015), by providing recipients with convergent (vs. divergent) evidence matching their thoughts (J. K. Clark et al., 2009; Clark et al., 2013), by highlighting the entitativity nature of their groups (Clark & Thiem, 2015), and merely by priming the concept of justice (Santos & Rivera, 2015). In all of these self-validation paradigms, thoughts were more likely to impact prejudiced attitudes under high (vs. low) confidence conditions.

In addition to generalising across different variables capable of validating thoughts, another advantage of considering a basic persuasion process such as validation is the potential to generalise the results across diverse stigmatised groups. Thus, research on attitude change through thought validation has been able to change prejudiced attitudes towards stigmatised groups beyond people with disabilities, including African Americans, and people with low socio-economic status (SES, e.g. Clark & Thiem, 2015; J. K. Clark et al., 2009).

Beyond extending across different validating variables and diverse outgroups, another important aspect of meta-cognitive validity is that it can apply to *any* accessible mental contents regardless of their specific content, valence, origin, or nature (Briñol & Petty, 2009). For example, P. Briñol et al. (2015) demonstrated that the impact of subliminally primed words related to the Black (vs. White) stereotype could be magnified when validated by having participants nodding their heads following the prime. Also in line with the idea that any mental content can be validated, recent research has shown that meta-cognitive confidence can improve the ability of group identity to guide behaviour. That is, Paredes and colleagues (2019) demonstrated that assessing confidence in people's identity fusion responses improved the ability of the fusion measure to predict extreme pro-group outcomes (for additional examples, see Santos et al., 2019; Shoots-Reinhard et al., 2015).

Cognitive and Affective Validation

As noted earlier, people can decide that their thoughts are valid to use for two general kinds of reasons. That is, people can rely on their thoughts because they believe their thoughts are correct (cognitive validation) or because they feel good about them (affective validation). People make inferences of correctness when they are feeling certain in the validity of their thoughts such as when the thoughts are inspired by social consensus (R. E. Petty et al., 2002), by an expert source (Tormala et al., 2007), and by convergent evidence (J. K. Clark et al., 2009). People presumably feel good about their thoughts when they are feeling happy following thinking (R. E. Petty & Briñol, 2015). If thoughts were positive, making people feel especially good would increase persuasion compared to a sad state. However, feeling good can also magnify the impact of negative thoughts thereby decreasing persuasion (Briñol et al., 2007; Huntsinger, 2013, 2014). Although happiness is clearly associated with feeling good (pleasantness), according to appraisal theories of emotion, it is also associated with certainty (e.g. C. A. Smith & Ellsworth, 1985). Because of this, it is not clear whether affective or cognitive validation was responsible for the validation effect in the initial happiness studies.

In order to demonstrate that validation can occur via both cognitive and affective routes, recent research examined emotions that have the potential to affect certainty (related to correctness) and pleasantness appraisals differently. For example, anger and disgust are unpleasant emotions that are associated with certainty, whereas surprise and awe are more pleasant emotions that are associated with doubt and uncertainty. Consistent with our *differential appraisals hypothesis* (P. Briñol et al., 2018), it was demonstrated that each of these emotions are capable of inducing either more or less thought use depending on which appraisal (certainty or pleasantness) is dominant. This approach concurs with previous frameworks in highlighting the importance of appraisals (Lerner & Keltner, 2000), but introduces some novelties such as predicting that different appraisals can be relevant when varied even within the same emotion.

In the most recent illustration of this paradigm relevant to promoting egalitarian attitudes, undergraduates were asked to think about the positive or negative aspects of a proposal to hire people with disabilities in an organisation (Requero, Briñol et al., 2020). Following this thought valence manipulation, participants were assigned to write about personal episodes in which they felt either hope or hopelessness. Naturally, geneating positive thoughts about people with disabilities might lead people to feel hopeful regarding this group and negative thoughts to feeling hopeless. However, in this paradigm participants are randomly assigned to feel hopeful or hopeless *following* the positive or negative thought generation so that the independent effects of thought valence and emotion can be determined. This work focused on hope and hopelessness because for these emotions the confidence and pleasantness appraisals are mismatched. Hope is a pleasant state that is associated with uncertainty, whereas hopelessness is unpleasant though associated with confidence.

After participants generated their thoughts and received the emotion induction, they were exposed to an appraisal manipulation designed to focus them on a specific appraisal of the emotion (pleasantness or confidence; P. Briñol et al., 2018). Specifically, participants were required in this study to respond to questions that contained words related to pleasantness (pleasantness appraisal) or questions that contained words related to confidence (confidence appraisal). Finally, after the three manipulations (positive versus negative thoughts induction; hope versus hopelessness induction; pleasantness versus confidence appraisal induction), participants reported their attitudes towards the proposal to hire people with disabilities in an organisation.

In line with the self-validation hypothesis, the resutls revealed that feeling hopeless or hope following thought generation can lead to different (and opposite) effects on the use of thoughts. This effect depends on whether the confidence or the pleasantness appraisal of these emotions was made salient. As predicted, when individuals were focused on the confidence/doubt appraisal of the emotion, then feeling hopeless led to more thought use than hope because experiencing hopelessness is associated with an appraisal of confidence that was misattributed to feeling sure about the accuracy or correctness of one's thoughts relative to feeling hope, an emotion associated with uncertainty (cognitive validation). In contrast, when individuals were focused on the pleasantness/unpleasantness appraisal of the emotion, then experiencing hope led to more thought use than feeling hopeless because experiencing hope is associated with an appraisal of pleasantness that was misattributed to feeling good about or liking one's thoughts relative to feeling hopeless, an emotion associated with feeling unpleasant (affective validation).

Beyond the potential to transform our understanding of the hope-hopeless continuum, this novel approach based on highlighting different appraisals within the same emotion can be relevant to designing process-based practical applications promoting positive attitudes towards more diverse organisations and individuals. Furthermore, this research on differential appraisals of emotions can contribute to inspiring future research on reducing prejudiced attitudes as a fuction of phenomenon such as wishful thinking (a pleasant but uncertain state, Villegas-Gold & Yoo, 2014) and realistic pessimism (an unpleasant but certain state, Kaiser et al., 2004).

Perceiving Cognitions and Meta-Cognitions of Others

After showing that what and how much people think (elaboration) and what people think about their own thoughts (validation) both play a role in prejudiced attitudes, we introduce a new line of research examining to what extent the perceived cognitions and meta-cognitions of others can also influence prejudiced attitudes. Specifically, this research tested the impact of thinking about the cognitions and meta-cognitions of out-group members, including Syrian refugees, South American immigrants, and Gypsy people (Santos et al., 2020).

This research compared the impact of thinking about how members of out-groups usually think (perceived primary cognition) and how members of those out- groups think about their own thoughts (perceived secondary cognition). These two types of cognition were compared because they mapped well onto the elaboration and validation research described earlier, and also because there is some previous evidence suggesting that the distinction between primary and secondary emotions is useful in the domain of dehumanisation. This work has shown that prejudiced evaluations can take the form of attributing stigmatised groups the ability to have mostly primary emotions (i.e. brief, physiologically embedded affective reactions such as anger or joy) but denying they are capable of having secondary emotions (i.e. affective reactions that are the result of social construction through the attachment of meaning to experiences such as admiration or remorse; Kteily et al., 2015; Loughnan et al., 2010).

Just as distinguishing between primary and secondary emotions has been useful in this domain, this work examined whether separating perceiving primary versus secondary cognition in others also can be useful when evaluating others. In two studies, Santos et al. (2020) randomly assigned undergraduates to one of three different experimental conditions. In the primary cognition treatment, participants had to answer questions about the primary thinking processes of out-group members. Specifically, participants in this condition were required to respond to 10 questions asking to what extent a particular group had primary thoughts. For example, in one study they responded to whether they thought that: "Syrian refugees tend to think about the world," "Syrian refugees are able to process information," or that "Syrian refugees are able to comprehend different ideas." In the secondary cognition treatment, participants answered questions about meta-cognition. That is, the questions focused on the ability of refugees to reflect on their own thoughts, and thinking processes. Examples of the items include, "Syrian refugees have a window into their minds," "Syrian refugees realize there are things that they don't know," and "Syrian refugees like to think about the validity of their thoughts." The effect of these two treatments on prejudiced attitudes was compared against a control group, in which participants answered 10 equivalent questions but that were unrelated to primary or secondary cognition (e.g. "Syrian refugees wear socks").

As expected, compared to the control group, the two treatments reduced prejudiced attitudes towards Syrian refugees as well as South American immigrants and Gypsy people. That is, thinking about how out-group members think and how they think about their thoughts both produced more positive attitudes towards these groups compared to controls. In these studies, the two treatments did not differ from each other, but were superior to control groups. Future research can benefit from work aimed at understanding *when* and *for whom* these two different treatments might be more effective alone or in combination in promoting deeper appreciation for the sophisticated mental processes of other groups.

Elaboration and Validation: Specifying Conditions

So far, this review focused on two fundamental mechanisms of reducing prejudiced attitudes – elaboration and validation. As noted, these two mechanisms are critical for predicting whether change occurs in the desired direction and how consequential it is. Given that many variables (e.g. group identity, stereotypes) can affect judgements and behaviours through these two processes, a natural concern is how to distinguish between them. Fortunately, a number of methods have been identified for both separating out and predicting when different processes occur. This section focuses on two moderating conditions: Amount of thinking and timing. Stereotypes are used here as an example describing next how the effects of stereotypes can be predicted *a priori* based on these two contextual factors.

In most of the research on stereotyping and prejudiced attitudes, group category membership (e.g. the race of the target) is learned *before* acquisition of individuating information. When such information precedes processing, research has shown that stereotypes can influence attitudes and performance in the various ways articulated earlier including serving as a simple cue when thinking is relatively low, biasing thoughts when thinking is high, and affecting elaboration when it is unconstrained by other variables (e.g. Wegener et al., 2006). As noted, any variable can influence prejudiced attitudes by one of the five key processes outlined by the ELM. Importantly, learning of someone's group membership "after the fact" allows group stereotypes to influence perceptions in a completely different way – by affecting validation processes.

For example, when a source serves in a validation role, it might matter if the thoughts are about the source him or herself rather than a proposal the source is advocating. Imagine reading a message about some unidentified person that you suspect is a woman. If you then learn that the source is indeed a woman, your thoughts about the source would be validated whereas if you learned that the source was a man, your thoughts would be invalidated. In general, people are likely to have more confidence when the content of their thoughts matches or fits the nature of the source that is revealed rather than when the content does not fit or mismatches. Thus, thought confidence might be increased if a person high in prejudice generated negative thoughts towards a job candidate and then learned that the candidate came from a stigmatised group with low performance expectations rather than from a non-stigmatised group with higher performance expectations. This suggests that sources with low (vs. high) status can affect judgements by validating (rather than invalidating) thoughts under some circumstances such as when the source is the object of the thoughts, and when thoughts are stereotypical or match the nature of the source.

In two experiments examining this idea (Clark et al., 2009), two hundred and nine university students received information about a child who performed either reasonably well or poorly on an intelligence test. The good performance information would lead people to have positive thoughts about the child's intelligence whereas the poor performance report would lead people to have negative thoughts about the child's intelligence. Following the information, participants listed their thoughts about the child and then learned that the child was either from a low socio-economic statue (SES) household or a high SES household. When the SES information matched (vs. mismatched) the performance expectations (i.e. poor performance with low SES and high performance with high SES), participants had more confidence in their thoughts. They also used their thoughts more in forming their judgements of the intelligence of the child. Importantly, the obtained findings on intelligence were mediated by thought confidence and have been replicated several times with different materials (e.g. Clark et al., 2012). This research is also consistent with work on stereotype threat revealing that stereotype-related thoughts can be validated by priming people with convergent (vs. divergent) evidence matching their thoughts (J. K. Clark et al., 2015; Clark et al., 2017; Clark et al., 2018).

In addition of showing the relevance of validation processes to stereotyping, this work also illustrates the importance of considering *timing* as a key variable for understanding process. That is, the confidence that emerges from matching with stereotypes should be salient *following* (or at least, during) thought generation rather than prior to thought generation. By varying the timing of experimental inductions, research on self-validation demonstrated the consequences for evaluation and performance of two different psychological processes: stereotypes affecting the generation of thoughts when preceding the reception of information and affecting the use (validation) of those thoughts when following the message (Clark et al., 2012; J. K. Clark et al., 2015; see also Briñol et al., 2007). These findings provide evidence in favour of the idea that the same variable (stereotypes) can have different (and opposite) effects on judgements depending on when the manipulation of the variable is introduced.

Testing Processes of Elaboration and Validation for Sources in Minority Status

Beyond stereotypes about SES, other variables associated with stigmatised sources such as being in a numerical minority can influence attitudes by the same processes of elaboration and validation depending on the timing, and the background level of elaboration. When elaboration is not constrained by other variables to be high or low, the numerical status of the source can determine the amount of information processing in which people engage. Thus, persuasive proposals that are presented by Black (vs. White) sources often receive more attention (as indicated by greater impact of strong vs. weak arguments) and result in more consequential attitudes (White & Harkins, 1994), at least among relatively unprejudiced individuals (R. E. Petty et al., 1999). Also, whether an idea is delivered by a source that belongs to the numerical majority or minority can influence how people evaluate that proposal (J. Horcajo, Petty et al., 2010a). When elaboration is unconstrained, majority/minority source status influences the extent of elaboration (Erb et al., 2002; Martin & Hewstone, 2008; Moscovici, 1985).

In one relevant study (Horcajo, Briñol et al., 2010b) eighty-two undergraduates were first assigned to receive a message arguing to change the institutional colour of the participants' university flag. The message came from a source in the numerical majority or minority. The minority status source increased the argument quality effect on attitudes relative to the majority source, which suggests that the minority source led to greater thinking, consistent with Moscovici's (1985) conversion theory (see also, Martin & Hewstone, 2008). Furthermore, as predicted, the argument quality effect obtained for attitudes was mediated by a change in the profile of message-consistent thoughts.

In that experiment, source information about numerical status preceded the presentation of the message information and elaboration was not set to be high. However, if source information were to follow information processing under high thinking conditions, source status should affect validation rather than elaboration. In a test of this hypothesis, Horcajo et al. (2010b) exposed one hundred and ten undergraduates to a persuasive message composed of either strong or weak arguments about the organisational regulations of a new company. After receiving and processing the message, the communication was attributed to either a person whose position was supported by the majority or a person whose position was supported by a minority of others. The majority source increased the confidence with which the recipients held their thoughts in response to the message compared to the minority source. As a consequence, the majority source increased the impact of argument quality on attitudes compared to the minority source. Importantly, the confidence with which participants held their thoughts mediated the effects of source status on attitudes, whereas the thoughts generated by participants did not.

As a final illustration, consider another study manipulating extent of thinking in the domain of minority influence. In this study with one hundred forty-four undergraduates, J. Horcajo et al. (2014) first manipulated the level of elaboration (low vs. high) using a manipulation of personal relevance to affect motivation to process the message (R. E. Petty & Cacioppo, 1979). Then, participants received a persuasive message composed of strong or weak arguments. Finally, they learned that the message was from a source in the numerical majority or minority and reported their attitudes towards the proposal.

In this study, only under high elaboration conditions did the majority source status increase the argument quality effect on attitudes compared to the minority source. This finding is consistent with the prediction that source

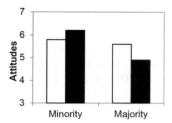 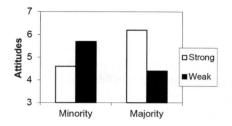

Figure 4. Attitudes as a function of argument quality and source status presented after a message under low thinking conditions (left panel) and high thinking conditions (right panel). Adopted from J. Horcajo et al. (2014).

status can validate thoughts under high thinking conditions (see Figure 4, right panel). In contrast, under low elaboration conditions, source status was predicted and found to influence attitudes by serving as a peripheral cue. That is, the majority source increased persuasion compared to the minority source irrespective of argument quality (see Figure 4, left panel). In sum, source status can influence attitudes by processes of primary cognition (e.g. serving as a cue, affecting elaboration) and processes of secondary cognition (validating thoughts) depending on timing and the background level of thinking.

Ambivalence Affects Elaboration and Validation

The evaluative structure of recipients' pre-existing attitudes can also influence how they evaluate and respond to individuals from different groups. This section describes research on attitudinal ambivalence in the domain of prejudiced attitudes.

When people endorse both positive and negative reactions to a particular out-group, they report feeling conflicted, indecisive, and mixed about individuals and information relevant to that group (Glick & Fiske, 1996; Katz & Hass, 1988; Priester & Petty, 1996). This form of psychological conflict is called *explicit ambivalence* and occurs when people have an attitude object linked in memory to both positivity and negativity and they further believe that both of these reactions are valid (see R. E. Petty et al., 2007). There are several other antecedents to feelings of ambivalence, including interpersonal disagreement (Priester & Petty, 2001) and having attitudes that are different from those one wants to have (e.g. wanting to be more positive about the elderly; DeMarree, Wheeler et al., 2014b).

In other cases, a person does not report being conflicted or mixed about the object, but he or she can nevertheless feel generally uncomfortable when considering the object because unendorsed gut feelings (implicit evaluations) conflict with endorsed (explicit) evaluations (Rydell et al., 2008). This is called *implicit ambivalence* (e.g. R. E. Petty et al., 2006). In implicit ambivalence, a person also has an attitude object linked to both positivity and negativity in memory, but one of these reactions is tagged as invalid (Petty & Briñol, 2006). This person does not report being ambivalent because the person does not consider both reactions to be valid. A person's evaluative reaction to an attitude object might be seen as invalid for a number of reasons including that: (1) the person believes the reaction is a mere cultural association (e.g. from the media) and does not represent what they truly believe (e.g. I have a negative reaction to Hispanics because they are portrayed as criminals on TV, but I know that is not true) and (2) the reaction represents a prior attitude (e.g. I used to be a bit prejudiced towards this particular group, but now I no longer am; P. Briñol et al., 2006; R. E. Petty et al., 2006, 2012).

Both explicit and implicit ambivalence are important because they are associated with increased elaboration of relevant messages. In one study examining explicit ambivalence, G. R. Maio et al. (1996) measured participants' attitudinal ambivalence regarding immigration to Canada and then exposed them to a discrepancy-relevant message favouring immigration from Hong Kong to Canada that contained either strong or weak arguments. The extent to which participants processed the message information was assessed by examining the extent to which the quality of the arguments made a difference in post-message immigration attitudes. Consistent with the idea that ambivalence increases elaboration, G. R. Maio et al. (1996) found that being ambivalent increased the impact of argument quality on attitudes suggesting that ambivalent individuals engaged in enhanced scrutiny of the issue-relevant information presented. Subsequent research has provided further support to the idea that explicit ambivalence increases elaboration and improves accuracy in decision making (Kleiman & Hassin, 2013; G. R. Maio et al., 2001; Rees et al., 2013; Savary et al., 2015).

In a study examining how implicit ambivalence can enhance elaboration, I. Johnson et al. (2017) showed that as the discrepancy in students' implicit and explicit racial (black versus white) attitudes increased, they engaged in more scrutiny of a message if delivered by an African-American (vs. White) source even if the message content itself was race-irrelevant. In another study, they found that people high in implicit ambivalence more carefully scrutinised a message related to racial issues (Affirmative Action) even if delivered by a White source. As illustrated in Figure 5, the results of both studies combined (a total of two hundred eighty-five undergraduate participants) showed that the greater the discrepancy between implicit and explicit racial attitudes, the greater the argument quality effect on attitudes to the message. This means that among individuals who were relatively low in explicit prejudice, it was those who were also relatively high in implicit prejudice who were more likely to process messages from or relevant to

Blacks. Similar enhanced scrutiny effects occurred for people who were relatively high in explicit prejudice if they were also relatively low in implicit prejudice. That is, the direction of the discrepancy didn't matter. What mattered was the degree of discrepancy in implicit versus explicit racial attitudes. If both explicit and implicit prejudice were relatively low or high, then the scrutiny of information was relatively low.[6]

These findings are important because earlier research on prejudice and persuasion showed that White individuals tended to engage in greater elaboration when information was presented by a Black rather than a White source (White & Harkins, 1994). Subsequent research showed that this enhanced processing of Black over White sources extended to greater processing of Black over White targets (Fleming et al., 2005). Importantly, the research by I. Johnson et al. (2017) showed that the enhanced processing of Black over White sources and targets was most likely to occur among individuals who were low in their explicit prejudice. It was assumed that because these individuals would be concerned about being prejudiced when assessing information from or about Blacks, they would guard against this possible prejudice by processing the information very carefully (R. E. Petty et al., 1999). Contemporary research suggests that many White individuals who score low in explicit prejudice also harbour automatic negative reactions to Blacks and that they might wish to overcome these negative reactions in order to act in an unprejudiced way (Monteith, 1993; Plant & Devine, 1998). These automatic negative reactions are captured in contemporary implicit measures of racial attitudes such as the IAT (Greenwald et al., 1998). The research on implicit ambivalence provided evidence that rather than the

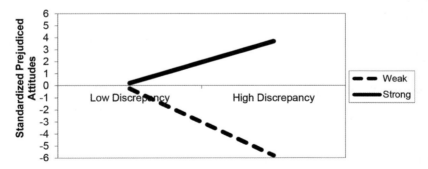

Figure 5. Standardised prejudiced attitudes as a function of argument quality and difference scores (i.e. Standardised explicit minus standardised implicit). Adopted from.I. Johnson et al. (2017)

---

[6]In another study, the discrepancy between implicit and explicit attitudes was manipulated rather than measured yielding similar results (R. E. Petty et al., 2006). That is greater implicit ambivalence was associated with a greater impact of argument quality on attitudes.

processing effects being driven solely by a desire to watch out for one's own possible prejudice – when explicit prejudice is lower than implicit prejudice – the processing also occurred when explicit prejudice was higher than implicit prejudice. That is, the processing was tied to implicit ambivalence which is the only framework that predicts that either direction of discrepancy between implicit and explicit prejudice would produce feelings of conflict and thereby increase information processing.

Although we focused on research showing that both explicit and implicit ambivalence lead to elaboration, it is important to note that ambivalence also can relate to validation processes (Clarkson et al., 2008; Luttrell et al., 2016). In fact, ambivalence can serve both as an antecedent and also as a consequence of both processes. For example, by elaborating on information relevant to the object of ambivalence one can expect psychological conflict to be reduced (e.g. G. R. Maio et al., 1996; Rydell et al., 2008).

Furthermore, validation processes also can be helpful in reducing ambivalence through a number of paradoxical possibilities, such as enhancing confidence in just one side of the mixed thoughts (K. G. DeMarree et al., 2015) and invalidating all of one's mixed thoughts (Durso et al., 2016). For example, in one study it was shown that low certainty can attenuate the typical effect of ambivalence (Luttrell et al., 2016). Unlike these studies that relied mostly on college student samples, the most recent research on moderating ambivalence effects has provided convergent evidence showing that ambivalence and certainty interact to predict attitude stability outside the lab using real-world populations and settings (Luttrell et al., in press).

Changing Automatic Prejudiced Attitudes with Elaboration and Validation

In the previous section we have seen that explicit measures of prejudice can differ from what is shown on implicit measures. For example, a person can express a positive evaluation of a minority group on an explicit self-report measure, but the automatic evaluations of this person can be negative. Thus, beyond understanding how the processes of elaboration and validation are capable of changing explicit attitudes, it is also important to understand the impact these processes can have on implicit measures of attitudes. Therefore, this section briefly describes recent research showing that automatic evaluations relevant to stigmatised individuals from minority groups can be affected by processes of primary cognition such as elaboration (e.g. C. T. Smith & De Houwer, 2014; Wyer, 2016), as well as processes of secondary cognition such as validation (e.g. Hahn & Gawronski, 2019; I. Johnson et al., 2017; Johnson et al., 2018; Maddux et al., 2005; Mann & Ferguson, 2016; Sassenberg & Wieber, 2005; Lai et al., 2013).

In initial work on affecting implicit measures of prejudice, automatic evaluations of Blacks were shown to be affected by a number of low thinking processes such as mere exposure to various exemplars of admired Black individuals (see, Gawronski & Bodenhausen, 2006, for a review). In general, research has shown that automatic measures of attitudes can be affected by relatively low thought attitude change processes. In fact, implicit measures of attitudes have sometimes been assumed to change only or to a greater extent as a result of low rather than high thought processes (e.g. Rydell & McConnell, 2006).

However, other work contradicts the general idea that automatic attitude measures respond only or mostly to simple persuasion techniques under relatively low thinking conditions. For example, recent research has shown that automatic evaluations can be affected by thoughtful processing of persuasive messages, advertisements, marketing campaigns and other treatments involving effortful processing of verbal information (e.g. Brannon & Gawronski, 2017; Horcajo, Petty et al., 2010a; Mann & Ferguson, 2016; Mann & Ferguson, 2016; C. T. Smith & De Houwer, 2014; Wyer, 2016; for a review, see R. E. Petty & Briñol, 2010). Thus, the most accurate conclusion is that like explicit measures, implicit measures can be affected by both automatic and deliberative processes. Furthermore, research in this domain is consistent with the idea that the greater the elaboration that goes into processing a message, the more consequential implicit measures become in terms of stability, resistance, and spreading – the same consequences as for explicit measures (e.g. Gawronski et al., 2017; Horcajo et al., 2010a; Ratliff & Nosek, 2011; Schultz & Maddox, 2013; Ye & Gawronski, 2016).

A final point is that research has shown that changes on implicit measures of attitudes are sometimes related to change on explicit measures, but sometimes they are independent of each other (e.g. R. E. Petty et al., 2006; Gregg et al., 2006). In general, deliberative/explicit measures are more likely to correspond with automatic/implicit measures when participants complete the explicit measures after being told to "trust their intuition" (Jordan et al., 2007) or "go with their gut" before responding (Ranganath et al., 2008). Such instructions apparently free participants to report evaluative stirrings of which they are aware but may not report spontaneously on an explicit measure due to uncertainty regarding their origins or appropriateness (Loersch et al., 2011).

Practical Recommendations

As noted throughout, maximising the chances of designing effective procedures to reduce prejudiced attitudes depends in part on understanding the psychological processes that are likely to underlie the impact of any practical interventions. Therefore, a natural concern is how researchers, practitioners, and institutions can explain and test the effects of interventions in a given context. Fortunately, as argued throughout our review, the effects of variables (such as stereotypes, majority influence, Black versus White message sources, etc.) can be predicted *a priori* based on contextual factors, such as the general levels of elaboration in the persuasion context as well as the order in which events occur. Therefore, agents of influence can target a particular process (elaboration, validation) by manipulating the amount of thinking, and by varying the time at which variables are made salient.

In addition to intentionally managing the situation, a number of measures can be useful to diagnose how variables affect persuasion. As noted, measuring both the type and the number of thoughts that participants generate and/ or manipulating argument quality can help assess the role of elaboration processes that could be involved in initiatives designed to reduce prejudiced attitudes. Beyond including methods of assessing how much actual thought participants are engaged in, it is also important to assess how much people perceive they have thought (subjective elaboration) because perceptions of thinking can have effects in addition to actual thinking. For example, in one study, participants merely led to believe that they had engaged in more thinking (even though they did not) became more confident in their attitudes and more willing to act on them (Barden & Petty, 2008). Thus, assessing subjective elaboration with a self-report single-item measuring how much people believe they have thought can be helpful in predicting who is more likely to use their attitudes to guide behaviours.

A third tip related to elaboration processes involves assessing both objective indicators of attitude strength to understanding long term consequences of induced changes (e.g. attitude stability, resistance) and also subjective indicators of attitude strength (e.g. perceived attitude importance, subjective knowledge, felt ambivalence). Relatively simple question such as to what extent the attitude is perceived to remain the same in the future (Cárdaba et al., 2013), and to what extent the person would like to have a different attitude (DeMarree et al., 2014b) can be useful to understand short and long term consequences of changes. We have also noted that taking into consideration the generalisation of change by assessing prejudiced attitudes in other domains (even attitudes only indirectly or distally related to the domain of prejudice) can provide researchers with a subtle, practical tool (Moreno et al., 2020).

In regard to validation processes, assessing participants' confidence and liking for their thoughts can have practical value. Thus, as another step, we recommend the use of these measures (e.g. judgemental confidence) as a moderator of the effect of any mental content (thoughts, attitudes, goals, traits) on behaviour (e.g. discrimination) because of their ease of use and efficiency, and because measures of meta-cognitive confidence and/or liking can increase the predictive validity of any mental construct. Questions about thought confidence or liking are easy for practitioners to use as they require only asking only one simple question, and people should find it easy to respond. As noted, there is value in asking these questions not only with regard to people's own thoughts but also when it comes to the thoughts of out-group members (Santos et al., 2020; see also DeMarree et al., in press).

Finally, we recommended assessing the psychological meaning of variables (e.g. is having confidence good or bad? is egalitarianism desirable or undesirable?). First, practitioners and institutions can benefit by considering the meanings that people associate to the presumably positive variables introduced in various interventions (P. Briñol et al., 2020; R. E. Petty & Briñol, 2020). For instance, one could expect that variables like power, self-affirmation, and a happy mood will produce a beneficial impact when, actually, it can produce a detrimental impact, and we have explained when and why this could occur (e.g. Briñol et al., 2018). Moreover, because the meaning of subjective states used in various interventions is personal and can also differ depending on the situations and the culture, we suggest that persuasive agents evaluate this important factor by asking a simple question regarding what people think key aspects of a treatment mean. Of course, beyond assessing its natural variations, confidence and meaning can also be manipulated to produce the desired levels of validity.

Summary and Future Directions

This review has focused on how a wide variety of seemingly diverse variables (e.g. stereotypes, stigmatised sources, group identity, minority sources) can affect prejudiced attitudes by the same two underlying psychological processes. These processes refer to how extensively people think in response to a stimulus (elaboration) and whether or not those thoughts are used in forming judgements (validation). The operation of these processes depended on a number of other factors, such as a person's overall motivation and ability to think in the situation, and whether the variable affecting the persuasion process preceded or followed the stimulus to be evaluated. Variables are more likely to impact amount of thinking when the level of elaboration in the situation is not already set to be very high or low by other variables and when the variable precedes the stimulus to be processed. In contrast, validation processes are more likely when elaboration is set high enough for individuals to both generate thoughts and consider their validity, and when the variable of interest occurs during or after the stimulus to be processed rather than before.

It is important to note that increasing elaboration does not necessarily imply that the thinking that takes place will be objective and bias free. As noted, one of the five processes outlined by the ELM refers to biased processing. Thus, high thinking can make the effect of biasing variables such as stereotypes even stronger than when thinking is low (e.g. Wegener et al., 2006; see Petty, 2001). Furthermore, although the focus was on actual thinking, as we noted earlier, how much people think they are thinking is also important (Barden & Petty, 2008). In a recent line of research in the domain of prejudiced attitudes focused on subjective elaboration (Moreno et al., 2020), undergraduates first read a message advocating in favour of hiring people with disabilities. Then, perceived elaboration was manipulated by having participants answer a misleading questionnaire in which the responses were framed to imply low or high degrees of thinking about the message. Finally, attitudes towards the proposal and behavioural intentions were measured. One behavioural measure involved having participants receive the vita of a job candidate with disabilities and indicating whether or not they were willing to defend that candidate in a forthcoming meeting. In a second measure they reported their intentions to hire the candidate for their university. The perception of having thought more about the proposal led participants to use their attitudes in guiding these choices. Along with assessing subjective perceptions of thinking, future research in this context can also examine the extent to which people find elaboration to be associated with pleasantness and confidence.[7]

Similarly, greater confidence in thoughts does not imply that thoughts are any more accurate or unbiased. People can perceive accurate thoughts to have low validity and believe that biased thoughts have high validity. In fact, in many cases confidence is often overly high and not well calibrated to accuracy since it can be affected by unrelated incidental variables such as the non-verbal indicators of the source delivering the information (Guyer et al., 2019), and the non-verbal responses occurring in the recipient (P. Briñol et al., 2018).

As noted, a key aspect of validation is that confidence and doubt can be attached to anything in mind, including prejudice-related thoughts, group identity, and stereotypes. We have argued that assessing confidence and doubt in responses to prejudice scales have the potential to improve the predictions made by those scales. Validity is not only likely to apply to individual differences in evaluations of minority groups, but also to the associated motivations to control for prejudice towards these groups. We argue that the ability of instruments such as the Motivation to Control Prejudiced Reactions scale (Dunton & Fazio, 1997), and the Internal and External Motivation to Respond without Prejudice scale (Plant & Devine, 1998) to predict differences in public and private endorsement of stereotypes

---

[7]Future research should also take into consideration the goals underlying elaboration. In the research described throughout this review, most participants were likely to be motivated by their need to know. Recent research has examined an alternative motive in which people aim to process information to be entertained (cf., Moyyer-Guse´, 2008) (e.g. Cancela et al., 2020; Wilson et al., 2019). This research has shown that the same variable (e.g. personal relevance) that can enhance elaboration when people have a knowledge goal can decrease elaboration when people have an entertainment goal.

as well their capacity to predict motivation to correct one's social judgements is likely to be improved as meta-cognitive confidence in participants' responses to those scales increases.

Beyond measuring meta-cognitive confidence, assessing subjective indicators of attitude strength such as perceived knowledge can be also useful for future research. For example, in a recent research, Paredes et al. (2020) examined how perceived knowledge influenced the propensity to make hiring decisions about job candidates. In one of the studies of this series, actual job candidates were interviewed by personnel selection professionals for real job offers. After each interview, the interviewers reported their perceived knowledge about the candidate, their attitudes towards the candidate, and whether or not the candidate was actually hired or not was recorded. As expected, these real-world interviewers used their attitudes to hire actual job candidates to a greater extent when they perceived themselves as having more knowledge about the candidates. Having more knowledge about the candidate likely reflected greater confidence in attitudes towards the candidates. Importantly, this effect of perceived knowledge on attitude-impact was present even when the actual amount of information presented was held constant, and it was replicated when job candidates were presented as individuals with disabilities.

In closing this review it is important to make two final remarks. First, in most research covered in this review, persuasion variables (e.g. numerical status, group identity, stereotypes) have been studied in isolation. However, variables associated with the person and the situation can be examined in combination, interacting with each other to influence elaboration and validation processes. It is especially likely that person and situational variables together will affect the extent of elaboration or validation when they match in some way. Some forms of matching capable of operating through elaboration and validation include matching person and social roles (e.g. agent vs. recipient in expressing and receiving information, Xu et al., 2019), matching personal identity and occupation (Schmader & Sedikides, 2018), and matching virtually any dispositions and situations more generally (Teeny et al., in press).

Second, elaboration and validation are two general processes capable of accommodating virtually any change in judgement caused by social and contextual factors. This includes changes in prejudiced attitudes, but it also can include changes in group identity, changes in stereotypes, and many others. The most recent of these applications has examined change within the domain of expectations (Geers et al., 2019). Although this work focused on amplifying placebo expectations and minimising nocebo expectations, we think that the same basic processes (elaboration and validation) are relevant for understanding changes in expectations in other domains, including expectations about academic performance of members from disadvantaged groups (Murphy et al., 2018), self-fulfiling prophecies (Madon et al., 2018), and even changing expectations related to mental and physical stigmas (P. Briñol, Petty, Belding et al., 2017; Durso et al., 2020).

Funding

This work was supported by the National Science Foundation [0847834]; Ministerio de economía, industria y competitividad (ES)[PSI2017-83303-C2-1-P].

References

Allport, G. W. (1954). *The nature of prejudice*. Addison-Wesley.
Ashton-James, C. E., & Tracy, J. L. (2012). Pride and prejudice: How feeling about the self influence judgmetns of others. *Personality and Social Psychology Bulletin*, 38 (4), 466–476. https://doi.org/10.1177/0146167211429449
Barden, J., & Petty, R. E. (2008). The mere perception of elaboration creates attitude certainty: Exploring the thoughtfulness heuristic. *Journal of Personality and Social Psychology*, 95(3), 489–509. https://doi.org/10.1037/a0012559
Bem, D. J. (1972). Self-perception theory. In L. Berkowitz (Ed.), *Advances in Experimental Social Psychology*, (Vol.6, pp. 1–62). New York: Academic Press. doi:10.1016/S0065-2601(08)60024-6
Bergh, R., Akrami, N., Sidanius, J., & Sibley, C. G. (2016). Is group membership necessary for understanding generalized prejudice? A re-evaluation of why prejudices are interrrelated. *Journal of Personality and Social Psychology*, 111(3), 367–395. https://doi.org/10.1037/pspi0000064
Blankenship, K. L., Wegener, D. T., & Murray, R. A. (2015). Values, inter-attitudinal structure, and attitude change: Value accessibility can increase a related attitude's resistance to change. *Personality and Social Psychology Bulletin*, 41(12), 1739–1750. https://doi.org/10.1177/0146167215609063
Bogdan, R., & Taylor, S. J. (1989). Relationships with severely disabled people: The social construction of humanness. *Social Problems*, 36(2), 135–148. https://doi.org/10.2307/800804
Brannon, S. M., DeJong, A., & Gawronski, B. (2019). Determinants of lateral attitude change: The roles of object relatedness, attitude certainty, and moral conviction. *Social Cognition*, 37(6), 624–658 DOI: 10.1521/soco.2019.37.6.624
Brannon, S. M., & Gawronski, B. (2017). A second chance for first impressions? Exploring the context (in)dependent updating of implicit evaluations. *Social Psychological and Personality Science*, 8(3), 275–283. https://doi.org/10.1177/1948550616673875
Briñol, P., & Petty, R. E. (2009). Persuasion: Insights from the self-validation hypothesis. In M. P. Zanna (Ed.), *Advances in experimental social psychology* (vol. 41, pp. 69–118). Elsevier.
Briñol, P., DeMarree, K. G., & Petty, R. E. (2015). Validating a primed identity leads to expectations of group-relevant outcomes. *International Journal of Social Psychology*, 30(3), 614–630. https://doi.org/10.1080/02134748.2015.1065086
Briñol, P., Petty, R. E., & Barden, J. (2007). Happiness versus sadness as a determinant of thought confidence in persuasion: A self-validation analysis. *Journal of Personality and Social Psychology*, 93, 711–727.

Briñol, P., Petty, R. E., & Belding, J. (2017). Objectification of people and thoughts: An attitude change perspective. *British Journal of Social Psychology*, 56(2), 233–249. https://doi.org/10.1111/bjso.12183

Briñol, P., Petty, R. E., Gandarillas, B., & Moreno, L. (2020). Are positive interventions always beneficial? *Spanish Journal of Psychology*, 23(e23), 1–9. https://doi.org/10.1017/SJP.2020.21

Briñol, P., Petty, R. E., Santos, D., & Mello, J. (2018). Meaning moderates the persuasive effect of physical actions: Buying, selling, touching, carrying, and cleaning thoughts as if they were commercial products. *Journal of the Association for Consumer Research*, 2(4), 460–471. https://doi.org/10.1086/693561

Briñol, P., Petty, R. E., Stavraki, M., Lamprinakos, G., Wagner, B. C., & Díaz, D. (2018). Affective and cognitive validation of thoughts: An appraisal perspective on anger, disgust, surprise, and awe. *Journal of Personality and Social Psychology*, 114(5), 693–718. https://doi.org/10.1037/pspa0000118

Briñol, P., Petty, R. E., & Wagner, B. C. (2009). Body postures effects on self-evaluation: A self-validation approach. *European Journal of Social Psychology*, 39(6), 1053–1064. https://doi.org/10.1002/ejsp.607

Briñol, P., Petty, R. E., & Wheeler, S. C. (2006). Discrepancies between explicit and implicit self-concepts: Consequences for information processing. *Journal of Personality and Social Psychology*, 91(1), 154–170. https://doi.org/10.1037/0022-3514.91.1.154

Brown, R., & Hewstone, M. (2005). An integrative theory of intergroup contact. *Advances in Experimental Social Psychology*, 37, 255–343. DOI: 10.1016/S0065-2601(05)37005-5

Cacioppo, J. T., & Petty, R. E. (1982). The need for cognition. *Journal of Personality and Social Psychology*, 42(1), 116–131. https://doi.org/10.1037/0022-3514.42.1.116

Cancela, A., Briñol, P., & Petty, R. E., (2020). Hedonic vs. epistemic goals in processing persuasive communications: Revisiting the classic personal involvement by argument quality interaction. *Unpublished Manuscript*. Universidad Autónoma de Madrid

Cárdaba, M. M. A., Briñol, P., Horcajo, J., & Petty, R. E. (2013). The effect of need for cognition on the stability of prejudiced attitudes toward South American immigrants. *Psicothema*, 25(1), 73–78. https://doi.org/10.7334/psicothema2012.107

Cárdaba, M. M. A., Briñol, P., Horcajo, J., & Petty, R. E. (2014). Changing prejudiced attitudes by thinking about persuasive messages: Implications for resistance. *Journal of Applied Social Psychology*, 44(5), 343–353. https://doi.org/10.1111/jasp.12225

Carpenter, C. J. (2015). A meta-analysis of the ELM's argument quality X processing type predictions. *Human Communication Research*, 41(4), 501–534. https://doi.org/10.1111/hcre.12054

Chaiken, S. (1987). The heuristic model of persuasion. In M. P. Zanna, J. M. Olson, & C. P. Herman (Eds.), *Social influence: The Ontario symposium* (Vol. 3, pp. 143–177). Hillsdale, NJ: Erlbaum.

Clark, J. K., & Thiem, K. C. (2015). Group communicators, perceived entitativity, and persuasion: A self-validation analysis. *Journal of Experimental Social Psychology*, 61, 5–11. https://doi.org/10.1016/j.jesp.2015.06.005

Clark, J. K. & Thiem, K. C. (2018). Stereotype validation and intellectual performance: Negative implications for future achievement. *Self and Identity*, 17, 37–55.

Clark, J. K., Thiem, K. C., Barden, J., Stuart, J. O., & Evans, A. T. (2015). Stereotype validation: The effects of activating negative sterotypes after intellectual performance. *Journal of Personality and Social Psychology*, 108(4), 531–552. https://doi.org/10.1037/a0038887

Clark, J. K., Thiem, K. C., & Kang, S. (2017). Positive Stereotype Validation: The Bolstering Effects of Activating Positive Stereotypes After Intellectual Performance. *Personality and Social Psychology Bulletin, 43*, 1630–1642.

Clark, J. K., Wegener, D. T., Briñol, P., & Petty, R. E. (2009). Discovering that the shoe fits: The self-validating role of stereotypes. *Psychological Science, 20*(7), 846–852. https://doi.org/10.1111/j.1467-9280.2009.02375.x

Clark, J. K., Wegener, D. T., Sawicki, V., Petty, R. E., & Briñol, P. (2013). Evaluating the message or the messenger? Implications for self-validation in persuasion. *Personality and Social Psychology Bulletin, 39*(12), 1571–1584. https://doi.org/10.1177/0146167213499238

Clarkson, J. J., Tormala, Z. L., & Rucker, D. D. (2008). A new look at the consequences of attitude certainty: The amplification hypothesis. *Journal of Personality and Social Psychology, 95*(4), 810–825. https://doi.org/10.1037/a0013192

Crites, S., Fabrigar, L., & Petty, R. E. (1994). Measuring the affective and cognitive properties of attitudes: Conceptual and methodological issues. *Personality and Social Psychology Bulletin, 20*(6), 619–634. https://doi.org/10.1177/0146167294206001

Cvencek, D., Meltzoff, A. N., Maddox, C. D., Nosek, B. A., Rudman, L. A., Devos, T., Dunham, Y., Baron, A. S., Steffens, M. C., Lane, K., Horcajo, J., Ashburn-Nardo, L., Quinby, A., Srivastava, S. B., Schmidt, K., Aidman, E., Tang, E., Farnham, S., Mellott, D. S., Banaji, M. R., & Greenwald, A. G. (2020). Meta-an. alytic use of balanced identity theory to validate the implicit association test. *Personality and Social Psychology Bulletin.* https://doi.org/10.1177/0146167220916631

DeMarree, K. G., Briñol, P., & Petty, R. E. (2014b). The effects of power on prosocial outcomes: A self-validation analysis. *Journal of Economic Psychology, 41*, 20–30. https://doi.org/10.1016/j.joep.2012.07.005

DeMarree, K. G., Briñol, P., & Petty, R. E. (2015). Reducing subjective ambivalence by creating doubt: A metacognitive approach. *Social Psychological and Personality Science, 6*(7), 731–739. https://doi.org/10.1177/1948550615581497

DeMarree, K. G., Petty, R. E., Briñol, P., & Xia, J. (in press). Documenting individual differences in the propensity to hold attitudes with certainty. *Journal of Personality and Social Psychology.* http://dx.doi.org/10.1037/pspa0000241

DeMarree, K. G., Wheeler, C. S., Briñol, P., & Petty, R. E. (2014). Wanting other attitudes: Actual-desired attitude discrepancies predict feelings of ambivalence and ambivalence consequences. *Journal of Experimental Social Psychology, 53*, 5–18. https://doi.org/10.1016/j.jesp.2014.02.001

Devine, P. G. (1989). Stereotypes and prejudice: Their automatic and controlled components. *Journal of Personality and Social Psychology, 56*(1), 5–18. https://doi.org/10.1037/0022-3514.56.1.5

Dixon, J., Durrheim, K., Tredoux, C., Tropp, L. R., Clack, B., & Eaton, E. (2010). A paradox of integration? Interracial contact, prejudice reduction and black South Africans' perceptions of racial discrimination. *Journal of Social Issues, 66*(2), 401–416. https://doi.org/10.1111/j.1540-4560.2010.01652.x

Dixon, J., Levine, M., Reicher, S., & Durrheim, K. (2012). Beyond prejudice: Are negative evaluations the problem and is getting us to like one another more the solution? *Behavioral and Brain Sciences, 35*(6), 411–466. https://doi.org/10.1017/S0140525X11002214

Dovidio, J. E., Schellhaas, F. M. H., & Pearson, A. R. (2019). The role of attitudes in intergroup relationships. In D. Albarracín & B. T. Johnson (Eds.), *Handbook of Attitudes* (Vol. 2, 2nd ed., pp. 419–454). Routledge.

Dovidio, J. F., Gaertner, S. L., & Kawakami, K. (2003). The contact hypothesis: The past, present, and the future. *Group Processes and Intergroup Relations*, 6(1), 5–21. https://doi.org/10.1177/1368430203006001009

Dunton, B. C., & Fazio, R. H. (1997). An individual difference measure of motivation to control prejudiced reactions. *Personality and Social Psychology Bulletin*, 23(3), 316–326. https://doi.org/10.1177/0146167297233009

Durso, G., Petty, R. E., Briñol, P., Hinsenkamp, L., Sawicki, V., & Siev, J. (2020). *Predictably unpredictable people: Expecting ambivalence in social evaluation* [unpublished manuscript]. Ohio State University

Durso, Geoffrey R. O.., Briñol, P., & Petty, R. E. (2016). From power to inaction: Ambivalence gives pause to the powerful. *Psychological Science*, 27, 1660–1666.

Ehrke, F., Berthold, A., & Steffens, M. C. (2014). How diversity training can change attitudes: Increaing perceived complexity of superordinate groups to improve intergroup relations. *Journal of Experimental Social Psychology*, 53, 193–206. https://doi.org/10.1016/j.jesp.2014.03.013

Erb, H., Bohner, G., Rank, S., & Einwiller, S. (2002). Processing minority and majority communications: The role of conflict with prior attitudes. *Personality and Social Psychology Bulletin*, 28(9), 1172–1182. https://doi.org/10.1177/01461672022812003

Fazio, R. H. (1990). Multiple Processes by which Attitudes Guide Behavior: The Mode Model as an Integrative Framework. In M. Zanna (Ed.), *Advances in experimental social psychology* (Vol.23, pp. 75-109). San Diego, CA: Academic Press.

Fleming, M. A., Petty, R. E., & White, P. (2005). Stigmatized targets and evaluation: Prejudice as a determinant of attribute scrutiny and polarization. *Personality and Social Psychology Bulletin*, 4(4), 496–507. https://doi.org/10.1177/0146167204271585

Forscher, P. S., & Devine, P. G. (2014). Breaking the prejudice habit: Automaticity and control in the context of a long-term goal. In J. Sherman, B. Gawronski, & Y. Trope (Eds.), *Dual-process theories of the social mind* (pp. 468–482). Guildford Press.

Gandarillas, B., Requero, B., Briñol, P., & Rojo, B. (2014). El efecto de la responsabilidad organizacional sobre las actitudes hacia la contratación de personas con discapacidad. *Universitas Psychologica*, 13(4), 1615-1624. doi:http://dx.doi.org/10.11144/Javeriana.UPSY13-4.eroa

Gawronski, B., & Bodenhausen, V. (2006). Associative and propositional processes in evaluation: An integrative review of implicit and explicit attitude change. *Psychological Bulletin*, 132(5), 692–731. https://doi.org/10.1037/0033-2909.132.5.692

Gawronski, B., Morrison, M., Phills, C. E., & Galdi, S. (2017). Temporal stability of implicit and explicit measures: A longitudinal analysis. *Personality and Social Psychology Bulletin*, 43(3), 300–312. https://doi.org/10.1177/0146167216684131

Geers, A. L., Briñol, P., & Petty, R. E. (2019). An analysis of the basic processes of formation and change of placebo expectations. *Review of General Psychology*, 23 (2), 211–229. https://doi.org/10.1037/gpr0000171

Glaser, T., Dickel, N., Liersch, B., Rees, J., Süssenbach, P., & Bohner, G. (2015). Lateral attitude change. *Personality and Social Psychological Review*, 19(3), 257–276. https://doi.org/10.1177/1088868314546489

Glick, P., & Fiske, S. T. (1996). The ambivalent sexism inventory: Differentiating hostile and benevolent sexism. *Journal of Personality and Social Psychology*, 70(3), 491–512. https://doi.org/10.1037/0022-3514.70.3.491

Greenwald, A. G. (1968). Cognitive learning, cognitive response to persuasion, and attitude change. In A. Greenwald, T. Brock, & T. Ostrom (Eds.), *Psychological foundations of attitudes* (pp. 148–170). Academic Press.

Greenwald, A. G., McGhee, D. E., & Schwartz, J. L. K. (1998). Measuring individual differences in implicit cognition: The implicit association task. *Journal of Personality and Social Psychology, 74*(6), 1464–1480. https://doi.org/10.1037/0022-3514.74.6.1464

Gregg, A. P., Seibt, B., & Banaji, M. R. (2006). Easier done than undone: Asymmetry in the malleability of implicit preferences. *Journal of Personality and Social Psychology, 90*(1), 1–20. https://doi.org/10.1037/0022-3514.90.1.1

Guyer, J. J., Briñol, P., Petty, R. E., & Horcajo, J. (2019). Nonverbal behavior of persuasive sources: A multiple process analysis. *Journal of Nonverbal Behavior, 23*, 211–229. DOI: 10.1007/s10919-018-00291-x

Hahn, A., & Gawronski, B. (2019). Facing one's implicit biases: From awareness to acknowledgement. *Journal of Personality and Social Psychology, 116*(5), 769–794. https://doi.org/10.1037/pspi0000155

Haugtvedt, C. P., & Petty, R. E. (1992). Personality and persuasion: Need for cognition moderates the persistence and resistance of attitude changes. *Journal of Personality and Social Psychology, 63*(2), 308–319. https://doi.org/10.1037/0022-3514.63.2.308

Horcajo, J., Briñol, P., & Petty, R. E. (2010b). Consumer persuasion: Indirect change and implicit balance. *Psychology and Marketing, 27*(10), 938–963. https://doi.org/10.1002/mar.20367

Horcajo, J., Briñol, P., & Petty, R. E. (2014). Multiple roles for majority versus minority source status on persuasion when source status follows the message. *Social Influence, 9*(1), 37–51. https://doi.org/10.1080/15534510.2012.743485

Horcajo, J., Petty, R. E., & Briñol, P. (2010a). The effects of majority versus minority source status on persuasion: A self-validation analysis. *Journal of Personality and Social Psychology, 99*(3), 498–512. https://doi.org/10.1037/a0018626

Horcajo, J., Santos, D., Guyer, J. J., & Moreno, L. (2019). Changing attitudes and intentions related to doping: An analysis of individual differences in need for cognition. *Journal of Sports Sciences, 37*(24), 2835–2843. https://doi.org/10.1080/02640414.2019.1665876

Hovland, C. I., Janis, I. L., & Kelley, H. H. (1953). *Communication and persuasion: Psychological studies of opinion change*. New Haven, CT: Yale University Press.

Huntsinger, J. R. (2013). Incidental experiences of affective coherence and incoherence influence persuasion. *Personality and Social Psychology Bulletin, 39*(6), 792–802. https://doi.org/10.1177/0146167213482588

Huntsinger, J. R., Isbell, L. M., & Clore, G. L. (2014). The affective control of thought: Malleable, not fixed. *Psychological Review, 121*(4), 600–618. https://doi.org/10.1037/a0037669

Johnson, I., Petty, R. E., Briñol, P., & See, Y. H. M. (2017). Persuasive message scrutiny as a function of implicit-explicit discrepancies in racial attitudes. *Journal of Experimental Social Psychology, 70*, 222–234. https://doi.org/10.1016/j.jesp.2016.11.007

Johnson, I. R., Kopp, B. M., & Petty, R. E. (2018). Just say no! (and mean it): Meaningful negation as a tool to modify automatic racial attitudes. *Group Processes and Intergroup Relations, 21*(1), 88–110. https://doi.org/10.1177/1368430216647189

Jordan, C. H., Whitfield, M., & Zeigler-Hill, V. (2007). Intuition and the correspondence between implicit and explicit self-esteem. *Journal of Personality and Social Psychology, 93*(6), 1067–1079. https://doi.org/10.1037/0022-3514.93.6.1067

Kaiser, C. R., Major, B., & McCoy, S. K. (2004). Expectations about the future and the emotional consequences of perceiving prejudice. *Personality and Social Psychology Bulletin, 30*(2), 173–184. https://doi.org/10.1177/0146167203259927

Katz, D. (1960). The functional approach to the study of attitudes. *Public Opinion Quarterly, 24*(2), 163–204. https://doi.org/10.1086/266945

Katz, I., & Hass, R. G. (1988). Racial ambivalence and American value conflict: Correlational and priming studies of dual cognitive structures. *Journal of Personality and Social Psychology, 55*(6), 893–905. https://doi.org/10.1037/0022-3514.55.6.893

Kim, J. Y., Fitzsimons, G. M., & Kay, A. C. (2018). Lean in messages increase attributions of women's responsibility for gender inequality. *Journal of Personality and Social Psychology, 115*(6), 974–1001. https://doi.org/10.1037/pspa0000129

Kleiman, T., & Hassin, R. R. (2013). When conflicts are good: Nonconscious Goal conflicts reduce confirmatory thinking. *Journal of Personality and Social Psychology, 105*(3), 374–387. https://doi.org/10.1037/a0033608

Kteily, N., Bruneau, E., Waytz, A., & Cotterill, S. (2015). The ascent of man: Theoretical and empirical evidence for blatant dehumanization. *Journal of Personality and Social Psychology, 109*(5), 901–931. https://doi.org/10.1037/pspp0000048

Lai, C. K., Hoffman, K. M., & Nosek, B. A. (2013). Reducing implicit prejudice. *Social and Personality Psychology Compass, 7*(5), 315–330. https://doi.org/10.1111/spc3.12023

Legault, L., Gutsell, J. N., & Inzlicht, M. (2011). Ironic effects of anti-prejudice messages: How motivational interventions can reduce (but also increase) prejudice. *Journal of Experimental Social Psychology, 33*(November), 244–275. DOI: 10.1177/0956797611427918

Leippe, M. R., & Eisenstadt, D. (1994). Generalization of dissonance reduction: Decreasing prejudice thought induced compliance. *Journal of Personality and Social Psychology, 67*(3), 395–413. https://doi.org/10.1037/0022-3514.67.3.395

Lerner, J. S., & Keltner, D. (2000). Beyond valence: Toward a model of emotion-specific influences on judgement and choice. *Cognition & Emotion, 14*(4), 473–493. https://doi.org/10.1080/026999300402763

Lick, D. J., Alter, A. L., & Freeman, J. B. (2017). Superior pattern of dectectors efficiently learn, activate, apply, and update social stereotypes. *Journal of Experimental Psychology: General, 147*(2), 209–227. https://doi.org/10.1037/xge0000349

Loersch, C., McCaslin, M., & Petty, R. E. (2011). Exploring the impact of social judgeability concerns on the interplay of associative and deliberative attitude processes. *Journal of Experimental Social Psychology, 47*(5), 1029–1032. https://doi.org/10.1016/j.jesp.2011.03.024

Loughnan, S., Haslam, N., Murnane, T., Vaes, J., Reynolds, C., & Suitner, C. (2010). Objectification leads to depersonalization: The denial of mind and moral concern to objectified others. *European Journal of Social Psychology, 40*(5), 709–717. https://doi.org/10.1002/ejsp.755

Luttrell, A., Petty, R. E., & Briñol, P. (2016). Ambivalence and certainty can interact to predict attitude stability over time. *Journal of Experimental Social Psychology, 63*(december), 56–68. https://doi.org/10.1016/j.jesp.2015.11.008

Luttrell, A., Petty, R. E., & Briñol, P. (in press). The interactive effects of ambivalence and certainty on political opinion stability. *Journal of Social and Political Psychology*.

Maddux, W. W., Barden, J., Brewer, M. B., & Petty, R. E. (2005). Saying no to negativity: The effects of context and motivation to control prejudice on automatic evaluative responses. *Journal of Experimental Social Psychology*, *41*(1), 19–35. https://doi.org/10.1016/j.jesp.2004.05.002

Madon, S., Jussin, L., Guyll, M., Nofziger, H., Salib, E. R., Willard, J., & Scherr, K. C. (2018). The accumulation of stereotype-based self-fulfilling prophecies. *Journal of Personality and Social Psychology*, *115*(5), 285–844. https://doi.org/10.1037/pspi0000142

Maio, G. R., Bell, D. W., & Essess, V. M. (1996). Ambivalence in persuasion: The processing of messages about immigrant groups. *Journal of Experimental Social Psychology*, *32*(6), 513–536. https://doi.org/10.1006/jesp.1996.0023

Maio, G. R., Greenland, K., Bernard, M., & Esses, V. M. (2001). Effects of intergroup ambivalence on information processing: The role of physiological arousal. *Group Processes and Intergroup Relations*, *4*(4), 355–372. https://doi.org/10.1177/1368430201004004005

Maio, G. R., Haddock, G., & Verplanken, B. (2019). *The psychology of attitudes and attitude change*. Sage.

Maio, G. R., Pakizeh, A., Cheung, W., & Rees, K. J. (2009). Changing, priming, and acting on values: Effects via motivational relations in a circular model. *Journal of Personality and Social Psychology*, *97*(4), 699–715. https://doi.org/10.1037/a0016420

Major, B., Hunger, J. M., Bunyan, D. P., & Miller, C. T. (2014). Ironic effects of weight stigma. *Journal of Experimental Social Psychology*, *51*(March), 74–80. https://doi.org/10.1016/j.jesp.2013.11.009

Mann, T. C., & Ferguson, M. (2016). Reversing implicit first impressions through reinterpretation after a two day delay. *Journal of Experimental Social Psychology*, *68*(June), 122–127. https://doi.org/10.1016/j.jesp.2016.06.004

Martin, R., & Hewstone, M. (2008). Majority versus minority influence, message processing and attitude change. *Advances in Experimental Social Psychology*, *40*, 237–326. DOI. 10.1016/S0065-2601(07)00005-6.

McGuire, W. J. (1981). The probabilogical model of cognitive structure and attitude change. In R. E. Petty, T. M. Ostrom, & T. C. Brock (Eds.), *Cognitive responses in persuasion*, (pp. 291–307). Erlbaum.

Meleady, R., Crisp, R. J., Hodson, G., & Earle, M. (2019). On the generalization of intergroup contact: A taxonomy of transfer effects. *Current Directions in Psychological Science*, *28*, 430–435. https://doi.org/10.1177/0963721419848682,

Monteith, M. J. (1993). Self-regulation of prejudiced responses: Implications for progress in prejudice-reduction efforts. *Journal of Personality and Social Psychology*, *65*(3), 469–485. https://doi.org/10.1037/0022-3514.65.3.469

Moreno, L., Briñol, P., Petty, R. E., & Paredes, B. (2020). The impact of elaboration on spreading and generalization of attitude change. *Unpublished Manuscript*. Universidad Autónoma de Madrid

Moscovici, S. (1985). Social influence and conformity. In G. Lindsey & E. Aronson (Eds.), *The handbook of social psychology* (Vol. 2, 3rd ed., pp. 347–412). Random House.

Moyyer-Guse', E. (2008). Toward a theory of entertainment persuasion: Explaining the persuasive effects of entertainment-education messages. *Communication Theory*, *18*(3), 407–425. https://doi.org/10.1111/j.1468-2885.2008.00328.x

Murphy, M. C., Kroeper, K. M., & Ozier, E. (2018). Prejudiced places: How contexts shape inequality and how we can change them. *Policy Insights from the Behavioral and Brain Sciences*, 5(1), 66–74. https://doi.org/10.1177/2372732217748671

O'Brien, G. V. (2003). People with cognitive disabilities: The argument from marginal cases and social work ethics. *Social Work*, 48(3), 331–337. https://doi.org/10.1093/sw/48.3.331

Paluck, E. L., & Green, D. P. (2009). Prejudice reduction: What works? A review and assessment of research and practice. *Annual Review of Psychology*, 60(1), 339–367. https://doi.org/10.1146/annurev.psych.60.110707.163607

Paolini, S., Crisp, R. J., & McIntyre, K. (2009). Accountability moderates member-to-group generalization: Testing a dual process model of stereotype change. *Journal of Experimental Social Psychology*, 45(4), 676–685. https://doi.org/10.1016/j.jesp.2009.03.005

Paredes, B., Santos, D., Briñol, P., Gómez, A., & Petty, R. E. (2019). The impact of meta-cognitive certainty on the relationship between identity fusion and endorsement of extreme pro-group behavior. *Self and Identity*. DOI: 10.1080/15298868.2019.1681498

Paredes, B., Santos, D., Briñol, P., Guyer, J. J., Moreno, L., & Petty, R. E. (2020). The influence of perceived knowledge on hiring decisions of job candidates. *Unpublished Manuscript*. Universidad Autónoma de Madrid.

Pettigrew, T. F. (2009). Secondary transfer effect of contact: Do intergroup contact effects spread to noncontacted outgroups? *Social Psychology*, 40(2), 55–65. https://doi.org/10.1027/1864-9335.40.2.55

Pettigrew, T. F., & Tropp, L. (2006). A meta-analytic test of intergroup contact theory. *Journal of Personality and Social Psychology*, 90(5), 51–783. https://doi.org/10.1037/0022-3514.90.5.751

Petty, R. E., & Wegener, D. T. (1991). Thought systems, argument quality, and persuasion. In R. S. Wyer & T. K. Srull (Eds.), *Advances in social cognition* (Vol. 4, pp. 147–161). Erlbaum.

Petty, R. E., Haugtvedt, C., & Smith, S. M. (1995). Elaboration as a determinant of attitude strength: Creating attitudes that are persistent, resistant, and predictive of behavior. In R. E. Petty & J. A. Krosnick (Eds.), *Attitude strength: Antecedents and conseqeunces* (pp. 455–488). Erlbaum.

Petty, R. E. (2001). Subtle influences on judgments and behaviors: Who is most susceptible? In J. Forgas & K. D. Williams (Eds.), *Social influence: Direct and indirect processes* (pp. 129–146). Psychology Press.

Petty, R. E., & Briñol, P. (2010). Attitude structure and change: Implications for implicit measures. In B. Gawronski & B. K. Payne (Eds.), *Handbook of implicit social cognition: Measurement, theory, and applications* (pp. 335–352). Guilford Press.

Petty, R. E., Briñol, P., & Johnson, I. (2012). Implicit ambivalence. In B. Gawronski & F. Strack (Eds.), *Cognitive consistency: A fundamental principle in social cognition* (pp. 178–201). Guilford Press.

Petty, R. E., & Briñol, P. (2012). The Elaboration Likelihood Model. In P. A. M. Van Lange, A. Kruglanski, & E. T. Higgins (Eds.), *Handbook of theories of social psychology* (Vol. 1, pp. 224–245). Sage.

Petty, R. E., & Briñol, P. (2020). A process approach to influencing attitudes and changing behavior: Revisiting classic findings in persuasion and popular interventions. In J. P. Forgas, W. D. Crano, & K. Fiedler (Eds.), *Applications of social psychology: How social psychology can contribute to real world problems* (pp. 82–103). Psychology Press.

Petty, R. E., & Briñol, P. (2006). A meta-cognitive approach to "implicit" and "explicit" evaluations: Comment on Gawronski and Bodenhausen (2006). *Psychological Bulletin, 132*, 740–744.

Petty, R. E., & Briñol, P. (2008). Persuasion: From single to multiple to meta-cognitive processes. *Perspectives on Psychological Science, 3*(2), 137–147. https://doi.org/10.1111/j.1745-6916.2008.00071.x

Petty, R. E., & Briñol, P. (2015). Emotion and persuasion: Cognitive and meta-cognitive processes impact attitudes. *Cognition and Emotion, 29*(1), 1–26. https://doi.org/10.1080/02699931.2014.967183

Petty, R. E., Briñol, P., & DeMarree, K. G. (2007). The meta-cognitive model (MCM) of attitudes: Implications for attitude measurement, change, and strength. *Social Cognition, 25*(5), 657–686. https://doi.org/10.1521/soco.2007.25.5.657

Petty, R. E., Briñol, P., & Tormala, Z. L. (2002). Thought confidence as a determinant of persuasion: The self-validation hypothesis. *Journal of Personality and Social Psychology, 82*(5), 722–741. https://doi.org/10.1037/0022-3514.82.5.722

Petty, R. E., & Cacioppo, J. T. (1979). Issue involvement can increase or decrease persuasion by enhancing message-relevant cognitive responses. *Journal of Personality and Social Psychology, 37*(10), 1915–1926. https://doi.org/10.1037/0022-3514.37.10.1915

Petty, R. E., & Cacioppo, J. T. (1986). Communication and persuasion: Central and peripheral routes to attitude change. New York: Springer-Verlag.

Petty, R. E., & Cacioppo, J. T. (1990). Involvement and persuasion: Tradition versus integration. *Psychological Bulletin, 107*(3), 367–374. https://doi.org/10.1037/0033-2909.107.3.367

Petty, R. E., DeMarree, K. G., Briñol, P., Horcajo, J., & Strathman, A. J. (2008). Need for cognition can magnify or attenuate priming effects in social judgment. *Personality and Social Psychology Bulletin, 34*(7), 900–912. https://doi.org/10.1177/0146167208316692

Petty, R. E., Fleming, M. A., & White, P. H. (1999). Stigmatized sources and persuasion: Prejudice as a determinant of argument scrutiny. *Journal of Personality and Social Psychology, 76*(1), 19–34. https://doi.org/10.1037/0022-3514.76.1.19

Petty, R. E., Harkins, S. G., & Williams, K. D. (1980). The effects of group diffusion of cognitive effort on attitudes: An information processing view. *Journal of Personality and Social Psychology, 38*(1), 81–92. https://doi.org/10.1037/0022-3514.38.1.81

Petty, R. E., & Krosnick, J. A. (Eds.). (1995). *Attitude strength: Antecedents and consequences.* Erlbaum.

Petty, R. E., Ostrom, T. M., & Brock, T. C. (Eds.). (1981). *Cognitive responses in persuasion.* Erlbaum.

Petty, R. E., Tormala, Z. L., Briñol, P., & Jarvis, W. B. G. (2006). Implicit ambivalence from attitude change: An exploration of the PAST Model. *Journal of Personality and Social Psychology, 90*(1), 21–41. https://doi.org/10.1037/0022-3514.90.1.21

Petty, R. E., Wells, G. L., & Brock, T. C. (1976). Distraction can enhance or reduce yielding to propaganda: Thought disruption versus effort justification. *Journal of Personality and Social Psychology, 34*(5), 874–884. https://doi.org/10.1037/0022-3514.34.5.874

Phills, C. E., Kawakami, K., Tabi, E., Nadolny, D., & Inzlicht, M. (2011). Mind the gap: Increasing associations between the self and Blacks with approach behaviors. *Journal of Personality and Social Psychology, 100*(2), 197–210. https://doi.org/10.1037/a0022159

Pinel, E. C., & Long, A. E. (2012). When I's meet: Sharing subjective experience with someone from the out-group. *Personality and Social Psychology Bulletin, 38*(3), 296–307. https://doi.org/10.1177/0146167211433878

Plant, A. E., & Devine, P. G. (1998). Internal and external motivation to respond without prejudice. *Journal of Personality and Social Psychology, 75*(3), 811–832. https://doi.org/10.1037/0022-3514.75.3.811

Priester, J. R., & Petty, R. E. (1996). The gradual threshold model of ambivalence: Relating the positive and negative bases of attitudes to subjective ambivalence. *Journal of Personality and Social Psychology, 71*(3), 431–449. https://doi.org/10.1037/0022-3514.71.3.431

Priester, J. R., & Petty, R. E. (2001). Extending the bases of subjective attitudinal ambivalence: Interpersonal and intrapersonal antecedents of evaluative tension. *Journal of Personality and Social Psychology, 80*(1), 19–34. https://doi.org/10.1037/0022-3514.80.1.19

Ranganath, K. A., Smith, C. T., & Nosek, B. A. (2008). Distinguishing automatic and controlled components of attitudes from direct and indirect measurement methods. *Journal of Experimental Social Psychology, 44*(2), 386–396. https://doi.org/10.1016/j.jesp.2006.12.008

Ratliff, K. A., & Nosek, B. A. (2011). Negativity and out group biases in attitude formation and transfer. *Personality and Social Psychology Bulletin, 37*(12), 1692–1703. https://doi.org/10.1177/0146167211420168

Rees, L., Rothman, N. B., Lehavy, R., & Sanchez-Burks, J. (2013). The ambivalent mind can be a wise mind: Emotional ambivalence increases judgment accuracy. *Journal of Experimental Social Psychology, 49*(3), 360–367. https://doi.org/10.1016/j.jesp.2012.12.017

Requero, B., Briñol, P., & Petty, R. (2020a). Appraisals of hope vs. helplessness are capable of moderating the effect of thoughts on attitudes and behavior. *Unpublished Manuscript.* Universidad Autónoma de Madrid.

Requero, B., Santos, D., Paredes, B., Briñol, P., & Petty, R. E. (2020b). Attitudes toward hiring people with disabilities: A meta-cognitive approach to persuasion. *Journal of Applied Social Psychology, 50*(5), 276–288. https://doi.org/10.1111/jasp.12658

Rohmer, O., & Louvet, E. (2018). Implicit stereotyping against people with disability. *Group Processes and Intergroup Relations, 21*(1), 127–140. https://doi.org/10.1177/1368430216638536

Rucker, D. D., Tormala, Z. L., Petty, R. E., & Briñol, P. (2014). Consumer conviction and commitment: An appraisal-based framework for attitude certainty. *Journal of Consumer Psychology, 24*, 119–136. 1

Rudolph, A., & Hilbert, A. (2017). The effects of obesity-related health messages on explicit and implicit weight bias. *Frontiers, 7*, 2064. https://doi.org/10.3389/fpsyg.2016.02064

Rydell, R. J., & McConnell, A. R. (2006). Understanding implicit and explicit attitude change: A systems of reasoning analysis. *Journal of Personality and Social Psychology, 91*(6), 995–1008. https://doi.org/10.1037/0022-3514.91.6.995

Rydell, R. J., McConnell, A. R., & Mackie, D. M. (2008). Consequences of discrepant explicit and implicit attitudes: Cognitive dissonance and increased information processing. *Journal of Experimental Social Psychology, 44*(6), 1526–1532. https://doi.org/10.1016/j.jesp.2008.07.006

Saguy, T., Tausch, N., Dovidio, J. F., & Pratto, F. (2009). The irony of harmony: Intergroup contact can produce false expectations for equality. *Psychological Science, 20*(1), 114–121. https://doi.org/10.1111/j.1467-9280.2008.02261.x

Santos, D., Briñol, P., Petty, R. E., Gandarillas, B., & Mateos, R. (2019). Trait aggressiveness predicting aggressive behavior: The moderating role of meta-cognitive certainty. *Aggressive Behavior, 45*(3), 255–264. https://doi.org/10.1002/ab.21815

Santos, D., Requero, B., Martínez, R., Briñol, P., & Petty, R. E. (2020, February). Changing prejudiced attitudes through meta-cognitive processes of persuasion. *Presented at the Attitudes Preconference of the Society for Personality and Social Psychology*. Vegas, Nevada.

Santos, D., & Rivera, R. G. (2015). The accessibility of justice-related concepts can validate intentions to punish. *Social Influence, 10*(3), 180–192. https://doi.org/10.1080/15534510.2015.1031170

Sassenberg, K., & Wieber, F. (2005). Don't ignore the other half: The impact of ingroup identification on implicit measures of prejudice. *European Journal of Social Psychology, 35*(5), 621–632. https://doi.org/10.1002/ejsp.267

Savary, J., Keliman, T., Hassin, R. R., & Dhar, R. (2015). Positive consequences of conflict on decision making: When a conflict mindset facilitates choice. *Journal of Experimental Psychology: General, 144*(1), 1–6. https://doi.org/10.1037/a0038551

Schmader, T., & Sedikides, C. (2018). State authenticity as fit to environment (SAFE): Implications of social identity for fit, authenticity, and self-segregation. *Personality and Social Psychology Review, 22*(3), 228–259. https://doi.org/10.1177/1088868317734080

Schultz, J. R., & Maddox, K. B. (2013). Shooting the messenger to spite the message? Exploring reaction to claims of racial bias. *Personality and Social Psychology Bulletin, 39*(3), 346–358. https://doi.org/10.1177/0146167212475223

Scroggins, W. A., Mackie, D. M., Allen, T. J., & Sherman, J. W. (2016). Reducing prejudice with labels: Hared group membership attenuate implicit bias and expand implicit group boudaries. *Personality and Social Psychology Bulletin, 42*(2), 219–229. https://doi.org/10.1177/0146167215621048

Sherman, J., Gawronski, B., & Trope, Y. (2012). Dual-process theories of the social mind. New York, NY: Guildford Press.

Shoots-Reinhard, B. L., Petty, R. E., DeMarree, K. G., & Rucker. D. D. (2015). Personality Certainty and Politics: Increasing the Predictive Utility of Individual-Difference Inventories. *Political Psychology, 36*(4), 415–430.

Smith, C. A., & Ellsworth, P. C. (1985). Patterns of cognitive appraisal in emotion. *Journal of Personality and Social Psychology, 48*(4), 813–838. https://doi.org/10.1037/0022-3514.48.4.813

Smith, C. T., & De Houwer, J. (2014). The impact of persuasive messages on IAT performance is moderated by source attractiveness and likeability. *Social Psychology, 45*(6), 437–448. https://doi.org/10.1027/1864-9335/a000208

Stark, T. H., Flache, A., & Veenstra, R. (2013). Generalization of positive and negative attitudes toward individual to outgroup attitudes. *Personality and Social Psychology Bulletin, 39*(5), 608–622. https://doi.org/10.1177/0146167213480890

Tausch, N., Hewstone, M., Kenworthy, J. B., Psaltis, C., Schmid, K., Popan, J. R., Cairns, E., & Hughes, J. (2010). 'Secondary transfer' effects of intergroup contact: Alternative accounts and underlying processes". *Journal of Personality and Social Psychology, 99*(2), 282–302. https://doi.org/10.1037/a0018553

Teeny, J. D., Siev, J. J., Briñol, P., & Petty, R. E. (in press). A review and conceptual framework for understanding personalized matching effects in persuasion. *Journal of Consumer Psychology*.

Tesser, A. (1978). Self-generated attitude change. In L. Berkowitz (Ed.), *Advances in experimental social psychology* (Vol. 11, pp. 289–338). Academic Press.

Tormala, Z. L., Briñol, P., & Petty, R. E. (2007). Multiple roles for source credibility under high elaboration: It's all in the timing. *Social Cognition, 25*(4), 536–552. https://doi.org/10.1521/soco.2007.25.4.536

Tormala, Z. L., & Petty, R. E. (2001). On-line versus memory based processing: The role of 'need to evaluate' in person perception. *Personality and Social Psychology Bulletin, 12*(12), 1599–1612. https://doi.org/10.1177/01461672012712004

Turner, R. N., & Crisp, R. J. (2010). Imagining intergroup contact reduces implicit prejudice. *Social Psychology, 49*(December), 129–142. https://doi.org/10.1348/014466609X419901

Villegas-Gold, R., & Yoo, H. C. (2014). Coping with discrimination among Mexican American college students. *Journal of Counselling Psychology, 61*(3), 404–413. https://doi.org/10.1037/a0036591

Vornholt, K., Uitdewilligen, S., & Nijhuis, F. J. (2013). Factors affecting the acceptance of people with disabilities at work: A literature review. *Journal of Occupational Rehabilitation, 23*(4), 463–475. https://doi.org/10.1007/s10926-013-9426-0

Walther, E. (2002). Guilty by mere association: Evaluative conditioning and the spreading attitude effect. *Journal of Personality and Social Psychology, 82*(6), 919–934. https://doi.org/10.1037/0022-3514.82.6.919

Wegener, D. T., Clark, J. K., & Petty, R. E. (2006). Not all stereotyping is created equal. Differential consequences of thoughtful versus non-thoughtful stereotyping. *Journal of Personality and Social Psychology, 90*(1), 42–59. https://doi.org/10.1037/0022-3514.90.1.42

White, P., & Harkins, S. G. (1994). Race of source effects in the elaboration likelihood model. *Journal of Personality and Social Psychology, 67*(5), 790–807. https://doi.org/10.1037/0022-3514.67.5.790

Wilson, T. D., Westgate, E. C., Buttrick, N. R., & Gilbert, D. (2019). The mind is its own place: The difficulties and benefits of thinking for pleasure. *Advances in Experimental Social Psychology, 60*(January), 175–221. DOI: 10.1016/bs.aesp.2019.05.001.

Wyer, N. A. (2016). Easier done than undone ... by some of the people some of the time: The role of elaboration in explicit and implicit group preferences. *Journal of Experimental Social Psychology, 63*(March), 77–85. https://doi.org/10.1016/j.jesp.2015.12.006

Xu, N. M., Wright, N., Petty, R. E., & Briñol, P. (2019). Individual differences in the specific motivations to evaluate: Learning and expressing. *Unpublished Manuscript*. Ohio State University.

Ye, Y., & Gawronski, B. (2016). When possessions become part of the self: Ownership and implicit self-object linking. *Journal of Experimental Social Psychology, 64* (May), 72–87. https://doi.org/10.1016/j.jesp.2016.01.012

Author index

Aaker, J. L., 195
Abakoumkin, G., 133, 143, 146
Abcarian, R., 26
Abele, A. E., 232, 244, 256
Abeyta, A. A., 124, 132
Abou-Zeid, A., 40
Abrams, D., 78, 80, 81, 90, 93, 94, 96, 98, 99, 110, 111
Abu-Lughod, L., 40
Acharya, K., 321, 329
Acquisti, A., 11
Adams, G., 67
Adewuya, A. O., 325
Agaibi, C. E., 317
Aguiar-Conraria, L., 77
Aikman, S. N., 240
Ajzen, I., 2
Akerlof, F. G., 78
Alais, D., 286
Ali, R. S., 127
Allen, A. M., 108
Allport, D. A., 293
Allport, G. W., 272, 283, 293, 296, 300
Allum, F., 75, 82, 111
Alowidy, D., 159
Altemeyer, B., 160, 256
Alves, H., 220, 231–234, 237, 240, 242, 243, 246, 249–252, 253
Ambrose, M. L., 135
Ames, D. R., 94
Anderson, C. A., 11, 12, 25, 59
Anderson, C., 202
Anderson, D. L., 124
Anderson, G. T., 124
Andrews, F. M., 225
Anisman, H., 335
Antoniewicz, F., 293
Antonovsky, A., 318
Archer, J., 324
Argyris, C., 27
Arin, C., 42
Armour, M. P., 326
Arndt, J., 124, 127, 129, 134, 140, 158
Arnold, M. B., 230

Aron, A., 145, 146, 334
Aron, E. N., 145, 334
Arrighi, R., 286
Asch, S. E., 217
Aschersleben, G., 283
Asendorpf, J. B., 15
Asher, S. R., 134
Ashton, M. C., 222
Aslani, S., 43, 66, 67
Ataca, B., 42, 46, 57, 85
Augustine, A. A., 222, 223
Aune, R. K., 124
Aust, F., 280
Aveyard, M., 286
Avnet, T., 175, 204
Awh, E., 283
Axelrod, R., 236
Ayanian, A. H., 85, 154

Baas, M., 175
Bäcker, A., 206
Baden, D., 124
Baeyens, F., 272, 276, 280, 281, 296, 297
Bagli, M., 42
Bai, L., 81
Bak, P., 288
Bakan, D., 244
Bakarou, M., 133
Balabanis, G., 151
Balas, R., 300
Baldwin, G. C., 195
Baldwin, M., 125, 150, 155–157
Banaji, M. R., 27, 78
Banfield, E. C., 83, 97
Bar-Anan, Y., 4, 299, 300
Bargh, J. A., 27, 79, 231, 273, 289, 300
Barnes, C. D., 68, 86, 88, 92, 98, 108
Barnes-Holmes, D., 273
Barrett, F. S., 14, 127, 135, 137, 138, 140, 148
Barsalou, L. W., 294
Bartels, D. M., 13
Bartur, L., 328
Başoğlu, M., 321
Batailler, C., 155

AUTHOR INDEX

Batcho, K. I., 124, 132, 134, 140
Batson, C. D., 148
Bauman, C. W., 13
Baumeister, R. F., 10, 27, 130, 218, 257
Beaulieu-Pelletier, G., 159
Becker, D., 194
Becker, E. S., 294
Becker, J. C., 338
Beckers, T., 280, 297
Beersma, B., 43
Begley, C. G., 24
Behnke, M., 178
Beilock, S. L., 294
Beiser, M., 124
Belopolsky, A. V., 283
Bem, D. J., 4
Bennett, M., 98
Bentham, J., 238
Berg, J., 237
Bergeman, C. S., 159
Berger, W., 317
Berinsky, A. J., 12
Berman, L., 218
Berntsen, D., 127, 142
Berntson, G. G., 294
Berry, J. W., 159
Berscheid, E., 244
Best, D., 327
Betts, K. R., 133
Bialobrzeska, O., 124
Biernat, M., 125
Billig, M., 9
Birney, S., 124
Bisconti, T. L., 159
Blader, S. L., 77
Blank, H., 276, 278
Blascovich, J., 175–178, 180, 207, 209
Blask, K., 272, 273, 275, 281–294, 296, 297
Bless, H., 87, 182, 188, 233, 242
Blok, A., 82, 86, 97, 108
Bluemke, M., 293
Boals, A., 333
Boddez, Y., 280
Bodenhausen, G. V., 289, 300
Bohlmeijer, E., 128
Bohner, G., 260
Boiger, M., 66
Bolland, M. J., 22
Boluk, P., 43
Bonanno, G. A., 159, 312

Bond, C. F., 25
Bond, R. N., 175
Booth, R. J., 132
Borkenau, P., 228
Borkowski, W., 45
Bosson, J., 68
Boucher, J., 218, 222, 223
Bouvrette, S. A., 53
Bowdle, B. F., 43, 86
Bower, J. E., 333
Bowers, J., 3
Bowling, A., 145
Bowman, J., 93, 103
Bowman, N. D., 125
Boym, S., 124
Bradley, M. M., 222, 234
Bradshaw, D., 337
Brand, R., 293
Brandimarte, L., 11
Brandt, M. J., 22
Brandt, V., 4, 11
Brans, K., 225
Branscombe, N. R., 322, 333, 334
Bratslavsky, E., 218
Brazy, P. C., 179, 202, 204
Breakwell, G. M., 8
Brebels, L., 137
Breckler, S. J., 10
Brédart, S., 285
Brendl, C. M., 184
Brennan, K. A., 134
Breslau, N., 317
Brett, J., 66
Breuer, J., 125
Breugelmans, S. M., 43
Brewer, M. B., 101, 107, 253
Brewer, W. F., 275
Brewin, C. R., 311
Brim, O. G., 19
Britt, S. H., 5
Brodribb, W., 327
Brown, E. M., 139
Brown, R., 101, 145
Brown, R. P., 43, 86
Bruckmüller, S., 20, 232, 256
Brunstrom, J. M., 278
Brunswik, E., 218, 258, 261
Bryant, F. B., 128
Brysbaert, M., 234
Buhrmester, M., 12

392 AUTHOR INDEX

Bui-Wrzosinska, L., 67
Burgess, C., 223
Burgess, P., 324
Burr, D., 286
Burt, M. R., 333
Burton, F., 78
Buschini, F., 8
Bushman, B. J., 25
Bybee, J., 227
Byrnes, D., 228

Cable, D. M., 142, 205
Cacioppo, J. T., 134, 257, 294, 336
Cacioppo, S., 134
Cadamuro, A., 334
Cahoon, M. B., 127
Cairns, E., 147
Calhoun, L. G., 317, 333, 334
Calvert, J., 8
Camacho, C. J., 180
Camerer, C., 237
Campbell, D. T., 151
Campbell, H., 106, 108
Campbell, J. K., 44
Campbell, R., 335
Campbell, W. K., 132, 140
Canetti, D., 329
Cannizzaro, G., 83
Cantor, N., 51
Cantril, H., 5
Capozza, D., 101
Cappeliez, P., 124
Carey, B., 26
Carlson, R., 11, 13
Carlston, D. E., 244, 259
Carney, D. R., 15
Carr, C., 331
Carvacho, H., 77
Carvallo, M., 68
Castano, E., 150
Cernat, V., 155
Cesario, J., 15, 25, 28
Chaiken, S., 231
Chalabaev, A., 178, 209
Chandler, J., 12
Chandler, M. J., 144, 158
Chang, C. H., 175
Chang, M. X.-L., 337
Chartrand, T. L., 27
Charuvastra, A., 317, 318, 324, 325

Chen, F. F., 81
Chen, X., 125
Cheng, B-S., 81
Cheston, R., 125
Cheung, W. Y., 127, 140, 148, 154, 155, 158
Chisholm, B. J., 135
Chiu, C. Y., 58
Chonody, J. M., 145
Chou, L-F., 81
Christakis, N. A., 12
Christopher, G., 125
Chung, C. K., 132
Cialdini, R. B., 14, 26, 217
Cilibrasi, R. L., 240
Ciziceno, M., 83
Clark, E. V., 227
Clark, H. H., 227
Clark, M., 85, 335
Clarke, F., 124
Clipp, E. C., 333
Cloitre, M., 317, 318, 324, 325
Cohen, D., 39, 40, 41, 43–45, 50, 53, 56, 59, 62, 66, 80, 85, 86, 89
Cohen, J., 3
Cohen, L. H., 317
Cohen, T. R., 149
Cohen-Mansfield, J., 328
Coles, M. G. H., 283
Collins, R. L., 333
Colquitt, J. A., 137
Combs, B., 257
Conlon, D. E., 135, 137
Conner, A. C., 19
Constantin, T., 293
Coon, H. M., 80
Cooper, M. L., 5, 53
Cooper, W. H., 244
Coppock, A., 12
Cordaro, F., 133
Cordaro, P., 134
Corneille, O., 242, 272, 273, 278, 280, 281, 300
Costa-Lopes, R., 75, 77
Cotterill, S., 77
Coultas, J. C., 12
Cowen, A. S., 125
Cox, C. R., 125, 139
Craig, R. T., 9
Crandall, C., 5
Crandall, R., 18

Crawford, E., 336
Crawley, L., 334
Creamer, M., 324
Creighton, L. A., 300
Crocker, J., 53, 150, 152, 322, 328
Crombez, G., 272, 276
Cross, S. E., 41, 46, 50, 57, 59, 62, 63, 65, 66, 67, 85
Crow, M., 223
Crowe, E., 175, 179, 182, 204, 209
Cruwys, T., 312, 327, 330, 335, 337, 339
Csikszentmihalyi, M., 226
Cuddy, A. J., 15
Culmer, M. J., 93
Cumming, G., 3–5, 25
Curtain, M., 334
Curtis, M., 94
Cury, F., 178
Cuthbert, B. N., 234
Czapinski, J., 218, 244

Dabbs, J., 223
Daftary, T., 127
Dahan, N., 299
Dahlem, N. W., 135
Dalgleish, T., 311
Daniele, V., 76
DaRin, M. L., 132
Davey, G. C., 282
Davies, M., 324
Davis, C. G., 333
Davis, D. D., 27
Davis, F., 124, 133, 139, 142
De Almeida, I., 39
de Barra, M., 12
De Clercq, A., 296
De Cremer, D., 136–138, 152
De Gilder, D., 335
de Houwer, J. D., 184, 272, 273, 275, 278, 280–283, 296, 297, 299, 300
De la Rey, C., 8
de Lange, M. A., 195
De Schryver, M., 300
De Vicq, P., 297
de Vries, A., 225
Deci, E. L., 144
Dedonder, J., 281
Deffenbacher, K. A., 7
Dekel, S., 333
DeKeseredy, W. S., 42

Den Hartog, D. N., 197
Denrell, J., 238, 246
Deutsch, R., 242, 243
Devos, T., 147
Devue, C., 285
Dhillon, S., 294
Dhont, K., 101
Di Blasi, M., 83
Di Piazza, S., 79
Diamantopoulos, A., 151
Díaz, E., 296
Dickel, N., 260
Dickerhoof, R., 238
Dickhaut, J., 237
Dickinson, A., 297
Diener, C., 225
Diener, E., 225
Dimitriadou, M., 151–153
Dingle, G. A., 312, 327, 330, 337
Dion, K., 244
Dodds, P. S., 224
Dodman, T., 124
Donchin, E., 283
Dotsch, R., 242
Dovidio, J. F., 75
Downes, C., 317, 323
Druckman, J. N., 11, 12
Drury, J., 323, 334, 336
Drury, L., 100–102, 104, 106, 109
Duarte, J. L., 20
Dudo, A., 22
Duesing, J., 275
Dugard, P., 337
Duncan, J., 286
Dunning, D., 259
Dunton, B. C., 148
Dutton, J. E., 335

Ebert, I., 297
Eckaus, R. S., 112
Eckstein, D., 283
Eder, A. B., 282, 294
Edgerton, R. B., 41
Edwards, D., 149, 153
Edwards, J. R., 205
Eelen, J., 294
Eelen, P., 184, 276, 281, 288, 296
Ehrhardt, J., 225
Eich, E., 5
Ein-Dor, T., 333

Eiser, J. R., 238
Ekman, P., 230
El Sarraj, E., 328
Elder, G. H., 333
Ellemers, N., 15, 43, 152, 187, 205, 335
Eller, A., 93
Eller, A. D., 110
Ellin, N., 124
Elliot, A. J., 124, 139, 140, 141, 175
Ellis, L. M., 24
Ellsworth, P., 230
Ellsworth, P. C., 125, 128
Elms, A. C., 5, 6, 11, 27
Emler, N., 109
Engber, D., 24
Ennis, M., 140
Epstude, K., 126
Erbs, J., 228
Eriksen, B. A., 286
Eriksen, C. W., 283, 286, 287
Eriksson, K., 12
Ernst, J. M., 177
Esteves, F., 285
Etherton, J. L., 284
Evans-Campbell, T., 332
Everaert, T., 296
Eyre, H. L., 94

Fabrigar, L. R., 25
Fahey, J. L., 333
Falvello, V. B., 242
Farh, J-L., 81
Farley, G. K., 135
Faye, C., 6
Fazio, R. H., 148, 231, 238, 276, 281, 288, 292
Feather, J., 9
Feather, N. T., 93
Federico, C. M., 75
Fehr, B., 51
Fehr, E., 154
Ferguson, R. W., 231
Feshbach, S., 156
Fetter, R., 137
Fetterman, A., 191, 192, 196
Feyers, D., 285
Fiedler, K., 29, 218–220, 231–233, 240, 242, 258, 260, 278, 299
Field, A. P., 282, 290
Filipas, H. H., 325

Finckenauer, J. O., 81
Findley, C. V., 41
Fine, C., 27
Finkenauer, C., 175, 218
First, M. B., 315
Fischbacher, U., 154
Fischer, A. H., 43, 47, 85
Fischer, D. H., 41
Fischhoff, B., 257, 259
Fishbach, A., 12
Fishbein, M., 2
Fisher, S., 124
Fishman, D. B., 3
Fiske, A. P., 77, 86
Fiske, D. W., 151
Fiske, S. T., 145
Fletcher, J., 41
Flykt, A., 285
Foa, E. B., 324
Fong, G. T., 143
Förderer, S., 299
Forgas, J. P., 232, 233, 242
Förster, J., 61, 175, 188, 190, 202, 208, 209
Fortune, D. G., 316, 331, 335
Foschi, R., 83
Foster, D., 8
Fox, E., 283
Fraboni, M., 146
Fraley, R. C., 3, 134
Francis, G., 25
Francis, W., 222
Francken, G., 296
Frazier, P., 339
Frederick, C., 144
Fredrickson, B. L., 224
Freedman, J. L., 3
Freeman, P., 178
Freese, J., 12
Fresc, L., 5
Freyd, J. J., 325
Friedman, M. J., 315
Friedman, R., 175
Friedman, R. S., 188, 202, 209
Friese, M., 293
Friesen, W. V., 230
Frijda, N. H., 126
Frings, C., 272, 283–285, 291
Frings, C. F., 275, 295
Fritsche, I., 206
Fritz, U., 228

AUTHOR INDEX

Fuentenebro de Diego, F., 124
Fukuyama, F., 82
Fultz, J., 148
Funder, D. C., 10
Furnham, A., 110

Gaertner, L., 158
Galinsky, A. D., 335
Gallagher, S., 314, 316, 326, 331
Gambetta, D., 82, 84, 85
Gamble, G., 22
Gao, D.-G., 134, 136
Garcia-Marques, T., 260
Gardner, W. L., 133
Garza, A., 135
Gast, A., 282, 291, 296, 298, 300
Gastil, R. D., 41
Gati, I., 254
Gawronski, B., 272, 273, 276, 278, 280, 281, 289, 295, 296, 300
Geertz, C., 79
Gelfand, M. J., 43, 45, 53, 58, 67, 81
Gentile, D. A., 59
Gentner, D., 239
George, E. W., 124
Gercek-Swing, B., 57, 67, 85
Gergen, K. J., 2, 7, 8
Gernsbacher, M. A., 14
Gheorghiu, M., 147
Giesen, C., 294
Gifford, R. K., 221, 257
Gigerenzer, G., 3, 258
Gilbert, D., 15
Gilboa, E., 126
Giles, H., 145
Gill, A. K., 86
Gille, Z., 155
Gilmore, D. D., 44
Gilovich, T., 127
Giner-Sorolla, R., 3, 5, 94
Giofré, D., 5
Giordano, C., 83, 84, 111
Gkinopoulos, T., 132
Gladwell, M., 14
Gocłowska, M. A., 335
Godfrey, H. P. D., 135
Godin, B., 8
Goffman, E., 329
Goldacre, B., 23
Goldberg, D., 321

Goldberg, L. R., 222
Goldinger, S. D., 231
Goldstein, D. G., 27
Goldstein, N. J., 217
Goldstone, R. L., 239
Gonzalez, A., 132
Gonzalez, R., 3, 127
Goodman, N., 239
Göritz, A. S., 128, 130
Gortner, E. M., 132
Gosling, S. D., 12
Gotlib, I. H., 126
Gottman, J. M., 224
Govender, R., 231
Grace, J. J., 335
Gräf, M., 244, 245, 256
Graham, J., 79
Graham, S., 230
Grant, A. M., 242
Grant, P. R., 98, 99
Grapendorf, J., 194
Grassegger, H., 26
Gratton, G., 283
Gravani, M., 147
Gray, J. A., 230
Grealy, M., 336
Green, C. S., 297
Green, J. D., 140, 142
Greenberg, J., 140
Greenwald, A. G., 3, 27
Gregg, A. P., 40
Gregg, G. S., 140
Greifeneder, R., 260
Greving, H., 191–194, 196
Grey, A., 22
Griffiths, T. L., 240
Grignolo, A., 24
Gronwall, D. M. A., 326
Gruenfeld, D. H., 202
Grynkewich, A. G., 78
Guastella, A. J., 232
Guimond, S., 8
Guindon, M., 124
Gul, P., 41, 85
Güngör, D., 68
Günsoy, C., 41, 63, 64, 67, 85
Guthrie, D., 3
Guveli, A., 43

Hacker Hughes, J., 16

AUTHOR INDEX

Haesen, K., 280
Haidt, J., 79
Halbeisen, G., 273, 280, 281, 282, 285–287, 296–298, 300
Hallett, D., 144
Halligan, S. L., 311
Halloran, M. J., 95
Hamilton, D. L., 221, 257
Hamilton, W. D., 236
Hammack, P. L., 328
Hamstra, M. R. W., 175, 185, 196–200
Hanson, L. R., 244
Hardin, C. D., 78
Hardin, G., 236
Harford, T., 14
Hargreaves, D. J., 154
Harinck, S., 43
Harré, R., 7
Harris, C. B., 127
Harris, R., 3
Hart, C. M., 132, 152
Harter, S., 319
Harvey, O. J., 256
Harvey, R. D., 322
Harwood, J., 145
Hase, A., 178
Haslam, C. J., 323
Haslam, C., 312, 315, 320, 323, 326, 327, 330, 331, 337, 339
Haslam, S. A., 81, 97, 312, 318, 321, 323, 325, 327, 330, 335, 337, 339
Häusser, J. A., 326
Hayes, A. F., 155
Hazan, H., 328
He, W., 9
Heaphy, E. D., 335
Heatherton, T. F., 130
Hefferon, K., 336
Hegarty, B., 3
Hegarty, P., 20
Heider, F., 184
Heider, G. M., 184
Heider, N., 280
Heine, S. J., 12, 40
Helmreich, R., 7
Hendrickson, B., 124
Henkel, L. A., 124
Hennes, E. P., 78
Henrich, J., 12, 40
Henson, R. N., 283, 285, 293

Hepper, E. G., 132, 143, 146, 147, 159
Hermans, D., 184, 288, 296
Hernandez, I., 45
Herrera, M., 337
Hertwig, R., 27, 260
Hertz, D. G., 133
Herwig, A., 293
Herzog, S. M., 260
Hess, H., 81, 97
Hewstone, H., 145
Hewstone, M., 101, 145, 147
Higgins, E. T., 175, 176, 179, 180, 182–185, 187, 196, 197, 204, 207, 209
Higgs, S., 278
Hill, P. B. E., 100
Hills, M., 9
Hillyard, D., 149, 153
Hilton, D. J., 158
Hinch, R., 42
Hinchy, J., 297
Hinsz, V. B., 133
Hirsch-Hoefler, S., 316, 329
Ho, M. D., 225
Hobfoll, S. E., 318
Hobsbawm, E. J., 107, 108
Hodges, S. D., 254
Hodson, G., 101
Hofer, J., 124
Hoffman, R. R., 7
Hofmann, W., 272, 296
Hofstede, G. J., 80
Hofstede, G., 80
Hogg, M. A., 81, 318
Holmes, T. H., 326
Holt, C. A., 27
Hommel, B., 272, 275, 283, 284, 292–295, 298, 300
Hood, W. R., 256
Hoogervorst, N., 138
Hook, D., 124
Hopkins, N., 81, 95
Horner, A. J., 283
Houghton, G., 285
Hout, M. C., 231, 232, 247
Houwer, J. D., 238
Huang, I., 129
Huang, M-P., 81
Huang, X., 129
Huber, G. A., 12
Huddy, L., 96

Hughes, S., 146, 273, 275, 280–282, 292, 293, 299
Hunter, J., 226
Hunter, S. B., 209
Hunyady, O., 90
Hurling, R., 282
Hütter, M., 278, 280, 299, 300
Hynie, M., 42

Idson, L. C., 175, 180, 182, 195
Igou, E. R., 154
Imara, D. A., 93
Imhoff, R., 242
Imura, M., 86
Inzlicht, M., 129
Ipeirotis, P., 12
Ipser, J., 8
Ireland, M., 132
Ismail, S. U., 125, 160
Issenberg, S., 26
Ito, T. A., 257
Iyer, A., 94, 158–160, 315, 327, 330
Izard, C. E., 229, 230

Jackson, J. W., 101
Jacoby, J., 175
James, W., 230
Janata, P., 140
Janiszewski, C., 299
Janoff-Bulman, R., 324
Jarodzka, H., 180
Jetten, J., 155, 156, 158–160, 312, 315, 320, 325–327, 330
Jing, Y., 81
John, O. P., 288, 292
Johnson, E. J., 27
Johnson, N. D., 237
Johnson, R. E., 175
Johnson-Laird, P. N., 230
Jonas, K. J., 15, 202, 204, 207
Jones, C. R., 276, 278, 290
Jones, J. J., 330
Jones, J. M., 316, 331, 333, 335
Jones, M. N., 240
Jordan, C. H., 187
Joseph, C., 79
Joseph, S., 311, 312, 317, 333
Jost, J. T., 75, 78–90
Judd, C. M., 13, 155, 281
Juhl, J., 124, 133, 134, 158

Juslin, P., 258–260

Kaczmarek, L. D., 178
Kagitcibasi, C., 42
Kahneman, D., 3, 10, 14, 26, 127
Kalamaras, D., 132
Kam, C. D., 11
Kanouse, D. E., 244
Karasawa, M., 67
Kardam, F., 42
Kardes, F. R., 231, 288
Karremans, J. C., 298
Kaschak, M., 286
Kashima, E., 95
Kasinitz, P., 149, 153
Kaslow, N. J., 15, 16, 21, 23
Kattenstroth, M., 326
Kattner, F., 296, 297, 300
Katz, B. L., 333
Kavanagh, L. C., 294
Kearns, M., 316, 330
Keller, J., 182, 188
Keller, P. A., 175
Keller-Allen, C., 10
Kellezi, B., 324, 325, 337
Kelsey, R. M., 178
Keltner, D., 125, 202
Kemeny, M. E., 333
Kemmelmeier, M., 80
Kenney, K., 336
Kenny, D. A., 13
Kenny, M., 156
Kenworthy, J., 145, 147
Kerr, N. L., 24
Kersten, M., 125, 139
Khan, S. S., 337
Khan, T., 68
Khatib, N., 96
Kibler, J., 177
Kim, B. K., 125
Kim, H., 44, 54
Kim, Y. J., 135
Kinderman, N., 16
Kinsella, E. L., 316, 334, 335
Kinzie, J. D., 159
Kirby, L. D., 178
Kitayama, S., 5, 21, 39, 46, 80
Klandermans, B., 93, 321
Klauer, K. C., 288, 294, 300
Klein, R., 175

398   AUTHOR INDEX

Knight, N., 90
Knight, R. G., 135
Knowles, M. L., 133
Koch, A. S., 220, 231–234, 242, 243, 246, 249, 253, 260
Kocks, J., 134
Komischke, M., 278
Koopman, P. L., 197
Koranyi, N., 298
Korn, J. H., 27
Kortekaas, P., 152
Korteweg, A., 67
Kosterman, R., 156
Koval, P., 225
Krauskopf, C. J., 13
Krauss, D. A., 11
Krauss, K., 124
Kris, A., 124
Krishna, A., 282
Krogerus, M., 26
Krosnick, J. A., 281
Krüger, T., 231
Kruglanski, A. W., 175
Krumhansl, C. L., 232
Krummenacher, J., 283
Kruskal, J. B., 129
Kteily, N., 77
Kucera, H., 222, 223
Kuhl, J., 175
Kunda, Z., 187, 256, 257
Kuperman, V., 223, 228, 234
Kuppens, P., 225
Kuppens, T., 281
Kurutaş, M., 63
Kutlaca, M., 338
Kutzner, F., 240
Kwang, T., 12
Kwon, K.-M., 158

Labonte, R., 9
Lagravinese, R., 112
Lalonde, C. E., 144
Lalonde, R., 42
Laloyaux, C., 285
Lam, B. C. P., 327
Lammers, J., 157
Lanaj, K., 175
Landau, M. J., 125
Landkammer, F., 175
Lang, P. J., 222, 234, 235

Langer, T., 276, 278, 279
Langston, C. A., 238
Lantz, G., 152
Larsen, J. T., 257
Larsen, R. J., 222
Larson, J., 333
Lasaleta, J. D., 124, 133
Latané, B., 221
Laub, R., 284
Laubscher, L., 124
Lauriola, M., 83
Lavezzi, A. M., 76
Lavie, N., 292
Layman, M., 257
Leach, C. W., 5, 94, 99, 108
Leary, M. R., 8, 140
LeBel, E. P., 4, 24
Lecours, S., 159
Ledgerwood, A., 4, 78
Lee, A. Y., 175, 195
Lee, J. M., 81
Lee, K., 222
Lee, S. W., 66
Lee, Y., 158
Leeper, T. J., 12
Lehmann, D. R., 175
Leising, D., 218, 221, 228, 229, 233, 240, 242, 256
Leitten, C. L., 178
Lenes, J., 68
Lenz, G. S., 12
Lepage, J., 300
Leung, A. K. Y., 27, 40, 43, 44, 50, 53, 66, 80, 85
Leunissen, J. M., 137, 149, 158
Levey, A. B., 275
Levi, P., 339
Levin, S., 68, 77
Levine, J. M., 81
Levine, M., 325
Levy, C., 9, 95
Lévy-Leboyer, C., 9
Lewin, K., 184, 240, 261
Lewis, R., 336
Li, R. M., 10
Liberman, N., 175, 182
Lichtenstein, S., 257, 259
Lickel, B., 94
Lieberman, J. D., 11
Lilienfeld, S. O., 14

AUTHOR INDEX   399

Lim, Y. L., 225
Limbaugh, R., 29
Linardatos, E., 24
Lindsay, D. S., 5
Lindsay, J. J., 25
Linley, P. A., 312, 317, 333
Linville, P. W., 318
Lipp, O. V., 297
Liu, J. H., 158
Livingstone, A. G., 97, 99, 108
Lock, A. J., 337
Locke, K. D., 218
Lockwood, P., 134, 187, 190
Loeb, S., 152
Logan, G. D., 284, 293
Long, W., 8
Louis, W. R., 106
Loveland, K. E., 124, 133
Lovibond, P. F., 278, 279
Low, C. A., 333
Lowe, R. D., 323, 329
Ludolph, R., 195
Luger, L., 180
Luhtanen, R., 150, 152, 322, 328
Luhtanen, R. K., 53
Luminet, O., 278, 281
Lunardi, R., 286
Lund, K., 222
Lykken, D. T., 3
Lyubomirsky, S., 126, 238

Maciejovsky, B., 151, 153
MacKenzie, S. B., 137
Mackie, D. M., 96, 146, 243, 319
Maddox, W. T., 195
Madoglou, A., 132
Magalhães, P. C., 77
Magerøy, N., 329
Magurean, S., 293
Mahadevan, N., 140
Mainieri, T., 27
Mair, H., 124
Maitner, A. T., 96
Major, B., 9, 10
Makel, M. C., 3
Malkinson, R., 328
Malle, B. F., 77, 160
Manstead, A. S. R., 43, 47, 85, 128
Marani, U., 76
Marine, S., 336

Markman, A. B., 195
Marks, M., 25
Markus, H. R., 9, 44, 46, 54
Marques, J. M., 81, 96
Marsh, N. V., 135
Marshall, H., 75, 84
Martens, S., 286
Martin, I., 275, 276
Martinovic, B., 150, 155
Mason, V., 297
Matheson, K., 335
Matlin, M. W., 218
Maton, K. I., 8
Matsumoto, H., 46
Matthews, A. M., 24
Mavelli, L., 75, 82, 87, 88, 111
Mayer, D. M., 138
Mayeux, L., 86
Mcaleer, C. A., 13
McCabe, K., 237
McCann, R., 145
McDougall, W., 230
McFarlane, A. C., 324
McGraw, A. P., 13
McGregor, H. A., 175
McGuire, W. J., 18
McLaughlin-Volpe, T., 146
McWhiney, G., 41
McWhirter, L., 319
Meaney, S., 326
Medin, D. L., 8, 239
Medvec, V. H., 127
Meeker, M. E., 42
Meertens, R. W., 148
Mehl, M. R., 222, 223
Meinerling, K., 297
Melnikoff, D. E., 300
Memelink, J., 284, 298
Memon, A., 8
Mendes, W. B., 184, 209
Mermelsteon, J., 332
Mesquita, B., 67
Metting, E., 134
Mewhort, D. J., 240
Meyer, A. D., 9
Meyrick, J., 125
Michels-Ratliff, E., 140
Middleton, D., 149, 153
Mikulincer, M., 134, 140
Miller, G., 13

400 AUTHOR INDEX

Miller, W. I., 44, 59
Milligan, M. J., 149
Minkov, M., 80
Mischel, W., 51
Mislin, A. A., 237
Mitchell, C. J., 278, 300
Mitchell, G., 25
Moeller, B., 284
Moeller, K., 209
Moghaddam, F. M., 7
Mojzisch, A., 326
Molden, D. C., 182
Mols, F., 156
Moon, C., 80
Moore, A. C., 290
Moore, L. J., 178
Moorman, R. H., 137
Moran, T., 300
Mori, I., 153
Morling, B., 46
Morrone, C., 286
Morsella, E., 273, 280
Mortensen, L., 10
Moscovici, S., 7
Motyka, S., 185, 195
Mowrer, O. H., 230
Msetfi, R. M., 330
Mueller, P., 12
Mulcahy, A., 329
Mulders-Jones, D., 86
Muldoon, O. T., 311–339
Muller, D., 155
Müller, H. J., 283
Mullet, E., 132
Mullinix, K. J., 12
Munafò, M. R., 3
Murch, R. L., 317
Murdock, T., 324
Musch, J., 288
Müsseler, J., 283, 294
Mussweiler, T., 61
Mutrie, N., 336

Nagengast, B., 272, 281, 300
Nairn, A., 27
Nam, H. H., 78
Nam, J., 158
Napier, J. L., 75
Naughton, C. M., 314, 323, 325, 337
Nave, A. M., 132

Nederveen Pieterse, A., 200
Neigher, W. D., 3
Nelson, L. D., 4
Neto, F., 132
Neuliep, J. W., 18
Neumann, D. L., 297
Ng, K. Y., 137
Nicks, S. D., 27
Niedenthal, P., 294
Nijstad, B. A., 175
Nisbett, R. E., 43, 45, 56, 85, 86, 90, 272
Nishi, A., 12
Nolen-Hoeksema, S., 126, 127, 333
Norasakkunkit, V., 46
Norenzayan, A., 12, 40
North, M. S., 145
Nosek, B. A., 4
Nowak, A., 45
Nuerk, H. C., 209

O'Brien, A., 325
O'Brien, J., 178
O'Connor, F., 320
O'Donnell, A. T., 314, 323, 325
O'Donnell, J. M., 7
Oakes, P. J., 318, 321
Oatley, K., 230
Öhman, A., 285
Olds, J. M., 260
Olson, M. A., 276, 281
Ong, A., 159
Oosterhof, N. N., 242
Organ, D. W., 137
Orne, M. T., 2
Ortmann, A., 27
Ortony, A., 229, 230
Osgood, C. E., 218, 222, 223, 234
Osterman, L. L., 86
Ostrovski, O., 228
Oyserman, D., 66, 80

Packard, V., 27
Paladino, M. P., 150
Panksepp, J., 230
Paolacci, G., 12
Paoli, L., 74, 75, 81, 82, 83, 93, 96, 100, 111
Paolini, S., 145
Paquette, J. A., 134
Park, B., 226
Park, C. L., 317

Parker, I., 7
Parkinson, B., 128
Parrott, W. G., 94
Patterson, J., 325
Pauketat, J. V., 96
Paulhus, D. L., 136
Pavia, L., 83
Peacock, E. J., 187, 194
Pedersen, A., 94
Peer, E., 12
Peerbux, S., 93
Peeters, G., 218, 244
Penna, S., 325
Pennebaker, J. W., 132, 147, 223
Penrod, S. D., 8
Pereira, C. R., 75
Peristiany, J. G., 41, 44, 53
Perugini, M., 25, 272, 273, 282
Peters, K. R., 24
Peters, M., 15
Peters, R., 124
Peterson, R. A., 11
Pettigrew, T. F., 8, 101, 148
Pham, M. T., 204
Philippe, F. L., 159
Phillipov, M., 124
Pickett, C. L., 133
Pielke, R., 7
Pierro, A., 175
Ping, R. M., 294
Pinotti, P., 76
Pinto, I. R., 81, 96
Pitt-Rivers, J., 40, 44, 53, 85
Platow, M. J., 81, 326
Pleyers, G., 278, 281, 290, 300
Plucker, J. A., 3
Plutchik, R., 230
Podsakoff, P. M., 137
Poehlman, T. A., 79
Poldrack, R. A., 281
Poppi, F. I. M., 79, 88, 96
Porter, C. O. L. H., 137
Porter, J. M., 242
Posse, B., 293
Postmes, T., 97, 318, 327
Potter, T., 242
Poulsen, J. R., 101
Powell, M. C., 231, 288
Praharso, N. F., 327
Pratkanis, A. R., 5

Pratto, F., 68, 77, 160, 231, 288, 292
Prestwich, A., 101, 282
Pretorius, S., 24
Price, J., 223
Priester, J. R., 294
Prinz, W., 272, 283, 292, 293, 295
Puente, S., 45
Punamki, R. L., 328
Pupavac, V., 337
Putnam, R. D., 83
Pyszczynski, T., 140

Qouta, S., 328
Quinn, R. E., 335

Rafaeli-Mor, E., 318
Rahe, R. H., 326
Rai, T. S., 86
Ramanathapillai, R., 324
Ramirez Marin, J., 43, 66, 67
Rand, D. G., 12
Randsley de Moura, G., 78, 81, 90, 94, 96
Ranehill, E., 15
Rantilla, A. K., 45
Rapaport, C., 329
Rasmussen, A. S., 127
Ratliff, K., 140
Ratner, R. K., 125
Rauthmann, J. F., 217
Ray, D. G., 179
Razran, G. H., 275
Reber, R., 260
Reicher, S. D., 81, 95, 99, 109, 318, 337
Reid, C. A., 142
Reid, D. G., 124
Reis, H. T., 4, 238
Rescorla, R. A., 276, 298
Rhodes, G., 242
Richard, F. D., 25
Richeson, J. A., 189
Richetin, J., 282
Richter, J., 300
Riddle, T. A., 273
Rieger, D., 125
Riggs, D. S., 324
Righetti, F., 175
Rijsman, J., 7
Rinck, M., 294
Ritchie, T. D., 132
Roberti, F., 84

AUTHOR INDEX

Roberts, J. E., 126
Roberts, K., 86
Roberts, L. M., 335
Robertson, S., 132, 149, 150, 151
Robins, R. W., 136
Robinson, M., 5
Robitaille, A., 124
Roccas, S., 68
Rodriguez Mosquera, P. M., 43, 45–47, 53, 57, 59, 61, 68, 85, 90, 92, 96, 108
Roese, N. J., 126, 246
Roets, S., 280
Roll-Hansen, N., 8
Rom, S. C., 260
Ropp, S. A., 146
Rosch, E., 131
Rosen, G., 123, 124
Rosenberg, M., 321
Rosenthal, R., 2, 24
Roskos-Ewoldsen, D. R., 292
Rossnagel, C., 288
Rothbart, M., 226
Rothbaum, B. O., 324
Rothermund, K., 184, 282, 283, 288, 291, 294, 298
Routledge, C., 124, 127, 129, 132–135, 137–140, 148, 158
Rovenpor, D. R., 329
Roylance, C., 132
Royzman, E. B., 218
Rozin, P., 218
Rubin, D. C., 142
Rude, S. S., 132
Ruggiero, V., 75
Ruiz, G., 296
Rusbult, C., 175
Russo, G., 80, 90, 94
Russo, R., 88
Rusting, C. L., 126
Ruys, K. I., 242
Ryan, R. M., 144
Rye, M. S., 127
Ryff, C. D., 144

Sacchi, S., 150
Saleem, F., 59
Saleem, M., 59
Sally, D., 237
Salomon, K., 209
Saltstone, R., 146

Samat, S., 11
Sanbonmatsu, D. M., 231, 288
Sand, E., 134
Sands, J., 82
Sani, F., 156
Saribay, A., 63
Sarrazin, P., 178
Sassenberg, K., 174, 175, 179, 180, 182, 185, 187, 191–194, 196–198, 200, 202, 204–207, 209
Sassenrath, C., 179, 180, 182, 187–189, 196, 206
Sava, F. A., 293
Saviano, R., 88, 112
Scarnier, M., 94
Schaller, M., 15
Scheepers, D., 182, 187, 205, 209
Scheiter, K., 179
Scherbaum, S., 218
Scherer, K. R., 128
Schimel, J., 140
Schimmack, U., 4, 225
Schlenger, W. E., 328
Schmader, T., 94
Schmid, K., 313, 322–324
Schminke, M., 135
Schmitt, M. T., 322
Schneider, J. C., 75, 76, 78, 83–85, 87, 95, 101, 105–107, 108, 111
Schneider, K. K., 283
Schneider, P. T., 75, 78, 83–85, 87, 101, 105–107, 108, 111
Schoenrade, P. A., 148
Scholl, A., 174, 180, 205, 206, 209
Schönbrodt, F. D., 25
Schopenhauer, A., 271
Schuettler, D., 333
Schulz, P. J., 195
Schuster, M. A., 328
Schwartz, B., 22, 242
Schwartz, J., 51
Schwarz, N., 43, 66, 86, 224, 226, 260
Sciarrone, R., 76
Scott, B., 135
Seabright, M. A., 135
Sears, D. O., 3, 11, 109, 226
Sebastian, K., 336
Secord, P., 7
Sedikides, C., 123–134, 136, 137, 140, 142–144, 147–149, 151–154, 158, 159

AUTHOR INDEX 403

Sedlmeier, P., 3, 272, 294
Seehusen, J., 126
Seery, M. D., 176–178
Seibt, B., 190, 208
Selya, A., 68
Semnani-Azad, Z., 66
Sev'er, A., 42
Severance, L., 43, 67
Seymour-Smith, M., 327
Shafa, S., 43, 67
Shah, J. Y., 175, 179, 202, 204
Shakespeare, W., 43
Shanks, D. R., 273
Shaver, P. R., 134, 140
Shaw, R., 325
Sheehy-Skeffington, J., 77
Sherif, C. W., 261
Sherif, M., 7, 11, 256
Sherman, J. W., 4, 254
Shmotkin, D., 328
Shook, N. J., 2, 238
Shteynberg, G., 58
Sidanius, J., 68, 77, 160
Silva, R. R., 260
Silverman, I., 1, 7
Silverman, S. F., 84
Simmons, J. P., 4
Simms, L. J., 242
Simonsohn, U., 4
Skaperdas, S., 75, 82, 84, 85
Skjelsbaek, I., 324
Skokan, L. A., 333
Skowronski, J. J., 244, 259
Slovic, P., 257
Smallman, R., 246
Smeekes, A., 149, 150, 154–156
Smith, C. A., 125, 128
Smith, C., 27
Smith, E. R., 96, 147, 319
Smith, M. B., 7, 13
Smith, N. C., 2, 3
Smith, N. K., 257
Smith, R. H., 94
Smollan, D., 145
Snyder, M., 9, 18
Sokol, B. W., 144
Solnit, R., 332, 338
Solomon, S., 140
Solomon, Z., 333
Son, J. Y., 239

Soureti, A., 147
Sousa, L., 238
Spellman, B. A., 4
Spencer, S. J., 143, 144
Spitzer, R. L., 315
Spreitzer, G. M., 335
Spruit, A., 280
Spruyt, A., 296
Stahl, C., 272, 273, 280, 300
Stallworth, L. M., 77, 160
Stam, D., 199–201
Stang, D. J., 218
Stanton, A. L., 333
Stark, C., 327
Stathi, S., 147
Steffens, N. K., 81, 327, 335
Steinberg, J., 318
Stephan, E., 125, 129, 139, 141, 142
Sterling, T. D., 3
Stern, C., 78
Steward, J. M., 333
Stewart, F. H., 41, 45, 59
Stewart, N., 12, 259, 260
Stewart-Brown, S., 325
Steyvers, M., 240
Stiller, J., 4
Stillman, S., 26
Stillwell, A. M., 130
Stokes-Zoota, J. J., 25
Stollberg, J., 206
Stone, L. D., 132
Storti, L., 76
Stovall-McClough, C., 325
Strange, C., 86
Strange, S., 75, 78, 82
Strauman, T., 175
Stroebe, W., 7, 298
Stroessner, S. J., 243
Suci, G. J., 234
Sullivan, D., 150
Summerfield, D., 317
Summerville, A., 126
Sumner, P., 22
Sunbay, A., 46, 57
Sunbay, Z., 85
Sundet, P., 332
Sung, H-E., 83
Surgenor, P. W., 330
Sutherland, E. H., 102
Sweldens, S., 278, 299, 300

404 AUTHOR INDEX

Syropoulos, C., 76, 84

Tajfel, H., 95, 98, 221, 253, 257, 318
Tam, T., 145, 147
Tamborski, M., 86
Tan, L., 59
Tannenbaum, P. H., 234
Tarrant, M., 154, 339
Tarrow, S., 84
Tashiro, T., 10
Tassell, N. A., 337
Tausch, N., 85, 154, 338
Tavassoli, N. T., 285
Taylor, S. E., 333
Tear, M. J., 327
Tedeschi, R. G., 317, 333, 334
Tell, R. A., 24
Tenenbaum, J. B., 240
Terhorst, K. M., 297
Theeuwes, J., 283, 285
Thomas, D. L., 225
Thomas, S., 272
Thompson, J. B., 79
Thompson, M., 333
Thoreson, R. W., 13
Thorndike, E. L., 244, 246
Thrash, T. M., 139–141
Thurber, C. A., 124
Tipper, S. P., 285
Todd, P. M., 258
Todorov, A., 242
Todorova, M., 155
Tomaka, J., 175–178, 180, 188, 207
Tomkins, S. S., 230
Topolinski, S., 242, 243
Toros, H., 74, 82, 87, 88, 111
Tosto, C., 83
Tracy, J. L., 136
Trafimow, D., 25
Trasselli, C., 272, 282
Travaglino, G. A., 74, 78–81, 83, 84, 89–96, 98–104, 107–110
Trawalter, S., 189
Treisman, A. M., 292
Tressoldi, P. E., 5
Trew, K., 313, 319
Treynor, W., 127
Triandis, H. C., 80, 81, 158
Trifiletti, E., 101

Tropp, L. R., 101, 145
Trzesniewski, K. H., 136
Tsal, Y., 292
Tsivrikos, D., 327
Tullett, A. M., 129
Turner, E. H., 24
Turner, J. C., 77, 257, 318, 321, 335
Turner, R. N., 101, 143, 145–147
Turner, T. J., 229
Turner-Zwinkels, F., 97, 138
Tversky, A., 3, 231, 254
Tyler, T. R., 75–78, 103, 136

Uchida, Y., 39
Uhlmann, E. L., 79
Ullman, S. E., 325
Unkelbach, C., 220, 221, 231, 232, 242–246, 249, 253, 256, 260, 278, 299, 300
Uskul, A. K., 39, 40, 42, 45–47, 54–57, 59, 62, 64–67, 80, 85, 90, 108, 189

Valiente Ots, C., 124
Van den Bergh, O., 276, 281
Van Den Bos, K., 137
van der Hoef, H., 318
Van der Molen, T., 134
Van der Toorn, J., 78
Van Dessel, P., 282
van Dick, R., 326
van Dijk, J., 83, 137, 138, 158
Van Dijke, M. H., 137, 138, 158
Van Enkevort, E. A., 125, 139
Van Gulick, A. E., 240
van Knippenberg, A., 195
van Knippenberg, D., 199
Van Laar, C., 77
Van Muijen, J. J., 197
van Osch, Y., 43, 56, 67
Van Osselaer, S. M., 299
Van Quaquebeke, N., 137
Van Tilburg, W. A. P., 124, 125, 128–131, 144, 149–151
van Valkengoed, A. M., 318
Van Yperen, N. W., 185, 196–200
van Zomeren, M., 97, 106, 338
Vanaelst, J., 296
Vandello, J. A., 45, 86
Vankov, I., 3
Vansteenwegen, D., 296

AUTHOR INDEX

Varese, F., 81
Vazire, S., 3, 5, 25
Veenhoven, R., 225
Velez, J. A., 125
Velikonja, M., 124
Verduyn, P., 225
Verhaeghen, P., 240
Verkuyten, M., 149, 150, 155
Verplanken, B., 158
Versari, A., 334
Vervliet, B., 296
Verwijmeren, T., 298
Vezzali, L., 101, 334
Viki, G. T., 93, 240
Vingerhoets, A. J. J. M., 125, 144
Vitanyi, P. M. B., 240
Vitellin, R., 27
Voci, A., 145
Vogel, T., 240
Vohs, K. D., 10, 218
Von Lampe, K., 75, 81, 83, 111
Vonofakou, C., 101, 145
Vormedal, K., 325
Voss, A., 184

Wagnild, G. M., 160
Wakefield, J. C., 315
Wakefield, J. R., 337
Walasek, L., 259, 260
Walker, J., 324
Wallace, K. A., 159
Waller, N. G., 134
Walsh, R. S., 316, 331, 332, 334, 339
Walsh, W., 324
Walster, E., 244
Walther, E., 271–273, 275–278, 280–283, 285–287, 295–297, 299
Walton, E. A., 124
Wan, C., 58
Wang, J., 175
Wang, M. T. M., 22
Wänke, M., 293
Ward, L. M., 25
Ward, R., 286
Warner, R. H., 333
Warren, C., 13
Warriner, A. B., 223, 228, 234, 235
Wasco, S. M., 335
Washington, G., 127
Waszak, F., 283, 293

Watson, J. B., 221, 230, 260
Webber, D., 18
Weber, M., 75, 76, 78, 100
Webster, J. D., 128
Webster, J. M., 94
Wegener, D. T., 25
Wegner, D. M., 4
Weich, S., 325
Weigelt, O., 272
Weil, R., 275, 278, 281, 285
Weiner, B., 230
Weinstein, N., 144
Weisbuch, M., 178
Wells, G. L., 8
Wenger, H. D., 13
Wentura, D., 184, 283, 288, 292
Werman, D. S., 126
Wesson, M. J., 137
West, T., 5
Westerhof, G. J., 128
Westerman, D. L., 260
Westfall, J., 13
Wetherell, M. S., 318
Wheatley, J., 81
White, B. J., 256
White, M., 150
Wichmann, L. J., 318
Wicker, A. W., 2
Wieber, F., 204
Wielgosz, J., 294
Wiener, R. L., 11
Wiers, R. W., 300
Wigboldus, D. H., 298
Wikan, U., 42, 53
Wildschut, C., 133
Wildschut, R. T., 132
Wildschut, T., 123–137, 139, 142–144, 147–154, 158, 159
Wilkes, A. L., 221
Williams, D., 189
Williams, P., 321
Williams, T. F., 242
Williamson, V., 20
Wilson, J. P., 317
Wilson, K., 313, 321
Wilson, T. D., 272
Winkielman, P., 294
Wisco, B. E., 126
Wish, M., 129
Wisse, B., 185, 196–200

406 AUTHOR INDEX

Witte, E. H., 4, 11
Wittenbrink, B., 281
Wojciszke, B., 244
Wolf, E. R., 79, 80, 106
Woltin, K. A., 174, 175
Wong, P. T., 187, 194
Woud, M. L., 294
Wright, M. O. D., 336
Wright, R. A., 178
Wright, S. C., 145, 146
Wrzesniewski, A., 282
Wu, T-Y., 81
Wühr, P., 290
Wulf, T., 125
Wyatt-Brown, B., 89
Wyer, Z. T., 129

Xanthopoulos, P., 132
Xu, A. J., 66

Yamagishi, T., 58
Yamaguchi, S., 67
Yao, J., 66
Yap, A. J., 15
Yaworsky, R. R., 132
Yaxley, R., 286
Ye, Y., 299

Yehuda, R., 311
Yellen, J., 78
Yetkili, O., 81
Yoder, N., 189
Youn, N., 158
Young, H. M., 160
Ysseldyk, R., 335
Yuki, M., 101, 107
Yurdakul, G., 42, 67
Yzerbyt, V., 150, 155, 278, 281, 300

Zajonc, R. B., 223
Zanna, M., 143
Zauberman, G., 125
Zeelenberg, M., 43
Zelditch, M., 77
Zerhouni, A., 300
Zhou, H., 12
Zhou, X., 124, 134, 136
Zimet, G. D., 135
Zimmermann, J., 218
Zinchenko, A. V., 124
Zorbas, P., 325
Zou, X., 58, 142
Zwaan, R., 286

Subject index

Locators in bold refer to figures/tables.

action control theory, 175, 283–284, 295
action research, 8
aggressive responses, 41, 56, 59, 62, 68, 108
Alan Alda Center for Communicating Science, 23
Amazon Mechanical Turk (AMT), 11–12
American Psychological Association (APA), 7, 13, 15
amoral familism, 83
AMT, *see* Amazon Mechanical Turk (AMT)
appraisal theory, 125, 128–129
Association for Psychological Science, 23
attitude formation, 272–273, 278, 280, 286, 289, 292–293, 295–298
Australian Psychological Society, 23
authority, 77

Behavioral Insights Team, 26
behavioural research, 14
Behavioural Science Policy Association (BSPA), 19
Biopsychosocial Model, 175–176
 integration, 180–182
 motivational states, outcomes of, 183–184
 threat/challenge in, 175–179
BPS, *see* British Psychological Society (BPS)
British Psychological Society (BPS), 16

Center for Open Science (COS), 4
coercion, 77, 85
cognitive EC accounts
 holistic account, 276
 implicit misattribution account, 276–278
 issues, 280–281
 propositional account, 278–280
 referential account, 276
collective nostalgia, *see* national nostalgia
communication relevance, criticism, 6, 13–16
 incentives for, 21–24
conditioned stimuli (CS), 272
conditioning phase, **274**, 294
consequences, positive information's evidence

higher frequency, 224–226
similarity and diversity, 229
consumer ethnocentrism, 151–153
Contingencies of Self-Worth Scale, 53
criminal organisation, 74. *See also* masculine honour values
 attitudes towards, 88–93, 95–97, **100**
 cultural honour, 85–87
 cultural values, 105–107
 culture and political action, 106–107
 definition, 74–75, 81–82
 governance and, 82
 Italian context, 81–82
 mafia-type groups, 107–108
 members contacts and, 99–102, **103**
 moral emotions, 94–95
 omertà, 83–85, 109–111
 regional identity and social change, 97–99
 regional membership, 95–97
 as social bandits, 107–108
 social identity, 95–97
 theoretical implications, 102–109
crisis, 2. *See also* relevance crisis
 of evidence, 2–5
 of relevance, 1–2
cultural affordances, 46
cultural honour
 background on, 40–41
 construction of, 45–46
 contributions and limitations, 65–68
 definition, 85–87
 factors, **53**
 intracultural appropriation theory, 87–88
 origins of, 41–43
 overview, 39–40
 prototypes approach, 50–54
 research on, 65
 situational approach, 46–50, **48**
 theoretical foundations of, 43–45
 threats, responses to, 54–65
cultural values, 76
 criminal organisations and, 105–106
 of honour, 86, 108
 and intracultural appropriation theory, 78–81, **79**, 87

406 SUBJECT INDEX

in shaping individuals, 101, 107, 110
culture
definition, **79**, 79–80
and political action, 106–107
culture as ideology, 76–77
intracultural appropriation theory, 78–81, **79**
unequal social arrangements, 77–78
"culture shift," 23

dignity cultures, 43–44, 46, 65
domestic country bias, 151

EC, *see* evaluative conditioning (EC)
EC action control perspective, 271–272
attitude formation, 293–294
emergence of, 286–290
evaluative conditioning, 283–285
implications and limitations of, 295–300
processing of CS and US, 285–290, **286–287**
scores, difference, 288–289, **289**
selection condition, 287–288, **288**
stimulus and response, 290–293
Economic and Social Research Council
(ESRC), 23
empirical evidence, 186
action control perspective implications, 285–
290
for contexts, roles, and groups, 197–207
masculine honour values and criminal
organisations, 88–93
on outcomes of motivational states, 191–196
regulatory focus and threat–challenge, 186–
207
threat/challenge appraisals, 189
on transitions *vs.* motivational states, 186–
191
evaluative conditioning (EC), 272. *See also*
cognitive EC accounts
accounts, 275–283
action-control perspective on, 283–285
functional perspective, 273
investigations, 273
evaluative information ecology (EvIE), 216,
218–221
benefits and drawbacks of, 259–261
direct assessments, 229–234
frequency of information, 221–226
implications, 243–257
information, positive and negative, 217–221
models, 257–259
similarity and diversity, 226–229

structural properties of, 236–243
evaluative learning effects, **274**
event-file, 284
Event Reflection Task, 132, 137, 140–145,
149, 152, 159
evidence crisis, 1
overview of, 2–3
EvIE, *see* evaluative information ecology
(EvIE)

Facebook, 64–65, 88
frequency and valence, 249–253
functional accounts, 281–282
issues, 282–283
funding environment, incentives, 21

General Health Questionnaire, 321
group membership, social identity approach,
318–319
group support, 150–151

halo effects, 244–246
"helping others," 52
holistic account, 276
Honor Ideology for Manhood scale, 88, 92
Honor Ideology for Womanhood scale, 92
honour cultures, *see* cultural honour
"honour killings," 42
honour-threatening/honour-enhancing
situations
behavioural responses, 58–65
consequences of, 66
emotional responses to, 54–55
feedbacks, **60**
retaliatory responses to, 56–58
sensory stimuli, **62**
Honour Values Scale, 53, 61, 92

ICAT, *see* intracultural appropriation theory
(ICAT)
Identity Continuity Hypothesis, 315
Identity Revitalisation Hypothesis, 315
ideologies, 77
IMEV, *see* Integrative Model of Eagerness
and Vigilance regulation (IMEV)
implications, EvIE's
frequency and valence, 249–253
halo effects, 244–246
intergroup biases, 253–256
similarity and liking, 246–249
implicit bias, 14

SUBJECT INDEX   407

implicit misattribution account, 276–278
Inalienable Worth Scale, 53
incentives
  communication relevance, 21–24
  question relevance, 16–20
  and relevance, 16–24
  sample relevance, 20–21
individuals behaviour, 43–46
ingroup, personal sacrifice, 153–154
ingroup evaluations and approach
    orientation, 149–150
inspiration and nostalgia, 139–142, **141**
Integrative Model of Eagerness and Vigilance
    regulation (IMEV), 181–182. *See also*
    promotion/prevention focus; threat/
    challenge focus
intergroup biases, 253–256
intersecting regularities, 273
intracultural appropriation theory (ICAT),
    74, 76, 78–81, **79**, **104**, 105, 111
  masculine honour and criminal
    organisations, 87–88
  omertà, model of, 109–111
Italian criminal organisations, 75–76, 81–82,
    85, 105, 111–112
Journal of Applied Psychology (JAP), 17
*Journal of Personality and Social Psychology
    (JPSP)*, 3–4, 11
"law of silence," *see* omertà
leadership, promotion/prevention focus,
    197–202

legal authority, 77
legitimising ideologies, 77
"life changing," *see* trauma
limitations, nostalgia research, 158–160
lingering issues, nostalgia, 160–161
Linguistic Inquiry and Word Count (LIWC),
    132–133
LIWC, *see* Linguistic Inquiry and Word
    Count (LIWC)
loneliness and nostalgia, 134–135
luncheon technique, 275

mafias, 82, 84, 87–88, 96–97, 100, 105, 107–
    108, 110
mafia-type groups, 84, 97, 100, 106–108
masculine honour values, 88–89, **100**
  and criminal organisations, 87–93, **103**,
    108–109
  cultural values of, 76, 85–86

moral emotions, 94–95
  and omertà, 93–94
  regional identification, 95–96
  social identity theory, 95
media
  honour-related behaviour, 63–64
  relevance crisis, 14–16
meta-psychologies, 14
Monitor on Psychology, 15
moral behaviour, 52, **53**
moral emotions, 94–95
motivated performance situations, 177–179
motivational states, 176, 179. *See also*
    promotion/prevention focus; threat/
    challenge focus
  contexts, roles, and groups, evidence, 197–
    207
  outcomes of, 183–186
  transitions, evidence on, 187–191
  transitions between, 182–183
  valenced stimuli, evidence, 191–196
multidimensional scaling, 129–131, **131**
multiple group memberships, 326–327

national nostalgia
  consumer ethnocentrism, 151–153
  group support, 150–151
  ingroup, personal sacrifice, 153–154
  ingroup evaluations and approach
    orientation, 149–150
  outgroup attitudes, 155–156
  promotes collective action, 154–155
  rejection/exclusion, outgroup, 156–157
  strengthen intergroup, 155–156
negative information, 217–221
neutral *vs.* negative feedback, honour
    threatening, **60**, 60–61
nostalgia, 125–126, **136**. *See also* national
    nostalgia; sociality and nostalgia
  functional property of, 133
  inspiration, 139–142, **141**
  linear regression analyses, **149**
  loneliness and, 134–135
  organisational hardship and, 135–139
  prejudice reduction, 145–148
  procedural justice/injustice, **138**
  prototype theory, 131–132
  self-continuity and, 142–144, **143**
  social connectedness, 139–149, **141, 143**
  as social emotion, 128–131
  social exclusion and, 133–134

408 SUBJECT INDEX

"nudge unit," 26

omertà, 76, 83–85
  criminal organisations and, 109–111
  model of, **90–91, 104**
  passivity and fear accounts, 83–84
  shortcoming of, 84–85
one-way influence, 8
organisational hardship and nostalgia, 135–139
outgroup rejection/exclusion, collective
  nostalgia, 156–157

personal sacrifice, collective nostalgia, 153–154
philosophical messages, 14
physiological threat-challenge-index, 178
positive information, 217–221
  frequency of, 221–222
  similarity and diversity, 226–236
positive information, higher frequency
  consequence evidence, 224–226
  from evolutionary necessities, 236–237
  from hedonic sampling, 238–239
  psycho-lexical evidence for, 222–224
  from reinforcement learning, 237–238
positive information, similarity and diversity
  of
  from affective influences, 242–243
  consequence evidence, 229
  from co-occurrences, 239–240
  direct assessments of, 229–234
  psycho-lexical evidence for, 227–229
  from range principle, 240–242
post-traumatic growth (PTG), 312
post-traumatic stress disorder (PTSD), 312
post-traumatic stress (PTS), 311
  social identity continuity, 328–330
  social identity gain, 330–332
prejudice reduction and nostalgia, 145–148
promotion/prevention focus
  classification of, **181**
  integration, 179–182
  leadership, 197–202
  motivational states, outcomes of, 183–184,
    186
  self-regulation approach, 176–186
  social contexts, roles, and groups, 185–186
  transitions, 182–186
  valenced stimuli, 184–185
propositional account, 278–280

prototypes approach, honour, 50–54
prototype theory, 131–132
psycho-lexical evidence, positive
  information's
  higher frequency, 222–224
  similarity and diversity, 227–229
*Psychological Science and Journal of
  Experimental Social Psychology (JESP)*, 4
PTG, *see* post-traumatic growth (PTG)
PTS, *see* post-traumatic stress (PTS)
PTSD, *see* post-traumatic stress disorder
  (PTSD)
PTSD risk and resilience theories, 317–318

question relevance criticism, 6–10
  incentives for, 16–20

real-world relevance, criticism, 20, 28
referential account, 276
regional identity, 97–99, **100**
regional membership, 95–97
Regulatory Focus Theory, 175, 179–180
  evidence on transitions, 187–190
  measures, **187**
  motivational states, outcomes of, 195
  promotion and prevention, 179–180
  social power, 202–207, **203**
relational model theory, 77
relevance crisis, 1–2, 19. *See also* incentives
  communication, 6, 13–16
  vs. evidence, 24–29
  question, 6–10
  sample, 6, 10–13
response formation phase, **274**, 294

SAM, *see* sympathetic adrenomedullary axis
  (SAM)
sample relevance, criticism, 6, 10–13
  incentives for, 20–21
secret power, 75–76
  intracultural appropriation theory, **79**
self-assessment, 44
self-categorisation theory, 320–321
self-continuity and nostalgia, 142–144, **143**
self-regulation, 174–175
  promotion and prevention, 179–180
  threat/challenge, 176–179
self-respect, 52, **53**
SES, *see* socioeconomic status (SES)
shared cultural values, **79**, 80, 107

SUBJECT INDEX   409

similarity and diversity, positive
  information's, 226–227
 direct assessments, 229, **231, 233, 235**
 evidence from consequences, 229, **230**
 psycho-lexical evidence for, 227–229
SIT, *see* social identity theory (SIT)
situation sampling approach, honour, 46–50,
  48
Social and Behavioral Sciences Team, 26
social bandits, 107–108
social change beliefs, 97–99, **100**
social contexts, roles and groups
 motivational states, 185–186
 promotion and prevention focus, 197–202
 social power, 202–207
social dominance theory, 77
social embedding, 8, 80–81, 87
social exclusion and nostalgia, 133–134
social identification, 312
 to criminal organisations, 95–97
 to trauma, 312, **313–314**, 320–326
social identity continuity, 327–330
social identity gain, 330–332
Social Identity Gain Hypothesis, 315
*Social Identity Model of Identity Change
  (SIMIC)*, 315
social identity model of traumatic identity
  change (SIMTIC), 312–315, **316**, 328
social identity resources, 312
social identity revitalisation, 332–336
social identity theory (SIT), 95
sociality and nostalgia
 appraisals and emotions, 128–129, **129–130**
 collective nostalgia and outcomes, 149–157
 issues, 160–161
 judging, 128–131
 limitations, 158–160
 multidimensional scaling, 129–131, **131**
 proneness and social functions of memory,
  126–128
 research, 133–139
 social connectedness, 139–149
 summary, 157–158
social power, 202–207
Social Psychology Insight (SPInsight), 23–24
social status/respect, 53, **53**
Society for the Psychological Study of Social
  Issues (SPSSI), 18–19, 23
socioeconomic status (SES), 80
SPInsight, *see* Social Psychology Insight
  (SPInsight)

stereotype threat, 190
strategic exploitation, 78, **79**, 80, 87
structural properties of EvIE
 positive information, frequency of, 236–239
 similarity and diversity of positive
  information, 239–243
suppressor situation, **136**
sympathetic adrenomedullary axis (SAM),
  177
system justification theory, 78

TESS (Time-sharing Experiments in the
  Social Sciences), 21
test phase, **274**, 294
threat/challenge focus
 appraisals, 189–190
 biopsychosocial model of arousal regulation,
  176–179
 classification of, **181**
 evidence, 187–190
 integration, 180–182
 outcomes of, 183–184, **186**
 social contexts, roles, and groups, 185–186
 transitions, 182–186
 valenced stimuli, 184–185
Time-sharing Experiments in the Social
  Sciences, *see* TESS (Time-sharing
  Experiments in the Social Sciences)
total peripheral resistance (TPR), 177
TPR, *see* total peripheral resistance (TPR)
traditional authority, 78, 100
transactional leadership, 197–199, **199**
transformational leadership, 197–199, **199**
translational goals, 9
translators, 13
Transparency and Openness Principles
  (TOP), 4
trauma, 312, **313–314**
 concepts and theories, 315–326
 group membership, 318–320
 and psychological sequelae, 315–317
 PTSD risk and resilience theories, 317–318
 resources, social identity, 323–326
 responses to, group, 320–323
 self-categorisation, 320–321
 social identity approach to, 318–326
 social identity change, **316**, 326–336
 symptoms, 317
 two-way influence, 8

unconditioned stimuli (US), 272

410   SUBJECT INDEX

valenced stimuli, processing of, 176, 184–185
  evidence on, 191–196
  motivational states impact, 196
  regulatory focus, 195
  threat *vs.* challenge, 191–194, **193**

WEIRD (Western, Educated, Industrialized, Rich, Democratic), 12

European Review of Social Psychology
Contents of Volumes 17–28

Volume 17, 2006

1 Collective guilt: Emotional reactions when one's group has done wrong or been wronged
Michael J. A. Wohl, Nyla R. Branscombe and Yechiel Klar

38 Deservingness and emotions: Applying the structural model of deservingness to the analysis of affective reactions to outcomes
N. T. Feather

74 Unresolved problems with the "I", the "A", and the "T": A logical and psychometric critique of the Implicit Association Test (IAT)
Klaus Fiedler, Claude Messner and Matthias Bluemke

148 Multicultural recognition and ethnic minority rights: A social identity perspective
Maykel Verkuyten

185 "Better to be safe than to be sorry": Extinguishing the individual - group discontinuity effect in competition by cautious reciprocation
Hein F. M. Lodewijkx, Jacob M. Rabbie and Lieuwe Visser

233 Individuality and the prejudiced personality
Katherine J. Reynolds and John C. Turner

271 Social dominance theory and the dynamics of intergroup relations: Taking stock and looking forward
Felicia Pratto, Jim Sidanius and Shana Levin

321 Threatened identities and interethnic interactions
J. Nicole Shelton, Jennifer A. Richeson and Jacquie D. Vorauer

359 The social functions of ingroup bias: Creating, confirming, or changing social reality
Daan Scheepers, Russell Spears, Bertjan Doosje and Antony S. R. Manstead

397 Author index

412 Subject index

Volume 18, 2007

1 From social projection to social behaviour
Joachim I. Krueger

36 Pervasiveness and correlates of implicit attitudes and stereotypes
Brian A. Nosek, Frederick L. Smyth, Jeffrey J. Hansen, Thierry Devos, Nicole M. Lindner, Kate A. Ranganath, Colin Tucker Smith, Kristina R. Olson, Dolly Chugh, Anthony G. Greenwald and Mahzarin R. Banaji

89 Attitudes in social context: A social identity perspective
Michael A. Hogg and Joanne R. Smith

132 Self-interest and fairness in coalition formation: A social utility approach to understanding partner selection and payoff allocations in groups
Ilja Van Beest and Eric Van Dijk

175 Explanations of interindividual - intergroup discontinuity: A review of the evidence
Tim Wildschut and Chester A. Insko

212 Reducing prejudice via direct and extended cross-group friendship
Rhiannon N. Turner, Miles Hewstone, Alberto Voci, Stefania Paolini and Oliver Christ

256 Behaviour variability and the Situated Focus Theory of Power
Ana Guinote

296 Another view of "we": Majority and minority group perspectives on a common ingroup identity
John F. Dovidio, Samuel L. Gaertner and Tamar Saguy

331 Superordinate identities and intergroup conflict: The ingroup projection model
Michael Wenzel, Amélie Mummendey and Sven Waldzus

373 Author index

386 Subject index

Volume 19, 2008

1 The social neuroscience of intergroup relations
David M. Amodio

55 Attributing and denying humanness to others
Nick Haslam, Stephen Loughnan, Yoshihisa Kashima and Paul Bain

86 Emotion in inter-group relations
Aarti Iyer and Colin Wayne Leach

126 Group-based self-regulation: The effects of regulatory focus
Kai Sassenberg and Karl-Andrew Woltin

165 Emerging perspectives on the structure and function of attitude strength
Asia A. Eaton, Elizabeth A. Majka and Penny S. Visser

202 Forgiveness in personal relationships: Its malleability and powerful consequences
Johan C. Karremans and Paul A. M. Van Lange

242 Improving intergroup attitudes and reducing stereotype threat: An integrated contact model
Richard J. Crisp and Dominic Abrams

285 When and why do implicit measures predict behaviour? Empirical evidence for the moderating role of opportunity, motivation, and process reliance
Malte Friese, Wilhelm Hofmann and Manfred Schmitt

339 Understanding dieting: A social cognitive analysis of hedonic processes in self-regulation
Esther K. Papies, Wolfgang Stroebe and Henk Aarts

384 Author index

403 Subject index

Volume 20, 2009

1 Self-enhancement and self-protection: What they are and what they do
Mark D. Alicke and Constantine Sedikides

49 Source factors in persuasion: A self-validation approach
Pablo Briñol and Richard E. Petty

97 Implicit volition and stereotype control
Gordon B. Moskowitz and Courtney Ignarri

146 Three decades of lay epistemics: The why, how, and who of knowledge formation
Arie W. Kruglanski, Mark Dechesne, Edward Orehek and Antonio Pierro

192 Social neuroscience evidence for dehumanised perception
Lasana T. Harris and Susan T. Fiske

232 The unconscious unfolding of emotions
Kirsten I. Ruys and Diederik A. Stapel

272 An integrative review of process dissociation and related models in social cognition
B. Keith Payne and Anthony J. Bishara

315 The dynamics of self-regulation
Ayelet Fishbach, Ying Zhang and Minjung Koo

345 Unravelling the motivational yarn: A framework for understanding the instigation of implicitly motivated behaviour resulting from deprivation and positive affect
Martijn Veltkamp, Henk Aarts and Ruud Custers

382 Author index

399 Subject index

Volume 21, 2010

1 Interpersonal behaviour and social perception in a hierarchy: The interpersonal power and behaviour model
Marianne Schmid Mast

34 The dual pathway to creativity model: Creative ideation as a function of flexibility and persistence
Bernard A. Nijstad, Carsten K. W. De Dreu, Eric F. Rietzschel and Matthijs Baas

78 The cognitive miser's perspective: Social comparison as a heuristic in self-judgements
Katja Corcoran and Thomas Mussweiler

114 On graves and graven images: A terror management analysis of the psychological functions of art
Mark J. Landau, Daniel Sullivan and Sheldon Solomon

155 Compensation between warmth and competence: Antecedents and consequences of a negative relation between the two fundamental dimensions of social perception
Nicolas Kervyn, Vincent Yzerbyt and Charles M. Judd

188 From imagery to intention: A dual route model of imagined contact effects
Richard J. Crisp, Senel Husnu, Rose Meleady, Sofia Stathi and Rhiannon N. Turner

237 A social neuroscience approach to self and social categorisation: A new look at an old issue
Jay J. Van Bavel and William A. Cunningham

285 Contingency learning and stereotype formation: Illusory and spurious correlations revisited
Thorsten Meiser and Miles Hewstone

332 Author index

348 Subject index

Volume 22, 2011

1 Splitting consciousness: Unconscious, conscious, and metaconscious processes in social cognition
Piotr Winkielman and Jonathan W. Schooler

36 A trans-paradigm theoretical synthesis of cognitive dissonance theory: Illuminating the nature of discomfort
Jared B. Kenworthy, Norman Miller, Barry E. Collins, Stephen J. Read and Mitchell Earleywine

114 Emotion is for influence
Gerben A. Van Kleef, Evert A. Van Doorn, Marc W. Heerdink and Lukas F. Koning

164 Culture as situated cognition: Cultural mindsets, cultural fluency, and meaning making
Daphna Oyserman

215 Stereotypes and stereotyping: What's the brain got to do with it?
Susanne Quadflieg and C. Neil Macrae

274 A process model of intuition
Sascha Topolinski

316 Understanding in close relationships: An interpersonal approach
Catrin Finkenauer and Francesca Righetti

364 Interpersonal perception in cross-group interactions: Challenges and potential solutions
Tessa V. West

402 Author index

426 Subject index

Volume 23, 2012

1 Future thought and behaviour change
Gabriele Oettingen

64 We are human, they are not: Driving forces behind outgroup dehumanisation and the humanisation of the ingroup
Jeroen Vaes, Jacques-Philippe Leyens, Maria Paola Paladino and Mariana Pires Miranda

107 A goal model of catharsis
Markus Denzler and Jens Förster

143 Effective regulation of affect: An action control perspective on emotion regulation
Thomas L. Webb, Inge Schweiger Gallo, Eleanor Miles, Peter M. Gollwitzer and Paschal Sheeran

187 A social-psychological perspective on tacit coordination: How it works, when it works, (and when it does not)
Erik W. de Kwaadsteniet and Eric van Dijk

224 Psychological effects of risk glorification in the media: Towards an integrative view
Peter Fischer, Joachim I. Krueger, Tobias Greitemeyer, Kathrin Asal, Nilüfer Aydin and Evelyn Vingilis

258 The social identity theory of leadership: Theoretical origins, research findings, and conceptual developments
Michael A. Hogg, Daan van Knippenberg and David E. Rast III

305 How to achieve synergy in group decision making: Lessons to be learned from the hidden profile paradigm
Stefan Schulz-Hardt and Andreas Mojzisch

344 A social mind: The context of John Turner's work and its influence
Stephen D. Reicher, S. Alexander Haslam, Russell Spears and Katherine J. Reynolds

386 Statement of Retraction

387 Author index

403 Subject index

Volume 24, 2013

1 We are sorry: Intergroup apologies and their tenuous link with intergroup forgiveness
Matthew J. Hornsey and Michael J. A. Wohl

32 Humour in advertising: An associative processing model
Madelijn Strick, Rob W. Holland, Rick B. van Baaren, Ad van Knippenberg and Ap Dijksterhuis

70 Racial healthcare disparities: A social psychological analysis
Louis A. Penner, Nao Hagiwara, Susan Eggly, Samuel L. Gaertner, Terrance L. Albrecht and John F. Dovidio

123 Inaction inertia
Marijke van Putten, Marcel Zeelenberg, Eric van Dijk and Orit E. Tykocinski

160 Morality and behavioural regulation in groups: A social identity approach
Naomi Ellemers, Stefano Pagliaro and Manuela Barreto

194 How the disadvantaged appraise group-based exclusion: The path from legitimacy to illegitimacy
Jolanda Jetten, Aarti Iyer, Nyla R. Branscombe and Airong Zhang

225 Social identity, group processes, and helping in emergencies
Mark Levine and Rachel Manning

252 A functional-cognitive framework for attitude research
Jan De Houwer, Bertram Gawronski and Dermot Barnes-Holmes

288 Author index

302 Subject index

Volume 25, 2014

1 Indirect emotion regulation in intractable conflicts: A new approach to conflict resolution
Eran Halperin, Smadar Cohen-Chen and Amit Goldenberg

32 Beyond terror: Towards a paradigm shift in the study of threat and culture
Leonard L. Martin and Kees van den Bos

71 Media violence use as a risk factor for aggressive behaviour in adolescence
Barbara Krahé

107 Power, negotiations, and the anticipation of intergroup encounters
Tamar Saguy and Nour Kteily

142 Living in a multicultural world: Intergroup ideologies and the societal context of intergroup relations
Serge Guimond, Roxane de la Sablonnière and Armelle Nugier

189 Conceptions of national identity in a globalised world: Antecedents and consequences
Kumar Yogeeswaran and Nilanjana Dasgupta

228 What's really in a Name-Letter Effect? Name-letter preferences as indirect measures of self-esteem
Vera Hoorens

263 The strategic role of language abstraction in achieving symbolic and practical goals
Monica Rubini, Michela Menegatti and Silvia Moscatelli

314 Improving intergroup relations with extended and vicarious forms of indirect contact
Loris Vezzali, Miles Hewstone, Dora Capozza, Dino Giovannini and Ralf Wölfer

390 Author index

405 Subject index

Volume 26, 2015

1 The person-based nature of prejudice: Individual difference predictors of intergroup negativity
Gordon Hodson and and Kristof Dhont

43 A dynamic model of engagement in normative and non-normative collective action: Psychological antecedents, consequences, and barriers
Julia C. Becker and Nicole Tausch

93 Intergroup reconciliation: Instrumental and socio-emotional processes and the needs-based model
Arie Nadler and Nurit Shnabel

126 Things we (don't) want to hear: Exploring responses to group-based feedback
Anna Rabinovich and Thomas A. Morton

162 The presence of the past: Identity continuity and group dynamics
Anouk Smeekes and Maykel Verkuyten

203 How self-regulation helps to master negotiation challenges: An overview, integration, and outlook
Andreas Jäger, David D. Loschelder and Malte Friese

247 The role of self-evaluation and envy in schadenfreude
Wilco W. van Dijk, Jaap W. Ouwerkerk, Richard H. Smith and Mina Cikara

283 Cognition is a matter of trust: Distrust tunes cognitive processes
Ruth Mayo

328 A sociocultural framework for understanding partner preferences of women and men: Integration of concepts and evidence
Marcel Zentner and Alice H. Eagly

374 Author index

392 Subject index

Volume 27, 2016

1 Mnemic neglect: Selective amnesia of one's faults
Constantine Sedikides, Jeffrey D. Green, Jo Saunders, John J. Skowronski and Bettina Zengel

63 Changing people's views of outgroups through individual-to-group generalisation: meta-analytic reviews and theoretical considerations
Kylie McIntyre, Stefania Paolini and Miles Hewstone

116 Applying processing trees in social psychology
Mandy Hütter and Karl Christoph Klauer

160 The social psychology of disordered eating: The Situated Identity Enactment model
Tegan Cruwys, Michael J. Platow, Elizabeth Rieger, Don G. Byrne and S. Alexander Haslam

196 The question-behaviour effect: A theoretical and methodological review and meta-analysis
Sarah Wilding, Mark Conner, Tracy Sandberg, Andrew Prestwich, Rebecca Lawton, Chantelle Wood, Eleanor Miles, Gaston Godin and Paschal Sheeran

231 Cooperation in repeated interactions: A systematic review of Centipede game experiments, 1992–2016
Eva M. Krockow, Andrew M. Colman and Briony D. Pulford

283 Understanding defensive and secure in-group positivity: The role of collective narcissism
Aleksandra Cichocka

Volume 28, 2017

1 Stereotypes as Pseudocontingencies
Florian Kutzner and Klaus Fiedler

50 Disgust as embodied loss aversion
Simone Schnall

95 Doing emotions: The role of culture in everyday emotions
Batja Mesquita, Michael Boiger and Jozefien De Leersnyder

134 Suppress for success? Exploring the contexts in which expressing positive emotion can have social costs
Katharine H. Greenaway and Elise K. Kalokerinos

175 Creating shared reality in interpersonal and intergroup communication: the role of epistemic processes and their interplay
Gerald Echterhoff and E. Tory Higgins

227 To what degree do situational influences explain spontaneous helping behaviour? A meta-analysis
G. Tyler Lefevor, Blaine J. Fowers, Soyeon Ahn, Samantha F. Lang and Laura M. Cohen

257 A motivational perspective on punishment in social dilemmas
Stefan Pfattheicher and Johannes Keller

288 Identifying "types" of ideologies and intergroup biases: Advancing a person-centred approach to social psychology
Danny Osborne and Chris G. Sibley

333 Visualising mental representations: A primer on noise-based reverse correlation in social psychology
L. Brinkman, A. Todorov and R. Dotsch

362 Author index

377 Subject index

383 Contents of previous volumes

392 Instructions to Authors

Volume 29, 2018

1 Cultural concerns: How valuing social-image shapes social emotion
Patricia M. Rodriguez Mosquera

38 The role of social identity processes in mass emergency behaviour:
An integrative review
Patricia John Drury

82 Objectifying objectification: When and why people are cognitively reduced to
their parts akin to objects
Philippe Bernard, Sarah J. Gervais and Olivier Klein

122 Integrating who "we" are with what "we" (will not) stand for: A further
extension of the *Social Identity Model of Collective Action*
Martijn van Zomeren, Maja Kutlaca and Felicity Turner-Zwinkels

161 Disparate roads to certainty processing strategy choices under need for
closure
*Małgorzata Kossowska, Ewa Szumowska, Piotr Dragon, Katarzyna Jaśko and
Arie W. Kruglanski*

212 An experimental approach to Intergroup Threat Theory: Manipulations,
moderators, and consequences of realistic vs. symbolic threat
Kimberly Rios, Nicholas Sosa and Hannah Osborn

256 Why conspiracy theories matter: A social psychological analysis
Karen M. Douglas and Robbie M. Sutton

299 Confirmation as coping with competition
Fabrizio Butera, Nicolas Sommet and Claudia Toma

340 Stress and the stability of social systems: A review of neurophysiological
research
Patricia M. Rodriguez Mosquera

Volume 30, 2019

Article

1 From crisis of evidence to a "crisis" of relevance? Incentive-based answers for
social psychology's perennial relevance worries
Roger Giner-Sorolla

39 The social and cultural psychology of honour: What have we learned from
researching honour in Turkey?
Ayse K. Uskul and Susan E. Cross

74 How criminal organisations exert secret power over communities: An intracultural appropriation theory of cultural values and norms
Giovanni A. Travaglino and Dominic Abrams

123 The sociality of personal and collective nostalgia
Constantine Sedikides and Tim Wildschut

174 Linking regulatory focus and threat–challenge: transitions between and outcomes of four motivational states
Kai Sassenberg and Annika Scholl

216 The evaluative information ecology: On the frequency and diversity of "good" and "bad"
Christian Unkelbach, Alex Koch, and Hans Alves

271 An action control perspective of evaluative conditioning
Eva Walther, Katarina Blask, Georg Halbeisen, and Christian Frings

311 The social psychology of responses to trauma: social identity pathways associated with divergent traumatic responses
Orla T. Muldoon, S. Alexander Haslam, Catherine Haslam, Tegan Cruwys, Michelle Kearns, and Jolanda Jetten

INSTRUCTIONS FOR AUTHORS

Aims and Scopes

The *European Review of Social Psychology* (ERSP) is an international open-submission review journal, published under the auspices of the European Association of Social Psychology. It provides an outlet for substantial, theory-based reviews of empirical work addressing the full range of topics covered by the field of social psychology. Potential authorship is international, and papers are edited with the help of a distinguished, international editorial board.

Articles published in *ERSP* typically review a programme of the author's own research, as evidenced by the author's own papers published in leading peer-reviewed journals. The journal welcomes theoretical contributions that are underpinned by a substantial body of empirical research, which locate the research programme within a wider body of published research in that area, and provide an integration that is greater than the sum of the published articles. *ERSP* also publishes conventional reviews and meta-analyses.

All published review articles in this journal have undergone rigorous peer review, based on initial screening and refereeing by the Editors and at least two independent, expert referees.

Manuscript submission

Before preparing your submission, please visit the Journal's homepage at www.tandfonline.com/PERS for full instructions for authors.

Most manuscripts are commissioned by the Editors, who invite contributions based on the authors' recent, original, empirical articles in leading peer-reviewed journals. However, the Editors welcome spontaneous submissions and suggestions for manuscripts either direct from the authors, or indirectly from other scholars. Authors with a concrete proposal should provide approximately a 5 page outline, with a full listing of their own prior primary publications, which will form the basis of the proposed submission.

All full submissions should be made online at the *ERSP* Editorial Manager website at http://www.editorial manager.com/pers. New users should first create an account. Once logged on to the site, submissions should be made via the Author Centre. Online user guides and access to a helpdesk are available on this website. Submission enquiries may be directed to PERS-peerreview@tandf.co.uk. Manuscripts may be submitted in any standard editable format, including Word and EndNote. These files will be automatically converted into a PDF file for the review process. LaTeX files should be converted to PDF prior to submission because Editorial Manager is not able to convert LaTeX files into PDFs directly. All LaTeX source files should be uploaded alongside the PDF.

The author's covering letter must include the corresponding author's full contact details (including email), the manuscript title and a copy of the submission checklist.

Example proposals and a checklist for completion before submitting a first draft to *European Review of Social Psychology* are available at http://www. tandfonline.com/PERS.

All manuscripts must be accompanied by a statement confirming that it has not been previously published elsewhere and that it has not been submitted simultaneously for publication elsewhere.

Invitation to submit a manuscript to *ERSP* does not imply that the manuscript will ultimately be accepted for publication. All manuscripts will be externally peer reviewed. As a result, some will be rejected and others have to undergo more or less extensive reviews. For more information about anonymous peer review, please visit http://authorservices.taylor-andfrancis.com/what-to-expect-during-peer-review/

Copyright and author's rights

To assure the integrity, dissemination, and protection against copyright infringement of published articles, you will be asked to assign to European Association of Social Psychology, via a Publishing Agreement, the copyright in your article. Your Article is defined as the final, definitive, and citable Version of Record, and includes: (a) the accepted manuscript in its final form, including the abstract, text, bibliography, and all accompanying tables, illustrations, data; and (b) any supplemental material hosted by Taylor & Francis. Our Publishing Agreement with you will constitute the entire agreement and the sole understanding between European Association of Social Psychology and you; no amendment, addendum, or other communication will be taken into account when interpreting your and European Association of Social Psychology rights and obligations under this Agreement.

Copyright policy is explained in detail at http://author services.taylorandfrancis.com/copyright-and-you/.

Free article access

On publication, you will be able to view, download and check your article's metrics (downloads, citations and Altmetric data) via http://authorservices.taylorand francis.com/my-authored-works/. This is where you can access every article you have published with us, as well as your free eprints link at http://authorservices.taylor andfrancis.com/ensuring-your-research-makes-an-impact/ so you can quickly and easily share your work with friends and colleagues. For enquiries about reprints, please contact the Taylor & Francis Author Services team at reprints@tandf.co.uk. To order a copy of the issue containing your article, please contact our Customer Services team at Adhoc@tandf.co.uk.

Abstracting and indexing

European Review of Social Psychology is abstracted/indexed in: Current Contents/Social and Behavioral Sciences; PsycINFO; Social Sciences Citation Index; Social Scisearch

For further information about Taylor & Francis journals please visit www.tandfonline.com.

If you are unable to access our websites, please write to: *European Review of Social Psychology*, Editorial Department, Taylor & Francis, 4 Park Square, Milton Park, Abingdon, Oxon, OX14 4RN, UK.